THE

TUNISIA

THE REAL GUIDE TUNISIA: CREDITS

Text Editor: Richard Trillo
Proofreading: Margaret Doyle
Production: Susanne Hillen and Kate Berens
Typesetting: Gail Jammy and Andy Hilliard

Real Guides Series Editor: Mark Ellingham

Continuing thanks for invaluable help on the first edition goes to: Joyce Brown, Catherine Cole, Mark Ellingham, the Ezzine Family, Jenny Hughes, Ghislaine Morris, and many others in England and Tunisia.

Many people have helped on the third edition, either directly during the research, or by writing with update information. Daniel Jacobs, revisions author on the third edition, particularly wants to thank:
Keith Barclay, Amanda Bishop, Samir Bouzekri, CJ Bradbeer, Jonathan Bousfield, Sue Carpenter, Debbie Collis, Trevor E Corner, WJ Cowler, L Crowhurst, Matthew Cullen, Kieron Devlin, David Doff, S De Souza, R Edwards, David Evans, Philip Foster, Martin Godfrey, Jerry Graham, Malcolm Gunter, Susan Haynes, CS Hilliard, Susan Hodder, Brenda Keatley, Micheal Oldrieve, Niels-Oluf Larsen, Joe Lembo, Matt Limb, RA Ludlow, Lindsay Maginn, Justin McGuiness, Denis J Muir, Paul O'Rourke, Karin Oswald, MZ Pelcis, C Pogmore, BE Polley, Pieter Schram, Tony Shephard, Joe Silke, DJ Slade, Ernst Spaan, Mike Stapleton, D Stockham, Jacqui Tilt, Shirley Vollweiler, Zeineb C Whatford, Lucy Williams, Ron Wright and Paul Zandbergen.

A number of organisations have also given a great deal of assistance in the preparation of this edition. To all concerned, we extend our warmest thanks: ASM Bizerte, ASM Le Kef (in particular Mr Mohammed Tlili), ASM Sfax, ASM Tunis, Association pour la Sauvegarde de l'Ile de Jerba, Commonwealth War Graves Commission, Maghreb Association (in particular Mr Mohammed Ben Madani), ONTT London (in particular Mr Moncef Battikh), ONTT Bizerte, ONTT Gafsa, ONTT Tozeur.

Publishing acknowledgements

We are grateful to Oxford University Press for permission to reprint two lines of Keith Douglas's poem *Remember me when I am dead*, © Marie Douglas; and to Penguin Books for the extracts from *The Odyssey*, translation © EV Rieu, *The Aeneid*, translation © The Estate of WF Jackson Knight, and *Salammbô*, translation © AJ Krailsheimer.

The publishers and authors have done their best to ensure the accuracy and currency of all information in *The Real Guide Tunisia*; however, they can accept no responsibility for any loss, injury or inconvenience sustained by any traveller as a result of information or advice contained in the guide.

Typeset in Linotron Univers and Century Old Style to an original design by Andrew Oliver.
Printed in the United Kingdom by Cox & Wyman Ltd (Reading).

Illustrations in Part One and Part Three by Edward Briant.
Basics and Contexts page illustrations by Henry Iles.

Published in the United States by
Prentice Hall General Reference
A division of Simon & Schuster Inc.
15 Columbus Circle
New York, NY 10023

400pp. Includes index.

Cataloguing-in-Publication Data is available from the Library of Congress.

ISBN 0-13-761750-X

THE REAL GUIDE
TUNISIA

Written and researched by

**Peter Morris, Daniel Jacobs,
Charles Farr and Adrian Fozzard**

With additional research and accounts by
Pete Raine, Linda Cooley and Lindsay Maginn

Edited by
Richard Trillo

PRENTICE HALL TRAVEL

NEW YORK LONDON TORONTO SYDNEY TOKYO SINGAPORE

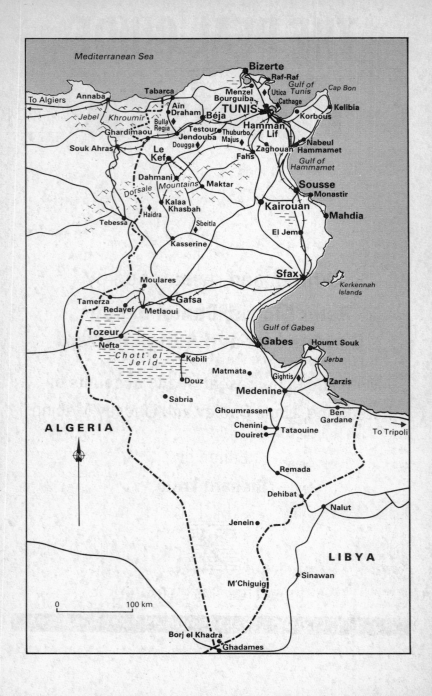

CONTENTS

Introduction vi

INTRODUCTION

Tunisia, the Arab world's most liberal nation, is recognisably Mediterranean in character and, in the north at least, predominantly European in style. Indeed, its image seems, at times, to verge on blandness, dominated as it is by the package holiday clichés of reliable sunshine, beautiful beaches and just a touch of the exotic. If this seems predictable, however, be assured that it is only one side of the picture. Beyond the white sands of Jerba and Hammamet, there is a great deal to encourage more independent-minded travel: sub-Saharan oases and fortresses, medieval Islamic cities like Kairouan, and some of the finest of all surviving Roman sites. And the Western aspects – the legacy of a half-century of French colonial rule – work to your advantage, undeniably, in talking to people, with French remaining a widely spoken second language. Being such a compact territory, especially when compared to its North African neighbours, Tunisia is also very easy to get around. Even with a fortnight's holiday, it is quite feasible to take in something of each of the county's aspects of coast, mountains and desert. The journey from **Tunis**, the capital on the north coast, to Tataouine, in the heart of the desert, can be made in little over ten hours by bus or shared taxi and, while most trips are considerably shorter, the majority of journeys in Tunisia leave an impression of real travel in the transformation from one type of landscape and culture to another. This **immediacy** makes the country very satisfying to explore – an accessible introduction to the Arab world, and to the African continent.

The **country**, sited strategically at a bottleneck in the Mediterranean, has long played an important role in the region's history. In antiquity it was the centre of Carthaginian civilisation – the ruins of Carthage lie just outside modern Tunis – and, as that empire folded, it became the heartland of Roman Africa. Later, as Islam spread west, it was invaded and settled by Arabs, providing, in the cities of Kairouan, Tunis, Sousse and Sfax, vital power bases for North Africa's successive medieval dynasties. By the fifteenth century, the Europeans and Turks were also turning their attentions to Tunisia – a process that ultimately resulted in French colonisation in the nineteenth century. Today, in its fourth decade of independence, Tunisia is a fully established modern nation and, by regional standards, relatively prosperous.

TUNISIA: FACTS AND FIGURES

With an **area** of 163,610 square kilometres (63,170 square miles), Tunisia is slightly larger than England and Wales, or Florida. The **population** stands at around eight million, of whom some 650,000 live in Tunis. The official languages are **Arabic**, spoken by almost everybody, and **French**, spoken by most school-educated people. English is not widely spoken but more and more young people are studying it at school. About 99 percent of the population are Muslims, with tiny minorities of Jews and Christians. On the economic side, Tunisia's main **exports** are crude oil, textiles and phosphates and its main trading partners are France, Italy and Germany. Inflation is currently less than ten percent. The head of **state**, President Zine el Abidine Ben Ali, took office on November 7, 1987. He succeeded the founder of modern Tunisia, Habib Bourguiba, who led the country to independence (March 20, 1956) from French colonial rule. There is an elected National Assembly and a number of legal political parties – though Islamic fundamentalism is outlawed.

Where to go

If the diversity of Tunisia's past cultures and their legacy of monuments comes as a surprise to most first-time visitors, the range of **scenery** can be even more unexpected. In the north you find shady oak forests reminiscent of the south of France; in southern Tunisia the beginning of the Sahara desert, with colossal dunes, oases and rippling mirages. Between the extremes are lush citrus plantations, bare steppes with tabletop mountains, and rolling hills as green and colourful (in spring) as any English shire. Just offshore lie the sandy, palm-scattered islands of Jerba and Kerkennah.

In terms of **monuments**, the **Roman sites** of the north are the best-known, and, even if your interest is very casual, many are quite spectacular. At **El Jem**, in the Sahel, an amphitheatre which rivals Rome's Colosseum towers above the plain; at **Dougga** you can wander around a marvellously preserved Roman city, complete with all the accoutrements and buildings of second- and third-century prosperity; and there are sites, scarcely less grand, at **Utica**, **Bulla Regia**, **Maktar** and **Sbeitla**, as well as the legendary, extensive and much-battered **Carthage**. They're all atmospheric places to visit and at the smaller sites, off the excursion routes, you'll find yourself, as often as not, enjoying them alone.

Islamic Tunisia has a varied architectural legacy, taking in early Arab mosques – most outstandingly at **Kairouan**, the first Arab capital of North Africa – and the sophisticated Turkish buildings of **Tunis**, as well as the strange Berber fortresses of the south. The latter are accompanied by equally weird structures known as *ghorfas*, honeycombed storage and living quarters, and, at **Matmata**, by underground houses. All reward the small effort it takes to get off the more beaten tracks.

For more hedonistic pleasures, the **coast** is at its most beautiful – and most commercialised – around **Hammamet**, **Sousse-Monastir** and the island of **Jerba** (connected by causeway to the mainland). Hammamet is a genuinely international resort and its satellites are spreading, but by Spanish or Italian standards, developments remain relatively small-scale and unusually well-planned. Escaping them entirely is not hard either: even within sight of Hammamet, on **Cap Bon**, there is still wild coastline; **Bizerte**, on the north coast, has good sands and more character; whilst the **Kerkennah islands** still retain genuine fishing villages.

Your time should ideally include a spell in the **desert and mountains** as well as on the coast. The **oases** at **Nefta and Tozeur** are classically luxuriant, while further south, the *ksour* (extraordinary, fortified granaries) around **Tataouine** and dunes around **Remada** give the region an almost expeditionary feel (indeed, many people choose to go on organised "safaris", easily arranged locally). In the mountains of the northwest, **Le Kef** is an ideal place to rest up for a few days.

All of this ignores one of Tunisia's best facets – its **people**. While the hassle of some tourist areas (particularly for women) shouldn't be underestimated, visitors are often startled – and exhilarated – by the sheer hospitality which they're shown when away from the major resorts. Few independent travellers leave Tunisia without having been invited, quite spontaneously, to stay with a family. Even during the 1991 Gulf War, when the government did not support the US and allied forces, and there was a certain amount of anti-Western rhetoric on the street, the slogans were usually transcended by Tunisians' extraordinary pleasure in meeting vistors. The politics of the wider world rarely hinder personal contact.

Climate and seasons

Tunisia follows usual Mediterranean patterns of **climate**. The best time to travel, from a scenic point of view, is **spring**, when the south has not yet reached full heat and the north looks astonishingly fertile – above all, around the orchards and vineyards of Cap Bon. Be warned, though, that March and April are the dampest months of the year in the south and it can bucket down in the north.

Summer has mixed virtues. **July and August** are much the hottest months of the year – if only slightly more so than in the southern parts of Italy or Greece – and the one time you really do need to lapse into a local way of life, for example resting through the midday hours at a café, or taking a siesta at your hotel. Obviously this goes above all for the deep South and the *ksour* (see Chapter Nine). On the more exposed beaches of the north coast, midsummer is actually a pull – some of them are only warm enough for swimming from around May until October. If you wait until **autumn,** you get the best of both worlds, with warm swimming and few crowds, even at the big resorts.

In **winter**, the north and the Tell can get distinctly cold; Aïn Draham, the highest mountain town, commonly has a metre of snow, and in 1985 it snowed at Bizerte (on the Mediterranean coast) as well. Tunis, Cap Bon and Sousse are not so much cold in winter as dull, with sporadic rains. But this is an ideal time for covering the ancient sites at leisure and then migrating south to Jerba's beaches and the Sahara.

AVERAGE TEMPERATURES AND RAINFALL												
	Jan	Feb	Mar	Apr	May	Jun	Jul	Aug	Sep	Oct	Nov	Dec
Tunis												
Min night °C	6	7	8	11	13	17	20	21	19	15	11	7
Max day °C	14	16	18	21	24	29	32	33	31	25	20	16
Rainfall (mm)	64	51	41	36	18	8	3	8	33	51	48	61
Days with rainfall	13	12	11	9	6	5	2	3	7	9	11	14
Gabes												
Min night °C	6	7	9	12	16	19	22	22	21	17	11	7
Max day °C	16	18	21	23	26	28	32	33	31	27	22	17
Rainfall (mm)	23	18	20	10	8	0	0	3	13	31	31	15
Days with rainfall	4	3	4	3	2	0	0	1	3	4	4	4

PART ONE

THE

BASICS

GETTING THERE

Flying is likely to be both the fastest and the cheapest way to get to Tunisia, with most of the best deals originating in London, no matter where you're starting from. In the case of package charter flights you may well find that accommodation (in other words the full holiday) is hardly any more expensive. Using a package for a few nights accommodation, and breaking out on your own for the rest, usually offers good value for money. If you're determined to travel quite independently, then surface options like ferry plus train, bus, car or even hitching are all feasible means of getting to the country.

FLIGHTS FROM BRITAIN

Many high street travel agents will sell a flight without accommodation, though you have to accept the limitations of a **charter flight** (a return flight of one to four weeks, arriving at Monastir rather than Tunis). From London you can find something suitable at any time of the year, though prices are much higher in July–August (usually between £160 and £250) than out of season, when they may plummet to £100 or less. All-inclusive winter packages (for example, 2 weeks with flight and accommodation for under £200) are an absolute bargain. At this sort of price, even if you're only wanting to travel one way, it makes sense to buy a charter seat (though selling the return portion of a charter ticket is not really on – tickets are non-transferable and

boarding cards are matched with passports at the departure gate).

Contact the Tunisian National Tourist Office, (77a Wigmore Street, London W1H 9LJ; ☎071 224 5561) and ask for their list of agents handling Tunisian holidays, then phone round for the best deal. You'll find adverts for numerous other operators and bucket shops in the travel pages of the Saturday *Daily Telegraph, Independent* and *Times* and, on a Sunday, the *Sunday Times* and *Observer*. If you're in London, also check the London listings magazines *Time Out* and *City Limits*, and London's free magazines for Australasians and commuters – *TNT, Southern Cross, Ms London, Midweek* and *G* – which can be picked up at tube stations. You can also come across last-minute cheap charters in the London *Evening Standard.*

SCHEDULED FLIGHTS

Two airlines operate **scheduled flights** from London to Tunisia – *GB Airways* (inquiries c/o *British Airways* ☎081 897 4000) and *Tunis Air* (25 Sackville Street, London W1X 1DA; ☎071 734 7644/5; and 6 Vigo Street, London W1X 1AH; ☎071 437 6236). Flying on a scheduled service is useful if you want to stay longer in Tunisia or continue onwards. Both airlines have Apex returns for £212 in summer, £182 in winter, or excursions open for a month at £392; the full economy return fare is £580! The problem with an Apex (advance purchase excursion) ticket is that you cannot change your reservation and if you cancel you only get fifty percent of the cost back. *Tunis Air* also has occasional cheap deals on one-way seats. *GB Airways'* flights leave for Tunis on Monday and Thursday from Gatwick. *Tunis Air* fly to Tunis on Fridays and Sundays from Heathrow.

Alternatively, KLM has some good deals on three-month and one-year validity return tickets, available through selected agents. Services hub through Amsterdam, but there are connections from British regional airports.

FLIGHTS FROM IRELAND

Ireland has no direct flights to Tunisia, so the cheapest way to get there is to pay a tag-on fare and go via Britain or France. Among agents worth

contacting are *Joe Walsh Tours*, 8–11 Lower
Baggot Street, Dublin (☎01 789555), who are
usually good for budget fares, and *UIST*, 7
Angelsea Street, Dublin (☎01 778117), who
specialise in student/youth deals.

FLIGHTS FROM MAINLAND EUROPE

The flight situation **from Amsterdam** is similar
to that in London, with *Tunis Air* running a weekly
flight from Schipol to Tunis, and a Saturday one
to Monastir, while *KLM* fly to Tunis twice a
week.

There are also plenty of charters in season.
Charters are also available in **the rest of
Europe**, though they may be more expensive.

FLIGHTS BACK FROM TUNISIA

Flying one-way back to Europe from Tunisia is
not cheap. Unless you strike lucky with a
surprise spare seat on a charter flight (direct
approach to the resort reps is the only means of
finding out), the most practical cheap solution is
to fly to Marseille and work your way back from
there; flights can be found for as little as £60
from *Tunis Air* or *Air France (see* Tunis Listings,
p.75). There are also sometimes spare seats
available on return flights from the regional
airports at Monastir, Jerba, Sfax and Tozeur.

There are direct scheduled flights to Tunis
twice daily from Rome and Paris, daily from
Geneva and Marseille and at least weekly from
several places in France and Germany, as well as
Athens, Barcelona, Brussels, Madrid, Milan,
Palermo, Prague, Vienna and Zurich. Direct sched-
uled flights reach **Monastir** from Brussels,
Frankfurt, Geneva, Luxembourg, Lyon, Marseille,
Nice, Paris and Rome; **Jerba** from Brussels,
Geneva, Frankfurt, Paris and Zurich; and **Sfax
and Tozeur** from Paris.

OVERLAND FROM BRITAIN

You won't save any money by **going overland**
between London and Tunis but the routes are
obviously worth considering if you have the time
to take in something of France and/or Italy on the
way. And if you're under 26, there are bargains to
be had on rail tickets.

The route through **Italy** is probably the most
popular. By train it takes around thirty hours from
London to Genoa or fifty hours to Trápani, the two
Italian ferry terminals for Tunis. An alternative
route, with shorter land portion, is to travel down
to Marseille (twenty hours), for the longer ferry
crossing from France. Alternative, very roundabout routes, are via Spain, Morocco and Algeria,
or Greece, Egypt and Libya; for more on these
possibilities, see the *Onwards* section on p.380.

OVERLAND BY TRAIN

Standard **train** tickets for London–Marseille run at £91 single/£141 return; to Genoa they are £109/£171; you cannot buy a through ticket to Trápani in London, but London–Palermo is £139/£230; details of routes and timetables from the *European Rail Centre* at Victoria Station (☎071 834 2345). If you're **under 26,** the options are slightly cheaper. A *Eurotrain/Transalpino* rail ticket (available from student/youth travel agents) costs around £71/£128 for Marseille, £75/£135 for Genoa, and £98/£182 for Palermo. These have two months' validity and allow as many stopovers as you like along the (specified) route. An **InterRail pass** can be even better value at £175 if you're under 26, £235 over 26, for a month's unlimited travel on European trains, though you'll have to pay fifty percent for the first stage (from London and across the channel). Tunisia itself is not included on the InterRail scheme, but for anyone considering the Italy–Tunisia–Algeria–Morocco–Spain loop you will only be paying around £30 extra for the journey from Tunis through Algeria to Oujda; InterRails are valid in Morocco. Note, however, that virtually every train you will want to use in Spain charges a supplement, as do many in France.

OVERLAND BY BUS

Buses from London to Marseilles, Genoa or Rome take about the same time as trains but can cost substantially less. *Eurolines* (52 Grosvenor Gardens, London SW1W 0AX; ☎071 730 8235 or ☎071 730 0202), for example, run coaches to Marseille for £64 single/£108 return; and to Genoa for £83/£126. There are slight reductions for under-25s. You may find other offers in the travel pages of the London magazines mentioned on p.3 under *Flights from Britain*.

OVERLAND BY CAR

Driving or hitching, the fastest route down is via Turin, Rome and Naples across to Sicily on the Reggio–Messina ferry, and over to Tunis by ferry from Trápani. If you're hitching, whatever you do, don't let yourself get sucked down to the south of France, where you could get stuck for days. Instead, steer a course more to the north-east, skirting the Alps.

A more expensive but somewhat more relaxed option is to pick up a connection for the Tunis ferry at Genoa or Marseille, but if you've got a car you'll need to book ahead in season.

There are ferries to Tunisia from **Cagliari** (Sardinia), **Trápani** (Sicily), **Genoa** and **Marseille**, and sometimes from **Malta**. The Trápani–Tunis crossing is the shortest and generally the most straightforward. Ferries from Genoa and Marseille are in some respects more convenient and certainly more pleasant (they lack a certain "attitude" to Arab passengers and a feeling of being herded like cattle) and the Genoa crossing, which works out at only slightly more than the one from Trápani, is certainly worth considering for pedestrians. Car drivers, however, will need to make reservations three or four months in advance for summer crossings from Genoa or Marseille. For foot passengers, an alternative and quicker approach is the **hydrofoil** service from Trápani to Kelibia on Cap Bon, which runs in the summer only.

The monthly *ABC World Shipping Guide*, available from ABC Publications (Church St, Dunstable, Beds LU5 4HB; ☎582 600111) or at any public reference library or good travel agent, should carry current information on these ferries, but isn't always up to date.

FERRIES FROM TRÁPANI

From Trápani, two companies operate to La Goulette (the port for Tunis). *Tirrenia Navigazione* run one ferry a week all year round leaving Trápani at 9am on Tuesdays and La Goulette at 8pm the same day. *Alimar/Aliscafi SNAV* run one ferry a week in winter and up to three in summer. Their schedule tends to vary a lot from season to season and year to year so you should check with them before setting out. The crossing takes roughly eight hours.

In midsummer especially, you'll need to be prepared for a harassed and frantic time buying tickets in Trápani (if you haven't done so in advance). *Alimar*'s office there (in Piazza Garibaldi, opposite the dock) opens for last-minute sales only about an hour before scheduled departure time, but there is no need to panic since the boat is always late.

If you're **taking a car** across any time between mid-June and mid-September it's essential to book in advance. Foot passengers, at least on the outward leg from Sicily, have less of a problem since deck class tickets (£37.90 in winter, £44.80 in summer) are sold pretty much without restriction. But if you're planning to

---

FERRY OPERATORS

Alimar/Aliscafi SNAV:– Livorno–Trápani–Tunis (La Goulette); Trápani–Kelibia.

Livorno (Leghorn): Stazzione Marittima (Boat Station) (☎0586 880733).

Rome: Via Appia Antica (☎06 780 6728).

Naples: 22 Viale Gramsci (☎081 761 2348).

Trápani: 1 Via Torre Arsa (☎0923 27101).

Tunis: c/o *Tourafric*, 52 av Bourguiba (☎01 341488).

Compagnie Tunisienne de la Navigation (*CTN* or *Cotonav*):– Genoa–Tunis (La Goulette); Marseille–Tunis (La Goulette).

London: c/o *Southern Ferries*, 179 Piccadilly, W1V 9DB (☎071 491 4968) – handle the Marseille route only, not Genoa.

Amsterdam: c/o *Hoyman and Schuurman*, 124 De Ruyterkade (☎020 241677).

Brussels: c/o *SNMCM*, Bureau 314, Centre International Rogier (☎02 2194 788).

Frankfurt: c/o *Karl Geuther & Co*, 9 Heinrichsraße (☎069 730471).Marseille: c/o *SNMCM*, 61 bd des Dames (☎9156 3200).

Genoa: c/o *Tirrenia*, Ponte Colombo (boat station), (☎010 26981).

Tunis: 122 rue de Yougoslavie (☎01 242801), or c/o *Navitour*, 8 rue d'Alger (☎01 249500).

Tirrenia Navigazione:– Cagliari–Trápani–Tunis (La Goulette).

London: c/o *Serena Holidays*, 40/42 Kenway Rd SW5 0RA (☎071 373 6548/9).

Frankfurt: c/o *Karl Geuther & Co*, 9 Heinrichsraße (☎069 730471).

Cagliari: c/o *Agenave*, 1 Via Campidano (☎66065/6/7/8).

Trápani: Corso Italia 52/56 (☎0923 27480).

Naples: 2 Rione Sirignano (☎081 720 1111).

Palermo: 385 Via Roma (☎091 585733).

Tunis: c/o *Tourafric*, 52 av Bourguiba (☎01 341488).

---

return from Tunis you would be well advised to get a full return ticket in advance, especially if you're travelling during the **last two weeks of August**, when the boats are packed with returning migrant workers.

Tirrenia's Trápani–La Goulette service in fact starts in **Cagliari** (Sardinia) and can be picked up there. It leaves Cagliari at 7pm on Mondays, and the journey takes some 24 hours.

The thrice-weekly summer-only **jetfoil from Trápani to Kelibia** is operated by *Aliscafi SNAV*. At four hours, it's twice as fast as the ferry, but also more costly (around £60 one way) and often heavily booked. If the weather is rough, sailings can be unpredictable; it's not unknown for the captain to put in at Pantelleria for a couple of days until conditions improve.

FERRIES FROM MAINLAND ITALY

Alimar usually run a service from **Naples** in the summer. This service is sometimes suspended but *Alimar*'s Trápani–La Goulette service does run to and from **Livorno** (Leghorn) once a week, taking an extra day, but costing only some forty percent more than Trápani. The *Compagnie Tunisienne de la Navigation* (*CTN*, or *Cotonav*) run one ferry a week in winter and up to five a fortnight in summer between **Genoa** and La

Goulette. It's a comfortable crossing and an economic one, too, at least in "Tourist Class" — four-berth cabins for little more than the cost of a seat on the Trápani ferry. However, it's a heavily oversubscribed service in season – and if you're thinking of taking a car in summer, forget it: bookings need to be made sometimes five months in advance, and no London agents handle this route.

FERRIES FROM MARSEILLE

A ferry service from **Marseille** to La Goulette, again operated by *CTN*, also runs weekly in winter and up to five times a fortnight in summer – though car drivers need, if anything, more forward planning than for Genoa. Reaching Marseille from Britain is reasonably cheap (£71 one way with *Transalpino/Eurotrain*) though inevitably ferry prices are higher than for Trápani or Genoa – by about forty percent: £80 one-way steerage, £140 with a cabin and meals. To take a car will cost around £200 single, £320 return though the London agents offer special deals out of season. For summer crossings, car drivers should ideally try to book as soon as the summer tickets become available, usually in February; pedestrians stand more chance, though don't count on seats.

PACKAGE OPERATORS

Several companies either specialise in Tunisia or run specialist or unusual Tunisian trips:

Panorama Tunisia Experience, 29 Queens Road, Brighton BN1 3YN (☎0273 202391), the main specialists with flights from Heathrow, Gatwick and Manchester. As well as the usual package tours, they offer self-catering, and "à la carte" holidays where they help you put together your own itinerary. Their hotels are in Hammamet, Sousse, Port el Kantaoui and Jerba.

Tunisian Travel Bureau, 304 Old Brompton Road, London SW5 9JF (☎071 373 4411). London flights only and rather expensive, but offer the

Cadogan, Cadogan House, 9–10 Portland Street, Southampton SO9 1ZP (☎071 831 1616). Upmarket firm with a personal approach, using scheduled flights and selected hotels in Hammamet and Port el Kantaoui.

Swann Hellenic, 77 New Oxford Street, London WC1A 1PX (☎071 831 1616). Offer a thirteen-day tour of Tunisia's Roman sites guided by a guest expert. Departures twice yearly (spring and autumn). The price is quite high, over £1000 per person, but is absolutely all-inclusive.

Alternatively, try phoning round the following mainstream tour operators:

Airtours, Wavell House, Helmshore, Rossendale BB4 4NB (☎0706 260000).

Cosmos, Tourama House, 17 Homesdale Road, Bromley, Kent BR2 9LX (☎061 480 5799).

Horizon, Broadway, Edgbaston Five Ways, Birmingham B15 1BB (☎021 632 6282).

Intasun, 2 Cromwell Avenue, Bromley, Kent BR2 9AQ (☎0274 760022).

Martin Rook's, Groundstar House, London Road, Crawley, Sussex RH10 2TB (☎0293 519222).

Thomson, Greater London House, Hampstead Road, London NW1 7SD (☎081 200 8733).

FERRIES FROM MALTA

Services from **Malta** are rather sporadic, but at time of writing *CTN* are running one ferry a week via Catania, taking twelve hours.

PACKAGE HOLIDAYS

If you're planning a **last-minute holiday** or extended travels without much preparation, a short-notice package from the UK (try the *Evening Standard* if you are in London) could cost little more than a charter flight, and you won't have to worry where to stay on your first night.

If, on the other hand, you're specifically interested in a **package holiday,** with everything thrown in and sorted out, there is plenty of choice. Almost all the major British operators offer Tunisian holidays, mainly on the Nabeul–Hammamet or Sousse–Monastir coasts. For more variety, including the chance of smaller, more local resorts, there are a couple of specialist operators (see box).

ADVENTURE TRIPS

A more adventurous package alternative, until recently, was to take one of a limited number of North African **expedition tours**. These involved overland travel for several weeks by adapted

Land Rover or truck. Covering Morocco and Algeria as well as Tunisia, the routes themselves are both authentic and exciting, cutting across minor *piste* roads in the Sahara and mountains. At one time there were several operators covering the "North African loop" of Morocco–Algeria–Tunisia, but as of the beginning of 1992 none were offering trips along the circuit. Partly this is a result of the Gulf War; the situation is likely to change in the near future. For up-to-date information, contact an Africa specialist agent such as *Africa Travel Centre* or *STA Travel's Africa Desk* (see box on p.4).

Once in Tunisia, you may be able to do a trip with the **Tunisian YHA**, which sometimes organises tours of southern Tunisia by Land Rover. For further details about these "Saharan Adventures", write to: ATAJ, 10 rue Ali Bach Hamba, BP 320, 1015 Tunis (☎353277).

GETTING THERE FROM NORTH AMERICA

No airline operates direct flights from the USA and Canada to Tunisia: the cheapest solution if you're a student or count as a youth (usually under 26) is to get a discount ticket to Italy and make your way on from there by train and ferry (see p.5–6).

For student discount tickets in the USA, try *CIEE* (☎800 223 7401) or *STA* (☎800 777 0112); in Canada, try *Travel Cuts* (☎416 979 2406). Another possibility in both countries is *Nouvelles Frontières* (☎212 764 6494).

You should also try the **discount travel** clubs such as *Moment's Notice* in New York (☎212 668 2182), *Stand Buys Ltd* in Chicago (☎800 255 0200), or *Worldwide Discount* in Miami (☎305 534 2082). *Airhitch* in New York do last-minute standbys (☎212 864 2000).

Failing any of these, *Alitalia* and other airlines do SuperApex tickets to Italy from New York, Boston, Chicago, LA, Montreal, Toronto and Vancouver. The onward seat to Tunis won't cost much in comparison.

GETTING THERE FROM AUSTRALASIA

There are no direct **flights from Australia** or **New Zealand** to Tunisia. Your best bet is probably via London or Athens; alternatively, you could go via Singapore and pick up a *Royal Jordanian* flight, changing again at Amman. Serious adventurers might consider flying to Harare (the only African city with a direct air link to Australia) and heading north overland. Reliable agents to try for flights to London (and connections on to Tunisia) are the independent travel specialists *STA Travel*, who have offices throughout Australia and New Zealand, the principal ones being:
AUCKLAND: 10 High Street (☎09 309 9723)
SYDNEY: 1A Lee Street (☎02 519 9866)
MELBOURNE: 256 Flinders Street (☎03 347 4711)

VISAS AND RED TAPE

British citizens need no visa for a stay of up to three months, and British Visitors' Passports are valid for Tunisia. Irish and Canadian nationals, Maltese, Scandinavians, Japanese, Austrians and Swiss also need no visa for a ninety-day stay, while Americans may stay for up to four months with no visa. Among European **Community nationals, only citizens of the Netherlands, Belgium and Luxembourg need visas. You're not supposed to be allowed entry if you have Israeli or South African stamps in your passport, but in practice this does not seem to matter.**

Australians and New Zealanders need visas. Following the 1991 Gulf War, new visa

TUNISIAN EMBASSIES AND CONSULATES

ALGERIA 11 rue du Bois de Boulogne, Hydra, Algiers (☎02 601567);
6 rue Emir Abdelkader, Annaba (☎08 824448);
BP 280, Tébessa (☎08 974480).

BELGIUM 278 av Tervueren, Brussels 15 (☎02 771 7395).

CANADA 515 O'Connor St, Ottawa (☎613 237 0330).

DENMARK Strandboulevarden 130, Copenhagen, DK2100 (☎01 625010).

EGYPT 26 Sharia el Jazira, Zamalek, Cairo (☎02 340 4940).

FRANCE 25 rue Barbet de Jouy, 75007 Paris (☎1 4555 9598);
8 bd Athènes, 13001 Marseille (☎9150 2868).

GERMANY 2 Godesbergerallee 103, 5300 Bonn (☎0228 376983).

ITALY 7 Via Asmara, Rome (☎06 839 0748);
2 Piazza I Florio, Palermo (☎091 628996).

JAPAN 29-2 Ichibancho – Chiyoda-Ku, Tokyo102 (☎03 262 7716).

LIBYA Sharia Bashir Ibrahimi, PO Box 613, Tripoli (☎021 31051).

MALTA Dar Carthage, Qormi Road, Attard (☎498853).

MOROCCO 6 av de Fès, Rabat (☎07 30636).

NETHERLANDS Gentsestraat 98, The Hague (☎070 512251).

SPAIN Plaza Alonzo Martinez 3, Madrid (☎91 447 3516).

SWEDEN Drottningatan 73, Stockholm 11136 (☎08 236470).

UNITED KINGDOM 29 Prince's Gate, London SW7 1QG (Knightsbridge tube; ☎071 823 7749).

USA 1515 Massachusetts Ave, Washington DC 20005 (☎202 234 6644);
3401 Sacramento Street, San Francisco (☎415 922 9222).

restrictions were introduced. Visas are no longer issued at ports or borders, and applications take **two to three weeks** to process. Visas cost around £4 sterling, plus two photos and two forms to fill.

VISA EXTENSIONS

The practice for **extending a visa** varies, but is rarely easy. Go to the police in good time, with some proof that you have a reason for staying in the country and evidence that you can support yourself (take along all your exchange slips). Extensions usually take between two weeks and a month to process, during which time you will be without your passport. Once granted, they usually give three months' residence. An alternative and in many ways much simpler means of getting a renewal is to make a trip over the border to Algeria, Libya or even Sicily so that you can get a new tourist stamp on re-entry.

COSTS AND MONEY

The cost of travel in Tunisia compares well with Southern Europe – and increasingly so with Italy. You can get by quite easily on £80 a week, including good meals, reasonable hotel rooms and a fair amount of transport, while on £120 you would be moving into relative luxury. At the bottom end, camping out or staying in the cheaper medina hotels, you could survive on as little as £40.

Rooms are the most variable factor. A basic (unclassified) hotel will generally charge around £2–5 single and £4–7 double while one-star or two-star places may vary from £4–15 single, £7–20 double. A set **meal,** with (excellent) wine, in most local restaurants will put you back only around £6 a head, or you can fill up in hole-in-the-wall cafés for less than half that. **Transport** costs are moderate, and distances are not very great: Tunis–Sfax, perhaps the longest single journey you might think of making, costs under £7 by bus, train or *louage* – the shared taxis which are a standard way of getting around the country.

THE TUNISIAN DINAR

The **Tunisian dinar (TD)** is a soft currency – illegal to export from (or import into) the country. The **exchange rate** is fixed daily on a national basis (you can find it in the newspapers under *Cours des Devises);* at present one dinar is worth about 65p sterling, US$1.20, or FF6.50, which makes prices generally cheap for overseas visitors.

An **initial source of confusion** is the way the dinar is written. It is divided into 1000 millimes and small, fractional prices are usually expressed in terms of **millimes** – 1,500, for example, instead of 1.5. "Whole" dinar prices, however, are usually written as "1TD", rather than "1,000TD". For the sake of clarity, prices in the guide are all expressed in dinars so that, for example, seven hundred millimes appears as "0.7TD".

BRINGING MONEY

You are allowed to bring in unrestricted amounts of **foreign currency** and **travellers' cheques.** Thomas Cook, Visa and American Express are the best known cheques and are accepted at most banks and many hotels. **Credit cards** are of limited use outside tourist resorts, though they can sometimes be used for cash advances and are handy for items of major expense such as car hire – indeed sometimes essential for car hire deposits. They are also accepted by most hotels of two or more stars, and by the more upmarket restaurants. For some reason, Diners Club is the best known, but American Express, Visa and Access/Mastercard are all usable in the right places.

BANKS AND EXCHANGE

Bank **opening hours** are irritatingly limited: in summer (July to September) Mon–Fri 8–11am, closed in the afternoon; in winter, Mon–Thurs 8–11am and 2–4.15pm, Fri 8–11am and 1.30–3.15pm. In tourist areas banks will sometimes open outside standard hours for **money exchange** and you can often fall back on hotels (the bigger, posher ones are naturally most likely to change money for you). Always retain the receipts from your transactions for re-exchanging when you leave the country.

Away from tourist areas, exchange facilities can be few and far between and you'll sometimes find banks don't have the essential exchange rates. The local *STB* (Tunisia's "national" bank) is generally most reliable, and some *STB* branches will let you draw cash on Access/Mastercard. As a very last resort, if you have hard cash, you could try asking around the local *louage* (shared taxi) station, especially if it runs to any destinations beyond Tunisia's borders.

Carrying some **foreign currency** around with you in cash (French francs and US dollars rather than sterling) is a good idea. Any bank will take them and plenty of individuals too. Post offices will also often change cash, including Scottish banknotes.

Finally, it's as well to know that the **black market** offers rates only marginally better than official ones. If you're buying something expensive like a carpet, however, you may be able to get the price down by offering foreign exchange instead of dinars.

LEAVING TUNISIA

There are strict regulations about the quantity of dinars that you can **change back when leaving** the country. You're allowed to reconvert up to thirty percent of the total amount you can prove you have changed since being in Tunisia – with an upper limit of 100TD. This means keeping an eye on the number of dinars you're likely to have on you when you leave, particularly if you've changed large amounts. It also means you should keep all the **exchange receipts** you're given.

Note too, that if you leave by air or sea on a ticket purchased in Tunisia, you will require a **Bon de Passage**, which is a slip of paper certifying that the ticket was bought with money changed in a bank. You will first have to get a form from the ticket agent to give to the bank. But before changing your money, make sure the bank in question will issue you with the *bon*, as you cannot buy the ticket without it. The money you change when getting a *bon de passage* cannot count as part of the sum from which you're allowed to reconvert thirty percent, so it's best not to change money for other business in the same transaction.

HEALTH AND INSURANCE

Inside the country, most drugs are available but expensive; take any basics you might need, including stomach pills, suntan lotion and similar ordinary items. **Travel insurance, especially to cover your health, is a basic precaution.**

INOCULATIONS AND HEALTH ISSUES

Doctors vary about which **inoculations** they advise but many will suggest protection against typhoid, hepatitis A, cholera, polio and tetanus. The cholera jab, in particular, is now considered to be next to useless by many authorities, but many GPs like to keep their patients up to date with polio and tetanus as a matter of course. In any case, most visitors survive quite happily without having the full works, but the injections are a small price to pay for the security they provide. Tunisia is on the fringe of the **malaria** risk zone, too, and weekly pills are probably worthwhile.

You may also consider the new **rabies** jab. It's expensive but if you're travelling by bicycle or walking, when you might attract the attention of dogs, it may be a wise precaution. The alternative – if you get bitten – is a course of painful jabs in the stomach. Remember, any mammal can carry the disease, which, if untreated, is a certain killer, and a scratch is enough to transmit it.

MEDICAL CARE IN TUNISIA
Medical care is of a high standard (most doctors are trained in France or Belgium). But state hospitals are filthy and overcrowded and basic services like food are not provided. Minor problems can be dealt with by any *infirmerie* (a surgery with a nurse) of which there's one in every town, and several in bigger ones. The larger towns all have hospitals, and also *cliniques* (small private hospitals, usually more pleasant than state-run ones). **Pharmacies** administer most kinds of medicine, including some only available on prescription in Europe, and can often advise you about minor ailments too. Pharmacists usually speak French but rarely English so you should learn a few appropriate phrases if you have special needs.

COMMON COMPLAINTS
Two complaints in particular are liable to afflict pampered constitutions: stomach upsets and heat. Most people experience some kind of **stomach problem** during a visit but, short of starving, there's little you can do to avoid it – unfamiliar micro-organisms are present in everything you consume. Some people drink only bottled water, or use water purifying tablets, and still have trouble; others drink tap water and come through unscathed. The best policy is probably just to avoid obviously dirty food, wash all fresh fruit and vegetables, always try to wash your hands before eating and otherwise hope for the best.

If you do go down with diarrhoea, it's essential to **replace the fluid which is lost** because dehydration can strike very quickly. Hot, sweet Tunisian tea is ideal, as are prickly pears. In serious cases, or with children, remember that dissolving rehydration salts in water helps your body absorb it. Failing that, half a teaspoon of table salt with four of sugar in a litre of water per day should see you alright. If symptoms persist for several days, especially if you get painful cramps too, or if blood or mucus appear in your stools, seek medical advice.

Never underestimate **Tunisia's heat**, especially in the south. A hat is an essential precaution and, especially if you have very light skin, you should also consider taking a suntan lotion with a very high screening factor: this far south the sun really is higher (and therefore stronger) than in northern latitudes.

HIV INFECTION
Although sexual encounters between Tunisians and tourists are not particularly common – or likely – it's as well to know that the incidence of **HIV infection** and full-blown AIDS in Tunisia is almost certainly far higher than officially known or declared. Returning emigrant workers are particularly at risk. From the point of view of travellers, a **holiday affair** in one of the resorts is more likely to put you at risk. Take condoms with you.

INSURANCE
You'll have to pay for any **health treatment** you receive in Tunisia so, at around £20 for a month's cover, a policy really does make sense. You can buy travel insurance from all travel agents, but it's a good idea to phone around for the best deal. Remember, it may cover you for **risks against which you're already insured** (for example, theft of or damage to your property, which may be covered under an "All Risks" clause if you have a household policy). Be sure to keep a note of your policy number somewhere safe; **notify the insurance company** if you intend to make a claim; and keep your receipts or other evidence of treatment paid for. The same goes for theft of property: you'll need to produce documentary evidence from the local police – basically a copy of their official report.

MAPS AND INFORMATION

Included in the guide are maps and plans of the main towns, cities and sites – and most other places where we think you'll need one. They can be supplemented with free hand-outs from the Organisation National de Tourisme Tunisien (ONTT), who print a reasonable general map of the country and a number of local town plans. Also availa-

ble, though to be read with occasional irony, are a range of glossy pamphlets and reasonably full lists of hotels (usually including most of the unclassified ones).

The ONTT have a main office in Tunis (1 av Mohamed V; ☎341077) and others throughout the country, but you can pick up most of their material in advance before setting out.

There are also locally run tourist information offices called **Syndicats d'Initiative**, which give out information and are often friendlier and more informative than the ONTT.

MAPS

It's worth buying a large-scale map of Tunisia. The most reliable of these are the Austrian *Freytag & Berndt* Tunisia, the *Michelin* (no. 972: Algérie-Tunisie), and the German-produced *Hildebrand* Tunisia. They are best bought in advance. In Britain – and probably worldwide – the best map shop is *Stanfords*, 12–14 Long Acre, London WC2 (☎071 836 1321).

ONTT OFFICES ABROAD

UNITED KINGDOM: 77a Wigmore Street, **London** W1H 9LJ (☎071 224 5561).

BELGIUM: Galerie Ravenstein 60, **Brussels** 1000 (☎02 511 1142).

GERMANY: Am Hauptbahnhof 6, **Frankfurt** 6000 (☎0609 231891/2); Steinstraße 23, **Dusseldorf** 4000 (☎0211 84218).

NETHERLANDS : Muntplein 2111, **Amsterdam** 1012 WR (☎020 224971/2).

SWEDEN: Almlövsgatan 3, **Stockholm** 11451 (☎08 66 71765).

ONTT also have offices in the Tunisian embassies in **Washington DC** (☎202 234 6644), **Ottawa** (☎613 237 0330) and **Tokyo** (☎03 262 7716).

GETTING AROUND

Many visitors to Tunisia are discouraged from exploring the country by the high cost

of car hire – around £300 a week – but it's possible to reach almost nearly every town detailed in this guide by some form of scheduled transport. Admittedly, this may be slow, sometimes infrequent, and occasionally very crowded, but it's reliable enough and distances are relatively short.

The one general warning to bear in mind is that transport services tend to stop at around 5pm – except in the far south, where local transport can dry up even

earlier, but buses for Tunis leave either late at night or early in the morning. On remote routes your only choice may be the early-morning market bus.

BUSES

Buses, the most popular form of transport, are comprehensive but complicated. They are run by different companies: **SNTRI** (*Société Nationale de Transport Rural et Interurban*) and several regional rivals known as **SRT**s (*Société Régionale des Transports*). These usually have predictable names such as *SRT Beja*, or *SRT du Gouvernorat de Medenine*, but one or two are called things like *SORETRAS* (Sfax) and *SOTREGAMES* (Gabes).

SNTRI run services in and around Tunis, linking Tunis to almost every town in the country at least once a day. Each *SRT* runs local services within its own region, and some northern ones also run services to Tunis. Only a few long-distance services don't end up in Tunis (such as Sousse–Le Kef), making it much easier to move towards or away from Tunis than across the country.

The different companies often refuse to recognise each others' existence, so it's important to ask at each individual office to be sure of finding all the buses on a given route. Some bigger towns have a central bus station but often the companies operate from their own separate locations (detailed in the guide). *SNTRI* generally have departure lists displayed – with most others it's a case of persistent questioning. On some routes there are *Confort* class services. These are less crowded and faster than the standard buses and the premium is slight, about twenty percent on top of the normal fare.

When travelling in the daytime, it's a good idea to consider which side of the bus the sun will be on, and choose a seat accordingly. Going from east to west, the sun will be on the left; from north to south, it will be on the left in the morning and the right in the afternoon.

LOUAGES

Louages – large shared taxis, usually battered Peugeot estates – are the fastest form of long-distance transport as they operate non-stop. They leave as soon as the full complement of five passengers has appeared, or when the driver gets tired of waiting. If the car moves off without a full complement and you are the only passenger(s), make sure the driver realises you are paying only

the rate for one *place*. Allowing for five passengers the fares are fixed at a rate a little higher than for buses. The routes are also fixed, though of course you can hire a *louage* privately to go to a specific destination. If you think a *louage* driver is overcharging you, ask to see the official *tarif* (price list), which all louages must carry by law.

The louages operate from informal stations, liable to be elusive to the uninitiated foreigner – often a particular garage or backstreet yard. In larger towns, there are different terminals for different destinations. Once you've found the right place (they are detailed in the text, but they often change), ask for your destination – the signs in the cars only indicate where they are licensed. If you make enough noise, someone will find you a car or show you where to wait. Competition for seats can be fierce: you may find yourself joining a tense group of twenty people awaiting the next arrival, in which case the time-honoured technique is to sprint for the car when you see it in the distance, grab a door-handle, and hang on until the car stops. If you're carrying luggage, your only chance in this situation is to abandon it in the struggle for a seat then load it when the dust has settled. If this is too much for you, someone may get you a place for a little backsheesh. *Louages* will only stop for you on the road if they have a spare seat – the police are tough on drivers who carry more than the legal limit of five passengers.

In addition to inter-city *louages*, local **pick-up vans**, known officially as *transports rurals*, run from large towns to the surrounding villages. These have no limit on passenger numbers and are very cheap, but rather uncomfortable.

TRAINS

Only a small proportion of the railway lines (built by the French) have passenger **trains**. They're run by the **SNCFT** (*Société Nationale des Chemins de Fer Tunisiens*) and cost about the same as *louages*, slightly more than buses and usually run more-or-less on schedule. Some routes, like the air-conditioned service down the coast, are excellent – and a real boon in summer. Prices are graded according to the type of service, and all have First and Second Class. Most long-distance services, especially the *climatisé* (air-conditioned), can get crowded in midsummer and should be booked in advance if possible. Even for ordinary services, turn up early to be sure of buying a ticket – if you board without, you have to pay double. The only train actually called an

"Express" is the *Trans-Maghreb* to Algiers (see p.380). Thomas Cook's Overseas Timetable gives a complete and up-to-date list of services. You can consult it in any public reference library.

As well as *SNCFT* services, there is a local railway called the TGM from Tunis to some of its suburbs (see p.43), and a metro in the city itself.

HITCHING

Hitching is generally good in Tunisia, for men at least. There are no problems with officialdom, and although there is remarkably little traffic, in remote areas almost anything that passes will stop. In some of these areas, hitching is a semi-institutionalised form of public transport – especially in the ubiquitous Peugeot 404 pick-up trucks (*Quatre cents quatre bachées*), and a small contribution is expected. If there are other passengers, watch how much they pay. If you're on your own, you can either try to agree on a price in advance or risk disagreement at the end just in case the driver tries to rip you off; in fact this is very unlikely and waiving payment is much more common. There are no hard and fast rules, but the fare should be a little less than you would pay by bus. Outside remote areas like this, Tunisians do not often hitch, but traffic will usually stop for you anyway, and rarely charge you.

It can be hard to hitch out of **Hammamet**, and you have to walk a long way out of **Tunis** and **Sfax**, but other routes are fairly unproblematic. In the remote areas of the south, particularly the Ksour, local people get around by a wide and miscellaneous variety of means, details of which are given in the relevant chapters. **Women** hitching alone or together can pick up lifts with car-hiring tourists around Cap Bon or Jerba – but elsewhere it's not advisable unless you join up with at least one male.

BIKES

Tunisia's terrain and climate are ideally suited most of the year to **bicycles and motorbikes** (though you may get soaked in winter and spring, and strong winds can make cycling hard work). The only drawback is maintenance: there are very few motorbikes in the country (though thousands of mopeds), and bicycles are common but basic, so you'll have to bring any specialised spare parts along. Bicycles and occasionally mopeds can be hired in big towns, but, frustratingly, only for use in the town or along the beach. If you're staying some time in Tunisia and want a motorbike for transport it's cheaper to buy abroad and import than buy locally. **Trains** will carry a bicycle for about the same fare as a passenger; **buses** usually charge about half the passenger fare.

DRIVING AND CAR HIRE

In such a small country **driving** ought to be the ideal way to get around. If you can afford to bring a car with you this is true. Unfortunately **car hire charges** in Tunisia are phenomenal – among the highest on the Mediterranean. Even the smallest Renault will set you back 400TD a week and officially, at least, it's illegal to carry more than three passengers. Even at this price they'll give you a clapped-out car and if it breaks down that's your problem. Nor is petrol cheap at prices very similar to those in Britain. If you decide to go ahead, you'll need to be over 21 and have held a licence for at least a year. You should also check the insurance and the small print very thoroughly. From this point of view, if not price, it might be a good idea to go for a big agency such as *Europcar*. There are cheap private companies (*Garage Lafayette*, 85 Ave de la Liberté, Tunis, for instance) but few bargains: if a car is cheap to hire it may not be very well maintained.

Despite these hassles and expenses driving has many **advantages**. You can visit the smaller and remoter villages seen only through dusty windows by those trapped in public transport and you can make rewarding contacts with local people, especially if you pick up hitch-hikers.

To bring **your own vehicle**, you will have to be over 21 and carry documents proving your ownership of the vehicle, an acceptable driving licence (British for example) or an international one, and a green card covering Tunisia (if it doesn't, you can buy insurance at the frontier).

DRIVING CONDITIONS

Main **roads** are straight and surfaced, often lined with shady eucalyptus trees, and driving is not as bad as people tend to make out, except, perhaps, in the crowded cities – Tunis in particular is best avoided. Tunisia **drives on the right** and vehicles coming onto a roundabout or traffic circle have right of way over those already on it. **Speed limits** are (in theory, and unless otherwise indicated) 90km/hr (55mph) in the country and 60km/hr (37mph) in built-up areas, 110km/hr (68mph) on the country's only motorway from Tunis to Bir Bou Rekba, and 70km/hr (43mph) on the isle of

Jerba. However fast you're going, though, it's customary to slow down when passing **highway patrols**. It's a good idea to have your papers available because there are frequent road checks, especially in the south and around Gafsa, and if you get stopped for speeding you have to pay on the spot. One practice that's initially disconcerting is that the police often flag down drivers to get a lift. It's best not to argue, and if you're not going their way they won't force the matter.

The biggest potential problem is the state of some of the **rougher roads,** especially in the south. Some are obviously difficult, but drifting sand on others can be insidious. Also, tarmac can be rather narrow and lorries tend to force cars off the edge of the road, accepted practice but a little worrying at first. Another hazard, especially when passing through towns, is the apparent lack of road sense among pedestrians, cyclists and moped riders, who all seem to meander quite happily down the middle of the road as if they'd never heard of the automobile; you will almost certainly end up using your horn more than you do at home, but you will also have to reduce speed and keep your eyes peeled, especially at dusk.

In the south, many of the routes are **unsurfaced roads**. Their condition varies and many are passable in any ordinary car, while others require an off-road vehicle. In any case, you will not be able to drive down them at the same sort of speed as on a tarmac road: even if it seems quite easy, remember that the road surface can change unexpectedly, and boulders can appear as if from nowhere. Car hire firms don't permit their vehicles to be driven on unsurfaced roads, and can hold you liable for "any damage caused to the vehicle through driving on dirt tracks". If you intend driving into the desert, see the box on p.314.

In case of **breakdown**, always carry a good supply of water and, if you're planning a longer journey, food and blankets. There are plenty of places that will repair a puncture cheaply: look out for workshops with tyres outside, especially on the way into and out of towns. Mechanics are cheap and can sort out most problems.

FLIGHTS

Tunisia's size makes **internal flights** something of an extravagance. For the time saved, you will miss out on the satisfaction of seeing the scene changing from one region to another. However, flights are worth bearing in mind for the odd journey back to Tunis, say from the south. Tickets are relatively cheap (under £15 from Jerba to Tunis) if also, in summer at least, sparse; to rely on a flight it's wise to book well ahead.

TRANSPORT IN TOWNS

The cheapest way to get around big towns is by **local bus.** These can be very crowded (you often have to fight your way on and off) and stops are not always sign-posted. Useful routes are indicated in the text of the guide, but it's often easier and more interesting to walk.

Taxis are very good value for small groups. They all have meters so there's no need to fix a price before you go, except that rides are not metered at night, and can cost a lot more then, depending on your bargaining skills. You can arrange a tour (around several sites for example) by renting the taxi for the day. In this case, fix the price first. By law taxis can only take four people but if there are more of you it is possible to use a larger (and more expensive) estate car, a *louage* for example.

SLEEPING

Tunisia's more expensive hotels are geared primarily to the package holiday trade. The country is adapting to the growth in independent travel – but it's a slow process. In all the main tourist centres, and in most sizeable towns in the interior, you can find rooms in all hotel categories, but in smaller places there may only be a choice between a very basic or a fairly pricey hotel. And in midsummer, any kind of room in the more

HOTEL CLASSIFICATION

Classified hotels, officially considered suitable for tourists, are graded from 1 to 4 stars, with widely ranging prices within each category:

1-star, approximately 10TD–20TD a double, often including breakfast.

2-star, approximately 15TD–30TD a double, including breakfast.

3-star, approximately 25TD–50TD a double, including breakfast.

4-star, approximately 50TD–80TD a double, including breakfast.

Deluxe (*4*L*), 60TD upwards, not always including breakfast.

popular towns can be hard to find on the spot – though if you get really stuck someone local will probably invite you to stay rather than see the country's reputation for hospitality diminished.

CHEAP HOTELS

Below the 1-stars there is a range of hotels very suitable for budget travellers, even if not officially regarded as suitable for tourists. These **unclassified hotels**, usually concentrated in a town's *medina* – just ask for an *auberge* (inn) or *Hôtel Tunisien* – differ widely. The best of them, often colonial relics, have high ceilings and creaking fans, and are very respectable: the equivalent of a D-class, say, in Italy or Greece and charging 3–10TD for a double room. Many of the cheapest ones (2TD per person), though, can be more rough – and they're sometimes closed to, or dangerous for, "unaccompanied" women. In these you'll often be expected to share a room, or fill it, or even pay for any beds (as many as four) which remain empty. However, there are good (and perfectly safe) places even in this range – price is no guide – and, for men at least, they're a useful standby as you can nearly always find a bed.

Women will have to play it by ear much of the time. If Tunisian women are staying in a hotel, that should be a good sign: if all the clientele are men, think again. Male fellow travellers may be prepared to help out by posing as "husbands" or "brothers", but this may not excise some nuisances such as the presence of peeping

Toms when you use the hotel's shared shower – and relying on male tourists can, obviously, plunge you into just the compromising situations you were trying to avoid.

PENSIONS AND YOUTH HOSTELS

Hotels are supplemented by two other cheap forms of accommodation: *pensions* and youth hostels. **Pensions** are found mainly in the Cap Bon area. At their best these really are *pensions familiales* – cheap and friendly places – and even at their worst they're quite adequate.

There are some thirty **youth hostels** in Tunisia, five of them run by Tunisia's Youth Hostel Association and the rest attached to youth centres (*Maisions des Jeunes*) run by the Ministry of Culture. These charge 4TD a night, as much as a cheap hotel, and are usually situated on the edge of town near the municipal stadium. They tend to look like barracks and feel like changing-rooms, operate curfews and turf you out early in the morning. They usually seize your passport on arrival so you have to track it down before you can leave, and can't easily use it for changing money while staying. Women's accommodation is separate – which is a boon if you're a woman travelling alone – and they can be excellent places for meeting young Tunisians, many of whom are dying to practise their English. YHA hostels charge less than *Maison des Jeunes* hostels; they often have food, and tend to be better run, less heavy-handed with the rules and regulations, more central and often housed in interesting old buildings. Recommended in particular are the hostels in **Tunis Medina**, **Gabes** and **Houmt Souk** (Jerba). Those at **Remel** (Bizerte), **Kelibia** and **Aïn Soltane** (near Ghardimaou) are also a cut above the norm.

CAMPING

Although there is a mere handful of official **campsites** in the country, there are many unofficial ones and it's almost always possible to arrange something. The official sites cost around 2TD a head; unofficial ones often a little less. Many youth hostels and hotels will also let people camp in their grounds and **camping sauvage** ("wild") – with a minimum of discretion – is often a positive option. While **sleeping out** on the main tourist beaches (Hammamet, Nabeul, Sousse, Monastir) is either expressly forbidden or likely to be cut short by the police, there should be few problems elsewhere and it's common practice around Bizerte, Raf Raf and other places. In the interior it's a good idea to ask the permission of the land owner. If you can't find the owner, ask the local police, who are very unlikely to say no, or will suggest an alternative site. Informing the police of your presence will also help avoid misunderstandings, especially if you're in a sensitive area such as an international frontier.

MUSLIMS, ARABIC SPEAKERS AND JEWISH PILGRIMS

For **Muslims** or anyone who **speaks Arabic** the opportunities for cheap accommodation are wider. Most likely you will move from one hospitable family to another but if you're ever stuck, try the **local mosque or zaouia.** They often have hostel accommodation where pilgrims can stay – always an interesting place to meet people. **Jews** on pilgrimage, particularly in Jerba (see p.290) may find similar help from the local Jewish community.

PRICES QUOTED IN THIS BOOK

The pricing system for official hotels is complicated, with supplements for singles, high season, and even sea views. As far as possible, the guide gives the following information for each hotel: its **star rating** if it's classified (eg 1*: one star),

prices for a normal **single and double room** (eg 5TD/8TD), in low and high season if appropriate (there's a mid-season too: see box), and whether that includes breakfast (b&b) and any extra charges. Special rates are sometimes available for **half board** (HB: dinner, bed and breakfast) and **full board** (FB: all meals).

Out of the high season, prices can fall quite dramatically, occasionally by as much as half. Every hotel must display its official prices, usually in the form of a price per person in a double room, with a supplement for single occupancy. You have to multiply the first figure by two for a double room, and add the two figures together for the single occupancy price. Prices quoted, however, are the *maximum legal tariff* for foreign tourists. They may, however, charge less, so every price, especially out of season, is open to discussion, something **bargaining** enthusiasts can test out for themselves.

SEASONS

Seasons apply in general only at beach resorts. They vary slightly but are roughly as follows:

Low season: November to March.

High season: mid-June to mid-September (or sometimes only July–August).

Mid-season: April to June, and September to October.

EATING AND DRINKING

"Chilis were essential to the full glory of Kuss Kussu; but he did not expect mere Europeans to rise to such heights. And yet he'd known one really great Englishman, a

certain Captain Gordon, who could eat more chilis than any Arab."
Reginald Rankin, Tunisia (1930).

RESTAURANT MEALS

Eating out is not really an Arab tradition but the French presence and tourism have made inroads and there are now three distinct levels of eating establishment. In big cities and tourist centres you'll come across smart, essentially French **restaurants** offering meals of several courses; these can be excellent and are usually very good value. Every town also has less elaborate restaurants serving main dishes which are virtually indistinguishable from one place to the next – simple meat, chicken, fish and vegetables which

GLOSSARY OF TUNISIAN FOOD

French and Arabic names are given where possible, but often the French is used rather than the Arabic.

BASICS

L'addition/el fatura or el hisab	The bill	Couteau/sekina	Knife	Poivre/filfel	Pepper
Bouteille/darbooza	Bottle	Cuiliere/mirafa	Spoon	Sel/melha	Salt
Pain/khobs	Bread	Fourchette/farchita	Fork	Sucre/sukar	Sugar
Beurre/zibda	Butter	Huile/zit	Oil (invariably olive)	Cassecroûte/cassecroûte	Sandwich
Ouefs/adhma	Eggs			Salade/salata	Salad
Verre/keson	Glass	Olives/zitoun	Olives	Table/taula	Table

FISH

(in general, the French name is used, even when speaking Arabic)

Rouget/ trilya	Red mullet	Huîtres/ babush	Oysters	Homard/ fakrun b'har	Lobster
Thon/ ton	Tuna	Clovisses/ babush	Clams	Langouste/ fakrun b'har	Crawfish (rock lobster)
Mulet/ bowri	Mullet	Moules/ babush	Mussels		
Merou/ manani	Grouper	Crevettes/ qambri	Shrimp or prawns	Calmar/ subia	Squid
Loup de Mer/ karus	Perch			Poulpe/ qarnit	Octopus

MEAT AND POULTRY

Poulet/djaj	Chicken	Biftec/habra	Steak
Mouton or agneau/houli	Mutton or lamb	Foie/kibda	Liver
Boeuf/bakri	Beef	Brochette/ safud	Small kebab

VEGETABLES

Pommes frites/batata	Chips	Pois chiche/houmous	Chick-peas (garbanzo beans)
Pommes de terre/batata	Potatoes		
Haricots/loobia	Beans	Oignons/b'sal	Onions

TUNISIAN DISHES

Brik a' l'oeuf	One of Tunisia's great culinary curiosities – an egg fried inside a pastry envelope, the eating of which demands considerable ingenuity to avoid getting egg on your face. Sometimes made with tuna or vegetables, briks vary a lot in quality.
Chakchuka	Vegetable stew based on onions, peppers and chick-peas, usually topped with a fried egg.
Chorba	Soup. There are many varieties, but most are spicy and delicious.
Couscous (cousk-see)	The classic North African dish – steamed semolina grains, served with meat or fish, and vegetables.
Harissa	Hot red chilli sauce added liberally to almost everything.
Kamounia	Meat (lamb, beef and/or liver) stewed in a thick cumin sauce.
Kefteji	A vegetable stew like a spicy ratatouille, often served with meatballs.
Lablabi	Bread soaked in chick-pea broth, usually with a raw egg scrambled into it to cook, and spices added on top, sometimes with tuna. Very cheap – the worker's staple – and made in front of you so you can ask them to hold back on this or that.
Mechoui	Grilled meat.
Merguez	Spicy sausage – eat it well cooked!
Mermez	Mutton stew.
Ojja	Similar to a chakchuka, with egg scrambled into it .
Salade mechouia	Not a salad in the usual sense, but a mashed, spicy mix of roasted vegetables served cold.
Schewarma	Marinaded lamb kebab on a vertical spit, carved and served in a pitta bread. Looks like a doner kebab but is insulted by the comparison.
Tajine	No relation to its Moroccan namesake, Tunisian tajine is a kind of baked omelette or quiche.

SWEETS

Baklava	Honey-soaked flaky pastry with a honey-soaked nut filling – hazelnut is best.	Ftair	A Ghoumrassen speciality – deep-fried batter pancake, between a doughnut and a fritter, usually available in the morning.
Kab el ghazal (corne de gazelle)	A Tataouine speciality – pastry horn stuffed with chopped almond filling.	Halva	Sesame-based sweet common throughout the Middle East.
Draw	Lukewarm, dark grey porridge, topped by a strip of halva, spoonfuls of various coloured powders and a hunk of cake: served by some city cafés for breakfast and worth trying at least once.	Loukoum	Turkish delight.
		Mesfuf	Sweet couscous.
		Millefeuille	French cream pastry.
		Makroudh	A Kairouan speciality – honey-soaked semolina cake with a date centre.
		Youyou	Ring doughnut.

FRUIT AND NUTS

Dattes/t'mar	Dates	Grenade/rouman	Pomegranate
Orange/burtukal	Orange	Melon/battikh	Melon
Pomme/tufah	Apple	Fraises/fraulu	Strawberries
Citron/limoun	Lemon or lime	Cerises/hbmluk	Cherries
Raisins/ainab	Grapes	Pêche/khoukh	Peach
Figues/kermus	Figs	Amandes/louze	Almonds
Abricots/mishmash	Apricots	Noix/zouze	Walnuts
Figues de Barbarie/ hendi	Prickly pears (Barbary figs)	Pistaches/fozdok	Pistachios
		Cacahuètes/kakawiya	Peanuts

DRINKS

Bière/birra	Beer	Lait/halib	Milk
Thé/té or shai	Tea	Citronade/citronade	Real lemonade
Café/qahwa	Coffee	Lait de poule/halib djaj	Milk shake with egg-white
Eau/ma	Water	Jus/'asir	Juice
Vin/sharab	Wine		

are kept warm through the day. You soon learn to recognise these places, known throughout Tunisia as **gargotes**. Last and cheapest are the **rôtisseries** which despite their name do more frying than roasting: if you have a low tolerance of grease, you'll probably prefer the restaurants.

Rôtisseries are usually open all day, their food laid out behind the counter so you can just point at what you want. Restaurants are open mainly in the evening, and almost always display a menu – if it's in Arabic you can ask to go and look at the dishes; cheaper restaurants begin to close around 9pm, and the most popular dishes are often finished some time before then.

If there is a **starter** at a restaurant it will probably be soup (*chorba* – oily and very spicy), Tunisian salad (basically a finely chopped green salad), or a more specifically Tunisian dish such as *brik à l'oeuf* or *salade mechouia*.

TYPICAL MEALS

There are two levels of **main course**. For around 1TD you can get a starch-based dish (couscous, spaghetti, or beans) with only a little meat and a hot peppery sauce. Unexciting, but very filling, this is what most families eat at home. Paying anything from 1.5TD upwards, you get more meat or fish, usually served with a separate plate of fried potatoes. Both grilled meat *(brochettes)* and fish can be delicious. Bread (*khobs*) is always included, along with a little plate of hot, red sauce (*harissa*). There is rarely much to follow the main course except perhaps seasonal fruit.

VEGETARIAN FOOD

How you fare as a **vegetarian** in Tunisia depends on how strictly you avoid animal products. If you are completely vegan, you're going to have a very hard time of it. About the only things you'll be able to eat ready-cooked are chips and *lablabi* (and even then, you'll have to watch that no eggs or tuna get into it). You can get pizzas made up without cheese or you could live on a diet of bread and olives, but you're best advised to take a spirit stove and do your own cooking. Staples such as rice, dried beans and pasta are available at grocers and supermarkets, fresh vegetables are easy to find in markets, and "burning alcohol" (*alcool à brûler*) is widely available at hardware shops (camping gas cannisters much less so).

If you eat **eggs and dairy products**, you're increasing your range considerably: *brik*, *tajine*, and omelettes all become possible, and you have even more choice if you are prepared to eat fish and cheese. Even so, you will have to be watchful as the concept of vegetarianism is completely alien to most Tunisians, who may well not understand what you want.

Muslims eat meat with every meal (or aspire to) and you won't meet any Tunisian vegetarians. Nor do Tunisians exhibit much concern about animal welfare: at *Aid el Adha* most families will slaughter their own sheep and in abattoirs and markets animals are slaughtered *halal*, their throats cut without being stunned. So when you try to explain that you don't want meat with your couscous don't be surprised if you get a blank look. And don't be surprised either if you find meat added to vegetable dishes to "improve" them. You may also ask for a dish without meat, only to find that it's a meat dish with the lumps of meat (but not the gravy) removed. The fussier you are about this sort of thing, the harder it will be for you to eat out and the more you should consider taking a stove and cooking for yourself.

There is one other possible problem: **hospitality** is an extremely important part of Arab civilisation, and if you enter a Tunisian home, you're bound to be offered something to eat. Moreover, your host may be insulted if you don't eat it. Do bear this in mind if invited into someone's house.

PATISSERIES, SNACK FOOD AND BREAKFAST

Cafés are beginning to merge with **patisseries**, French-style pastry shops which serve elaborate cakes along with *citronade*. This is a refreshing drink made by putting whole lemons, skin and all, through a blender with sugar and water and straining the result. *Citronade* is a lifesaver in the summer heat, but only as safe as the water that goes into it. Some patisseries also serve other fresh fruit drinks made with a blender, including *lait de poule* ("chicken's milk"), a fresh fruit milkshake with egg white. If you don't want sugar in juices or milk shakes, make it clear from the start.

The pastries served by patisseries are rapidly replacing more traditional Arab and Berber sweets, usually soaked in honey. Patisseries and cafés are also becoming institutionalised as the place to eat **breakfast** – a croissant or dry cake with coffee. In less sophisticated areas some cafés still provide the traditional *ftair* and *draw*.

The **perennial snack meal** is a *cassecroûte*, a thick chunk of French bread filled with vegetables, olives, oil, and either egg, tuna or sausage. It's automatically spread with *harissa* sauce, a concentration of red peppers which makes the average curry taste anaemic; if you prefer to go without, specify *sans piquant* or *bilesh harissa*. *Cassecroûtes* can be bought at most *rôtisseries* and many bakeries.

Alternatively, grocers will often make up a **sandwich** for you when you buy the ingredients. Cheese is generally disappointing, though the soft white sheep's milk *maasoura*, similar to Italian *ricotta*, is worth a try, and sardines or tuna are other possible fillings.

The other ingredient of picnic meals, **fruit**, is one of Tunisia's greatest delights. Depending on the season you can gorge yourself on fresh oranges, figs, grapes, melon, dates, pomegranates, prickly pears, strawberries and cherries. Pomegranates are often served as a dessert, broken up in a dish with the bitter yellow pith removed; if you don't want sugar on top, say so when you order. The prickly pear, or "Barbary fig", was introduced into North Africa by the Spanish in the sixteenth century, after they brought it over from the Americas. In summer they are sold by the thousand from barrows –

immensely refreshing and, surprisingly perhaps, the first remedy to try for upset stomachs.

If you want to snack while you're out and about, **nuts** are available from shops everywhere – usually open quite late.

DRINKING

Wine, when available in restaurants, is good, and even the most expensive brands rarely cost more than £3 a bottle. *Haut Mornag, Sidi Rais* and *Koudjat* are all excellent table wines; *Grombalia* and *Tardi* very rough standbys, while Kelibia in Cap Bon produces a distinctive and unusual **dry muscat**. Except in the tourist hotels, wine is not served in restaurants on Fridays.

Other local drinks include the rather watery *Celtia* **beer**, ubiquitous **mineral waters** (*Safia, Aïn Garci* or *Aïn Oktor*), standard fizzy drinks generically known as *gazouz;* and two **strong spirits**. Unless you have an asbestos throat it's best to drink *boukha* (derived from figs) in the standard combination with Coke; *thibarine*, a date liqueur, is more palatable. *Laghmi* (palm wine) is the sap of the date palm milked from the tree. It ferments in 24 hours, and both fresh and fermented versions are available around the oases in season. If you're offered *laghmi* down south be sure it's okay before drinking as it is sometimes mixed with dirty water or left too long. *Sirops*, distilled from fruit (pomegranate, orange, lemon, fig, and even pistachio), are rather sickly in taste and garish in colour but make good mixers.

You may find alcohol at a few westernised cafés, but most Tunisian drinking is done in **bars** – exclusively male and still with an air of the bootleg about them, dense with smoke and invariably deafening. Still, they often serve excellent little snacks (melon, olives, even *brochettes)*. In the European-style bars of the bigger hotels the drinks are more expensive but the atmosphere more relaxed and even Tunisian women can

sometimes be seen. If you're a lone drinker you can buy alcohol in the larger supermarkets but you mustn't carry the bottles around town in public view; take a bag which you can close.

COFFEE AND TEA

Coffee-drinking in the ubiquitous card-playing cafés is a national pastime. Perhaps as a result of French colonialism, the coffee can be very good. Coffee (*qahwa* in Arabic, *café* in French) comes in several forms. *Express* is Italian-style espresso and almost as good as across the water. *Café au lait, café crème* or *qahwa bi halib* is usually not espresso, and comes with a lot of milk. If you want an espresso version of this, ask for a *crème express*. *Capucin* is not a cappuccino, just an espresso with a little milk, like a Spanish *cortado* or Italian *macchiato*. Finally, *Café Maure* or *Café Turc* is Turkish coffee – finely ground coffee brought to the boil and served with the grounds still in it, often perfumed with rose water. Two spoons of sugar are usually assumed – to avoid them, ask for *sukar kalil* (a little sugar) or *bilesh sukar* (without sugar).

Tea is either black (*té ahmar* in Arabic, *thé rouge* in French) or green with mint (*té akhdar* in Arabic, *thé vert* in French). The latter is sometimes served with pine nuts or almonds. Unfortunately, it is most commonly made by boiling the leaves in water, then pouring it into a pot with massive quantities of sugar and leaving it to stew for hours on a charcoal stove (*canoun*) which every household possesses for the purpose. The result is a powerful brew of almost pure tannin and sugar – said to result in cases of "tea poisoning" and even death – and too pungent for most unhabituated tastes.

Tunisian cafés still supply the traditional **hookah pipe** (*chicha*), filled with half-burned tobacco mixed with honey. It is something of an acquired taste, but if you smoke you should certainly try it.

DISABLED TRAVELLERS

Facilities for people with disabilities are little developed in Tunisia, and disabled Tunisians are often reduced to begging, although families are usually very supportive. Blindness is more common than in the West, and sighted Tunisians are generally used to helping blind people find their way

and get on and off public transport at the right stop. Wheelchairs, on the other hand, are unusual, and there is little in the way of wheelchair access, though the Sfax–Kerkennah ferry is an exception.

Bus and train travel will be difficult because of the steps that have to be negotiated, but *louage* travel is more feasible if you can stake a claim on the front seat, assuming there is a helper to get you in and out. You should also be able to get on and off planes with a lift, but check this with the airline or tour operator.

You're likely to find travel with a package tour much easier than full independence. *Thomson's* run a "Care Line" on ☎071 387 9697 ext. 4242, to advise people with disabilities on specific travel arrangements with them. *Panorama Tunisia Experience, Cadogan, Cosmos, Horizon, Intasun* and *Sunspot* also claim to cater for travellers with disabilities, but you should contact any operator and inform them of your exact needs before making a booking. You should also make sure you are covered by any insurance policy you take out.

The following hotels claim to cater for disabled people: The *Médi Sea* (☎01 293030) in Borj Cedria (Greater Tunis), the *Lido* (☎02 85786) and *Le Prince* (☎02 85470) in Nabeul, and the *El Hana Beach* (☎03 26900) and *Marhaba Beach* (☎03 40112) in Sousse. Again, you should check with them before booking. If you use a wheelchair, beach hotels are generally much more practical than cheap city centre ones, which tend to have steep staircases and narrow corridors.

Useful contacts include: in the UK, *RADAR*, 25 Mortimer Street, London W1N 8AB (☎071 637 5400) for information, and *Holiday Care Service*, 2 Old Bank Chambers, Station Road, Horley, Surrey RH6 9HW (☎0293 774535), who may be able to match you up with a helper/travelling companion. In Tunisia, the dispiritingly named *Association Générale des Insuffisants Moteurs* (*AGIM*), 1 rue Vergers, Khaznadar, Tunis (☎01 520365) is worth contacting if you have specific enquiries.

TRAVELLING WITH CHILDREN

Tunisians, even more than other Mediterranean people, love kids. Travelling with small children in Tunisia, you may find that people will frequently come up to admire them, to compliment you on them, and to caress them. Children are very important, and numerous, in Tunisian society, and people are not really considered complete adults until they have at least one child.

Hotels in Tunisia usually give a reduction of thirty to forty percent for children aged under eight or ten, though this varies with each hotel and you may have to negotiate: obviously, a child staying in your room will cost much less than a separate room. Beach hotels often have facilities like playgrounds and children's pools; city hotels are far less likely to cater specifically for children.

Of items you might consider taking, **disposable nappies** – *Peaudouce* is the commonest brand – are available at most chemists and larger pharmacies stock a wider range of items. You may want to take along some **dried baby food** just in case; you can mix this with hot water which any café will supply you with. Bear in mind that Tunisian food can be very spicy, and you will probably want them to hold back on the *harissa* when serving your children. Remember to take high factor **sunscreen** for delicate skins.

For touring, hiking or walking, child-carrier **backpacks** such as the *Tommy Lightrider* are ideal, start at £30 and can weigh less than 2kg. If the child is small enough, a fold-up buggy is also well worth packing – especially if s/he will sleep in it (while you have a meal or a drink…).

MEDIA

Tunisia is almost completely bilingual, so if you're competent in either national language you can keep in close touch with what's happening. You should have little trouble following international news in the local newspapers or on radio or TV – though the quality in terms of real reporting and

analysis is not high. Foreign newspapers, and even TV, are available in any case.

NEWSPAPERS AND MAGAZINES

The three daily **French language newspapers**, *La Presse, l'Action* and *Le Temps* stay close to the Party line: *l'Action* almost slavishly, *La Presse* less so. *Le Temps* is perhaps the most substantial. They all carry listings of cultural events, exchange rates, bus, train and plane departures from Tunis, and TV and Tunis cinema listings.

Periodicals, less restricted than the daily press, carry interesting items from a more radical standpoint: *Jeune Afrique*, published weekly in France but with a Tunisian editor, is excellent (its credibility enhanced by occasional government bannings). The bi-monthly Women's Journal, *Nissa*, which began publication in 1985, is in Arabic and French.

Foreign newspapers can be bought, a day late, at newsagents and big hotels in all tourist areas (*Le Monde* almost everywhere). In the resort areas, most British national dailies are available, as is the *Herald Tribune*.

RADIO AND TV

There are plenty of **French-language radio stations**. *Radio Monte Carlo* is popular for music. The *BBC World Service* in **English** can be picked up from 05.00–23.15hrs GMT on 15.07MHz (19.91m), but you may get better reception morning and evening on 12.095MHz (24.8m) or in the evening on 9.41MHz (31.88m).

There are two **local TV channels**: one in Arabic, one in French. The latter is a Tunisian version of the French *Antenne 2*. The news programme, *Téléjournal*, is at 8pm. The Italian station *RAI Uno* is also available, and other French and Italian channels can sometimes be picked up. TV schedules are published daily in *La Presse*, *l'Action* and *Le Temps*.

POST AND PHONES

Post and telecommunications in Tunisia are easily up to international standards and you should have little cause to complain. Letters arrive reasonably quickly and rarely go astray, while international phone calls are a piece of cake with direct dialling, immediate connection and reasonable charges. Indeed, Tunisia compares very favourably in this respect with much of southern Europe.

POST OFFICE HOURS AND POSTAL SERVICES

Post offices (PTT; "pé-té-té") in large towns tend to follow **city opening hours** (Mon–Sat 8am–6pm in summer, 7am–1.30pm in winter; Sun 9–

11am all year), while those in villages and small towns follow **country opening hours** (winter Mon–Thurs 8am–noon & 3–6pm, Fri & Sat 8am–12.30pm; summer Mon–Sat 7.30am–12.30pm). During **Ramadan**, post offices are open Mon–Sat 8am–2pm, with Sunday hours unaffected.

Postal services are very reliable; **letters** to Europe and Britain rarely take more than a week, to North America and Australasia around two weeks. The parcel service is slower but equally reliable.

For **Poste Restante** address letters clearly "Tunis R.P., Rue Charles de Gaulle, Tunis" (the main post office) or to any local post office, marked "R.P." (for *Recette Postale*). To collect it, you'll need some form of identification.

PHONE CALLS

It is almost as easy to make an **international phone call** as a local one. In most towns you can dial direct on a coin phone (save up those dinar coins) at the PTT or a "Taxiphone" office. The latter is a sort of shop where you can phone Tunisian or international numbers; they're usually open later than the PTT and have plenty of change on hand. In one or two places, you make the call without coins and then pay on completion. Either way, it's rarely difficult. Three minutes to the British Isles currently costs around 3TD, to North America 6TD, and to Australasia 9TD. First dial the international code (see box), followed by the

TUNISIAN PHONE CODES

The 01 zone has six-digit numbers; others are five-digit.

☎01 – Tunis region

☎02 – Bizerte to Nabeul

☎03 – Sousse to Mahdia

☎04 – Sfax region

☎05 – Gabes and all points south

☎06 – Gafsa region

☎07 – Kairouan region

☎08 – Le Kef and region

INTERNATIONAL PHONE CODES

From Tunisia to:

UK	☎00 44
Irish Republic	☎00 353
USA and Canada	☎00 1
Australia	☎00 61
New Zealand	☎00 64

To Tunisia from:

UK	☎010 216
Irish Republic	☎010216
USA and Canada	☎ 011 216
Australia	☎0011 216
New Zealand	☎00 216

area code – leaving out any initial zeros. An occasional problem in larger towns is waiting for a booth: in summer, 2–5pm is an off-peak period.

Internal calls are not expensive: you will need hundred-milleme coins, which are taken by all local pay phones. The system is fairly efficient, with area codes used in the normal way (see box).

To call Tunisia from abroad, dial the international access code plus 216 for Tunisia, plus the local code, omitting the zero.

MOSQUES, MUSEUMS AND SITES

Westerners may visit mosques and religious buildings in Tunisia (unlike Morocco) but it is not, and never has been, an easy business. A few of the major tourist attractions are open at specified hours, but in 1972 a law was passed forbidding non-Muslims entrance to the prayer-halls of mosques. This concession to religious feelings was the result of the behaviour of some tourists, who still parade in the Great Mosque at Kairouan as though it were a zoo.

VISITING ISLAMIC BUILDINGS

For some well-touristed mosques you don't even have to be decently dressed, but obviously you show a serious lack of respect if you wander into a mosque in scanty attire. At Kairouan you're given a gown to cover arms, legs and (sometimes for women) head.

According to **religious regulations**, a woman entering a mosque should be covered from her neck to her ankles and wrists; she should also cover her hair and not wear trousers. A man should be covered from his torso to below his knees (so T-shirts, but not shorts, are all right for men).

Mosques **off the tourist trail** can be more tricky, and older people will often flatly refuse you entry. Students and younger people are more helpful and often if you hang around outside someone will ask if you want to be taken in. Chances are your guide will have to argue with an older guardian – but at least while this is going on you can take a look round before gracefully retreating. Occasionally, you'll be allowed into a prayer hall, in which case you must take off your shoes. Remember, mosques are ritually clean and no Tunisian would consider entering without washing thoroughly. It is a bad idea to try to visit mosques against the will of local people: religion is taken very seriously here.

The **zaouias** – cult centres – are slightly different in that they are private institutions. Unless Arabic-speaking or Muslim, you're most unlikely to be allowed into a *zaouia* which is still in use, but many are disused and either deserted or used as domestic residences. This goes too for **medersas** – Islamic colleges. How much you impose on the occupants of secularised buildings is a personal decision: a courteous enquiry, however, can't do any harm, and many people are only too pleased to show visitors around.

ARCHAEOLOGICAL SITES AND MUSEUMS

Archaeological sites are generally open Tues–Sun 8am–5pm. Most are closed on Mondays (sometimes Sundays) and on Muslim holidays. **Museums** vary but Tues–Sun 9am–4pm is quite typical. A student card *may* get you free admis-

sion, but it's unpredictable. For **photography** in museums you have to buy another ticket, and tripods (and any other professional-looking equipment, including sometimes flash) can only be used with special authorisation (write to the *Institut National d'Archaeologie*, Dar Husayn, Tunis). Many of the **lesser sites** out in the country have neither entry charge nor permanent guardian and even some of the larger ones are only nominally fenced off, so outside official opening hours you can often just walk in.

HAMMAMS

It's difficult to understand the horror of an English woman in the 1850s who wrote that "a Moorish bath is one of the tortures with which the traveller in the East must make acquaintance". A hammam, or Turkish bath, is not only civilisation at its most refined, it's also a bargain: less than £1 for treatment which would cost twenty times as much in the West, and which leaves you feeling seriously clean and totally relaxed. There is rarely, if ever, any sexual implication in visiting a hammam, any more than, say, a swimming pool.

Most Tunisians have at least one hammam a week, and for men Friday night at the hammam is the great social gathering. For women travellers, the hammam is the best place to make contact with Tunisian women (see p.356). Most hammams have different hours for men and women. Women usually bathe in the afternoon, men morning or evening. Sometimes, especially in Tunis, hammams are exclusively for the use either of males or females, who can therefore use it all day. There are two mixed hammams, both very expensive and for tourists only, at the *Hôtel Palmariva* at Aghir (Jerba), and the *Hôtel*

Chems el Hanna in Sousse, both after about 7pm. To find a hammam just ask around: there are plenty of them, but they tend to be well hidden and usually have signs only in Arabic if at all (hammam is spelt حمّام in Arabic).

Some of them have a distinctive red and green front door. Bear in mind that in Islam cleanliness is often quite literally next to godliness, and foreigners tend not to be welcome in hammams attached to mosques – which are used for ritual washing before prayer.

Hammams usually have secure lockers to leave any valuables, but an important thing to remember is that total nudity is not acceptable in Tunisia. You have to change discreetly, and wrap a linen towel (a *kassa*, which is provided) around your waist. Once you're suitably attired you head for the hot room to sit in or around a very hot bath. Before long, people start scratching, using the sweat that's being induced to rub off as much dead skin as possible. This process is finished by the masseur or masseuse, who first gives an expert massage, then uses abrasive gloves to remove every last particle of dead skin and dirt. After your bath, you may care to wrap yourself up in several *kassa* and relax for a while.

TRADITIONAL COSMETICS

Suek Walnut bark or root, used for cleaning teeth and reddening lips and gums, giving a slight, and not unpleasant, burning sensation.

Harqus Black skin dye used by women to decorate their hands and faces. At weddings, a spot of it is worn on the cheek.

Chab White stone used as a deodorant and to stop shaving cuts bleeding.

Henna Powdered leaves made into a paste and used for conditioning hair, and for colouring hair, hands and feet. The best henna comes from Gabes.

Tfal Fine earth used as shampoo and traditionally kept in a container called a *tafalla*.

Kohl Eyeliner made from ground antimony, sometimes with the addition of other materials.

SOUVENIRS AND BARGAINING

There are all sorts of souvenirs you might consider buying, depending on your taste, purchasing power and weight limit. The most popular seem to be soft toy camels – useful for young relatives perhaps but, like many items sold as souvenirs, not something a Tunisian would buy. Traditional craftwork, such as carpets and ceramics, have more lasting – and adult – appeal, but you may find that items of everyday Tunisian life make better, cheaper and more impressive souvenirs of the country.

If you're going to buy arts and crafts, it's probably worthwhile paying a visit to the local **crafts shop** run by the **ONA** – the crafts organisation, *Organisation National de l'Artisanat*. They have a number of workshops and a showroom and shop in most big towns – listed in the guide for each town under *Practicalities*, or in the town *Listings*. Their goods are generally of a high quality, and a little overpriced, but they are worth a visit to get an idea of what sort of crafts are available and how much they should cost, and to help you weed out the imposters in the field – like the cheap Moroccan pottery sold as "Souvenir of Tunisia".

OPENING HOURS

The smarter the shop, the more likely it is to follow this timetable: winter, 8.30am–12noon and 3–6pm; summer, 8.30am–12noon & 4–7pm.

POTTERY AND CERAMICS

Of the two main pottery centres (whose wares you can find throughout Tunisia), **Nabeul** on Cap Bon specialises in pottery glazed in the Andalusian style, for which tourists are the main customers. Good buys include plates, vases and tiles which can be made up into a wall panel. In the other main centre, **Guellala** on the island of Jerba, ordinary Tunisians are still the main customers, and the best buys are more utilitarian. If you can cart it home, you might go for a huge "Ali Baba" jar – with room to hide at least one thief. Otherwise, you could try a "magic camel" water jug, which is filled from the bottom, but can be poured only through the spout. An

alternative souvenir from here is an octopus trap (see p.288) but if you'd prefer a used one, you should have no trouble persuading a fisherman to sell it to you. Tunisia's third ceramics centre is **Sejenane**, with its own style of "naive" ceramic sculpture, not available outside the region.

CARPETS, RUGS AND BLANKETS

There are two main regions of **carpet production**: Kairouan in the centre, and Gafsa and the Jerid in the south. In **Kairouan**, where carpets are more finely knotted (quality being measured in knots per square metre), they usually have geometric designs and deep colours. **Jerid** carpets are more psychedelic, with bright colours and stylised images. In **Tozeur** you may find carpets with the same distinctive designs used in the traditional brickwork on the houses. Other places where carpets are sold include Gabes and Jerba. *Kelims*, sold particularly in the south, are woven rather than knotted. Before buying a carpet, always check to see that it carries the government seal of approval. For further details about carpets in Kairouan, see p.174.

JEWELLERY

Tunisia's **jewellery** trade was traditionally run by Jews, most of whom have now emigrated. Still, the Jewish village of Hara Kebira on Jerba, and the jewellery shops of Houmt Souk (often still in Jewish hands), are the best places to buy silver or gold pieces, or to have them made up. The Berber regions of the south also specialise in chunky silver jewellery, often set with semi-precious stones. This, however, is less openly on sale, and you may have to ask around to find something good. One typical piece is the **khlal**, a buckle consisting of a pin attached to a silver crescent and used to fasten clothes. In Tabarca, you'll find a lot of **coral** jewellery on sale, though perhaps you should consider the plight of its source before buying.

Common **motifs** in Tunisian pieces include the hand of Fatima and the fish. Both are good-luck symbols used to ward off the evil eye (see p.346), though some say the fish was originally a phallic fertility symbol.

WOODWORK, BASKETWORK AND METALWORK

There are masses of wood carvings around, but the best buys are made of **olive wood**. Especially attractive here are salad bowls – and not made at the expense of southeast Asia's teak forests!

Basketwork is common throughout the country, made from esparto grass, rushes or palm fronds. Baskets, hats and table mats are among the items produced. Another craft worth investing in is **hammered metal**. There are some excellent plates and trays available, but also a lot of shoddy rubbish. Rather than buying from tourist shops, seek out places where Tunisians might buy, and check the artistry.

CLOTHING AND LEATHER

Traditional Tunisian **clothes** can look rather silly on foreigners, especially men, so be sure it fits your style before buying. *Chechias* (red felt hats) are one possibility, or a handsome, camel hair *burnouse* (heavy men's cloak), but these are expensive. If you go for a *sifsari* (light women's shawl and head covering), get a cotton one. A cheaper way to obtain clothes is to buy the fabric and have a tailor make you something to order. Alternatively, you could try the second-hand clothes markets in most *medinas*. Although much of the clothing is European, there are some outrageous garments among them. Also available are the blue jackets (called *blusa*) that North African workers all seem to wear.

Leather can be good, but it can also be awful, so check the quality before buying, especially any stitching. Western-style gear such as jackets and handbags can be very shoddily made; more traditional items such as poufs and *babouche* slippers are usually better. **Sheepskins** are also widely available – make sure they're well cured.

ODDS AND ENDS AND ITEMS OF EVERYDAY LIFE

Often the things which will remind you best of Tunisia are everyday items sold in ordinary shops and markets. A *canoun* (charcoal stove), while not of much practical use back home, can't fail to remind you of all those cups of stewed tea you drank while waiting for *louages*. Alternatively, you could get a Tunisian **teapot** or a pot for making Turkish coffee (very finely ground coffee

traditionally brought to the boil seven times). You could always buy a *chicha* (water pipe). Failing that, esparto mats, used in pressing olives, make great table mats. Olive oil and *harissa* (chilli sauce) are almost required and cooks could try their hand at some real Tunisian cookery with a *couscoussier* (couscous steamer). If you own a car, don't forget some Hand of Fatima stickers to plaster it with.

There are all sorts of other odds and ends you might go for, from the ornate **birdcages** sold especially in Sidi Bou Said to **sea sponges**. Other possibilities include **darbouka drums**, typical of Tunisia. Try the drum souk in Tunis for these, though if you need one good enough for a serious musician, you will probably want it made to order. **Sand roses** are the commonest souvenirs sold down south, and very cheap, especially around Nefta, Tozeur and Douz. They can be rather bulky but all sizes are available and you can get several very small ones for a dinar.

In the way of **antiques**, there are a lot of colonial remnants about, but none especially cheap. In Tunis, Rue des Glacières by Place de la Victoire, and the market area around Souk des Armes and Place du Marché du Blé, are likely hunting grounds for this sort of thing. Around Roman sites, hawkers offer "Roman" and "Byzantine" coins and "old" oil lamps. Some of them are genuine (coins found after rain and left overnight in a glass of gut-rot to clean them), though worthless; most, however, are artificially aged fakes.

BARGAINING

Whatever you buy, you will almost always be expected to **haggle over the price**. There are no hard-and-fast rules – it's really a question of how much something is worth to you. It is a good plan, however, to have an idea of how much you want to pay. Don't worry too much about initial prices. Some guidebooks suggest paying a third of the opening price, but it's a flexible guideline: you may end up paying only a tenth or less of the opening price, or, on the other hand, not be able to get the seller much below it. If you bid too low, you may be bustled out of the shop for offering an "insulting" price, but this is all part of the game and you will no doubt be welcomed as an old friend if you return the next day. Prices for food, cigarettes, buses and hotels are usually fixed. All hotels display government-regulated

DEALING WITH SALES TECHNIQUES: A TYPICAL SCENARIO

Veterans of countries like Morocco, Egypt and India will find Tunisia tame by comparison. In general, you won't be hassled endlessly by salesmen, nor will people attach themselves to you and then demand payment for having been your "guide". But some **hard selling** is now creeping into some of the more touristed areas, notably the tourist ghettos of Cap Bon, and the *medinas* of Kairouan and Sousse. If you're going to play the game, it pays to know the rules.

A salesman invites you into his shop, maybe **"for tea"** because it is his birthday, or "the birthday of the shop" (this is common on Jerba). You make it quite clear (and this is **fundamental**) that you don't want to buy anything, even if you half think you might. The salesman insists you should come in just to have a look. Of couse, you may not want to go in. The Arabic for "no thank you" is "*la shookran*": say it with a smile, then no one can take offence. A more definitive tactic is to say you already have whatever is being offered.

A **typical scenario**, if you do enter, begins as he shows you the ceiling to demonstrate what an old house he has – a "museum of carpets" (or carv-

ings, or silver, or antiques); he shows you people at work; he sits you down and calls for tea. A large number of carpets are brought and rolled out in front of you. As well as being a tradition, the tea and hospitality may make you feel obliged to him. In a way, charming and pleasant as he may be, he has deceived you by saying that he wouldn't try to sell you a carpet, for that's exactly what he now begins to do. He shows you examples of the different styles, tells you how much they would be worth in your country, shows you the government seal of approval, tells you how little it will cost to send one home and demands to know why you don't want one. He brings out smaller and cheaper examples and keeps up the fluent spiel.

Finally, as you apologise and make to leave, he demands to know, of the carpets he has shown you, which you like. He will now probably tell you his **final price**, but any sign of interest on your part will raise it: if you're genuinely interested, you can always shop around and return any time you like. Hostility or abusiveness at this stage is still unusual, but it happens, along with claims that you're a time-waster.

maximum tariffs, but you can try haggling anyway. You can sometimes get a better price for souvenirs by bartering: Levis and the latest trainers are always in demand.

There are certain rules of the game to remember. Never start haggling for something if in fact you do not want it, and **never** let any figure pass

your lips that you are not prepared to pay. It's like bidding in an auction. Having mentioned a price, you are obliged to pay it. If the seller asks how much you would pay for something, and you don't want it, say so. And never go shopping with a **guide**, who will get a commission on anything you buy, which means a higher price to you.

FESTIVALS AND HOLIDAYS

The great national festivals of Tunisia are all related to Islam and so are calculated according to the Muslim calendar. This is a lunar system so dates recede against the Western calendar by about eleven days a year.

Ramadan, the month-long fast required of all good Muslims every year (see p.347), sounds like a disastrous time to travel, and if you need food or drinks during the day it can be hard outside the resorts. But it is an exciting time, too. If those observing the fast sometimes get a little sluggish and short-tempered during the day (nothing may pass the lips between sunrise and sunset), the riotous night-time compensation more than makes up for it. Eating, drinking and smoking – with a day's consumption packed into a few hours – go on until two or three in the morning, and, for the only time in the year, café nightlife really takes off. Lights are strung up and you'll find music, occasionally belly dancing, and even puppet shows. In Tunis, the best places to look are Place Bab Souika and Bab Saadoun. If you're lucky enough to see a puppet show, it may well feature a character called Karagoz, enacting a tradition which arrived with the Turkish rulers in the sixteenth century. Ramadan ends with a flourish in a feast called the **Aid el Fitr,** or **Aid es Seghir.**

The other great national festival, the feast of Abraham known as **Aid el Adha** or **Aid el Kebir,** is more of a family affair, the equivalent of a western Christmas perhaps. Every family which can afford it celebrates the willingness of Abraham to sacrifice his son Ishmail by slaughtering its own sheep and roasting the meat: you can

tell the Aid is approaching by the sheep which begin to appear tethered by almost every house. It's a grisly business: children treat the family sheep as a pet all the time looking forward to seeing its throat cut as if waiting for Father Christmas. There's a gradual movement away from actually slaughtering to just buying the meat, but the festival is still the time when families gather and transport is packed all over the country.

Other religious festivals are less widely observed, though the Prophet's birthday, **Mouled,** is a great event at Kairouan (see p.175).

It's impossible to predict **festival dates** in the lunar calendar exactly since they are set by the religious authorities in Mecca, where the new moon is sighted (see box). In addition, there are fixed **national secular holidays,** all to some extent celebrations and all meaning the closure of banks, most shops and offices (see box). Other secular holidays are **local events,** and mainly

APPROXIMATE DATES FOR THE MAIN RELIGIOUS FESTIVALS

	1992	1993	1994	1995
1st of Ramadan (not a holiday)	March 8	Feb 25	Feb 14	Feb 3
Aid es Seghir (two days' holiday)	April 7	March 27	March 16	March 5
Aid el Kebir (two days' holiday)	June 12	June 1	May 20	May 9
Islamic New Year	July 3	June 23	June 12	June 1
Mouled	Sept 10	Aug 31	Aug 20	Aug 9

ANNUAL SECULAR HOLIDAYS

January 1	New Year	**May 1**	Labour Day
March 20	Independence Day	**July 25**	Republic Day
March 21	Youth Day	**August 13**	Women's Day
April 9	Martyrs' Day	**November 7**	New Era Day

LOCAL FESTIVALS AND HOLIDAYS

February Olive Festival, Kalaa Kebira (near Sousse, see p.161).

March Hammam Festival, El Hamma de l'Arad (see p.259).

April–May Orange Blossom Festival, Menzel Bou Zelfa (see p.114).

May Matanza, Sidi Daoud (see p.111–12); Jewish pilgrimage, Hara Sghira (Jerba, see p.111–12).

May–June Drama performances in Roman theatre, Dougga (see p.203).

June Falconry Festival, El Haouria (see p.110); Malouf Music Festival, Testour (see p.202).

July Sidi Bou Makhlouf Festival, Le Kef.

July–August Various tourist-orientated "cultural" festivals at resorts and Roman sites around the country.

August Festival du Borj, Gafsa (see p.233).

September Wine Festival, Grombalia (see p.114); Wheat Festival, Beja.

October Liberation Day, Bizerte (see p.121 & 126).

November Date Festival, Kebili (see p.252); Matmata Festival; Carthage Film Festival (biennial, 1992, 1994, mainly in Tunis).

December Tozeur Festival (see p.245); International Festival of the Sahara, Douz (see p.256).

recent creations designed to bolster tourism or agriculture. They are covered in the relevant chapters but, again, see the box on p.29.

WEDDINGS

In the country, life for most of the year revolves around a cycle of regular markets and occasional weddings. **Weddings** are extraordinarily public celebrations – almost the only chance people get to let their hair down and enjoy themselves, and they make the most of it. Cavalcades of pick-up trucks loaded with people playing pipes and drums, drive round the town (in Tunis, Mercedes hoot up and down av Bourguiba); a solemn procession carries the bride's dowry through the streets; and the celebrations, dancing and feasting can go on for several days. Sadly, you can

now sign up at the big hotels for an evening at a "Tunisian wedding". Avoid these like the plague but don't decline the genuine invitations you're bound to receive if you spend any time away from the big towns.

WEEKLY MARKETS

The rest of the year, life in the country revolves around a cycle of weekly **markets,** always colourful affairs. The Sousse and Nabeul markets have been comprehensively "discovered"; but it's well worth timing a visit to other towns to coincide with the weekly event which for many of them is the mainstay of the economy. Testour and Fahs are particularly worthwhile. Market days in most regions are listed in a box at the beginning of each chapter.

WOMEN'S TUNISIA

Women travellers will come across problems with Tunisian men that don't affect their male counterparts. Some can be avoided or overcome; others are inescapable. They can range from comments as you pass by in the street to persistent chatting, following you or touching; on occasions, however, friendly overtures may suddenly give way to demands for sex as if you knew what they were after all along.

Gay women are not likely to find any hint of a community in Tunisia. Lesbianism is more or less invisible and its existence

denied – though what is true about friendships between men (see opposite) applies even more so between women.

HARASSMENT

While some women compare it favourably with southern Europe, there's no doubt that general **harassment in Tunisia** is much more commonplace than in northern Europe or the English-speaking world. While you'll probably face a lot of minor hassles rather than anything seriously threatening, if you do feel you're in danger, don't be afraid to ask for help from passers-by or to make a scene. No Tunisian man would get away with treating a Tunisian woman in this way: the Arabic word *shooma*, meaning "shame on you!" should – if shouted loudly in a public place – embarrass any man into leaving you alone.

A number of readers have pointed out that some Tunisian men seem unable to distinguish between ordinary civility and making a pass. There's a cultural difference here: Tunisian women are generally coy or aloof towards men, any other attitude being considered sluttish and taken as an invitation (two areas where this is *not* the case are the big cities, notably Tunis and Sfax, where European sexual attitudes are emerging, and in parts of the far south, where women have always been more assertive).

The best solution is to be as stand-offish as possible, even if your attitude may be misunderstood as an insult – and even if, as occasionally happens, you're accused of racist sexual preferences or it appears obvious that the "misunderstanding" is deliberately disingenuous.

For more in-depth coverage of these issues, two **personal accounts** by women travellers are included in the "Women in Tunisia" section in *Contexts* (see p.354), as is some background on issues facing Tunisian women in modern society.

MEN'S TUNISIA

Generally, men experience few problems in Tunisia related to their sex. There are several issues to be aware of, however, and gay men, certainly, should be prepared for Tunisian attitudes.

Men should **beware of talking to Tunisian women alone**, especially in more traditional communities. All might seem well at the time but the family may regard it as a breach of confidence and afterwards make life difficult for the woman. Male English teachers for instance are requested not to talk to female students alone behind a closed door.

GAY ATTITUDES

Male tourists and travellers can expect the occasional **sexual proposition** by Tunisian men. A polite refusal should put an end to the matter. If you find it annoying, remember what women have to put up with. **Attitudes to male homosexuality** are very different from those in the West, but

equally neurotic. Because of the sexual segregation endemic to Islam, homosexuality is very widespread, but not necessarily seen as such. Friendships are far closer than in the West and much more physical: you will often hear Tunisians say of their friends, "I love him like a brother". With such brotherly love about, the point where affection ends and a sexual relationship begins is not perhaps very significant. What's clear enough is that taking the passive role in intercourse is considered a disgrace, yet no such stigma attaches to the other role, and men will boast quite openly about their prowess. There are not many special centres for gay contacts – any café or bar may lead to introductions – but calls for money or "presents" tend to be more common than sincerity.

Responses to the dangers of **HIV infection** have so far been limited but there's little doubt the problem is as grave in Tunisia as it is almost everywhere else in the world and the need for safe sex no less pressing (see "Health").

POLICE AND THIEVES

You are unlikely to run into any trouble in Tunisia beyond that covered in the preceding section or caused by "guides" and the hard-sell techniques covered on p.28. The police are invariably polite and helpful to tourists. Thieving, though it obviously goes on, is a lot less common than in most of Europe or North America.

THE POLICE

There are two main **types of police**: the *Sûreté* and the *Gendarmes*. The *Sûreté*, who wear grey uniforms, are the normal police force, and the people you should go to if you need to report a

crime, or to let them know if you're camping out. They usually speak good French and should be able to give you directions if you're lost. The khaki-uniformed *Gendarmes* patrol the roads in rural areas. Drawn from conscript soldiers, they may stop you if you're driving in remote areas or near borders, ask to see your passport and question you about where you're going and why, but they won't give you any trouble.

It is just possible, though unlikely, that you will be stopped and asked for **identification** on the street (Tunisians are issued with state identity cards which they carry at all times), but you'll be okay if you can take a police officer to your hotel and show your passport.

The **National Guard**, a branch of the military, are the people you should inform if driving across the desert.

Tunisians are generally honest and law-abiding and **stealing** from a visitor is considered shameful. Nonetheless, the odd isolated case of mugging does take place, in large towns, in unlit deserted areas at night, so these are the places to avoid. There have also been a number of incidents of **bag-snatching** in the *medina* at Sousse, and of "guides" outside the tourist office in Kairouan leading tourists deep into the *medina* and demanding large sums of money to lead them out again.

Many hotels operate a deposit for valuables; otherwise, wearing a body belt (cotton, with room for your passport, which you should put in a plastic bag to stop it getting saturated in sweat) might be good for your peace of mind.

DIRECTORY

Abortion Women from certain European countries come to Tunisia for abortions, which are legal, inexpensive (around £100), and as safe as they are in the West.

British Tunisian Society, c/o Tunisian Embassy, 29 Prince's Gate, London SW7 1QG. *Council for the Advancement of Arab-British Understanding*, 21 Collingham Road, London SW5 0NU (✆ 071 373 8414). *Maghreb Studies Association*, c/o The Maghreb Bookshop, 45 Burton Street, London WC1H 9AL (✆071 388 1840).

Cigarettes Tunisian brands are cheap but rough: *20 Mars* are strong, *Caravanes* medium and *Cristal* weaker. Western brands, widely available, cost about four times as much, slightly more than in Britain.

Cinemas Tunisians like going to the movies. French films and English-language films dubbed into French are especially popular in Tunis. Arabic films, including a few made in Tunisia, are usually a mixture of American-style soap and musical; they're more popular in rural areas and in the cities' cheaper cinemas and, even if you don't understand the plot (probably an advantage), can be fun. Indian movies are usually subtitled in French and Arabic, but British, American and Hong Kong films are invariably dubbed into French (still, if you've never seen Jackie Chan or Sylvester Stallone speak French . . .). Long films are not so much cut as slashed (leave out a reel or two!).

Clothes Two things to bear in mind are the heat, especially in the desert, and the modesty demanded by Islam. You will certainly want a light sun-hat, especially in summer, and light, loose-fitting cotton clothes. In winter, especially in the north, you will want at least one warm sweater. Be aware that many people, especially older people, can feel seriously intimidated or affronted by scantily dressed tourists wandering around town. Don't walk around the *medina* in a swimsuit or bare-chested, nor in shorts or short skirts.

Contraceptives Known as *Chapeaux Americains*, condoms are available from most chemists in large towns; so too are some brands of the Pill (la Pilule). If you get diarrhoea, remember that oral contraceptives may not stay in your system long enough to be absorbed and may thus become ineffective.

Duty Free: The duty free allowance into Tunisia is the usual 400 cigarettes and a litre of spirits plus two litres of wine, a quarter litre of perfume, and a litre of toilet water. Tunisian duty free shops (often open at airports on arrival as well as departure) do not take dinars, so don't bother to save any for a bottle on your way home.

Electricity Generally 220v 50Hz, as in continental Europe, with double round-pin sockets. British, Irish and Australasian plugs will need an adaptor (double round-pin electric shavers will be all right though). American and Canadian appliances will need a transformer too unless multi-voltage. One or two old places, especially in Tunis, still have 110v voltage – check before plugging in!

Emergencies The national emergency telephone number is ☎197.

Film Most of the major brands of film are widely available, but they're expensive, so it pays to bring a supply. Speeds other than 100ASA are hard to come by. Videotape for cameras is expensive or unobtainable.

Hashish This is not Morocco or Egypt: in fact, Tunisia is more like rural France in its attitude to dope. There is hardly any tradition of hashish or other drug use (though *kif* was smoked during the Ottoman period), and no sign of one emerging. Use of cannabis is frowned on, both officially and popularly, and is extremely clandestine with very stiff penalties in force for possession of it or any other illegal drug.

Laundry There are no self-service laundromats, but many towns have places which do washing by weight. Ask at hotels.

Luggage consignment Many hotels (particularly cheaper ones) and most large railway stations take left luggage or have a safe room where you can leave belongings, sometimes even when you are away – ask for the *consigne*. Tourist offices may also be able to help for a short period of time, and staff at bus stations are often willing to keep an eye on your baggage for you while you wander around town between buses – often just as a favour without charge.

Odd Essentials For reasons that soon become apparent, it's a good idea to carry a stock of toilet paper around with you – it can be bought in most towns.

Stoves Camping gas stoves are widely available, but the refills (*cartouches*) much less so. Ironmongers (*quincailleries*) and supermarkets should stock them, but supplies are sporadic. Street sellers sometimes have them when the shops have run out. In Tunis, rue al Jazira is the place to look – especially pl Cheikh el Bourzouli, where the street traders sometimes have them

when the shops run out. Much more sensible is to take a spirit stove, since burning alcohol (*alcool à brûler*) is widely available. A petrol stove is also a possibility, though somewhat messier.

Student Cards There are reductions (in theory) for students under 32 at sites and museums and on quite a lot of flights. Many of the flights also have under-26 discounts.

Tampons Available from pharmacies in all except the remotest towns.

Time Tunisia is one hour ahead of GMT all year round, which means that the time is the same as in Britain and Ireland during the summer, an hour ahead in winter. Crossing from France or Italy, there is no time difference in winter, but you have to put your watch back an hour in summer.

Tipping In smarter hotels and restaurants tipping follows western practice: service is often included, and ten to fifteen percent is a normal tip for waiters. Porters and chambermaids expect something depending on the price bracket of the hotel and the length of your stay. Taxi drivers do not necessarily get a tip, but always appreciate one. Backsheesh is also expected for small services such as loading your baggage onto buses or finding you a place in a *louage*.

Work A work permit is officially required for all foreign citizens working in Tunisia: in the present state of the economy permits are hard to come by. **English teaching** is expanding rapidly, though: try writing to the *British Council* (10 Spring Gardens, London SW1A 2BN) or direct to the *Bourguiba School of Modern Languages* in Tunis (47 av de la Liberté). Private conversation classes are sometimes possible to arrange on an informal (and illegal) basis. For almost anything else you will need at least competent French; but because the tourist industry is so highly organised there's little of the fringe market found elsewhere. The best way to see the country for free is to join one of the **international work camps** which are run most summers. In Britain, contact *International Voluntary Service*, 53 Regent Road, Leicester (☎0533 541862); in the USA: *Civil Service International*, POB 3333, NY 1085; in Australia: *SCI*, 21 Saint George's Terrace, Battery Point, Hobart, Tasmania 7000. The Tunis headquarters are in the *Party Building* on Boulevard 9 April 1938.

USEFUL THINGS TO TAKE

● Suntan lotion with a high screening factor.

● A wide-brimmed cotton sun-hat for protection against sunstroke; in the intense heat of the desert, you can drench it in water and stick it on your head to cool you down.

● A water bottle is a must, especially if you plan to do any walking. If you plan to do any driving in the desert, it's a good idea to bring one of the five-litre roll-up water bags, available at camping shops.

● A pocket alarm clock – vital for catching those crack-of-dawn buses.

● A mini-padlock for your baggage.

● Insect repellant.

● Film, especially fast film (useful in the dark nooks and alleyways of city *medinas*) or slow film (if you are into some serious landscape photography in the desert south).

● A sheet sleeping bag is a good safeguard against dubious sheets in cheap hotels.

● A body belt of some sort with room for your passport (which you should wrap in a plastic bag to prevent it getting soaked in sweat).

● An all-purpose knife and bottle opener – few bottles are screw-top.

PART TWO

THE

GUIDE

BIZERTE
AND THE
NORTH

CAP
BON

TUNIS
AND
AROUND

Mediterranean Sea

THE TELL

KAIROUAN
AND THE
SAHEL

ALGERIA

THE JERID

GABES
AND
MATMATA

JERBA AND
THE SOUTH-EAST
COAST

THE KSOUR

0   100 km

LIBYA

CHAPTER ONE

TUNIS AND AROUND

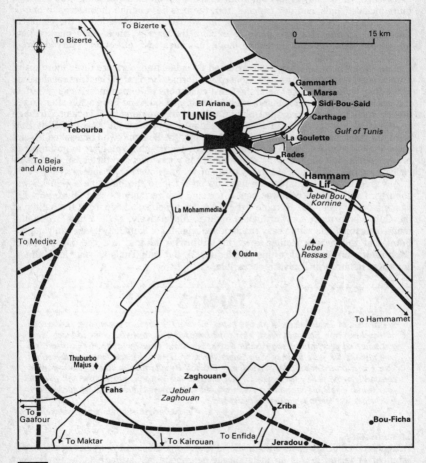

Tunis is very much a capital city – home to over a tenth of Tunisia's population, the base of government and power, and the centre of virtually all that happens in the country. It is not an attractive city, at least on first impressions. The old colonial centre is becoming increasingly submerged by anonymous housing suburbs, and the streets have a rather westernised air. But stay a few days and you'll find that behind this unexceptional facade there is a real allure. The old Arab town, the

Medina, shelters monuments spanning six hundred years of Arab and Turkish endowment, and the French-built **Ville Nouvelle** is beginning to acquire a period value of its own.

These distinct parts and phases of the city's development are intricately linked in a manner which is somehow symbolic of Tunisia's ability to blend cultures. Moving from ninth-century mosque to eighteenth-century Turkish palace to nineteenth-century French boulevard seems almost a natural progression. And it's one you'll be able to experience without any great compromises made to tourist sightseeing. Few package tours include Tunis, and day trippers from the beaches confine themselves to one or two standard streets and monuments in the Medina. The rest is left to the people of Tunis and anyone else who cares to explore the narrow lanes, busy markets and unrestored **monuments**, including huge mosques and elaborately carved street fountains.

Away from the centre, but easily reached by public transport, are three more major attractions. The **Bardo Museum**, housed in a former Beylical palace (the royal palace of the Bey, or Regent), has one of the finest collections of Roman mosaics anywhere in the world, best visited once before seeing the Roman sites and once again after. In the other direction, overlooking the Gulf of Carthage, are the remains of ancient **Carthage** itself and, a little further in the same direction, the picturesque resort of **Sidi Bou Said**. Carthage can be somewhat underwhelming: the Romans (who ransacked it), and then simply time itself, were such thorough conquerors that you have to go prepared to use your imagination. On the other hand, the views over the turquoise Gulf, especially those from Sidi Bou Said, easily make up for any lingering disappointment.

Any free time in Tunis can be used up on a trip to the other, less well known, suburbs. **La Goulette**, with its Spanish fort and fish restaurants, and **Hammam Lif**, nestling below Jebel Bou Kornine – the mountain which stands guard at the bottom of the Gulf – both make for worthwhile outings. Alternatively, catch a bus to one of a range of destinations within easy reach of the capital. For simplicity's sake, only a few – **Fahs** and the nearby Roman town of **Thuburbo Majus**, and the hill resort of **Zaghouan** – are included in this chapter (p.92), but with Tunis as your base almost anywhere in northern Tunisia is accessible.

TUNIS

We arrived at Tunis, object of all our hopes, focus of the flame of every gaze, rendezvous of travellers from East and West. This is where fleets and caravans come to meet. Here you will find everything a man could desire. You want to go by land? Here are endless companions for your journey. You prefer the sea? Here are boats for every direction. Tunis is a crown whose every jewel is a district, its suburbs are like a flower-garden constantly refreshed by the breeze. If you come to her watering-places, she will quench your thirst; if you fall back on her resources, she will cure your problems; her gardens are like brides, her worth is written in many books.

El Abdari, thirteenth-century traveller.

Some history

Tunis is rooted firmly in an Arab medieval past. For a thousand years before the establishment of Islam, it was an insignificant neighbour of Carthage (although in fact founded earlier) and its only historic role was as a base for invaders laying siege to the larger city. The Arabs, however, preferred Tunis's less exposed site and, as early as the ninth century, the **Aghlabids** (for a full glossary of names and epochs see p.371) built the Great Mosque which still stands at the heart of the Medina. In the last years of their rule, from 894 to 909 AD, Tunis served as the Aghlabid imperial capital.

Largely ignored by the **Fatimids**, the city really came into its own following the **Hilalian** invasion of the eleventh century when Abdelhaq Ibn Khourassane established a principality here. Amid the chaos of the time, this **Khourassanid** state was such an island of stability that by the time it fell to the **Almohads** a hundred years later, it had become the country's natural power centre. When the **Hafsids** declared complete independence in 1236, it was a capital once again.

Under the Hafsids, and especially after the fall of Baghdad to the Mongols in 1258, Tunis became the Arab world's leading metropolis – a great Mediterranean marketplace at a time of expanding trade between Christian Europe and the Muslim East. Culture flourished in the cosmopolitan atmosphere, and the university in the Great Mosque – the Zitouna Mosque – was rivalled only by those of al-Azhar in Cairo and the Kairaouine at Fez. The Hafsids' own building programmes included the first *medersas*, or Islamic colleges, many of the purpose-built souks (markets) around the Great Mosque, the Kasbah with its mosque, and the city walls. It was this city that El Abdari is describing in the quotation opposite.

As Arab rule wavered before the **Ottoman Turks**, Tunis changed in appearance – becoming enclosed by fortifications – and in character, as a more foreign-dominated era emerged. Wealth from trade and piracy poured into the city, financing the building of more mosques, *medersas* and palaces. Christian traders were allowed to settle, and since many of the "Turkish" officials ruling the new **Regency** were *Mamelukes*, slaves of Greek or Eastern European origin taken as children, several of the buildings and even a few mosques have a strong European flavour.

Until the nineteenth century, Tunis still consisted essentially of the **Medina** and *faubourgs* – poor suburbs outside the walls – with a few elaborate palaces, such as the Bardo, set in gardens further away. The *Bab el Bahr*, the Sea Gate, was just that, with the waters of Lake Tunis lapping right up against it. But by the 1860s several thousand European traders and advisers were living in Tunis and their presence was influential. The International Financial Commission set up by the colonial powers virtually ran the government, and newly found wealth gave merchants considerable power over the impoverished Beys. At this time a new European city – the **Ville Nouvelle** – began to develop outside the city walls, and with **the French** occupation in 1881, they set about draining the marshy land on the edge of the lake to extend this new colonial domain. Today its wide avenues, jammed with traffic and beginning to crumble, still feel thoroughly *Belle Epoque* with their pavement cafés, iron balconies and fancy stucco work.

PHONE CODE

☎01 for the whole of Greater Tunis

The city: orientation and getting around

Initially, Tunis's setting can be confusing (see "Around Tunis" map on p.78). **The city** itself lies on the shore of a large, shallow lake – **Lac Tunis** – which stretches between the town and the Gulf of Carthage. Along the Gulf shore, north and south of the narrow entrance to the lake, stretches a chain of suburbs easily reached by public transport from the city centre. An independent light railway, the **TGM** (Tunis, La Goulette, Marsa) crosses the lake on a causeway to the northern shore's suburbs, which include **Carthage** and **Sidi Bou Said**. This journey is so quick and convenient that for all practical purposes there's no gap at all. A normal railway runs from the mainline station to the less attractive southern suburbs of **Rades** and **Hammam Lif**.

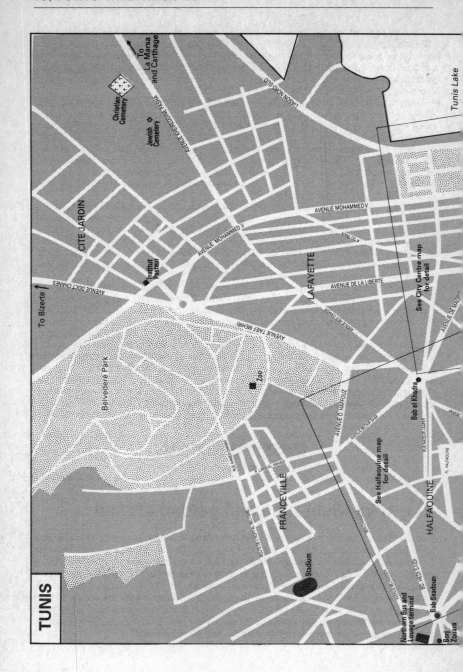

TUNIS

To Bizerte

CITE JARDIN

AVENUE DOCT CHANES

Institut Pasteur

Jewish Cemetery

Christian Cemetery

To La Marsa and Carthage

AVENUE MERECURE PASHA

LIAISON NORD-SUD

AVENUE MOHAMMED V

AVENUE MOHAMMED V

LAFAYETTE

AVENUE DE LA LIBERTE

See City Centre map for detail

AVENUE DE MADRID

Tunis Lake

AVENUE TAIEF MEHIRI

Belvedere Park

Zoo

AVENUE O. HAFFOUZ

Bab el Khadra

RUE NACER JAAFER

See Halfaouine map for detail

HALFAOUINE

FRANCEVILLE

Stadium

Northern Bus and Louage terminal

BD. HEDI SAIDI

Bab Saadoun

Borj Zouara

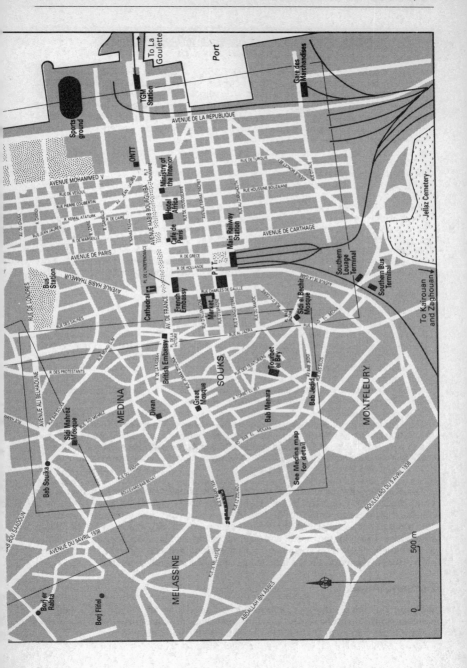

Port

To La Goulette

Gare des Marchandises

TGM Station

AVENUE DE LA REPUBLIQUE

Sports ground

ONTT

AVENUE MOHAMMED V

Ministry of the Interior

RUE DE TURQUIE

Jellaz Cemetery

RUE DE VESOUL

RUE PIERRE COUBERTIN

Hotel Africa

Café de Paris

Main Railway Station

AVENUE DE PARIS

AVENUE DE CARTHAGE

Bus Station

P.T.T.

Southern Louage Terminal

Southern Bus Terminal

RUE DE LONDRES

French Embassy

Cathédrale

Market

Sidi el Bechir Mosque

To Kairouan and Zaghouan

SOUKS

British Embassy

Tourbet el Bey

MEDINA

Divan

Great Mosque

Bab Jedid

MONTFLEURY

Bab Menara

Sidi Mahrez Mosque

AVENUE ALI BELHAOUNE

Bab Souika

See Medina map for detail

500 m

MELASSINE

AVENUE DU 9 AVRIL 1938

BOULEVARD DU 9 AVRIL 1938

Borj er Rabta

Borj Filfel

0

ABDALLAH BEN ABBES

POINTS OF ARRIVAL AND DEPARTURE

By Air

■ **Tunis Carthage Airport** (☎288000/235000/236000) is 8km – a 15-min drive – northeast of the city centre on the shore of the lake, served by both buses and taxis (the TGM station misleadingly called "aeroport" has nothing to do with the airport and is nowhere near it).

■ **Buses** The #35 runs roughly from 5am to 10pm, quite frequently, and takes about 30min. Set-down/pick-up points are: the bottom of **av Habib Thameur**, where it becomes rue de Rome; **av Bourguiba** south side near the corner of rue 18 Janvier; **Tunis Marine** bus station; **pl Palestine** behind République metro station.

■ **Taxis and car hire** A taxi to or from the airport will be less than 2TD on the meter, but at least 5TD at night when you have no choice. Several **car hire** firms also operate from the airport and you should be able to rent a car as soon as you arrive.

■ **Airport tips** Remember you need a **bon de passage** (see p.10) before buying an international air ticket. On flying out, note that the **duty free shop** at the airport only takes hard currency, so don't save any dinars to spend in it. If you're **flying in at night**, join the queue at the "all-night" currency exchange immediately and leave baggage collection till later. Because of the currency regulations, you'll have to change some money immediately and the exchange service, while reliable, is slow. You should also carry some cash as they occasionally refuse to change travellers' cheques. They are sometimes closed at night, so you may have to get a taxi to somewhere you can change cash (try the *Hôtel Africa* or the *Majestic*). Or you could ignore the currency regulations and bring a few dinars with you.

By Sea

Ferries dock at La Goulette, the port in the northern suburbs.

■ **Arriving in Tunis**, the cheapest way into town from here is by TGM (the urban railway) across the lake to av Bourguiba. To find the TGM, come out of the ferry terminal, go straight ahead past the *poste de douane* and follow the road round to the left. From here it's more or less straight on past the Kasbah (on your right) and another 300m or so down to the line. Turn right here and the station is 100m ahead. If that sounds too complicated or your baggage is too heavy, take a taxi. In a car, head for the TGM but instead of turning right for the station, cross the line and take a left (a left before the line takes you to the Rades ferry) across the causeway into town.

■ **Departing Tunis**, get off at the TGM's second stop, Goulette Vielle, and walk back alongside the track towards Tunis for 100m or so to the main road. Then turn left and continue for some 300m, past the Kasbah (on your left) until you come to a roundabout where the beach is to your left. Turn right here and continue, following the road round to the left by the *STAM/CTN* building and the *BNT* bank. The ferry terminal is right in front of you.

Once in the city itself, orientation couldn't be simpler. **Avenue Bourguiba**, the great central artery, flanked by ministries, smart hotels and shops, and divided by a tree-lined promenade, links the **Medina** in the west to **the lake** in the east. To either side stretches the grid-plan of the French-built **modern city**, bounded by the hilltop **Belvedere Park** in the north and the sprawling **Jellaz Cemetery** in the south. Everything in this central area is within easy walking distance and, with the exception of the **Bardo Museum**, there's little to be seen in the straggling suburbs.

Getting Around

Walking isn't simply the most interesting way of getting around the city centre. In summer, when the traffic seizes up in the streets and the atmosphere in the buses is as steamy as any hammam, it's often quickest and most comfortable.

■ Remember you will need a **bon de passage** (see p.10) before buying an international ferry ticket. **Ferry schedules** and **ticket office addresses** are given in *Basics* on p.6. In the summer, things can get hectic at the offices, so it may be wise to leave plenty of time for queuing and struggling, or get your ticket in Bizerte, Sousse or Sfax instead.

By Rail

■ The mainline **railway station** (☎244440) is on Place Barcelone, right at the centre of the main hotel area, south of av Bourguiba (metro lines 1 and 2). Most train services run every day but a few are non-operational on Sundays and public holidays. To secure a seat, it's a good idea to turn up at the station an hour or so before departure, to stake your claim as soon as the train arrives. Full details are given in **"travel details"** at the end of this chapter.

■ The central Tunis **TGM** station is at the port end of av Bourguiba, next to Tunis Marine bus and metro (line 1) stations. Trains from here run every twenty minutes or so across Lake Tunis, linking the city with La Goulette, Carthage, Sidi Bou Said and La Marsa. Last service is at around 1am.

By Road

■ Both the intercity **bus terminals – Bab Saadoun** for the north of the country and **Bab Alleoua** for the rest – are well connected to the centre by city bus (#3 for Bab Saadoun) and have **metro stations** of the same names fairly nearby. If you're not too weighed down, neither terminal is too far from the city centre to walk. Bab Alleoua is a modern terminal at the bottom of rue Sidi el Bechir (from Bab Jazira) and av de Carthage. Bab Saadoun terminal is actually a couple of hundred metres past Bab Saadoun itself, up av 20 Mars and to the right, down av Bougatfa. City bus #50 runs constantly between the two terminals, though, again, it stops by the Bab Saadoun city gate rather than outside the northern bus terminal.

■ If you miss your bus, there are **louages** very close by. Most *louages* arrive at and depart from locations right by the bus terminals (Bab Saadoun's *louage* station adjoins the bus station; Bab Alleoua's is across rue Sidi el Bechir). The exceptions are the international ones serving Libya and Algeria, which have their main parking lots at **Garage Ayachi** at Bab Souika (Libya) and **rue al Jazira** at Place de la Victoire/Porte de France (Algeria and Morocco). *Louages* usually make departures from Tunis between about 4am until about 6pm (the later departures are mostly local). It's better to start earlier the further your destination. One or two important destinations (for example, Sfax) have *louages* all night but bear in mind that you have to wait for them to fill up before leaving: this can take a long time in the small hours.

Buses

Bus rides in the city generally cost around 250 millimes. If you plan to do a lot of travelling by bus, buy a book of tickets from the office at the Tunis Marine bus station at the end of av Bourguiba, near the TGM station. It's also possible to buy a sheet of TGM tickets at the TGM station. The main urban **bus stations** are at Jardin Thameur, pl Barcelone, and Tunis Marine by the TGM.

Metro

More an overgrown tram than an underground train, the fairly new **metro** system runs down the middle of the street and obeys traffic lights. Outside rush hours and lunchtime, it's not as frequent as it might be nor very fast, and its lines are so arranged that almost any journey requires at least one change. At present, line #5 is not yet in operation and line #4 only runs as far as the 20 Mars station.

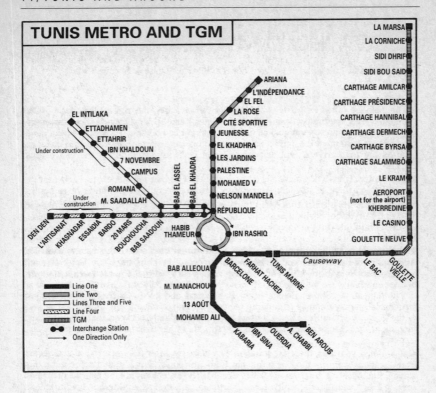

TUNIS METRO AND TGM

Line One
Line Two
Lines Three and Five
Line Four
TGM
●● **Interchange Station**
→ **One Direction Only**

USEFUL BUS LINES

#1: circles the Medina
#5 and **#38:** Tunis Marine–Belvedere Park
#20: Jardin Thameur–La Marsa
#20b: Jardin Thameur–Gammarth
#21 and **#26:** Place Barcelone–Mornag
#27: Jardin Thameur–Raouad

#30: Tunis Marine–Bardo
#35: Tunis Marine–Airport
#40: La Marsa–Gammarth
#44: Place Belhaouane–Kalaat El Andalous
#50: connects the two intercity bus terminals (Bab Saadoun–Bab Alleoua)

USEFUL METRO STATIONS

Barcelone (lines #1 and 2): train station and interchange
République (lines #2, 3, 4 and 5): interchange
Tunis Marine (line #1): TGM station
Bab Alleoua (line #1): southern intercity bus station
Palestine (line #2): UK and Algerian consulates, US embassy

Jeunesse (line #2): football ground
Cité Sportive (line #2): Olympic swimming pool
Bab Saadoun (lines #3, 4 and 5): northern intercity bus station
20 Mars (line #4): nearest stop to the Bardo Museum until its own station opens

Taxis

Taxis in Tunis are hailed in the street in a fairly conventional way and metered. By day you'll rarely pay more than 2TD for a ride in the city centre. They cost more at night, when meters are off and you have to negotiate the price.

Accommodation in Tunis

On arrival, the **ONTT Tourist Office** on pl 7 Novembre is of limited use in finding a place to stay. Although they provide a list of hotels (omitting some of those in the listings that follow), they're unable to handle bookings. Many travel agencies, particularly those at the airport, offer a booking service, usually for the more expensive, classsified hotels with a few selected 1-star choices at the lower end of the scale.

On the whole, the best way to find a room is just to start walking. Central Tunis has dozens of **cheap hotels**, though in midsummer the more **recommended addresses** tend to fill up disconcertingly quickly and it's wise to start looking as early as possible. If you're mightily organised you could also try to book in advance by telephone – certainly worth the price of the call. If everything appears to be full (*complet*) it's worth knowing that at the height of the season a few hotels let people sleep on the roof. This is cheaper, and also more comfortable with the humidity, but officially illegal. The only real alternative to a hotel in Tunis is the rather good **youth hostel** in the Medina – again, you should try to book.

The following listings cover the cheaper hotels in the French city and the Medina, district by district, followed by the city's posher options for those who value and can afford their comforts. Hotels are unclassified unless otherwise indicated – though classification is rarely an indication of value for money. In some you pay to use the shower and you may or may not find breakfast included, so it's important to check what the price actually includes. The **cheapest hotels** of all are in the Medina and at its edges. Some of these can be extremely insalubrious and women travelling alone are advised to steer clear.

Lastly, in order **to camp** you have to leave the city completely to find a place to pitch a tent. The campground at Hammam Plage/Borj Cedria, southeast of the city, is almost certainly still closed after the attack on the nearby PLO office. The possibility still exists of "wild" camping on Raouad beach north of the city – though it's not exactly a peaceful getaway in midsummer when there are lots of families here.

Hotels in the Ville Nouvelle

The densest concentration of hotels – though they're also the most likely to be full – lies in the French quarter of the city **between the Medina and av de Carthage**, which cuts across **av Bourguiba** about halfway down. If you have the energy there are other cheap places to check out further south **around Bab Jazira**, especially on rue d'Alger and av Bab Jedid. Numbered hotels are keyed on the city centre map (see overleaf).

Av Charles de Gaulle

Hôtel Cirta (1), 42 av Charles de Gaulle (☎241582). A favourite with Tunisians and tourists alike. Friendly, good value and the nearest thing in Tunis to a travellers' hotel. Recommended. 5/7TD, shower 0.5TD.

Hôtel de l'Agriculture (2), 25 av Charles de Gaulle (☎246394). Opposite the *Cirta* and very similar. 3.5/6.5TD, shower 0.6TD.

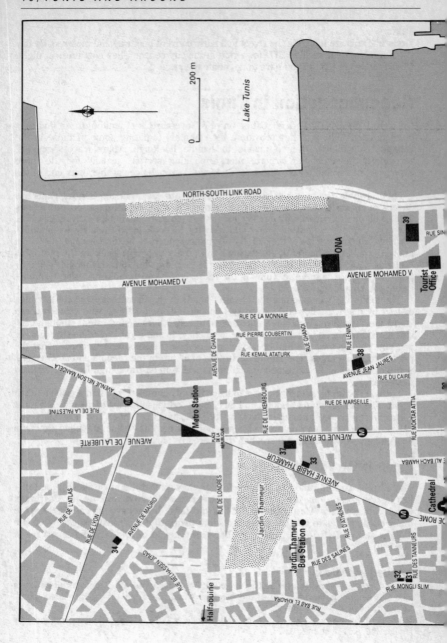

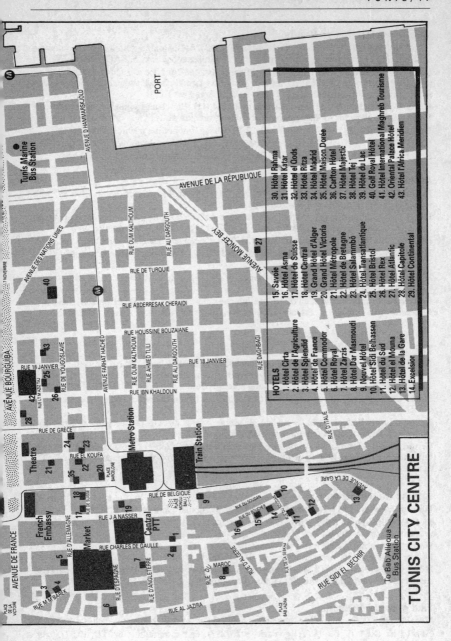

TUNIS CITY CENTRE

PORT

AVENUE DE LA RÉPUBLIQUE

AVENUE MONCEF BEY

Tunis Marine
Bus Station

AVENUE D'HAMMARSKJOLD

RUE OUM KALTHOUM

RUE ALI DARGOUTH

RUE DE TURQUIE

RUE ABDERRESAK CHERAIDI

RUE HOUSSINE BOUZAIANE

RUE OUM KALTHOUM

RUE AHMED TLILI

RUE ALI DARGOUTH

RUE 18 JANVIER

RUE IBN KHALDOUN

RUE DAGHBAGI

AVENUE DES NATIONS UNIES

NOVEMBRE

AVENUE BOURGUIBA

RUE DE YOUGOSLAVE

RUE L'MAZDI TAJ

RUE 18 JANVIER

AVENUE FARHAT HACHED

RUE DE GRÈCE

RUE EL KOUFA

PLACE
BARCELONE

Theatre

Metro Station

Train Station

RUE DE BELGIQUE

PLACE
MONGE
BALI

RUE D'ITALIE

AVENUE DE LA GARE

French
Embassy

Market

Central
PTT

RUE D'ALLEMAGNE

RUE DE SUISSE

RUE J A NASSER

RUE CHARLES DE GAULLE

RUE D'ANGLETERRE

RUE D'ESPAGNE

RUE M M'BAREK

PLACE
DE LA
VICTOIRE

AVENUE DE FRANCE

RUE DU MAROC

RUE AL JAZIRA

PLACE
BAB JAZIRA

RUE DU SOLDAN

RUE DU SOUFRE

RUE DE LA SEBKA

RUE DE L'AGHCHE

RUE SIDI EL BÉCHIR

To Bab Alleoua
Bus Station

HOTELS

1. Hôtel Cirta
2. Hôtel de l'Agriculture
3. Hôtel Splendid
4. Hôtel de France
5. Hôtel Commodor
6. Hôtel Royal
7. Hôtel Zarzis
8. Hôtel Dar Masmoudi
9. Nouvel Hôtel
10. Hôtel Sidi Belhassen
11. Hôtel du Sud
12. Hôtel el Mouna
13. Hôtel de la Gare
14. Excelsior
15. Savoie
16. Hôtel Asma
17. Hôtel de Suisse
18. Hôtel Central
19. Grand Hôtel d'Alger
20. Grand Hôtel Victoria
21. Hôtel Métropole
22. Hôtel de Bretagne
23. Hôtel Salammbô
24. Hôtel Transatlantique
25. Hôtel Bristol
26. Hôtel Rex
27. Hôtel Atlantic
28. Hôtel Capitole
29. Hôtel Continental
30. Hôtel Rahna
31. Hôtel Katar
32. Hôtel el Oods
33. Hôtel Ritza
34. Hôtel Madrid
35. Hôtel Maison Dorée
36. Carlton Hôtel
37. Hôtel Majestic
38. Hôtel Tej
39. Hôtel du Lac
40. Golf Royal Hôtel
41. Hôtel International Maghreb Tourisme
42. Oriental Palace Hôtel
43. Hôtel l'Africa Meridien

West of av Charles de Gaulle

Hôtel Splendid (3), 2 rue Mustapha M'barek (☎242844). Rooms quite clean if somewhat sombre. Has a certain seedy charm and a style reminiscent of Cairo. 5/8.4TD, bath 1.5T.

Hôtel de France (4), 8 rue Mustapha M'barek (☎245876). Nice big old-fashioned rooms, many with bathroom (about 1.5TD extra). Would be a great place if the management weren't so downright rude and unpleasant. 1* 8.4/10.2TD, breakfast 1.7TD.

Hôtel Commodor (5), 17 rue d'Allemagne (☎244941). Big clean rooms but rather gloomy. 1* 6.8/12TD, more for rooms with bath or shower, breakfast1.3TD.

Hôtel Royal (6), 19 rue d'Espagne (☎242780). Cheap, but not the friendliest. 3/4.5TD.

Hôtel Zarzis (7), 20 rue d'Angleterre (☎248031). Not exactly welcoming. 3TD per person.

Hôtel Dar Masmoudi (8), 18 rue du Maroc (☎342248). Overpriced. 1* 14/19TD b&b.

Around av de la Gare

Nouvel Hôtel (9), 3 pl Mongi Bali (☎243879). Very much a station hotel: friendly, with rather Dickensian rooms and big iron beds. 4/6TD.

Hôtel Sidi Belhassen (10), 23bis av de la Gare (☎256928). Cheery sort of place, but small rooms. 4/6TD low season, 8TD with bath; 7TD/8TD high, 14TD with bath, b&b.

Hôtel du Sud (11), 34 rue du Soudan (☎246916). Cheap and basic. 5TD double.

Hôtel el Mouna (12), 64 rue de la Sebkha (☎343375). A new place, spacious and spotless. 10TD double with bathroom.

Hôtel de la Gare (13), 25 av de la Gare (☎256754). Friendly with clean if rather bare rooms. 4.5/7TD, shower 0.7TD.

Rock-bottom alternatives, all on rue du Boucher. For around 2–3TD per person, these are: **Excelsior (14)** at No. 7, **Savoie (15)** at No. 13 (☎243779), and **Asma (16)** at No. 17 (☎340940).

East of av Charles de Gaulle

Hôtel de Suisse (17), 5 rue de Suisse (☎243821). In an alley joining rue d'Hollande and rue Jamel Abdel Nasser. Pleasant rooms, a slightly grubby kitchen available and promises of a 10 percent discount for anyone brandishing a Rough Guide. 1* 6.5/9.5TD, 10.5TD with bath.

Hôtel Central (18), 6 rue de Suisse (☎240433). A bit on the seedy side but quite clean. 6.5TD double, shower 1TD.

Grand Hôtel d'Alger (19), 5 rue de Belgique (☎246429). On pl Barcelone. Cheap and grotty with peculiar management. 2.5/5TD, shower 0.8TD.

Grand Hôtel Victoria (20), 79, rue Farhat Hached (☎342863). Not that grand perhaps, but with large rooms and right on pl Barcelone – handy for bus, train and metro. 6.5TD double.

Around rue de Grèce

Hôtel Métropole (21), 3 rue de Grèce (☎241377). Popular place. 1* 7/14TD b&b.

Hôtel de Bretagne (22), 7 rue de Grèce (☎242146). Dirty and unfriendly with dubious security. 3.5/6TD, shower 0.6TD.

Hôtel Salammbô (23), 6 rue de Grèce (☎244252). Great old-fashioned rooms and a TV lounge to hang out in. Recommended. 1* 8/12TD b&b, shower 1TD.

Hôtel Transatlantique (24), 106 rue de Yougoslavie (☎240680). Pleasantly colonial-style rooms and a beautifully tiled lobby. Again, recommended. 1* from 8/10.5TD.

East of av de Carthage

Hôtel Bristol (25), 30 rue Lt Mohamed el Aziz Taj (☎244836). Reasonable value. 4/6TD.

Hôtel Rex (26), 65 rue de Yougoslavie (☎257397). Fair to middling. 6/9TD, 10.5TD with bath. **Hôtel Atlantic (27)** 27 rue Daghbagi (☎246430). A very basic hotel in an industrial part of town but pleasantly run. Rooms clean but spartan and rather poky; no showers. 2.5/4TD.

Av Bourguiba and north

Hôtel Capitole (28), 60 av Bourguiba (☎244997). Slap bang in the middle of av Bourguiba along with the restaurant, bar and cinema of the same name. In the centre of things, but still overpriced for what it is. 1*12.8/19.3TD, extra 4.6TD with bath.

Hôtel Continental (29), 5 rue de Marseille (☎259834). Nothing to write home about but quite adequate. 5/6TD, shower 0.7TD.

Hôtel Rahma (30), 5 rue Qadiciyah (☎255566), an alley behind *La Parnasse* cinema. Reasonable place with small rooms. Avoid the neighbouring *Quercy*. 3.5/6.5TD, shower 1TD.

Hôtel Katar (31), imp 6, rue des Tanneurs (☎241222). Cheap and dingy. 2.5/5TD, shower 0.5TD.

Hôtel el Qods (32), imp 6, rue des Tanneurs (☎340404). Next door to the *Katar* and preferable. Ask for a room with balcony. 2.5/5TD.

Hotel Ritza (33), 35 av H. Thameur (☎245428). Recently redecorated but not very personable. 7/9TD.

Hôtel Madrid (34), 24 rue Belhassen Jerad (☎353216). On the corner of av de Madrid. Great decor – tiles and painted ceilings – but no alcohol allowed. 9/15TD, 15/20TD with bath.

Medina Hotels

Hotels in the **Medina** tend to be the cheapest, but also the dirtiest and very stuffy in summer. Apart from the first, and the ones on bd Bab Menara, they are not recommended to women on their own. On the other hand, a stay in the Medina throws you headlong into a world that would completely pass you by in the safe hostelries of the Ville Nouvelle. If you want to experience the real Tunis, you might think about sacrificing a little comfort and security for a dose of authenticity, to see how the other half lives.

Hôtel Medina, 1 pl de la Victoire (☎255056). Nicest hotel in the Medina – clean, conveniently situated and naturally very popular. 7.5TD double, shower 0.5TD.

Hôtel de Bonheur, 32 rue de la Kasbah (☎254758). Very suspect but preferable to the *Soleil* next door. 4TD double.

Hôtel Riadh, 57 rue Mongi Slim (☎257330). On the edge of the Medina, rooms rather poky and airless. 4/7TD, shower 0.8TD.

Hôtel Hammami, 12 rue el Mechnaka (☎260451). Large grubby rooms in a huge and very impressive mansion near Place Bab Carthajana. 2.5/4.5TD, shower 0.5TD.

Hôtel les Amis, 7 rue Monastiri (☎565653). Basic but clean, with kung fu videos in the TV room. 2TD per person.

Hôtel Sfax, 5 rue de l'Or (☎260275). Near pl Bab Souika. No shower but a men's hammam nearby. The beds are in a bit of a state. 2.5/4.7TD.

Hôtel el Massara, 5 bd Bab Menara (☎ 263734). On the western edge of the Medina. Clean but miniscule rooms. 3.5/7TD.

Hôtel de la Victoire, 7 bd Bab Menara (☎261224). Neighbour to the *Massara*. Cool and airy if rather noisy. Friendly management and a painting in every room. 4/8TD, shower 1TD.

Medina Youth Hostel

Dar Saida Ajoula (YHA Tunis Medina), 25 rue Saida Ajoula (☎567850). Clean, friendly and well run but still subject to rules and curfew (10pm winter, midnight in summer and closed 10am–3pm in July–Aug). The building is a former palace and fills up quickly in summer so book ahead. 2TD bed, 2.5TD b&b, 6.5TD FB, plus YHA card or 2TD daily membership.

North of the Medina proper: Halfaouine

Hôtel El Khir, 24 rue Souki Bel Khir (no phone). Between Bab El Khadra and pl Halfaouine. Slightly musty but not bad. 3/4TD.

Hôtel 20 Mars, 9 rue Sidi El Aloui (☎266924). Men only – and even if you are only a man hardly recommended – but at 1TD per bed in 5-berth rooms, the cheapest in town. 1TD.

Upmarket Addresses

Tunis's luxury offerings stand comparison with any and several offer good value if you're in this league. You won't find large numbers of tourists in competition for their services, either, as few packages put clients up in the capital. Numbers refer to the city centre map key.

Hôtel Maison Dorée (35), 3 rue el Koufa (☎240632). Backs onto rue de Hollande. Spotless and rather formal. 2* 12TD/13.9TD b&b, 19/21TD with bath.

Carlton Hôtel (36), 31 av Bourguiba (☎258167/8). Friendly and well situated. 2* 12.5TD/16TD, 15/20TD with bath, breakfast 1.5TD.

Hôtel Majestic (37), 36 av de Paris (☎242848/9). Elegant colonial architecture, especially the foyer, but the hotel in general is getting a bit shabby. 3* 15/22TD b&b.

Hôtel Tej (38), 14 rue Lt Mohamed el Aziz Taj (☎344899). Claims to offer a "three-star service for two-star prices". Well, actually the prices are three-star, but the service matches, and the breakfasts are great. 2* 20/30TD b&b.

Hôtel du Lac (39), rue Sinbad (☎258322). Discreet and tasteful it is not, but the inverted pyramid is now a landmark on the Tunis skyline and not a bad place to stay if you like a bit of luxury. 3* 22.5/34TD b&b, 28/45TD FB.

Golf Royal Hôtel (40), 51–53 rue de Yougoslavie (☎344311). Business-class place with a/c and TV, but not many other facilities. 3* 38/48TD b&b.

Hôtel International Maghreb Tourisme (41), 49 av Bourguiba (☎254855). Not what you'd call a classy joint, in spite of the deluxe rating. 4*L 50/62TD.

Hilton Tunis, Notre Dame (☎282000). Out above the Belvedere, miles from the city centre but with a great view over it and, except in rush hours, only 10 minutes away by taxi. 4*L 66/80TD b&b.

Oriental Palace Hôtel (42), 29 av Jean Jaures (☎348846). This place has style. The decor is completely over the top and worth taking in if you're just passing by. 4*L 66/74TD, American-style breakfast 4.5TD.

Hôtel l'Africa Meridien (43), 50 av Bourguiba (☎347477). A monstrous carbuncle, yes, but the best hotel on av Bourguiba. 4*L from 68/75TD, American-style breakfast 6TD.

The French City and Parks

When the French arrived in 1881, Lake Tunis came right up to Bab el Bahr in Place de la Victoire. The centre of today's city is built on land reclaimed by them from the lake. Down the middle of it runs **Avenue Bourguiba** and, off that, the streets more or less follow a grid pattern. The city's main chunk of greenery is the massive **Belvedere Park** which overlooks it: Tunis's other parks are in rather a sorry state.

Avenue Bourguiba

Avenue Bourguiba (now officially av 7 Novembre) is the centre of Tunis in every way. People converge here from all over the city to sit in cafés, stroll under the trees, buy a nosegay made of jasmine buds – above all, just to see and be seen. There's something very continental about its life, quite at odds with the privacy of the Medina's cramped narrow streets.

Along the avenue: the Cathedral, Theatre, and Ambassade de France

The first landmark along the avenue – or to be more accurate on av Bourguiba's prede-cessor, av Jules Ferry – is the **Cathedral**, built in 1882 and, like its companion on the Byrsa hill at Carthage, a monstrous, bizarre mixture of Romanesque, Byzantine, and Oriental styles. But if ever the authorities decided to do the decent thing and demolish it, there's no doubt it would leave an irreplaceable gap.

Just across from the cathedral, the old French **Theatre**, with its bulging layers of white stucco and fantastic carved figures supporting the balcony, has just been refur-bished and plays host to regular and highly recommended Arabic and classical music concerts. Here, in 1896, the Marquis de Morés made a speech condemning British imperialism in the Sudan (remarkably hypocritical, given France's colonial adventur-ism at the time), before making his fateful expedition to bring military aid to the Mahdi (see p.304).

Beyond the theatre is the **French Embassy**, quite modest by contrast. Built in 1862 as the advance guard of growing French influence, and as the *Residence Générale*, the centre of the Protectorate administration from 1881, many of the important decisions of Tunisia's recent history have been made within its unassuming walls.

Modern architecture

The embassy and theatre and other old colonial buildings still set the avenue's tone – as, too, do the arcades of av de France – but they're slowly being overshadowed by post-Independence additions. The *Hôtel Africa* in particular was a planning disaster which succeeded in ruining Tunis's skyline at a stroke, and caused a national policy in favour of low buildings. The equally brazen *Hôtel du Lac,* an upturned pyramid at the eastern end of av Bourguiba, is at least bizarre enough to be interesting.

CHRISTMAS CAKE COLONIAL ARCHITECTURE

Tunis has some buildings in the same league as any in Algiers, Marseille, Casablanca, or even Barcelona. These are some of the more outstanding examples around the city centre:

South of av Bourguiba Have a look at 9 rue Charles de Gaulle and 114 rue de Yougoslavie. The block of 35-37 rue Ahmed Tlili and 40-42 rue Oum Kalthoum is also quite striking, while 55 av Carthage looks decidedly askew nowadays.

Av Bourguiba There is the theatre of course, and no. 48 is also quite impressive if you cast your eyes above the *Tunis Air* office.

North of av Bourguiba Some other fine confections are to be seen at 1 rue des Tanneurs (on the corner of rue de Rome), 11 av de Paris, 30 rue Ghandi (on the corner of rue de Paris), and 5 rue de Luxembourg.

Av de la Liberté No. 130 catches the eye, as to a lesser extent do no. 22 and the *Hôtel Majestic* at no. 36. Nearby, 11 rue de l'Atlas is rather hidden away for such a splendid piece of stucco; notice too the hand of Fatima, dated 1929, on the building opposite.

Rue de Londres There are several interesting **doorways** here. No. 4, on pl de la République, is quite impressive, and nos. 32 and 55-57 are also worth checking out, as are the faces above the doors of nos. 22-28.

Off Avenue Bourguiba

South of the Avenue are most of the restaurants, night-clubs and cinemas. The most lively area of French Tunis, this also contains the huge **food market** on rue d'Allemagne, selling every conceivable kind of produce. Beyond the railway station, the grid plan begins to lose its grip near the Medina, and the same thing happens **north of the Avenue**, where the area immediately adjoining rue Mongi Slim and rue Bab

Souika, the old **Maltese and Jewish quarters**, is agreeably chaotic. The thirteenth-century **Zaraia Mosque**, on the corner of rue Zarkoun and rue Mongi Slim, is the area's main "sight". The further you get from the Medina, the stronger the European influence. Avenue de Paris and av de la Liberté would be anonymous were it not for the wonderful examples of colonial architecture, ranging from turn-of-the-century *kitsch* (some marvellous carved heads – eagles, lions, old men – peer over the doorways) to provincial 1930s Art Deco. Towards the end of av de la Liberté things get more sombre, as you move into a zone of embassies and government buildings.

The Parks

The **Belvedere Park** provides an excellent reason for coming this far north, though. Breathing space has always been a problem in Tunis. An anonymous "English lady" of the 1850s, author of *Letters from Barbary*, reported asking to be shown a garden. Her guide led her some way through the streets, then "halted before two trees, growing against a wall, and surrounded by a plot of about four foot wide, perhaps: and this, he told us, was the biggest garden in the town." Most people today escape the summer humidity by catching the TGM to Carthage or Sidi Bou Said, but the Belvedere park, with its green lower area kept heavily watered, is a peaceful and accessible alternative. Vegetation grows much more sparsely as you climb the hill, but there's an excellent view from the top over Tunis to Bou Kornine (see p.90). The elaborate **koubba** ("dome") standing about halfway up was built in 1798 for a palace in the suburbs and transplanted here in 1901.

At the bottom of the park (just above its main entrance) the old Casino has been converted into a **Museum of Modern Art and Cinema**, and its terrace is used for theatrical performances in summer as part of the Carthage Festival. The museum is being reorganised, and the cinema is due to open soon. Further round to the south is the **Zoo**, where some distressingly small cages provide an eyeball-to-eyeball perspective on the fiercer species; look out, too, for that exotic native of the northern wastes – the Shetland pony. Also here is the **Midha**, an early seventeenth-century fountain for pre-prayer ablutions, brought here from its original site at Souk et Trouk in the Medina. The **cafés** in the middle of the zoo and on the lake just outside are two of the most relaxed in the city.

One or two other **parks** are worth mentioning only to save disappointment. The *Jardin Habib Thameur*, just off av de Paris, is green but small and fume-laden; and the *Parc Kennedy*, which looks so tempting on out-of-date maps, is no more. The *Jardin el Gorjiani* by Montfleury, southwest of the Medina, provides a much-needed patch of green in that part of town. Otherwise, the **cemeteries**, of which Jellaz (see p.68) is the biggest, provide patches of open space for a walk or a rest.

The Medina

"White, domed, studded with minarets, honeycombed with tunnel-like bazaars": until about 100 years ago the **Medina**, with its few *faubourgs* surrounding it, *was* Tunis. Porte de France, the old gate now standing isolated in Place de la Victoire, was then an important lakeside entrance to the city (and is still called *Bab El Bahr:* the "Sea Gate").

The French built their new capital on reclaimed land, and although they made no deliberate attempt to eradicate local culture (as they did in Algiers), the Medina inevitably declined. After Independence in 1956 a plan was raised to drive a continuation of av Bourguiba through the heart of the Medina to the government offices on the far side, which would have destroyed the quarter for ever, but fortunately this was abandoned and the ASM (*Association de Sauvegarde de la Medina*) was set up to try to preserve the old city's heritage. But however much the physical fabric is preserved, the original way of life is gone. Putting government offices in the Medina (just below the site of the former Kasbah) was an important gesture, but most of Tunis's everyday life continues outside its confines. What's left for the Medina is a suburban existence in the remoter corners and a good deal of tourist-oriented activity, which helps to support some traditional crafts, in the central area.

So much for the prosaic reality. Tunis's Medina still offers visitors an intense and vibrant experience quite unlike anything to be found in Europe. The narrow streets, alternately bustling with crowds and quietly lined with historic monuments and palaces, bear comparison with any other great Middle Eastern city. The most distinctively Tunisian elements are the magnificent **doorways** which, according to El Bekri, were already famous in the thirteenth century: blue or beige, set with black studs and a "hand of Fatima" knocker, and surrounded by intricately carved stone frames (see *Tunisian Architecture*, p.339–341). In many ways it's best just to wander randomly, stumbling on unexpected sights; but the following itineraries are the only way to find the full wealth of historic interest.

The **divisions** below are artificial, and purely for convenience. If you're short of time, try at least to see the central area, where the interest is most concentrated. The other routes go through quieter districts, but include a number of significant and beautiful monuments. The **Dar Ben Abdullah Museum** in the south is a must, for the sumptuous palace building as much as the exhibits; and the big Turkish-style **Mosques of Sidi Mehrez** and **Hammouda Pasha** in the north offer a fascinating and little-appreciated contrast to the Tunisian ones of the centre.

One note of caution: avoid wandering around after dark, when the Medina is deserted, ill-lit and dangerous. Although old men are hired as watchmen (they stand on corners of the main thoroughfares with baseball bats calling out the all clears at regular intervals), they hardly inspire confidence for nocturnal jaunts. More tangibly, the main danger in the Medina after dark is being hit by flying rubbish. It's flung from windows in the evenings for the early morning street cleaners, who supposedly arrive before the tourists and brush it all up. All very medieval, but then there's not much space for dustbin lorries.

The centre and the souks

With the Great Mosque and souks set squarely in the middle, the **central section of the Medina** was once the heart of the old city. Here the Medina is at its most intense and the concentration of streets, shops and people at its greatest. At some times of day, the main streets into the Medina from pl de la Victoire are so chock-a-block you can hardly move down them. On the downside, the Medina's main industry nowadays is tourism, usually of the daytrip variety, with most tour groups "doing" the same streets, the same sights and the same souvenir shops. The result is that the centre of the Medina can feel very commercial, even artificial, and the streets like a gauntlet of traders, albeit mostly amiable ones.

Rue Jemaa Zitouna

Two main streets lead in from the pl de la Victoire, but before taking the left-hand fork (rue Jemaa Zitouna) just stand for a moment and soak in the difference between western symmetry and eastern activity. The contrast is really less fundamental than it at first seems, but it's an impression that remains striking.

Rue Jemaa Zitouna leads directly to the Great Mosque, and, as the main tourist highway, has turned into a cauldron of overflowing stalls and overeager proprietors. You can buy everything more cheaply elsewhere, but the shops are a useful training ground for bargaining techniques, and the stall on the corner of rue Sidi Ali Azouz often has interesting old metal items.

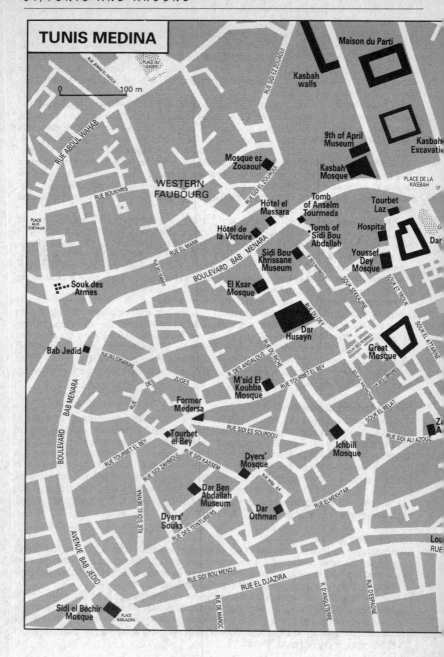

TUNIS MEDINA

RUE JEMAA EL HAOUA

PLACE DU LEADER

RUE SIDI EZ ZOUAOUI

RUE EZ ZOUAOUI

Maison du Parti

Kasbah walls

0   100 m

RUE ABDUL WAHAB

9th of April Museum

Kasbah Excavation

Mosque ez Zouaoui

WESTERN FAUBOURG

RUE BOUKHRIS

RUE EL MARR

Kasbah Mosque

PLACE DE LA KASBAH

Tomb of Anselm Tourmeda

Tourbet Laz

PLACE AUX CHEVAUX

Hôtel el Massara

Hôtel de la Victoire

Tomb of Sidi Bou Abdallah

Hospital

Dar

RUE EL MENARA

BOULEVARD BAB MENARA

Sidi Bou Khrissane Museum

Youssef Dey Mosque

RUE SI MAHROUK

El Ksar Mosque

RUE DES TORNES

SOUK SEKKAJINE

SOUK ET TROUK

Souk des Armes

RUE DU DEY

Dar Husayn

SOUK DES HOMMES

Great Mosque

SOUK EL ATTARINE

Bab Jedid

RUE DES FORGERONS

R. DES ANDALOUS

RUE DU RICHE

SOUK EL KACHACHINE

BOULEVARD BAB MENARA

RUE DES JUGES

M'sid El Koubba Mosque

RUE TOURBET EL BEY

SOUK EL FALAKINE

Former Medersa

RUE SIDI ES SOURDOU

SOUK EL BELAT

Za A

Tourbet el Bey

RUE SIDI ALI AZOUZ

RUE TOURBET EL BEY

RUE SIDI ZAHMOUL

RUE SIDI KASSEM

Dyers' Mosque

RUE EMLA 44

Ichbili Mosque

Dar Ben Abdallah Museum

Dar Othman

RUE EL MEKHTAR

RUE SIDI EL BENNA

AVENUE BAB JEDID

Dyers' Souks

RUE DES TEINTURIERS

Lou RUE

Sidi el Bêchir Mosque

PLACE BABJAZIRA

RUE SIDI BOU MENDJI

RUE DE MAROC

RUE EL DJAZIRA

R. D'ANGLETERRE

RUE D'ESPAGNE

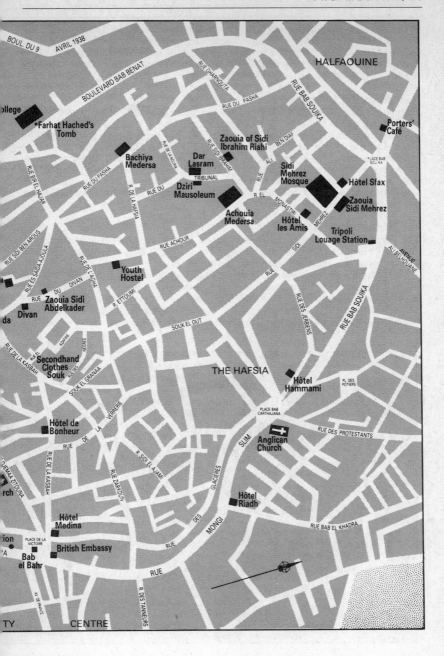

BOUL. DU 9 AVRIL 1938

HALFAOUINE

RUE GHARNOUTA

BOULEVARD BAB BENAT

RUE BAB SOUIKA

RUE DU PASHA

ollege

•Farhat Hached's
Tomb

Porters'
Café

PLACE BAB
SOU KA

RUE BIR EL HAJAR

RUE DU PASHA

RUE DE LA HAFSIA

Bachiya
Medersa

RUE DE M'NDRA

RUE SIDI IBRAHIM

RUE DU

Dar
Lasram

TRIBUNAL

Zaouia of Sidi
Ibrahim Riahi

RUE ALI

BEN DIAF

RUE EL

Sidi
Mehrez
Mosque

Hôtel Sfax

RUE SIDI BEN AROUS

RUE ES SAIDA AJOULA

RUE DE LA KASBAH

Dziri
Mausoleum

Achouia
Medersa

R. EL

MONASTIR

MEHREZ

Zaouia
Sidi Mehrez

Hôtel
les Amis

SIDI

Tripoli
Louage Station

AVENUE ALI BELHOUANE

RUE DU DIVAN

RUE DE L'AGHA

Youth
Hostel

RUE ACHOUR

RUE ACHOUR

RUE

da

Divan

RUE

Zaouia Sidi
Abdelkader

R. ETTOUMI

SOUK EL OUT

RUE DES JEBBENS

RUE BAB SOUIKA

RUE DE LA KASBAH

R. EL

Secondhand
Clothes
Souk

SOUK EL GRANAA

SPADAS

THE HAFSIA

Hôtel
Hammami

PL. DES
POTIERS

RUE DE LA VERRERIE

Hôtel de
Bonheur

RUE DE LA

PLACE BAB
CARTHAJANA

RUE DES PROTESTANTS

RUE

RUE DE LA KASBAH

R SIDI EL AJAMI

RUE ZARKOUN

GLACIERES

SLIM

Anglican
Church

Hôtel
Medina

Hôtel
Riadh

RUE BAB EL KHADRA

RUE DES

rch

ion

PLACE DE LA
VICTOIRE

British Embassy

MONGI

RUE

A

Bab
el Bahr

RUE

AV DE FRANCE

R. DES TANNEURS

TY

CENTRE

No. 14 rue Jemaa Zitouna (on the left) was the **first church in Tunis** when it was built in 1662. In the 1860s it became a sanctuary, protected by the French, and the source of repeated confrontation between them and the Beys. Time after time the Beys had to back down and accept that the criminals and enemies who escaped here were outside their jurisdiction.

Hammouda Bey's barracks

Hammouda Bey (1777–1813) was faced with problems of a different sort when, in 1811, his Ottoman troops mutinied. Hammouda responded by recruiting as auxiliaries tribal warriors from among the Zouaoua Berbers. He built them five sets of barracks in Tunis. The fine door at no. 55 belongs to the **Sidi Morjani Barracks**, the third set he built. At the end of rue Jemaa Zitouna, no. 73, now the **National Library**, was originally the second barracks; entrance to the library is through the Souk el Attarine. The first of Hammouda Bey's barracks is now Aziza Othmana Hospital (near pl du Gouvernement, see p.59), another is in rue Sidi Ali Azouz, just off rue Jemaa Zitouna, and the fifth has been demolished.

The Zitouna Mosque

The **Great Mosque** brings rue Jemaa Zitouna to an abrupt halt. It is known as the Zitouna ("olive tree") because it stands on the site of an olive tree under which its founder apparently preached and taught the Koran.

The Mosque's massive size is exaggerated by the cramped alleys around it, an effect which must have been even greater when it was completed under the Aghlabids' rule in the ninth century. Most of the Great Mosque's present structure is theirs – part of the scheme which included mosques at Kairouan, Sfax and Sousse – but with considerable additions and refurbishments. The original minaret, for example, has

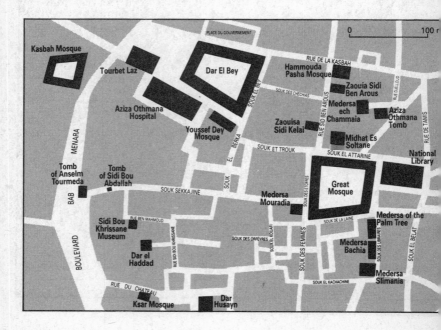

been restored since the thirteenth century, along the lines of the Kasbah Mosque (see p.69). For such a huge building, it has an extraordinarily spiritual quality which later disappeared from Islamic architecture, especially in Spain and North Africa, under a welter of ornamentation.

In its day, the **university** based in this mosque was one of the greatest in the world, rivalled only by al-Azhar in Cairo (which was itself founded in 970 after the Fatimid invasion from Tunisia). Hundreds of years before European universities had even been thought of, students were coming to Tunis from throughout the Islamic world. Tradition records that each professor had his own column, next to which he always did his teaching. Even in the 1950s there were 10,000 students here, but during the 1960s the university was brought into line with the national educational system, and theological students moved elsewhere. Visiting hours for the mosque are 8am–noon (closed Fri).

Three Medersas

Coming out of the mosque, turn right along **Souk des Libraires**, one side of which is lined by a series of interconnecting *medersas* built in the early eighteenth century – the **Medersa of the Palm Tree** (no. 11), the **Bachia** (no. 27) and, on the corner, the **Slimania**. The *medersa* is a type of residential Islamic college found all over the Muslim world, and here each has the classic form of a courtyard surrounded by students' cells. Expensive institutions, *medersas* were usually endowed at times of domestic prosperity. These three are part of a series founded in Tunis in the eighteenth century, and the story behind two of them typifies the instability of the Husaynid dynasty. The Bachia was founded in 1752 by Ali Pasha, and only two years later he dedicated the Slimania to the memory of his son Suleiman, who had been poisoned by a younger brother. There's also a **hammam** here (no. 30).

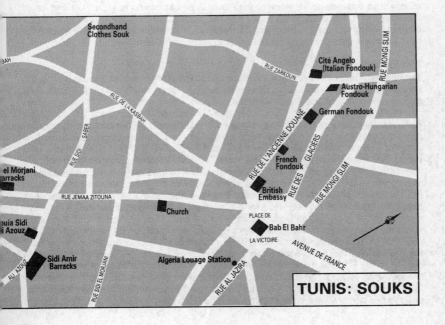

The main souks

Back at the Great Mosque, turn left along the **Souk de la Laine** – Wool Market – which runs up the near side. There's not much wool here anymore, but a few traditional tailors and, at **no. 21**, a doorway into the mosque improvised out of Roman blocks. Opposite no. 9 is the Rue de Béjà, where most of the wool and cotton weaving seems to have moved to. It's interesting to watch the weaving – most of the textiles are still made on hand looms. At the end of this street, a brief detour takes in some of the more remote souks.

Left along Souk des Femmes, you cross the Souk du Coton to a junction with **Souk el Kachachine** (this is where to find noisy wholesale bargaining for rugs and garments). Turn right at this corner, then first right (onto Souk el Kouafi) and first left into **Souk des Orfèvres**. True to its name, this is still the home of gold jewellers, whose tiny shops on narrow streets reflect their need for security. First right and then second right among the gold jewellers, and you should find yourself back at the corner of the mosque, at the meeting of Souk de la Laine and Souk des Etoffes.

Souk des Etoffes – Cloth Market – with its deep stalls set behind arcades of red and green barbershop columns, is the most spacious in the Medina: elegant and refined, it comes to an end at the far corner of the mosque. At no. 37, the **Mouradia Medersa** was built in 1673 by Mourad Bey, son of Hammouda Pasha, whose mosque is referred to on p.53.

The close link between Islam and commerce could hardly be better represented than by these purpose-built souks. Even the hierarchy of trades was symbolised by their respective positions: the closer to the mosque, the more "noble" the trade. Thus the Souk des Etoffes (cloth) and Souk el Attarine (perfume) were right next to it; messier businesses such as dyeing and metalwork were relegated to the suburbs. Unfortunately, the **Souk el Attarine**, which slopes down one side of the mosque, no longer specialises in perfume: in the sixteenth century it used to stay open until midnight in order to serve women, who took their hammams at night. On the left of this street as it descends, steps lead up to the **Midhat es Soltane**, a fifteenth-century bathing facility attached to the Great Mosque, whose builder, apparently desperate for popular credit, even arranged for hot water to be provided in winter.

The Slave Souk

Turning back up Souk el Attarine, continue up the hill along **Souk et Trouk**, built in the seventeenth century for Turkish (hence the name) tailors, past the *M'Rabet Restaurant* (pricey, see p.72, but you can sometimes just have a tea) and past the *Musée des Turcs* carpet shop with its terrace view over the Medina. At the top, turn left into *Souk Kebabjia*. An open space a little way along here is the **Souk el Berka**, once the market place of Tunis's slave trade. Slaves were brought here – the most unfortunate from their dungeons in the Kasbah at La Goulette – and displayed to prospective buyers, who would first check their teeth, because unskilled slaves ended up working the corsair galleys and being fed entirely on hard biscuits. Most of the slaves were captured at sea, as far away as the English Channel, but there were also frequent raids on coastal towns in Italy, France and Spain. It was a brutal business, though Western tradition has been happy to ignore the equally ferocious Christian corsairs supplying the great slave markets at Pisa, Genoa and other European trading cities. Piracy and slavery were generally accepted (even if not officially) as a lucrative adjunct of Mediterranean trade.

By the end of the eighteenth century, European fleets had forced the corsairs from the sea. Initially the Trans-Saharan trade compensated for the declining Mediterranean supply. In the 1790s as many as 6000 African slaves were sold in Tunis every year. Over the following decades, however, taxation, competition from Tripoli's markets and wars in the south ruined the trade. Then in 1846 Ahmed Bey, building his reputation as an enlightened ruler, abolished the slave trade and the markets were closed. The Africans have remained. In the past they suffered discrimination and were often reduced to the status of domestic servants, but today they are an integral part of Tunisian society.

Around place du Gouvernement

Back and round from the Souk el Berka, the **Mosque of Youssef Dey**, dating back to 1616, is distinguished by its octagonal minaret – the first built in Tunis. The Malekite school, dominant in North Africa since the Arab invasion, built square minarets, and the appearance of this octagonal design signalled the arrival of the new Turkish rulers, who were mainly Hanefites. The Italianate use of marble on the facade is another characteristic feature of an increasingly cosmopolitan Turkish culture.

Continuing on up past the mosque, you emerge from the Medina into **pl du Gouvernement**. Formerly a royal guest house, the **Dar el Bey** is now the Prime Minister's office, which means – since the thirteenth century the Hafsid Kasbah stood just above here – that government in Tunis has returned to its original site. You can see the excavations, over the road and above them the gleaming PSD Party building, while to the left is the **Kasbah Mosque** (see p.69 for more on this area).

Also in the pl du Gouvernement is the **Tourbet Laz**, the tomb of a seventeenth-century Dey and his family. These *tourbets* (tombs) were very fashionable among rich Turkish families of the time and Tunis has several (the Tourbet of Ahmed Kouja Dey is across the street, opposite the **Aziza Othmana Hospital**.

Souk des Chechias

Heading back past Youssef Dey's mosque, the street on your left behind the Dar el Bey is the **Souk el Bey**, suitably grand with its broad, pillared arcade. Third right off here is the **Souk des Chechias**, another eye-catching market. *Chechias* are the characteristic Tunisian skullcaps, made from wool by a complicated process of carding, moulding and dyeing. During the eighteenth century this was one of Tunisia's most important industries, since *chechias* were worn all over the Middle East. In 1835 the British Consul, Sir Thomas Reade, watched a procession carrying 200,000 *chechias* to La Goulette for export to Constantinople. The manufacturers, usually of Andalusian origin, were among the richest people in Tunis. In the mid-eighteenth century, however, European factories flooded the market with cheap imitations and the Tunisian industry, reduced to the luxury end of the market, was ruined. By the 1920s the remaining manufacturers faced another recession as the wealthy turned to Western dress. Now it is a disappearing industry – few Tunisians under the age of forty own or wear a *chechia* – and so the souk sits quiet and dignified. In its centre, Tunis's oldest café sells thick Turkish coffee.

Rue Sidi Ben Arous

Right at the end of the souk (at no. 23 rue Sidi Ben Arous) is the **Zaouia of Sidi Ben Arous**, a fourteenth-century native of Cap Bon who brought back Sufi teaching (see p.246) from Morocco. A *zaouia* is the meeting place of a religious fraternity, founded after the death of an individual master to propagate his teachings. The buildings which house the fraternities often date from long after the teacher's death, and though some are still in use, others have lapsed into poor repair. Built in 1437, this particular *zaouia* quickly became too popular with women for the authorities' liking and was closed – only to be promptly re-opened in the face of the ensuing uproar. On the opposite side of the street (at no. 18) is another Hafsid *zaouia*, the **Zaouia of Sidi Kelai**, and the shocking pink marble facade of the **Tourbet of Hammouda Pasha**, attached to the **mosque** of the same name. Built in 1655, soon after Youssef Dey's mosque, this also has an octagonal minaret, and even more ornate Italian decoration. Hammouda Pasha's father was one of many Italians in the service of the Turks who converted to Islam in order to further his career. Italians and Greeks in Turkish service were despised as *arrivistes* by the longer-established Georgians and Circassians.

Along rue de la Kasbah

Going down **rue de la Kasbah**, the other main street running across the Medina, the first proper street you cross is **rue Jelloud**. A dead end to the right off here surprisingly contains two important monuments. At no. 4, the **Medersa ech Chammaia**, founded by the Hafsid Sultan Abu Zakariya in 1249, was the first *medersa* built in Tunis. At the end of the same impasse (no. 9), the **Tomb of Aziza Othmana** belongs to a princess renowned for her generosity. Just before her death in 1669, she liberated her slaves and left her estate to charitable causes – funds to liberate slaves and prisoners, and a fund for poor girls who couldn't otherwise afford to marry. She's buried next to her grandfather Othman Dey (who built the Dar Othman in the south of the Medina), and the tomb itself was built by Husayn, founder of the Husaynid dynasty and Aziza Othmana's son-in-law. The world of the Tunisian ruling classes was a small one.

The foreign foundouks

Rue de la Kasbah continues downhill and out of the Medina. Just before emerging into the pl de la Victoire, a tiny alley on the left – rue de l'Ancienne Douane – leads to the site of the first **French Consulate-cum-trading post** (marked by a plaque on the wall just before the Guersin baths). Along the same street are the Italian, Austro-Hungarian, and German embassy buildings, whose first-floor balconies still bear their national insignia, the only clue to their erstwhile importance. Originally known as *fondouks* (trading posts where foreign merchants were obliged to live), they're today all *oukala*, houses divided up to accommodate several families. This is one of the most rundown areas of the Medina – rue Zarkoun at the end of the alley is a kind of flea market and just beyond you'll find yourself in a street of brothels. The only consular building left is the **British Embassy** on the corner of pl de la Victoire. When other nations were moving out to the suburbs the British obstinately stayed in the centre of town, rebuilding the embassy on the same site at the turn of the century.

It was Hammouda Pasha in 1659 who gave permission for the *fondouks* to be built. These were still dangerous times for foreigners in Tunis: in 1678 Francis Baker, the English Consul, reported that one Sidi Mohammed Bey "did…forceably and violently seize on Charles Gratiano, Consul for the French, together with ourselves…swearing by the Soule of his deceased he would cut us to pieces…". Fortunately Mohammed Bey fled when his brother Ali Bey returned, and the Consul lived to tell the tale in one (nervous) piece.

Place de la Victoire

Bab el Bahr, or Porte de France as it is also known, stands alone in the middle of **pl de la Victoire**. Not a triumphal arch, it was once the city's seaward gate, the present structure built in 1848 to replace its Hafsid predecessor. Its adjoining walls were demolished in the 1950s. Facing it is a large Italianate building with shabby columns and stucco decoration. In the late nineteenth century this was the office of the International Financial Commission that supervised the bankrupt Bey's administration. These French, Italian, and British commissioners forced the government to grant foreigners privileges and concessions that caused much resentment at the time, and on several occasions the building was attacked by mobs.

From the pl de la Victoire the **rue des Glacières** leads up to the north. Here, in the eighteenth and nineteenth centuries, huge blocks of ice, shipped from the Alps, were stored to be sold at vast profit during the summer months. Today the street's main attractions are the shops selling second-hand furniture and bric-à-brac. Most of the stuff was left by the French in the mid 1950s – Art Deco statuettes and nineteenth-century portraits of long-forgotten soldiers. If you're tempted to buy something, you'll find out why it's all still there: the prices asked are astronomical. Better just to wander through what is really an informal museum of the colonial past.

Northern Medina

The **northern part of the Medina**, largely free of tourists, leaves you feeling more a visitor than a punter, especially as the shops here sell goods that ordinary Tunisians buy. There are fewer sights as such, though the Mosque of Sidi Mehrez is as familiar to Tunisians as the Zitouna Mosque, but this is a much better part of the Medina if you just want to wander.

From the Divan to Dar Lasram

Turning off **rue de la Kasbah** along rue Saida Ajoula, the first left is rue Onk el Jemal, in which no. 5, the **Onkiya Medersa**, was founded by a Hafsid princess in 1341. Backtracking, duck left right off rue Saida Ajoula into **rue du Divan**. No. 3 on the right is the **Divan** itself, home of the Divan council which at first played a major role in the power structure of the sixteenth–seventeenth-century Turkish Regency of Tunis. As authority gradually passed into the hands of individual Beys, though, the council's function became more that of a religious court. Further on at no. 16 is the **Zaouia of Sidi Abdelkader**, built in 1851 as the seat of the Kadria brotherhood, a Sufi group.

At the end of the rue du Divan, just up to the left, is an area of **second-hand clothing stalls**, where bundles of unsorted clothes arrive regularly from European and American charities to be sold off at auction. Prices are ridiculously low – you can get virtually brand-new clothes for next to nothing – but the aid organisations seem to have overlooked the impact of these cheap imports on the local clothing industry. Tunisians wear flared jeans and ludicrous second-hand suits because there's no economical alternative: traditional dress has become a luxury. Nearby, at 9 rue des Nègres, is a *medersa* founded in 1435 by the Hafsid Sultan el Mustansir. The seventeenth-century Zaouia of Sidi Braham around the corner in rue el Azafine is famous for its collection of **ceramic tiles**.

Follow the rue de l'Agha up to the left into the little square where it finishes and have a quick look up at the amazing set of **Ottoman windows** through the arch ahead of you in rue Bir el Hajar. Then head off to your right, down **rue du Pasha**, a tidy cobbled street which was the main thoroughfare of the Turkish residential quarter, with graceful doorways befitting the homes of important officials. No. 40, on the left, is the eighteenth-century **Bachiya Medersa**, not to be confused with the Bachia Medersa in Souk des Libraires. Opposite no. 64 in the street there's a passageway into **rue de la Nouria**, which has to be the narrowest lane in the Medina. On the left as you bear left into rue du Tribunal is **Dar Lasram**, home of the Tunis *Association de Sauvegarde de la Medina* (ASM). Until twenty years ago, this palace was still owned by the descendants of its original owner, who came to Tunis in the fifteenth century from Yemen. Allies of the Husaynid Beys, the Lasram family were one of the most powerful political families of the eighteenth and nineteenth centuries. Opposite, at no. 27, is the nineteenth-century **mausoleum** of the landowning Dziri family.

Sidi Mehrez

At the end of rue du Tribunal runs rue Sidi Ibrahim. Just to the left at no. 11 is the **Zaouia of Sidi Ibrahim Riahi**, an eighteenth-century religious propagandist. Follow the street the other way and a dog-leg to your left at the end brings you into rue el Monastiri. Around the corner in rue Achour is the seventeenth-century **Achouria Medersa**. Rue el Monastiri runs down into **rue Sidi Mehrez**, the last incarnation of one of the main north–south arteries of the Medina. A busy shopping street, it houses the **Zaouia of Sidi Mehrez**, fronted by a long passage.

Sidi Mehrez is still revered as a patron saint of Tunis for his efforts in the tenth century. After the city's sufferings during the revolt of Abu Yazid, it was he who took the situation in hand and oversaw its revival. And at a time of Shiite Fatimid domination, he was also a champion of the Malekite rites of the Sunni majority. The original tomb has shared many of Tunis's ups and downs, and the present building is mainly eighteenth and nineteenth century. Traditionally, boys come to drink from its well before their circumcision ceremony.

Opposite the *zaouia*, though not visible from the street, is the **Mosque of Sidi Mehrez**, one of Tunis's most distinctive landmarks. A little beyond the *zaouia* on the right, you can climb some steps for the best look at its heap of white domes. Dotted with pigeons, they stand out for miles in any rooftop view of the Medina and are the city's only example of Imperial Ottoman (Turkish) building styles. Perhaps Mohamed Bey, who founded it, wanted to stamp a truly Turkish presence on the city, but after his early death, the assassination of his brother, and the rise of the Husaynids, the mosque was left unfinished and is even named after the *zaouia* opposite rather than its own founder. The pottery shops at nos. 96 and 97 warrant a quick mention here: although they don't sell the fancier souvenir products, they do have a wide range of plates, cups, pots and ashtrays, all at very low prices.

Rue Sidi Mehrez emerges from the Medina into **pl Bab Souika**, once a place of public execution, and more recently the area of the liveliest **cafés** during Ramadan nights. It was recently more like a building site as a row of rather twee boutiques went up on its southern side, but by now it should have returned to its bustling self, once again vying with pl Bab Jazira as the place to hang out in the evening.

The Hafsia

A left turn out of rue Sidi Mehrez along the eastern edge of the Medina and down rue Bab Souika takes you past the Anglican church of Saint George. The large open space opposite marks the site of the **Hafsia**, the Jewish ghetto. At one time the Hafsia was separated from the rest of the town by a wall and its gates were closed at night. Before the status of Jews was regularised in 1861 there were many other **petty restrictions**: Jews had to wear black clothes of a traditional style – European dress was forbidden; they were not allowed to ride horses or own land outside the Hafsia. Jews had their own civil courts, but in their dealings with Muslims were subject to Islamic law, and they faced burning at the stake if found guilty of a capital offence. Although protected as a "people of the book" (those who share with Islam a reverence for the Old Testament), many Muslims regarded them as heathen and treated them as such. Occasionally riots broke out and the Hafsia was wrecked by Muslim mobs, but for most of the time the Jews lived in peace, however restricted.

It was the **immigration of Maltese and Italian Jews**, citizens of powerful European states, that allowed the Jews to escape these repressive laws. By the 1870s their wealth and connections with European governments gave them considerable power and new freedoms. Then, under the Protectorate, they joined the middle class and many left the Medina for the suburbs. Nevertheless, when the Germans arrived in 1942 the Hafsia was still very crowded. The Gestapo used the ghetto as an assembly point for Jews from other parts of Tunisia before sending thousands to their deaths. After the war most of the survivors emigrated to Israel. The Hafsia, an embarrassing eyesore for the French, was pulled down in 1953 and the remainder of the Jewish community dispersed into the suburbs.

Southern End of the Medina

In the southern areas too, you get much more a feeling of being in the "real" Medina than you do around the main souks. Compared with the northern end, however, the south has a greater density of specific places of interest including palaces, tombs and historic mosques.

Around the Mosque of the Dyers

Climbing up rue Jemaa Zitouna from the pl de la Victoire, you come to **rue Sidi Ali Azouz** and, turning right, at no. 7 a **zaouia** of the same name. Sidi Ali Azouz was born in Fez in Morocco in the seventeenth century and settled in Zaghouan after returning from pilgrimage to Mecca. Like Sidi Mehrez, he is one of the patron saints of the city of Tunis. The *zaouia* built to house his cult dates from the nineteenth century and is currently under restoration. A little further, on the southern side of rue Sidi Ali Azouz, the **Sidi Amir Barracks** was one of those built by Hammouda Bey at the beginning of the nineteenth century as mentioned on p.56.

Continuing, the street merges with a dark tunnel of the Souk el Belat (mainly food). To your right, on the corner of Souk el Belat and rue Trèsor, is the tenth-century **Ichbili Mosque** with its squat fourteenth-century minaret set well back. A little further along rue Sidi Ali Azouz, bear right where the street forks and you're on **rue des Teinturiers** (Street of the Dyers). Ahead rises the minaret of the **Mosque of the Dyers**, also known as the New Mosque and centre of a sizeable complex. The octagonal minaret recalls those of Youssef Dey and Hammouda Bey near the Great Mosque, though it was built a century later than Youssef Dey's, in 1716. The mosque was commissioned by Husayn Bin Ali, founder of the Husaynid dynasty, as his own memorial, and he lavished great expense on it, importing tiles for the prayer-hall from Iznik in Turkey. In the *tourbet* attached to the mosque, Husayn buried two holy men, Sidi Kassem Sababti and Sidi Kassem El Beji, reserving the space between them for his own use. Things didn't quite work out, however: Husayn was driven from power by his nephew Ali Pasha, who buried his own father in the position of honour. A *kouttab* and a *medersa* were later added to the complex, making it an impressive, if abortive, memorial. You can see the tombs through a window, if it's open, in rue Sidi Kassem.

Two palaces

Almost opposite the mosque, down the passage-like rue M'Bazaa, stands the superb doorway of **Dar Othman**, a palace which Othman Dey (ruled 1598–1610) built to escape the intrigues and insecurities of life in the Kasbah. Gates closed off the street so that the palace could be defended if necessary. Although the courtyard inside is occupied and slightly run-down, the facade remains striking in its contrasting black and white stone. At present the house is being restored, but it's still possible to enter, though backsheesh may be demanded for the privilege.

Close by is the **Dar Ben Abdallah**, one of the finest old palaces in the Medina and now converted into the *Museum of the Traditional Heritage of Tunis* (Mon–Sat, 9.30am–4.30pm; closed Sun). From rue des Teinturiers turn right into rue Sidi Kassem, then left through an arch on rue Dar Ben Abdallah. The palace has a classic design – a *driba* (entrance hall) lined with stone benches for waiting guests, opens onto a *skifa* (passage) leading into the house proper. In a military context (as at Mahdia, see p.180) a *skifa* was narrow and obliquely angled for ease of defence, but here, in a domestic setting, it isolates the inner house from the world outside.

The florid **decoration** of the door that leads from *driba* to *skifa* is once again typical of the Italianate styles which became increasingly popular from the eighteenth century – as, too, is much of the ornamentation in the courtyard (look out for the grotesque little dolphins hanging upside down on the fountain). T-shaped reception rooms open off the courtyard; the cupboard-like rooms at the angles were sometimes used as bedrooms.

The exhibits consist mainly of costumes and **ephemera**. It's clear how even the simplest items, such as pen-cases and perfume-sprinklers, are imbued with an Islamic sense of design. And look out for the elaborate old rifle-rack, carved with wooden stalactites.

The Dyers' Souk and the Tourbet el Bey

Returning to rue des Teinturiers, there's an old **hammam** on the left which proclaims itself "most elegant establishment of bathing baths in marble". In fact it's a bit of a dump, but the building is interesting. Opposite to nos. 92 and 104 open the actual **Souks of the Dyers**, after whom the street is named. At one time, as part of the clothing industry, dyeing was a vital part of Tunis's economy, but now it's just one more threatened traditional craft. The first of the souks has been taken over for making drums: piles of their clay bodies line the walls and skins are tanned before being stretched over them. The other souk is still used for a limited amount of (rather gaudy) dyeing.

Continue along rue des Teinturiers to the end, and you'll emerge from the Medina at Bab Jazira. Alternatively, turn right on **rue Sidi el Benna**, then right again on **rue Sidi Zahmoul**, past a huge palace with lazy palm trees to the **Tourbet el Bey**. As its name suggests, this royal mausoleum, built by Ali Pasha II (1758–82), contains most of the Husaynid dynasty which followed him. Leaden, ornate and uninspired, the building almost totally lacks the usual Tunisian feel for delicacy and balance.

Nearby, no. 44 rue Sidi Essourdou was once a **medersa** founded by Husayn bin Ali, the first Husaynid Bey.

Bab Jedid – and the house where Ibn Khaldoun lived

Turning left from the Tourbet el Bey onto the street named after it, a small detour can be made taking a left down rue des Juges and then a right up rue des Forgerons (since the thirteenth century the blacksmiths' souk), bringing you out of the Medina at **Bab Jedid**, a gate built in 1276 as part of the Hafsid city wall. Up some stairs next to it is a tiny mosque, the Khalouet Sidi Mehrez, where the Hafsid sultans used to pay homage to the city's patron saint.

Returning to rue Tourbet el Bey and continuing along it, no. 41 is the tiny **M'sid el Koubba Mosque**, where the great historian **Ibn Khaldoun** used to teach. Born in 1332, at no. 33 in the same street, Ibn Khaldoun revolutionised his field of study and was the first historian to suggest that history repeats itself in cycles. In his greatest work, *el Muqaddima*, he introduced the idea of *'asabiyah* (group solidarity), which he says is the foundation of a society. As *'asabiyah* rises and declines, so does civilisation. After writing *el Muqaddima*, he moved to Egypt, where he became a teacher at al-Azhar university and died in 1406.

Sidi Bou Khrissane

Backtracking slightly, go left onto **rue du Riche**, then right into **rue des Andalous**, both streets with a scattering of magnificent doorways. This is where wealthier Andalusian immigrants settled while the less well-off had to petition for land in the country on which to found towns like Testour (see p.201). A left turn on rue du Dey then another on rue Mohsen will bring you into a small square. On your left is the **Dar Husayn**, a palace built originally in the twelfth century and enlarged in the eighteenth. Once the town hall, then the French army headquarters during colonial rule, it's now used by the National Institute of Archaeology, who will be pleased to let you have a look inside – something well worth doing. Across the square is the **el Ksar Mosque**, founded around 1106 by the Emir **Ahmed Ibn Khourassane**. The minaret, an interesting blend of Ottoman and Andalusian styles, was added in 1647.

Ibn Khourassane's family, the Khourassanids, who ruled Tunis from 1059 to 1159, have their mausoleum just around the corner. Turn right out of the square into rue Sidi Bou Khrissane then left into rue ben Mahmoud. On your right is the **Sidi Bou Khrissane Museum** (officially open 9am–noon Mon–Sat, but you'll be let in at any reasonable hour if you knock – donation expected). Part of a cemetery dating back to the ninth century, it is really more a garden full of old tombstones than a museum. The Khourassinid emirs are interred under a cupola at the back.

On the way to the museum, at the end of impasse de l'Artillerie, a blind alley off rue Sidi Bou Khrissane, the sixteenth-century **mansion of the Andalusian Haddad family** will be open to the public when restoration work on it finishes.

Bab Menara
Rue ben Mahmoud finally runs out into Souk Sekkajine. Buried in a red and green box in the middle of the street on your left is **Sidi Bou Abdallah**, who died on this spot while defending Tunis against the invading Spanish. A Spaniard, however, is buried only a few metres further on, under an olive tree at Bab Menara, where Souk Sekkajine emerges from the Medina. He is **Anselm Tourmeda** (aka Abdallah Tourjman), a fourteenth-century Majorcan who came to Tunisia, converted to Islam and wrote religious propaganda in Arabic and Catalan.

The Faubourgs

As well as an inner wall around the Medina, the Hafsids built an outer rampart to enclose the city's **residential suburbs**. Today, these **faubourgs** have become the most distinctive parts of Tunis with a strong local character and sense of community. They are often referred to by the names of former Medina gates: thus Halfaouine is in the *Rbat Bab Souika* and Montfleury in the *Rbat Bab Jazira*.

Halfaouine

Halfaouine has achieved a certain fame due to Férid Boughedir's **film** of the same name, which ran away with most of the prizes at the 1990 Carthage Festival. In fact, it is one of Tunis's most fascinating areas, with a style completely its own. See the film if you get the chance and see how many locations you recognise.

Place Halfaouine
On the north side of pl Bab Souika, a vaulted entrance leads into the **food markets** of rue Halfaouine. Just on the right as you leave pl Bab Souika is the **Abu Mohamed Mosque**, a fine example of architecture from the Hafsid era, erected by public subscription. Associated with this mosque is a tradition of religious discussion meetings during Ramadan on the subject of the *hadiths* – sayings of Mohammed.

Rue Halfaouine eventually emerges into pl **Halfaouine**. Having begun life as one of the commodity markets common on the edges of the old city, this square had become, by the eighteenth century, an exclusive district, thanks largely to the efforts of **Youssef Sahib et Tabaa**. A former Moldavian slave, Youssef rose to become Hammouda Pasha's top civil servant: he commissioned the mosque here, as well as the neighbouring Souk Jedid, site of his personal palace. Later in the century another high official built a palace on the square (the large Italianate building in the northeast corner), and the surviving trees, benches and cafés create an air of decaying elegance, belying the fact that this quiet backwater was once notorious for nationalist demonstrations against the French. The **Sahib et Tabaa Mosque** itself, begun in 1812, is one of the most beautiful and unusual in Tunisia, closer to a Venetian *palazzo* than to the Great Mosque of Kairouan. The interaction of eastern and Italian styles is at its most developed, with metal railings, classical columns and sophisticated use of polychrome marbles. Thanks to a story that the successful builder would be rewarded with death, the minaret was only completed in 1970.

Behind the mosque, at 9 rue du Salut, is the crumbling **Zaouia of Sidi Ali Chiha**, off rue Sidi el Aloui, which leads into an elongated square full of palm trees. Cross rue Bab Saadoun at the other end of the square and in front of you is the **En Nefefta**

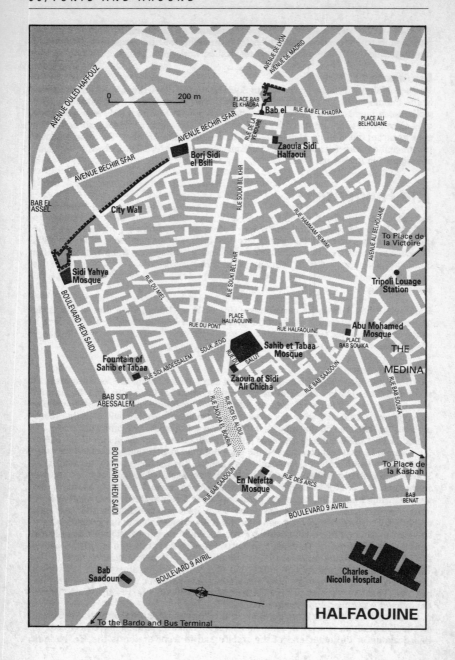

AVENUE OULED HAFFOUZ

AVENUE DE LYON

AVENUE DE MADRID

PLACE BAB
EL KHADRA

Bab el

RUE BAB EL KHADRA

PLACE ALI
BELHOUANE

AVENUE BECHIR SFAR

RUE DE LA
VERDURE

Zaouia Sidi
Halfaoui

AVENUE BECHIR SFAR

Borj Sidi
el Bsili

RUE SOUK BEL KHIR

BAB EL
ASSEL

City Wall

RUE SOUK BEL KHIR

RUE HAMMAM REMMIMI

AVENUE ALI BELHOUANE

To Place de
la Victoire

Sidi Yahya
Mosque

RUE DU MEL

Tripoli Louage
Station

PLACE
HALFAOUINE

RUE HALFAOUINE

Abu Mohamed
Mosque

RUE DU PONT

SOUK JEDID

Sahib et Tabaa
Mosque

PLACE
BAB SOUIKA

THE

BOULEVARD HEDI SAIDI

Fountain of
Sahib et Tabaa

RUE SIDI ABDESSALEM

RUE EN SALUT

MEDINA

RUE BAB SOUIKA

Zaouia of Sidi
Ali Chicha

RUE BAB SAADOUN

BAB SIDI
ABESSALEM

RUE ZAOUIA EL BOKRA

RUE SIDI EL AJOU

To Place de
la Kasbah

En Nefetta
Mosque

RUE DES ARCS

BAB
BENAT

RUE BAB SAADOUN

BOULEVARD 9 AVRIL

BOULEVARD HEDI SAIDI

Bab
Saadoun

BOULEVARD 9 AVRIL

Charles
Nicolle Hospital

To the Bardo and Bus Terminal

HALFAOUINE

0   200 m

Mosque on the corner of rue des Arcs and impasse de la Mosquée. The building you see is modern but the mosque was founded in the fifteenth century and parts of the interior structure still date back to that period.

Around Bab Sidi Abdessalem

In the northwest corner of pl Halfaouine (where rue Sidi el Aloui starts), is the Souk el Jedid, a vaulted passage leading out into rue Zaouia el Bokria. The souk, commissioned by Sahib et Tabaa, now specialises in clothes. As you emerge, keep straight ahead along **rue Sidi Abdessalem**. A small room known as a *sabat* crosses the street here at first floor level; it houses a *kouttab* (Koranic school) attached to the *masjid* (small mosque). This complex of buildings is characteristic of old Medina quarters – the local primary school attached to the parish church, as it were. Right at the end of rue Sidi Abdessalem on a sliver of open space stands the bulbous-domed **Fountain of Sahib et Tabaa**, another of his municipal works in this quarter. The fountain was originally located just inside one of the Hafsid city gates, **Bab Sidi Abdessalem**, so that travellers arriving from the country could refresh themselves, and it's usually surrounded by a flea market.

Bab Saadoun and some Ottoman forts

Beyond the fountain runs bd Hedi Saidi, where you can pick up a bus going west to the Bardo Museum (see p.69). A few hundred metres to the left, **Bab Saadoun**, once one of the city's outer gates but now a traffic island at a major road junction, looks rather lost. Beyond it is the bus station serving the north of the country.

South of Bab Saadoun is Rabta Hill, site of two Ottoman forts, **Borj Flifel** and **Borj er Rabta**, both built in the mid-eighteenth century. Nearby, yet another fort, **Borj Zouara** (or Borj el Andalous), dates back to the seventeenth century.

Bab el Assel

Heading in the other direction (eastwards) from Bab Sidi Abessalem, bd Hedi Saidi takes you to Bab el Assel, site of yet another of the city's gates. As you approach it, you'll see the **Sidi Yahya Mosque** on your right. Built as a *masjid* in the fourteenth century by the saint whose name it bears, it was elevated to the status of *jemaa* (Friday mosque) by the Hafsids because of its strategic position. Turn left just before the mosque and have a look round behind it, and you will see the entrance to the old Bab el Assel fort at 25 rue du Fort, now a private house. Above the doorway, a plaque dates it at 1216AH (1801AD).

Here too begins a huge chunk of the **old wall**, currently undergoing restoration. It starts just past the Sidi Yahya Mosque, and then runs by the Bab el Assel sports centre, where you get a good view of it through the perimeter railings. Follow the pavement round into av Bechir Sfar and take the first right into rue du Miel. The entrance to the sports centre is on your right if you want a closer look; otherwise take a left down a little street full of carpenters' workshops. You'll be walking parallel with the wall, still there behind the houses on your left. The street emerges at another of the old fortifications, **Borj Sidi el Bsili**, again dating back to the turn of the nineteenth century. The Ministry of Culture has plans to restore it and open it to the public.

Bab el Khadra and rue de la Verdure

A left turn here down av Bechir Sfar brings you, after 100m or so, to perhaps the city's oddest gate, **Bab el Khadra**. This double-doorwayed piece of a fairytale castle is not – no surprise – the fourteenth-century original, but a rebuilt version dating back to 1881.

Behind the right-hand doorway is **rue de la Verdure**, a name referring, like that of the gate, to the "greenery" of the countryside which used to start outside it. Halfway along rue de la Verdure, the impasse de Sidi el Halfaoui (left) leads to the **Zaouia of**

Sidi el Halfaoui, containing the tomb of the seventeenth-century saint after whom the Halfaouine district is named. Non-Muslims can't enter, but you can glimpse the saint's tomb through a grill by the door.

Rue de la Verdure runs onto a square from which rue Hammam Remimi will take you straight back to Bab Souika. Much better, however, is a stroll down rue Souiki Bel Khir, straight ahead, which runs past various interesting cul-de-sacs and under the odd *sabat* (room crossing the street at first-floor level) to end up back in pl Halfaouine.

Bab Jazira and the West

Like Halfaouine, **Bab Jazira** is an ancient district of the city whose appearance hasn't changed in centuries. Less compact than the northern *faubourg*, it stretches from the vast Jellaz Cemetery in the south, over the shore of Sebkhet Sejoumi, the salt lake west of the city, to the administrative quarter by the site of the Kasbah.

Jellaz Cemetery
Place Bab Jazira, the big square at the southern tip of the Medina, is dominated by the fourteenth-century **Mosque of Sidi el Beshir**, with its Andalusian-style minaret. Rue Bab el Fellah leads from here southwards to the **Jellaz Cemetery**, a huge and very pleasant hillside burial ground founded in the thirteenth century. According to legend, the founder was a saint whose servant bought the land from a Jew so that poor Muslims could be buried there. In 1911 it was the scene of the first mass demonstration against the French when the municipal council threatened to requisition the land for development. A shot was fired – some say by an Italian spectator, others by a French officer – killing a young boy. In the riot that ensued nine Frenchmen, five Italians and over thirty Tunisians died.

The cemetery is dominated by the seventeenth-century **Borj Ali Raïs**, an Ottoman fortress visible from the whole city but, unfortunately, closed to the public. It's also known as Borj Sidi Bel Hassen after the nearby **Zaouia of Sidi Bel Hassen**, which was built in 1815 but dedicated to a thirteenth-century marabout said to have introduced coffee into Tunisia.

Montfleury and the markets around Bab Jedid
Returning from the cemetery up rue Bab el Fellah, turn left down rue Sidi Mansour through the Montfleury quarter. The street ends up in rue Hajjamine which leads (right) into a square surrounded by tombs of eighteenth- and nineteenth-century worthies. Near the end of rue Hajjamine is another square, the **Souk des Armes**. Once a weapons market, it now trades in food, and is a lively area in the evening. In one corner a tree stands next to the small fourteenth-century **Mosque of El Helaak**, traditionally held to have been founded in 1375 by a black slave who sold his gold jewellery to pay for it.

Otherwise, head uphill along Souk Saida Manoubia, beside the mosque, to two more open spaces, **pl du Marché du Blé** and, higher up, **pl aux Chevaux**. Today these play host to great junk markets, where you can pick up anything from old shoe buckles to metal utensils; in the past, they were the markets where city merchants would meet and deal with farmers bringing in grain and animals from the countryside.

Place du Leader
From pl aux Chevaux, rue Abdul Wahab bears away to the right, opening eventually on to a square with a formal garden and a clumsy name – **pl du Résidence du Leader**, after Habib Bourguiba, who lived for a time at 6 rue Jemaa el Haoua nearby. The thirteenth-century **mosque** of the same name (also called the Taoufiq Mosque) stands at

the top of the square. It was founded by Queen Atif, wife of the Hafsid Sultan Abu Zakariya.

Across the square is the pyramidal green-tiled roof of the **Zaouia of Sidi Kassem Jelizi**: this fifteenth-century Andalusian tile-maker was buried just inside where the gate into the western suburb originally stood, and the building was enlarged in subsequent centuries. The pyramidal roof is a classic Andalusian touch.

Beyond the square you reach **bd du 9 Avril 1938**, a major highway of the city. As it runs along the top of the ridge there's a good view down over the **Sebkhet Sejoumi** (salt lake), round to the Jellaz Cemetery and beyond to Lake Tunis. Standing on the top of this ridge overlooking the Medina it's easy to understand Tunis's attraction for early Arab rulers from the point of view of security; equally, the city's appalling climate is explained – "low, hot and damp" is how eighteenth-century traveller James Bruce described Tunis (see "Books" in Contexts, p.363).

The Kasbah site

A couple of hundred metres up bd 9 Avril, you'll find a small piece of the Kasbah wall and an old city gate (Bab Sidi Abdallah) on the corner of rue 2 Mars 1934. You're now entering Tunis's government district, with various ministries down to your right, behind the wall. Across rue 2 Mars are the headquarters of the RCD, the party founded by Bourguiba in 1934 as the Neo-Destour, renamed in 1956 and 1988, and until recently the country's only legal political party. Below that are the meagre excavations of the Hafsid **Kasbah**.

Some 200m down rue 2 Mars on the right is the **9th of April Museum**, devoted to Habib Bourguiba and the struggle for independence (see p.332), complete with one of the many prison cells where the great man resided under French rule. Entry is free but, unless you happen to be passing and speak Arabic (the displays are in Arabic), not really worth the effort.

The **Kasbah Mosque** (built in 1235) was part of the same Hafsid building programme as the Kasbah itself. Its minaret, with geometric relief patterns, owes a good deal to Moroccan architecture, but the general style – elegant but not over-elaborate – quickly set a standard which has endured in Tunisia. Perhaps because of its elevated position, the mosque signals to the rest of the city for the call to prayer: five times a day a white flag is hung out from the minaret.

The impressive-looking building over the other side of the excavations is **Sadiki College**, founded by Kherredin in 1875 and invariably described as Tunisia's Eton, where Bourguiba and other future leaders were educated. Below it, on bd Bab Benat, is the **tomb of Farhat Hached**, the trade union leader murdered by reactionary French colonialists in 1952 (see p.332).

The Bardo and other museums

Housed in the former Beylical Palace, the **BARDO** (9.30am–4.30pm, closed Mon; 1TD entry plus 1TD to take photos) is one of those museums which are almost too well endowed. Its encyclopaedic collection of Roman mosaics is really too much to take in on a single visit, but even a glimpse of some of the designs will flesh out the Roman sites in the country, and a second visit afterwards will complete the picture.

The museum is a fine palace in its own right (as you wander around note the ceilings especially) – one of a collection of buildings dating from various periods and surrounded by gardens full of Roman and Punic stones. Just next door is the National Assembly, guarded by traditionally garbed soldiers who defend the Assembly from overzealous tourist–photographers.

Getting there

The museum is a thirty-minute bus ride from the city centre: take the #3 from av Bourguiba, or the #3c, 4, 4c, 4d, 23, 23b, 23c, or 23t from Jardin Thameur, or several from Bab Saadoun. The metro (line 4) runs to 20 Mars station, a short walk away, and should soon be extended to the museum's own station.

On the way up av 20 Mars from Bab Saadoun, look out for the old **aqueduct** near Bouchoucha metro station (you may also notice it down the back route to Bab Saadoun bus station if you're travelling by *louage*). A branch of the old Zaghouan–Carthage aqueduct, it was built by the Hafsids in the thirteenth century and restored in the seventeenth.

THE BARDO'S LAYOUT

Many of the rooms are named after the particular sites which produced most of their exhibits, and they're grouped roughly according to period. In summer it's a good idea to begin at the top, so that you don't arrive there just as it receives the full attention of the sun. If time is limited, you could take in the Punic rooms (1–4); the early Christian (5); rooms 9, 10, 11, 14 and 15 of the Roman period, with 17 to 22 for the Mahdia sculptures; with time left over for a quick look at the Islamic section.

Roman mosaics

Africa's **Roman mosaics**, of which the Bardo has by far the largest collection, are arguably the most colourful and vivid images left behind by a Roman Empire better known for its monumental feats of engineering. Like an album of colour snapshots, they offer a direct and beautiful visual record of what was considered important by this extraordinarily successful civilisation. Native Romans at home in Italy painted their walls so colourfully that they preferred their floor mosaics in monochrome black-and-white. In Africa, though, wall-painting was never widespread, and mosaics developed as almost the only form of domestic decoration.

Seeing the mosaics in such exuberant quantity, there's a danger of taking them for granted. These were the Persian rugs of the ancient world, requiring enormous time and skill to lay out, and the fact that most were privately commissioned for homes says a good deal about the status-conscious social structure of the time.

The **subjects** were probably also chosen by the commissioner, so the emphasis on (broadly speaking) entertainment is significant. Hunting, fishing, the amphitheatre and, to a lesser extent, theatrical themes, are all indicative of the leisure enjoyed by the wealthy. Even the mythological and religious scenes have a strongly hedonistic slant: **Bacchus**, the god of wine and sensual pleasure in general, features heavily, often shown triumphant over the forces of evil. **Venus**, goddess of love, usually has her vampish side strongly emphasised. Most noticeable of all, though, is the feeling of abundance. The sea is always shown crammed with endless varieties of fish (including the lobsters which wave in the god Ocean's hair), rural farming scenes are a constant, and lush vines weave their way through and around almost every scene. The mosaics evoke a life of sensual gratification and plenty, neatly summed up in an inscription found at Timgad in Algeria: "To hunt, to bathe, to gamble, to laugh, that is to live".

Towards the end of the Roman era, and into the Byzantine, the increasingly tense stylisation of the mosaics reflects a less carefree society, permeated by a stricter spiritual discipline intended to preserve it in a hostile world. Although there's nothing here to match the early Byzantine mosaics of Ravenna, the tauter styles can come as a relief after the more florid Imperial mosaics.

Further highlights: statues and Islamic art

Because it had to be expensively imported, **marble statuary** was less common in Africa than in other parts of the Roman world. Carthage, though, was richly stocked with figures of all types, primarily important men and women: generals, senators, sponsors, emperors and other worthies. The museum has a fine, though typically damaged selection: it's worth pointing out that the systematic **de-nosing and emasculation** of male statues was the routine work of invading Vandals, presumably mutilating and castrating their enemies in stone as well as flesh. The absence of any other kinds of representation would have endowed these statues with a significance verging on the divine that's hard to imagine in our image-glutted century.

There is also a stunning collection of bronze and marble figures and domestic furniture, recovered from the so-called **"Mahdia wreck"**. In 1907 fishermen off Mahdia found this ancient shipwreck, dating from the first century BC. The cargo gives an impression of the baroque style in which contemporary Romans lived.

Islamic art, which shuns the human image, is at the other extreme. The ban on the human form has not always been total, and the rooms here contain one or two rare, early exceptions. But for the most part Islamic artists have concentrated on decorative pattern and colour, a combination most brilliantly exemplified in a room of ceramic **tiles** taken from inside old mosques. The best are those brought by the Turks from Iznik, with their vegetal designs and bright colours still fresh after hundreds of years. There are others from Tunisia itself, in characteristic blues, greens and yellows, and from Morocco, distinguishable by the tighter geometric patterns.

Other Museums

Apart from the **Dar Ben Abdallah Regional Museum** in the Medina (see p.63), Tunis's other museums are very small beer. The recently renovated **Museum of Modern Art** in Belvedere Park (see p.52), is eye-catching but short on work of real merit. It would be just as interesting to see the city's collection of works (mainly by foreign artists) painted during the **Protectorate**: there are occasional exhibitions of them in various galleries (see Listings, p.77) and a Protectorate Art Museum is projected for the future. The **Postal Museum**, a dark and dusty part of the main post office (entrance in rue d'Angleterre), is for ardent philatelists only, and the **Coin Museum** at 27 rue de Rome is, equally, of interest only to numismatists. Nor would many go out of their way to visit the **Ninth of April Museum** near the Kasbah, devoted to Habib Bourguiba and the independence struggle (see p.332).

Eating and Drinking

Eating out and drinking in Tunis are activities concentrated on **av Bouguiba** and the streets to either side. Since the **Medina** itself closes down fairly early in the evening, there are fewer restaurants there than you might expect, though Bab Jazira and Bab Souika, at its northern and southern tips respectively, are pretty lively in the evenings, especially during Ramadan, with enough tea shops and cheap restaurants to satisfy any appetite.

Even **fairly smart restaurants** are very cheap by European standards, and you can get a memorable meal (with wine) for about 10TD. Some of these restaurants also offer set menus, often at extremely reasonable prices. Naturally there are plenty of **inexpensive eateries** too, most of which will fill you up for 2–3TD. Cheaper still, almost every street in the city has a *rôtisserie*, where you either eat a plate of fried food standing up or take away a sandwich (*cassecroûte*). There are several around the junction of rue Ibn Khaldoun and rue de Yougoslavie.

Ordinary Tunisian restaurants

The following tried and tested **cheapies** are mostly good as well as cheap. Don't go expecting refinements, however, in the style of service or surroundings.

Abid, 98 rue de Yougoslavie. No-nonsense nosh at no-nonsense prices (around 2TD a meal).

Erriadh, 9 rue Ibn Khaldoun. Around the corner from the above and almost identical.

Carcassonne, 8 av de Carthage. The 2.2TD four-course set menu will stuff you full and must be one of the best deals in the country. Recommended.

Istanbul, 4 rue Pierre Courbetin. In case you wondered if there was anywhere cheaper than the *Carcassonne*.... This place does a four-course set menu for 1.8TD, and not a bad one.

Le Neptune, 3 rue du Caire. A less satisfying four-courser for 2TD.

Goulue, 3 rue de la Monnaie. Off av Bourguiba by pl 7 Novembre. Self-service, all stainless steel and glass. 3TD for a three-course set menu.

Capitole, 60 av Bourguiba. Downstairs from (but otherwise unconnected with) the hotel of the same name. 3TD brings you three courses served in style.

Le Marhaba, 166 rue de la Kasbah. Dirt cheap spit 'n' sawdust joint in mid-Medina.

Mic Mac, 96 rue Yougoslavie (on the corner of rue Ibn Khaldoun). A *rôtisserie* that's a cut above the rest. Pizzas, chips and *schewarma* sandwiches to take away.

Upmarket Tunisian restaurants

The best way to find **fancier establishments** is to wander along streets south of av Bourguiba, such as Hollande, Yougoslavie and Grèce, and, on the northern side, the early stretches of av de Paris and rue de Marseille, until you find something suitable – most places display a price-list and menu. If you've had a recommendation, you'd do well to book in advance.

L'Orient, 7 rue Ali Bach Hamba (☎242058). A long-time favourite, still going strong.

M'Rabet, Souk et Trouk (☎261729). Situated in the heart of the Medina and built over the tombs of three holy men. Probably the most stylish place in town to splurge seriously, a meal and the accompanying show (belly-dancing or similar entertainment) will cost around 15TD a head.

Le Palais, 8 av de Carthage (☎256326). Delicious food at reasonable prices.

Mehdoui, rue Jemaa Zitouna. Right by the Great Mosque and something of an institution, this is open lunchtime only but it does the best couscous in town.

Le Malouf, 108 rue de Yougoslavie (☎243180). Similar fare and prices to the *M'Rabet* but less style. Live malouf music.

Majestic, 36 av de la Liberté (☎242666). Part of the hotel of the same name, the *Majestic*'s 5TD set menu remains ever-popular.

Smart French-style restaurants

Fine dining is one of the **legacies of French rule**, and Tunis is peppered with elegant Gallic establishments. The food and ambience in these places is everything you would expect from their equivalents in France, but far cheaper.

Le Cosmos, 7 rue Ibn Khaldoun (☎241610). Around 10–12TD for good food in a a pleasant atmosphere. Recommended for a splurge.

Chez Nous, 5 rue de Marseille (☎243043). The 7TD four-course set menu is excellent value and includes chocolate mousse. Mohammed Ali, Michael York and Edith Piaf are among the celebs who've patronised it and whose photos deck the walls.

Chez Slah, 16 rue Pierre Coubertin (☎258588). Discreetly tucked away in a small street, and possibly the best restaurant in town. Reservation recommended.

Le Petite Hutte, 102 rue de Yougoslavie (☎244959). One of Tunis's most highly regarded eateries with posh nosh for around 12TD.

Gaston's, 73 rue de Yougoslavie. Specialises in seafood at around 12TD. Has a set menu for 5TD weekday lunchtimes.

Restaurant des Margaritas, 6 bis rue d'Hollande (☎240632). Attached to the *Hôtel Maison Dorée*. 12TD à la carte, but 4TD for a three-course set tourist menu.

L'Etoile, 3 rue Ibn Khaldoun (☎240514). Good value at under 10TD a meal.

Ethnic cuisine

Non-Tunisian food is thin on the ground – though rather awful pizzas are widely available – and your basic choice is still between French and Tunisian. The following are notable exceptions to what you might expect.

Le Robinson, 14 av de Madrid (☎249051). Tunisia's only kosher restaurant, doing Sephardic Jewish specialities such as stuffed tongue and *boulette* (a sort of meatball) as well as kosher versions of normal Tunisian dishes. About 6TD a meal.

Shogun, 80 av Hedi Chaker. If you really can't live without a Chinese, this, apparently misnamed, establishment is one of the nearest to the city centre.

Hong Kong, 85 av Taieb Mehiri (☎285311), up near the Belvedere. More renowned than the *Shogun*.

Vietnamien, 26 rue Amine el Abassi (☎282251). Better and more expensive than either of the Chineses.

La Mamma, 11bis rue de Marseille (☎241256). Your best bet for Italian food short of crossing the water. Pizzas, pasta and similar fare for around 7TD a meal, and pizza only for 3–4TD.

Patisseries and cafés

Patisseries can be found all over the city, most heavily concentrated on rue Charles de Gaulle. They tend to get cheaper as you move away from av Bourguiba. As well as cakes, they often do sandwiches and other savoury snacks, sometimes even ice-cream, coffee and fruit juice. The **Ben Yedder** at 7 rue Charles de Gaulle is a bit pricey but makes up sandwiches to order.

A lot of patisseries are becoming like cafés in fact, and it's sometimes hard to know if a place is one or the other, although you won't see a *chicha* at a patisserie. Again, Bab Jazira and Bab Souika are the places to head. The **Capitole** bar at 60 av Bourguiba is open 24 hours, seven days a week, serving up crêpes, freshly pressed fruit juice and *lait de poule*. Seedy though it looks, this is the best and cheapest place on the avenue to get these things, and a lifesaver for insomniacs.

Bars

There are two kinds of bar in Tunis, as elsewhere in the country: Tunisian and western-style. Tunisian bars – small, crowded and very male-dominated – can be found mostly around the railway station, though there are others scattered through the new city (especially along av de la Liberté) on street corners. They usually close around 8.00pm. After that you have to turn to the western-style bars, generally attached to the bigger hotels or cafés and considerably more expensive. Try the *International Hotel* on av Bourguiba or the *Majestic* (36 av de Paris). Alternatively, you can get away with drinking in some restaurants provided you order a plate of something solid too, though this can work out just as expensive as ordering your beer in a posh hotel.

Festivals and Nightlife

Tunis's **cultural life** is fairly low-key, with the exception of **Ramadan** (see p.347). The city, normally dead by 11.00pm, acquires a new lease on (night)life for the month of Ramadan: eating, drinking and making merry until the early hours of the morning. The centre of all this activity is **Place Bab Souika** at the Medina's northern end, though construction of the underpass and new shops here has, for the time being at least, dampened the excitement. Otherwise, try Bab Jazira at the other end of the Medina.

Music and culture

At other times, Tunis's nightlife is limited. Crowds stroll along av Bourguiba, and mill around the streets to either side, but facilities in the city centre are limited. **Discos** – try the *Pub Sandwich* (av de Carthage) though there are others – don't offer a very exciting alternative to just sitting at a café and watching the world go by; the more sophisticated places are out at the suburbs of La Marsa and Gammarth.

You're more likely to find **local music** at Sidi Bou Said (see p.86) than in the city centre, but with money to burn, the cabaret shows at restaurants such as *Le Malouf* (108 rue de Yougoslavie), *M'Rabet* (Souk et Trouk in the Medina), *Carstop* (73 rue de Yougoslavie) and *Le Palais* (8 av de Carthage) offer a slick version of "Oriental" entertainment. Watch out, too, for events such as concerts of Arabic and western classical music at the **Théâtre Municipal** on av Bourguiba. These can be surprisingly cheap, especially if you flash a student card and don't mind sitting in the vertigo-style upper circles. Occasional one-off performances by **foreign groups** are sponsored at a government level. Many use the *Maison de la Culture Ibn Khaldoun* (16 rue Ibn Khaldoun), which also mounts seasons of **classic movies**.

Films

Cinema-going is a popular pastime in Tunis, with some twenty cinemas dotted around town (see "Listings" p.76). Matinées start around 3pm and there are usually shows at around 6pm and 9pm. Listings are published every day in *La Presse*.

The **Carthage International Film Festival**, a celebration of Arab and African cinema alternating yearly between Tunis and Ouagadougou (Burkina Faso), takes over the capital's cinemas every other November (1992, 1994) – probably your best chance to see some Tunisian films. Events are listed in *La Presse* and *Le Temps*.

Moving On

Buses and louages leave Tunis regularly for all the country's main towns, as well as direct to Libya, Algeria, Morocco and sometimes even Egypt. There are **trains** to some of these places too, but they are slower, less frequent and not much cheaper. Almost everywhere in Tunisia being within twelve hours of the capital by land, internal **air travel** is a bit of an unnecessary luxury, and internal flights are not in any case very regular. But if you're feeling flush or short of time, and happen to coincide with a flight in your direction, it might be worthwhile. Full details of **leaving Tunis** by public transport are given at the begining of this chapter. The run-down of travel times and connections is given, as usual, at the end of the chapter.

Tunis Listings

American Express agent c/o **Carthage Tours**, 39 and 59 av Bourguiba (☎254304). Mail service very efficient (open mornings, Mon– Sat); money service less so.

Arabic courses The Bourguiba School (47 av de la Liberté) runs the cheapest residential Arabic course in the Middle East, costing about 120TD for an eight-week intensive course in July–August, with the possibility of renting accommodation in the university for around 80TD for the course, and eating in the college canteen for about the same. Alternatively, the school does non-intensive courses of 4hr a week at 70TD for the academic year.

Banks Banks along av Bourguiba tend to get crowded in summer. Less-packed locations include: Franco-Tunisian Bank, 13 and 8 rue d'Alger; Banque du Sud, 45 av de la Liberté (next to the Bourguiba School); BIAT, 21 rue d'Algerie (by Bab Jazira). The STB next to the *Hôtel Africa* opens late and at weekends. Outside banking hours, you can change cash at the

AIRLINE OFFICES

Aeroflot, 24 av Habib Thameur (☎341888)
Air Algérie, 26 av de Paris (☎341587)
Air France, 1 rue d'Athènes (☎341999)
Egyptair, 49 av Bourguiba, in the back of the *Hôtel International* (☎341182) (*Gulf Air* are at the same address).
GB Airways, 17 av Bourguiba (☎244261)
Iberia, 17 av Habib Thameur (☎340238)
KLM, 50 rue Lucie Faure (☎341309)
Libyan Arab Airlines, 49 av de Paris (☎341646)

Lufthansa, Complexe Hôtel el Mechtel, bd Ouled Haffouz, El Omrane (☎893515)
Royal Air Maroc, 45 av Bourguiba (staircases C and D, 3rd floor) (☎249016)
Sabena, Centre Commercial, Hôtel Abou Nawas, av Mohamed V (☎259845)
Swissair, 45 av Bourguiba (☎342122)
Tunis Air, 48 av Bourguiba (☎785100)
Tunisavia, c/o Tunisian Travel Service, 19 av Bourguiba (☎254239)
TWA c/o *Tunis Air*

EMBASSIES AND CONSULATES

Australians are represented by the Canadian Embassy; **Irish**, **New Zealand** and most **Commonwealth** nationals by the British Embassy (the British Consulate issues visas on behalf of **The Gambia**, **Nigeria**, **Sierra Leone** and other Commonwealth countries). The Côte d'Ivoire Embassy issues visas for **Niger**. The French Embassy issues visas for **Burkina Faso**, **Centrafrique** and **Togo**.

Algeria, 136 av de la Liberté. Open for visa applications 8.30–11.30am Mon–Sat. At present, unwilling to issue visas to nonresident Westerners. See p.380.

Austria, 16 rue Ibn Hamdiss, BP 23, el Menzah (☎238696).

Belgium, 47 rue 1 Juin, BP 1002 (☎781655).

Canada, 3 rue de Sénégal (☎286557).

Côte d'Ivoire (Ivory Coast), 84 av Hedi Chaker (☎283878).

Denmark, 5 rue de Mauritanie, BP 541 (☎282600).

Egypt, 16 av Essayouti, el Menzah (☎230004). Open Mon–Fri 9am–noon. Visas cost 40TD plus one passport photo and take 2–3 days to issue.

Finland, 67 rue Oum Kalthoum (☎252806).

France, rue de Yougoslavie, at the corner of rue de Hollande (☎245700). Open 8am–1pm. Issues visas on behalf of several francophone African countries for 10TD plus two passport photos. Allow 24hr and expect long queues. No visa service for Mali or Chad.

Germany, 1 rue el Hamra, Mutuelleville (☎786455).

Greece, 3 rue el Birouni, BP 58, Mutuelleville (☎288890).

Italy, 37 rue J A Nasser (☎247486).

Japan, 10 rue Mahmoud el Matri, BP 95, Belvedere (☎285937).

Libya, 48bis rue 1 Juin (☎236666). Probably still no visas for tourists, but you could try. Your best bet is to get the necessary stamp from your embassy in Tunis, then stop off in Sfax for your visa on the way south. For full information on Libyan visas, see p.382.

Mauritania, 17 rue Fatma Enneshi, BP 62, el Menzah (☎234935).

Morocco, 39 av 1 Juin (☎782775).

Netherlands, 6-8 rue Maycen, BP 449, Belvedere (☎287455).

Portugal, 2 rue Sufetula, Belvedere. (☎893981).

Senegal, 122 av de la Liberté (☎282544). Open 9am–2.30pm Mon–Fri. Visas cost 5TD plus three photos, issued the next working day. Letter of introduction required from your embassy.

Spain, 22 av Dr E Conseil, Cité Jardin (☎280613).

Sweden, 87 av Taïeb Mehiri, (☎283433).

Switzerland, 10 rue ech Chenkiti, BP 501, Mutuelleville (☎281917).

UK Consulate, 141–143 av de la Liberté (☎287293; visas Mon–Fri 8–11.30am; consular services 8am–1pm). NB, for most practical purposes it is the consulate you want, not the embassy itself on pl de la Victoire. Conditions of visa issue vary but they cost the equivalent of £30 sterling and can usually be processed in 24hr.

USA, 144 av de la Liberté (☎782566).

Yugoslavia, 4 rue de Libéria (☎281032).

Zaire, 11 rue Tertullien, Notre Dame (☎281833). Visas for Tunisian residents only.

PTT and the *Hôtel Africa*. You might also try the *Hôtel Majestic*. Travellers' cheques are trickier but you could ask around the big hotels. You are supposed to be able to change money at the airport all night, but don't count on it. As a last resort, you may find someone at one of the international *louage* stations who will change cash for you.

Beaches The Gulf shore, north from La Goulette and south from Rades, is virtually one beach, but not a very pleasant one. In summer, even Raouad beach, the furthest (out beyond Gammarth), is crowded, and unofficial reports claim the whole Gulf of Tunis is polluted.

Birdwatching Keen ornithologists will find the city of Tunis is nowhere near the bottom of the list. Belvedere Park has quite a range of **small birds**, and you can't miss the huge **sparrow** roost on the trees of av Bourguiba – extremely noisy around dusk. **Barn owls** sometimes come to hunt here at night. The cathedral shelters breeding colonies of common, pallid and little **swifts**.

Books *Claire Fontaine* (4 rue d'Alger)is very French and there's a short shelf of English books here and in another large bookshop at 5 av de Carthage. *Editions Alif* (5 rue d'Hollande) is also worth a browse, even though they have nothing in English. They sell their own publications, including a pop-up Medina book....For books in English, you're better off trying the second-hand bookshop at 10 rue d'Angleterre near the PTT. *Sapi*, next to the US Cultural Centre, is good for guides, as is the *Hôtel Africa*'s stall (at inflated prices).

Car hire There are several agencies on av Bourguiba and in the big hotels. The main ones also have a desk at the airport (☎288000 for all of them). The smaller agencies are usually cheaper but their cars may be older. *Hertz* are said to have the newest cars. Read that small print! City centre offices include:

Africar, 35 rue Alain Savary (☎782017)

Avis, 90 av de la Liberté (☎781795) – also in *Hôtel Africa*

Ben Jemaa, 53 av de Paris (☎240060)

Express, 49bis rue de la Monnaie (☎354099)

George Lafayette, 84 av de la Liberté (☎280284)

Hertz, 29 av Bourguiba (☎248559)

InterRent/Europcar, 17 av Bourguiba (☎340308) and 99 av de la Liberté (☎287235)

Car repair Any French make, and Land Rovers, can be handled at most garages. British and American dealers are in very short supply.

Churches St George's Anglican church is at pl Bab Carthajana on the edge of the Medina: very friendly weekly service. Catholics can go to Mass in the **Cathedral** – irregularly in English – or at Ste Jeanne d'Arc church on pl Palestine where there's an English service at 10am every Sunday. The Greek Orthodox church is on rue de Rome (round the corner from the cathedral) and worth a visit just to see the icons. There's a Russian Orthodox church at 12 av Mohamed V, currently out of use.

Cinemas The *Afrah* (1 rue 18 Janvier), the only art-house cinema, costs more than the others and usually subtitles Tunisian movies in French. There are daily listings in *La Presse*. Screens nearest the city centre include: *ABC*, 8 rue Ibn Khaldoun; *Afrah*, 1 rue 18 Janvier; *Alhambra*, 28 rue al Jazira; *Biarritz*, 32 rue Lt Mohamed el Aziz Taj; *Capitole*, 60 av Bourguiba; *Cinemonde*, 19bis rue Marseille; *Cine Soir*, pl de la Victoire; *Colisée*, 45 av Bourguiba (in the arcade); *Le Globe*, 12 rue Marseille; *Hani Jawharia*, 10 rue Ibn Khaldoun; *Le Palace*, 54 av Bourguiba; *Parnasse*, 63 av Bourguiba (in the arcade); *Rio*, 94 rue de Yougoslavie.

Emergencies Police: ☎197. *Protection civil* (fire brigade): ☎198. Ambulance: ☎341250/341280 (other medical numbers under Medical Facilities, below).

Excursions Trips of various lengths and prices are available from Tunis's travel agencies, but the best deal, if you can get in on it, is the YHA's "Saharan Adventure" (see p.7).

Football Tunis has two clubs, Ésperance Sportif and Club Africain, sharing the El Monza ground up in the Cité Olympique, where they play at home alternate weeks, usually Sunday at 2pm or 4pm, depending on time of year. The best way to get up to El Monza is by metro to Jeunesse (line 2), or you could walk – you may in any case have to walk back into town as it's not unknown for the metro to stop running when the fans come out at the end of a match. To avoid the mad scramble for tickets, you're advised to arrive well before the match.

Galleries The following galleries sometimes run interesting exhibitions:

Maison de la Culture Ibn Rashiq, 20 rue de Paris

Galerie Yahia, av Mohamed V, 200m from pl 7 Novembre, next to the ONA and in a similarly makeshift building

Maison de la Culture Ibn Khaldoun, 16 rue Ibn Khaldoun

1, av de France, next to the cathedral

Ministry of Information, pl de l'Independence

Alif, 5 rue de Hollande

Hammams Ubiquitous but well hidden – ask at your hotel for the nearest. Hammams in Tunis are usually single-sex, which means that you can use them all day. One of the oldest is at 75 rue des Tinturiers (men only, rather a dump, open 4am–midnight or 24hr during Ramadan). Also for men are the Hammam Kachachine at 30 souk des Librairies (5am–5pm), and one at 6 rue Bab el Khadra. There's a women's hammam in Souk el Belat, one at 1 rue Noria (open 6am–9pm) and one in rue des Femmes off bd Bab Menara. Further away, there's another at 45 av Lyon (8am–5pm).

Laundry Best solution is the *Laverie* at 15 rue d'Allemagne, which charges by the kilo.

Left luggage/baggage check In the railway station.

Libraries US Cultural Centre (1 av de France): a very prominent presence in the centre of Tunis. Mainly technical literature for students, but become a member (passport and two photos) to read the US papers. **British Council Library** (ground floor of embassy building, closed through the summer). In theory this isn't open to tourists, but has a more interesting selection of books for the long-term visitor.

Medical facilities Emergency ambulance: ☎341250/341280.

For minor complaints or injuries, an *infirmerie* – basically a nurse with a surgery – should be able to sort you out. A wound dressing and tetanus jab, for example, will cost around 3TD. There are *infirmeries* at: 23 rue Ibn Khaldoun, 20 av de la Liberté, 32 av Bab Jedid, 59 rue al Jazira and 150 rue Bab Souika. Failing that, ask your hotel receptionist for the nearest *clinique*. The best hospital is the **Hospital Charles Nicolle**, bd 9 Avril 1938 (northwest of the Medina by Bab Benat) (☎664215 illness/664211 accident). For specialised treatment, ask your consulate for a list of doctors; in an emergency try the phone numbers listed in *Le Temps* or *La Presse* which also list *pharmacies de service* – weekend and all-night chemists (for example at 43 av Bourguiba, 20 av de la Liberté, 44 av Bab Jedid and 47 av Ali Belhouane).

Newspapers A wide range of foreign papers can be bought at the stands under the trees in the middle of av Bourguiba.

ONA (Organisation National de l'Artisanat) Craft goods showroom in what looks like a jerry-built warehouse on av Mohamed V about 200m up from the tourist office: prices are high but it's worth a look if you are planning to buy crafts elsewhere.

Passport photos A lot of places do these fast and cheaply, for instance: 23 rue J A Nasser (near the PTT), 32 rue al Jazira (on the corner of rue Ecosse), 59 rue Mongi Slim, av de France (next to the cathedral, on the corner of Rue de Rome), and several places up av de la Liberté on your way to the embassy zone.

Post and phones The main PTT, for stamps and Poste Restante, is on rue Charles de Gaulle. Mail is kept in Poste Restante for only two weeks and there is a 0.2TD charge for each item. Entrance to the telephone section is off rue J A Nasser (open 24 hours a day). If this is crowded, try the smaller one on rue d'Angleterre round the corner. The **parcels** office (*Colis Postaux*) is on av de la République just off av Bourguiba. There is a branch PTT at 1 av Habib Thameur, and a very helpful one in Bab Alleoua bus station.

Postcards *Tanit* at 3 rue d'el Houdaybiyah near the cathedral have a massive selection.

Swimming Municipal pools, like the one in Belvedere Park, are often closed. Hotels like the *International* or *Africa* (5th floor) may not mind or notice non-residents using the pool.

Tourist information The main tourist office is on pl 7 Novembre (Mon–Thurs 8.30am–1pm and 3–5.45pm; Fri & Sat 8.30am–1.30pm). Free maps and booklets. Other offices are at the airport and railway station. 51 av de la Liberté is ONTT's head office, and will provide posters. There is also a Syndicat d'Initiative on av Bourguiba at the junction with av Carthage and av de Paris, but its opening hours are erratic.

Travel agencies The many travel agencies which line av Bourguiba are all very similar, offering combinations of car-hire, organised tours, flights, ferry tickets, hotel bookings and so on. As for student travel agents, the only official organisation is *Sotutour* (2 rue de Sparte), but its special deals are not spectacularly cheap. Many ordinary agencies will give a 25 percent discount for a student card, as will *Tunis Air* and some other airlines if you're under 31.

Visa extension Ask at your consulate or the Ministry of the Interior near the bottom of av Bourguiba. Note: you must show evidence of sound finances and reasons for wanting to stay.

GREATER TUNIS

On a hot summer evening, there's no better way of enjoying Tunis than getting out of it, catching the TGM across the lake to one of the suburbs on the shore of the Gulf where the sea breezes clear away the city's oppressive humidity.

Carthage gave its name to a modern suburb built over and among the remains of the ancient capital of the Carthaginian Empire, later second city of the Roman world. The physical extent of the ruins can be disappointing, but not the sense of history or the scenery. And, when you've seen enough, you can take your pick of the other suburbs: **La Goulette** with its Kasbah fortress and fish restaurants; **Sidi Bou Said**, a cliff-top village of considerable charm; **La Marsa**, **Gammarth** and **Raouad** for swimming and nightlife.

The suburbs of the southern shore are distinctly downmarket, with *bidonville* shanties spreading out beyond the bd du 9 Avril 1938. But **Hammam Lif**, a turn-of-the-century resort dominated by Jebel Bou Kornine, retains some character of its own.

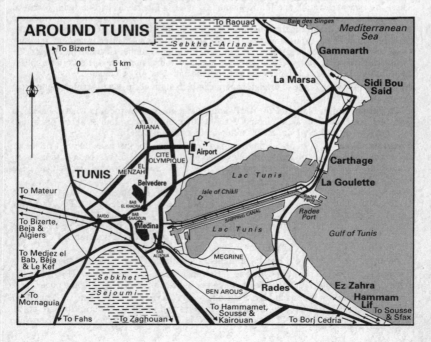

BIRDWATCHING ON LAKE TUNIS

Lake Tunis offers the chance of sighting some of Tunisia's more exciting **birds**. Forget the northern half of the lake, the edges of which are now being reclaimed for hotel and other developments, and head instead for the southern half, which attracts flamingoes, waders, gulls and terns. Numbers are particularly high in spring and autumn when they're swollen by migrants. The best vantage point is the lake's southeastern corner; take the TGM to La Bac and the ferry across to Rades port, from where you can stroll 3km down into Rades along the lakeshore.

Crossing Lake Tunis

The **causeway** on which you cross Lake Tunis was built in the 1870s to carry the **TGM railway**. The story goes that it was ordered by the Bey for the British consul so that he could get easily from his La Marsa residence to the embassy in pl de la Victoire (it originally ran all the way down what is now av Bourguiba). A deep channel, created by the dredging of material for the construction of the causeway, runs next to it on the southern side, allowing access for shipping to Tunis.

On the **Isle of Chikli**, north of the causeway, Fort St Jacques, built by the Spanish in the sixteenth century, sits mysteriously. Once used as a prison, it is now a stopover for migrating birds – who alone have the right to visit it.

Tunis Port: La Goulette

LA GOULETTE (the gullet, or throat) is the port of Tunis and increasingly a dormitory suburb for the capital. However, it still has a lively atmosphere of its own, and some excellent **fish restaurants** – the main reason for coming here, along with the ferries. The cheaper restaurants line the main avenue, more expensive ones are down quieter sidestreets.

Sights

The road from the causeway and TGM towards the port (from Goulette Vielle TGM station, head back towards Tunis for 100m then turn left at the *Esso* garage) passes, on the left, a rather run-down area reminiscent of a poor district in southern Europe, complete with church. If you're not going on to Italy, this is probably about the closest you will get to a *Mezzogiorno* slum. In the middle of the same road is La Goulette's **city gate**, part of the Spanish king Charles V's walls but now standing alone, shored up with concrete. It looks even more miserable than Bab Saadoun in Tunis.

The **Kasbah**, a massive fortress built in 1535 by Charles V to defend his bridgehead in Tunisia, is a little further on the left and really the only monumental sight here. As a key strategic point in the sixteenth century struggle for control of the western Mediterranean, it saw some torrid times, finally falling in 1574 to "four hundred and seventy-five thousand" Turks, Moors and Arabs – the figure quoted by Miguel de Cervantes, author of *Don Quixote*, who fought in its defence. Despite being captured, he and many others were glad to see the Kasbah lost – it was a "breeding-place and cloak of iniquities, a glutton, sponge and sink" of all the money spent on it in a futile policy of prestige. Over the next centuries the Kasbah was used as a dungeon for prisoners who would be taken from here to the Souk el Berka in the Medina to be sold into slavery.

Recently, an **International Museum of the Ram** (open summer only) has been installed in two of the rooms. Its literature proclaims it "probably unique in the world" – though mainly for an unrivalled collection of miscellaneous *kitsch* including an appalling reproduction of a group of Romans using a battering ram against the besieged Jews of Masada in Palestine.

Practicalities

Straight on from the museum leads to the port (see p.42), but to go into La Goulette **town**, take a left up av Farhat Hached immediately after the Kasbah. This leads to pl 7 Novembre where, if you need a room, you'll find the unclassified *Hôtel Beau Rivage* (on the right, first floor, entrance round the back). This is the main area of fish restaurants and there's a great variety, from very cheap to very upmarket. *Restaurant Venus* on pl 7 Novembre is one of the smartest, charging around 10TD a head.

From pl 7 Novembre, av Bourguiba splits to the left and av Franklin D Roosevelt to the right. Food-wise, FD Roosevelt is better (av Bourguiba has a *"Wimpy"*) with cheap places around the 3–4TD mark like the *Stambli* and the *Guitoune* alongside posher, 10–15TD establishments such as the *Monte Carlo*, the *Avenir*, the *An 2000* and the *Labidi*.

Carthage

> *[Walking around the city as it was being built]*, Aeneas looked wonderingly at the solid structures springing up where there had once been only African huts, and the gates, the turmoil, and the paved streets. The Tyrians were hurrying about busily, some tracing a line for the walls and manhandling stones up the slopes as they strained to build their citadel, others siting some building and marking its outline by ploughing a furrow.... At one spot they were excavating the harbour, and at another a party was laying out an area for the deep foundations of a theatre; they were also hewing from quarries mighty pillars to stand tall and handsome beside the stage which was still to be built.... Aeneas looked up at the buildings. "Ah, fortunate people," he exclaimed....

Ever since Virgil wrote the *Aeneid* in the first century BC, **CARTHAGE** has been suffused in a legendary aura of romance, power, cruelty and decline. "Any man who could survey the ruins of Carthage with indifference," wrote E. Blaquière, a typical nineteenth-century traveller, "or not call to mind the scenes of its past glories and misfortunes must, indeed, be devoid of sensibility." The image is made that much more potent by the yawning gap which separates the myth from the pitiful reality. Today's remains consist of a series of widely spaced sites, only a little of which stands above ground level, lurking among the plush villas of Tunis's wealthier commuters.

Still, if you approach Carthage with some imagination and a willingness to be impressed, it has a good deal to offer – not least the wide views over the Gulf and back to Tunis. It only takes a moment's thought to bring the bare bones to life, and judicious use of the TGM railway allows you to see as much or as little as you want; if you get tired just go on to Sidi Bou Said for the evening, where the mood of dusk falling over the Gulf often revives the romance.

The Site

The two main obstacles to **excavating** Carthage are that the original city was thoroughly destroyed by the Romans in 146 BC – and what was left of the Roman city after the Vandal and Arab invasions was used either for building material or, more recently, buried under commuter housing. Nonetheless, a UNESCO-inspired project involving Tunisian, French, German, British, Canadian and American archaeologists has excavated areas of the Carthaginian and Roman cities for some 5–6km along the shore on either side of the TGM railway.

Carthage tickets

A logical way to visit Carthage's rather sprawling collection of sites is in one continuous **route**, which would make a good day's leisurely ramble. An alternative would be to pick and choose, using the TGM whenever possible (trains run about every 20

CARTHAGE LEGENDS AND HISTORY

Carthage (*Qart Hadasht*, or New City) was founded, according to legend, in 814 BC by Phoenicians from the Eastern Mediterranean. One of a number of such settlements on the North African coast, it gradually became the most important of them, especially after a 507 BC treaty with Rome banned foreign shipping from the others.

Dido and Aeneas

According to a myth which plays on the Phoenicians' celebrated **commercial astuteness**, their queen, **Dido**, landed on the North African coast and requested as much territory as could be enclosed by an ox-hide. The request willingly granted, she proceeded to cut the hide into a long strip which gave her room for a city. According to Books 1 and 4 of Virgil's epic poem the *Aeneid*, **Aeneas** – sole survivor of the Greek destruction of Troy and charged by the gods with a mission to found a new Troy in Italy – turned up while she was building the city. Taken in and sheltered by Dido, Aeneas became increasingly torn between his divine mission and his love for the Carthaginian queen. All this was probably intended as high-class **propaganda** explaining the rivalry between Rome and Carthage, and Rome's superiority. But Virgil found himself unable to depict Aeneas as the sort of brainless Roman hero required by the official line, and the episode became the first classic tragic love story in European literature. Historically there's no chance of it being true – Troy was destroyed five centuries before Carthage was built.

Carthage in history

Remarkably little is known about the appearance of the **historical Carthage**, except that it grew up around the ports on the shore and the acropolis on the Byrsa Hill. The first detailed accounts come from the Romans, who gleefully described how thoroughly they destroyed the city in 146 BC.

Having left Carthage in ruins, the Romans made Utica capital of their African province, but in 46 BC **Julius Caesar** refounded Carthage as a symbol of the planned resurrection of Africa, and it grew to a huge size – the second city of the Empire after Rome. Estimates of its population range from 200,000 to 700,000, and it was as cultured as it was cosmopolitan, with a large university. As the Empire's moral and military foundations began to tremble, Christianity became the voice of the Establishment, trying too late to halt the decline. Regarded as a typically **decadent Roman city**, Carthage was a natural target for Christian abuse. Saint Augustine lambasted a group of its citizens: "Up to very recently these effeminates were walking the streets and alleys of Carthage, their hair reeking with ointment, their faces powdered white, with enervated bodies moving along like women, and even soliciting the man on the street for sustenance of their dissolute lives."

The ancient Moral Majority would feel themselves vindicated by history. Although the Vandals and Byzantines tried to keep up the Imperial lifestyle, time was running out. The Arab invaders made almost as thorough a job of destroying Carthage as the Romans had done, and what was left was carted away over the next centuries for buildings in Tunis, Kairouan and elsewhere. "In the beginning of the sixteenth century," according to Edward Gibbon, "the second Capital of the West was represented by a mosque, a college without students, twenty-five or thirty shops, and the huts of five hundred peasants, who, in their abject poverty, displayed the arrogance of the Punic senators."

minutes), and perhaps combining Sidi Bou Said and La Marsa with a couple of sessions at Carthage.

The problem with either of these approaches is that entry to all the major sites is by ticket only (2TD plus 1TD to take photos), and tickets are only available from three places: the **Carthage museum**, the **Antonine Baths**, and the **Villa de Volière** site: you'll have to begin to one of those to get one. In addition, tickets cover your entry to the **Paleo-Christian museum**, the **Punic Ports**, the **Tophet**, the **Magon Quarter**, the **Roman theatre** and the **Basilica of St Cyprian**, in theory, only for the one day – but you'd be unlucky to find a *gardien* so pedantic as to refuse you entry the following day.

If you have a **student card**, officials at some of the sites with no ticket office may let you in free. Maybe by the time they clamp down on that, it will be realised how inconvenient the system is, and tickets will be made available at all the sites.

The Carthage Museum

You can get up Byrsa Hill to the **museum** (N°1 on the ticket, which is available here) quite easily from Dermech or Hannibal TGM stations. From Dermech, stop for a breather on the terrace of the *Reine Didon* hotel, from where you can survey the whole area. The entrance to the museum (open 7am–7pm summer, 8am–5pm winter) is on the far side of the hill beyond the cathedral. Beware of guides here charging outrageous rates for their services.

Housed in the former headquarters of the White Fathers missionaries, the museum houses a display illustrating life at Carthage over more than a thousand years. Look out for a pair of **stone sarcophagi**, with a man and a woman carved lifesize on the lids, which graphically illustrate the cultural *mélange* of the ancient Mediterranean. Their clothing styles, and the fact that they were found here, suggest that they were Carthaginian; but the realism of the sculpture is almost pure Greek – the man's head would not be out of place on the statue of a fourth-century BC Greek philosopher. The **garden** is full to overflowing with various fragments: pillars, capitals, arms, legs, even an elephant. Some subterranean vaults on the far side probably supported the terrace of a massive Roman structure.

The Cathedral of Saint Louis

The **Cathedral** is a pseudo-Oriental Gothic heap which reminded Herbert Vivian in 1899 of "a glorified Brixton villa". It was built in 1890, and dedicated to Saint Louis, the thirteenth-century French king who died at Carthage while laying unsuccessful siege to Tunis in the hope of converting the Hafsid ruler El Mustansir: "Instead of a proselyte, he found a siege," wrote Gibbon. "The French panted and died on the burning sands; Saint Louis expired in his tent." In 1930 the French Catholic Church held a grandiose conference here to proclaim a revival of Africa's great Christian tradition, which is said to have played an important part in arousing Bourguiba's nationalist feelings.

The Romans left their mark even more noticeably on the Byrsa than usual, but incidentally helped to preserve what they replaced. At some point after they sacked the Carthaginian city, the top of the hill was levelled to provide a larger platform for their architects. Carthaginian quarters which were clustered around the top of the hill were buried under the rubble tipped over the sides, and saved for the present exemplary **French excavations** on the south side. These have revealed a domestic quarter similar to Kerkouane, almost the only other known example. Here the buildings were as many as five storeys high and the streets narrow, as in the Medina. Each house had its own cistern and a rudimentary drainage system. The scorched material found above these foundations has proved that vindictive Rome did indeed burn Carthage to the ground after the siege.

Behind the hill

The **amphitheatre** below the hill, in sketchy but recognisable condition, was the site of numerous early Christian martyrdoms. Perhaps most notorious were those of saints Perpetua and Felicitas, victims in 203 AD, who were brought into the arena, stripped naked and placed in nets. Even Romans were horrified when they saw that "one was a delicate young girl, and the other a woman fresh from childbirth with the milk still dripping from her breasts", so they were taken out to be brought back again, "dressed in unbelted tunics"; Perpetua was killed by a heifer, Felicitas by a gladiator's sword.

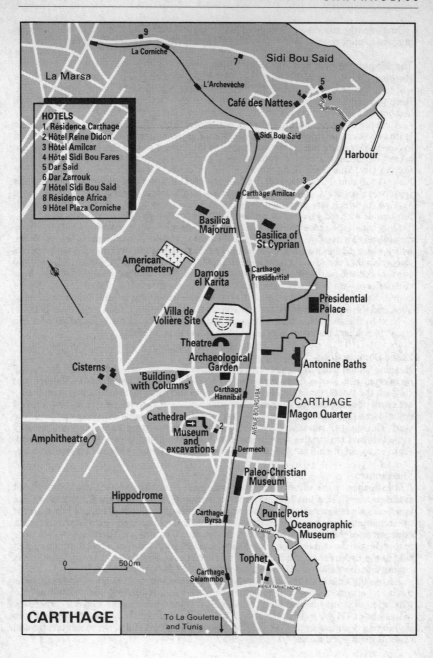

La Corniche

9

Sidi Bou Said

7

La Marsa

L'Archevêche

5

4

6

Café des Nattes

HOTELS
1. Résidence Carthage
2 Hôtel Reine Didon
3 Hôtel Amilcar
4 Hôtel Sidi Bou Fares
5 Dar Said
6 Dar Zarrouk
7 Hôtel Sidi Bou Said
8 Résidence Africa
9 Hôtel Plaza Corniche

Sidi Bou Said

8

Harbour

Carthage Amilcar

3

Basilica
Majorum

Basilica of
St Cyprian

American
Cemetery

Damous
el Karita

Carthage
Presidential

Presidential
Palace

Villa de
Volière Site

Theatre

Cisterns

Archaeological
Garden

Antonine Baths

'Building
with Columns'

Carthage
Hannibal

CARTHAGE
Magon Quarter

AVENUE BOURGUIBA

Cathedral

Museum
and
excavations

2

Amphitheatre

Dermech

Paleo-Christian
Museum

Hippodrome

Punic Ports

Carthage
Byrsa

AVENUE 2 MARS

Oceanographic
Museum

Tophet

0   500m

1

Carthage
Salammbo

AVENUE FARHAT NACHED

CARTHAGE

To La Goulette
and Tunis

Just over the road is a collection of huge **cisterns**, some inhabited and others decaying, which once received part of Carthage's water supply from the Zaghouan aqueduct.

The Magon Quarter and Antonine Baths

Heading directly seawards from Hannibal TGM station, cross av Bourguiba and you will find the **Magon Quarter** (Nº7 on the ticket, not available here) on your right. Here you can see a few bits of excavation done by a German team: neat, tidy and well laid-out, but not really very interesting; open 8am–5pm daily.

A couple of blocks north, and also sign-posted from Hannibal TGM, the **Antonine Baths** (Nº2 on the ticket, available here) are the most extensive example of their kind in North Africa, and were once the largest in the Roman world. The entrance to the site takes you through a sort of archaeological park, whose paths follow the streets of the Roman city. You enter along *Kardo* no. 16 (a *kardo* is a north–south Roman street). Nos. 17, 15 and 14 run parallel, and all are crossed after two blocks by Decumanus (east–west street) 4. Left from the entrance are a *schola* (young men's club) and a *basilica* (in which was found a poignant inscription from the Epistle to the Romans, "If the Lord is with us, who can be against us?"); the baths are right on the beach.

Once again it's a case of using your imagination, since what remains is only the basement level of a massive complex. Baths like these provided for the mass urban leisure which was a distinctive feature of Roman Imperial civilisation, and they became a pervasive symbol of the imperial presence from Morocco to Britain to Turkey. Inside, they were decorated with mosaics and statuary, and their soaring vaulted ceilings bear comparison with Western cathedrals or large mosques. It's almost impossible to convey the original size, but the central pool alone was as big as an Olympic swimming pool, and the enormous *capital* on the roundabout on the main road came from here.

Next to the site is a modern **Presidential Palace**, one of many found all over the country. Soldiers stationed here do not like cameras pointed at it.

Some Roman villas

Heading inland from the baths, cross av Bourguiba at the roundabout with the capital mentioned just above, carry on under the railway line and the **Villa de Volière** site (Nº3 on the ticket, available here) is 50m up on the right. It's really little more than a series of foundations of Roman villas and an "Antiquarium" where a few stunted columns and statues have been collected to make a foreground for photographs of the Gulf. The sight of modern villas below is hardly new – over 1500 years ago wealthy Tunisians and expatriates were already making this idyllic stretch of coast their own. Right on top of the hill are the bare foundations of the Roman **Odeon**, a type of theatre.

The theatre

A little further up the same road on the same side is the **theatre** (Nº8 on the ticket, not available here). This has been extensively restored for the modern Carthage Festival and bears scant resemblance to the original. Carthage's theatres became infamous for the immorality they portrayed and encouraged; several hundred years later a Christian critic wrote of the last days of the African Empire: "The arms of Barbarian people were resounding against the walls of Carthage; and yet the Christian population was going wild in the theatres and enjoying itself in the circuses. Some were having their throats cut outside the walls; others were fornicating inside the walls."

Across the street, a small **archaeological garden** with a few Roman odds and ends might be a good place for a breather. Further up, a "**building with columns**", or what's left of it, may be the Baths of Gargilius where St Augustine called a conference of bishops in 411 AD to trick the dissident Donatist church into being a party to its own prohibition. Continuing further will take you behind Byrsa Hill to the amphitheatre and cisterns mentioned above.

The American cemetery and northern sites

Taking a left at the "building with columns" – or from the Villa de Volière site climbing over a fence on the far side of the Odeon and cutting across the fields – gives access to the **Damous el Karita Basilica**; the name is an Arabic corruption of the Latin *Domus Caritatis*, or House of Grace. With its nine aisles, this is the largest of the churches surviving here.

The **American cemetery** beyond (cross the road and take a short cut between the fields on the other side) is more interesting. Most Americans killed in action in Tunisia during the Second World War are buried here and, in contrast to the Commonwealth and other war cemeteries elsewhere in the country, it goes all out for size and grandeur, submerging individuals in the national identity. Grandiose and patriotic with a huge flagpole, it's open 8am–5pm every day. The caretaker is something of an authority on the war in Tunisia.

One or two minor sites are scattered around Amilcar station. An old Byzantine basilica, alleged to be the **Basilica of St Cyprian** (not listed on the ticket, but you may need to show it anyway) lies southwards and towards the sea. Heading inland, not much is left of another old church, the **Basilica Majorum**.

The Tophet

Meanwhile, at the other end of Carthage, a short hop on the TGM will take you to Salammbô station, from where av Farhat Hached heads seawards. About 200m down, rue Hannibal leads off to the left, and 50m down that on the right are the remains of the **Tophet**, or sanctuary, of the Carthaginian divinities Tanit and Baal (N°6 on the ticket, not available here). A rare patch of undeveloped suburban land, dug down into deep pits and scattered with Punic stelae (headstones), this conceals a lurid past. According to legend, the Carthaginians eagerly and frequently brought their children here to be ritually slaughtered. Urns containing the ashes of children have been found on this site, but the practice was almost certainly not as common as Roman propagandists would have us believe.

The Punic Ports

The **Punic Ports** begin just 50m away, at the end of rue Hannibal (or straight down av 2 Mars from Byrsa TGM station). All that's left of these docks now, once the foundation of Carthaginian prosperity and power, are two rather nondescript lagoons. The northern one was the naval harbour, linked by a passage to the merchant docks to the south. The Ports were the responsibility of the British under the UNESCO project, and they left behind a lifelike model in the small building near the naval harbour – you can occasionally find someone to let you in. Part of the southern lagoon's shore is half-heartedly fenced off to include some holes in the ground passing as excavations (these are N°5 on the ticket, not available here).

Cross the bridge over the channel joining the two ports and you come to the **Oceanographic Museum** – which was opened in 1924, and frankly looks its age: some tanks of grumpy groupers and sad turtles, a fine collection of stuffed birds, but little else. Opening hours are Tues–Sun 2.30–5.30pm and also Sunday morning 10am-noon. Entrance is on a separate ticket costing 0.2TD (0.1TD for students).

The Paleo-Christian museum

On av Bourguiba, between Byrsa and Dermech TGM stations, is a site described as a "**Paleo-Christian museum**" after early Christian remains unearthed here (7am–7pm summer and 8am–5pm winter; N°4 on the ticket, not available here). It includes excavations and a building housing some fragments of mosaic and a cute statuette of Gannymede – the beautiful Trojan youth who was cupbearer to the gods – cuddling an eagle. There are explanations in English.

THE CARTHAGE INTERNATIONAL FESTIVAL

The **Carthage International Festival** is Tunisia's biggest cultural celebration (June–Aug). Events of all sorts – dance, cinema, music, theatre – are staged at the restored Roman theatre in Carthage (and also on the terrace of the old Casino in the Belvedere Park in Tunis). The events are largely in French and are well advertised on hoardings and in the press – tickets can be bought at the theatre. For details of the biennial **"Carthage Film Festival"**, see p.74.

Accommodation in Carthage

There are not many **places to stay** in Carthage and nowhere cheap at all. Most inviting is the two-star *Résidence Carthage* at 16 rue Hannibal (☎731072), near the Tophet (1 on the map). This little place does singles/doubles at 16.5TD/24TD b&b low season, 23TD/37TD high. It also has a rather classy little restaurant. The three-star *Hôtel Reine Didon* (☎275344), on Byrsa Hill(2), is a much more grandiose affair, priced accordingly (29.5TD/43TD b&b low, 35TD/52TD high), but only worth the difference for the view. Definitely not recommended is the rather packagey three-star *Hôtel Amilcar* (☎740788) on the beach up towards Sidi Bou Said (3), though it's cheaper at 14.7TD/21TD b&b low, 30.2TD/46TD high, and has a pool.

Beyond Carthage

As you move **up the coast from Carthage**, you are also moving towards upmarket resorts that tend to cater for the more sedate variety of French tourist looking for a more refined alternative to staying in Tunis. Remember, however, that as beach resorts, half of Tunis converges on them in summer, especially at weekends. The TGM will get you as far as La Marsa, but past there you will depend on buses if you do not have your own wheels.

Flora and fauna

If you have the time or inclination to **walk**, on the other hand, some of the fields between Carthage and Sidi Bou Said have wonderful wildflower displays in spring; look for yellow chrysanthemums, scarlet poppies, blue borage and pink campions. Brilliant **goldfinches** are common in the area, while butterflies include swooping **swallowtails** and **orange tips** and, in spring, hundreds of migrating **painted ladies** feeding on the sea stocks at the back of the beach.

Sidi Bou Said

Somehow, **SIDI BOU SAID** shrugs off its two-and-a half centuries as a tourist trap and remains a place of extraordinary charm. The first building on this strategic cliff-top was a *ribat* or monastic fortress built in the early years of Arab rule, part of the chain stretching through Sousse and Monastir to Tripoli in Libya and over whose foundations the modern lighthouse is built. The village grew up around the tomb and *zaouia* of the thirteenth-century holy man Sidi Bou Said, still celebrated in the central mosque (there's an August **festival**). According to one inventive but unlikely story, the saint was none other than Saint Louis, fresh from defeat at Carthage (see p.82) who retired here incognito to marry a local girl. Around the beginning of the century the village was discovered by wealthy French and other expatriates, who bought houses and went to great lengths to "preserve" its character. As a result, there's very little here which is not Tunisian in origin – and nowhere else in Tunisia quite like it.

You certainly won't see such a concentration of **wealthy residents and visitors** anywhere else in Tunisia: Sidi Bou is as chic as they come. In 1939 **Sacheverell Sitwell** was told that Sidi Bou Said was the finest town in all Tunisia in which to see the harem ladies in their silken dresses, but gold jewellery and tanned flesh are more the style now, especially around the expensive, central **Café des Nattes**.

It seems every artist and every writer visiting Tunisia spent some time in this square: **Cervantes, Paul Klee, Simone de Beauvoir, André Gide** and **Foucault** have all passed this way. **Walter Bayes**, the English painter, told how he was brought a cup of coffee when working here. Noticing that there was a dead scorpion floating on the surface, Bayes sent it back and asked for another cup. On draining this one, he found the scorpion at the bottom. The café doesn't appear to have suffered any drop in its reputation – it's still pretty snooty.

Orientation and practicalities

The TGM leaves you five minutes from the town centre. To get there, head uphill towards the sea (it's a cliff-top), until you get to pl 7 Novembre. Just off that square is a bank, the **PTT** (country hours), *Star* rent-a-car and a *Magasin Général* supermarket. A left here up rue Dr H Thameur takes you to the town's main square, passing the *Comité Culturel*'s gallery at no. 13. From the main square, rue el Hadi Zarrouk continues on to end at Cap Carthage, from where, on a clear day, you can see right across the bay to KORBOUS. Below, the rain has exposed several fragments of **Punic flooring**, indicating the presence of villas here even in the third century BC.

A little way from the main square down rue el Hadi Zarrouk on the right, opposite the *Hôtel Dar Said* and next to the *Dar Zarrouk*, steps lead down to the marina and beach – be careful not to trip over any courting couples on the way. Back at the main square, you could take a left up the steps of rue Sidi Bou Fares, then left again up av Taieb Mehiri for 200m, and you suddenly have a great view on your left over Carthage to La Goulette and beyond. To your right is Sidi Bou Said's lighthouse.

Eating and cafés

A stop at the *Café des Nattes* in the main square is a must, but the *Café Sidi Chabaane* further on along rue el Hadi Zarrouk and down to the right is less oppressively trendy. A steep series of narrow terraces set spectacularly in the cliff overlooking the Gulf, it's the perfect place in town to relax in romantic company with a glass of pine-nut tea

.Even with the summer evening crowds, you can have Sidi Bou to yourself by wandering through the silent back streets past white, cubic houses and their blue studded doors. **Eating** can be tailored to your budget – the cheapest places, like the *Bagatelle* with its local cooking, are around pl 7 Novembre – but doughnut fans should try a *bonbalouni* from the stall just past the *Café des Nattes*. Opposite, the *Restaurant Chergui* is a cheap café where you can fill up for 4–5TD; for a more elaborate meal, try *Pirates* at the bottom of the cliff by the marina, said to be one of Tunisia's best restaurants.

Accommodation

There's no budget **accommodation** in Sidi Bou Said, but you will find some excellent little retreats, in pleasant contrast to the noise and grime of Tunis. Be aware however that everywhere here is booked up months in advance in season, so plan ahead. The most economical is the *Hôtel Sidi Bou Fares* (☎740091) in the stairway of the same name off the main square (4 on the Carthage map). It's set around a fragrant fig tree branching all over a peaceful patio and its owner something of a musician – a bargain at 8.5TD/13TD b&b. Also off the main square, on rue el Hadi Zarrouk, are two very pleasant 2* places, both more upmarket – the *Dar Said* (☎740295) on the left (5), and the *Dar Zarrouk* (☎740912) on the right (6). Both charge 14TD/18TD b&b Sept–June, 18TD/26TD July–Aug. Former palaces, once occupied by the Zarrouk family – the prime ministers under the Beys – they are peaceful and jasmine-scented. *Dar Zarrouk* is usually open only as a restaurant out of season.

With a little less charm, the jet-set 4* *Hôtel Sidi Bou Said* (☎740411), round the cape past the lighthouse and a kilometre or so out of town (7), has high-class accommodation (31TD/42TD b&b low season, 45TD/66TD high). *Résidence Africa* (☎740600), down by the marina at the bottom of the cliff (keyed "8" on map, access down steps beside the *Dar Zarrouk*), offers bungalows from 18.5TD/dbl low season, 45TD/dbl high, with lower negotiable prices for long stays or more people sharing.

La Marsa

LA MARSA, next in the long chain of suburbs along the northern shore, is a place of some antiquity. In past centuries when transport was less easy, the entire court moved out here for the summer. "It is adorned with a royal palace, and pleasant places", wrote John Ogilby in 1670, "whither the rulers of Tunis in the summer go to take their pleasure, and keep their court." Behind the PTT are the remains of an early palace, but in the nineteenth century, when the last of Tunisia's independent Beys favoured La Marsa, many other Beylical palaces and those of their ministers were built inland. Two of the best are the residences of the British and French ambassadors, both sadly inaccessible.

Today La Marsa is easy to get to on the TGM and, in summer, has become a weekend resort for all Tunis, or so it seems. The long **beach**, with an attractive palm-lined corniche road, is what draws the crowds, and though it is slightly less crowded than those further down, you still feel like a lemming.

If for some reason you don't want to take the TGM from Tunis, buses #20 and 20d will take you to La Marsa from Jardin Thameur, or #20g from pl du Gouvernement.

Orientation and practicalities

La Marsa is quite a large town compared with Sidi Bou Said. The **TGM station** is at the southern end of the **corniche**, heading up which – past a pedestrian arcade on your left and sweeping majestically above the beach on your right – you come to the French ambassador's residence where av Bourguiba heads off to the left. At the other end of av Bourguiba is pl 7 Novembre, where you'll find the **PTT**, banks, *Tunis Air*, chemists and **buses** #20, 20d and 20g to Tunis. Bus #40 for Gammarth leaves from the TGM station and can be picked up along the corniche.

Accommodation

Should you want to stay here, options are limited. *Pension Prendl*, 1 rue Mohamed Salah Malki (☎270529, 8TD/bed plus 1TD/breakfast) is off av Bourguiba about 100m from the French ambassador or 300m from pl 7 Novembre. Not the easiest place to find, it compensates with the cosiest family atmosphere of any *pension* in Tunisia. Alternatively, there's the *Hôtel Plaza Corniche* (☎270099) at 22 rue du Maroc (9 on the Carthage map), five minutes walk from the station back towards Sidi Bou Said. Officially also a *pension*, it's more expensive at 30TD/38TD b&b low season, 40TD/48TD high, but gets booked solid in season – call ahead.

Food and drink

La Marsa's **cheap eateries** are off the corniche around the av 20 Mars arcade. The restaurants *el Hana* and *du Peuple* do meals for around 2TD, and the *Chez Scofe* opposite *du Peuple* has Lebanese sandwiches (including felafel) for a similar price. **Midrange** possibilities include two just by the bridge where the corniche crosses rue Mongi Slim and begins to skirt the beach. Above is the *Restaurant des Palmiers* doing pizzas, crêpes, fish and similar fare for about 5TD a meal. Down below, there's nothing notably Mexican about the *Restaurant Mexicaine*, apart from the name and the cacti opposite. **Upmarket** places include the *Hôtel Plaza Corniche*'s restaurant at about 12TD a head and *Le Baalbek* on the beach at the bottom of rue Mongi Slim – an amazing Art Deco hulk that manages to look like it's escaped from Brighton Pier – serving Lebanese-ish cuisine at 10.5TD for the *menu* and much more à la carte.

The most interesting place in town for a **mint tea or Turkish coffee** is the *Café Saf Saf*, around the corner from av 20 Mars, opposite the mosque. Built around a **public well** dating back to the Hafsid period, this is still worked in summer by a camel wearing fluffy blinkers – not a unique phenomenon (see p.173), but something of a curiosity.

Gammarth

GAMMARTH, (bus #20b from Jardin Thameur in Tunis, or a #40 from La Marsa) is the next instalment of suburb. It grew up around the series of beaches dubbed *Baies des Singes* (Bays of the Monkeys) by local fishermen – reputedly after the Europeans who sunbathed in the nude there in the 1950s…. Up on the hill is a cemetery of the free French killed during the Second World War.

Hotels at Gammarth are aimed at the business community, and priced accordingly. The deluxe 4* *Hôtel Abou Nawas* (☎741444), for example, charges 75TD for a double in high season. The 3* *Cap Carthage* (☎741724) and *Megara* (☎740366) charge 60TD and 52TD respectively (though the *Cap Carthage* halves its prices *hors-saison*), and the vacation village of *Dar Naouar* (☎741000) charges 50TD. The cheapest place in Gammarth is the 1* *Tour Blanche* (☎271697) at 17TD/25TD b&b.

Raouad

Beyond Gammarth, civilisation is almost at an end. The road runs between a salt flat and **RAOUAD BEACH**, a broad expanse of sand where families camp *en masse* in summer. As there are few, if any, facilities, the water becomes almost visibly unhygienic in the peak season. You could camp out or look for a place at a vacation village such as the *Noria* (☎270904), 21TD/28TD b&b, but frankly there are much more attractive places in Tunisia to do this.

The Southern Suburbs

Easily reached by train from Tunis's main station at pl Barcelone, the **suburbs along the southern shore of the Gulf** are for the most part shapeless areas of less affluent commuter housing, with warehouses and light industry filling in the gaps between what were once smart resorts. One slightly out-of-the-way natural highlight is the mountainous national park of **Bou Kornine**.

Rades and Ez Zahra

One of the formerly smart resorts was **RADES**; after the Arab conquest there was even a *ribat* here, as at Sidi Bou Said. Its **beach** is the beginning of one long strand running all the way round the south bay of the Gulf of Carthage to SIDI RAIS on Cap Bon; but at Rades it's crowded and dirty. With the opening of a pleasant new youth hostel in Tunis, there seems little reason to stay at the **Maison des Jeunes** here (☎483631), especially as it is more expensive at 4TD per person, and won't let you check in or leave your baggage before 7pm. Rades Port, 3km out of town, has a free **ferry** service to La Goulette (5min) which runs every 15min from 7am to 8.45pm.

EZ ZAHRA, the next suburb down the coast, is a little quieter than the other southern suburbs. There are two hotels here, the 4* *Hôtel Ez Zahra* (☎482550) and the unclassified *Hôtel La Siesta* (☎480776) and also a youth hostel (☎481547), or, in summer, *La Pinède* holiday village (☎206036).

Hammam Lif

Once the last stage on the caravan route from the south, where merchants paid tax before entering the capital, **HAMMAM LIF** was a popular spa in Carthaginian and Roman days, and emerged again as a resort under the Protectorate. Palm-lined avenues and an old seafront casino give the town a seedy sort of allure in its dramatic setting under Jebel Bou Kornine, but it rarely throws off its rather listless, Sunday-afternoon feel – except perhaps on a Sunday, market day, probably the busiest time of the week. The **Casino** (☎290010) is now a bar/restaurant – an excellent place to pop in for a beer and where women need have no worries. As for the decor, as one reader remarked, "The interior was obviously done by Elvis Presley on acid". If you want time to inspect this display, there are a few unclassified **hotels** in which to stay: the *Bon Repos*, 14 rue Ibn Rochd (☎291458) at 6TD/8TD; and the similarly priced *Hôtel des Thermes*.

Jebel Bou Kornine National Park

The imposing mountain of **Bou Kornine** is a national park, heavily forested lower down, but with a more open *maquis* vegetation at the top. To get there from the Hammam Lif station, walk south to the main road, turn right, and then left up rue Essoudess near the *Chalet Vert* sign. From here, a succession of winding tracks lead you up the mountain through pine forests, rosemary, rock roses and orchids. At the summit, the pines give way to scrubbier, more open vegetation, where you have the chance to see the rare **Bonelli's eagle** – a large species with a black band across its underwing – and get a terrific view over the Gulf of Tunis up to Sidi Bou Said.

Borj Cedria

BORJ CEDRIA, a last desultory resort before Soliman Plage which houses the PLO headquarters, lacks even Hammam Lif's doubtful attractions. In 1985, to the political embarrassment of the Americans, who had been instrumental in finding a home here for the PLO after their removal from Beirut, Israeli air force jets carried out a "surgical strike" (they bombed it) on the PLO complex but failed to kill Yasser Arafat, their presumed target. Should its history fail to deter – or even intrigue you – **hotels** in Borj Cedria include the 3* *Salwa* (☎290830) and *Médi Sea* (☎293030; with facilities for disabled visitors), the 2* *Dar* (☎290188), the unclassified *Younes* (☎293013) and the *La Pinède* "vacation village" (☎206036).

AROUND TUNIS

Tunisia is such a small country that this geographical division is even more arbitrary than most. The Roman site of **Thuburbo Majus**, and **Zaghouan** with its green mountain setting, both 60km from Tunis, make excellent day trips from the capital. Alternatively, if you're heading south to Kairouan or Sousse – or beyond – you could aim first for an overnight stay at either place.

La Mohammedia, Fahs and Thuburbo Majus

Sixteen kilometres from Tunis, on the road to Fahs, Ahmed Bey (1837–56) built a summer palace that he hoped would surpass even Versailles in its grandeur. Given the initial expectations, **La Mohammedia**'s present state of ruin is a little disappointing. All the roofs have collapsed and most of the tiles have been pillaged, but the site still has the bare outlines of the palace buildings and associated barracks. Tunisia has a large number of redundant and ruined Beylical palaces, probably because of the superstition that it was unpropitious for a Bey to rule from the palace of his predecessor.

A few kilometres beyond La Mohammedia, the road runs parallel to the Roman **aqueduct** which carried water from Zaghouan to Carthage. First built in the second century AD, it was reconstructed by the Byzantines after the Vandal invasion, and later by the Fatimids and Hafsids. Where the road meets the aqueduct an 8-km track leads directly to the minimal remains of Roman **OUDNA** – some excellent mosaics have gone to the Bardo, leaving (most recognisably) a Byzantine fortress.

If you're going by **bus** or **louage** you have to pass these sites to reach **FAHS**, a sizeable but nondescript market town. The only reason to come down this way is to see the Roman site of **Thuburbo Majus**, 3km north of Fahs; the town has few attractions of its own. If you do pass through, though, try to coincide with the **Saturday market**, one of the largest in the area and devoid of tourist coaches. The market place is next to the railway line and buses and *louages* stop nearby on the main road.

Thuburbo Majus

The ruins of **Thuburbo Majus** lie behind a low rise north of Fahs on the Tunis road. If you walk from the town, don't follow the signpost for the site – which seems to take you halfway round northern Tunisia – but walk up instead to the dip between the two small hills, the eastern edge of the Roman city. Thuburbo Majus – sounds more like a jazz singer than a Roman name – was a Berber-cum-Carthaginian settlement long before the Romans arrived, playing much the same role in this fertile district as modern Fahs. The Romans brought prosperity and their own characteristic building styles, but the site was abandoned after the seventh-century Arab invasion and only rediscovered in 1875.

The Forum

The town's great buildings, the expression of its citizens' collective pride, date from the great imperial era of the second to third century AD. The **Forum** – the paved open space at the centre of the site, laid out between the years 161 and 192 AD – was its most characteristically Roman feature, something that any self-respecting imperial town had to have. A colonnade ran around three sides, the fourth left open for the **Capitol temple**, which catered for the Imperial cult of Jupiter, Juno and Minerva. The podium and the vertical emphasis of the columns are very much the norm, and if you walk round behind it's easy to see just how much effort had to go into giving the temple a massive base so that it would dominate the Forum in the prescribed manner. In fact, the whole of one side of the Forum had to be raised on an artificial platform to create the required level space. The area of housing behind the Capitol was later converted into **oil factories** – you can see the cisterns and treading basins, and in the distance one of three surviving **triumphal arches** on the outskirts of the town.

The Temple of Mercury

Behind the colonnade on the other three sides of the Forum stood temples and municipal buildings. On the right-hand side as you look from the Capitol is a curious **Temple of Mercury**, built in 211 AD, according to the local, not the Roman pattern: an outer courtyard – circular, with niches making corners – leading into the sanctuary. Mercury was the god of trade (as well as of thieving), and the three courtyards below the temple on split levels formed the town's **market**, where stalls can be made out. The Mercury temple looks out over an area of jumbled streets and houses, predating the forum, in a layout that was anathema to the Romans. Several hundred metres beyond, towards another triumphal arch in the distance, is a second residential quarter with regular streets, a Roman addition as the town expanded. In many ways, the contrast between the two areas is similar to the difference in modern Tunisia between *medinas* and French grid plans: like the Romans before them, the nineteenth-century colonial powers imported their own ideas of organisation.

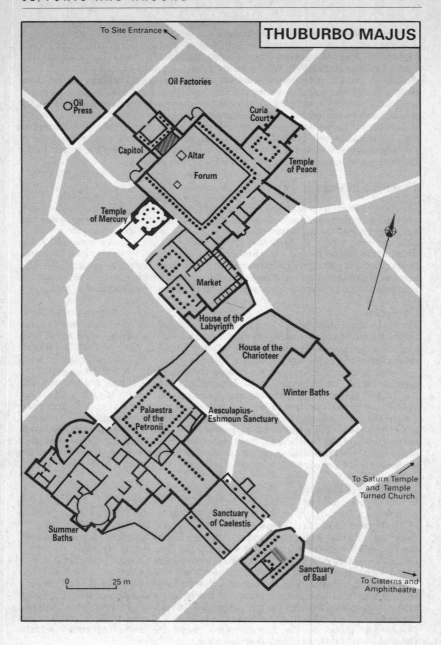

THUBURBO MAJUS

To Site Entrance

Oil Factories

Oil Press

Capitol

Curia Court

Altar

Forum

Temple of Peace

Temple of Mercury

Market

House of the Labyrinth

House of the Charioteer

Winter Baths

Palaestra of the Petronii

Aesculapius-Eshmoun Sanctuary

Summer Baths

Sanctuary of Caelestis

To Saturn Temple and Temple Turned Church

Sanctuary of Baal

To Cisterns and Amphitheatre

0   25 m

The Palaestra and some hybrid temples

The impressive semi-circular **portico** over the immediate housing is not, as you might expect, the facade of some grand public building, but the front of the public latrines. Behind is a large complex, the **Summer Baths**, remodelled in the year 361 and confused in plan. The row of blue-grey columns alongside were part of the **Palaestra of the Petronii**, where young men exercised by boxing, wrestling or running before going on to the Baths. Letters carved in the paving of its southern corner make up the Roman game of **"36 letters"**, used to improve knowledge of the alphabet.

Nothing could be more Roman than the Palaestra, but three hybrid centres of worship show just how much of a cultural blend Roman Africa was. In the far corner of the Palaestra is a small **shrine** to the healing god Aesculapius, here worshipped under the joint name of Aesculapius-Eshmoun. An inscription reveals that those wishing to enter the sanctuary had to observe a three-day ritual: they were forbidden sexual relations, beans and pork, and bathing and shaving. A street leads off to the right here towards a small temple podium. This **sanctuary of Baal**, the top deity in the Phoenician pantheon, was erected in the second century under Roman rule. The courtyard just over the street (with its entrance re-erected) was a **sanctuary of Caelestis**, the Roman version of Carthaginian Tanit. Later it was used as a church.

Other curiosities

Ruins discernible on the hillside south of the Baal temple comprise perhaps the most monumental **cistern** to be seen in Tunisia, even boasting an inner gallery around the top of the deep storage tank. An **amphitheatre** above is just recognisable – there's a fine view from here of Jebel Zaghouan dominating the whole region, and across to the eastern **gate** of the town on the next hill. Above the gate are the remains of a **temple of Saturn**, the Roman equivalent of Baal whose temples tend to be near the city boundaries, as at Dougga. A **church** between the temple of Saturn and the centre of town was fashioned out of another large temple and the path leads on past the **Winter Baths**, mediocre except for their impressive facade.

Zaghouan

Almost alpine in feel, with its green slopes and the grey crags above, **ZAGHOUAN** is perhaps the most refreshing town in Tunisia. The old town's steep, narrow streets criss-cross a low ridge of Jebel (Mount) Zaghouan – not the highest in the country, but easily the most spectacular. Cold water gushing from its springs used to supply Carthage via a 70-km aqueduct, and now splashes from taps at every street corner.

One end of the ridge is punctuated by the old church spire and the new mosque's minaret; nearer the middle are the nineteenth-century **Great Mosque** and the **Marabout of Sidi Ali Azouz** – patron saint of Tunis, with a *zaouia* in the *medina* there.

Practicalities

Although a fair number of tourists stop by to see the Roman ruins, few stay long, leaving the town surprisingly unspoiled. If you have the choice, come on a Friday, **market day**. The cheapest **accommodation** is the *Maison des Jeunes* Youth Hostel (☎75265), a barrack-like affair on top of the next ridge over from the town centre. The only **hotel**, the *Nymphes* (☎75094), along the shady lane leading behind the town towards the ruins and high up among the trees, is expensive, but sometimes open to bargaining. This same road continues to a **café-restaurant** just below the remains where they may allow **camping** ("but there are wild boar, Monsieur"!). **Transport** in Zaghouan operates from the bottom of the old town near the Roman arch, with **buses** and **louages** to Tunis and occasionally NABEUL, Fahs and Enfida, plus two buses daily for SOUSSE.

Activities – Jebel Zaghouan and around

The café is the place to sit and enjoy the **view**, extending over the bare plain below and up into a gash of the mountain behind. The Roman **"temple"** here is little more than a backdrop – and not a temple at all, but a grand fountain of the type found in all Roman towns. The twelve niches above the basin once held a statue for each month of the year.

If you feel inspired to climb the craggy, limestone ridge of **Jebel Zaghouan**, either take the 16-km track leading to the relay station on the summit (from which there are superb views over the countryside), or scramble up directly from the temple in a couple of hours. It's very hard going, though, rough on exposed legs and a good place to twist an ankle, and the mountain is not a place to get caught out after dark.

The mountain, rising 1300m above the surrounding plains, is the most typical of the ranges that form Tunisia's "backbone". From a naturalist's point of view, its highlight is an abundance of **birds of prey** – up to a dozen species can be sighted in a few hours, including eagles, vultures, kites and falcons, wheeling around their nest sites, or soaring hundreds of metres before gliding out over the plains in search of food. They're active most of the day, but early morning and evening are the best times to watch.

The plain around the mountain repays leisurely exploration if you have time. If you want a **walk with an unusual goal**, eight tanks from the Second World War lie rusting among the trees 5km south of the village of HAMMAM JEDIDI, near the road from Zriba. The main road to ENFIDA winds round to the south, eventually passing rocky TAKROUNA: in the hills between this road and the sea, there's another spectacular mountain village, JERADOU. For Hammamet, most traffic follows a road left from ZRIBA to BOU FICHA on the coast.

Routes from Zaghouan to Tunis

Returning from Zaghouan to Tunis, a couple of routes are worth exploring. The main road, followed by buses and *louages*, climbs and descends the forested ridge of **Jebel Oust** before joining the P3 road from Fahs. On the left of the slope as you drop down is a brand new spa centre called **HAMMAM OUST**, built on the site of a Roman predecessor. If you get a chance to see the remains, they're worth a quick look, weirdly eroded into distorted shapes as though you're peering through wet glass.

A more interesting alternative is to hitch back via OUED EZ ZIT (to the east of Zaghouan), where a steep road winds left under the ominous "Lead Mountain" (Jebel Ressas) to the wine centre of MORNAG. It's only a short bus ride from here to Tunis.

travel details

For details of where to catch transport in Tunis see "Points of Arrival and Departure" (p.42).

Trains

FROM TUNIS TO THE SOUTHERN SUBURBS
Half-hourly from 4am–10pm to: **Rades** (20min); **Ez Zahra** (30min), **Bou Kornine** (35min), **Hammam Lif** (40min), and **Borj Cedria** (50min). Most trains to Sousse also stop at Hammam Lif.

FROM TUNIS TO:
Hammamet and Nabeul (1 direct train daily plus many connections via Bir Bou Rekba); **Fahs** (4 daily, 1hr 30min), some continuing to **Kalaa Kasbah** (3, 5hr 30min), and **Le Kef** (1, 4hr); **Mateur** (4, 1hr) and **Bizerte** (4, 1hr 40min); **Beja** (6, 2hr), some continuing to **Jendouba** (4, 2hr 30min), **Ghardimaou** (4, 3hr) and **Algiers** (1, 20hr) via Souk Ahras, Annaba and Constantine; **Sousse** (7, or 9 in summer, 2hr 15min), some continuing to **Monastir** (2, 3hr 10min), **Mahdia** (2 4hr); **El Jem** (4, 3hr 15min) and **Sfax** (4, 4hr 10min) some continuing to **Gabes** (2, 7hr), **Gafsa** (1, 8hr 40min) and **Metlaoui** (1, 9hr 30min). Note: *This last train splits, half going to Gabes, and the other half to Gafsa and Metlaoui (be sure you're in the correct carriage).*

LOCAL SERVICES AROUND TUNIS

TGM line trains run every 20min to **La Marsa** (45min), via **La Goulette** (20min), **Carthage** (30min) and **Sidi Bou Said** (35min). Last train after midnight.
Tunis–La Marsa *SNT* city buses #20, 20d, 20g; **Tunis–Gammarth** *SNT* bus #20b; **La Marsa–Gammarth** *SNT* bus #40.
Hammam Lif/Borj Cedria–Grombalia/Nabeul Frequent *SRTG Nabeul* buses.

Buses

The terminals in Tunis at Bab Alleoua and Bab Saadoun (see p.43) have services to almost every town of any size in the country at least once a day. **Bab Saadoun mostly serves the north and parts of the Tell; Bab Alleoua serves the rest** *of the country, principally the south, and international destinations. With few exceptions, the following destinations have departures during daylight hours. Most destinations are served by louages – journey times are roughly three-quarters the bus times.*

FROM BAB SAADOUN TO THE NORTH & WEST
Medjez el Bab (half-hourly, 1hr); **Testour** (hourly, 1hr); **Teboursouk** (hourly, 1hr 20min); **Beja** (hourly, 2hr); **Bizerte** (hourly, 2hr); **Le Kef** (hourly, 3hr); **Mateur** (8 daily, 1hr 30min); **Jendouba** (5 daily, 3hr); **Aïn Draham** (4 daily, 4hr); **Tabarca** (7 daily, 4hr).

FROM BAB ALLEOUA TO CAP BON :
Nabeul (half-hourly, 1hr 30min); **Hammamet** (hourly, 1hr 30min); **Kelibia** (hourly, 2hr 30min); **Zaghouan** (3 daily, 1hr).

FROM BAB ALLEOUA TO THE CENTRE & SOUTH:
Enfida (very frequent, 1hr 30min); **Kairouan** (18 daily, 3hr); **Sousse** (12, 2hr 30min); **Gabes** (10, 7hr); **Sfax** (9, 5hr); **Gafsa** (8, 6hr); **Kasserine** (6, 5hr); **Medenine** (4, 7hr); **Houmt Souk/Jerba** (3, 8–10hr); **Sidi Bou Zid** (2, 5hr); **Maktar** (2, 3hr); **Ras Ajdir(Libyan frontier)** (1, 9hr 30min).

FROM ZAGHOUAN TO:
Tunis (3 daily, 1hr); **Sousse** (2, 2hr); **Fahs** (3, 30min); **Nabeul** (3, 1hr 30min).

FROM FAHS TO:
Tunis (6 daily, 1hr 30min); **Maktar** (6, 2hr); **Kasserine** (6, 4hr); **Zaghouan** (3, 30min); **Nabeul** (3, 2hr); **Le Kef** (2, 3hr); and **Sousse** (2, 2hr).

International Buses

Subject to the vagaries of Maghrebian politics.
FROM BAB ALLEOUA TO:
Annaba, Algeria (daily, 5hr 30min), **Constantine**, Algeria (weekly, 9hr), **Algiers** (weekly, 18hr), **Tripoli**, Libya (four times a week, 17hr), **Cairo** and **Casablanca** (weekly or less).

International Louages

FROM TUNIS (PORTE DE FRANCE) TO:
Constantine (7hr), **Algiers** (15hr) and **Oujda**, Morocco (24hr);
FROM TUNIS (BAB SOUIKA) TO:
Tripoli (13hr).

Flights

Inside back page of Le Temps or La Presse has a full list each day.

DOMESTIC FLIGHTS TO:
Jerba (9 a week, 12 in summer), **Tozeur** (3 each week), **Monastir** (weekly) and **Sfax** (weekly), all on *Tunis Air*. *Tunisavia* fly a Twin Otter to **Sfax** (twice a week).

INTERNATIONAL FLIGHTS TO:
Paris (2 a day); **Rome** (2 a day); **Algiers** (daily); **Casablanca** (daily); **Marseille** (daily); **Geneva** (daily); **London** (4 a week); **Malta** (3 a week).

Ferries

FROM LA GOULETTE TO:
Trapani (2–4 sailings per week, 8hr); **Genoa** and **Marseille** (1–3 sailings, 24hr); **Livorno** (at least 1, 32hr); **Cagliari** (1, 24hr); **Naples** (summer-only, weekly, 24hr) and sometimes **Malta**.

PHONE CODE

Tunis area ☎01 Fahs & Zaghouan ☎02

CHAPTER TWO

HAMMAMET AND CAP BON

Protruding like a crooked finger into the Mediterranean, the **Cap Bon** peninsula is Tunisia's main resort area. Indeed, glancing at the brochures – with their staggering hotel capacities – it looks a little ominous, particularly around the Hammamet–Nabeul zone. But although **Hammamet**, the best known resort in the country, is international, developed and expensive, any images of a Spanish-like *costa*, with tourists crowded like cattle, don't apply. The beaches, for a start, are too big and too luxuriant, and the hotels are kept discreetly down to a few storeys, strung well out along the tree-lined shore. Half an hour away, **Nabeul** has less perfect beaches and a less glamorous image, but cheaper places to stay, and good transport links for visiting other areas of the peninsula.

Among these areas, one of the most worthwhile targets is **El Haouaria**, a village at the end of the peninsula with the off-beat twin attractions of a remote white strand and a cavern full of bats. **Kerkouane**, round the coast from here, is the largest Carthaginian site yet uncovered, while **Kelibia**, a few kilometres on, and dominated by a massive Spanish castle, is the quietest beach resort on the east coast. Over on the north side **Korbous** is the bestknown lure, an ancient spa town now heavily commercialised; if you're after seclusion and have transport, however, the coast beyond is literally one long and as yet undiscovered beach.

The peninsula is at its best in **spring**. An immensely fertile region, more so than anywhere else in Tunisia, it becomes a mass of colour with its fruit orchards and vineyards. If you can make it in April try to coincide with the **Orange Festival** at **Menzel Bou Zelfa**. By September the ground is parched – but then there's the tempting **Wine Festival of Grombalia**.

MARKET DAYS

Monday – Kelibia	Friday – Nabeul, El Haouaria
Tuesday – Menzel Temime	Saturday – Soliman
Thursday – Menzel Bou Zelfa, Hammamet	Sunday – Korba

Hammamet

At the turn of the century **HAMMAMET** was a small fishing village making some extra money by selling lemons from its dense citrus groves to Sicily for export to America. It was only in the 1920s, with the arrival of a Romanian millionaire, Georges Sebastian, that the town found its true vocation. Sebastian built a fabulous villa just above the beach, described by Frank Lloyd Wright as the most beautiful house he knew. Others followed, and soon Hammamet was part of the international legend of a sensual Tunisia

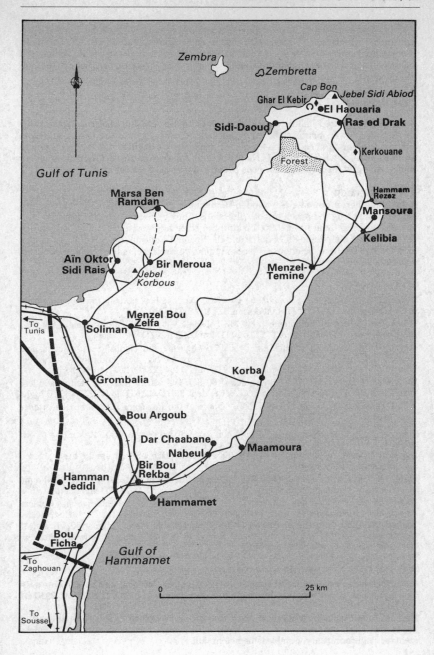

Zembra

Zembretta

Cap Bon

Jebel Sidi Abiod

Ghar El Kebir

El Haouaria

Sidi-Daoud

Ras ed Drak

Kerkouane

Gulf of Tunis

Marsa Ben Ramdan

Hammam Rezez

Mansoura

Kelibia

Aïn Oktor
Sidi Rais

Jebel Korbous

Bir Meroua

Menzel-Temine

Menzel Bou Zelfa

To Tunis

Soliman

Grombalia

Korba

Bou Argoub

Dar Chaabane

Maamoura

Nabeul

Bir Bou Rekba

Hamman Jedidi

Bou Ficha

Hammamet

To Zaghouan

Gulf of Hammamet

0   25 km

To Sousse

– somewhere between an intellectual resort and a luxurious Bohemia for Europe's pre-war moneyed classes. Today, with some sixty hotels and almost 20,000 beds, Hammamet is considerably less exclusive, but arriving from elsewhere in Tunisia you still feel as if you've landed in another world – St Tropez, say, with "Oriental" trimmings.

Practicalities

Hammamet's centre is a little cape sticking out into the sea. The **Medina** stands neatly on its point, newer quarters spreading out behind, with most of the hotels spaced to either side along the beach. The town's two main streets begin at the Medina: **Avenue de la République** heads towards Nabeul, becoming **Avenue de la Libération** further along, while **Avenue Bourguiba** goes inland towards the train station.

Accommodation

A large number of **hotels** claim to be in Hammamet, although most of them are spread out for miles along the beach in both directions. They generally cater for package tourists and some of them have started taking the same aggressively commercial attitude to tourists that put people off Majorca and the Spanish *costas* in the 1970s. If you book a package holiday here, be choosy. Places in the town itself are, at least, relatively cheap, especially out of season.

TOWN CENTRE

Pension Hallous, av de la République (☎80525). Not the best hotel in town but comparatively inexpensive. 12TD/16TD mid-season, 13TD/18TD high.

Hôtel Alya, 30 rue Ali Belhouane (☎80218). Polished, but overpriced in summer. Ask for a room with a view of the Medina. 1* 9TD/14TD low, 23TD/26TD high, b&b.

Hôtel Sahbi, av de la République (☎80807). Opposite the campsite and bus station. Described in their brochure as "Moorish style", rooms are big, clean and prettily furnished. Fills up with package tourists in summer. 2*9TD/14TD low, 23TD/26TD high, b&b.

Résidence Hammamet, 72 av Bourguiba (☎80733). Only 300m from the Medina and less from the beach. Four people sharing get a better deal. 8.6TD/12.6TD low, 27TD/45TD high.

Hôtel Yasmina, av Bourguiba (☎80222). Opposite the *Résidence Hammamet* and rather more expensive. 3* 18TD/33TD low, 34.5TD/55TD high, b&b.

EAST OF THE TOWN CENTRE

Pension Milano, rue des Fontaines (☎80768). A small place not far from the beach, closed out of season. 15TD per person.

Hôtel Olympia, av du Kowait (☎80662). Rather packaged but perfectly adequate and quite inexpensive by Hammamet standards. 2* 8.5TD/12TD low, 13.5TD/21TD high, b&b.

Nearby is the 2* **Hôtel les Charmes**, and further east, near the International Cultural Centre, the 1* **Pension Bennila** (☎80356). On the way, you pass the 4* deluxe **Hôtel Sinbad** (☎80122), then the 2* **Aladin** (☎80611), and the 3* **Parc Plage** (☎80111) and 3* **Continental** (☎80456). Further still, the 4* **Sheraton** (☎80555) is a cut above its business-class namesakes elsewhere in the world.

WEST ALONG THE BEACH: AV ASSAD IBN EL FOURAT

Hôtel Bellevue, av Assad Ibn el Fourat (☎81121). Seafront location, with most rooms overlooking the sea. Pleasant and modern but fills up in season. 2* 12.1TD/19.8TD low, 20.9TD/35.2TD high, b&b.

Baie du Soleil Vacation Village, av Assad Ibn el Fourat (☎80298). Quiet, leafy and right on the beach. 7.2TD per person low , 17TD high, b&b, in triple bungalows with 5.5TD supplement for single occupancy, payable if the hotel is full.

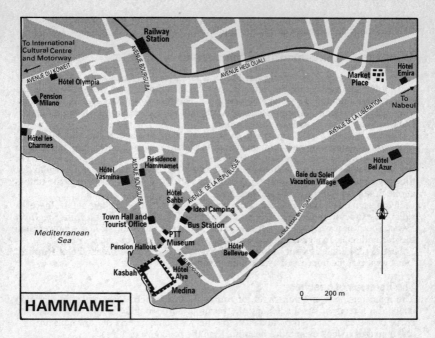

HAMMAMET

Hôtel Emira, on the Nabeul road leaving town (☎81720). One of the many hotels which line the beach all the way to Nabeul. 2*.

CAMPSITES

Ideal Camping, av de la République (☎80302). A pleasant little place with cold showers and laundry facilities. In general, lives up to its name. 1.5TD per person plus 0.8TD per tent.

Samaris campsite, out past the International Cultural Centre, on the Tunis road, in the grounds of this 1* hotel (☎80353).

Eating, drinking and entertainment

As you'd expect, **restaurants** are plentiful, both in the town and in most of the hotels – and if you're on a budget it's still surprisingly easy to find a cheap Tunisian meal around the town centre. Most of the places in av Bourguiba between the Medina and the Town Hall do seafood pizzas for about 3TD which are not very Italian but usually good (at the *Grill Etage* for example); however, these places are very tourist-orientated and the rest of their fare tends to be overpriced. Two cheaper options are the *Restaurant La Brise* at 2 av de la République, which will do you a solid Tunisian meal for about 3.5TD, and the *Snack Bar Khaltoum* in rue Ali Belhouane near the corner of av de la République, which has couscous from 2TD. More upmarket (around 9TD per head), the *Restaurant de la Poste "Chez le Chef"* in the main square opposite the Medina has excellent fish and soups and a very amiable polyglot staff. The *Berber Restaurant* nearby is pricier still, but good.

Most of the **discos** are out in the hotel zone on av Moncef Bey, or in the hotels themselves, notably the *Palm Beach* and the *Phoenicia*.

In July and August, a series of events at the International Cultural Centre are clustered together under the title **"festival"**. Although obviously directed at tourists, a lot of these are very interesting and it's worth getting hold of a programme from the ONTT here or in Nabeul to check out what's on.

Things to see and do around Hammamet

As far as sights go, the tiny walled **Medina** is surprisingly unspoiled once you get beyond the first rash of tourist emporia, and the fifteenth-century **Great Mosque** has an attractive minaret. The bionically restored **Kasbah** (open Oct–Apr 8.30am–6pm, May–Sept 8am–9pm, 1TD entry) can be safely ignored except for the view, though the Old Sea Gate below its walls is pretty enough.

Next to the PTT at 21 av de la République is what used to be the Municipal Museum. Though the museum itself has long since closed down, the building is sometimes still used as a **gallery**. Entry is free, and one or two relics remain inside. On the street corner next to it is an old olive oil press. The **Town Hall** on av Bourguiba, in the very centre facing the beach, used to be the *Hôtel de France* – packed to the rafters at one time with Europe's rich and famous.

If you want a very slow ride along the coast to Nabeul, via all the big hotels, there's a ridiculous **tourist road-train** ("Petit Train/Little Train/Kleiner Zug") from the *Hôtel Venus*, south of town, to Nabeul town centre (3 times a day, 2hr, 2.5TD) – slower than the bus and more expensive than a taxi: you pay for the fun of the ride.

Lastly, six kilometres out of town on the Sousse road is the Roman site of **Pupput**. Don't expect to be impressed by the limited remains.

The Hammamet beaches

The main business of Hammamet, of course, is **the beach**. Even with the fast food stalls, the forests of sunshades and the herds of bored-looking camels, the sheltered curve of the bay – backed by luxuriant greenery which conceals the low-built hotels – still manages to look even more beautiful than the brochure pictures.

The International Cultural Centre

There's little more to say about the seashore than that, but at some stage it's well worth following the signs on the road west of town to **Sebastian's villa**. This has been bought by the State and turned into an *International Cultural Centre* to host the annual summer **festival**. On Mondays, Wednesdays and Fridays (10am–noon and 3–5pm in summer only, though you may be able to persuade somebody out of season) you can look around the house and assess Frank Lloyd Wright's judgement: it really is fantasy material, with an arcaded swimming pool, a baptistery-like bath in solid marble built for four, and a nearby black marble poolside table. During the war, the villa was used by Rommel as his Tunisian HQ. If you can't make the visiting hours, wander into the grounds and look around the garden and the mock-Greek theatre built for the festival. Most of the events here are in French or Arabic – for programmes, ask at the Tourist Office.

Moving on – transport out of Hammamet

Buses stop on av de la République opposite the PTT, by *Ideal Camping*. There are departures every half-hour or so to Nabeul, 15min away (0.4TD), where you can change for other Cap Bon destinations, though there are some direct buses to these and twelve a day for Tunis.

There are no *louages* in Hammamet, though in theory you could share one of the **red and white taxis** that do the Nabeul run if you can find one (they're supposed to leave from the bus station). Yellow taxis out to the hotels wait for business in front of the Medina.

The **train station** is on av Bourguiba, near the junction of av Hedi Ouali. A number of trains ply to Nabeul every day, but there's only one service direct to Tunis – you can also change at Bir Bou Rekba on the main Tunis–Sousse line.

Hammamet Listings

Banks There are several banks on av de la République, and many shops and hotels (the *Alya* for instance) will change money out of banking hours.

Car hire Lots of firms to choose from including *Mattei* on rue Assad Ibn el Fourat at the corner of rue Taïeb el Azzabi (☎81322). *Avis* (☎80164) and *Topcar* (☎80767) are both on av du Kowait, and the rest are mainly out down av des Nations Unies on the hotel strip. These include *Interrent/Europcar* (☎80146), *Hertz* (☎80187) and *Intercar* (☎81423). *Locamop* in rue de Nevers (☎80339) hire out **mopeds**.

Hammams One is in the Medina; others at 82 av Bourguiba and at av Bourguiba's junction with av Hedi Ouali (three more along that road too). In general they're open for women from 1–5pm and for men in the mornings and evenings.

International phone calls The *Kaly Centre*, among the tourist boutiques opposite *Ideal Camping*, has coin-op direct-dial phones open 24 hours. You can't call abroad from the PTT.

Market Every Thursday near the junction of av Hedi Ouali and av de la Libération, heading out of town towards Nabeul.

Medical facilities All-night chemist at 80 av de la République. *Infirmeries* by the police station opposite 29 av Bourguiba (☎82333) and on av Assad Ibn el Fourat near *Hôtel Bellevue* (☎83160).

Newspapers British newspapers are available in av de la République near the Medina, and at *L'Artisane* by *Hôtel Résidence Hammamet* in av Bourguiba.

PTT Av de la République near the centre. Open country hours but also Sunday mornings. International phone calls not possible (but see above).

Supermarket *Magasin Général* on av de la République opposite the Medina (Tues–Sat 8am–12.30pm & 3–7pm; Sun 8am–1.30pm; Mon closed). There's also a large grocery at 1 av de la Libération and in rue Ali Belhouane opposite *Hôtel Alya*.

Tour agency If your hotel doesn't run **organised excursions**, *Holiday Travel Tunisia* in av de la République (☎81099) offers a 2-day tour of the south (dep. Wed 5.30am!) for 67TD all-inclusive, or a day trip to Tunis, Carthage and Sidi Bou Said for 22TD.

Tourist office ONTT in the town hall (*mairie*) building on av Bourguiba, facing the beach in the centre of town (☎80423). Open Sept–June: Mon–Thurs 8.30am–1pm & 3–5.45pm; Fri & Sat 8.30am–1.30pm. July & Aug: Mon–Sat 7.30am–1.30pm & 4–9pm.

Nabeul and Around

Between Hammamet and Nabeul, hotels continue right along the beach and more are being built all the time. A little way inland, the villagers of **Merazka** are encouraging tourists to take an interest in their glass-blowing activities. Signposts from the road direct you to workshops where you'll be welcome to watch and encouraged to buy.

NABEUL is the seat of a Governorate, a market centre and the pottery and stonework capital of Tunisia, with a busy working atmosphere quite different from Hammamet. With easier access to the fertile hinterland of Cap Bon, Nabeul has always been an industrious place. The inhabitants of Roman Neapolis supported themselves by manufacturing *garum*, a sort of fish sauce used as basic seasoning in almost every savoury dish. "Take the entrails of tunny fish", runs a second-century recipe, "and the gills, juice, and blood, and add sufficient salt. Leave it in a vessel for two months, then pierce the vessel and the *garum* will flow out." Potteries, too, are long established in this area and still the principal industry – along with tourism.

Practicalities

The Tunis road, **Avenue Bourguiba**, goes straight through the town almost to the beach (about a 15-min walk from the centre); the **town centre** is where av Bourguiba crosses the Hammamet road (**Avenue Habib Thameur**). The eastward continuation of av Habib Thameur (av Farhat Hached) is Nabeul's main tourist strip and leads to several cheap restaurants and *pensions* as well as the **Cap Bon louage station** and the Friday market site. A couple of blocks seawards, a giant pot built around a pine tree in the middle of the road at **Place 7 Novembre**, across from the railway station, is really the town's only landmark – the unsubtle symbol of Nabeul's craft.

Accommodation

As a major tourist resort, Nabeul is not short of **hotels**. The big ones are on the beach, but the town has acquired a welcome sprinkling of *pensions familiales*, along with two youth hostels and a campsite. Numbers in the following listings key the hotels to their locations on the map.

The only official **campsite** in Nabeul (1.3TD per person plus 0.9TD per tent plus 1TD for a hot shower) is attached to the 1* **Hôtel les Jasmins (6)** (☎85343) in rue Abou el Kacem Chabi near the *Pension Oliviers*. The hotel itself is not unreasonable at 10TD/15TD low, 14.5TD/24TD high, b&b, but is liable to be booked up in season.

PENSIONS AND YOUTH HOSTELS

Pension les Roses, (1) 3 rue Sidi Abd el Kader (☎85570). Just off av Farhat Hached. The cheapest of the *pensions* and not at all bad. 3.5TD/bed low season, 5TD high, shower 0.5TD.

Pension Mustapha, (2) av Habib el Karma (☎22262). A lovely little place, clean and welcoming. Recommended. 7TD/11TD low, 8TD/12TD high, b&b.

Pension Hafsides, (3) rue Sidi Maaouia (☎85823). Behind the hospital. Closed out of season. 8TD/9.5TD mid-season, 9.5TD/13TD high, b&b, shower 0.8TD.

Pension el Habib, (4) av H Thameur (☎87190). On the road to Hammamet by the *oued*. Clean and friendly with a small library of left-behind paperbacks. Recommended. 5TD/8TD low, 9.5TD/15TD high, b&b.

Pension les Oliviers, (5) rue de Havana, off rue Abdou el Kacem Chabi, out beyond the *el Habib* (☎86865). Closed in winter. 8.5TD/13TD mid-season, 11.9TD/17.8TD high, b&b.

YHA Auberge de Jeunesse, (7) av Mongi Slim (☎85547). Right by the beach, the location is great but that's about it. The hostel is completely full in summer and empty the rest of the year. 4.5TD HB, 6.5TD FB; you must pay for at least one meal.

Youth Hostel/Maison des Jeunes, (8) av Taïeb Mehiri (☎86689). The usual concrete splendour. Check-in after 5pm only – you can't leave your bags there in the meantime. 4TD.

NEARER THE TOWN CENTRE

Hôtel Résidence Imene, (9) av Bourguiba (☎22310). Very correct, with big comfy rooms, but impersonal and fraying slightly at the edges. 3* 11TD/16TD low, 24TD/40TD high, b&b.

Hôtel Monia Club, (10) on the "Route Touristique" (Hammamet beach road) opposite the site of Neapolis (☎85713). Officially a *pension*, really more a restaurant and bar with guests. You can play pool or pinball here. 9TD per person low, 14TD high, b&b.

Hôtel Club Aquarius, (11) (☎85777). French, *Club-Med*-style establishment with full facilities, fortified against any possible intrusion by anyone or anything remotely Tunisian. Near the *Monia Club*. 2* 17.5TD per person mid, 23.5TD high, FB only, closed Nov–Feb.

Other hotels in the centre of town include the 1* **Hôtel el Ons (12)** (☎86129), the 3* **Hôtel le Prince (13)** (☎85470), **Hôtel les Pyramides (14)** av Bourguiba (☎85444), and **Hôtel Nabeul Plage (15)** rue Jardin Neapolis (☎86111), 4* **Hôtel Khéops (16)** av Mohammed V (☎ 85902) and another *Club Med* imitator, the **Club Farah (17)** (☎85519).

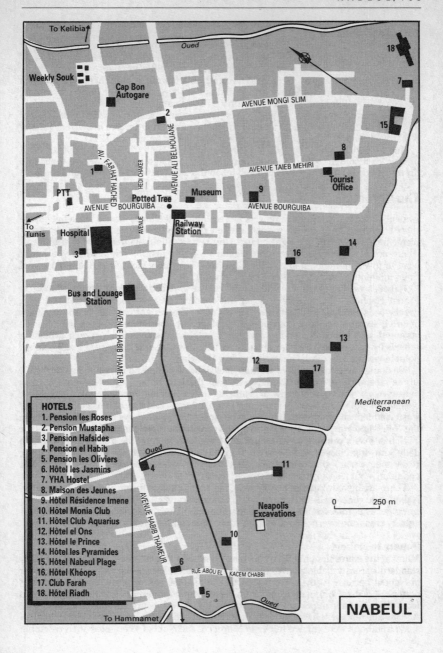

To Kelibia

Oued

18

Weekly Souk

7

Cap Bon
Autogare

AVENUE MONGI SLIM

2

15

AV - FARHAT HACHED

HEDI CHAKER

AVENUE ALI BELHOUANE

8

AVENUE TAIEB MEHIRI

1

Tourist
Office

PTT

Museum

9

Potted Tree

AVENUE

AVENUE BOURGUIBA

AVENUE BOURGUIBA

To
Tunis

Hospital

Railway
Station

14

3

16

Bus and Louage
Station

AVENUE HABIB THAMEUR

13

12

17

Mediterranean
Sea

HOTELS
1. Pension les Roses
2. Pension Mustapha
3. Pension Hafsides
4. Pension el Habib
5. Pension les Oliviers
6. Hôtel les Jasmins
7. YHA Hostel
8. Maison des Jeunes
9. Hôtel Résidence Imene
10. Hôtel Monia Club
11. Hôtel Club Aquarius
12. Hôtel el Ons
13. Hôtel le Prince
14. Hôtel les Pyramides
15. Hôtel Nabeul Plage
16. Hôtel Khéops
17. Club Farah
18. Hôtel Riadh

Oued

4

11

Neapolis
Excavations

0   250 m

AVENUE HABIB THAMEUR

10

6

RUE ABOU EL   KACEM CHABBI

5

Oued

NABEUL

To Hammamet

Eating and drinking

Nabeul's two main budget restaurants are to be found at the bend in av Farhat Hached by the *Pension des Roses*. Both the *Restaurant du Bonheur* and the *Restaurant de la Jeunesse* do pretty solid meals for around 3.5TD, with little to choose between them. The *Rôtisserie/Self-Service Berbère* at 34 rue Habib Karma is also cheap (1.3TD for a quarter chicken), but extremely greasy and not exactly pristine. For more refinement, the *Hôtel les Jasmins* has a restaurant with a 4TD set menu.

If you want to splash out, or you're living on a credit card, the *Restaurant de l'Olivier* at 6 av Hedi Chaker (corner of av Bourguiba: the numbering system in av Hedi Chaker is a little eccentric) is as good a place as any, with meals for around 12TD.

And for just a coffee, the *Café le Petit Chef* at 82 av Hedi Chaker is a popular hangout for local student types. If your French is good enough, you can peruse their little library of books and magazines to catch up on the latest news over your *té* and *chicha*.

The Attractions

Nabeul's **beach**, like Hammamet's, is increasingly hotel-lined but still attractive. Since there's nothing here except tourist-oriented cafés and restaurants, it's worth taking picnic meals if you're on a tight budget (the better-value restaurants are in the town). There are also plenty of watersport facilities – if you plan to stay a while you might want to invest in membership of the **Club des Trières**, which gives unlimited use of their equipment (subject to often heavy demand).

Nabeul's weekly **market** – Fridays, out on rue el Arbi Zarrouk, a continuation of av Farhat Hached – has become one of the country's biggest tourist attractions, with coach loads arriving from all over the country. There's nothing out of the ordinary about it except size and convenience – since the tourists have been coming it's sprouted an additional section specialising in holiday souvenirs. You can avoid the crowds by coming on Thursday evening for an early start next day – better still, make a point of visiting a less self-conscious market elsewhere.

No doubt the excavations of **Roman Neapolis** will soon be developed as a "sight". In the meantime, few of the tourists who pass through Nabeul are even aware of their existence. If you've seen any of Tunisia's other Roman remains, you may think Neapolis is not worth seeing, just a few fallen columns and bits of mosaic in a piece of wasteland fenced off by cacti. Officially it's closed but you can get in from the beach by the *Hôtel Aquarius*, or climb in by the gate opposite the *Hôtel Monia Club*.

Nabeul has a **municipal museum** at 44 av Bourguiba by the tree in the pot (open daily 9am–4pm; closed Mon; entry 0.6TD plus 1TD for cameras). It contains nothing really spectacular – the main exhibits are locally discovered mosaics, many in excellent condition – but it's worth a look if you're passing.

There are also two quaint but, in practical terms, useless forms of public transport in Nabeul: the **road-train** to Hammamet (3 times a day, 2hr, 2.5TD) and the horse-drawn *calèches*. The *calèches* are no more traditionally Tunisian than the road-train, and equally crass and overpriced. Children adore them both.

Pottery in Nabeul

Many of the souvenirs on display, such as "Sindbad's Palace" and "Aladdin's Cave", are standard wares available all over the country. But there's a special emphasis on **pottery** in Nabeul because, with Jerba, Nabeul is the national centre of the craft. In fact, the potters of Nabeul originally came from Jerba, attracted perhaps by the quality of the local clay. Another important influence was the arrival in the seventeenth century of Andalusian refugees, bringing with them the artistic traditions of Muslim Spain. The same traditions were carried to Fes in Morocco, and Nabeul's ceramics often resemble those of Fes.

Pottery has a long history in Tunisia – the Roman province of Africa exported standard red tableware all over the Empire – and thanks to the tourist trade it's one traditional craft that appears to have a healthy future, even if some of the more "artistic" products are in highly dubious taste. Most shops will be happy to show you to the workshop of one of their suppliers (ask about an *atelier*). The industrial potters, who make bricks, are not as glamorous or well known, but are no less interesting. Small humps dotted around the eastern edge of the town, especially near the market, are the ovens in which the bricks are fired, and when they're in operation (usually in the evening) they produce a thick black pall of smoke. You'll probably be invited to clamber down into the inferno-like subterranean chamber where the oven flames are kept fired through the night.

Stonemasonry and other crafts

Other crafts are worked in and around Nabeul. BENI KNIAR, a village just along the coast road, specialises in **wool products**, and ES SOMAA, just inland, in **mats**.

But the big craft, after pottery, is **stone carving**. This is less amenable to souvenir production, but flourishes thanks to the policy of incorporating traditional elements in modern buildings: not just in overtly traditional ones, but in hotels and private houses too. Doorways, columns and benches have long been carved in Tunisia with intricate geometric patterns – witness the Tunis Medina – and it's fascinating to watch the process. Most of the stonework is done in DAR CHAABANE, a small village to the east which is now virtually a suburb of Nabeul. Its main street is lined with workshops clinking to the sound of chisels, while a pile of raw stone on the pavement announces the trade.

Moving On

From the **railway station** opposite the potted tree, there are trains to Hammamet and connections on to Tunis, Sousse, Sfax, Monastir, Gabes and Gafsa.

Usually more convenient, however, is the **bus** station, off av H Thameur a five-minute walk down from av Bourguiba. There are loads of buses from here to Hammamet, north to the Gulf of Tunis and to Tunis itself, rather fewer to Fahs and Zaghouan, and a weekly bus to Korbous. **Louages** serve Tunis, Zaghouan, Fahs and Enfida and, if you're lucky, you may find a red and white **taxi** for Hammamet.

Buses and *louages* going **up the Cap Bon peninsula** leave from rue el Arbi Zarrouk, a continuation of av Farhat Hached, about 500m east of av Bourguiba. There are frequent departures for Kelibia via Korba and Menzel Temime, and plenty of *louages* on the same route. Note there are no buses or *louages* through to El Haouria; you have to change at Kelibia.

Nabeul Listings

Airline *Tunis Air*, 145 av Bourguiba (☎85193).

Alcohol The *Epicerie Fine*, 6 rue de Khartoum, hidden away down an alley off av H Thameur (parallel to av Bourguiba between it and the hospital), sells wine, beer and spirits to take away.

Banks There are lots on and around av Bourguiba, and there should be some open in the morning at weekends.

Bicycles The youth hostel rents out bicycles at about 2TD/hr.

Car hire Offices in central Nabeul include: *Express Car*, 148 av H Thameur (☎87014); *Mattei*, 54 av Bourguiba (☎85967); *Rent-a-Car*, 94 av Bourguiba (☎85948); *Royal Car*, 3 rue Sidi Maaouia; *TLS*, 3 rue Ibn Badis (☎85373); *Hertz*, av H Thameur, out of town (☎85027).

Cinema *Palace Cinema*, 43 av Hedi Chaker.

Festivals The summer "festival", a programme of cultural events for tourists, takes place over July and August in the open-air theatre at the beach end of av Bourguiba, the only time it's ever used. The Orange Blossom Festival around April or May (whenever the orange blossom appears) is also more directed at tourists than celebrated by Nabeulis. The ONTT should be able to supply programmes of events.

Hammams There's one at 42 av Hedi Chaker (men mornings, women afternoons), one at 37 rue Sidi Bel Aissa, and a women-only one, *Bain Sidi Maaouria*, at 19 av H Thameur.

International phone calls At the PTT, or a taxiphone office at 168 av H Thameur, open daily 7am–midnight.

Left luggage In the train station.

Medical facilities The regional hospital (☎85633) is in the centre of town on av H Thameur 100m from av Bourguiba. The night chemist is opposite at 37 av H Thameur. *Infirmeries* are at 80 av Hedi Chaker and 10 rue Ibn Badis.

Newspapers British tabloids are available at the Libraire de l'Avenir, 86 av Hedi Chaker, among other places.

ONA crafts shops 144 av Farhat Hached and 93 av H Thameur.

PTT On av Bourguiba, north of the junction with av H Thameur. City hours.

Supermarkets Big one at 30 av Bourguiba; small one in rue de Gafsa by the *louage* station.

Swimming pool If the sea isn't good enough, most of the hotels have pools. The *Imène* charges a whopping 5TD to use theirs.

Tourist office ONTT regional office on av Taïeb Mehiri not far from the beach: open July–Aug, Mon–Sat 7.30am–1.30pm & 4–9pm and Sept–June Mon–Thurs 8.30am–1pm & 3–5.45pm, Fri & Sat 8.30am–1.30pm.

North of Nabeul

Nabeul is the main transport centre of Cap Bon, and it's easy to reach most parts of the peninsula from here. For the market towns inland, and KORBOUS, beyond on the north coast, see p.112.

   North of Nabeul the coast is one endless stretch of white beach backed, as far as Menzel Temime, by unsightly salt flats, and after that by rich farmland. There are few towns, fewer places to stay, and little reason to stop off except for a minimal change of beach scenery. **MAAMOURA** and **TAZERKA** are all small settlements not far from the sea; Maamoura has a pricey beach club.

Korba

KORBA, the next town north, has an exclusive *Club Méditerrannée* resort as well as a Sunday souk and minor Roman remains. **Birdwatchers** should find it worth a stop in passing as there are lagoons and a salt marsh just to the north which hold flamingoes, spoonbills and avocets in the spring, a good range of migrants in spring and autumn and ducks over the winter. Should you need them, Korba has a PTT (country hours) and a couple of banks on the main Nabeul–Kelibia road through town.

Menzel Temime

MENZEL TEMIME has no special attractions, but its beach (albeit rather windy and some way from town) makes it a feasible alternative to the tourist ghettos of Nabeul and Hammamet. The **bus station** in town is a roundabout on the Nabeul–Kelibia road, av de la République. Running off it is the inevitable **Avenue Bourguiba**, along which the people at nos. 29 and 31 av Bourguiba have put a lot of work into their front doors so admire them as you pass. The **PTT** is at no. 39, and beyond that two **banks**, with another on the main square at the end. The main square is where **louages** hang out, plying to Nabeul, Kelibia, Menzel Bou Zelfa and Tunis. Also on the square, next to a cavernous café, the 2* *Hôtel Temime* (☎98296) offers pleasant, clean rooms (with a choice of bath or shower) for 9TD/15TD, b&b, rising to 10.5TD/17TD in the high season. If that's too steep, the *Maison des Jeunes* **youth hostel** behind (☎98116), signposted only in Arabic, is only 4TD. There's a **cinema** next door and a couple of cheap **restaurants** on the market square beyond that. On a Tuesday, turn left at the square for the **Tuesday souk**, spread out down a wide boulevard, and if you're in need of supplies at any other time, the opposite direction (the continuation of av Bourguiba) takes you to the *Monoprix* supermarket.

Kelibia

The next resort along the coast, **KELIBIA** hovers tantalisingly between full-blown tourist centre and quiet fishing port. It cannot be both, and how it strikes you depends in large part on when you visit, but for the moment it remains the most peaceful resort in the country. It offers quite good beaches, and reasonably priced places to stay – though try to arrive early if you come in midsummer. Unique to Kelibia is the **dry muscat wine** produced here: it's worth trying. Another Kelibia curiosity is its "English" population – they all bear the name *el Ingliis* meaning "Englishman" or "Englishwoman". By one account their common ancestor was an Englishman who came to work here during the Ottoman era, converted to Islam and stayed. Another story has it that they are all descendants of shipwrecked sailors.

The town centre focuses on **Place de la République**, from where **Avenue des Martyrs** heads down the two kilometres or so to the port. Dominated by the towering fortress, which adds an unexpected scenic accent, the **port area** consists of a few scattered shops and houses and a State Fishing School. Kelibia is the best **natural harbour** before Sousse – which explains the fortress. To get to the main **beach**, follow **Avenue Erriadh**, parallel with av des Martyrs, which runs down to it.

Practicalities

The **PTT** (country hours) is on av Bourguiba, and the **banks** are nearby, one on av Bourguiba, one on rue Ibn Khaldoun, and one in pl de la République. There's a **supermarket** on rue Ibn Khaldoun, and another close by in rue Ezzouhour (off av des Martyrs). The **night chemist** is at the beginning of av des Martyrs, opposite the Maison du Peuople, and the **cinema** is a couple of hundred metres down av Erriadh. There's a small food **market** where av Erriadh meets av des Martyrs, but the **Monday souk** takes place just north of av Ali Belhouane.

Accommodation

Pension Amis, off av Erriadh between the town centre and the beach (☎95777). Spotless, airy rooms (7, 9 and 10 have balconies). Bathrooms are shared but also squeaky clean. 9.5TD/13TD low, 13TD/20TD high, b&b.

Hôtel Florida, down the beach by the harbour (☎96248). An old favourite – rooms and bungalows cost the same but the bungalows are far better with *en suite* bathrooms. Owned by an exile from Franco's Spain, it serves cold beer to Maltese and British oil workers. 9.5TD/15TD low, 13TD/22TD high, b&b.

En Nassim/Ennacim, next door to the *Florida* (☎96245), is closed but may reopen.

Mamounia, some way along the beach (☎96219). More expensive, package-type establishment, having little in common with its Marrakesh namesake. 17TD/28TD low, 31TD/48TD high, b&b.

Youth Hostel/Maison des Jeunes – turn left at the port and it's on your right (☎96105). Drab, but convenient, unusually friendly and only 4TD per person. You can sometimes camp in the grounds and there's a small, unearthed Roman site in front of it.

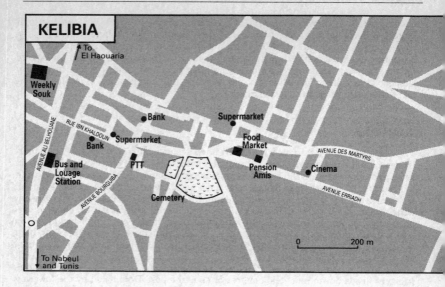

The fortress

Part of Kelibia's charm is the feeling that it's something of a backwater, but this was by no means always so. Some fine remains, which can be seen in the various patches of excavation around the town, bear witness to a sizeable Roman presence, and for the Byzantines, who built the first **fortress** here, *Clupea* (Kelibia) was reportedly the last place of refuge after the Arab invasion. Later, the town and fortress were sacked three times by the Spanish between 1535 and 1547.

The fortress is currently being restored and an Islamic museum is planned here. For the time being, it's open at any reasonable hour of the day and entrance is free (though contributions are appreciated). Photos are allowed, but not zoom lens shots as the fortress still has strategic significance, giving panoramic views over the whole southern coast of Cap Bon.

Eating, drinking, beaches and watersports

For **eating** and **drinking**, the *Florida* and the *Amis* both have excellent restaurants – the former slightly cheaper – where fish is the obvious thing to go for. Otherwise there's the attractive *Café Sidi el Bahri* right next to the port. For a change, catch a taxi from near the harbour to **Mansoura**, a series of beautiful coves just to the north, backed by a small but exclusive community nicknamed "Little Paris". There's an excellent café-restaurant here on a rocky promontory separating two of the coves, and the *Hôtel Mansoura* (☎96156) right on the sea for aspiring beach slugs.

North of Mansoura the shore runs in deserted and tempting swathes of white beach to the end of the peninsula. You can combine these with a visit to Kerkouane (see opposite) by taking some food and strolling back along the shore, though it is about four-and-a-half-hours' walk.

For **watersports** close to Kelibia, you could try and persuade the *Mamounia* you're a resident; the municipal club by the harbour also hires out sailboards not in use by local people.

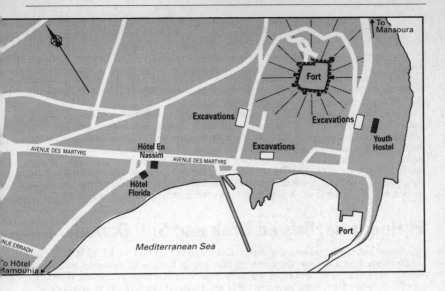

Moving On from Kelibia

Buses and, to a lesser extent, **louages** all leave from the *autogare* on av Ali Belhouane, with early departures to Sousse, Monastir and Mahdia, and every hour or so through the day to Nabeul, Tunis and El Haouaria.

It's worth noting that a summer **jet-foil** service runs from Kelibia to Trapani in Sicily, usually a four-hour journey but unpredictable, especially in rough weather. For more details ask around at the port, or contact *Tirrenia Navigazione* or their agents (in Tunis, *Tourafric*, 52 av Bourguiba, ☎01-341483). There used to be a fast catamaran service to Malta too, but it hasn't run for some time.

Kerkouane

Halfway between Kelibia and EL HAOUARIA, a sign-posted side road runs about a 1500m down to the Carthaginian site of **KERKOUANE**, discovered in 1952 and the first to produce more than a few funerary objects. There was great initial excitement about the streets and house-plans uncovered: at first no public buildings were found, and the eccentric theory was posited that this had been a fifth-century BC holiday resort, a sort of Carthaginian *Club Med*. Saner ideas eventually prevailed, and it is now thought that the town, founded in the fifth century BC, lived off both sea and land. The main industry seems to have been manufacturing a **purple dye** for which Carthaginians and Phoenicians were famous, named after a species of shellfish called *murex*. Hundreds of these creatures were collected and left in large pits in the ground to rot; the smell must have been overpowering, but the decomposed mess was somehow made up into the dye known by the Romans as "Tyrian purple" (after the Phoenician capital, Tyre), much beloved as the Imperial colour.

To get to Kerkouane, if you don't have your own transport, you can take a bus or *louage* from Kelibia to the turn-off, hire a taxi (for around 3TD – settle the price before you start) or even walk or hitch – the latter is certainly possible. Leaving the site, you'll probably have to take pot luck: hitch or hail a passing bus or *louage*.

The site

The **site** (9am–4pm; closed Mon; 1TD plus 1TD to take photos), includes a small adjoining **museum**, housing Punic jewellery and other artefacts, notably a wooden Punic statue found nearby.

Almost all the **houses**, whose foundations line the easy-to-follow streets, follow the same plan: a narrow corridor leading into a small courtyard, with a water well and sometimes an altar of the household gods. Kerkouane's houses are most famous, however, for their **baths**, neatly lined with reddish cement. Virtually every house has its own, which says something about Carthaginian society: while the Romans spent vast sums on public baths, the Carthaginians kept a private, introverted profile. The town was abandoned some time in the second century BC, after the destruction of Carthage, and never reoccupied by the Romans – which explains its remarkable state of preservation.

El Haouaria, Ras ed Drak and Sidi Daoud

Just below **Jebel Sidi Abiod**, the defiant last hump of Cap Bon, is **EL HAOUARIA**, a pretty village best known as the centre of **falconry** in Tunisia. In an annual festival that used to be held in April or May, young birds were caught on the mountain, trained for a month, then used for hunting game birds on the mountain and the heaths below. A shortage of game birds led to a temporary end to the festival, but it has started up again and is now held in mid-June. Two species of birds of prey are involved – sparrow hawks, which are trapped in nets on the mountain as they migrate, and peregrine falcons, which are taken as young from the nests on the rocky cliffs. The number of birds each falconer can catch is supposed to be strictly limited; they may not be sold, and the sparrow hawks are later returned to the wild; what happens to the peregrines is uncertain.

Fortunately, the perennial (and innocuous) attractions are also natural ones. The **caves of bats**, a short walk from the village, are what locals will assume you're visiting for. Further afield, one of the peninsula's prettiest beaches, **Ras ed Drak**, is a potent draw, while the bloody tuna harvest at **SIDI DAOUD** is a fine, photogenic spectacle – but a grisly and unpleasant business for nature-lovers.

Practicalities

If you need to change any money, El Haouaria has a **bank** in the main square. It also has at least one place to stay, the *Hôtel Dar Habib*, tucked away down the side streets but well sign-posted (follow the light blue arrows). Having tracked down the hotel, you may have to track down the proprietor, who charges 5TD per person. If it seems too basic, the *Hôtel l'Epervier* in the main street (av Bourguiba, of course) opened recently with a rather upmarket restaurant. Across the street, the *Restaurant de la Jeunesse* is more basic – salad and macaroni, for example – for under 2TD.

You may have to wait a while for **transport** to turn up, but it does come here in the form of *louages* to Kelibia and buses every hour or so to Kelibia, and less frequently to Tunis. For more local destinations like Kerkouane or the Sidi Daoud turn-off, you could hitch or share a taxi (0.4TD each to the Sidi Daoud turn-off).

To the caves

El Haouaria is pleasantly out of the way and all the villagers will assume you've come to see the two sets of **caves**. One of these, the *Ghar el Kebir*, is a complex of quarries right on the shore: follow the road straight through the village past the cemetery. About 500m out of the village, there's an extremely helpful and informative wildlife information centre, with particularly good information on birds of prey, run by the *Cellule Nature et Oiseaux*. The building is called the "Aquilaria", after the Latin for "eagle"; the name El Haouaria is supposed to be a corruption of the same root word.

Ten minutes' walk from here brings you to a group of pyramid-shaped chambers poised above crashing breakers. Operations started here by the Carthaginians were continued by the Romans and Byzantines – the latter installing a military garrison – and the stone was used for buildings all round the Gulf of Carthage. Chat to the residents and you'll hear vivid stories of slaves spending their whole lives in the caverns.

The other caves, up on the mountain, are full of **bats**. A 4km track leads from the village, but you'll need to ask around for a guide (mention *la grotte des chauves-souris*). You'll also need a torch to make a close acquaintance with the creatures. Even if bats don't appeal, the mountain is still a wonderful place for long windy walks.

Ras ed Drak

Just south of the cape itself, at the very beginning of Cap Bon's south coast, hides its most beautiful and least-known beach, **Ras ed Drak**. The white sands are sheltered here and given an extra dimension by the mountain's craggy shoulder. A sign-posted four-kilometre road leads from El Haouaria over heathland to the assortment of villas and farms on the slopes behind the beach where, in season, there's a small shop on the sand. **Camping** is feasible if you're happy with water from wells and food bought from the farms, which is how the villa-owners get by; otherwise you will have to stay back in El Haouaria. The futuristic complex on the shore to the south is a station on a gas pipeline from Algeria to Italy.

FLORA AND FAUNA AROUND EL HAOUARIA AND THE CAPE

The rocky hillsides around the mountain of **Jebel Sidi Abiod** are rich in **flowers**, as is the walk to the Ras ed Drak beach. The fields and field edges have abundant bird life, with many finches, buntings and warblers, along with stonechats – the black-headed males perching prominently on bushes and telegraph wires. Down on Ras ed Drak, the scrub behind the beach is often full of migrating birds, with the unusual blue rock thrush and Moussier's redstart both relatively common residents.

The **sea** is worth watching, too, and vast numbers of breeding pairs of the stiff-winged **Cory's shearwater**, as well as gulls and gull-billed and Sandwich terns, can often be seen flying past, the latter two species occurring as winter visitors and passage migrants.

The actual headland of Cap Bon is special because it is the last jumping-off point for **migrating birds** of prey before they cross the Mediterranean. April and May are the peak spring passage months, with lesser numbers coming back each autumn. Honey buzzards are the dominant species, although black kites, marsh harriers and common buzzards also occur in good numbers, together with a variety of migrating eagles, sparrow hawks and hobbies. Hobbies are small, rather dashing falcons, midway in size between kestrel and peregrine; since they prey mostly on swallows and the like, they simply follow the migrating swallow flocks up from Africa, catching a snack on the wing. The best place for viewing the migration is the top of Jebel Sidi Abiod. This requires a **permit** during the migration season: write in advance to the *Direction des Fôrets*, 30 rue Alain Savary, Tunis.

Sidi Daoud

Seven kilometres on past El Haouaria, heading west along the north coast of the peninsula, a turning on the right leads two kilometres to **SIDI DAOUD**, the sleepiest of sleepy fishing villages. Almost totally dormant for ten months of the year, it bursts into life around May for the **Matanza**, a spectacular if gory tuna harvest with a technique going back to Roman times. A huge net is laid about 4km out to sea, stretching from surface to sea bed to catch the fish as they migrate around the coast to reproduce. The net forms a series of chambers of decreasing size, and when the final one – the *corpo*, or death chamber – is full, it is closed. Then the boats converge around the net and raise it from all sides until the fish are virtually out of the water, at which point the fishermen jump into the net and set about the fish (some of which weigh as much as 250kg) with clubs and knives. Well and truly slaughtered, the fish are canned in the village's factory and distributed.

It used to be possible to get a **permit** from the National Fisheries Office to watch the Matanza from one of the boats, but after some disagreements with the tourist authorities this scheme has lapsed. If you're interested, it might be worth checking the permit situation with the *Commissariat Général de la Pêche* in Tunis (30 rue Alain Savary, ☎01–890761) before you come up here. Failing that, the local office is at the dockside. If you do get permission and decide to try it, be warned that the smell of fish lingers for some days afterwards.

OFF-LIMITS ISLANDS: ZEMBRA AND ZEMBRETTA

The islands of **Zembra** and **Zembretta** are also now off limits, having been declared a nature reserve under army protection. Zembra, with seabirds, beautiful scenery and excellent snorkelling, used to host a scuba diving centre run by the *Centre Nautique de Tunisie*. If you want to try for a permit to visit, you could write to the *Direction des Fôrets* (30 rue Alain Savary, Tunis) well in advance of your trip, stating reasons; don't expect success, but if you do get permission, the only access to the island is by fishing boat from Sidi Daoud. There's nowhere to stay so it'll have to be a day trip – don't forget to book your return journey.

South or west from Sidi Daoud

A road runs inland from Sidi Daoud through the forest of **Dar Chichou** to emerge on the south coast between Kerkouane and Kelibia. On the way, you pass a fenced-off **nature reserve** devoted, strangely enough, to **gazelles**; you should be able to glimpse some from the road, especially if you stop and wait quietly for a while.

From Sidi Daoud down the Cap Bon's northern coast to BIR MEROUA, the road stays several kilometres inland, skirting country that is surprisingly mountainous – even reminiscent of Scottish heathland. For most of the way, the coastline is one deserted beach backed by farmland. With your own transport, there's any number of possible tracks down to the shore – without it, supplies will be a problem.

There is no **public transport** from Sidi Daoud itself, but you may be able to pick up a bus or *louage* along the main road. Buses from El Haouaria to SOLIMAN and GROMBALIA run along it (local people will know current times), but *louages* are likely to be full, so you should have a shorter wait if you hitch.

BIR MEROUA is a small settlement where the road down Cap Bon's north coast splits. Straight on, the main road continues to Soliman; to the right, a new road runs on round the mountain of **Jebel Korbous** to KORBOUS or to MARSA BEN RAMDAM. Unfortunately there is no public transport on this new road: the old road into Korbous, more convenient if less spectacular, branches off 10km further south to skirt the other side of the mountain.

Korbous and the North Coast

The **old road** heads for the coast through thick plantations of oranges, one of them sheltering the inexpensive *Hôtel Chiraz* (☎93920), confusingly listed under Korbous in tourist leaflets. You hit the sea at the rickety settlement of SIDI RAIS, once a fashionable resort but now just a row of wooden houses on stilts.

Here the road climbs onto a ledge above the shore and soon passes the spring of **AÏN OKTOR**, where the 3* *Hôtel Aïn Oktor* (☎94522) offers thermal cures and views; outside, in a sort of concrete tent, it's possible to taste the water for free.

A few more winding kilometres and you drop into **KORBOUS** itself, set in a steep ravine where the Romans first came to take the waters at *Aquae Carpitanae*. At the end of the last century the modern spa was redesigned by a French civil engineer, who then retired to the precarious villa – now a Presidential Palace – perched on the rock overlooking the main street. There isn't a great deal to Korbous: a main street lined with souvenir stalls for the trippers on Sundays, and the fancy 3* *Hôtel les Sources* (☎94533) for those who can afford the supervised thermal cure ("The largest dose will be taken first thing in the morning while fasting in several successive swallows," according to the ONTT literature). An ancient **hammam** to the left of the street (men in the morning, women in the afternoon) is reputed to go back to the Romans and, between the Presidential Palace and the new hotel, the **Zarziha Rock** has been polished smooth by generations of women sliding down it to cure infertility. It's a pretty enough place, with waves crashing on to rocks below the Mount Korbous's craggy green slopes.

The new road

Once you've seen Korbous village, you'll need your own transport (or be prepared to hitch) if you want to follow the **new road** around the mountain. A few kilometres beyond the village a third spring called **Aïn el Atrous** shoots out of the mountain through a pipe below the road. There's a narrow strip of beach beyond where people **camp** (though it looks very exposed), and at this point the recent extension of the road takes off and before you know it you're hundreds of metres up on the mountain's north shoulder, then dropping down onto a high plain. Here you run through the village of DOUELA before meeting up again with the main road from Soliman at Bir Meroua. If you can find some way of getting down to the beach of **Marsa Ben Ramdam**, it's one of the most spectacular in the country: a track goes right about 3km outside Bir Meroua on the road to Korbous.

Soliman

Eighteen kilometres south of Korbous is **SOLIMAN**, a seventeenth-century Andalusian settlement whose **mosque** is almost the only remnant of that time, although the town still has a certain feel about it reminiscent of even modern-day Andalusia. The semi-circular tiles in the roof – the mosque's main distinctive feature – are invisible from street level.

Rue Habib Thameur runs from the town centre around the mosque to end up near the bus station. The **PTT** (country hours) is on it at no. 35. As for accommodation, there are **no hotels** in town, only at the beach settlement of Soliman Plage. There are no buses or *louages* for Soliman Plage: taxis leave from pl 7 Novembre, the other side of the town centre, or you could hitch or walk.

To get away, **buses** run regularly to Tunis, El Haouaria and Grombalia, and twice daily to Korbous. There are also **louages** to Tunis and Grombalia which leave from near the bus station.

Soliman Plage

There's not much of additional interest at **SOLIMAN PLAGE** (also known as Plage Ejjehmi), the beach resort 3km out of Soliman. It's not the most magnificent strand in Cap Bon, but it's more sheltered than those in Nabeul and Hammamet and there are good views of the mountains – Jebel Bou Kornine down the coast in one direction, and Jebel Korbous in the other. On a clear day, you can even see the white smudge of Sidi Bou Said across the bay.

At the end of the road from Soliman is a café where you could stop for a tea. The hotels are a few hundred metres up the beach to your left (to get straight to them, you turn off the Soliman road 500m before hitting the beach). Between the café and the hotels, straw beach cabins are used by Tunisian day-trippers during July and August when the beach is packed solid. The rest of the year, abandoned for the cows to browse, anyone could use them for a night on the beach.

Of the two hotels, both catering for European package tourists, the 1* *Hôtel el Andalous* (☎90199) is the cheaper, with bungalows at 12TD/18TD low season, 13TD/20TD high, for b&b, and waterskiing and riding, but no pool. Posher and rather Teutonic, the 2* *Hôtel Solymar* (☎90105), with its stone camel, has rooms from 11.5TD/16TD low season, 17.5TD/28TD high, b&b. Beyond the *Solymar*, the beach continues round to Borj Cedria (see p.90).

Grombalia, Menzel Bou Zelfa and Bou Argoub

Instead of going round the coast, excursions to some of the inland farming towns can be very lively, depending on the time of year. **GROMBALIA** is the centre of Cap Bon's vineyards and home of a week-long **Wine Festival** in September to celebrate the *vendange*, or harvest. It's on the main Tunis–Sousse railway line (several **trains** a day stop here) and frequent **buses and louages** also connect it and Menzel Bou Zelfa with Soliman and Nabeul. (In Grombalia, Tunis *louages* are based at the level crossing near the train station.)

MENZEL BOU ZELFA, 8km east of Grombalia, has an **Orange Festival** to celebrate the appearance of orange blossom in April or May, as well as an important seventeenth-century **zaouia**, a multi-domed feature in the centre of town.

Some ten kilometres south of Grombalia on the road to Hammamet is **BOU ARGOUB**. There's little enough to this tiny village but, in 1929, the Fascists of Tunisia's Italian community built Mussolini a villa here. Relations between Mussolini and the French were never good; the Italians always felt they had been cheated out of Tunisia in 1881 and had had to settle for second best with Libya; Mussolini was continually preparing to invade Tunisia and, with more Italian colonists in the country than French, this appeared no empty threat. Ultimately, however, the Abyssinian campaign distracted "Il Duce" and the villa, now a girls' school, was never occupied by him.

travel details

Nabeul is the main centre for transport in Cap Bon and anyone visiting the peninsula will probably pass through here. Alternative routes are by rail via Grombalia and Bir Bou Rekba (on the main railway line) or by road through Menzel Bou Zelfa, or up the north coast via Soliman.

Trains

FROM NABEUL AND HAMMAMET TO:
Bir Bou Rekba junction on the Tunis–Sousse line (9 trains daily in each direction, 7min from Hammamet, 25min from Nabeul, of which 1 is a **direct through-train to Tunis**, 1hr 30min from Hammamet; 1hr 45min from Nabeul).

FROM BIR BOU REKBA TO:
Tunis, (6 each day, 1hr, of which 4 go via **Grombalia**, 20min, and **Hammam Lif**, 50min); **Sousse** (5, 1hr 15min, some via **Enfida**, 30min); **Sfax** (3, 3hr 10min) via **El Jem** (2hr 15min); **Monastir** (3, 2hr); **Mahdia** (3, 3hr); **Gabes** (2, 6hr); **Gafsa** (1 overnight, 7hr 30min); and **Metlaoui** (1 overnight, 8hr 30min).

Note: None of the Nabeul–Bir Bou Rekba trains connect conveniently with the overnight trains to and from Gabes, Gafsa and Metlaoui: if heading south, you have to spend an hour waiting at Bir Bou Rekba.

FROM GROMBALIA TO:
Tunis (4 daily, 45min); **Bir Bou Rekba** (4, 20 min, with 9 daily connections to **Hammamet** and **Nabeul**); **Sousse** (3, 1hr 30min); **Monastir** (3, 2hr 15min); **Mahdia** (3, 3hr 15min).

Buses
All buses in this region are operated by SRTG Nabeul.

FROM NABEUL (AND HAMMAMET) TO:
Tunis (12 daily, 1hr 30min); **Grombalia** (frequent, 45min); **Borj Cedria** (frequent, 1hr); **Korba** (frequent, 15min); **Menzel Temime** (frequent, 45min); **Kelibia** (frequent, 1hr); **Fahs** (3 daily, 1hr 45min); **Zaghouan** (2, 1hr 30min); **Sousse** (2, 2hr 15min); **Soliman** (1, 1hr); **Kairouan** (1, 2hr); **Monastir** (1, 2hr 30min); **Mahdia** (1, 3hr 30min).

FROM KELIBIA TO:
El Haouaria (frequent, 30min); **Menzel Temime** (hourly, 15min); **Korba** (hourly, 45min); **Nabeul** (hourly, 1hr); **Menzel Bou Zelfa** (hourly, 1hr); **Soliman** (hourly, 1hr 15min); and **Tunis** (hourly, 2hr 30min). Early-morning buses to **Sousse** (1, 2hr 30min); **Monastir** (1, 3hr); and **Mahdia** (1, 4hr).

FROM GROMBALIA TO:
Soliman (frequent, 15min); **Tunis** (hourly, 45min); **Menzel Bou Zelfa** (frequent, 15min); and **Nabeul** (hourly, 45min).

FROM MENZEL BOU ZELFA TO:
Menzel Temime (hourly, 45min); **Kelibia** (hourly, 1hr); **Soliman** (frequent, 15min); **Grombalia** (frequent, 15min); and **Tunis** (hourly, 1hr).

FROM SOLIMAN TO:
Tunis (hourly, 45min); **Grombalia** (frequent, 15min); **Menzel Bou Zelfa** (frequent, 15min); and **Korbous** (2 daily, 20min).

Louages
DIRECT TO TUNIS (BAB ALLEOUA) FROM:
Nabeul/Menzel Temime/Kelibia/Soliman/Grombalia/Menzel Bou Zelfa

LOUAGES WITHIN CAP BON:
Along the **south coast** linking **Nabeul–Korba–Menzel–Temime–Kelibia** and, less frequently **Kelibia–El Haouaria**.
Inland, linking **Menzel Temime–Menzel Bou Zelfa** and **Menzel Bou Zelfa–Grombalia–Soliman**.

LOUAGES FROM NABEUL TO:
Zaghouan/Fahs/Enfida
Note: None to Hammamet.

Hydrofoil
Kelibia–Trapani, Sicily, with *Aliscafi Navigazione* (summer only, 3 times a week, 4hr).

PHONE CODES
The code for the whole Cap Bon region is ☎02

CHAPTER THREE

BIZERTE AND THE NORTH

S parsely populated, and with few roads, Tunisia's **northern region** has played little part in the country's tourist development. **Bizerte**, the one town of any size, is still more of a port than a resort – despite the excellence of the beaches in the area. Even if you get no further, Bizerte is worth a few days of your time – easily reached from Tunis, and with a monumental heritage covering centuries of strategic importance. Closer to the capital, and very much the preserve of Tunisians, are the superlative long white strands of **Raf Raf** and **Ras Sidi El Mekki**. Beaches with few equals, they are cut in two by the steep green flanks of Cap Farina with its crumbling old pirate base of **Ghar el Melh**. Inland, **Lac Ichkeul** is an ornithological highlight.

West of Bizerte along the coast, buses are infrequent and often informal, but it's possible to reach some beautiful and remote beaches poised between deep forested headlands. **Cap Serrat** and **Sidi Mechrig** are both feasible targets; **Tabarca**, already popular as a resort for independent travellers, is perhaps best of all, overlooked by a spectacular island-castle. Just inland from here, **Aïn Draham** is reckoned the coolest point in midsummer; and around, in the **Khroumirie Mountains**, there are some impressive hikes.

The **Medjerda Valley**, formed around the country's one permanent river, provides the main rail and road routes into Algeria. In contrast to the coast it has always had a considerable urban population. **Beja** is the most attractive of the modern centres, though more intriguing is the Roman city of **Bulla Regia** with its underground villas, unique in the ancient world.

MARKET DAYS

Monday – Aïn Draham	Thursday – Sejenane, Bou Salem
Tuesday – Beja, Bizerte, Ghardimaou, Souk es Sebt	Friday – Mateur, Tabarca, Ras Jebel
	Saturday – El Alia, Hammam Bourguiba
Wednesday – Jendouba, Menzel Bourguiba, Nefza	Sunday – Menzel Bourguiba, Thibar, Bezina, Fernana

---

THE COAST

To visit anywhere other than the major centres in this region without a car, you'll need to improvise your **transport**, either by hitching or fighting for a place in the occasional *louage*. **Trains** only run along the Medjerda Valley with a branch line up to Bizerte; otherwise the whole northern coastal region is somewhat inaccessible. The pay-off lies in the rugged, unspoiled shoreline and the sensation of being far from any form of tourist development. Soaking in the sun on the best beaches and stopping off to explore the historic sights could fill several weeks: on the whole, it's best not to hurry, taking leisurely trips and avoiding confrontation with the searing summer heat.

Between Raf Raf beach and Tunis the northern shoreline consists of barely inhabited alluvial farmland: beyond, the coast becomes thickly populated and culminates in

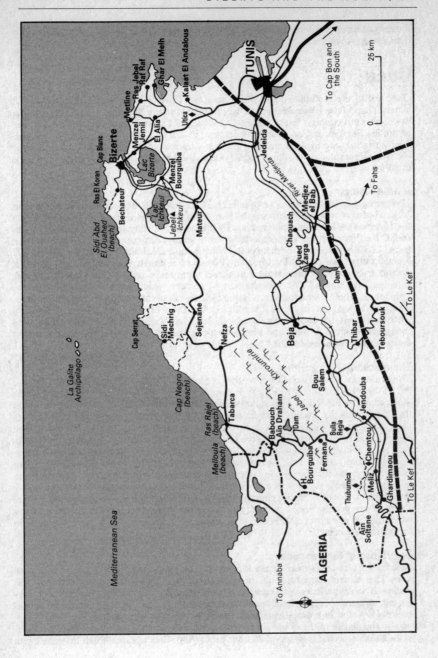

the port of Bizerte, where the population thins out again until Tabarca, itself little more than a large village.

Utica

Once out of the foothills surrounding Tunis, the Bizerte road drops on to the broad alluvial plain of the **River Medjerda**, whose banks, so Sir Grenville Temple reported in the nineteenth century, "were witnesses to the well-known combat between the forces of Attilius Regulus and an enormous serpent, in 225 BC." The river – the only permanently flowing one in the country – plays a vital part in irrigating the north, but for centuries it has also been silting up this section of the coast, locking in what were once great ports.

A little history

The greatest of the ancient ports was **UTICA**, former capital of the Roman province in Africa, but now a smallish site some 10km from the sea (a 2-km walk from ZANA on the Bizerte road). It was made famous by an incident during the Roman Civil War. In 46 BC the Younger Cato, a supporter of Pompeii, was in control of the city when he heard of Caesar's decisive victory at Thapsus, near Mahdia. Having decided to kill himself rather than surrender, he fell on his sword in time-honoured fashion; and when doctors tried to repair the damage, he thrust them aside and rent his innards asunder with his bare hands. This was the sort of gesture which went down well with the Romans and their later admirers: a statue of Cato was immediately erected, facing heroically out to sea, and in the eighteenth century the story inspired Joseph Addison to write a memorably awful play in which Act Five begins: "Cato alone, sitting in a thoughtful posture: in his hand Plato's Book on the Immortality of the Soul. A drawn sword on the table beside him."

The museum

The **museum** (open Tues–Sun 8am–5pm, entrance 1TD plus 1TD for photos) is on the left of the road just before the site. It contains mainly domestic and funerary objects illustrating the life led by Uticans over more than a thousand years. Utica was one of the first Phoenician trading posts in this area, and the Punic pottery and grave reliefs (note the angular Punic script) in the early rooms date from its first 600 years. The Phoenicians were traders and merchants, and when they weren't fighting the Greeks they were doing business with them: look out in Room I for a fine Greek *skyphos* (wine goblet) painted with a Maenad chasing a Satyr. The Roman relics, as so often, are prosaically domestic; but while lamps, nails and glass are only to be expected, the quantity of marble statuary is a clear indication of the city's wealth. None of it is of a very high standard – the Reclining Ariadne and Satyr (recognisable by his tail) in Room IV are poor versions of stock garden figures – but because North Africa has no white marble of its own all this had to be imported at great expense from elsewhere in the Mediterranean.

The House of the Cascade

Despite the size and wealth of the Roman city, its **site**, a little further on, is not extensive. The central monument is the **House of the Cascade**, whose doorway still stands. A private residence of some very well-off citizen, it gives an impression of staggering affluence even without walls or decoration. The ground floor was almost entirely devoted to entertaining, with the main complex of rooms to the right of the pool in the centre of the house. In the middle of this side, the *triclinium* (dining room) is identifiable by the U-shape of its floor decoration. Couches, on which Romans lay to eat their meals (Cato was a source of amazement because, Stoic that he was, he actually ate sitting up), occupied the three sides around the walls. Of the orange and green paving in the middle of the floor, the orange "Numidian" marble came from Chemtou (see p.148), while the green was imported from Euboea in Greece. On either side of the dining room is a garden well and another reception room: the further garden well contains the running fountain arrangement (all in mosaics) which gives the house its name. Other rooms around the central pool are smaller reception chambers, except for a stable to the left of the entrance (note the feeding troughs). The garage for the carriage which the horses pulled is on the other side of the entrance, with a wide doorway.

The rest of the site
Residences surrounding the House of the Cascade are less affluent, but part, all the same, of an exclusive district. The **Forum** was only a block away to the north (beyond the **Punic necropolis** excavated at a lower level), and not much further came the sea. No one knows for certain where the shore was when the Medjerda started silting it up, but it must have been close to the bottom of the slope – from the House of the Cascade's roof you could have watched ships sailing in from Spain, Carthage and Alexandria in the cool, clear air of the morning.

Kalaat el Andalous
KALAAT EL ANDALOUS is the village just visible to the northeast, on what was once another headland in the sea. Nothing distinctive is left now of this Andalusian foundation, but it's a pleasant walk across the rich river plain and there's a magnificent view from the steep cliff on the far side, ranging from Bou Kornine and Sidi Bou Said in the south to Cap Farina in the north. The #44 and 44a **bus** service from pl Belhouane in Tunis passes through here regularly.

Ras Jebel and the Raf Raf Coast

A beach of legendary beauty, **Raf Raf** is the best-known attraction on a stretch of coast that remains surprisingly undeveloped. Conventional tourist facilities are sparse in this area of conservative farmers, but the rewards are all the greater if you make the effort to explore.

    Transport to the Raf Raf area can be confusing until you master the local geography. All buses from Bizerte go through RAS JEBEL before backtracking to RAF RAF TOWN and then down to the beach (specify "Raf Raf Plage"). There are plenty of buses and taxis plying solely between Ras Jebel and Raf Raf. As for transport from Tunis, only one bus a day leaves for Raf Raf direct from the capital (Bab Saadoun), but nine go to Ras Jebel, and during the summer you can usually get a *louage* direct to the beach, though you'll have to fight for a seat at weekends.

    Buses to **Ghar el Melkh** operate through Ras Jebel, but to get to **Ras Sidi el Mekki**, you'll either have to hitch or end up walking from Ghar el Melkh.

Ras Jebel
At the centre of the region is **RAS JEBEL**, a farming town which makes few concessions to visitors – the only foreigners you're likely to see are American Peace Corps volunteers who come en masse in summer to study Arabic. The road into town divides before reaching the centre, with the **bus stop** on the left, the main square (with a towering minaret) straight ahead. A street drops to the right, passing a large café and the market on the left before reaching the **hotel** further round to the right. The town's single other notable, and rather unlikely, feature is a French Lee Cooper jeans factory.

Although Ras Jebel has its own **beach**, 2.5km down a sign-posted road, it's small and gets crowded in July and August when families camp on a long-term basis and conditions become less than hygienic. To avoid this, just walk along to the west until you find a deserted cove, though note that you'll have to carry water supplies.

Raf Raf Beach

The real attraction, though, is **RAF RAF beach**, an almost endless curve of white sand backed by dunes and forest, then steeply sloping fields of figs, vines and rustling cane. At its eastern edge is the long claw of Cap Farina, with the cliffs of its ridge hidden in shadow or gleaming in the sun; to the west a small, knobbly hill; and out in the bay the rocky islet of Ile Pilau.

The beach is popular, formidably so at weekends, but even then it's easy to escape from the crowds. The *Hôtel Dalia* (☎47077), with a friendly manager, costs 9.5TD/13TD low season, 11TD/15TD high, b&b, but you may prefer to try the **straw shacks** which can be hired (in season) for about 7TD a day, or you can sleep out if you're discreet. Keep your eyes open if you decide to camp: one of the few muggings of foreigners in Tunisia happened in the forest here.

If you feel an urge to do other than swim, sunbathe and eat grapes and figs (some of the best in the country), **Cap Farina** is a spectacular walk. The easiest way up is from Raf Raf town, along a track to the watchtower. More daring is to climb the gash of sand visible on the mountain from the beach. By the time you reach the top you feel like a suicidal salmon, but then the whole coast opens out beneath, west to Raf Raf's curve, east down to the lagoon of Ghar el Melkh and Ras Sidi el Mekki beach.

Ghar el Melkh

GHAR EL MELKH means "Cave of Salt", perhaps a reference to the lagoon which the River Medjerda has created around the town, ruining the harbour facilities which once made Porto Farina (as it was then called) a notorious haunt of pirates. In 1654 the English Admiral Blake, in an action described by Lieutenant Colonel Sir Lambert Playfair as "one of the most brilliant victories in the history of the British Navy", attacked and destroyed the port. By the next century, however, it had been rebuilt with three forts and an arsenal. Piracy and smuggling continued to be the town's main source of revenue well into the nineteenth century – carried out, for the most part, by British citizens, the Maltese. The government only clamped down in 1834, when a huge arsenal, kept by one of the Maltese smugglers in his basement, exploded, taking many of the surrounding houses with it. Ahmed Bey tried to turn the port to more legitimate trade, building new jetties and forts. But by this time the estuary had started to silt up, and today Ghar el Melkh is a quiet backwater: a small farming town half asleep under the green flank of the mountain, where the forts and the crumbling walls of the **old port** are steeped in a sense of nostalgic melancholy.

Ras Sidi el Mekki

Ghar el Melkh should really be left to slumber gently, but its peace is liable to be disturbed before long, as the beach at **RAS SIDI EL MEKKI**, 6km beyond at the tip of Cap Farina, becomes developed. The authorities like to call this beach "Polynesian", which does at least convey the stillness of the water and the isolation. In its different way, Ras Sidi el Mekki is as perfect as Raf Raf, just over the mountain. It's little known for the moment though, and its facilities consist of just a few straw cubicles and a café-restaurant so **camping** is the ideal solution. There are rumours of a grandiose project involving ten thousand beds and a Disneyland, so try to see the beach while you can.

Bizerte

BIZERTE, also called Benzert or Bizerta, is the most underrated of Tunisia's resorts – perhaps because it's not so much a resort as a historic port which happens to have beaches. These aren't as opulent as those of the east coast, but if you're looking for a town with both swimming and character, you won't find better. It stands at the mouth of **Lac Bizerte**, a salt-water lake connected to the sea by a canal, along which the modern port is located.

Some history

One of the great natural ports of the Mediterranean, Bizerte was exploited early by the **Phoenicians**, who improbably called their town **Hippo Diarrhytus** and dug the first channel linking the lake to the sea. When the Romans arrived they improved the existing facilities, and imperial prosperity gave the town its first taste of popularity: the Younger Pliny described it as "a town where people of all ages spend their time enjoying the pleasures of fishing, boating and swimming."

The Arabs changed the name to **Benzert** (still locally used), and under the Hafsids its prosperity continued, contemporary writers mentioning a great hunting park. Bizerte inevitably found itself in the front line during the Turco-Spanish struggles of the sixteenth century, and Charles V punished the town for supporting Barbarossa with a brutal raid in 1535; it went on absorbing large numbers of Andalusian immigrants, however, and was rewarded with considerable attention from the Turkish rulers, who added greatly to its amenities during the seventeenth and eighteenth centuries. **Piracy** was the order of the day but, with the demise of the slave trade and increasing European domination of the Mediterranean, Bizerte declined until the opening of the Suez Canal brought renewed strategic importance; the French set about building up the port's facilities – strictly for commercial purposes, they claimed. Even after World War II Bizerte inspired lust in the hearts of western strategic planners, and following Independence the French simply stayed on here. They still refused to evacuate when requested to do so after the bombing of Sakiet Sidi Youssef (see p.214) so, in 1961, Tunisian forces blockaded the town. When the French tried to break the blockade, the result was the Tunisian army's first military action. More than a thousand Tunisian lives were lost before the French finally withdrew in 1963, on October 15 – no longer a national holiday, but still a day for celebrations.

Thanks to the French legacy (and departure), the main thrust of Bizerte's development has been industrial. The naval arsenal has been converted into a vast complex including what was once North Africa's first blast-furnace. Tourism comes second place… which, after a moment's reflection, seems no bad thing.

Practicalities

Bizerte straddles a shipping canal built in the 1890s. The canal, crossed by a **liftbridge**, runs from the sea into Lac Bizerte, a large inland stretch of salt water. The bridge looks pretty impressive when raised, its middle section towering straight up and visible right across town, and the canal has prevented much encroachment on the town centre, which still consists of a **French new town** (wholly unscenic, but with a certain gritty charm) and a **medina**, the two meeting along **Avenue Bourguiba**, which divides the town conveniently in two. The new town is constructed on a grid pattern which makes it easy to find your way around, but unfortunately, street names are mainly posted in Arabic only and Bizertians don't seem to believe in numbering houses, so locating specific places can sometimes be a problem. Note that rue d'Alger and av d'Algerie are two different streets.

Accommodation

In Bizerte you can choose to stay in the **town centre**, on the **beaches to the north**, or at **Remel beach** south of town. The choice depends on what kind of hotel you want, with different types of accommodation concentrated in different areas. **Camping** out on the main northern beaches is usually tolerated.

TOWN CENTRE BUDGET HOTELS

Hôtel Continental, 29 rue 2 Mars (☎31436). On the corner of rue de Constantinople. Grubby but friendly with a certain run-down charm that hardened travellers enjoy. 4.5TD/6TD, cold shower 0.5TD.

Hôtel Africain, pl Slahedinne Bouchoucha (☎32903). Recently closed, but due to reopen.

Hôtel Zitouna, pl Slahedinne Bouchoucha (☎38760). A bit on the dingy side (ask for a room with a window). 3TD/5TD, shower 0.5TD.

Hôtel Saadi, rue Salah ben Ali (☎37528). A nice clean little place between av Farhat Hached and av Hedi Chaker with a hammam three doors down. Not all rooms have windows. 3.5TD per person, shower 0.5TD.

ON THE CORNICHE

More upmarket establishments are strung out along the Corniche for 5km. Take a bus from the "Cheik Driss" bus stop at the corner of bd Hassen en Nouri and av Bourguiba.

Hôtel Petit Mousse, Corniche (☎32185). Going back 40 years and exceptionally friendly – if you have the money and the good fortune to find an unbooked room, this is the place to stay. 2* 13.5TD/19TD low season, 15TD/22TD high, b&b.

Hôtel Corniche, Corniche (☎31844). Looks like a block of council flats – the North Bizerte estate? 3*12.5TD/16TD low, 21TD/30TD high, b&b.

Hôtel Nador, Corniche (☎31848). Rather pricey, especially in high season, and mainly geared to German package tours. 2* 11.1TD/17TD low, 25.7TD/40TD high, b&b.

Hôtel Jalta, Corniche (☎34276). Run by the Austrian-based *Club Dido*, with riding, windsurfing and other facilities. Friendly, too. 3* 9TD/14TD low, 19TD/31TD high, b&b.

Hôtel El Khayem, Corniche (☎32120). Cheapest of the beach hotels, and furthest from town. 4.5TD/6TD low, 7.5TD/11TD high, b&b.

YOUTH HOSTELS AND REMEL BEACH

Youth Hostel/Maison des Jeunes, Route de la Corniche (☎31608). Behind the Spanish Fort. The usual charmless monolith. Check in after 6pm. 4TD per person.

YHA Hostel/campsite, Remel Plage (☎40804). Formerly unofficial, now under YHA auspices. Sign-posted from the road near the #8 bus stop (20min service from Bizerte bus station). Silvan, peaceful, smelling of pine and eucalyptus. The sea is 300m through the trees and over a dune. 1.5TD per person in dorms; 3.5TD per tent plus 0.1TD per person camping. See p.125 under "Town beaches" for more on Remel Plage.

Hôtel Remel, off the Bizerte–Tunis road and sign-posted but not easy to find (☎40664). 13TD per person low, 20TD high.

Places to eat

Because it is so undeveloped for tourism, **restaurants** in Bizerte are rather thin on the ground, especially in the mid-range. On the other hand, there are enough cheap *gargotes* to keep you satisfied, and Bizerte is one of the best places in Tunisia for a real splurge too: just up the Corniche from the moderate eateries are two places to treat yourself.

GARGOTES

Restaurant la Cuisine Tunisienne, rue 2 Mars near the corner of rue de Constantinople. Silence a grumbling stomach for around 2TD.

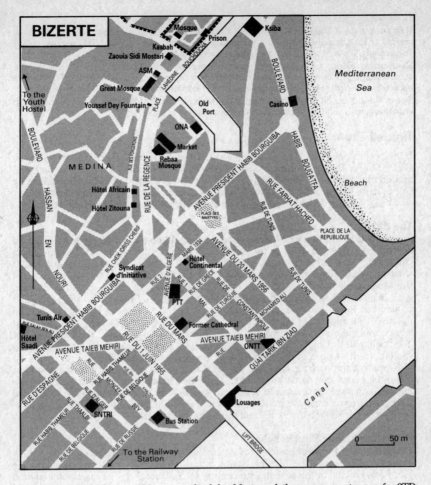

Restaurant Erriadh, rue 2 Mars towards pl des Martyrs. A three-course set menu for 2TD; seating is upstairs.

Restaurant de la Jeunesse, av Bourguiba near the corner of av Taïeb Mehiri. Another possibility, at similar prices, with good grub but limited choice.

MID-RANGE RESTAURANTS

Restaurant du Bonheur, av Thaalbi (near the corner of av Bourguiba). Around 4TD per person.

Tip Top Restaurant, rue de Belgique, near the corner of rue Moncef Bey. Around 5TD, but not as good as its name makes out.

Patisserie de la Paix, just opposite the *Hôtel Continental*. The best patisserie in town, well known for its excellent ice cream.

UPMARKET ESTABLISHMENTS

Restaurant de l'Hôtel Petit Mousse, (☎32185). An excellent meal here will set you back around 15TD (including wine), but on Sunday lunchtimes they do an 8.5TD set menu. Not surprisingly, it's very popular so get in there early or book.

Restaurant Eden, a few hundred metres closer to town. Another seriously classy joint specialising in seafood, and by all accounts the best in town. Again, at around 15TD which is a fraction of the price you'd be paying at a similar establishment in say London or New York.

Sport Nautique, bd H Bougatfa right at the harbour mouth (☎31495). Bizerte's third posh restaurant, with similar prices to the other two, but not as much style.

Around Town

If the post-colonial part of town is where you'll find the necessities of life, it's across av Bourguiba in Bizerte's **older quarters** where you will find the places of interest: around the Medina, the Andalusian Quarter and the city's ancient fortifications. Largely free of large tour groups, this is a city where you can enjoy a good, hustle-free wander. And if sightseeing doesn't appeal, you can always vegetate on the beach instead.

The Old Port

Surrounded by cafés, narrow streets and forts (and one particularly hideous block of apartments), the **Old Port** is the heart of Bizerte. Until the end of the nineteenth century it was a different shape, with two separate arms of the sea running through what's now the new town to the lake; one of these arms ran down the eastern edge of the Medina, along what is now pl Salahedine Bouchoucha, while the other crossed what is now av Bourguiba and took in modern-day pl des Martyrs, isolating an island around the Rebaa Mosque and the market, where the European population lived in detached splendour. At that time, the area south of the market island – the centre of what's now the new town – was part of Lac Bizerte and underwater; the canal had not been built and the inlet of the old port was the lake's only outlet to the sea. For a map of all this as it was, call at the ASM office in the Medina (see p. 125).

Nowadays the harbour comes to life **in the evening** when café tables are set out along the quays and, as darkness falls, illuminated boats chug off for the night's fishing, accompanied by the call to prayer. In the daytime, the quaysides are a peaceful retreat where you can have a coffee, or wander up to the bridge between the twin fortifications of the Kasbah on the left and the Ksiba on the right.

Place Salahedine Bouchoucha

Place Salahedine Bouchoucha and its continuation, rue de la Régence, is the town's commercial hub, and the Medina begins immediately behind. The **fountain** on the Place was erected in the seventeenth century by Youssef Dey – its inscription advises passers-by in both Arabic and Turkish to use its water until such time as the waters of Paradise become available to them – wise counsel, perhaps, but no longer apt as the fountain is dry. Across the square is a covered market, specialising in fish.

The Kasbah and Ksiba

Lurking just behind town, with an attractively compact minaret, the **Kasbah**, at the end of the quay, is hard to miss: like Youssef Dey's fountain it dates from the seventeenth century, when it dominated the harbour entrance, but its fascination now lies in the miniature old town neatly boxed within its walls: passages, arches and walls are all painted in pastel shades. Inside the Kasbah are an ancient prison, a hammam and a mosque.

On the other side of the harbour, the smaller **Ksiba**, another fort built to defend the port entrance, has been renovated and turned into an **Oceanographic Museum** (open 3–6pm daily, 0.2TD entry). Like the Kasbah, the Ksiba also has its own mosque.

The Medina

The best way to approach the Medina is to take the street directly opposite the entrance to the Kasbah, named (though the sign is only in Arabic) **rue des Forgerons**, "street of the ironmongers", which indeed it still is. The first monument you pass is the seventeenth-century **Zaouia of Sidi Mostari** on your left. Ahead of you, also on the left, is the **Great Mosque** built in 1652, its minaret of golden sandstone octagonal in the Ottoman (Hanefite) fashion. Just before it on the corner, the **Zaouia of Sidi Moktar** is now the headquarters of the local ASM (*Association de Sauvegarde de la Medina*), and is sometimes used by them to put on exhibitions about the Medina and their work in restoring and maintaining it. The ASM also produce a fascinating "Archaeological Map of Bizerte", showing the city as it was in 1881, before the new town or canal were built.

The Spanish fort

Yet another old fort dominates the hill behind Bizerte, standing four-square at the angle of the walls which run up its slope. This **"Spanish fort"** was actually built by Turks in 1573, then updated by Youssef Dey. Although it's occasionally used as an open-air **theatre**, all it really offers now is the **view** from its battlements, a couple of World War II Italian guns, and some rusty old **cannons** which were mentioned by Alexandre Dumas on his visit in 1848. Arriving for the first time in Tunisia, what struck Dumas most was the richness of the birdlife – which, instinctively, he came up here to shoot. "Our expedition lasted about two hours," he reported; "we saw fifty partridge, killed five or six, and finished our tour of the town."

The Andalusian Quarter and Bizerte's cemeteries

The **Andalusian Quarter** behind the Kasbah is also worth a wander round, with its whitewashed **mosque**, and its ornate doorways and window-grilles, designed to keep would-be suitors apart from the objects of their admiration. Like so many villages and city quarters in northern Tunisia, the quarter was founded by Muslims fleeing Spain after the Christian reconquest.

Cemetery buffs may be interested to know that Bizerte boasts several interesting graveyards. These include a **"Martyrs' Cemetery"** dedicated exclusively to those who fell during the liberation of Bizerte, which is a little way out of town (follow av Farhat Hached past the edge of town and take a left); an **international cemetery**, among whose dead are Serbian victims of World War I, at the end of rue Pasteur; and the cemeteries of **Sidi Ben Nur** (between the Kasbah and the Andalusian Quarter) and **Sidi Bou Hadid** (between the Andalusian Mosque and the Spanish fort) which are older and more traditional.

Town beaches

Bizerte's main beach is the **Corniche**, a strip of sand varying in width and crowdedness as it stretches the five kilometres from Sidi Salem by the old port bridge north towards Cap Bizerte. Buses up the Corniche stop in town at "Cheik Driss", a bus stop on bd Hassan en Nouri by the corner of av Bourguiba. Buses #1 and 2 also go up the Corniche from just north of the old port.

Three kilometres southeast of town, the beach of **Remel** (whose name means "sand") is definitely lusher, if a little exposed. This is where Bizerte's other youth hostel is situated, reached by bus #8 from the Menzel Jemil stop at the bus station. The **shipwrecks** on Remel beach can be seen from the bridge over the canal, and are about a 50-minute walk down the beach from the hostel/campsite away from town. Both hulls, it seems, are Italian vessels wrecked in 1940. For beaches further afield, see p.130.

Moving On

Transport in and out of Bizerte is plentiful (there's a detailed run-down at the end of the chapter). The *SRT Bizerte* **bus station** is at the bottom of av d'Algerie and rue Ibn Khaldoun, at the end of quai Tarak ibn Ziad. Buses to Tunis leave more or less half-hourly from here, and less-frequent departures for Menzel Bourguiba, Beja, Jendouba, Aïn Draham via Tabarca and one a day direct to Raf Raf (though there are plenty to Ras Jebel, where you can change for Raf Raf). Outside the bus station building is the Menzel Jemil (via Remel) and Menzel Abderrahman bus stop, with buses every twenty minutes or so. There are other buses for Kairouan, Sousse, Sfax and Jerba from *SNTRI*'s unpromising-looking depot in rue d'Alger (at rue H Thameur).

Apart from buses, **louages** hang out next to the lift-bridge on quai Tarak ibn Ziad, with loads of departures to Tunis and plenty to Mateur, Menzel Bourguiba and Raf Raf – but none to Tabarca. Finally, the **railway station** is at the end of rue de Russie and rue de Belgique by the docks, with trains for Mateur, Tunis, and Menzel Bourguiba.

Bizerte Listings

Airline *Tunis Air*, 76 av Bourguiba (☎32201/2).

Banks Spread around the grid-zone, they include: *UIB* on av Taïeb Mehiri (at rue Moncef Bey); *l'Habitat* on av Bourguiba (at av Taïeb Mehiri); *BIAT* on rue Moncef Bey (at rue 2 Mars); *du Sud* on rue H Thameur (at av Taïeb Mehiri); *BNA* on rue Mongi Slim (at pl 7 Novembre); *BT* on rue Ibn Khaldoun (at av d'Algerie).

Car hire *Avis*, 7 rue d'Alger (☎33076); *Budget*, 7 rue d'Alger (☎32174); *Hertz*, pl des Martyrs (☎33679); *Interrent/Europcar*, 52 av d'Algerie (☎39018); *Mattei*, 27 rue d'Alger. The *Hôtel Jalta* rents out bicycles at 2TD a day.

Cinemas *Casino*, pl des Martyrs; *Paris*, 43 av Taïeb Mehiri (at av Bourguiba); *Majestic*, rue de Tunis; *Colisée*, rue 1 Mai (at av d'Algerie).

Excursions Some of the big hotels, notably the *Hôtel Jalta*, run trips – for example, half a day in Raf Raf and Utica for 7.5TD. *Transtour* at the *Hôtel Nador* offer a day in Kairouan for 32TD and a 3-day "safari" (not a wildlife trip as such) in the south for 125TD. The island nature reserve of Cani, miles out to sea towards Sicily, is closed to all but "bona fide scientific expeditions".

Festivals Liberation Day is October 15, with street celebrations and a carnival of sorts to celebrate the city's 1963 liberation from the French. Sidi Selim is a saint's day, the date of which is fixed on the Islamic calendar.

Football The local club is CAB Bizerte, 1987 African Cup winners. Their ground is up by Porte de Bechateur and the Maison des Jeunes. Matches usually kick off at 2pm on Sundays.

Hammams The best one is hidden deep in the Medina. Another is in the Kasbah, and there's one in rue Salah Ben Ali near the *Hôtel Saadi*. Hours at all of these are 6am–noon and 6pm–9pm for men, noon–6pm for women.

International phone calls Rue 1 Mai (corner of rue 2 Mars), 8am–8pm every day.

Left luggage At the railway station.

Market day Tuesday, in pl du Marché in front of the Kasbah.

Medical facilities The regional hospital is up rue Ibn Khaldoun (☎31422), with a night-time *garde medicale* open 8pm–7am at 3 av Bourguiba near the Old Port (☎33673), and a night chemist around the corner at 28 rue Ali Belhouane.

ONA crafts shop Behind the market, facing onto the Old Port.

PTT Av d'Algerie (corner of rue 1 Mai), city hours, changes cash, phones in the side entrance.

Shipping companies *Tourafric*, 1 rue Salah ben Ali (☎32315). Tickets for Tunis–Sicily.

Supermarkets *Monoprix*, rue 2 Mars, at rue Ibn Khaldoun; *Magasin Haddad*, rue 2 Mars next to the *Hôtel Continental*.

Swimming pool There's a municipal pool on rue de la Corniche near the Maison des Jeunes. Otherwise, the *Hôtel Nador* is one with a pool – officially 2TD for non-residents out of season, 8TD in high season.

Tourist office ONTT, rue de Constantinople, corner of quai Tarak ibn Ziad (☎32703/32897). Very friendly and helpful. Syndicat d'Initiative in the *Club de Presse*, av Bourguiba, by the Esso station on the corner of rue Cheik Idriss Cherif (☎33802), Tues–Sat 9am–noon & 4–7pm; Sun 10am–noon & 6–7pm. Again, friendly, but not exactly swimming with info.

Around Bizerte and Lac Ichkeul

West of the town, the **beaches** run in shallow curves until they fetch up with a bump against Cap Blanc, 8km further along. Like all the beaches of the north coast, when the wind blows they can feel slightly exposed, but in summer it's never unpleasant. The Roman writer Pliny the Younger tells how a boy out swimming here was befriended one day by a dolphin so tame that it carried him out to sea for rides. It soon acquired a cult following, but this was too much for the local bureaucrats of the Roman Empire, who had the dolphin killed. More conventional watersports are available today at the big hotels.

The beaches and hills

Cap Blanc is a formidable hump. Often said to be the northernmost point in Africa, if you're standing on top, buffeted by the winds, it's easy to persuade yourself you're on top of a continent, although in fact Africa's most northerly point is really a few kilometres west at **Ras Angela** (aka Ras Ben Sekka). For a distant view of this cape, catch a #6 bus from bd Hassan en Nouri to the village of **BECHATEUR** – a side trip which reveals some of the unexpectedly bleak scenery behind the coast at this point. Bechateur itself is a tiny hamlet on a windswept hilltop which, almost unbelievably, was once inhabited by Romans; blocks of their masonry can be seen in the walls of the village here and there. The bus stops at Bechateur, but a track continues for 20km to the **beach of Sidi Abdel Waheb** – worth exploring, if you have some means of getting down. The area still yields **unexpected discoveries** – between Cap Blanc and Ras Angela, at AÏN DAMOUS, a recently discovered underwater cave is said to be the entrance of Roman catacombs leading all the way to Utica.

Menzel Abderrahman and Menzel Jemil

The lakeside villages of **MENZEL ABDERRAHMAN** and **MENZEL JEMIL** (short journeys from Bizerte's main bus station), are both ninth-century Aghlabid foundations and attractive places from which to get a view of **Lac Bizerte**. Menzel Abderrahman is actually on the shore, while Menzel Jemil perches on a hillside with a dapper old central square dominated by a fortress-like whitewashed mosque.

Menzel Bourguiba

On the south side of Lac Bizerte, **MENZEL BOURGUIBA** (formerly the French garrison town of Ferryville) is itself uninteresting, but it's the perfect base for exploring **Lac Ichkeul**, the country's best-known nature reserve.

The centre of Menzel Bourguiba is a pleasant square with a bandstand. The only hotel in town is the *Moderne* (☎60551) in rue d'Alger, which runs off the bandstand square towards the station. Cheap (2TD per person) but very basic and somewhat grubby, it has no showers – though there are three hammams nearby. The *Hôtel Moderne* is also an inexpensive eatery and the town's main bar and social focus, a pretty lively place in the evenings when they serve cold beer and wine until late (except on Fridays). During World War II, soldiers on both sides had occasion to drink here, and the venerable *patron* who served them still runs the place.

The other hotel in the area is *Hôtel Younes*, some way out of Menzel Bourguiba in Guengla (☎61606), right on **Lac Bizerte**. To get there, you could take a taxi or (infrequent) bus from Menzel Bourguiba town centre, or follow av de Palestine from the bandstand past the hospital and the craft centre opposite, turning left with the tarmac at the barracks entrance, and straight on for another 2km. The hotel is sign-posted on the right. Here, for 7.5TD per person b&b, you get a pleasant room in a tranquil setting with a new high-class restaurant (open to non-residents and about 10TD a meal). The proprietor also runs the *Tardi* wine company which bottles many of the region's wines and arranges visits to the cellars at Aïn Ghellal. **Wildlife** enthusiasts should note that the hotel is ideally placed for exploring Oued Tinja, the river that connects Lac Ichkeul with Lac Bizerte.

Transport and other practicalities

The **train station**, down rue d'Alger from the bandstand, has eight shuttles a day running to Tinja, four connecting for Mateur and Tunis, and four for Bizerte.

Turn left just before the station and continue for 100m to find the **Tunis louage station**, or cross the tracks and turn right to the site of Menzel's Wednesday and Sunday **market**, where you can pick up **louages to Mateur**.

To find the **bus station, and louages for Bizerte**, go back up rue d'Alger, turn left at the bandstand and go straight on past a six-way roundabout and monument to the November 1987 uprising, where you'll also find the **PTT** and *Monoprix* **supermarket**. There are regular buses to Tunis and Bizerte, plus two or three daily for Tabarca, Aïn Draham and Beja.

Lac Ichkeul National Park

Lac Ichkeul is linked with Lac Bizerte. The fact that it's too shallow to be navigable has made it ideal for fish and birdlife. In winter it's an ornithologists' delight and a haven for birds migrating from Northern Europe – those that make it across the killing fields of Italy and Malta. Non-tidal but slightly saline, the lake provides a unique ecosystem that the government has protected as a nature reserve. Unfortunately it's already under threat, due to heavy demand on its water, with two dams already constructed on its feed rivers, and a further four planned before the end of the century. The combined effect of these dams and of low rainfalls is that the water level in the lake is falling, causing salt water from Lac Bizerte to flow back into it. This, together with evaporation, means that the lake is growing more saline, killing off the water plants on which its delicate ecosystem depends.

Apart from its famous ornithological attractions (detailed p.129), the lake abounds in **frogs** and **toads**, including a very handsome, vocal species with green stripes down the back. There are **terrapins** too: the Sejenane marsh is a good place to look.

Transport and practicalities

Getting to the National Park is not easy by public transport. It's a good idea to visit the tourist office in Bizerte to get some advice and information. From Bizerte, the bus or *louage* to Mateur passes the southeastern corner of the lake; get off at the level crossing and hitch or walk past the southern end of the Joumine marsh. A turn to the right then takes you through the park gates and a track leads along the southern flank of the **Jebel Ichkeul** mountain to its northeastern spur (which pokes into the lake), on which peninsula a small **museum and interpretation centre** should now be open. Alternatively, for viewing the northern shore of the lake, the bus from Bizerte to

Sejenane passes along the water edge, passing both the Douimis and Sejenane marshes. If you're staying at the *Younes*, a local bus goes from Guengla to Tinja: hitch from there either along the north or, with more promise, the south side of the lake

Mountain and lakeside flora

The **flowers** up on Jebel Ichkeul are utterly dependent on the winter rains and you can walk through a carpet of colour or over barren straw, depending on the weather. As well as on the mountain, interesting flowers grow around the rivers feeding the lake – around the Douimis river on the north shore, for instance, you'll find a white **Star of Bethlehem** and a delightful, tiny wild **narcissus**. The **agricultural weeds** are spectacular even in a dry year, since many of the fields to the north of the lake are irrigated. Look out for fields ablaze with poppies and wild chrysanthemums, and for various colourful convolvulus species around the edges. **Honeywort**, with its strange pendulous yellow and brown flowers, is also common by the roadside, and there's a shocking pink **soapwort** in the fields.

Birdwatching on the lake

Waterfowl are the lake's highspot. Ducks feed on the extensive beds of pondweed and grey lag geese on the club rush. These plants, together with the sheer size of the lake (over sixty square kilometres), make it North Africa's principle wildfowl wintering ground with up to 150,000 birds at its winter peak.

Although huge flocks are present only between October and February, ducks remain in good numbers until the spring, with a few staying on and occasionally breeding over the summer. The birds move around the lake depending on the distribution of their food plants, but in general the best viewpoints are from the coast north of the mountain (there's a good track along it starting from the museum), or from the Douimis and Sejenane marshes on the north side. The latter marsh requires a walk along the river from the road.

As well as ducks and geese, the lake supports a variety of **wading birds** around its fringes. If the water level is high enough, both the Douimis and Sejenane marshes are good all year round for waders, with sizeable populations of avocets, black-winged stilts and Kentish plovers. These are augmented in winter by black-tailed godwits, redshanks and the smaller sandpipers. If wet, the edge of the Joumine marsh closest to the level crossing is a great spot to watch waders, but beware of the evil dogs around here. Herons and egrets breed amongst the reeds, with grey heron as a resident and purple heron as a summer visitor, and there's sometimes a colony of night herons in the reeds at the north edge of the mountain. The unmistakable white storks don't breed in the park but they nest close by and often feed around the lake edges.

The lake's **speciality birds** include the purple gallinule, a rarity rather like a huge red-billed coot, the marbled teal, a small, shy duck with a mottled brown plumage, and the white-headed duck, a universally rare bird which winters in small numbers on a few Tunisian lakes, including Ichkeul.

With all these water birds about, as well as small mammals, reptiles and amphibians, the lake also attracts **birds of prey**. Marsh harriers are the most dominant species, identifiable by their upturned wings as they drift over the reedbeds and surrounding fields in search of small prey. Of the falcons, peregrine, lanner and kestrel all breed on the mountain; Bonelli's and short-toed eagles wheel high in the sky, and long-legged buzzards breed here too.

Don't ignore the **smaller birds**, either. Reed warblers and great reed warblers breed here in summer, nightingales are common, and bee-eaters breed in the river banks and spoil heaps. Quail, the smallest game bird, breed in the park too; listen for their "whic whic" call from the surrounding fields in spring – they're notoriously hard to spot. Moussier's redstarts are common amongst the scrub on the mountain, and Sardinian warblers are everywhere. Woodchat shrikes perch on telegraph wires and lone trees in summer, and a related and very rare species, the black-headed bush shrike, breeds here in very small numbers. Boring bulbuls – like drab blackbirds but with a loud and mellifluous song – reach the most northerly part of their range in Tunisia (they're primarily Asian and African birds).

The mountain's wildlife

A superb limestone mountain, **Jebel Ichkeul**, rises directly from the southern edge of the lake. It used to be a royal hunting park in the thirteenth century and **wild boar** and **jackals** still live on its flanks, as do **porcupines**, **mongooses**, **otters**, **tortoises** and a small herd of **water buffalo** – descended, it's said, from a pair given to the Bey of Tunis by the king of Sicily in 1729. During the war, American troops stationed nearby developed a taste for the meat and the herd was virtually wiped out. Fortunately, enough animals survived to revive it.

West of Bizerte

The **coastline** between Bizerte and Tabarca consists of a series of isolated coves, backed by increasingly heavy forests, whose inaccessibility pays dividends to those in search of wilder shores: most are uninhabited, putting them beyond the reach of all but the most dedicated, but a few are viable even if you don't have your own transport. In order to get to them, though, you'll need plenty of time, and you'll probably have to hitch, negotiate a taxi fare or charter a *louage* from SEJENANE. To get to Sejenane, heading first to Mateur is likely to be your best bet, although it should also be possible from Tabarca and the west via Nefza.

MATEUR has little of interest apart from its transport connections. *SRT Bizerte* runs the bus station, but other services stop here, and one way or another there are plenty of departures for Tabarca, Sejenane, Beja, Bizerte and, of course, Tunis.

Sejenane

The base for any expedition to the beaches is **SEJENANE**, almost the only place of any size between Mateur and Tabarca. It's a peaceful country town, living off agriculture and mining, with its own unique "primitive" style of pottery. Pots aside, there's little reason to stop here (unless it's market day, Thursday) except to enquire about transport out again – which is mainly back to Mateur.

Some remote beaches

Cap Serrat is a promontory almost due north of Sejenane, with a tiny population in the valley behind. There's a small seasonal shop on the beach – enough to support anyone wanting to camp out.

Alternatively, the beaches of **Sidi Mechrig** and **Cap Negro** are both reached by a track which turns north off the main GP7 road some 10km west of Sejenane, then splits in two. **CAP NEGRO**, very remote and now uninhabited, used to be the site of a French coral-fishing establishment, the ruins of which (it was sacked in 1741 by the same expedition that attacked the Genoese fort at Tabarca) are still to be unearthed.

If you can't find a way of reaching these beaches, or prefer not to stay at them, it's relatively easy to pick up lifts in TABARCA (especially at the *Club des Pins*) from people going out for the day. There may also be lifts going to the beaches of **Jabbara** and **Ras Rajel**: tracks to these lead off the main road about 15km and 10km short of Tabarca, the second one from nearby Ras Rajel's **Commonwealth War Cemetery**.

Tabarca

The setting of **TABARCA** is all that anyone could ask for: the **Khroumirie mountains** subside suddenly into a fertile plain, and in one corner is the natural harbour first used by the Carthaginians, dominated by an offshore rock crowned by a **Genoese castle**. Tabarca's success as a resort in recent years has taken what's basically a sleepy country town by surprise. In July and early August it is almost swamped by tourists, though since they're mostly independent (there's only one package hotel, some way out of town) the atmosphere is more of a big easy-going campsite; towards the end of August the town settles back to being a market centre (Friday **souk** on the Bizerte road just out of town) and small fishing port. Alas, this all looks set to change. Tabarca is now part of a massive tourist development project due for completion in the mid-1990s. It will include a new international airport and lots of new hotels. (For a taste of its future in store, have a look at Monastir, then rush back to Tabarca while it's still worth visiting.)

Some history

Roman Tabarca was the main port of exit for Chemtou marble from south of the mountains (see p.148), and thanks to this and grain exports it became a substantial town – probably about the same size as today, and wealthy enough to produce the fine early Christian mosaics on display in the Bardo Museum in Tunis. Decline set in after the fall of the Empire, but the eleventh-century geographer El Edrisi was still impressed by "ancient monuments of fine construction". He found the town "much frequented by foreigners", and like everywhere else along the North African coast it was fiercely disputed during the course of the sixteenth century. The French colonials used Tabarca as a resort in a small way, for hunting rather than swimming, but it was still considered remote enough in 1952 to be a suitable place of exile for Bourguiba. After Independence, the isolation and charm remained, until recently, quite intact. **Coral** and **cork** (from the mountain forests behind), as well as fishing and farming, are the important industries.

TABARCA

Mediterranean Sea

To the Genoese Castle

HOTELS
1. Hôtel Corail
2. Hôtel de France
3. Hôtel de la Plage
4. Pension Mamia
5. Hôtel Mimosas

AVENUE HEDI CHAKER

Club de Plonger

To the Needles

AVENUE BOURGUIBA

RUE DES PECHEURS

3

Railway Station

2

1

RUE DU PEUPLE

Tourist Office

Excavations

Basilique

RUE FARHAT HACHED

SNTRI

RUE DU PEUPLE

AVENUE BOURGUIBA

To Bizerte

SRT Jendouba

4

Louages

Borj Messaoud

PTT

RUE DE TUNIS

RUE ALI ZOUAOUI

0   50 m

5

To Aïn Draham

Practicalities

The town is tiny – just the main street, av Bourguiba, and a few blocks on either side. Right in the middle of av Bourguiba is Tabarca's main square where you'll find a covered market and *Magasin Général* **supermarket** (8am–12.30pm & 3–7pm, closed Sun pm and all day Mon), as well as the Town Hall and a statue of Habib Bourguiba and his dog. Behind the statue is a mosque and a **bank** (others are at 30 av Bourguiba and opposite the Hôtel de France at 12 av Hedi Chaker); in front, some interesting-looking Roman remains are being unearthed.

From the main square, av Bourguiba heads in one direction towards Aïn Draham and Bizerte, and in the other to the beach, passing the ONTT **tourist office** (at no. 33) and the hotels *Corail* and *de France*. A left off av Bourguiba up rue Farhat Hached takes you past the **PTT** (country hours) and two **hammams** (men 5am–noon & 5–10pm; women noon–5pm).

In case of **medical emergency**, there's the Sidi Moussa Clinic at the beach end of av Bourguiba, and a **night chemist** at 5 rue Ali Zouaoui, which is off av Bourguiba the other side of the main square.

The *Hôtel Mimosas* organises **day trip excursions**. Prices per head for six people are Tunis 35TD, Bizerte 30TD, Bulla Regia and Dougga 25TD or Bulla Regia and Chemtou 16TD.

Accommodation

Two cheap **hotels** overlook av Bourguiba: the unclassified *Hôtel Corail* (1 on our map) on the corner of rue Tazerca (☎44455) is the cheaper of the two at 5TD per person, but cannot compete for fame with the 1* *Hôtel de France* (2) (7TD/10TD low season, 13TD/20TD high, b&b), a block beyond (☎44577), where Bourguiba stayed during his enforced sojourn in 1952, after a disagreement with the manageress of the *Mimosas*; the *France* has capitalised on this ever since, with a plaque ouside Bourguiba's old room commemorating their famous guest.

The best-value cheapie in town is neither of these, but the unclassified *Hôtel de la Plage* (3), hidden away at 7 rue des Pecheurs. Clean, bright, friendly, and 5TD per person, it definitely gets top recommendation. The only other budget alternative is *Pension Mamia* (4) at 3 rue de Tunis (☎44058), costing 6.5TD per person.

If none of these is up to scratch for you, the 3* *Hôtel Mimosas* (5) (16TD/24TD low, 27.5TD/39TD high, b&b), on the hill overlooking Tabarca and up its own road off av Bourguiba as you come into town (☎44500), should see you satisfied, with large well-furnished rooms and a certain amount of old-fashioned style.

Some 2km down the beach, the package-touristy 3* *Hôtel Morjane* is closed for rede-velopment, but should reopen soon. Lots of similar establishments are likely to join it.

Eating and drinking

Fish is the main dish of the day around these parts, and excellent it is too, with large, whole succulent ones being the rule, and a plate of bony tiddlers the exception, in cheap places as well as more expensive. Among the bargains, the *Restaurant Trikki* in rue Farhat Hached is one of the best (1.5TD for a fish course, or 1.7TD for steaks). At simi-lar prices, try the *L'Athiniki* at 7 rue Ali Zouaoui, the *Restaurant des Etoiles* at 19 rue du Peuple, or two more places at nos. 31 and 35 of the same street.

With a bit more style, the *Hôtel de France* does a set menu at 4TD – and you can have a beer with it: hard drinking is done in a small garden behind the *France*, where delicious brochettes are sometimes cooked outside. The *Hôtel Mimosas*' menu is dearer (7TD), but seafood pizzas are reasonable value at 3TD and the *Mimosas* is also good for a quiet drink – and they have a pool table. Also in this range, the *Café des Agriculteurs* at 43 av Bourguiba should cost about 5TD. If you want to chuck your money around, the *Restaurant Khemir* at 11 av Bourguiba provides superior service and higher bills to match.

For tea or coffee and a *chicha*, don't miss Tabarca's trendiest rendezvous, the *Café Andalous*, next to the *Hôtel de France*, with its bizarre, and rather atmospheric, collection of bric-à-brac.

Entertainment
Organised nightlife consists of discos at the *Mimosas*. In addition, there's the **Tabarca Festival** in July and August but, in truth, the cultural content of the festival is not spectacularly high – it's more an all-embracing term for the six-week party which takes over the town during the peak season. The festival slogan, exhorting people to do more than just sunbathe – "ne pas bronzer idiot!" – may not survive the redevelopment.

Coral and diving
Coral, Tabarca's favourite souvenir, was one of the luxury items exported from North Africa to Europe, and av Bourguiba is lined with shops selling jewellery made by local artisans out of the coral brought up by divers. Prices here are considerably lower than in Tunis. The coral is Mediterranean coral, a species which has been collected for jewellery use for centuries, with the result that it is now fast declining and has been listed as an **endangered species** – think twice, therefore, before buying a coral souvenir in one of the many shops in Tabarka (and throughout northern Tunisia).

The coral divers are trained locally by the **Club de Plonger**, near the fishing port, which also trains individuals. They offer a *"bapteme"* (first dive) for 12TD, training to the first grade for 100TD plus 12TD membership and a medical certificate (which the Sidi Moussa Clinic in town can sort out). The price includes ten dives and you must be over fifteen. They also hire out boats and equipment and do training up to the third grade.

Sights Around Town

Many of the events in the summer festival are put on in the garden of the so-called **Basilique**, just above the *Café Andalous*. This was actually a cistern supplying the Roman town, which the "White Fathers" converted into a church. Other patches of Roman excavation are dotted around the town, including the **Borj Messaoud** halfway up the hill behind, also originally a cistern but converted into a fort by French and Italian merchants in the twelfth century.

The Genoese Castle
Compared with the **Genoese Castle**, these minor monuments seem rather feeble. The castle's origins were as dramatic as its appearance is now: in 1541 the Turkish corsair Khair ed Din Barbarossa surrendered it to Charles V of Spain in return for his colleague Dragut, who had been languishing in a Christian jail, and the next year Charles sold the coral fishing rights and the island to a Genoese family called Lomellini. Having built the castle and enough of a town to support 1200 inhabitants, they managed to stay, despite Turkish control of the mainland, for two centuries. One of their main sources of income came from acting as agents for ransoming slaves in Tunis, a service for which they charged a three-percent commission. Then in 1741 they found themselves in need of agents when an Ottoman expedition sacked the outposts here and at Cap Negro, selling all the inhabitants into slavery.

The romance of this story was dealt a blow when the French built a causeway to the castle's island after World War II, but the castle on its rocky pinnacle has lost none of its allure – it's a fabulous place, especially at sunset when the sun sinks gingerly over the Needles. The castle is closed to the public but the lighthouse keeper has been known to invite people in depending on his mood.

WILDLIFE AROUND TABARCA

This region is one of the richest **natural habitats** in Tunisia, with the cork oak forests around Aïn Draham dropping down to the "coral coast" around Tabarca.

For a good **walk to the west of Tabarca**, go up rue Farhat Hached from av Habib Bourguiba, and then take a track off to the right which scrambles up to the road by the army camp. Turn left along this road, and follow it as it winds up through shrub-covered hillsides. The sandy rock doesn't support a great variety of flowers, but there are some unusual species – the Mediterranean **medlar tree** (a species of hawthorn) and heavily grazed **mastic trees** and **Kermes oaks**. Turn right off the road and head towards the coast. Look closely under the **white-flowered rockroses** on the hill and you'll find the extraordinary parasitic plant **cytinus**: with red and yellow waxy flowers and no green leaves, it gets its energy from its host plant, and is particularly common around here. In between the shrubs is **romulea**, an abundant and very beautiful tiny purple relative of the crocus. You can return along the cliffs to Tabarca, passing above the Needles. Blue rock thrushes are common on this stretch of cliffs.

A longer but more varied walk is **up the hill to the east of the town**, at the other end of the beach. Check out the **Oued el Kebir river** as you cross it – it's full of small birds at migration time, and **marsh harriers** are usually to be seen wheeling their way over the valley. **Nightingales** sing from the riverside shrubs, and the "tsip tsip" of **fan-tailed warblers** is constantly heard. The sand dunes behind the beach are covered in pines and windblown junipers, the resting zone of **stone curlews**. **Lesser kestrels**, which breed communally in the old Genoese fort, can be seen patrolling the sand dunes for mice and voles – they're very similar to the common kestrel but much noisier, and the male has an unspotted chestnut back.

Fork left after the road to the *Hôtel Morjane*, and a firebreak up the hill from the pines makes for an easy walk to the top of the ridge. The pines, junipers and cypress trees at the bottom soon give way to a typical *garigue* vegetation of sandy soils – cork and Kermes oaks above a shrubby layer including tree heath, strawberry bush and mastic tree. The **tree heath** and **strawberry tree** are both in the heather family, with bell-shaped white flowers (the fruits of the strawberry tree don't taste so wonderful). On the ground you wade through thickets of **French lavender**, its purple flowerheads making it one of the most conspicuous small shrubs in the region. At the bottom of the firebreak there is the inevitable rubbish dump – not a pleasant place, but positively swarming with **ravens**.

The beaches

West of town, the coast is a series of rocky coves whose beginning is marked by the grotesquely shaped **Needles**, jagged blades of rock standing in a row that juts out towards the castle.

In the other direction, the **beach** stretches 4km round the bay. A kilometre or so down towards the *Hôtel Morjane*, a few remnants of World War II wrecks just protrude from the water. You should be able to find some space on this beach, even at its most crowded. The presence of the coral makes for some of the best snorkelling in the Mediterranean.

If you want more isolation try some of the lonely coves that punctuate the coast in either direction. **Melloula beach** is 7km west; in the other direction, to the east, the coast is covered under "Sejenane" (see p.130).

Visits to La Galite

La Galite is a small volcanic archipelago 60km off the coast. The largest of the islands is only 5km long, with a tiny seasonal population which at one time included Bourguiba (on yet another of his bouts of exile). The seas here are rich in fish, with great snorkelling in summer if you get the chance, and this is the only place in the Mediterranean where it's possible to see the exceedingly rare Mediterranean monk seal

– numbered in the very low hundreds or even less. La Galite is now a strictly protected area and in theory closed to all except genuine scientific expeditions, although it is just possible the *Club de Plonger* in Tabarca could organise a trip if you wrote to them well in advance (Secretaire, Club de Plonger, Port de Pêche, 8110 Tabarca, Tunisia, ☎44478).

Moving on

Tabarca's **train station**, by the beach, has no passenger services at present, and the projected **airport** is due to open at some time in the future.

Meanwhile, there are two **bus** stations: *SNTRI* at 12 rue du Peuple (Tunis, either via Sejenane and Mateur, or via Beja), and *SRT Jendouba* at 72 av Bourguiba (Jendouba, Bizerte and Le Kef, and Aïn Draham). *SRT Beja* run two buses a day, which stop in Tabarca's main square, but if Beja is where you're headed, you may have to visit all three stops to see who has the next bus out.

Louages – most of them for Jendouba, though you may find one for Aïn Draham if you're lucky – leave from av Bourguiba, by the *Hôtel Mimosas* turn-off and the Esso station. Otherwise, **hitching** to Aïn Draham is pretty standard practice, but you're expected to contribute.

On to Algeria

The road across the frontier through the mountains via Oum Teboul is not very good, and there is no public transport; so if you want to go that way to **Algeria**, you'll have to hitch to El Kala, from where there are plenty of buses on to Annaba. It's a good precaution to check that the crossing is open before setting out.

Aïn Draham and the Khroumirie

Strictly speaking, the small eruption of forested mountains in the northwest corner of Tunisia is called the **Khroumirie**, but in practice you're more likely to hear the area called after its one sizeable village and effective capital, **Aïn Draham**. The region stretches from Tabarca on the coast to Fernana 50km south, and its mountains rise steeply from the sea to a height of over 1000m, covered with leafy forests of **cork oak** and ferns – and reputedly bristling with wild boar – before subsiding to the Medjerda valley at Jendouba. This sudden mountainous barrier precipitates enormous amounts of rain which never reach other parts of the country: in winter it's not unusual to find a metre of snow at Aïn Draham. In summer the mountain air is refreshing, and the town has become a resort in an unassuming kind of way. If you want to tie in your visit, **market day** is Monday.

CORK

Cork is made from the outer bark of the cork oak, which grows all around the western Mediterranean. The first cork, when the tree is about 15–20 years old, is harvested by making a careful cut – so as not to damage the layer of inner bark beneath the cork – around the trunk just above the ground, and another just below where the branches begin. Four vertical cuts are then made and the oblong panels of cork carefully removed. The outer bark regrows and can be harvested every eight to ten years. Trees continue producing cork for about 150 years. Cork's springy lightness is due to millions of tiny air pockets trapped within it which also make it waterproof and pretty well soundproof. It wasn't used to make bottle corks until the fifteenth century, but that was almost its only use until the veritable explosion – lifebuoys, table-mats, cigarette tips and, of course, floor and wall tiles – of recent times.

Aïn Draham

The French tried to recreate a small Alpine village in what was their equivalent of the British Simla in India, and many of the older buildings appear to have been spirited out of the Jura and Switzerland and plumped down on this remote mountain in North Africa. Today Aïn Draham is popular with those Tunisians who can afford to escape the heat of the capital – which means that prices have been pushed a little higher than usual (its name means, appropriately, "Springs of Money"). Most holidaymakers are here for a longish stay: they hire villas on the outskirts of the village, leaving the centre mostly unspoiled. The steep main street, av Bourguiba, lined with a few cafés and general stores, runs down the flank of **Jebel Bir** ("Well Mountain"), the highest point in the area at 1014m. It doesn't quite have the full Swiss Alpine atmosphere sometimes claimed, but the combination of forested slopes, fresh air and red tiled roofs is European enough for a minaret to look incongruous.

Practicalities

Most of the necessities of life are to be found somewhere along av Bourguiba. The Syndicat d'Initiative **tourist office** is at no. 57 (☎47115), and the **PTT** at no. 114 – open country hours with international phone calls from an open kiosk up the street towards Jendouba, between the *Hôtel Beauséjour* and the *Maison des Jeunes*. There are two **banks** on av Bourguiba too. The police station, halfway along, must be Aïn Draham's prettiest building.

Towards the northern end of town, av Bourguiba descends quite sharply. When it reaches the bottom, av 7 Novembre branches off left to the *autogare*. Past here, av Bourguiba climbs again, with av H Thameur the next left by the Esso station. Down here, you'll find the municipal **swimming pool**, the **ONA** crafts shop and the Clinique Sidi Abdullah. There is also a regional **hospital** (☎47047) not far from the *autogare*.

Accommodation

One drawback in Aïn Draham's lack of development is that **accommodation** is limited. The *Hôtel Beauséjour* (☎47005), near the top of av Bourguiba and a remnant of French hunting parties (stuffed boar heads on the walls), is almost certain to be stuffed with bores in high season (11TD/15TD low season, 15TD/22TD high, b&b). Slightly further on, the *Maison des Jeunes* **youth hostel** (4TD for the usual Colditz-like barracks; ☎47087) is also liable to be filled by group bookings in summer, but empty in the winter. Your passport is seized on entry and you have to track it down before leaving. Fortunately, there is now another youth hostel, the **Centre d'Acceuil**, or *Centre des Stages et de Vacances*, which looks much more promising (☎47126). It is situated right at the other end of town beyond the bus station, from which it is sign-posted. If you're on av Bourguiba, turn left at the Esso station and it's 100m down av H Thameur on the right.

A kilometre beyond the *Maison des Jeunes*, on the road to Jendouba, the 2* *Hôtel Rihana* (☎47391) charges 19TD/30TD b&b and is a very pleasant walk from town. Some five kilometres further is the 2* *Hôtel les Chênes* (☎47211), a State-run hotel training college with a nationwide reputation (14TD/22TD b&b). **Camping** is occasionally allowed in the grounds.

Eating and drinking

Aïn Draham is one of the few places in the country where you can eat **pork** – not sausage and bacon for breakfast perhaps, but you should find wild boar available in the *Hôtel Beauséjour* and other hunting-orientated hotels during the season. The *Beauséjour* does a set menu for 5TD.

Other town eateries are cheaper and more *halal*. Most of them are in av Bourguiba, including the *Restaurant el Qods* and the *Restaurant du Grand Maghreb* more or less opposite the *Beauséjour*, and, further down, the cheap and grotty *Restaurant de la Jeunesse* at no. 74 and the *Restaurant des Chasseurs* across the street at no. 113. None of these is especially recommended, but none of them should cost you more than 2TD for a meal.

Moving on

All **buses** leave from the *autogare* on av 7 Novembre, off av Bourguiba at the bottom of the hill. *SNTRI* operate services to Tunis via Beja, Tabarca, Jendouba, Bizerte, Le Kef, and Beni M'tir and Fernana. The **louage** station is at the other end of town opposite the *Maison des Jeunes*. Most vehicles are Jendouba-bound, though you might be lucky and get one to Tabarca. Otherwise, it's hitch and pay, very much the normal way of getting to Tabarca. To get to Babouch, you might have to take a taxi.

Walks around Aïn Draham

Coming here in summer, it's almost a shock to find exercise suddenly a pleasure instead of a penance. There are two standard **walks**. One is to **Col des Ruines**, the ridge opposite the village, which you can either scramble up directly, or gain access to from a side road two kilometres down the main Tabarca road. The other is the hike to the summit of **Jebel Bir**, which offers great views, east over mountains shaved with firebreaks like a reverse Mohican hairdo, north to Tabarca in its plain and west over more mountains into Algeria (you can make out El Kala as a white smudge on the horizon). A dirt road to the summit runs from the Jendouba road near the *Hôtel Rihana*: the pylon at the top is easy to spot and home in on.

Looking over the mountains it's easy to see why the **Khroumir Berber tribespeople** who lived here were virtually independent of the Beys. They had a reputation for ferocity, regularly raiding the surrounding tribes and even crossing into Algeria to steal herds. But, despite their strength, they kept clear of the dynastic quarrels that embroiled – and destroyed – other tribes. When Mohammed Bey's disgruntled nephew fled here after an abortive coup in 1867, he was sent packing. Fourteen years later, however, the Bey's inability to stop their cross-border raiding provided the French with the excuse they needed to invade Tunisia.

Around the Khroumirie

East below the mountain-top lies the lake of the Beni M'tir dam, surrounded by forests. A detour south of Aïn Draham leads down here before rejoining the main road just before **FERNANA**, which took its name from the only tree for miles around (now vanished), which stood near this bleak settlement (weekly souk on Sundays).

The tree's singularity gave rise to a **legend** about its special powers. On their annual tax-collecting rounds the Bey's officials never dared penetrate further into the Khroumirie than here. The story goes that the Khroumiris would consult the tree about how little they could get away with declaring, and it would rustle its answer. According to one tale, it was the tree's error of judgement which caused the French invasion.

North from Aïn Draham the road winds along the edge of the great natural bowl which surrounds the Tabarca plain, the only settlement it passes through being **BABOUCH**. Like Aïn Draham, Babouch was a great hunting centre in colonial times, and the last lion and leopard were shot here, eighty and sixty years ago respectively. *Louages* run from here to HAMMAM BOURGUIBA, a thermal resort (souk day is Sunday) used by the ex-President. If **heading for Algeria**, you're unlikely to get a seat on the Tunis–Annaba bus by the time it reaches Babouch. Most people take a taxi to the

Tunisian border post, walk 10km to the Algerian post, get another taxi from there to EL KALA, and then a bus to ANNABA. It might be easier to hitch, but traffic is scarce.

The 3* *Hammam Bourguiba* (17.5TD/24TD low season, 18.5TD/26TD high, b&b) (☎47217) is in the village of the same name, where you can also take the thermal cure.

Cork forest birdlife

Aïn Draham and Babouch are surrounded by **cork oak woodland**, and almost any walk from either of them will lead you through the forests; the valley leading from Babouch towards Hammam Bourguiba is one especially beautiful and rewarding area. This is the only large deciduous forest in Tunisia and the wildlife is distinctive. You may notice how individual woodland birds, familiar from northern Europe, are developing differences that will, in a few thousand or tens of thousand years, lead them to be classed as separate species – evolution in progress. The blue tit here has a black head; the chaffinch is pale, without a red breast; the green woodpecker is greyish and lacks the red "moustache"; and the jay is quite different, with a red, black and white head.

THE MEDJERDA VALLEY

The **Medjerda valley** is the most fertile and best-watered region of Tunisia. In Roman times it supplied much of the grain that fed Rome, its perennial river, unique in Tunisia, allowing the fields to be irrigated and the grain transported. During the 1930s and 1950s the French improved irrigation by building numerous dams, so harnessing the winter floods for the summer. More recently their engineering feats were surpassed by the Chinese, who built a canal that takes water to Cap Bon without a single pumping station en route. Most of the towns are prosperous market centres, but the region's main attractions are its **Roman ruins**, most spectacularly those of Bulla Regia. Inevitably and enticingly, the valley forms a stark contrast to the coastal route: and it's straightforward enough to combine both, in a looping, wandering journey starting and ending in Tunis.

Medjez el Bab

MEDJEZ EL BAB was a seventeenth-century Andalusian foundation on the Roman site of Membressa, but little remains of either except for the mosque just back from the main square and a few miscellaneous fragments in the garden of the town hall. Today it's a main crossing point over the Medjerda, one of a number of small farming centres dotted along the main roads of northern Tunisia.

Buses and *louages* stop in a square just across the bridge, where there are also two **banks**. There are frequent **buses** to Tunis, Beja, Jendouba, Testour, Teboursouk and Le Kef and **louages** to Tunis, Testour and Beja. There's also a **train station** 2km out of town on the left bank of the river, with trains to Tunis, Beja, Jendouba, Ghardimaou, and Oued Zarga.

If you want to stay, the *Hôtel Membressa*, on the west bank of the river overlooking the bridge (☎60121) is a bit grimy but quite adequate at 3TD/6TD. The hotel also has a rather raucous bar and restaurant where a meal will cost you about 2.5TD.

The bridge and the cemetery

Built in the seventeenth century (a plaque in the middle dates it at 1088 AH: 1677 AD), the bridge is the only real reminder of that period, but only by chance did it survive the

WAR GRAVES

The Imperial War Grave Commission, subsequently renamed the Commonwealth Commission, was set up after World War I to arrange for the burial of Britain's war dead in specially designed cemeteries. Its general principle was to bury the dead near where they died, and wherever possible in the countryside. Timeless English Pastoral was the desired atmosphere, and it comes as a shock to find **little pieces of England**, with lawns and trees, in the middle of Tunisia. This pastoral ethos creates the right contrast between now and then: as you move along the seemingly endless rows of names, it's impossible, and yet imperative, to imagine the nightmare they represent. An unnamed grave means that the remains were not enough to identify the body, and headstones are grouped together when several remains were indistinguishable. The cemeteries are moving places, their ethos summed up best in the words of a World War II poet, Keith Douglas, stationed in Tunisia in 1943: "Remember me when I am dead / And simplify me when I'm dead."

The Commonwealth War Graves Commission maintains cemeteries at Medjez el Bab, Messicault (1km east of Borj el Amri on the GP5 Medjez–Tunis road, some 30km from Tunis), Ras Rajel (see p. 130), Oued Zarga (see below), Beja (see p.140), Thibar (see p.143), Enfida (see p.153) and Sfax (see p.193). Indian servicemen are buried at Sfax, Jews at Borgel Jewish cemetery in Tunis, and victims of World War I in Bizerte International Cemetery (see p.125).

American servicemen killed in action in Tunisia (and a number of Commonwealth soldiers) are buried at Carthage American Military Cemetery (see p.85).

bitter battles for Medjez in the winter of 1942–3. A **Commonwealth War Cemetery**, 4km west along the Kef road, bears eloquent and emotional witness to the 2904 Commonwealth soldiers killed here, and a visit either to this (perhaps the most accessible site) or any of the other cemeteries scattered around the country is an experience you don't quickly forget. Probably the best way of getting there would be by taxi from Medjez *louage* station (around 5TD return), or, if you're in a group, by coming to an agreement with a *louage* driver. A bus would drop you off, but then you'd have to get another one to pick you up afterwards.

Around Medjez

After the War Graves it's a good idea to clear your head by taking a taxi-truck or bus up the road to Toukabeur and Chaouach, two villages high on the mountain wall to the north, for a magnificent view over the surrounding country and an understanding of why Medjez was so strategic a point. **CHAOUACH**, at the end of the road, is built on the site of a Byzantine fort on a rocky outcrop, the fort itself assembled from the remains of Roman Sua just below. **TOUKABEUR**, 3km below Chaouach on the same road, has more scant remains – the garage on the main square is a converted Roman cistern.

Oued Zarga

From Medjez westwards, the road hugs the north side of the Medjerda valley. When the huge **Sidi Salem dam** was completed, the river had to be diverted, and the people of **OUED ZARGA** were entirely rehoused in smart new houses. The old village was the site of a notorious massacre, in September 1881, when the French station master and ten other European staff were burnt alive in a sudden uprising by the local people. A conflagration more devastating by far is commemorated at Oued Zarga's **Commonwealth War Cemetery**, 2km west of town.

Beja and Routes South

West of Oued Zarga, after you climb over a high ridge, **BEJA** comes into view, spread over the slopes of a mountain rather like Le Kef to the south. It's an important grain town and although there's little of outstanding interest, it's well worth stopping off here if you're passing through, especially on a Tuesday when the **weekly souk** is held. Heading **south from Beja** out of the Medjerda valley towards the Tell (Chapter Five), there are several route options for getting over the Monts de Teboursouk range.

Some history

Since Roman times Beja has held the biggest **grain market** in the north, and has paid the price with a torrid history of destruction and recovery. The first of these cycles began in 109 BC, when a Roman garrison was massacred by a population keen to show its support for the Numidian **King Jugurtha**. The only survivor of the disaster, one Turpilius, turned out to have made a grave error of judgement, because when his supreme commander Metellus arrived and punished the town by razing it to the ground, he had Turpilius flogged and executed. "A man who in such a calamity could prefer dishonourable survival to an untarnished name must have been a detestable wretch," the historian Sallust explained helpfully.

The town recovered, only to be levelled again by the Vandals in the fifth century, Abu Yazid in the tenth, and the Banu Hilal in the eleventh. By 1154, however, according to El Edrisi, it was a "beautiful city, built on a plain extremely fertile in corn and barley, so that there is not in all the Maghreb a city so important or richer in cereals." Beja's importance as a centre for grain continues to this day.

Practicalities

Beja's backbone is **Avenue Bourguiba**, which climbs from a level crossing at the bottom of the hill up to the town's main square, with the **colonial church** on the right and the **Medina** behind that. Opposite, the bulk of the **modern town** begins just down av de France in pl de l'Indépendance. Above the main square, av Bourguiba winds up and out of town as it becomes the main road to Jendouba.

The **PTT** (city hours) is on av Bourguiba, just above the old church. Behind the church is a **cinema** and, opposite that, the **night chemist**. Also on av Bourguiba, there's a couple of **banks**, including one opposite the church. The regional **hospital** (☎51431) is a few hundred metres further up av Bourguiba, leaving town on the left.

There is a market to the left of av Bourguiba, between the level crossing and the main square, and a *Magasin Général* **supermarket** next to that. Another supermarket, *Bonprix*, is in pl de l'Indépendance.

Around Town

The large colonial population left an indelible mark on Beja. There are some strange churches left in Tunisia, but the huge and extraordinary **church** on the central square (now a "Complexe Culturel") has to be one of the most bizarre, built in a confusion of dimly remembered European styles with local additions – the tower looks like a minaret. Beja's outrageous **colonial architecture** includes the lilac house by the *Hôtel Vaga* in av Bourguiba, and the building (now a row of shops) dated 1912 immediately behind the ex-church opposite the top of rue Habib el Meddeb.

At the bottom of rue Habib el Meddeb, a left along av M ben Kahla (by the railway) brings you to the **Commonwealth Cemetery**, unusual for its position next to a housing estate; on its far side is a typical colonial cemetery, full of dynastic Italian family tombs now smothered in dust and cobwebs.

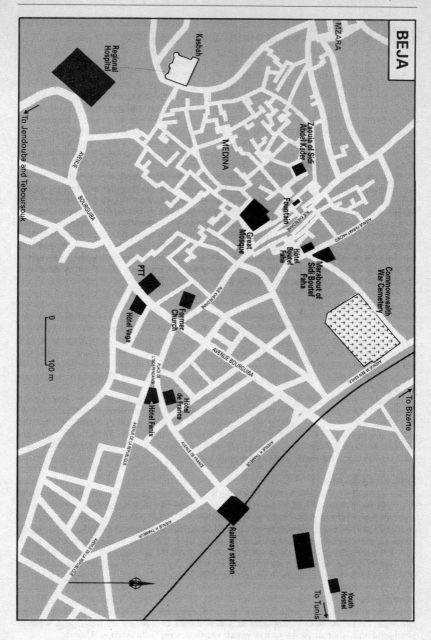

BEJA

MZARA

Kasbah

Regional
Hospital

Zaouia of Sidi
Abdel Kader

MEDINA

To Jendouba and Teboursouk

AVENUE

BOURGUIBA

Fountain

Great
Mosque

AVENUE HABIB MICHO

Hotel
Boutef
Faha

Marabout of
Sidi Boutef
Faha

Commonwealth
War Cemetery

PTT

RUE KHEREDINE

Hotel Vaga

Former
Church

RUE KHEREDINE

AVENUE BOURGUIBA

AVENUE M BEN KAHLA

0

100 m

PLACE DE
L'INDEPENDANCE

Hotel
de France

Hotel Fenix

AVENUE DE LA REPUBLIQUE

AVENUE DE FRANCE

AVENUE H. THAMEUR

To Bizerte

AVENUE DE LA REPUBLIQUE

AVENUE H. THAMEUR

Railway
station

To Tunis

Youth
Hostel

A walk in the Medina

Beja's **Medina**, run-down though it is, has survived largely intact. It is unusually full of mosques, as well as old fountains and busy market streets, and with the cool climate which seems to prevail here, it's one of the most pleasant to wander through in Tunisia.

Some 200m down **rue Kheredinne**, its main street, from behind the colonial church, **place Abdelkader** opens up on your left. Cross this square diagonally and take a left up rue Ali Bach Hamba to get to the front of the **Great Mosque**, Almohad in style, with an unusual red minaret. Rue de la Mosquée, behind it, emerges into a square as rue Blagui. Ahead, bearing right into pl Bab el Aïn, you pass a fountain on your left dated 1219 AH (1804 AD). To the left, in another square, the 1843 **Zaouia of Sidi Abdel Kader**, with its green tiled *koubba* dome, is now a kindergarten, but the people who work there (8am–5pm Mon–Sat as a rule) are welcoming and will almost certainly let you in to have a look.

Taking a right off pl Bab el Aïn, you're back on the main road at pl Khemais Bedda, the centre of the Medina. A couple of hundred metres further, rue Farhat Hached on the right sweeps round to give an impressive view of the countryside to the east, passing the **Marabout of Sidi Boutef Faha** on the left, to bring you back to the old church. Between rue Farhat Hached and rue Kheredinne is a **second-hand clothes market** where you can obtain all those ghastly 1970s fashions you missed the first time round.

Behind the Medina, the **Kasbah**, dominating the old town, was originally Byzantine, but what little remains is now occupied by the Army. The **Mzara** district, also above the old town, is said still to have one or two cave dwellings, but this is a very poor part of town and sightseers aren't especially welcome.

Accommodation

Officially, Beja only has two **hotels**. The 2* *Hôtel Vaga* on av Bourguiba, just above the main square, opposite the PTT (☎50818) at 8.5TD/14TD b&b, is friendly, with comfortable, pleasant rooms – if some rather bizarre decor. The unclassified *Hôtel Fenix*, at 8 av de la République just off pl de l'Indèpendance (☎50188), is adequate at 3TD per person. If no one is there, try the bar round the back, at 37 av de France. Note that the rooms at the end of the corridor on the right-hand side are rather dingy with little outside light.

In reality, a far better bet than either of these is the *Hôtel Boutef Faha*, opposite the marabout of the same name in rue Farhat Hached. At 3TD per person, rooms are basic but clean with a terrace, and you're right in the Medina. Other possibilities are the extremely grotty *Hôtel de France* in rue de France opposite the *Fenix*'s bar (3TD per person) and the *Maison des Jeunes* **youth hostel**, opposite the bus station (☎50621) – 4TD for the usual barracks-like accommodation.

Eating and drinking

As far as sustenance goes, you're not exactly spoiled for choice. There are a few cheap places in the Medina (the *Restaurant de la Victoire* at 31 rue Kheredinne, for example), and the restaurant of the *Hôtel Vaga* at around 7TD a head, but top recommendation, especially for their fish dishes, goes to the *Hôtel Fenix*'s restaurant (entrance in rue de France), where you'll get an excellent meal for 5TD. The only reservation here is that you enter through the *Fenix*'s rather raucous bar, which women may find intimidating. The bar itself is generally an all-male preserve but, if you qualify (or can handle it), one of the best places in Tunisia to knock back a few beers.

Moving on

From the **train station** (which, take note, does not have a left luggage office), trains run east to Tunis (either stopping at Oued Zarga or Medjez el Bab), and west to Jendouba and Ghardimaou – one of which continues right through to Algiers.

SRT Beja run the city's only **bus station**, also used by *SNTRI* and a few other regional companies.There are plenty of buses to Tunis and Medjez el Bab, and progressively fewer to Jendouba, Aïn Draham and Tabarca, Bizerte, Teboursouk via Thibar, Sousse and Siliana. **Louages** service Tunis, Medjez, Testour, Teboursouk, Thibar, Jendouba and Nefza (for connections to Sejenane).

Thibar and Trajan's Bridge

South of Beja, there are two routes down to TEBOURSOUK (see p.202). The tarmac road goes through the village of **Thibar**, with two buses daily, plus *louages* (on your way, look out at Borj Hamdoun, 12km before Thibar, for a farmstead that looks like a fort with an egg on top). A less commonly used route, unpaved, passes a **Roman bridge** attributed to the Emperor Trajan.

Thibar
THIBAR, 28km out of Beja on the main road to Teboursouk, is a pleasant little village with a farm set up by the "White Fathers" that's still very much in use. Thibarine liqueur and Thibar wine are made here and, if you're lucky, you may be able to visit the **wine cellars**. Behind the farm buildings, yet another **Commonwealth War Cemetery**, a small one this time, broods among trees full of birds.

There are some scant **Roman remains** south of the village, not really worth seeing but an excuse for a stroll. Head past the site of Thibar's **Sunday souk**, taking the right-hand fork in the road, sign-posted "Bou Salem". At the crossroads 1.5km further, turn right, again sign-posted. With vineyards on your left, then a peach orchard, you're now on an avenue of eucalyptus trees. After a kilometre or so, you pass a water-pumping station on your left and, 100m beyond, a path to the left takes you around a field and across an *oued*. The remains, such as they are, lie on the other side.

Trajan's Bridge
Those who feel strongly about Roman bridges will want to make the effort to reach **Trajan's Bridge**, 15km south of Beja over rough tracks (the C76 where it crosses the Oued Beja). Built to carry the main Carthage-Hippo Regius (Annaba) highway, this – with a well-preserved span of 70m – is the doyen of ancient bridges in Tunisia. It is even older than its name suggests as it was actually built a century before Trajan's reign. Unfortunately, public transport doesn't run here, so you'll probably have to get a taxi from Beja if you don't have your own wheels – and that means finding a taxi driver who's heard of the place.

Bulla Regia and other Western Sites

The impressive Roman site of **Bulla Regia** lies in the hills above the Medjerda valley, with the lesser remains of **Thuburnica** and **Chemtou** to the west. The nearby valley towns of Jendouba and Ghardimaou stand in disappointingly drab contrast. They do make ideal bases, however – and probably necessary transport hubs – if you're visiting the sites and are also the last stopping points in Tunisia if you're heading across the frontier into **Algeria**.

Jendouba

Important though it is, **JENDOUBA** is just about the least interesting town in the whole country. If you hit town on a Wednesday then at least you coincide with the **weekly souk**: otherwise, plan to move on quickly.

Arrival, accommodation and other practicalities

Travelling by bus or *louage*, you're likely to arrive at the main transport focus at pl 7 Novembre, to the west of the town centre (see below). If you're stuck out here, or want to find somewhere to stay immediately, right near the bus station is the 2* *Hôtel Smitthu* (☎31695), the best in town, with rooms at 16TD/24TD b&b.

Most of Jendouba's **hotels** can be found by taking rue Hedi Chaker off the roundabout at pl 7 Novembre towards the centre of town. About 100m down rue Hedi Chaker, in a little street on the left – bd Khemaïs el Hajera – the *Pension Saha en Noum* charges a mere 2TD per person. Continuing down rue Hedi Chaker, you come to pl des Martyrs, a monument to Jendoubans who died fighting the French for control of Bizerte in 1961 (see p.121), set in a small garden among Roman remains lifted from Bulla Regia. A left at this point down rue Taïeb Mehiri will take you to the town centre, with **PTT** (city hours, international call facilities), **banks** and the easily overlooked **train station**, tucked away in a corner by the police station, with daily departures to Beja and Tunis, Ghardimaou, and one across the border through to Algiers. If, from rue Hedi Chaker, you turn left just *after* pl des Martyrs, rue Ali Belhouane takes you past more banks, chemists (day and night), and the *louage* station for Tunis. A left at the end up rue 1 Juin leads to the *Hôtel Atlas* (☎30566), 9.9TD/13.8TD b&b (more for a room with bath), slightly cheaper and correspondingly less plush than the *Smitthu*.

Eating and passing the time

There are plenty of cheap **restaurants** in the town centre, and the *Smitthu* and *Atlas* hotels both do set menus (4TD and 5TD respectively). If your stay in town becomes prolonged, there's a flea market of sorts off pl 7 Novembre, at the end of bd Khemaïs el Hajera (the street with the *pension*) and a **cinema** 100m from pl 7 Novembre down the dual carriageway sign-posted "Le Gouvernorat".

Around Place 7 Novembre: moving on

The main focus for **bus and louage traffic** is pl 7 Novembre, a large roundabout on the western edge of town with two and a half Roman columns poised in its middle. On one side of this roundabout, by a level crossing, is the **louage** station for Aïn Draham and Tabarca (you can be dropped at the Bulla Regia crossroads for the site). On the other side are the *louage* stations for Le Kef, on the left, and Ghardimaou, on the right, and beyond them the **bus** station, with frequent departures for destinations to the north.

Bulla Regia

BULLA REGIA is one of the most extraordinary Roman sites to be seen anywhere in the world. Its distinctive feature, the **underground villas** built by wealthy inhabitants, have their modern parallel at Matmata (see p.269), but are unique in the Roman Empire. Equally important are the profusion of intact and beautiful mosaics left *in situ*, all too rare now that the museums have taken the best mosaics at other sites.

As with the troglodytes at Matmata, no one knows for certain why Bulla Regians went underground, but almost without doubt it was to escape the heat: by some geographical quirk, the plain surrounding Jendouba is one of the hottest areas north of Gafsa. This has always been an important region, though, and Bulla Regia played much the same market centre role as Jendouba does today. The *Regia* in its name refers to royal connections before the arrival of the Romans, when it was associated with one of the native Numidian kingdoms.

Access

The **site** itself (8am–6pm daily; 1TD plus 1TD to take photos) lies just north of Jendouba, 6km along the Aïn Draham road, then 2km, right, along a side road. A

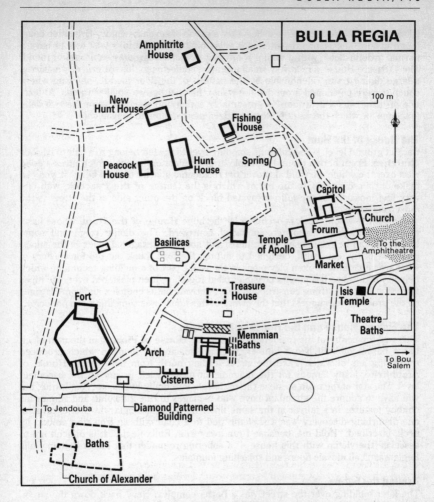

shared taxi from Jendouba to the site shouldn't cost more than 5TD from the flea market off pl 7 Novembre, or there are minibuses to the turn-off (*croisement*) for 0.4TD from the Aïn Draham *louage* station. Make it clear that it's just the *croisement* you want: if they think you want the site itself, they'll deny all knowledge and direct you to a taxi. From the crossroads, you have to walk the last 2km: take the opposite direction from the sign-posted route to Chemtou.

The Memmian Baths and Treasure House

The most prominent remains, the **Memmian Baths**, stand just by the entrance: their large central hall was a *frigidarium*. A Roman street leading past the entrance to the baths has been excavated, but instead take the track leading north; shortly on the left (keep your eyes peeled, some of these villas are easy to miss) is the first of the buried villas, the **Treasure House**, so called after a cache of seventh-century Byzantine coins found inside. The standard pattern for villas built in this curious way was to have a normal ground floor, with a dining room and perhaps bedrooms sunk underground. The Treasure House, a relatively small example, conforms to this pattern: downstairs is a large dining room (identifiable by the pattern of the floor mosaic, showing where couches were positioned around three walls), flanked by two smaller rooms. At least one of these was a bedroom, so presumably eating and sleeping were the two daily functions for which the wealthy Roman citizen most wanted to remain cool.

The House of the Hunt

Back at ground level, some columns standing over to the left belong to a pair of basilica **churches**. From here a mound is visible in the middle of the site, which gives a good view over the whole area and also over the residential quarter directly below it: you can make out a crossroads, to the left of which is the **House of the Peacock**, with one very fine mosaic. But the fully excavated block on the other side of the street is the most fascinating.

Almost the whole block is occupied by the huge **House of the Hunt**, whose basement even includes its own colonnaded courtyard. The dining room and some bedrooms can be recognised down here, and note the hexagonal holes in the superstructure of the courtyard, designed to lighten the load. Look out too for clusters of what are apparently broken clay pipes in the walls, part of a building technique which helped make these basements possible: piled together, then plastered over, the pipes formed a light but strong construction unit. A private baths complex and some latrines on the ground floor suggest that the owner of this house was something of a plutocrat.

The Fishing House and the House of Amphitrite

This was the centre of the residential quarter: the **House of Fishing** in the next block has a basement built like a bunker, with a semi-circular fountain which produced refreshing jets of water. Take the street leading north from here to the **House of Amphitrite**, justly famous for the magnificent mosaics left *in situ* on the basement level. The star of the main scene in the *triclinium* is actually Venus, not Amphitrite, but you have to admire the attendant Love who manages to ride a dolphin and admire his chubby features in a mirror at the same time. When Bulla Regia was first excavated, one disturbing discovery was a skeleton tied to a chair with an iron ring around its neck, inscribed: "Hold me, because I ran away from Bulla Regia." It is difficult not to associate the victim with this house – a sobering reminder that life in Roman Bulla Regia wasn't all mosaic floors and splashing fountains.

Around the Forum

The later building over the street was a **baths** complex. Head back down the street, then off left to the **spring** – as at SBEITLA (see p.221), the ancient source is still in use today. Beyond lies the administrative quarter of the town, the first open space being the **Forum**, flanked to the west by the Capitol, a true-blue Roman temple on a podium, and to the north by the temple of Apollo, in the African pattern of a courtyard with a small sanctuary opening off it. The best statues in Tunis's Bardo Museum were found here. A broad street leads south from the Forum, past the **market** on the right – an important facility in a town like this, its small shops around the sides could be locked up when not in use.

Continuing down the street, you pass another set of **baths** on the left, with an octagonal *frigidarium*, before reaching the back of the **theatre**. It's still possible to enter this by the original galleries, known graphically as *vomitoria*. The first three rows of seats, wider than the rest, were reserved for local dignitaries – who were separated from the proles behind by a solid railing. Bulla Regia's loose and immoral ways, focusing as ever on the theatre, were notorious. Saint Augustine preached a famous sermon here at the end of the fourth century, berating the citizens: he imagines them welcoming strangers to the town, "What have you come for? Theatrical folk? Women of easy virtue? You can find them all in Bulla."

The Temple of Isis

South of the theatre, blocked originally by the stage building, is a rectangular plaza. Making your way west from here, you pass the small podium of the **Temple of Isis**. Its remains are unremarkable, but the cult they served was a cosmopolitan one character-istic of the Roman Empire. Starting life as an Egyptian goddess, Isis was taken up as early as the first century BC by Romans searching for new deities to brighten up their spiritual lives. She brought unexpected problems, though: love poets are constantly complaining that their girlfriends deliberately tantalise them by pleading the purity which Isis's worship requires. Isis worship became heavily institutionalised, but always kept an air of mystery: in *The Golden Ass* (see p.364) it is Isis to whom Apuleius turns in his plea to be transformed back from a donkey to a man: "She is the shining deity by whose divine influence not only all beasts, wild and tame, but all inanimate things are invigorated; whose ebbs and flows control the rhythm of all bodies whatsoever, whether in the air, on earth, or below the sea."

Across the road

Beyond the temple you pass another open plaza on the way back to the site entrance. A jumble of ruins south of the modern road belongs to yet another set of **baths**, next to what is misleadingly called the **Church of Alexander**. An inscription from the Psalms was found over the door here ("May the Lord guard your coming in and your going out, now and for ever more, Amen."), and the trough-like stones (as at Kef, Haidra and Maktar) were probably connected with the distribution of food and commodities; 500m south of here is an area of pre-Roman **dolmens**.

Ghardimaou, Aïn Soltane and Thuburnica

GHARDIMAOU is a small border town – unglamorous but with a certain atmosphere about it. Its setting makes the place worthwhile: a misty river plain, overshadowed on three sides by mountains which pile up steeply towards Algeria. Trains run from here to **Souk Ahras** in Algeria, and thence (slowly) towards Algiers. If you intend to remain in Tunisia, however, the only real reason for coming here is to visit the minor Roman sites of **Thuburnica** and **Chemtou**, both set in fine hill locations.

In the mountainous **Forest of Feija**, a national park 20km northwest of Ghardimaou, there's a **youth hostel** at the village of **AÏN SOLTANE**, which is a good alternative to staying in Ghardimaou if you have time. You'll have to ask around for a lift to get there, and since it's very close to the border it's advisable to inform the Ghardimaou police or border officials of your intentions.

Ghardimaou and the border crossing

The **train station**, crawling with customs and immigration officials, is centrally placed. The **border** crossings, here and further north at Babouch, are the most heavily used in the country, and the most likely to remain open at times of tension. Be warned, though, that for 50km on the far side of the border, before the first Algerian town, Souk Ahras, the rugged countryside is more or less uninhabited. You hear stories of Algerian offi-cials offering lifts to hitchers, but it might be safer just to catch the daily Trans-Maghreb Express. (For visa requirements in Algeria, see "Onward" in *Contexts*.)

There's a single hotel in Ghardimaou, should you want to stay – the *Thuburnic* (7TD/9TD b&b), overlooking the station (☎45043). Some social life just about succeeds in happening in its bar and restaurant but, as a depressed resident admitted, "there's no *ambiance* in Ghardimaou."

When you're ready to leave, the **bus ticket office** is along av Bourguiba from the main square and **louages** to Jendouba depart from along the main road in the Jendouba direction.

Thuburnica

A good immersion in the district's **scenery** comes with a visit to the Roman site of **THUBURNICA** on the north side of the river plain; taxi-trucks leave regularly from the turning (across the bridge towards Algeria). The remains are an excuse for the journey, but there's a memorable little **bridge** carrying the track over one of the deep stream beds which hurries out of the foothills. The bridge's Roman builders are nearly two thousand years gone, but it still looks as if it might have been put up twenty years ago. The rest of the ancient town is scattered in smallish fragments over the hill to the west – a very fortress-like site of a Byzantine castle stands on top, and a fine two-storeyed **mausoleum** about halfway up.

Chemtou

The other Roman site in this region is **CHEMTOU** (free access), accessible at the end of the same track as Thuburnica, but more easily reached via a *louage* to OUED MELIZ (13km towards Jendouba). From there it's 1km further along the main road to a bridge, then left for 3km along a track sign-posted "*Groupement Interprofessionnel d'agrumes*". Chemtou can also be reached from the Bulla Regia turn-off on the Aïn Draham–Jendouba road, but it isn't within walking distance along that route.

Chemtou's marble

This apparently unremarkable corner of North Africa was once famous throughout the classical world as the source of "Numidian marble", a lurid red and yellow variety much in vogue with Imperial Roman builders. It came to be so closely identified with extravagance and luxury that when the poet Horace wanted to show how humble his lifestyle was, he wrote, "No beams of Athenian stone rest in *my* house on columns quarried in furthest Africa."

The quarries were first exploited in the second century BC, when the Numidian King Massinissa marked his newly won control over this area by building a massive **altar** (recently reconstructed) on top of the hill. Its magnificent decoration is kept in the excavation house, but you can see the ancient steps which were hacked in the living rock leading up to the altar: there's something powerful about this arcane high place of worship, which the civic dignity of official Roman religion came to lack.

The newly victorious Romans soon fell in love with the marble: it was first imported to Rome in 78 BC, and the industry supported a sizeable town – though little of it has been excavated.

The bridge and quarries

The huge **bridge**, whose massive remains in the river bed look like a giant's building blocks, carried the main Sicca–Thabraca (Le Kef–Tabarca) road along which much of the stone was hauled. Among the tangled ruins on the far bank, excavators found a unique feature: three parallel grooves in one large segment forced the flowing water to drive turbines, perhaps for grinding grain. The only other sizeable monument is the **theatre**, on the far side of the town's administrative quarter; the residential district lay beyond, around the corner of the slope.

The **quarries** are in the saddle in the middle of the hill – just gaping holes in the rock now, but their emptiness seems to preserve an indefinable memory of the skill and sheer hard work of so many men over so many years. The Romans had the industry highly organised: every block cut was stamped with the names of the Emperor, the Consul in office, and the local official, and with a production number, so that it wouldn't go missing or just fall off the back of a cart. The effort involved in transporting the stone from here in "furthest Africa" to its destination on the other side of the Mediterranean was enormous – it was either dragged all the way over the Khroumirie to be shipped from Tabarca, or floated down the Medjerda to Utica – but of course anything which added to the cost only enhanced its value as a status symbol. The Emperor Hadrian, a great devotee, once presented a hundred columns to Athens and twenty to Smyrna as marks of imperial favour. A number of remaining miscellaneous blocks graphically illustrate the Romans' **odd sense of colour**, a taste later shared in turn by the Byzantines and a nineteenth-century operation which revived the workings (and left the shell of a church on the hill). If you share this taste too, small carvings in Chemtou marble are sold as souvenirs.

Other remains

Below the northern slope of the hill is a broad area of remains, originally a first-century AD military camp but taken over and adapted by some sharp Roman entrepreneur into an on-site **factory** for the products of the quarries. Raw stone was delivered to the southern entrance of the camp and then passed along a primitive production line of workshops, ending up with the polishers. The finished articles – utensils, small statues – were despatched all over the Empire. It's well worth visiting the **Excavation House** of the joint Tunisian-German archaeological team, a farmhouse-like building south of the hill, for a glimpse of mosaics and reliefs found on the site.

Behind the site, there are several hundred metres of Roman aqueduct, too.

travel details

Trains

Two railway lines run through this region. There is no passenger service at present to Tabarca.

FROM BIZERTE TO:
Tunis (4 each day, 1hr 35min), via **Tinja** (20min, connecting for **Menzel Bourguiba**, 30min) and **Mateur** (35min).

FROM BEJA TO:
Tunis (6 daily, 1hr 50min) of which 3 call at **Oued Zarga** (20min) and 4 at **Medjez el Bab** (50min); **Jendouba** (5 daily, 55min) and **Ghardimaou** (5 daily, 1hr 10min) of which 1 continues to **Algiers** (18hr) via **Souk Ahras**, **Annaba** and **Constantine**.

Buses

There are three SRTs based in the region, at Bizerte, Beja and Jendouba, making these the main centres for bus transport. SRT Bizerte and SRT Beja both operate to Tunis (Bab Saadoun).

FROM BIZERTE TO:
Raf Raf (1 direct each day); **Ras Jebel** (frequent, 1hr, change for **Raf Raf**); **Ghar el Melkh** (2 daily, 1hr); **Tabarca** (1, early am, 4hr) and **Aïn Draham** (1, early am, 5hr); **Tunis** (frequent, 2hr); **Menzel Bourguiba** (8, 45min); **Beja** (2, 2hr); **Jendouba** (2, 3hr 30min, with *SRTJ*); **Le Kef** (1, 3hr); **Houmt Souk/Jerba** (2, with *SNTRI*, at 6am and 6pm, am via **Tunis** and **Kairouan**, pm via **Tunis**, **Sousse** and **Sfax**).

FROM RAS JEBEL TO:
Raf Raf (frequent, 30min); **Ghar el Melkh** (6, 45min); **Tunis** (5, 2hr).

FROM TABARCA TO:
Tunis via **Sejenane** and **Mateur** (5 daily, 3hr 45min, *SNTRI*, all before 4pm); **Tunis** via **Beja** (3, *SNTRI*, all before 4pm, more in summer); **Jendouba** (4, 2hr) and **Le Kef** (1, 3hr, early am, *SRT Jendouba*); **Bizerte** (1, early am, 4hr, *SRT Jendouba*); **Aïn Draham** (5, more in summer, 1hr); **Beja** (2, *SRT Beja*).

FROM AÏN DRAHAM TO:
Tunis (4 daily, 5hr, via **Beja**, *SNTRI*); **Tabarca** (4, 1hr); **Jendouba** (3, 1hr); **Bizerte** (1, 5hr); **Le Kef** (1, early am, 2hr); **Beni M'tir** and **Fernana** (1, noon); **Hammam Bourguiba** (2, 30min); **Annaba (Algeria)** (2, 4hr).

FROM MEDJEZ EL BAB TO:
Tunis (frequent, 1hr); **Beja** (frequent, 1hr); **Le Kef** (frequent, 2hr); **Jendouba**, **Testour**, and **Teboursouk** (all frequent).

FROM BEJA TO:
Tunis via **Medjez el Bab** (frequent, 2hr); **Jendouba** (10, 1hr); **Aïn Draham** (4, 3hr); **Tabarca**, (6, 1hr 30min); **Bizerte** (4, 2hr); **Teboursouk** via **Thibar** (2, 1hr); **Sousse** (1, 4hr 30min); **Siliana** (1, 3hr).

FROM JENDOUBA TO:
Tunis (10, 4hr); **Ghardimaou** (4, 1hr); **Aïn Draham** (3, 1hr, of which 1 continues to **Tabarca**); **Bizerte** (1, early am); **Le Kef** (6, 1hr 10min); **Beja** (8, 1hr 30min).

Louages
TO TUNIS DIRECT FROM:
Bizerte; **Beja**; **Jendouba**; **Medjez el Bab**; **Mateur**; **Menzel Bourguiba**; **Ras Jebel** and (in summer) **Raf Raf**.

LOUAGE ROUTES ACROSS THE REGION:
Bizerte–Mateur–Sejenane/Beja–Nefza–Tabarca–Aïn Draham/Jendouba.
Bizerte–Mateur–Beja–Jendouba–Ghardimaou–Aïn Draham/Tabarca.
Tabarca–Jendouba (occasionally Aïn Draham).
Aïn Draham–Jendouba (occasionally Tabarca).
Medjez el Bab–Tunis, **Testour**, and **Beja**.
Beja–Tunis, **Testour**, **Teboursouk** and **Thibar**
Beja–Medjez, **Jendouba** and **Nefza** (for connections to **Sejenane**).

LOCAL SERVICES:
Bizerte–Menzel Bourguiba and Raf Raf.
Beja –Thibar and Medjez el Bab.
Beja–Testour and Teboursouk.
Medjez el Bab–Testour.
Jendouba–Le Kef.

PHONE CODES

Two codes cover the region: The coastal region, northeast of the Tunis–Sejenane road, including Bizerte, is ☎02. The rest of the region, including Medjez el Bab, Beja Tabarca, Aïn Draham, Jendouba and Ghardimaou, is ☎08.

CHAPTER FOUR

KAIROUAN AND THE SAHEL

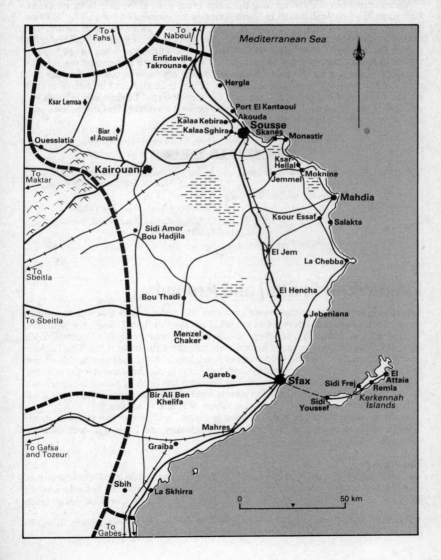

Mediterranean Sea

To Fahs

To Nabeul

Enfidaville
Takrouna

Hergla

Ksar Lemsa

Port El Kantaoui
Akouda

Kalaa Kebira
Kalaa Sghira

Biar
el Aouani

Sousse
Skanes

Monastir

Ouesslatia

Ksar
Hellal

Moknine

Jemmel

To
Maktar

Kairouan

Mahdia

Ksour Essaf

Salakta

Sidi Amor
Bou Hadjila

El Jem

La Chebba

To
Sbeitla

Bou Thadi

El Hencha

Jebeniana

To Sbeitla

Menzel
Chaker

Agareb

Sfax

Sidi Frej

El
Attaia
Remla

Bir Ali Ben
Khelifa

Sidi
Youssef

*Kerkennah
Islands*

Mahres

To Gafsa
and Tozeur

Graïba

Sbih

La Skhirra

0   50 km

To
Gabès

Kairouan – the Holy City – is only the most obvious attraction in **the Sahel***, an area that is central in every way to Tunisia. Ranging back from the east coast these fertile plains have long been the heartland of the country's agriculture, and a focus during each shift of power. The Romans planted millions of olive trees throughout the region and, under Arab rule, it was the base of the great Aghlabid dynasty which, from the port of Sousse, launched a successful invasion of Sicily in the ninth century.

Monuments from this and ensuing dynasties grace most of the Sahel's larger towns. **Kairouan**, the first Arab capital in North Africa, is pre-eminent – above all for its Great Mosque, justly Tunisia's most famous building as well as its spiritual centre. But **Sousse**, **Sfax**, **Monastir** and **Mahdia** are each highly rewarding for their architecture, and **El Jem** shelters what is arguably the Roman world's finest surviving amphitheatre.

Add to this an impressive series of beaches and it's easy to understand the region's popularity – and why the **Sousse–Monastir coast** is gradually becoming the country's most highly developed for tourism. However, this in itself shouldn't be reason to rush further afield. At **Mahdia** and still more on the near-deserted **Kerkennah Islands** you can find virtual isolation. Most independent travellers invariably find themselves staying for longer than originally planned.

MARKET DAYS

Monday – Kairouan, La Chebba, El Jem, Mahres, El Alia, Msaken

Tuesday – Ksar Hellal, Bir Ali Ben Khelifa, Remla (Kerkennah)

Wednesday – Moknine, Menzel Chaker, Agareb

Thursday – Ksiba el Mediouni, Sidi el Hani, Bou Thadi, Sbih

Friday – Mahdia, Sfax, Ouesslatia, Ej Jemaa, Jebiniana, Jemmel, Ksour Essaf, La Skhirra

Saturday – Monastir, El Hencha

Sunday – Enfida, Ksar Hellal, Sousse, Graïba

Enfida (Enfidaville) and Around

ENFIDA is the administrative centre for a vast and fertile **estate** that was an indirect cause of French colonial intervention in 1881. The estate's original owner, the reforming Turkish official Khaireddin, put it up for sale when he was recalled to Constantinople, and the Franco-African Company immediately submitted the highest bid. The Tunisian government tried to keep the estate out of French hands, but the attempt backfired, and helped to convince the French that the time had come to take full control in the country.

The estate is still heavily cultivated, but the town has been bypassed by the coastal road to Sousse, and its characterless streets would hardly be worth a visit were it not for a small museum and the breathtaking village of TAKROUNA nearby.

Leaving town, there are regular buses to Sousse and one or two to Hammamet/ Nabeul, while *louages* run to Sousse, Nabeul, Zaghouan, and Tunis. The train station is some way out of town.

The museum

The **museum**, in the old French church on the main street, has a collection of mosaic epitaphs and tombstones which vividly illustrate the mix of cultures and values prevalent here in ancient times – Berber, Carthaginian, Roman and Christian. Many tomb-

* The name "Sahel" means coast or margin and, in the case of the sub-Saharan Sahel, the edge of the desert; in Arabic, the word does not connote drought or famine.

stones are dedicated to priests of Saturn, a Roman transplant of the Carthaginian god Baal; hence the un-Roman symbols such as crescent moons. When Christianity came, the Berbers adapted once again, and names in the epitaphs like Filocalus, Gududa, Jades and Vernacla show that local people as well as overlords took to the new religion.

The war cemeteries
During World War II heavy fighting took place around Enfida in the final weeks of the Tunisian campaign as the retreating Germans attempted to hold a line here against the Eighth Army. The two **cemeteries** are a melancholy reminder of this: a Commonwealth one on the western edge of town (follow signs for Zaghouan) and, 3km further on, below the looming presence of Takrouna's rocky outcrop, one for the French forces. They stand interesting comparison – the French one is positively austere and militaristic, with a helmet placed on each grave, while the Commonwealth cemetery is green and rustic, just too neat to be an English churchyard.

Takrouna
The victims in these cemeteries died fighting for **TAKROUNA**, a Berber village perched high on a rock, whose inaccessibility had long made it a natural defensive position. The final Allied assault on it was made by thirteen New Zealanders, most of them Maoris. The dramatic site, crowned by a green-domed marabout, and the even more mind-blowing view – from the sinister gleaming blade of Jebel Zaghouan behind to the broad sweep of the coastline – have placed Takrouna firmly on the tourist map, and coachloads are rushed in and out along a specially built road. The Berbers have always cherished their independence, and this site is a typical one. Unfortunately, Takrouna's exploitation has led, naturally, to the villagers exploiting tourists, and today their friendliness comes at a price. The road which goes past Takrouna continues to ZAGHOUAN through some lovely remote heathland.

Sousse and Around

SOUSSE seems to have everything going for it: a historic **Medina** containing two of Tunisia's most distinctively beautiful monuments, an excellent **museum** second only to the Bardo, and endless stretches of white **beach**. Little wonder it has become Tunisia's most obvious resort: there's a brash, somewhat superficial feel about the place – but also the best nightlife in the country, good swimming, cultural events and plentiful places to stay.

A little history
Thanks to its natural harbour and central position on the fertile eastern seaboard, Sousse has been important to every civilisation occupying this stretch of North African coast, each remodelling it in their own image: Roman **Hadrumetum**, Vandal **Hunericopolis**, and Byzantine **Justinianopolis**. Even when the all-conquering Oqba Ibn Nafi, leader of the Arab invaders (see p.324), destroyed the town in the seventh century, it wasn't long before Susa – the Arabic name still most commonly used – revived. It was the main outlet to the Mediterranean for the Aghlabids ruling in Kairouan and they launched their invasion of Sicily from here in 827. It was later occupied by the **Normans**, in the twelfth century, and **Spaniards** in the sixteenth, and was bombarded in turn by the French and Venetians in the eighteenth century. By the end of the nineteenth century the resilient town was becoming increasingly important to the French colonists. Since then Sousse's growth has been impeded only by World War II and it's now the third largest city in the country, with textiles industries balancing its unpredictable earnings from tourism.

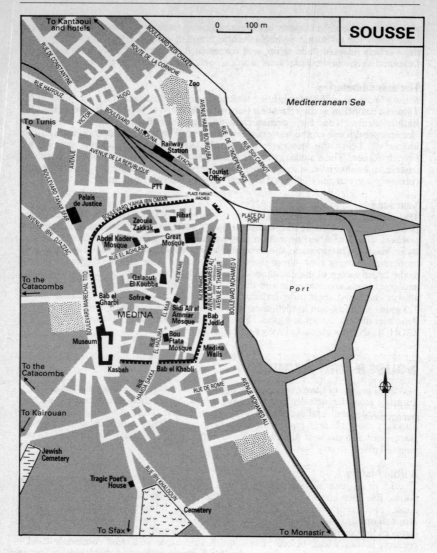

0   100 m

SOUSSE

To Kantaoui
and hotels

BOULEVARD HEDI CHAKER

ROUTE DE LA CORNICHE

RUE DE CONSTANTINE

RUE HAFFOUZ

HUGO

VICTOR

BOULEVARD HASOUNA

Zoo

AVENUE HABIB BOURGUIBA

RUE DE L'INDEPENDANCE

RUE SIDI CARNOT

Mediterranean Sea

To Tunis

AVENUE DE LA REPUBLIQUE

AVENUE

Railway
Station

AYACHI

Tourist
Office

BOULEVARD TAHAR SFAR

PTT

PLACE FARHAT
HACHED

PLACE DU
PORT

Palais
de Justice

BOULEVARD YAHIA IBN OMAR

AVENUE IBN DJAZZAC

Ribat

Zaouia
Zakkak

Abdel Kader
Mosque

Great
Mosque

RUE EL AGHLABA

Port

To the
Catacombs

Qalaout
El Koubba

RUE DE PARIS

AVENUE MOHAMED ALI

AVENUE H. THAMEUR

AVENUE MOHAMED V

Bab el
Gharbi

BOULEVARD MARECHAL TITO

Sofra

MEDINA

RUE DE FRANCE

Sidi Ali el
Ammar
Mosque

EL MAR

Bab
Jedid

Museum

Bou
Ftata
Mosque

RUE EL HADURA

Medina
Walls

To the
Catacombs

Kasbah

Bab el Khabli

RUE HAMDA SAKKA

RUE DE ROME

AVENUE MOHAMED ALI

To Kairouan

Jewish
Cemetery

Tragic Poet's
House

RUE IBN KHALDOUN

Cemetery

To Sfax

To Monastir

Practicalities – Orientation and Staying

The hub of the city is **Place Farhat Hached**, a huge "square" – if it can be called that – which becomes, on its outer fringes, variously pl des Martyrs, pl Sidi Yahia and pl du Port. Here all traffic and activity seem to converge; even the main railway line runs straight across it. To the north is the **new town** (almost entirely rebuilt since the war), and south the **Medina**. The port is so close that it's unsettling at night to see a large ship, all lit up, apparently being towed across the Place – a surreal image heightened when the train to Sfax edges its way through in front. The inevitable **Avenue Bourguiba** leads from here up to the beginning of the **corniche**, from which the **beach** stretches northwards all the way to **Port el Kantaoui**.

Accommodation

Most of the **cheaper places** are situated within the Medina. Options in the **ville nouvelle** tend to be classier. **Beach hotels** begin at the end of av Bourguiba: gleaming white monsters with none of Hammamet's discretion, they go on for miles. Almost all of them offer full board and an in-house disco, so you don't actually *need* to go into town at all.

There is also a **campsite** at CHOTT MARIAM, 18km north of Sousse, although this doesn't have official sanction and is more or less in the middle of nowhere. Camping isn't quite part of the Sousse image; it's strictly forbidden on most of the beach – though they may allow you to camp at the *Maison des Jeunes*.

MEDINA HOTELS

Hôtel Amira, 52 rue de France (☎26325). Clean and friendly, rooms with bath and balcony. Great views from roof terrace. 1* 8TD/10TD low season, 12.5TD/15TD high, b&b.

Hôtel Zouhour, 48 rue de Paris (☎28729). Smelly loos and hideous nylon sheets, but great staff. 5TD per room.

Hôtel des Perles, 71 rue de Paris (☎26609). Rather grubby. Ask for a room with a window. 3TD/6TD, shower 0.3TD.

Hôtel Gabes, 8 rue de Paris. A small place at the southern end of the Medina which doubles as a gay pick-up joint. 10TD/6TD.

Hôtel Medina, by the Great Mosque (☎21722). Pleasantly posher than the other hotels in the Medina but becoming a bit package orientated. 1* 8TD/12TD low, 11TD/16TD high, b&b.

Hôtel Ahla, opposite the Great Mosque (☎20570). Not amazingly clean, but looks onto the Mosque and the Ribat. 6TD/11TD.

Hôtel de Tunis, rue de l'Eglise. Near the back of the Ribat. Cheap but not exactly deluxe, nor recommended for women travelling alone. 3TD/4TD, or 2TD per person in dorm.

Hôtel de Paris, 15 rue du Rempart Nord (☎20564). Nice rooms, beautiful terrace, friendly management. 6TD/12TD, or 4TD on roof.

Residence Fatma, rue de Grèce (☎22198). A popular *pension* in the Medina, closed "for repairs" but may reopen.

HOTELS IN THE VILLE NOUVELLE

Claridge Hôtel, 10 av Bourguiba, just off pl Farhat Hached (☎24759). An old favourite, and city landmark, with central heating, shower or bath (but not loo) in every room. 1* 8.5TD/12TD low, 13TD/19TD high, b&b.

Hôtel du Parc, rue de Carthage (☎20434). Very comfortable with friendly young staff. 1* 8TD/12TD low, 10.5TD/17TD high, b&b.

Hôtel Mabrouka, 14 rue d'Italie (☎25883). On the corner of rue d'Alger. Not exactly welcoming. 7.5TD/10TD low, 9TD/13TD high, b&b.

Hôtel Hadrumète Palace, pl Farhat Hached (☎26292). Rooms not huge but clean and bright. 4th-floor rooms have balcony, some with a view of the port and square. 2* 8.5TD/13TD low, 15.5TD/25TD high, b&b.

Hôtel Linda, 5 rue Amilcar (☎27760). Near the "zoo". Spotless with en suite bathrooms and welcoming smiles. 14TD/10TD low, 26TD/17TD high, b&b.

Residence Massouada, 22 av Victor Hugo (☎22177). Clean, pleasant, friendly and quiet. 6TD/8TD low, 9TD/13TD high.

SEASIDE PACKAGE HOTELS – AND THE YOUTH HOSTEL

Hôtel Justinia, (☎26866), 3* 12.5TD/18TD low, 20TD/32TD high, b&b; **Hôtel Nour Justinia**, (☎26381), 3* 15.5TD/23TD low, 22.5TD/36TD high, b&b. The nearest beach hotels to the centre, and not at all bad.

Hôtel el Hana Beach, (☎26900), 3*19TD/26TD low, 30TD/49TD high, b&b; **Hôtel el Hana**, (☎25818), 4* 24TD/35TD low, 36TD/57TD high, b&b; **Hôtel Chems el Hana**, (☎28190), 4* 25TD/37TD low, 38TD/59TD high, b&b. About 2km from town, this threesome is the main focus of tourist beach action.

Youth Hostel/Maison des Jeunes, bd Taïeb Mehiri (☎27548). Situated roughly opposite the end of bd Mongi Slim near the *El Hanas* – almost certain to be full in summer. 4TD per person.

Hôtel Kaiser, av Taïeb Mehiri(☎28030). Opposite the *Maison des Jeunes*. Not too pricey, though not right on the beach. 2* 10.8TD/13.6TD low, 15.8TD/23.6TD high, b&b.

Hôtel Marabout, some 3km out of town (☎26245). Small, family-run and very friendly. 3* 19TD/26TD low, 28TD/44TD high, b&b.

Hôtel Salem, about 4km from town (☎41966). Good service and the usual amenities. 2* 15TD/25TD low, 23TD/36TD high, b&b.

Eating and drinking

Sousse has plenty of eateries appealing to both tourists and Soussis. The former provide European cooking and an ambience suited to their clientele: you'll find a number of places on the edge of pl Farhat Hached between the port and av Bourguiba, of which the *Restaurant Malouf* is probably the best, although the *Restaurant de Bonheur* is cheaper at 9–11TD a head. The Soussi-favoured haunts have much less in the way of finesse but the food is just as palatable, and the prices a lot more so.

CHEAP AND MODERATE RESTAURANTS

Restaurant Populaire, a very decent *gargote* on pl J ben Cherifa near the Great Mosque. The sign over the door is in Arabic only. Under 2TD a meal.

Restaurant National, start of rue el Aghlaba, near the Great Mosque. Around 2TD a head.

Restaurant Sidi Yahia, pl des Martyrs. Prime location, yet less than a dinar to fill you up.

Restaurant el Ferdaws, rue Braunschweig. Good food and good value at 2–3TD per head. Near the *Claridge Hôtel*.

Restaurant des Peuples, rue du Rempart Nord, next to the *Hôtel de Paris*. Inexpensive (around 2TD) and good.

Restaurant de la Jeunesse, rue Ali Bach Hamba. More mid-range, around 5TD per head.

Finally, a **cheap nameless restaurant**, av Victor Hugo near the corner of av de la République. 1–2TD but out of most things by the afternoon.

MORE UPMARKET RESTAURANTS

Le Lido, av Mohammed V. Lovely fresh fish at around 6TD a go.

Les Sportifs Restaurant, av Bourguiba. Better than most and around 10–12TD a head.

Restaurant le Khalife, 23 av Bourguiba, opposite the *Sportifs*, but cheaper and better value. The couscous is particularly recommended.

JUICE, SNACKS, PATISSERIE

Juice Bar, rue Braunschweig by the *Claridge Hôtel*. The best place in town for real fruit juice: compare their prices to all the tourist traps. Unfortunately, they only have what's in season – and sugar is always added liberally – but they also offer superb chocolate cakes....

Patisserie Cherif, av Bourguiba near the *Palace* cinema. Perhaps the best pastry shop in town, with equally delicious ice creams.

After sunset

Av Bourguiba provides a forum where people converge in the **evenings** to eat, drink, meet or simply stroll along the corniche. The *Topkapi* and *Atlantic* night clubs, opposite the *Claridge Hôtel,* are aimed at any foreigners who wander into town from their hotels. Most of the beach hotels run **discos**, though fairly tame ones. One place that does come highly recommended is *La Grotte*, a club well up the beach by the *Hôtel Tour Khalef.* Popular with Tunisians, it features Western and Arabic music, candle-lit tables and interesting variety acts.

The Medina

The monuments in the walled **Medina** testify to the city's long-lasting importance; in particular the Ribat and the Khalef Tower indicate Sousse's strategic importance, especially to the Aghlabids. You might expect the old city in a resort like Sousse to have lost all charm and character in a deluge of tacky souvenir shops. But while there are plenty of these, with a ready spiel for eager punters, and often abuse for less eager ones, the Medina, like the rest of town, wears its touristic status well, and maintains its individuality. There have been one or two cases of bag-snatching in the shopping areas of the Medina; you're advised to keep your eyes open and not dangle valuables temptingly about the place.

The Ribat

The **Ribat** at the Medina's northeastern corner (April–Sept, Tues–Sun, 9am–noon, 3–6.30pm; Oct–March, Tues–Sun, 9am–noon, 2–5.30pm; closed Mon, 0.8TD plus 1TD to take photos) was begun by the Aghlabids in 821.

It's a well-preserved example of a style peculiar to this period of North African history, when the Muslim inhabitants were under constant threat from marauding Christians based in Sicily. The word *ribat* is related to *marabout*, and the buildings served a religious as well as a military purpose, housing devout warrior troops broadly comparable to the crusading Christian orders such as the Knights Templar. When necessary, the men would fight – at times of peace they lived and studied in the bare cells around the Ribat's inner courtyard: the simplicity of the fort's form reflects the men's dedication to their second role. The only large communal room is the **prayer hall** over the entrance. Until superseded by the Khalef Tower at the opposite corner of the Medina, the Ribat's **tower** served as a look-out point and also to pass on beacon messages: towers could send a message from Alexandria in Egypt to Ceuta in Morocco in a single night. Although the Ribat was primarily defensive, only six years after it was begun the Aghlabids were strong enough to launch their successful invasion of Sicily. The defensive aspect remained important, however, against both Christians at sea and the Berbers inland – hence the thickness of the Medina walls on the western, inland side.

The Great Mosque

Opposite the Ribat stands the **Great Mosque**, Sousse's other great, early Islamic monument (open daily 9am–1pm, 0.3TD; dress with respect for the congregation and avoid prayer times). Although founded in the ninth century like the great mosques of Kairouan, Tunis and Sfax, this has a sparer quality, perhaps because it has received fewer later additions: the original conception of uncomplicated forms remains on view, giving added emphasis to the minimal decoration of the inscription around the wall of the courtyard. The little domed kiosk at one corner was added in the eleventh century to act as a minaret; its wide staircase is a feature more commonly seen further east.

Zaouia Zakkak and Kalaout el Koubba

Down a side street near the Ribat you should be able to see a curious open minaret, like stone crochet-work, which belongs to the **Zaouia Zakkak** – Turkish built, as the octagonal shape reveals. Nearby, rue el Aghlaba climbs to leave the Medina at Bab el Finga, passing en route the 1852 **Abdel Kader Mosque** opposite no. 29 and, a little further, the square, stone Tower of Sidi Ameur, like a minaret without a mosque. Moving on to rue d'Angleterre, parallel to the other main street, rue de Paris, head past the tourist stalls to an area of covered souks. Turn right here on rue Souk el Rba, and almost immediately on the right is the **Kalaout el Koubba**. No one really knows the original function of this building, though its features suggest it's eleventh-century Fatimid. It was once definitely a *foundouk*, later a café, now a council-run "cultural" exhibition gallery.

South of Souk el Rba

Souk el Rba leads directly out of the western wall of the Medina, with the museum away to the left. Alternatively, follow rue d'Angleterre on to where it joins rue de Paris in front of a hammam to become rue el Maar. Just beyond, on the left at no. 3, you can make out the delicately carved facade of the **Sidi Ali el Ammar Mosque**, another remnant of the Fatimid period though no longer in use. A turning to the right opposite the hammam entrance leads to a blank and impenetrable wall which surrounds the **Sofra**, an early Islamic cistern complex. Near the end of rue el Maar you pass a small, austere mosque on the left, named after one **Bou Fatata** and built, around 840, in a style that's in marked contrast to the incipient elaboration of the Fatimid buildings. From **Bab el Khabli**, gate of the southern wall of the Medina at the end of rue el Maar, it's a short climb up a windswept promenade to the museum in the kasbah.

The Kasbah and museum

The former **Kasbah** which houses Sousse's museum grew up around the **Khalef Tower**, built here in 859 at the highest point in the city to improve on the view given by the Ribat tower, put up thirty years earlier.

The **museum** (April–Sept, Tues–Sun, 9am–noon and 3–6.30pm; Oct–March, Tues–Sun, 9am–noon and 2–5.30pm; closed Mon; 1TD plus 1TD to take photos) is excellent: its exhibits – predominantly mosaics – are of consistently high quality, and unlike those of the Bardo don't threaten to overwhelm by sheer quantity. Many were found in the region's Christian catacombs and, distinguishable by their standard XP symbol, bear familial and domestic epitaphs. One long message reads:

> *"This was Eusebia, brothers, a rare and most chaste wife who spent with me a life of marriage, as time tells: sixty years, eight months and twenty days. God himself was pleased with her life, as I say. Truly a gentle wife of the rarest sort: I, Sextus Successus, lawyer, her husband, beg that you always remember her in your prayers, brothers."*

The earlier, more extroverted Imperial mosaics include some of the most stunning in the country. Don't on any account leave without seeing **Room 11**, across the courtyard, which contains an extraordinarily powerful group of amphitheatre scenes – almost all of them found in one villa.

Lastly, just south of the Kasbah, along rue Ibn Khaldoun and bearing right at the fork after 200m or so, is the **House of the Tragic Poet**, a tiny site with mosaics of dramatic themes along the lines of its namesake in the ruins of Pompeii in Italy.

The Beaches, Market and Catacombs

The modern town's sole pretence to culture is a small **zoo** west of av Bourguiba, but the real draw here is the **beaches**. Though inferior to Hammamet's – the shore is more exposed, urban and often windy – they have a more eminent literary history:

somewhere on the dunes underneath where the hotels now stand, the French novelist André Gide first faced up to his homosexuality.

You can take part in various **beach sports** up by the *Hôtel el Hana* and at other big hotels further up the beach and in Port el Kantaoui. Parascending (10TD a go), water-skiing (8TD) and windsurfing (5TD an hour) are all available. Beware of **petty thieving** from gangs of kids aged eight to fifteen, who will do the magpie on anything left lying around while you swim or doze. You can hire a locker on one of the guarded areas of beach to avoid this. For getting around in Sousse (at least along the beach) it's also worth hiring **bicycles**: one place which does this is a "minisouk" on the hotel road just outside the city.

If you're feeling slightly silly, you can take the **tourist land train** to Port el Kantaoui (1.2TD one way, 2TD return), departing every hour from 9am to 11pm from pl Boujaffar in Sousse, returning on the half-hour. Longer **excursions** are suggested in "Listings", p.160.

The market

Given the large numbers of tourists who come here, it was inevitable that the **market** in Sousse would be "discovered", and visions of huge camel sales are used to entice people. Market day is Sunday, and the site is a couple of kilometres out towards Sfax. Unfortunately, camels are no longer sold here, so if you were hoping to buy one you're out of luck.

The Catacombs

Another suburban attraction are the **Catacombs**, about the same distance to the west (times and prices as for the Ribat and Great Mosque). Access is via the Kairouan road from the Kasbah, first left onto rue 25 Juillet, then right into rue Abu Hamed el Ghazali and left after 600m. Alternatively, take rue Quatrième Tirailleur from Bab el Gharbi (the Medina's western gate), turn left after half a kilometre, then right onto rue Abu Hamed el Ghazali and left after 100m. Several chambers, stretching for over five kilometres, have been discovered, the burial place of early Christians from the third and fourth centuries. A total of over 15,000 tombs lie here. To see them, ask at the museum and arrange a time with the curator: make sure either you or he provides some sort of light.

Moving On

There are several **bus stations** in Sousse. Southbound *SNTRI* services stop by Bab Jedid, a gate in the Medina's east wall. Northbound services run from pl du Port, an extension of pl Farhat Hached over towards the port. Most **local services**, including those for HERGLA and the hill villages, run from pl Sidi Yahia by the Medina's north wall, but for Enfida you have to hike up to the *gare routière* on av Leopold Senghor (a continuation of av de la République). Bus departure times and fares are posted in the ONTT and Syndicat d'Initiative.

Louages for the Sahel districts leave from Bab Jedid and a few local ones go from pl Sidi Yahia, but for Tunis, Kairouan and elsewhere, they gather in a honking swarm under the Medina wall in pl des Martyrs, a stone's throw from the Great Mosque.

Mainline trains leave from the station in bd Hassouna Ayachi. There's also a fairly quick service known as the **"metro"** to MONASTIR via the **airport**, from 6am until 7 or 8pm, from a station 200m south of pl Farhat Hached on bd Mohammed V.

To get to Monastir **airport** at times when the metro isn't running, you will have to take a taxi, which will probably cost around 7TD, depending on your bargaining skills. Alternatively, you could try some of the package tour hotels to see if there are groups taking the same flight as you whose coach would give you a lift.

Sousse Listings

Airlines *Tunis Air*, 5 av Bourguiba (☎27955).

Banks There are plenty in av Bourguiba and always one or two open Sat and Sun am. A cure for the summertime queues is to try banks further afield (such as the *BNA* on av de la République near the corner of av Victor Hugo). There are also one or two places in the Medina and on av Mohammed V. After hours, try the big hotels.

Books The second-hand bookstalls by Sidi Yahia bus station have the odd English title.

Car hire *Avis*, rte de la Corniche (☎25901); *Ben Jemaa*, rue 2 Mars (☎24002); *Budget*, 63 av Bourguiba (☎27614); *Express*, 47 rue de Beja (☎24994); *Hertz*, av Bourguiba (☎25428); *Interrent/Europcar*, av de la Corniche (☎27562) and rte de la Corniche (☎26252); *Mattei*, 13 rue Ahmed Zaatir (☎25063); *Topcar*, rte de la Corniche (☎26070). In Port el Kantaoui, try *Kantaoui Rent* (☎41318).

Church services The church at 1 rue de Constantine has English Protestant/Anglican services Sundays at 10am, and regular Catholic masses.

Cinemas The *Théatre Municipal* on av Bourguiba shows arty films (as well as plays, classical concerts and other "culture"). Otherwise try the *Palace* a few doors up, the *ABC* on av H Thameur or the *Nejma* on the rte de la Corniche.

Excursions Try the big hotels, or else *Cartours* on the rte de la Corniche (☎24092), who do trips such as a 3-day "safari" (not a wildlife expedition) around the south for 80TD, or a day in Gabes and Matmata for 31TD. You should try to book a couple of days in advance.

Festivals Both Sousse and Port el Kantaoui have high-season programmes of cultural events for tourists known respectively as the "International Festival of Sousse" and the "El Kantaoui Festival". There's also an Olive Festival in Kalaa Kebira in Feb.

Hammams Hammam Sidi Bouraoui in rue Sidi Bouraoui (off rue Aghlaba by no. 23) is one of the oldest in the Medina (men 4am–3pm, women 3pm–midnight).

International phone calls Taxiphone office in rue du Caire, a little street behind the *Claridge Hôtel*, open 8am–11pm daily. Coin-operated phones.

Laundry The Vienna 1 at 37 rue Mongi Slim should sort you out.

Market Sunday, out of town on the Sfax road.

Medical facilities Farhat Hached University Hospital (☎21411) is on the Kalaa Kebira road, a continuation of av Ibn Jazzar from the back of the Medina, parallel with av Leopold Senghor 1km or so out of town. There is a night chemist at 38 av de la République and an out-of-hours emergency line (☎41333).

Newspapers British papers can be found at the stall in the main train station, and at *Cité du Livre* in av Bourguiba at the corner of rue Ali Bach Hamba.

PTT At the corner of av de la République and bd M Naarouf. Open city hours except in July, Aug and Sept when it opens Mon–Sat 7.30am–1pm and 4.30–6pm, Sun 9–11am. *Bureau de change* for cash.

Supermarkets *Monoprix* at the beginning of av Bouguiba by pl Farhat Hached, and two *Magasins Général*, one on rte de la Corniche and one behind pl Farhat Hached on rue de l'Indépendance.

Shipping companies *Tourafric*, 14 rue Khaled Ibn el Walid (☎32315). La Goulette–Sicily tickets and bookings.

Swimming pools If the Med isn't alluring enough for you, you could try the hotels. In town, the *Hadrumète Palace* charges 1TD for the use of its pool.

Tourist offices ONTT, 1 av Bourguiba, almost on pl Farhat Hached (☎25157/8), open Mon–Thurs 8.30am–1pm, 3–5.45pm, and Fri–Sat 8.30am–1.30pm only. Extremely helpful and organised, with loads of useful information posted up on a notice-board, including train and bus schedules and fares – quite the best tourist office in the country. There are also two Syndicats d'Initiative, both open, in theory, 8am–6pm daily, in pl Farhat Hached/pl Sidi Yahia (☎22331), and up in Port el Kantaoui (☎31799).

Around Sousse

Sousse is surrounded by the very old and the very new – the latter in the form of a massive tourist development at **Port el Kantaoui**; the former covering the cliff-top village of **Hergla** and a group of timeless hamlets in the hills a few kilometres inland. For amateur naturalists, too, the area is interesting, with marshland, mud flats and salt-pans all the way down the Sahel coast and round the bay of Gabes, attracting large numbers of wading birds and associated species. The best areas around Sousse to see these are the **Oued Sed** and **Sebkha Kelbia**.

Port el Kantaoui

If you want a glimpse of packaged tourism, 1990s-style, **PORT EL KANTAOUI** is 9km north of Sousse. With the help of Kuwaiti investment, a vast pleasure complex has been conjured out of a stretch of empty coast, including a "genuine" Tunisian yacht harbour in "authentic" Andalusian style. This is Tunisia without tears, built for the delectation of the international tourist – and a pretty anaemic version it is too. Buses and taxis head off there regularly from pl Sidi Yahia, or you could pay more and take the tourist land train.

Hill villages

Much more interesting are three hill villages inland – **KALAA SGHIRRA, KALAA KEBIRA** and **AKOUDA** – all of which date back to Aghlabid times. Kalaa Kebira has an **olive festival** at the beginning of February. To get to them, take the bus from pl Sidi Yahia in Sousse.

Seen from a distance, the villages are highly picturesque, each on its green hill topped by a mosque but, once inside, their attraction is more a sort of bustling venerability: the ancient winding streets and doorways are a bit decrepit, but full of the sense of a life that stretches far back into the past. In 1864 their tranquillity was shattered when the villagers joined forces with the tribes from the interior in a **revolt** against the Bey's demands for increased taxation. They came near to overthrowing the government but soon fell out amongst each other, giving **General Zarrouk** a chance to gather his troops and defeat them piecemeal. The retribution he exacted was terrible. Heavy fines were imposed on the villagers and those that could not pay were seized, tortured, and executed. Those that had no cash were forced to sell their land to merchants from Sfax, who had wisely remained loyal to the Bey, and thus the villagers became labourers rather than landowners. Many were totally impoverished. Even today, Zarrouk's name is remembered as synonymous with cruelty, and historians identify the year 1864 as the turning point in the region's economy. Thereafter a steady decline set in.

Hergla

HERGLA, a strange village ledged high above the coast about 30km north of Sousse, has a long history, including a time when it marked the boundary between two Roman provincial subdivisions – but this isn't what makes it so curious. The romantic setting should have belonged to a pirate's lair, but in fact the inhabitants have always made their living from weaving **esparto grass** (brought from as far inland as Kasserine) into filters used in pressing olives for oil. A fishing harbour has now been built, a spectacular place with whitewashed houses and topped, as in the hill villages, by a mosque. Built in the eighteenth century, but named after a local man called Sidi Bou Mendel (who, it's locally agreed, flew back from Mecca in the tenth century on his handkerchief), the mosque overlooks a cemetery and a drop to the deep blue sea. The paltry remains of Roman **Horrea Coelia** (a few mosaics) are a little way down the cliff road to the south. More interesting are the snorkelling possibilities around here.

Buses and *louages* serve Hergla from pl Sidi Yahia, passing on the coast road **CHOTT MARIAM**, a small settlement whose **unofficial campsite** may now be closed (the authorities will almost certainly tell you so).

Oued Sed

An interesting wetland area some 20km north of Sousse, the **Oued Sed** is a freshwater and reedbed area; the river flows under the main road and eventually ends up in **Sebkhet Halk el Menzel**, a salt lake close to the sea. Any bus heading north from Sousse can drop you off here.

As always, freshwater is a magnet for **birds** and, if there's enough water in the river and the salt lake, it's well worth a trip, with all the usual wading and waterside birds plus occasional sightings of purple gallinule and marbled teal. Peregrine falcons and marsh harriers hunt over the area – the latter feeding on the abundant frog population. **Flamingos** are present whenever there's enough water, and you can sometimes see large flocks of migrating cranes, too.

Sebkha Kelbia – dry wetlands

Sebkha Kelbia is a huge salt lake, lying inland of Sousse towards Kairouan. In the past it was a major site for wintering wildfowl and waders, but dams have been built on its feed rivers, and it has been completely dry since 1982. With a very wet winter, though, it would certainly be an outstanding site. The lake can be best explored from the village of DAR EL OUESSEF at the northern tip where the Oued Sed flows out, or (with a bit of a walk) from the village of BIR JEDID at the southwestern corner.

The fields around Kelbia are rich in **gypsum**, and, in spring, hold a very colourful and characteristic **flora**. Vast areas of the lake itself, in common with all *sebkhas*, are dominated by shrubby species of salt-resistant glasswort. Tamarisk bushes form a shrubby fringe, and are worth scouring for small warblers.

Monastir and Around

Coming to this area from almost any other part of the country, it's a shock to discover just how densely populated the small **triangle south of Sousse** is, with a thriving town every few kilometres. Even in Roman times this was so, and the coastline is still littered with vestigial remains of their many settlements. But it was under the Aghlabids, when the capital was Kairouan, that this area moved ahead of the rest of the country.

Most of the towns are virtually indistinguishable – crowded streets, and a purposeful atmosphere very different from the rest of the country. **MONASTIR**, however, has a special interest. Once a fishing port on the Sahel coast, it has never been allowed to

---

ARRIVING AT MONASTIR AIRPORT

Nearly everyone who takes a charter flight to Tunisia flies into **Monastir airport**, slap bang in the middle of the country's tourist haven. It's a convenient point of arrival: the airport is efficient and connected to both Monastir and Sousse by strings of coaches (which you may be able to catch a lift on) and the "metro" railway with its platform 100m from the air terminal. A number of car hire firms also operate from the airport, and you should be able to pick up a hire car immediately on arrival.

If arriving late at night, you'll probably have to take a taxi. With a bit of tough bargaining, you should be able to get to Sousse for around 7TD, and to Monastir for 5TD. As most things will be shut, your best bet might be to phone a hotel as soon as you arrive (or before you leave), check that they'll be open when you arrive, and get the taxi to take you straight there. You're unlikely to be allowed to sleep at the airport.

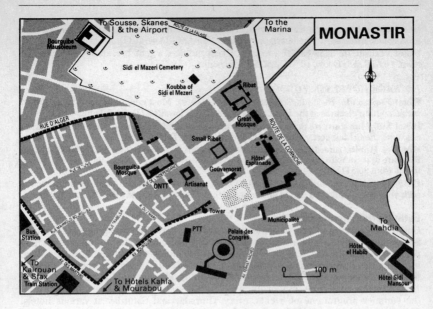

forget that **Habib Bourguiba** (born here August 3, 1903) emerged from its industrious middle class, which later provided his power base. With a festival every year on the ex-President's birthday, the Bourguiba family mausoleum, the Bourguiba mosque, and a much-used Presidential palace, Monastir has uneasily adjusted to a role in the national limelight. To add to its problems, the town has also had to cope with the international film industry and a level of tourist development which has all but swamped it. Needless to say, all this detracts somewhat from its older heritage.

Orientation and Practicalities

The heart of the town is its walled **Medina**, skirted to the north and east by rue d'Alger, to the south by av Bourguiba, and to the west by av des Martyrs, where both the train and bus stations are situated. The sea lies east of the Medina beyond the Ribat and the rte de la Corniche promenade. North of these are the marina and the Sidi el Mezeri cemetery containing the Bourguiba Mausoleum. Beyond, the rte de la Falaise heads towards Skanes and the main hotel area. The other way, the rte de la Corniche heads out past the fishing port to join up with the main road to Mahdia.

Accommodation

Hotels in Monastir are almost all reserved for charter tours. The following address is the only budget accommodation:

Youth Hostel/Maison des Jeunes, rue de Libye (☎61216). Near the bus station. Rather basic, but central and the cheapest place in town. 4TD per person.

MID-RANGE HOTELS

Hôtel Kahla, av 7 Novembre (☎64570). On a roundabout about 800m up the Ksar Hellal road from the junction of av Bourguiba and av des Martyrs. Self-catering apartments as well as rooms. 8TD/14TD low season, 11TD/20TD high, b&b.

Hôtel Mourabou, rte de Khniss (☎60111). A stone's throw from the *Hôtel Kahla*. Central heating and a free bus to the beach once a day. 8TD/16TD low, 10TD/20TD high, b&b.

Hôtel Yasmin, rte de la Falaise (☎62511). Clean and does a good breakfast, but 2km out of town. 10.5TD/16TD low, 16.5TD/25TD high, b&b.

PACKAGE HOTELS IN TOWN

Hôtel Esplanade, rte de la Corniche (☎61146/7/8/9). Most central of the hotels, almost within spitting distance of the Ribat. 3* 13.4TD/19.5TD low, 24.8TD/34.4TD high, b&b.

Hôtel Sidi Mansour, rte de la Corniche (☎62944). Beach holiday hotel with the usual facilities, near the fishing port. 4* 17TD/24TD low, 30TD/46TD high, FB.

Hôtel el Habib, rute de la Corniche (☎62944). 4* 37.5TD/60TD low, 51.5TD/84TD high, FB. Part of a complex which includes the 3* *Résidence el Habib*, where you can rent apartments from 36.5TD in season.

Hôtel Regency, Port de Plaisance (☎60033). Monastir's poshest gaff, right by the marina – park your yacht while you pop in for dinner. 4*L 30TD/40TD low, 45TD/70TD high, b&b.

Eating, drinking and nightlife

Good, cheap **eating** is hard to come by in Monastir. If you're staying here, you're best advised if possible to opt for full or half board (FB, HB). There are a couple of fast-food places opposite the ONA by the cinema, and one or two restaurants in the Medina, including the *Bonheur* in rue 2 Mars, which isn't too bad. Or, if you feel like a splurge, the *Hôtel Regency* does 10TD set menus which are good value by Monastir standards.

If you're here in June, July or August, you can seek **evening entertainment** from the summer programme of events, every Thursday and Saturday at various hotels. This, laid on by the ONTT and hotels, includes donkey racing, mock weddings, orchestras both traditional and less so, and an item billed mysteriously as "majorettes". For the rest of the year nightlife is typically low-key.

Around the Town Centre

To go with its new national prominence, the town centre has been emptied of habitation and replaced by a bleak esplanade designed to show off Monastir's **monuments** to the best advantage. The **Bourguiba Mausoleum** is undoubtedly the most eye-catching of these, unmistakable with its gilt cupola and twin minarets. It stands in a cemetery named after the **Koubba of Sidi el Mezeri**, the odoriferous tomb of a twelfth-century saint. The inscription on the gateway, apparently written by the saint, mentions one Princess Mona, and many believe that the town takes its name from her.

The Ribat

Compared to Bourguiba's monuments, the old **Ribat of Harthema**, overlooking the sea, is rather more restrained (open summer Tues–Sun 9am–noon, 3–6.30pm; winter Tues–Sun 9am–noon, 2–5.30pm; closed Mon, 1TD plus 2TD for photos). Begun in 796 it has undergone so many reworkings that even experts have difficulty in assigning its parts to the correct period. The core structure follows the same plan as at Sousse, however, with a courtyard surrounded by cells for the fighters, and on one side a prayer hall which is now used as a **museum** to display ancient Islamic writings, fabrics and pottery. Unfortunately for your chances of visiting the Ribat, its walls, towers and angles have in recent years become a favourite cinematic ancient world. Biblical epics are filmed by the dozen: Jesus trod the battlements in Zeffirelli's *Life of Christ*, as did Brian in *Monty Python*'s alternative scenario. The ninth-century **Great Mosque** stands next door, and a second, smaller, *ribat*, the **Ribat of Sidi Dhouwayeb**, between it and the Medina.

Other points of interest: the fishing port, Medina, museums and market

The **old fishing port** stands a few hundred metres to the east in a rocky inlet. It must have been a pretty place once, but the corniche is now so loaded with hotels that it looks distinctly out of place. In the other direction the road leads west along the coast past more resort development and Bourguiba's favourite **palace**. The house where Bourguiba was born is in pl 3 Août, way down the prom past the *Hôtel Sidi Mansour* towards the fishing port.

Inland from the Ribat, across the esplanade, lies the **Medina**. Some parts of its storybook walls are eighteenth century, others recent, and there are gratuitous additions in the 1980s Andalusian style used at Port el Kantaoui. This is acceptable at Kantaoui, where everything is avowedly fake, but when genuine and counterfeit are mixed indiscriminately you begin to wonder if the whole ensemble is just an extra to the film set. The **Bourguiba Mosque** in rue de l'Indépendance follows classic Hafsid design, but the rest of the Medina has been so blatantly Covent-Gardenised that it hardly even merits a stroll. In fact, the *real* Medina was originally the area around the Ribat; what is called the Medina today was a walled suburb, like the *faubourgs* of Tunis. One little curiosity is the **tower**, which protrudes, for no apparent reason, from the wall opposite the PTT.

Monastir's **museums** charge 0.8TD entry. The most interesting is the **Museum of Traditional Costume**, in rue de l'Indépendance by the ONTT (Mon–Sat 9am–noon, 2–5.30pm, closed Sun). Others include the **El Helm Museum** out on the rte de la Corniche past the fishing port – the collection of an amateur sculptor – and the **Museum of the National Movement** in rue Trabelsia in the Medina.

Monastir's Saturday **market** is a lively affair focusing around pl Guedir el Foul near the bus station.

Moving On

Monastir's **train station** is southwest of the Medina on av des Martyrs, near Bab el Gharbi (no left luggage facilities). The main service is by "metro" to Sousse via the hotel zone and airport – every hour or so from about 7am to 8pm.

The **bus station** is a short walk up the street, by the city wall, with limited bus departures to Tunis, Nabeul, Sfax and Sousse and **louages** to Tunis. The rest of Monastir's *louages* leave from south of the Medina (follow av des Martyrs past the station towards the hospital) but only go as far as Ksar Hellal, Moknine and Sousse.

To get to the **airport** (☎61314/5/6/7), the metro is the obvious means, although there are buses too. When none of those are running, you'll have to hire a taxi (around 5TD, depending on your bargaining skills), or try to get a lift with a tour group on the same flight as you. For details of flights out of Monastir, see "travel details" at the end of this chapter. It is occasionally possible to get a one-way ticket on a charter: try *Tunis Air* and the tour companies.

Monastir Listings

Airlines *Tunis Air*, in the *Hôtel el Habib* complex (☎64210/2).

Banks Near the PTT on av Bourguiba, and more on pl de l'Indépendance in the very centre of the Medina.

Car hire *Mattei*, pl de la Gare (☎61243).

Cinema Rue d'Alger, opposite the ONA crafts shop.

Excursions It's possible to visit the **Kuriat Islands**, a deserted archipelago 15km off the coast, from Monastir's diving centre, *Monastir Plongée et Loisirs*, down at the marina (☎62509). The minimum charge for a day trip – 200TD – probably means forming a large group.

Hammam Rue de Tunis, in the Medina (men 6am–1pm, women 1–5.30 pm).

International phone calls International calls can be made from the taxiphone office diagonally opposite the Central Bank of Tunisia next to the train station.

Medical facilities Regional Hospital, av Farhat Hached, out past the Sousse *louage* station (☎61144). Night chemist in rue Chedli Kallala, off av Bourguiba near the PTT.

ONA crafts shop Rue de l'Indépendance, on the corner of rue d'Alger.

PTT Av Bourguiba opposite the Medina wall (city hours).

Supermarkets *Magasin Général*, rue de l'Indépendance and *Monoprix* av Bourguiba. The latter is a better bet since it's open 8am–7pm Mon–Sat and 8am–1pm Sun.

Tourist office ONTT, rue de l'Indépendance, in a square opposite the Bourguiba Mosque (☎61960). Open Mon–Thurs 8.30am–1pm & 3–5.45pm, Fri & Sat 8.30am–1.30pm, and rather useless. There is another ONTT office just up the coast in Skanes, near Les Hotels metro station (☎61205).

South towards Mahdia

Direct public transport between Monastir and Mahdia being non-existent, any journey by road involves a change of vehicle at either **Ksar Hellal** or **Moknine**, though there is now also a rail link with eight trains a day (four on Sundays) calling at Lamta, Ksar Hellal, Bekalta and Moknine. The odd Roman site can be found en route if you really have to see every single one, but frankly, what's left of Leptis Minor (now the village of Lamta) and Thapsus, 6km off the main road at Bekalta, is not worth seeing even if you can find them.

Ksar Hellal

About twenty kilometres south of Monastir lies **KSAR HELLAL**. The town itself is not noteworthy but it is the last place in Tunisia where silk is made. The thread is dyed in large vats and handlooms are still used to weave the cloth. Sadly, the resulting article is disappointing – usually plain, with none of the geometrical designs that you find on coarser textiles, and very expensive. The town's other claim to fame is as the venue for a Neo-Destour Party Congress where Bourguiba emerged as leader. From here disciples went throughout the country encouraging strikes and civil disobedience that came close to overthrowing the Protectorate.

Moknine

Midway between Monastir and Mahdia, **MOKNINE** is an equally anonymous town, but one which happens to have a small regional **museum**. It's sign-posted on the main road coming in from Sousse, and 100m to the left there it is – a disused mosque exhibiting "Various things from different provenances": principally money, manuscripts, pottery and weapons from all periods. If the exhibits themselves fail to entertain, the labelling certainly will.

Kairouan

"What a Hell of a place to put a Holy City", wrote *The Times'* military correspondent of **KAIROUAN** in 1939; in midsummer, when the town bakes like a brick on its barren plain, it's hard to disagree. But Tunisia's oldest Arab city, Islam's fourth most holy centre after Mecca, Medina and Jerusalem, is an exceptionally rewarding place: its architectural interest is unrivalled, and the strong Eastern flavour it has retained is a particular shock after Sousse. All of this can best be appreciated by staying a while in its venerable Medina.

HISTORY OF KAIROUAN

Not surprisingly, perhaps, it was divine inspiration that led to the choice of this infernal site. In 670 **Oqba Ibn Nafi**, advancing west, called a routine halt here with his army. A golden cup was discovered on the ground, which he recognised as one he had lost at Mecca; then a spring was found, and declared to be connected to the holy well of Zem Zem at Mecca. The message was clear and, having first banished for eternity the "noxious beasts and reptiles" which had previously been in some abundance, Oqba founded his capital on the spot. There was sound strategic sense behind the inspiration, though: halfway between the seaborne threats of the Mediterranean and the mountainous homes of the rebellious Berbers, the new city was a reasonably secure and central base for the new rulers.

Despite this security, extremist **Kharijite** Berbers took the city in 757. Their behaviour (such as massacring their opponents and stabling horses in the Great Mosque) shocked more moderate Kharijites, who drove them out and installed one Abderrahman Ibn Rustam as their ruler. In 761, Egyptian forces loyal to the Caliph retook the city, and Ibn Rustam set up shop in Tahirt (Algeria), from where his family (the Rustamids) ruled the south of Tunisia.

As the **Aghlabid** capital, Kairouan quickly developed into one of the world's great cities, its monuments surpassed only by the level of its scholarship. There was a decline under the Fatimids, who moved the capital to Mahdia, and a low point was reached in 1057 when the town was sacked by the Banu Hilal. But although the Hafsids made Tunis their political capital, Kairouan has never lost its ancient, **holy status**. "The Arabs ascribe to this place extraordinary veneration," wrote John Ogilby in 1670, "many persons coming hither out of reverence, pull off their shoes when they enter into the city, as if it were a mosque." There arose a story that seven visits to Kairouan were equivalent to one pilgrimage to Mecca, and the town was jealously guarded from **infidels**. Before the arrival of the French, Christians needed a Beylical permit to enter the walls, and no Jew dared even approach them. Sir Grenville Temple in 1835 had a permit, and may have exaggerated in reporting that "if we were known to be Christians, whilst walking about, we might be torn to pieces by the infuriated populace". Members of the 1881 **French invasion force** were, indeed, distinctly apprehensive as the tribes assembled in a wide arc around the town. But when it came to the final battle their defence crumbled and, much to the surprise of the French column, the town surrendered without a shot being fired.

Modern Kairouan is a successful market centre for agricultural goods (apricots and almonds are grown in the district) and a major producer of carpets and *Caravanes* cigarettes. But it remains, too, intensely religious – a living centre of Islamic doctrine. Through the post-Independence years, its religious authorities periodically created friction over Bourguiba's attempts at secular reform. In 1960, when he urged national abandonment of the Ramadan fast (see p.333), Kairouan pointedly observed it a day later than the rest of the country – simultaneously with Egypt, in a gesture of Arab–Islamic solidarity. The town's av Bourguiba was only so named after the President made a visit of conciliation in 1969 (it has now been renamed again). Kairouan also has a special place in international Islamic consciousness, and representatives from all over the world converge on the city for the *Mouled* celebration of the Prophet's birthday.

Practicalities – Orientation and Staying

Kairouan's **Medina** stretches east to west, the Great Mosque at its far corner; to the north and west ancient suburbs; the new **French quarter** to the south. The last, as ever, contains the banks and administration, but most of the life of the town remains centred on the main street through the Medina, **Avenue Ali Belhouane** (formerly av Bourguiba). At one end of this is Bab Tunis, the main *louage* station and route to the hospital and the Aghlabid Pools north of town. At the other end of av Ali Belhouane is

> ## STREET NAMES AND CONFUSION
>
> Streets in Kairouan seem to change their names even more indiscriminately than else-
> where in Tunisia and many streets have two or more names. Thus, for example, rue
> Farhat Hached was formerly called av de la République; av de la République used to be
> av Zama el Balaoui; av Ali Belhouane was av Bourguiba; and bd Hedi Chaker (alongside
> the city wall between pl des Martyrs and rue de Gafsa) was av Ali Belhouane. Av Ali
> Zouaoui is also called bd Driss I. To add to the confusion, most maps of Kairouan are
> extremely inaccurate and name streets wrongly in any case. Great pains have been taken
> with the map opposite, but we would appreciate notification of any errors which may have
> crept in.

Bab ech Chouhada, by the **tourist office**, where you buy tickets for the monuments.
From here, av Bourguiba continues down to rue Farhat Hached, where a right takes
you to the PTT on a large roundabout.

To get to the Medina **from the bus station**, turn right outside the building and
walk straight on to the city wall, where you turn left for Bab ech Chouhada.

Accommodation

Hotels in Kairouan run the whole gamut from cheap and basic to four-star luxury.
There are good hotels in all categories and you should have no trouble finding one to
suit. Numbers in the following listings key the hotels to their map locations.

Hôtel Marhala, (1) 35 souk Belaghjia (☎20736).Well hidden inside the souk, a converted
Koranic students' hostel. Rooms with showers; shared but spotless loo (with paper). Ask for
a room right at the top. Recommended. 4.5TD per person.

Hôtel Sabra, (2) pl des Martyrs (☎20260). Excellent value, clean and spacious, hot showers, roof terrace (but no reduction for sleeping there). Recommended. 4TD/7TD b&b.

Hôtel Sidi Bel Hassen, (3) bd Sadikia (☎20351). Turn left just out of Bab Tunis for this,
the cheapest place in town. Basic but clean. 2.5TD per person.

Hôtel Barouta, (4) off av Ali Belhouane opposite Bir Barouta. A real dive with uncertain
security: dodgy in the extreme. 3TD/5TD.

Hôtel el Menema, (5) rue Moizz ibn Badis (☎20182). Clean and pleasant. 9TD/16TD b&b
plus 1TD for room with bath or shower.

Hôtel Tunisia, (6) av Farhat Hached (☎21855). Big clean rooms with choice of bath or
shower. 2* 10.5TD/16TD b&b.

Hôtel Splendid, (7) rue 9 Avril (☎20041). Off av de la République. Big rooms, and rather
classy if you ignore the linoleum floor. 3* 15TD/21TD b&b.

Hôtel des Aghlabites, (8) av de Fes (☎20855). A bit of fading grandeur, not to be confused
with the unclassified hotel of the same name in pl de Tunis. 3* 24.4TD/19.4TD b&b.

Hôtel Continental, (9) av el Moizz ibn Badis (☎21135). Near the Aghlabid Pools. The poshest hotel in town. 4* 25.5TD/38TD b&b.

Youth Hostel/Maison des Jeunes, av de Fes (☎20309). 4TD per person. Out near the
Hôtel des Aghlabites, midnight curfew but open all day.

Food

Buses between Tunis and the south often have to wait, even in the middle of the night,
while all the passengers get off at Kairouan to buy the **sweets** for which it is famous –
the best known of which is *makroudh*, a honey-soaked cake with a date filling. The
city's foremost patisseries are in the Medina along av Ali Belhouane.

For something more substantial, the **Restaurant Fairouz**, just off av Ali Belhouane
behind Bir Barouta, will feed you for about 3.5TD. Their couscous in particular is recommended. Otherwise, there's a number of cheap *rôtisseries* around the post office where,

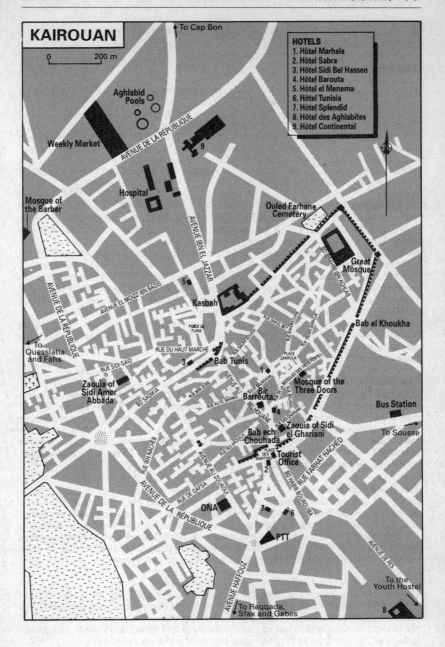

KAIROUAN

0   200 m

To Cap Bon

HOTELS
1. Hôtel Marhala
2. Hôtel Sabra
3. Hôtel Sidi Bel Hassen
4. Hôtel Barouta
5. Hôtel el Menema
6. Hôtel Tunisia
7. Hôtel Splendid
8. Hôtel des Aghlabites
9. Hôtel Continental

Aghlabid Pools

Weekly Market

AVENUE DE LA RÉPUBLIQUE

Hospital

Mosque of the Barber

Ouled Farhane Cemetery

AVENUE IBN EL JAZZAR

BD IBRAHIM IBN AGHLAB

Great Mosque

Kasbah

AVENUE EL MOIZZ IBN BADIS

AVENUE DE LA RÉPUBLIQUE

To Quesslatia and Fahs

PLACE DE TUNIS

RUE DU HAUT MARCHÉ

RUE SIDI GAID

Bab el Khoukha

RUE CASA EL BEY

RUE HAMDASSOS

MOSQUÉE DES TROIS PORTES

RUE TUAJ ZARROUK

PLACE ZARROUK

Bab Tunis

Zaouia of Sidi Amor Abbada

BD SADIKIA

RUE SIDI GAID

RUE BAB EDJO

RUE ALI EL BARREK

SOUK BLAGHJIA

RUE EL KA

RUE BLOVAS

RUE SIDI GHARIANI

Bir Barrouta

BEL HOUANE

Mosque of the Three Doors

RUE IBN NACHEB

AVENUE ALI ZOUAOUI

Bab ech Chouhada

Zaouia of Sidi el Ghariani

RUE DES AGLAUD

PLACE DES MARTYRS

Tourist Office

Bus Station

To Sousse

AVENUE DE LA RÉPUBLIQUE

RUE DE GAFSA

ONA

BD HABIB BOURGUIBA

RUE FARHAT HACHED

PTT

AVENUE DE FES

AVENUE HAFFOUZ

To Reqqada, Sfax and Gabes

To the Youth Hostel

for a dinar or two, you can fill up with a *schewarma* sandwich or a kebab. Classier places nearby include the **Restaurant el Karawan** in rue Soukhaine Bint el Houssein.

The City

Entrance to the most important of Kairouan's **monuments** is by a 2TD ticket which can only be bought from the tourist office opposite Bab es Chouhada (8am–5pm daily for tickets; Mon–Thurs 8.30am–1pm & 3–5.45pm, Fri & Sat 8.30am–1.30pm for general information). The ticket is valid, in theory, only on the day of issue, but you can usually get away with using it for a day longer. The seven places it covers are: 1) the **Great Mosque**, or Mosque of Oqba; 2) the **Zaouia of Sidi Sahab**, or Mosque of the Barber (aka the Mausoleum of Abu Zomaa el Balaoui); 3) the **Aghlabid Pools**; 4) the **Zaouia of Sidi el Ghariani**; 5) **the Museum of Islamic Art** at Reqqada; 6) the **Zaouia of Sidi Amor Abbada**; 7) **Bir Barouta**.

The Zaouia of Sidi el Ghariani

The way from Bab es Chouhada to the Great Mosque leads first past two other monuments: for the **Zaouia of Sidi El Ghariani**, turn right down rue Sidi Ghariani, just inside Bab es Chouhada, and you can't miss the formidable entrance. Although the building dates from the beginning of the fourteenth century, it is now named after a native of Gharian in Libya, who died 100 years later. In 1891, according to Sir Lambert Playfair, the hereditary governor of Kairouan was still one of Abd el Ghariani's descendants; since then the Zaouia has seen hard times, but it has been restored and is now the home of the ASM (*Association de Sauvegarde de la Medina*). Notice especially the green and black columns of the mihrab, and the typically dark wooden ceiling of the tomb.

The Zaouia is not where it's marked on most maps. That place, about 100m further along the street, is an old Beylical palace, now a carpet shop. The salesman will entice you in by asking for your ticket and claiming the shop is a museum. Go in if you like, but be prepared for the hard sell.

The Mosque of the Three Doors

If you turn left up rue Bouras (opposite the carpet shop) and then right down rue de la Mosquée des Trois Portes, you come to the **Mosque of the Three Doors**. This is closed to non-Muslims, but is a rare example of a small ninth-century mosque. Notice the inscriptions above the three doors: the top two bands date from the foundation, the lower band and minaret from later additions. Between the top two bands of inscriptions is a row of stones with floral decorations: notice that each stone is decorated quite differently, and no two are the same.

The Great Mosque

Heading east from here, through an old quarter of the city, will bring you to the **Great Mosque**, first impressions of which are of its relentless simplicity. Certainly, compared with the delicate elaboration of later periods, its massive buttressed walls feel more like a fortress; yet it's hard not to sense its enormously powerful and beautiful expression of faith. At least, that is, when it's not packed with coach parties: best times to visit are early or late morning (it closes for prayers at 12.35pm), or early afternoon.

THE LALLA RIHANA GATE

Only one of the several monumental entrances is now used, but the **Lalla Rihana Gate** on the east side, dating from 1294, deserves a quick detour. Typically Hafsid, with the characteristic arches and cupola, the gate is more than 400 years later than most of the present mosque, which was erected by the Aghlabid Ziyadatallah in 836 and greatly influenced the mosques built at the same time in Sfax, Sousse and Tunis.

THE GREAT MOSQUE

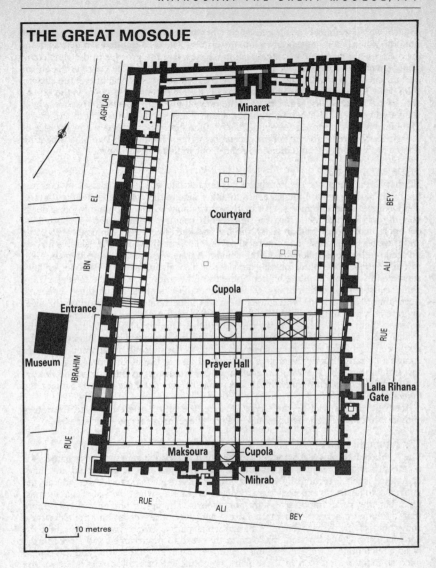

THE COURTYARD AND MINARET

Framed by Hafsid and Turkish colonnades, the vast **courtyard** was never just an aesthetic form. In a town so short of natural water sources, the courtyard was turned to use as a catchment area, with rainwater made to flow down to the curiously shaped drain in the centre and into huge cisterns below. The **drain**'s odd form is a gift for mischievous guides, who told their credulous employers for years that the curious notches were for animals coming to drink. They were actually designed to decant dust from the water before it went down into the cistern. The **well-heads** used to draw from the cisterns are made out of antique column-bases, and the grooves in the rims come from centuries of rope friction. The oversized **sundial clock** in the courtyard is one of two: the second, a smaller one for afternoon use, is on the superstructure of the eastern colonnade. Although the age of the **minaret** is disputed, its lowest storey is thought to date from 730, a century before most of the present mosque. This might explain why it stands off centre, and it certainly makes it the oldest surviving minaret in the world. The minaret's blunt form is more imaginative than first appears: notice how the size of the windows increases as that of the ascending storeys diminishes. Two blocks bearing Roman inscriptions are built into the minaret, one of them upside-down.

THE PRAYER HALL
Neither the minaret nor the courtyard is symmetrical, which emphasises by contrast the order of the **prayer hall**: six aisles to either side in the colonnade and eight in the hall itself, with the entrance set off by the cupola above. The elaborate wooden doors into the prayer hall date from the nineteenth century. With its roof supported by columns (mainly from Roman sites), the hall has been likened by centuries of pilgrims and travellers to a forest. The central aisle, higher than those on either side, is further marked out by stone reliefs below the ceiling. A transverse aisle, connecting the Gate of Lalla Rihana to another on the far side, is also distinguishable. Wooden pillows separate the capitals from the higher elements of the columns, designed to soak up any shifts caused by earth tremors. There are endless stories about these columns. According to one, anyone who counts them all will become blind; in another, the pairs operate as a sort of proverbial Muslim eye of the needle – those who cannot squeeze between them, it is said, will never reach Paradise. Dimly visible at the far end of the central aisle are 130 faience tiles around the mihrab, imported from Baghdad in the ninth century. The wooden *minbar* just next to the mihrab is another important example of early Islamic decorative arts, carved also in the ninth century by order of Ibn Aghlab himself. The wooden enclosure, or *maqsoura*, to the side of the *minbar* was installed by a Zirid ruler in 1022 so that he did not have to pray among the *hoipolloi*.

Just outside the wall by the Great Mosque, the little **Ouled Farhane Cemetery** with its whitewashed gravestones makes a pretty backdrop for souvenir snapshots.

The Aghlabid Pools
The **Aghlabid Pools** were wrongly ascribed to Roman engineers by many chauvinistic nineteenth-century French historians on the grounds that Arabs could not have completed such a technically complex project. Even after extensive restoration the pools are no aesthetic experience, particularly in summer when the water is at its most fetid, but they're an impressive sight nonetheless. The larger one is said to be more than a kilometre across – hard to believe – and the buttresses around the sides have something of the Great Mosque's monumental purity. Water was brought here by aqueduct from Jebel Cherichera, 36km to the west, to be decanted and stored in the basins. Such utilities were an essential feature of urban life in this area, and there were once as many as fourteen of these pairs (one smaller unrestored pair is just to the east). As well as holding the water, it was hoped that the pools would produce humidity over the town to relieve the summer heat. What, in retrospect, is sure enough, is that they were a terrific mosquito breeding ground and thus a source of malaria. The small stand in the middle of the larger pool held a pavilion in which the Aghlabid rulers could recline. Note that the pools and the Mosque of the Barber are in fact much further from the Medina than is apparent on most maps (ours is an exception).

The Mosque of the Barber

Following the main road (av de la République) west, you arrive at the Mosque of Sidi Sahab, more popularly known as the **Mosque of the Barber**. *Sahab* means companion, and Abu Zama el Belaoui, who's buried here, was one of the companions of the Prophet. His odd, distinguishing characteristic was that he always kept with him three hairs of the Prophet's beard: one under his tongue, one on his right arm, and one next to his heart – hence the (originally European) tendency to call him the Prophet's barber.

The mosque and its surrounding complex are still a much-venerated place of pilgrimage, and this is where you get the strongest impression of **Kairouan as a holy city**: families, both Berber villagers and prosperous town-dwellers, come to pay their respects. Most of the existing buildings date from the seventeenth and nineteenth centuries, and their elaborateness contrasts with the less fanciful form of the Great Mosque. The entrance to the main complex ducks under the Andalusian-style minaret, where an ornate passage (marble columns and Italianate windows at the end) leads to an equally rich courtyard, its walls and ceilings lined with green-blue tilework and white plaster stucco. In a small room to the left of the court is the tomb of Sidi Shrif Bin Hindu, the architect of the Great Mosque. Sidi Sahab himself lies buried in the room on the far side (closed to non-Muslims). This central court is a wonderfully peaceful place to sit on a hot afternoon, with the trees outside waving overhead. The carpets along one wall make it an unusually comfortable one, too (remember to remove your shoes before sitting on them). Carpets are uncommon in Tunisian mosques; this one has them due to a custom of each Kairouan girl presenting the first carpet she makes. The mosque is also a popular place to have sons circumcised, and the climax of the ceremony happens in this courtyard. Over the preceding weeks the boy's family will have filled a large jar with sweets and nuts before sealing it. At the moment of the big snip, the jar is smashed in the centre of the courtyard, and the watching children scramble for its contents.

The Zaouia of Sidi Amor Abbada

Outside the mosque to the west, before you reach a group of satellite marabouts, lies a pile of four huge **anchors** which used to belong to the **Zaouia of Sidi Amor Abbada**. This can be found by continuing southwards along av de la République for 500m or so and then taking a left down rue Sidi Gaid. (Sidi Amor Abbada was a nineteenth-century blacksmith who must have smithied very successfully to build this seven-domed tomb, now a museum of some of his artefacts.) As for the anchors by the Mosque of the Barber, he claimed that they had come from Noah's ark on Mount Ararat, and that they would anchor Kairouan to Tunisia forever. More prosaic rival theories suggest that they came from the silted-up port of Porto Farina (now Ghar el Melkh, see p.120).

The quarter you pass through to reach Bab Jedid (the way back to the Medina from here), one of the town's ancient suburbs, is particularly well endowed with **doorways** painted in the disturbing **colour combinations** which seem to be a Kairouan speciality.

Back into the Medina

Although the **Medina** can't compare in size with that of Tunis, it has a mystique which has always affected Western travellers. At the beginning of this century the artist Paul Klee remarked, somewhat patronisingly, that the Medina was "the essence of A Thousand and One Nights, with a 99 percent reality content". Still, it sent him into ecstasy: "Colour and I are one. I am a painter." Lurking just east of the av Bourguiba, the tunnel-like **souks** are surprisingly easy to miss, as is the **Bir Barouta**, which looks more like a mosque than a well. Up some stairs is an unlikely camel, clad in a natty set of green fluffy blinkers, tramping endless circles. Some say that this is the well connected to Mecca which Oqba found in 670; but the name refers to a holy man of the thirteenth century whose prayers for water were answered when his dog, Routa, scrab-

CARPETS

Carpets at Kairouan belong to a tradition going back many hundreds of years: if you're thinking of **buying one**, this is undoubtedly the place to do it. The authorities will tell you that every Kairouan woman – doctor, lawyer, or shop assistant – knows how to make them, and that 5000 families in the town are engaged in the industry.

The ONA shop
A good place to assess the range and general price levels is the local **ONA crafts shop** on av Ali Zouaoui, but you can usually bargain for better prices at the many shops on av Bourguiba. Some of these emporia offer tempting credit facilities as part of their hard sell – sceptical caution is advisable. The ONA organisation, however, is heavily involved in quality control, and every carpet for sale is inspected and awarded a rating which is then stamped on it: any carpet without this rating has not been passed. There are three ratings for design and overall quality: *Deuxième Choix*, *Première Choix* and *Qualité Supérieure*.

Knotted carpets
All the carpets are handmade, but there are two basic types. The more expensive ones, recognisable by the pile, are **knotted** to one of three standards: 40,000, 90,000 or 160,000 knots per square metre. These carpets are luxury items produced by a sophisticated urban culture: their designs are based on a central diamond-shaped lozenge derived originally from the lamp in the Great Mosque, but infinite variation is possible. Traditionally, each design is passed on and evolved from generation to generation within the family. An important subdivision is between *Alloucha* and *Zarbia*. *Alloucha* carpets use a range of colours which can be naturally derived from the wool – beiges, browns, whites and blacks, a recent innovation, perhaps in deference to Western "ethnic" tastes: the traditional *Zarbia* carpets use rich polychrome shades – deep blues and reds.

Woven carpets
Woven carpets, or *Mergoum*, come from a very different culture, the nomadic Berbers. Instead of being urban luxuries, they were literally the roof over a family's flocks. *Mergoum* use brighter colours, the sort of intense reds and purples which Berber women still wear, and more strictly linear geometric patterns. Because *Mergoum* are cheaper, they're more open to abuse, and designs of roofline silhouettes of mosques have very little to do with their traditional forms. For a look at some traditional designs, call in at the ONA, which has a small collection of old *Mergoum*.

The carpet market
If you're really committed to bargaining, it's possible to buy the carpets direct from the women who make them at the Saturday **carpet market**, held in **Souk Belaghjia**, near the *Hôtel Marhala*. Be aware, however, that the retailers don't like foreigners cutting into their business and if you don't speak Arabic you'll need a translator. The scene is fairly frenetic: a row of women sit on one side of the alley with their carpets and a row of merchants stand on the other; in between them runs an independent auctioneer who takes bids for the carpet on offer. The whole thing is done at feverish pitch and the atmosphere is electric. It's well worth a look, even if you don't intend to buy. If you do, then prices can be less than half those in the shops – though watch out, the nicest old lady can be a shark and you could easily pay good money for junk. Around 1–2pm Saturday is the best time to go.

bled in the ground until water gushed forth. A taste of the water, it's said, will bring you back one day to Kairouan.

The Medina **walls** were originally built by the Zirids on foundations dating from 761, but it was only a few years before they were wrecked by the Hilali invasion, and they have undergone repeated destructions and restorations ever since. The most recent depredation was during World War II, when the Germans needed to build an airfield in a hurry.

Oldest of the Medina's remaining gates is **Bab el Khoukha**, just south of the Great Mosque, which was originally called the "Sousse Gate" when built in 1705.

Moving On from Kairouan

The **bus station** is southeast of the Medina, on av Assad ibn el Fourat. Kairouan is pretty central and there are buses to most parts of the country run by most of the country's bus companies. Loads of them go to Tunis, even at night, many en route from the south. **Louages** for Tunis, Sfax and Sousse leave from place Bab Tunis, just outside the Medina walls at the northern end of av Ali Belhouane. For MAKTAR and SBEITLA, they go from a T-junction 400m down the GAFSA road. There are no *louages* for EL JEM: you have to go via Sousse.

Kairouan Listings

Airline *Tunis Air*, rue de Fes at the corner of bd Bourguiba (☎220442).

Banks There are several in the centre around Bab es Chouhada and rue Farhat Hached. One of them should stay open weekend mornings.

Car hire *Budget*, 17 av de la Victoire (☎20258); *Mattei*, rue Hafidha ben el Khattab (☎20210).

Cinema *Casino Municipal*, on the same roundabout as the PTT.

Festival The Mouled festival, to celebrate the Prophet's birthday, is a big event in Kairouan. A seasonal pudding called *assida* is a speciality of the celebration, which follows the Islamic calender (see p.29).

Hammams Men can use the hammam attached to the *Hôtel Sabra* (5am–4pm). Women can only use it by arrangement after 4pm, if there's a group of you. Failing that, you will have to find the women's hammam alleged to be close by, but very well hidden. There is another hammam in the Medina near Bir Barouta.

International phone calls Taxiphone office in av Haffouz (opposite the PTT across the roundabout) 8am–1am daily. Also in av Zama el Balaoui near Sidi Sahab Mosque 7am–9pm daily.

Market day Monday.

Medical facilities The Ibn el Jazzar University Hospital is on av Ibn el Jazzar (☎20036), near the *Hôtel Continental* and the Aghlabid Pools. There's a night chemist on av Ali Zouaoui, less than 100m north of the junction with bd Hedi Chaker, on the right.

ONA crafts shop On av Ali Zouaoui (see box).

PTT On the big roundabout where av de la République meets av H Thameur. City hours. *Bureau de change* for cash.

Supermarket *Magasin Général* on bd Bourguiba behind the tourist office.

Swimming pool 2TD to use the pool in the *Aghlabites* or the *Continental*.

Tourist office The ONTT and the Syndicat d'Initiative share a building in pl Chouhada (☎20452 or 21797). Open 8am–5pm daily, but sometimes only for the sale of the ticket to the monuments. Beware of "guides" offering their services outside the tourist office – they occasionally lead unsuspecting tourists into the rougher sections of the Medina and demand large sums of money to lead them out again.

Outside Kairouan

On the flat plain surrounding Kairouan are the remains of some of the palace complexes built by the ninth-century Aghlabid rulers, testimony to their feelings of insecurity even at such a prosperous period. The minimal remains are hardly worth a visit for their own sake, but those at **Reqqada** could be combined with a visit to the National Museum of Islamic Art. To the northwest, the old mountain fastness of Ouesslatia is more of an excuse for some stiff hiking.

Reqqada

The main reason for visiting **REQQADA** is the **National Museum of Islamic Art**, which recently opened to great fanfare in a former presidential palace and is included on the ticket issued by the tourist office in Kairouan. Actually, it's a bit of a let-down. Exhibits include ancient Koranic manuscripts, old gold and silver coins from the earliest period of Arab rule, ceramics, glassware and stonework. Explanations are in Arabic only (failing some comprehension of which, little in the museum makes much sense).

To get there, a bus for students (available to others) leaves every hour between 8.15am and 11.15am from av Haffouz by a hexagonal kiosk about 200m down on the right from the PTT. Otherwise, there are buses and *louages* 200m further on. When you arrive at the stop, the museum is a kilometre further, sign-posted to the right.

Just as you walk towards the museum from the bus stop , you'll find, in a field on the right, the minimal remains of the **palace** built in 876 by the Aghlabid sovereign Ibrahim II. The Aghlabids' reasons for wanting a palace out of town included avoiding troop rebellions, and being able to have a reasonably pleasurable lifestyle beyond the withering gaze of Kairouan's religious lobby. Another reason for choosing Reqqada was its agreeable climate, believed to have dynamic powers: "Every time the doctor Zian Ibn Khalfoun left Kairouan for Reqqada," wrote El Bekri, "he took off his turban in order to receive directly on his head the beneficial effects of this atmosphere."

More ruined palaces – El Abbasiya and Sabra

Reqqada's predecessor was **El Abbasiya**, built 5km southeast of Kairouan after a troop rebellion of 809, in which Kairouanis had joined. Even less remains of this than of the palace in Reqqada, but it has given rise to an intriguing theory: El Bekri's description of a minaret which once stood there fits that of the Leaning Tower of Pisa, itself built in 1174. The theory leads to the question of whether this is more than a coincidence, given that Pisan ships took part in the Norman campaign in Tunisia from 1141 to 60.

Scanty remains of another old palace, **Sabra**, are left off the Reqqada road a couple of kilometres out of Kairouan, and not easy to find. The palace was built for the Fatimid ruler El Mansour on the site of his final victory over the Kharijite rebel Abu Yazid (see p.325) in 947. Abu Yazid is said to have died of his wounds exactly a year later.

Jebel Ousselat

From the western battlements of Kairouan you can just make out the **Jebel Ousselat**, a ring of steep mountains enclosing a fertile plateau. In the eighteenth century, and for hundreds of years before, these mountains were the home of the eponymous Ousselatia, a tribe that, like the Khroumirs, remained outside government control. In the dynastic quarrel of the 1730s they made the mistake of backing Husayn Pacha, and on his death in 1740 the mountain was taken by his rival, Ali. The chronicler Mohammed Seghir Ben Youssef describes how the victorious Bey destroyed all the villages, cut down all the olive trees, and exiled the survivors to the corners of the Regency from where they were never allowed to return. Despite its fertility the mountain is still deserted, its empty villages having remained untouched for 200 years. If you like a good walk it's worth the effort. The town of **OUSSELATIA** and the road to it are both off the mountain; a bus service also runs from Kairouan – ask to be dropped off nearby, as there are no official stops.

Roads north to Fahs: Byzantine forts

Alternatively, with transport, you could take the **direct road to Fahs** (GP3). About 20km along the route at BIAR EL AOUANI, you suddenly come across a perfect **Byzantine fortress**, turreted at each corner and quite unexpected on the bare mountainside. There's a museum here, with a curator so isolated that he rushes up to greet any car that stops. The isolation makes the site all the more attractive.

This region turns out to be quite rich in unexpected antiquities. Some 20km further north, at HENDI EZ ZITOUN, are the remains of a **Roman bridge**, and 36km north of Ousselatia, on the C99 road from Kairouan via Ousselatia to Fahs, another Byzantine fortress crowns the remains at **Ksar Lemsa**, once the Roman town of Limisa.

Mahdia

Georges Sebastian, whose fabulous villa made Hammamet into an internationally famous resort, thought **MAHDIA** was the only place in Tunisia which could compare. So it is: one of the most beguiling and historic towns in the country, and as yet attracting no more than a trickle of visitors. In fact, Mahdia is nowadays rather insulted by the comparison with Hammamet. Charming, friendly and relaxed, it is totally unspoilt by tourism despite its monuments, its historical fame and its proximity to such tour industry bastions as Sousse and Monastir.

SOME HISTORY

Set on a narrow peninsula in the belly-like bulge of the Sahel coast, Mahdia's geographical position has defined its **history**. After defeating the last of the Aghlabids in 909, the new Fatimid ruler of Tunisia, the self-styled *Mahdi* (see p.371), needed a capital to provide security from the hostility of the Sunni majority. The heretical Fatimids overthrew the complacent Aghlabids with the aid of Berber dissidents, but were neither popular nor concerned to be so: they just wanted Tunisia as a base to conquer Egypt and Iraq, the heart of the Arab world. It was with this in mind that the historian Ibn Khaldoun later called Mahdia a "dagger held in the fist".

Mahdia made the ideal capital, its entrance easily closed off by the massive **wall** begun in 916. Behind the wall the Mahdi built a Great Mosque, a harbour, a palace and other installations: everything else was relegated to a suburb outside the wall. A few merchants were allowed to trade inside, but they had to live outside: the Mahdi claimed that his aim was to separate them from their wives during the day and their goods at night.

For the next 600 years, Mahdia was to be one of the most formidable fortresses in the Mediterranean. Its first test came with a siege in 944–5 by Abu Yazid, "the man on a donkey" (see p.325), and his Kharijite revolt from Tozeur, but this was soon beaten off. After the Fatimids left for Cairo in 970, Mahdia shared the chequered fortunes of other coastal towns. In 1057, the Zirids, supposedly the country's rulers, were forced to take refuge here by the invading Banu Hilal, and thirty years later, a joint Genoese/Pisan force seized the city, and the Zirids had to buy it back. Taken again by the Norman king Roger II of Sicily in 1148, the return to Islamic control in 1160 brought prosperity through trade and piracy and, in 1390, another unsuccessful siege by French, English and Genoese. The wars of the sixteenth century, however, brought Mahdia's great period to an end. In 1547 the corsair Dragut made the town his centre of operations, causing the Spanish to storm it in 1550. Rather than have to do this again, when they left in 1554 they blew the walls down. Since then – apart from routine pillagings by the Spanish in 1597 and the Knights of Malta in the seventeenth century – Mahdia has been a peaceful fishing port.

Practicalities: Orientation and Staying

The old town, on a peninsula poking out to sea, is only a tiny quarter now of what's otherwise a typical, thriving Sahel town. You pass through areas of new housing and light industry before reaching the modern **fishing port** (the fourth biggest in Tunisia)

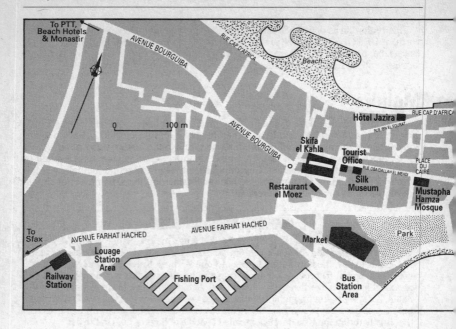

and the site of the ancient walls. Next to it is a main square, with town hall, police station and entrance to the **Skifa el Kahla** gate/tunnel (see p.180). This is really the centre of town. To one side lies the Medina and to the other the modern town. There are plenty of **banks** nearby, as well as the **tourist office** (8.30am–1pm Mon–Sat & 3–6pm Mon–Thurs, ☎81098) just through the *Skifa*. Also by the port, the *Maison de la Culture* is the local **cinema**.

Most of the peninsula itself is rocky, but some steps going down from the *Café de la Grotte* on the southern corniche road provide good **swimming** off the rocks. The daily fish **market** by the port and the weekly (Friday) regular market are both lively affairs: look out especially for octopus, which is sold by the bunch, rather like grapes. They're caught by boys who can be seen any morning picking their way round the shallow rocky pools on the peninsula's shore with spiked canes.

Stretching off into the **new town** is av Bourguiba, up which you will find the **PTT** (after about 500m on your left – city hours with international phone and cash exchange facilities) and a *Magasin Général* **supermarket** (at no. 63, about halfway to the PTT on your left – open Mon–Sat 8am–noon & 2.45–7pm, Sun 8am–12.45pm). Parallel with av Bourguiba, a block to your left, the **beach** stretches northwards, passing Mahdia's unobtrusive ventures into the mass tourist market: its three upmarket hotels. Also in the new town is the **regional hospital** in rue Mendes France (☎81005).

International phones calls can be made, when the PTT is closed, from the *Hôtel Mehdi* or the Shell station in the main square.

Accommodation

The first in the following listings is the only hotel in the Medina. For all the others, head out along av Bourguiba. If you want the beach without the luxury prices, there's also an unofficial **campsite** between the *Sables d'Or* and the *Mehdi* hotels.

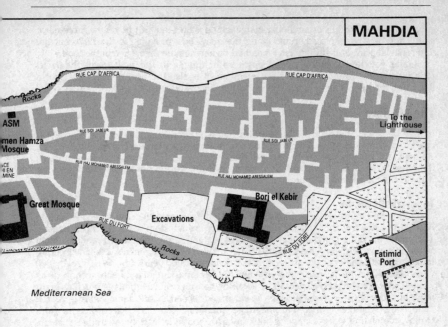

TOWN HOTELS

Hôtel Jazira, 36 rue Ibn el Fourat (☎81629). The only hotel in the Medina with lovely bedrooms but horrid bathrooms. To find it, walk straight into the Medina (see p.180) and when you get to the middle of pl du Caire, take a left and go straight on until you reach the sea. The *Jazira* is just to the right. 3TD per person.

Hôtel Panorama, av Bourguiba, opposite the PTT (☎80039). Formerly the *Grand*, with spotless rooms with showers; shared toilets. 9.5TD/14TD low season, 12TD/18TD high, b&b.

Pension Rand, 20 av Taïeb Mehiri (☎80448). Just 300m from the beach. 4TD/6TD low, 5TD/8TD high.

BEACH HOTELS

This is where you will find the rest of Mahdia's hotels, all a lot more expensive and quite a way from town, but all offering full or half board (FB/HB) if you want it.

Hôtel Sables d'Or, (☎81137). Rooms or roomy bungalows. A little bit run-down, but friendliest of the beach trio. 1*11TD/17TD low, 15TD/24TD high, b&b.

Hôtel Mehdi, (☎81300). Rather snooty, but cheaper than the *Sables d'Or* for FB. Way overpriced in season. 3* 11TD/18TD low, 22TD/34TD high, b&b.

Hôtel Cap Mahdia, (☎80300). Way out beyond the other beach hotels, in both price and location. 3* 25TD/40TD low, 46.5TD/69TD high, FB.

Places to eat

You don't have to stray far from the main square by the port to get some great food – and at prices you won't believe if you've just come down the coast from Sousse or Monastir. In the *Restaurant el Moez*, in a passage parallel with the *Skifa*, you can fill up on excellent fish soup and a deliciously spicy *kamounia*. For not much more, the *Restaurant de la Medina*, in the same building as the market, does some seriously succulent fish served by a handlebar-moustachied waiter in a bright yellow three-piece suit. There are posher restaurants along the quay, best of which is the *Lido*, but the difference in price and attitude isn't matched by any notable difference in the food.

Should you find yourself struck down with hunger in the new town, the *Hôtel Panorama*'s restaurant does a 3.5TD set menu. It is also the best place in town for a drink and the beer is served, unusually, with Spanish-style *tapas* snacks on the house.

The Medina

It may be small, but **Mahdia's Medina** has a maritime atmosphere which sets it apart from Tunisia's other old cities. The sea provides the dominant smell and even the stones in the houses look more seaworn than weather-beaten. The dominant sound, on the other hand, is not the breaking of waves, but the working of looms, since weaving is the main cottage industry here.

The Skifa el Kahla
The old town begins with the **Skifa el Kahla** gate, a sixteenth-century reconstruction of what the departing Spaniards blew up in 1554, which dominates the main square. The gate – once the only entrance to the city – stood in the middle of a wall, as much as ten metres thick, stretching right across the neck of the peninsula. It's a staggering thought that the defences destroyed by the Spaniards, 400 years ago, were already 600 years old. The *Skifa* in particular had quickly become legendary: each section of its vaulted passage could be closed off by lowering an iron grill weighing as much as eight tons; but it was the narrow passage itself, immortalised in the name *Skifa el Kahla*, "The Dark Passage", which became most notorious: "So dark," according to John Ogilby, translating Olfert Dapper's book of 1670, "that it is terrible to strangers, seeming rather a murdering den than an entrance into a city." Nowadays the murdering den is an informal souk, and you can climb to the top (Mon–Sat 8am–noon & 2–6pm, entry 0.6TD) for a view over the town.

Into the Medina
The street on the far side of the *Skifa* leads past a **Museum of Silk** (now closed) and a renovated souk, on the left, to the **Place du Caire**, one of the most perfect little squares in all Tunisia. Sitting at the café here under the small minaret, the only reminder of time passing is the tortoise-like movement of old men who shift their seats slowly round the square in pursuit of shade.

If you're interested in **weaving**, you'll notice that the Medina is full of workshops with looms whose sound can be heard all over the old town. Most of the weavers are very friendly and usually happy to chat about their job to passing tourists.

Also worth a visit if you want to know more about the Medina are the local **ASM**, who've set up shop in an old palatial residence on rue Cap Africa near the *Hôtel Jazira*.

The Great Mosque
Straight on from the pl du Caire, beyond another Turkish mosque on the left, the **Great Mosque** dominates an open plaza. By the 1960s the whole building was so decrepit that it was entirely reconstructed – what you see now is a 20-year-old version of the 1000-year-old original built by the Mahdi in the tenth century, incorporating some characteristic Fatimid elements. Most obvious of these is the monumental **entrance**, a Fatimid innovation which owes its form to Roman triumphal arches and its function to the elitism of Fatimid doctrine. Only the Mahdi and his entourage were allowed to use the main entrance, and the same distinction carried over to the prayer hall, where the central aisle was reserved for those in the ruler's favour. Deep niches, used in the entrance gate and in the prayer hall facade, represent another Fatimid inno-

vation which they pursued to great effect in Cairo. The two bastions at either corner of the north wall were once thought to be bases to twin minarets, but in fact there never was a minaret, and these were cisterns for collecting water from the roof. The courtyard was used as a cemetery by the Spaniards in 1551 – when they left in 1554 they exhumed the bodies and took them to Palermo. In theory visiting hours for the mosque are 10am–noon and 3–6pm, but these should only be taken as approximate: if you turn up at 3pm the *gardien* will give a charming smile, unlock the door, and forbid you to enter – it's prayer time. As some consolation though, he may give a live solo performance of the *muezzin*'s call to prayer, wonderful to hear echoing off the empty courtyard.

The Borj el Kebir

The hilltop **fort** in the middle of the peninsula, the *Borj el Kebir* (Mon–Sat 8am–noon & 2–6pm, 0.8TD), dates only from 1595. When it was first built it was just a simple rectangle, the corner bastions being added in the eighteenth century. As forts go, this one is bleak and uninteresting, but it does offer a great view over the town (mornings are best for photography). The *gardien* will probably tell you that a subterranean tunnel off the narrow entrance passage leads to El Jem: the story is that elephants carried the building blocks for the amphitheatre from the port at Mahdia to the middle of the Sahel. In fact it is most unlikely that there was any Roman settlement here: the crumbling **port** below the fortress was built by the Fatimids, with a tower on either side of the entrance and a chain suspended between them (which Christian attackers broke through in 1088). Long obsolete, the old harbour and the few confused remains of the Mahdi's palace almost breathe melancholy, an impression not helped by the fact that the end of the peninsula is a large cemetery.

Moving on – transport details, Ksour Essaf and south

Public transport hangs out by the port, with **buses** on one side by the market, and **louages** on the other side. There are regular buses to Sousse and towns en route with several to Tunis, and one to Nabeul and Kelibia. **Louages** run to Sousse, Sfax, Ksour Essaf, La Chebba and El Jem. There are no direct *louages* to Monastir – you'd have to take one to Moknine or Ksar Hellal and change there. The **train station**, with trains to Monastir, Sousse and Tunis, is a little further past the *louage* stand, opposite the *Maison de la Culture*.

South of Mahdia

About ten kilometres south of Mahdia, **KSOUR ESSAF** was the birthplace of Bourguiba's Neo-Destour Party in 1934; there's little to distinguish it from any other textile town in the Sahel, but it's the jumping-off point for **SALAKTA**, a small village on the site of Roman **Sullecthum**. The **ruins** are really only for the enthusiast, though it's a pleasant enough place with a new fishing harbour. Taxis ferry to and fro between Ksour Essaf and the shore. Right on the beach is a Roman cemetery, next to a new **museum** containing the smaller finds. South along the shore are other vestigial remains: baths, houses, walls, some of them actually in the sea. A little further on are the **Catacombs of Arch Zara**: ask someone for precise directions – they're about 3km south of the harbour, a little way inland. Like the complex at Sousse, they served as Christian cemeteries.

South of Ksour Essaf the coast road runs, with little passing interest, several kilometres inland from a bare coastline, to SFAX. LA CHEBBA has been earmarked for future resort development, but for the moment it's a tedious town. Some 5km away, by the sea, is RAS KABOUDIA, where a **tower** is the only remnant of a sixth-century Byzantine presence.

El Jem

The extraordinary **amphitheatre** at **EL JEM** (sunrise to sunset, 1.5TD plus 1TD for cameras) is the single most impressive Roman monument in Africa, its effect magnified by the sheer incongruity of its sudden appearance, surrounded by a huddle of small houses in the middle of the flat Sahel plain, halfway between Sousse and Sfax. There's a reasonable hotel here, but transport is good and there's no reason to stay longer than it takes to see the amphitheatre and the museum. If you do stay, however, you can get up early and visit the amphitheatre before the tour groups arrive – from 8am onwards.

A little history

Ancient El Jem was probably larger than the modern town, full of the luxurious villas of men who had grown rich on the proceeds of selling olive oil to Rome. As the Romans expanded from grain into oil, so the Sahel began to grow rich, and it was during the second century AD that **Thysdrus**, set here at a crossroads of the area, first started to expand so spectacularly. Prosperity brought luxury villas, mosaics and the amphitheatre – but eventually also the town's downfall. Some time in the 230s the citizens rose in revolt against the level of Roman taxation, killing the collector of taxes and proclaiming as Emperor of Rome an 80-year-old Imperial official called **Gordian**. This action introduced an unsettled period of 50 years for the Empire as a whole, but it did Thysdrus little good. The one memorial to Gordian's short rule (soon defeated, he committed suicide) is the amphitheatre, begun in his time and left unfinished at his death. According to an unlikely legend, the amphitheatre saw the last heroic stand of **Kahina**, Jewish prophetess and leader of **Berber resistance** to the Arab invasion in the seventh century. Certainly it would be even better preserved today if in 1695 Mohammed Bey had not blown up most of one side in order to evict followers of Ali Bey.

The amphitheatre

What is left still amounts to of one of the best preserved **amphitheatres** of its kind, however – finer than the Colosseum in Rome, and not a great deal smaller. It actually stands sixth in the league table of amphitheatre size, but such details lose all significance when you stand inside this artificial mountain. Estimates of its original capacity run to around 30,000, more than the total population of Thysdrus itself. People must have come from all around to watch the games here, a boost for the town's civic prestige. The ruined underground chambers in the middle of the arena held participants, people and animals alike, before they entered the fray (see box).

The museum and further ruins

The **museum** (8am–noon and 2–6pm daily), south of the amphitheatre by the road which swings past to Sfax, is full of mosaics which demonstrate El Jem's erstwhile prosperity. There's one small field of excavation next to the museum, with typical peristyle house plans and some mosaics in place.

Over the road from the museum, and across the railway track, are the remains of a **smaller amphitheatre**, hardly in the same state as the big one but open all the time, with no gates, no fences, no tour groups, and no charges. It was built before the big one.

Serious amateur archaeologists may like to note that even here, El Jem's Roman remains are not exhausted. If you want to find more, the easiest way is to take the SOUASSI road (av Hedi Chaker) westwards out of town for about a kilometre until you come to the last house on the right. Then turn sharp left up a track that heads straight back towards the big amphitheatre. There is a patch of **excavations** immediately on the left, and another 100m straight in front. A left turn there will take you to a third group, and beyond that a fourth. Frankly though, unless you want a walk in the sun for no apparent reason, none of these scattered bits of stone is really worth the effort.

ENTERTAINMENT – ROMAN STYLE

Circus shows were the opium of the Roman masses, used unashamedly by rulers to keep their huge urban proletariats happy, and the whole ritual played an important part in cementing the paternalistic relationship between rulers and ruled. A royal box was situated at each end of the arena (so that seasonal comfort could be assured) from where the beneficent sponsor of the show would watch the proceedings, and intervene when necessary. The defeated gladiator in a duel had the option of throwing himself on the mercy of the ruling official in his box, which he signalled by lying on his back and raising his left arm. If the crowd thought his courage had earned him his life, they would signal it by giving the thumbs-up sign – but the final decision was the official's alone: if *his* thumb was pointed down, the victim was killed on the spot. Doubtless prudent officials tended not to offend the crowd too often.

The only disadvantage of the shows as far as the rulers were concerned was their in-built **inflationary spiral**: the more spectacular the show, the higher the expectations next time. All they could do was to go on increasing the brutality quotient. **Wild animals** played a large part and since Africa was Rome's principal supplier they must have been plentiful here. They would be pitted against each other, or against gladiators, or else unarmed victims would be thrown in their midst; on the day Rome's Colosseum opened five thousand animals are said to have been slaughtered. But the public's appetite grew stronger and stronger for human blood. **Christians** were all too literally easy meat (see p.82 for martyrdoms at Carthage), but human life was sufficiently cheap for **armed gladiators** to be in plentiful supply. Most of them were prisoners or criminals, or even bankrupts on a contract which would pay off their debts – if they survived. Gladiators were surrounded by a macabre sort of glamour: they had their own fan clubs, and sometimes open banquets were put on at which the public could meet the next day's victims.

The most disquieting aspect of all this is that it would not have happened unless people enjoyed it: this really was **mass popular entertainment**, not in any way the freakish interest of a perverted minority. Ordinary concerns and interests circulated all around the slaughter: the poet Ovid describes, for example, how to pick up girls at the circus. And when a gladiator was on the point of dispatching his victim, the crowd would scream "Bene lava!" ("Wash yourself well [in blood]"), a homely little tag usually found in its literal meaning on the doorsteps of houses and public baths.

The modern town: transport out and other practicalities

The bulk of **modern El Jem** lies southeast of the main amphitheatre, around a central square planted with trees and shrubs. On one side of this is the **train station** with departures for Sousse, Tunis, Sfax, Gabes, Gafsa and Metlaoui. **Louages** cluster directly opposite, most of them headed for Mahdia, but some for Sousse and Sfax. *SNTRI* **buses** stop across the square, and *STS* (*SRT Sousse*) buses down the road in front of the archaeological institute by the museum. Note: there's no direct public transport to Kairouan.

If you want to stay in town, the *Hôtel Julius*, right next to the station (☎90044), is very respectable for its rates – 7.5TD/13TD b&b – and you can even ask for a room with a view of the amphitheatre. There are **banks** in town and the **PTT** (country hours) is on the way to the museum. **Market day** is Monday.

Sfax

The writer Ronald Firbank once took it into his head to call **SFAX** "the most beautiful city in the world", for which he has been ridiculed ever since by travel writers, their readers, and at least one mayor of the town. Granted some exaggeration, Sfax *is* a much more attractive place than is usually supposed. Somehow everything seems a little easier here, from bureaucratic operations to just asking people questions: a certain no-nonsense attitude that other Tunisians dislike can seem quite a plus to travellers. Indeed, with its two excellent museums, and consistently underrated Medina, Sfax can claim to be the most sophisticated and relaxing town in the country. Ferries also run regularly to the **Kerkennah Islands**, another good reason for passing through.

SFAX IN HISTORY

Sfax's lack of interest in tourism is significant: as the wealthiest and most successful city in the country, it has no need to rely on tourists either for revenues or for self-esteem. Founded in 849 AD near the site of a small Roman town, Taparura, Sfax took its name from a species of cucumber (*faqous* in Arabic) and made its money from a trading fleet and the products of the Sahel's olive trees. By the tenth century it was already wealthy.

During the Hilalian invasion, a member of the Zirid family, one Ibn Melil, set up a principality in Sfax, with hopes of reuniting Tunisia around it, but the Normans already had their eyes on it, and it fell to them in 1148. The Sfaxians plotted their resistance and began manufacturing arms in secret. Posing as beggars, they went from door to door recruiting fighters. As a signal they would be given beans of a number corresponding to the number of combat-worthy men in the house. Then, on New Year's Eve 1156, celebrated by the Christians with fireworks and a procession of bejewelled cows, they mingled with the Normans and surprised them mid-carnival, retaking the town. With money from the cows' gold, they built the "Cisternes des Vaches" a few hundred metres northwest of the Medina, and even today, New Year's Eve is celebrated in Sfax with beans and fireworks.

In 1546, under the crumbling rule of the Hafsids, Sfax again became a principality under the cruel adventurer El Mokkani. It was rescued fifteen years later by the pirate Dragut, who reunited it with the rest of Tunisia. Here began the period of Sfax's greatest prosperity, at its height in the eighteenth century. When the French came in 1881 they met fiercer resistance here than anywhere else, and the city was bombarded by nine iron-clads and four gunboats. Having taken Sfax, the French proceeded to sack the city, profane its mosques, and kill hundreds of its inhabitants. Later it produced two heroes of the nationalist movement in Hedi Chaker and Farhat Hached, the UGTT leader gunned down in 1952 by French terrorists.

Today, Sfax occupies a unique position in Tunisia. Politically, the Sfaxian lobby is a very powerful one, its clout coming from its commercial pre-eminence, which by now is Tunisian lore. Sfaxians are known as "the Jews of Tunisia" (a hint of residual anti-Semitism), and the stories and proverbs about their competitive nature are endless: according to one of them, if a Jerban grocer (Jerbans are the other notoriously sharp operators) sets up in Sfax, two locals will immediately move in on either side to squeeze him out. Feelings about Sfax in the rest of the country consist of a mixture of admiration, envy and resentment. Meanwhile, the Sfaxians just go about their business, happy to ignore claims that the city is ugly because they know, and everyone else knows, that it is successful.

Practicalities: orientation, accommodation and eating

At first the city seems to vindicate all criticism with its sprawling suburbs of housing and industry, but the centre is as compact as that of Sousse: the **Medina** separated from the port by a French grid-plan **new town** which contains almost everything you need. **Boulevard de l'Indépendance** connects the Medina's main entrance at **Bab Diwan** (by the main *louage* station) to the main thoroughfare of the new town, **Avenue Bourguiba**, that runs straight across the new town from the railway station and PTT at one end towards the main bus stations and the port for Kerkennah near its other end.

Accommodation

There are plenty of cheap and basic hotels in the Medina for those on a budget, and a couple of classy joints in the town centre for those who are not. Mid-range, you get a slightly wider choice, and if town centre hotels are full, there are others further afield, notably to the west of town. Numbers in the listings key the hotels to their locations on the city map. The locations of Medina hotels are shown on the Medina map.

MEDINA HOTELS

The **cheapest hotels**, as ever, are in the Medina – mostly very basic and mostly unsuitable for women travelling alone (*Hôtel Medina* may be an exception if a contingent of Tunisian women is staying). Note: it's not peculiar to Sfax, but normal practice here, for the most basic hotels is to put a price on each bed – so if you want a room to yourself you pay for all the beds in it. There are two main groups of hotels in the Medina: four in rue Mongi Slim, and four in rue Borj el Nar by Bab Diwan:

Hôtel el Andalous, 64 rue Mongi Slim (☎20903). Grotty but friendly. No shower but two hammams nearby. 2TD per bed.

Hôtel el Jemia, 89 rue Mongi Slim (☎21342). Marginally less grotty and correspondingly less friendly than the *Andalous*. 2TD per bed.

Hôtel el Medina, 53 rue Mongi Slim (☎20354). Sometimes puts up groups of Tunisian women, in which case probably the best cheap bet for women travellers. 3TD per person, shower 0.5TD.

Hôtel el Jerid, 61 rue Mongi Slim (☎23890). Miniscule rooms but reasonable value. 2.5/5TD, shower 0.5TD.

Hôtel el Magreb, 18 rue Borj el Nar (☎20057). Best and friendliest of the four hotels in this cluster. 5TD/6TD.

Hôtel Essaada, 19 rue Borj el Nar (☎20892). Extremely sleazy. 5TD/6TD.

Hôtel Besbes, 23 rue Borj el Nar (☎27271). Rather a dive, but no worse than the rest. 5TD/6TD shower 0.5TD.

Hôtel el Habib, 25 rue Borj el Nar (☎21373). Rude and unfriendly. 6TD/8TD.

Hôtel du Sud, 42 rue Dar Essebai near the Dar Jellouli museum. Not easy to find, especially if you've just arrived in town. 4TD per person.

MID-RANGE HOTELS

Hôtel le Paix, (1) 17 rue Alexandre Dumas (☎21436). Best of this bunch but tends to fill up early. 7TD/10TD, shower 1TD.

Hôtel Alexandre, (2) 21 rue Alexandre Dumas (☎21911). Next door to the *le Paix* and rather more sedate. 1* 9.5TD/15TD b&b.

Hôtel Colisée, (3) 32 av Taïeb Mehiri (☎27800). Very adequate but a bit impersonal. 2* 14.5TD/21TD b&b.

Hôtel Mondial, (4) 46 rue Habib Maazoun (☎26620). Another rather anonymous city-centre hotel. 2* 14TD/20TD b&b.

Hôtel Thyna, (5) 35 rue Habib Maazoun (☎25317). Rather pricey for its standards. 1* 15TD/24TD b&b.

YOUTH HOSTEL/CAMPSITE

Youth Hostel/Maison des Jeunes, route de l'Aeroport (☎43207). Somewhat hard to find. Head for the beginning of the airport road, but instead of going up it, look to your left: a *Novotel Syphax* sign points straight at it, but the sign over the entrance is in Arabic only. Closed 8am–6pm, curfew 10pm in winter, midnight in summer. 4TD per person in dorm, or 2TD for **camping**.

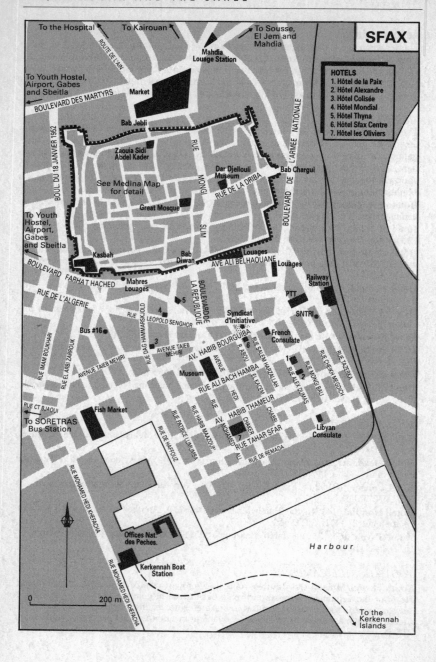

SFAX

To the Hospital
To Kairouan
To Sousse, El Jem and Mahdia

ROUTE DE L'AIN

Mahdia Louage Station

To Youth Hostel, Airport, Gabes and Sbeitla

BOULEVARD DES MARTYRS

Market

BOUL. DU 18 JANVIER 1952

Bab Jebli

Zaouia Sidi Abdel Kader

Dar Djellouli Museum

Bab Chargui

See Medina Map for detail

RUE DE LA DRIBA

BOULEVARD DE L'ARMEE NATIONALE

RUE MONGI SLIM

Great Mosque

To Youth Hostel, Airport, Gabes and Sbeitla

Kasbah

Bab Diwan

Louages

AVE ALI BELHAOUANE

Louages

BOULEVARD FARHAT HACHED

Mahres Louages

Railway Station

RUE DE L'ALGERIE

PTT

BOULEVARDE DE LA REPUBLIQUE

SNTRI

Bus #16

RUE DAG HAMMARSKJOLD

RUE LEOPOLD SENGHOR

4
5
3

Syndicat d'Initiative

French Consulate

6

AVENUE TAIEB MEHIRI

AV. HABIB BOURGUIBA

RUE SALEM HARZALLAH

RUE ABOU

1

RUE MONGI BALI

RUE CHEIKH MEDIOCH

RUE TAZERKA

RUE ALEX DUMAS

RUE IMAM BOUKHARI

RUE EL ARBI ZARROUK

AVENUE TAIEB MEHIRI

Museum

RUE ALI BACH HAMBA

AVENUE HEDI CHAKER

EL KACEM CHABBI

RUE CT BJAOUI

Fish Market

To SORETRAS Bus Station

RUE HABIB MAAZOUN

RUE PATRICE LUMUMBA

RUE MOHAMED ALI

AV. HABIB THAMEUR

7

RUE TAHAR SFAR

RUE DE REMADA

Libyan Consulate

RUE DE HAFFOUZ

Offices Nat. des Peches.

RUE MOHAMED HEDI KHEFACHA

Kerkennah Boat Station

Harbour

To the Kerkennah Islands

0   200 m

HOTELS
1. Hôtel de la Paix
2. Hôtel Alexandre
3. Hôtel Colisée
4. Hôtel Mondial
5. Hôtel Thyna
6. Hôtel Sfax Centre
7. Hôtel les Oliviers

HOTELS OUT OF THE CENTRE

Hôtel Hannibal, route de Mahdia (☎34329). Sfax's only *pension*, and an out-of-town alternative if the city's hotels are all full. 8TD/12TD b&b.

Hôtel Amin, rue Mejida Boulila (☎45600). In a rather industrial zone west of town. 1* 12.5TD/24TD b&b.

Hôtel Ennaim, 46 rue Mauritanie, near the corner of rue Alger (☎27564). Near the *Amin*, but rather more basic. 6.5TD/9TD, shower 0.7TD.

Hôtel Essourour, av Farhat Hached (☎23172). A place to try on your way to the above two.

UPMARKET ADDRESSES

Hôtel Sfax Centre, (6) av Bourguiba (☎25700). Opposite the Syndicat d'Initiative. Very business-oriented. 4*L 36TD/46TD b&b.

Hôtel Syphax, route de Soukra (☎43333). Way out of town and at the price (without breakfast), hardly worth the effort. 4* 40TD/54TD.

Hôtel les Oliviers, (7) av Habib Thameur (☎25188). On the corner of av Hedi Chaker. Has seen better days, but retains a certain old-fashioned charm. 3* 16TD/24TD b&b.

Eating, drinking and hanging out

As with accommodation, the **Medina** is the place to go if your **budget** takes precedence. On the other hand, if you feel like treating yourself, you'll find the expense well worth it: Sfax has some first-class restaurants at prices that are ridiculously cheap by Western standards.

CHEAP MEDINA EATERIES

Restaurant Saada, 22 rue Mongi Slim. Best of the cheapies at 2TD-odd.

Restaurant Tunisien, 23 and 16 rue Bab el Nar. Two cheap and basic diners with the same name just inside Bab Diwan. Around 2–3TD.

Restaurant PP, 17 pl du Journée de Tunis. Also just inside Bab Diwan. Couscous for 1.5TD, a meal for around 2TD. A bit of a greasy spoon, but quite adequate, especially at the price.

Various cheap places in the food market just outside Bab Jebli, serving *lablabi*, beans and other workers' staples.

MID-RANGE RESTAURANTS

Restaurant des Amis, 34 rue Dag Hammerskjold. About 3TD a meal.

Restaurant Carthage, 63 av Ali Belhouane. Handily, more or less opposite Bab Diwan. About 4.5TD a meat meal, 6TD for tasty fish. The octopus in sauce is good.

Restaurant Colombia, rue Tazerca. By *SNTRI* and opposite the train station, so a convenient place to grab a bite before travelling.

Chaine Hamburger, rue Tahar Sfar (at rue Abou el Kacem Chabbi). Offers "hot fast food and not dear." Ketchup on everything.

Restaurant Au Bec Fin, pl 2 Mars (by the side of pl de l'Indépendance opposite the police station). Pleasantly situated and about 3.5TD a meal.

UPMARKET DINING

Restaurant Baghdad, 63 av Farhat Hached (☎23856). Around 7TD a head for some excellent Tunisian dishes.

Chez Nous, 26 rue Patrice Lumumba. Good food and meticulous service, but it's the latter you pay for: about 6TD for a meat meal, 8TD for fish.

Le Corail, 39 rue Habib Maazoun (☎27301). Fairly chic, with fine food and cabaret-style entertainment.

Le Printemps, 55 av Bourguiba (☎26973). Sfax's most exclusive eatery. French and around 8TD.

Hôtel Alexandre, 21 rue Alexandre Dumas (☎21911). If none of the others are expensive enough, you should be able to stretch the bill here to 10TD if you order enough wine.

DRINKS AND SNACKS
For a cup of tea or coffee after your meal (or any other time), head for the **Café Diwan**, off rue de la Kasbah – an amazing place, actually inside the city wall. Go upstairs for a better view. With pine-nut tea, rose-watered Turkish coffee and a relaxed atmosphere, it's recommended for women as well as men. Other coffee bars, and alcohol bars, are around bd de la République. When these are shut, you'll get your last beer of the evening in the **Hôtel les Oliviers**, where you pay a bit more for it.

If you're suddenly attacked by a craving for **cakes or chocolate**, remember that several **patisseries** in rue du Grande Mosquée do fresh waffles with chocolate sauce.

Around the New Town

Sfax's grid-plan zone is more agreeable than that of Tunis. It is newer, with much of it rebuilt after heavy bombardment during World War II, and less crowded, and there are paved esplanades, genuinely green spaces and tree-lined streets. Being right on the sea, the climate is also less oppressive, and there's a large port with a busy daily **fish market**. If you need a sponge for your bathroom, there's a warehouse at 1 rue M Hedi Khefacha on the corner of av Bourguiba where they sit around trimming them and will be happy to sell you one if you stop by.

The Archaeological Museum
Very stylish, if a touch incongruous, is the French-looking clock tower on the Town Hall (pl Hedi Chaker), which houses the excellent **Archaeological Museum** (9am–1pm and 3–6pm; closed Monday; 0.8TD). There are only six rooms of exhibits, but for variety and quality they're hard to beat. **Room 1** (the entrance hall) holds Islamic antiquities; **room 2** has early Christian relics from La Skhirra and Thyna including a magnificent stylised Daniel in the lions' den; **room 3** contains Roman relics, including – unusually – wall paintings (a fine leering face) and delicate glass; **rooms 4, 5 and 6** are also Roman; and **room 7** (under the stairs) contains prehistoric stone tools from near Gafsa, evidence of the Capsian culture.

Sfax Medina

The **Medina of Sfax** differs from many in the rest of Tunisia in that it is still a thriving community. There are no souvenir stalls or tour groups trailing after a guide: this is no tourist spectacle, but a real city where people live and work. Not that you'll be made to feel in any way unwelcome. On the contrary, the ordinary pleasant reaction you get in ordinary shops where Sfaxians make routine purchases comes as a refreshing contrast to the tedious "Kommen Sie hier mein freunde" of Tunis and Kairouan's souvenir emporiums.

Another difference is Sfax Medina's near-complete **walls**, which make for a dramatic first impression. In view of the many bombardments which the city has endured, the walls are in remarkable shape and some parts go back to the ninth century – although these do co-exist with later additions. If you want to walk around the walls on the inside, the best place to do it is in the Medina's western corner from Bab Gharbi round to Bab Jedid: you can follow them all the way.

One curious feature of the Medina is the multitude of first floor **workshops**: narrow staircases lead up to these cramped rooms, where small businesses – tailors, shoemakers, engravers – beaver away in an almost Dickensian atmosphere. Few of them mind being interrupted, and their terraces offer wonderful rooftop views.

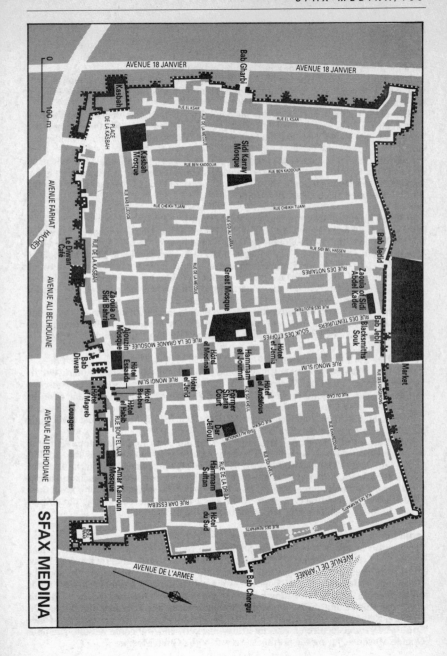

From the Kasbah to Bab Diwan

The **Kasbah** is in the Medina's southern corner. Originally a *ribat*, later the governor's residence and the headquarters of the town's militia, it has now been restored and is used for theatrical presentations and cultural exhibitions.

To its north, the **Sidi Karray Mosque** has what is considered the most typical doorway in Sfax, decorated in pink Gabes stone. The mosque is the focus of Sfax's Mouled festivities to celebrate the Prophet's birthday.

Rue de la Kasbah runs alongside the southern wall from the Kasbah, past the *Café Diwan*, into pl de la Journée de Tunis. On the corner as you come into the square is the **Zaouia of Sidi Bahri**. Note the double inscription above the door, again in pink Gabes stone.

As you cross the square, the multiple arches of **Bab Diwan**, the Medina's main entrance, are to your right. Only its westernmost, horseshoe entrance is ancient, going back to the fourteenth century. As at Tunis, Bizerte and Sousse, this main gate into the Medina was once much closer to the sea.

The Amar Kamoun Mosque and the Borj Ennar

To your left, opposite the inward side of Bab Diwan, is the Ajouzin Mosque, restored in the last century. Rue de la Grande Mosquée runs next to that, up towards the Great Mosque, and a little further, rue Mongi Slim also branches off left. Straight on down rue Borj el Nar, the **Amar Kamoun Mosque** – right, after about 150m – is between nos. 50 and 52. Look out for its small stone minaret. The mosque was rebuilt, like so many of Sfax's monuments, in the eighteenth century when the city became a major commercial centre. But the style of the minaret gives away its fifteenth-century origins.

Another 200m along the same street to the end, then a right, and a right at the end again, brings you to the entrance of the **Borj Ennar**, a fortress built to guard the Medina's eastern corner, now open to the public and the headquarters of the ASM.

To the Dar Jellouli Museum

Continue past the Borj's entrance down some cobbled steps into a small square. On the left is a gateway out of the Medina; on the right a small archway brings you back into rue Borj el Nar, emerging between nos. 76 and 78. Cross rue Borj el Nar and take the street ahead of you (rue Dar Essebai). At the end, turn left into rue de la Driba, past Hammam Sultan on your left, and you will see the Dar Jellouli Museum just to the right ahead of you, in rue Cheikh Sidi Ali Ennouri.

The **Dar Jellouli Regional Museum of Popular Arts and Traditions** is not to be missed, housed in a seventeenth-century residence as interesting as the exhibits (Tues–Sun 9am–4.30pm; closed Mon; 0.8TD, plus 1TD for photos). As in the Dar Ben Abdallah museum in Tunis, these illustrate local life, with costumes, utensils and manuscripts. One exhibit demonstrates how rose water is made, another shows how Tunisian women traditionally prepare their *kohl* eyeliner. There's even an old *kif* pipe similar to the ones still used in Morocco (though not Tunisia) today.

From the museum to the Great Mosque

Leaving the museum, turn left and continue up rue Cheikh Sidi Ali Ennouri, which brings you to a small square. Rue Sidi Khelil, left off the square under a small archway, takes you past the former *sharia* courthouse on the left (nos. 36–40) and the **Hammam el Joumni** at Nº25 opposite – one of Sfax's oldest bathhouses, restored in the eighteenth century but dating back to way before then. Just beyond the hammam, you cross **Rue Mongi Slim**, one of the Medina's main thoroughfares and perpetually bustling. Rather than get caught up in the flow, however, carry straight on past **Place Souk el Djemaa** (centre of a hectic Friday market), and you come out into rue de la Grande Mosquée, facing the northeastern wall of the Great Mosque.

The Great Mosque

Sfax's **Great Mosque**, though at first sight lower and less imposing than its contemporaries at Kairouan and Sousse, repays closer inspection. Unfortunately, it is not possible to enter the Great Mosque unless you are a Muslim, but you can see in through the windows, which are normally open.

Begun in 849 by the Aghlabids, it was extensively rebuilt in the tenth century under heavy Fatimid influence, and remains one of the most distinctive buildings left from that era – more so even than Mahdia's own Great Mosque. The most characteristic feature is the series of niches on the east facade, crowned by tooth-like rims – a form of articulation quite foreign both to the simple Aghlabid style and to the later, more sophisticated calm of the Hafsid styles.

This love of movement in external decoration is even more apparent in the **minaret**, whose wedding-cake-like layers of decoration are highly unusual for this region: the geometric bands, round windows and religious inscription seem almost frenzied compared to the Kairouan minaret. You can see the minaret from the northern corner of pl Souk el Djemaa, or climb up a terrace for a clearer view.

A curiosity worth looking out for is the stone embedded above the fourth window from the left in the northeastern facade: originally Byzantine, it depicted two peacocks surrounded by grapevines and small birds with a Greek inscription above. Such obvious pictures of animals and plants are very rare in Islamic architecture, but the spirit of the inscription was considered sufficiently Muslim for its inclusion in the mosque.

Into the souks: cloth, jewellery, food

Heading northwards from the Great Mosque, you pass under an arch into rue des Aghlabites, on the other side of which is the area of the main souks. More or less straight ahead is the **Souk des Etoffes**, specialising in fabrics, with rich garments all around, gradually giving way to carpets as you move up the souk. Parallel, one street to the left, is the **jewellers' souk** (rue des Bijoutiers). Cross rue Okba at the end of souk des Etoffes, and follow rue des Teinturiers (once the dyers' souk) until you come to **Bab Jebli**, which leads out of the Medina into the incredibly busy food market.

The blacksmiths' souk

Before leaving the Medina, there are other interesting visits to make. Just to the right is the **Zaouia of Sidi Abdel Kader**, over-carved in the pinkish-red Gabes stone already seen in Dar Jellouli. In the other direction, opposite no. 19 in rue des Forgerons, under a sign advertising coffee, an archway leads through to the **blacksmiths' souk**, where the smiths are hard at work amid the noise and grime. A glance at the upper storey, however, reveals that this was once a *foundouk* and dates back to the tenth century. It was associated with Bab Jebli, outside which was a marshalling point for trans-Saharan caravans, whose passengers would stay overnight at the *foundouk*.

Coming out of the blacksmiths' souk, a right turn brings you to the end of rue Mongi Slim, which leads straight back to Bab Diwan. Opposite the end of rue Mongi Slim, crowds squeeze through a narrow Medina entrance in a crush worthy of Cairo. On the other side of it is a large market complex, one of the most successful modern uses of the old vaulted forms to be seen in Tunisia, and, unlike so many other new market buildings, a delight to wander through.

Moving On from Sfax

Public transport out of Sfax – buses and *louages* especially – is complicated by the multiplicity of parking areas and *louage* stands. The **train station**, at least, is easy to find, right at the eastern end of av Bourguiba, with services to El Jem, Sousse, Tunis, Gabes, Gafsa and Metlaoui.

As for **buses**, city **bus #16**, which serves the war cemetery and nearly reaches the Thyna turn-off, can be picked up in rue Haffouz near the corner of rue Leopold Senghor every twenty minutes during the day. Otherwise, *SNTRI* **buses** stop opposite the train station in rue Tazerka with departures for Tunis, Gabes, Sousse and Houmt Souk (Jerba), and night departures to various southern destinations. **Two more bus stations**, which happen to be next to each other, are both down near the other end of av Bourguiba, in rue Commandant Bjaoui opposite the end of rue du Rabat. *SORETRAS*, Sfax's *SRT*, runs the main one, also served by other *SRT*s. There are regular buses to most large towns in the centre and south.

The **louage** situation is even more confused, with *louages* for Tunis, Sousse, Gabes, Medenine, Tataouine and Kebili (and some for Tripoli) leaving from bd de l'Armée at the corner of av Ali Belhouane across the road from Borj Ennar at the southeast corner of the Medina and, just 100m away, in front of Bab Diwan, the *louage* station for Gafsa, Sidi Bou Zid and Tripoli (plus some to Gabes). It's worth checking both if you're bound for Gabes or Tripoli, especially since Libyan *taxi binnasser* (*louages*) don't wait for each other to fill before touting for their own passengers (there may be two or more half-full vehicles). The Mahres *louage* park is further down av Ali Belhouane, at the corner of bd Farhat Hached in front of Bab Kasbah. Mahdia, too, has its own *louage* station on the other side of the Medina in bd des Martyrs, just north of the food market in front of a building with a "Sfax 2000" sign on it.

Ferries for the Kerkennah Islands leave six times a day in winter, four times daily in summer – free for foot passengers, 3.5TD for a car and 1.5TD for a motorbike. Unusually, there is easy access for wheelchairs.

Sfax's **airport** (☎40879) is not very well connected, but it offers three weekly flights to Tunis, two to Paris and one to Tripoli. Otherwise there are charters – including an occasional one to London. The airport is 7km west of town on the route de l'Aeroport. Bus #14 drops you 1km or so short, but your best bet is to take a cab, which shouldn't cost more than 3TD or so.

Sfax Listings

Airlines *Tunis Air*, 4 av de l'Armée (☎28628); *Tunisavia*, 51 rue Habib Maazoun (☎29828); *Air France*, rue Taïeb Mehiri (☎24847).

Banks Plenty, mainly concentrated on av Bourguiba and bd de la République.

Car and moped hire *Avis*, rue Tahar Sfar, at rue H Maazoun (☎24605); *Ben Jemaa*, route el Aïn (☎44325); *Hertz*, 47 av Bourguiba (at rue P Lumumba, ☎23553); *Interrent/Europcar*, 14 rue Coomandant Bajaoui (opposite the bus station, ☎26680); *Locar*, 67 rue H Maazoun (☎23738); *Mattei*, rue P Lumumba (☎96404); *Rentacar*, rue H Maazoun (☎23728); *Solvas*, rue H Maazoun, at rue Tahar Sfar (☎29882). Mopeds can be hired in the middle of rue Ali Belhouane, opposite the Borj Ennar, at the southeast corner of the Medina.

Cinemas *Baghdad*, 14 av Farhat Hached (at rue H Maazoun); *Le Colisée*, 27 rue Tahar Sfar (at av Hedi Chaker); *Atlas*, rue Hedi Chaker; *Etoile* and *Theatre*, opposite each other in bd de la République.

Consulates Belgium, 55 rue Haffouz (☎28096). France, 9 av Bourguiba (on the corner of rue A Dumas, ☎20788). Italy, rue Tahar Sfar (☎20052). Libya, 35 rue A Dumas (☎23332/8) open 8am–2pm Mon–Sat. Very friendly and much more likely to give you a visa than their counterparts in Tunis. If you arrive early enough, you can even pick it up the same day.

Football Sfax's main club, CSS (*Club Sportif de Sfax*), have their ground about 3km up the airport road. Matches are usually on a Sunday.

Hammams One of the oldest is the *Hammam el Joumni* at 25 rue Sidi Khelil (off rue Mongi Slim), open for men 6am–noon and 5pm–midnight, and for women 1–5pm. The nearby *Hammam Sultan* at 78 rue de la Driba is also open 6am–midnight, but women get longer hours: 9.30am–4.30pm (men before and after).

International phone calls In the PTT 8am–10pm daily; in a booth by the Syndicat d'Initiative 8am–11pm daily; and in another booth on bd de la République, supposedly 8am–11pm daily – but don't count on it. All are coin-operated.

Left luggage At the railway station.

Market day Friday in pl Souk el Djemaa and around the Great Mosque.

Medical facilities Main hospital, route de l'Aïn west of the town centre (☎44511); night chemist, 24 rue Leopold Senghor; *infirmerie*, 21 av Farhat Hached; *Polyclinique Ettawfik*, bd des Martyrs near Bab Jebli (☎41105).

Newspapers British papers are available at a kiosk on the corner of av Bourguiba and bd de la République, in a little square diagonally opposite the Town Hall.

ONA crafts shop Rue S Harzallah at rue Lt Hamadi Taj. Open 9am–noon and 3–7pm.

PTT At the eastern end of av Bourguiba. City hours and full range of services.

Shipping companies *CTN*, 75 rue H Maazoun (☎28020); *Sonotrak* (Kerkennah ferry company), Porte de Kerkennah, rue M Hedi Khefacha (☎22216); *Tourafric* (*Alimar's* agent), 35 av Hedi Chaker (☎29089).

Supermarkets *Monoprix* has a branch at 12 rue Abou el Kacem Chabbi, open Mon–Sat 8am–noon & 3–7pm, Sun 8am–2pm. Their other branch, in bd des Martyrs near the Mahdia *louage* station, is open Sat–Thurs 8am–7pm, closed Fridays.

Swimming pool The municipal pool, in route de l'Aerodrome near the Maison des Jeunes, is open rather ridiculous hours: Mon–Sat noon–3pm and Sun 10am–2pm. Entry costs 1TD per hour, 0.5TD for students.

Tourist office The Syndicat d'Initiative in pl d'Indépendance (☎24606) is open Mon–Sat 8.30am–1.30pm and Mon–Thurs 3–5.45pm, closed Sun. They're friendly and knowledgeable, with useful information posted on the door even when closed. If their HQ looks like a bandstand, that's what it was originally was, when first built at the turn of the century.

War cemetery 4km south of town on the Gabes road and served by bus #16. Hindu servicemen have their own cemetery behind the main one.

Around Sfax

The most popular **beach** around Sfax is 10km north at SIDI MANSOUR (where there are festivities around the marabout in September). THYNA, site of Roman Thaenae and source of some of the mosaics in the museum, is the other well-known nearby attraction but the **saltpans** just to the south of Sfax are a serious magnet for ornithologists. Out on the roads radiating from Sfax, it's all **olives** as far as the eye can see. The resort of MAHRES offers few reasons to break the trip to GABES; LA SKHIRRA maybe more.

The saltpans

The outstanding **saltpans of Sfax** stretch almost continuously from Sfax to THYNA. They produce some 300,000 tonnes of top-grade sea salt a year, but more significantly, they're the Mediterranean's single most important site for **wintering wading birds** and a site of internationally renowned scientific interest. The combination of a shallow coast and a tidal range of between one and two metres – a highly unusual feature in the largely tideless Mediterranean – exposes huge areas of **mudflats** at low tide, rich in the small creatures which form the bulk of a wading bird's winter diet. In addition, the area supports high winter populations of **flamingos**, rare **spoonbills**, and a variety of **herons**, **egrets**, **gulls** and **terns**. The whole area offers exceptional birdwatching, partly because of the sheer numbers and range of species, but mostly because the birds have become used to saltpan workers and shell fishers and this has made them very approachable. If you're remotely interested in wildlife, it's not a site to pass up.

Access to the saltpans is south down av Bourguiba and, after less than 2km on the Gabes road, left at a road sign-posted to the fishing port. Walk up that, and the mudflats start on your right just before the port. The entrance to the saltpans has a gate and a high wire fence and is clearly marked *Cotusal*. But while the mudflats are public land, they're unsafe to walk across, as well as being foully polluted with Sfax's effluent, and the best way to see the birds is to wander along the banks on the seaward side of the saltpans – private land, for which you'll need to ask **permission** to enter at the gate. The birds are found on the mudflats at low tide, and just a chosen few of the saltpans, depending on their salinity. There are fifteen square kilometres of saltpans, so it may take some time to find the birds' location.

Take a look at the little **inlet closest to Sfax** first, which, for aesthetic reasons alone – the sight of hundreds of wading birds amongst the shell fishers in the early morning sunlight – is magical. Although the biggest numbers of birds are recorded from November to the end of February, many are still present through to April, and some species (such as avocet, blackwinged stilt and redshank) stay on to breed in the coastal salt marshes surrounding the mudflats.

The feeding grounds in the mudflats beyond the saltpans are the actual reason why the birds congregate at Sfax, and a few hours watching the area gives a fascinating insight into their **feeding habits:** from flamingos doing their inverted side-to-side sieving of the shallow water with their huge bills, to spoonbills with their own usefully shaped mouthparts; from herons and egrets standing poised, ready to pounce, to the true waders (stints and dunlins, curlews and godwits) probing the mud, each species to a different depth and for different prey.

As well as the waders, Sfax is a good place to watch for **seabirds**, including the region's largest tern, the Caspian, with its long red beak. In winter, you can also see hundreds of **black-necked grebes**, bobbing on the water like miniature, round ducks.

Thyna

Off the Gabes road, about 10km south of Sfax, the **THYNA** turn-off is sign-posted but not too conspicuously, so keep your eyes peeled. Any bus bound for Gabes or Mahres should drop you there (ask for the Thyna *croisement*), and city bus #16 leaves you 1km short. From the turn-off, follow the Thyna road left towards the sea until you see a lighthouse; go straight on towards it, but take a track off to the right just before the lighthouse entrance (an arrow directs you). This track brings you to the main relic, a bathhouse. There were some mosaics here, but these are being chopped up and carted off to the museum in Sfax. Other bits and pieces are scattered about between the bathhouse and the lighthouse, but some are in a military zone, so be careful not to trespass on it – and avoid taking photographs.

Olives

Whether you find the roads out of Sfax scenically appealing depends on your reaction to row upon row of **olive trees** – the age-old industry of the Sahel ever since the Romans introduced them to replace grain. It was in the early nineteenth century, however, that the olive plantations really came into their own. Most of the olive oil was shipped to Europe where, too coarse and strong tasting for dainty European palates, it was made into soap. The markets seemed bottomless and the price high, encouraging many Sfaxians to occupy lands belonging to the surrounding Methelith tribes in order to plant trees. By the 1830s the German traveller Prince Puckler-Muskau, claimed that the trees already stretched further than the eye could see.

Most of the trees are planted a standard twenty metres apart, the optimum distance, and the harvest begins in November. As it has to be done by hand, the process is highly labour-intensive: teams of seven comb the branches, protecting their fingers with hollowed-out goat horns (more recently with plastic substitutes). An average tree around Sfax produces 50kg of olives a year, almost all of them sent to factories on the outskirts of the city which convert them into 15kg of oil.

Unfortunately, recent increases in productivity and production, not only in Tunisia but throughout the Mediterranean, have led to overproduction. In the last decade prices have tumbled and after a good harvest Tunisia can't sell the bulk of its oil, whatever the price. Now the government encourages farmers to uproot the older plantations and plant cereals: history has turned full circle.

Mahres

Once you emerge from the olive ranks there's little of interest on any of the main roads away from Sfax before El Jem, SBEITLA, GAFSA or GABES. On the way to Gabes you pass through **MAHRES**, an unexciting beach resort with a couple of hotels: the 2* *Marzouk* 10.5TD/16TD b&b (☎90231), and the unclassified *Younga* (☎90334) at 7TD/10TD without breakfast. Mahres has a Monday market and a Byzantine fortress – **Borj Younga**, 11km south of town.

La Skhirra and Kneiss Island

Further south, **LA SKHIRRA** is a big oil terminal for pipelines coming from Algeria and Tunisia. Just over 100 years ago this "town" was simply a summer camp for the Mehadhaba tribes. Then, in 1871, Perry Bury Co of Lancashire began exporting esparto grass for paper manufacture from here. It quickly became one of the region's most important commodities and the town grew up on this British link. There is an archaeological site, many of whose finds are now in the museum in Sfax, but the site is within the bounds of the oil terminal and off-limits to the public.

If you're lucky, you might be able to get someone down at the port to take you over to KNEISS ISLAND, a few hundred metres offshore, for some isolated birdwatching, but check with the port police first.

The Kerkennah Islands

Throughout history the **KERKENNAH ISLANDS** have been a place of exile: the Carthaginian General Hannibal, awkward Roman customers, adulterous Muslim wives and Habib Bourguiba have all been sent here at one time or another. Now the isolation is an attraction for tourists. Conventionally promoted as the poor folk's Jerba, the islands are distinctively quieter – the ideal spot for doing nothing for a few days, or a few weeks.... Even energetic swimming is out of the question because the sea is so shallow.

The islands' name came from the nymph Circe who, according to legend, imprisoned Odysseus here because she could not bear to let such a handsome hero leave. Since then, the only **historical events** interrupting the islands' calm were their 1286 seizure by Roger de Lluria, the Catalan ruler of nearby Sicily, their 1335 repossession by the Hafsids, and an attempt to occupy them in 1510 by the Spanish. At the time, the Spaniards held Tripoli and felt they needed a back-up base. They tried to take Jerba without success, leaving 400 men on Kerkennah to occupy it. All were massacred by the Kerkennians within the next year. They failed to hold Tripoli for very long either.

Island nature

Strictly speaking there are two inhabited islands, but the channel between them was bridged by a causeway in Roman times, so for all practical purposes there's only one: a hypnotic expanse of wind-blown date palms on sandy ground that never rises more than three metres above sea level. The trees are rather tatty, but many people think this the most beautiful spot they know, and return year after year. Apart from the dominant palms, there are some interesting **flowers** – in particular a small type of asphodel and another, a low plant with sprawling thin leaves and a beautiful flat purple flower with the inelegant name *Fagonia*. Other common seaside plants include dandelions and cottonweed with yellow "everlasting" flowerheads and covered with fine silvery hairs. Both of these species combine with pale blue sea lavender to form a fine carpet of colour at the edges of the beaches and rocks.

Island people

Many of the islands' people, understandably, find the desert island atmosphere less appealing than do the tourists, and depopulation has been a problem for some years. In the early 1960s a company called *Somvik* was set up to exploit the tourist potential and revive the islands' fortunes, but this has done little more than bring a small strip of low-key hotels, so isolated that unless you're staying in one it would be easy not to notice them at all. Happily, there are signs that the economy is picking up, and the island people remain some of the most hospitable in the country.

Arrival on Gharbi/Melita

There are six daily **ferries** to and from SFAX in summer (one every two hours in daylight) and four in winter (see p.198).

Island **buses** connect with the boats and run to Remla, Sidi Frej and El Attaia. The other way, they leave Remla and Sidi Frej an hour before the boat's scheduled departure time (although the journey only takes twenty minutes). The bus from the ferry to Sidi Frej runs on to Remla and there is also a minibus service from the *Grand* and *Farhat* hotels in Sidi Frej once a day to Remla and three times a day to meet ferries.

On Kerkennah the ferry docks at SIDI YOUSSEF, the westernmost tip of the first island, called either **Gharbi** ("Western") or **Melita** after the village at its centre. One of Kerkennah's three sights is a crumbling **Turkish tower** 3km along the north shore of this island. Meanwhile, the single bus line rumbles along the single road and over the causeway to the next island, **Chergui** ("Eastern"). A turning to the left serves the **hotel strip**, known as SIDI FREJ. If you're headed this way, make sure you take the right bus when you get off the ferry, otherwise you could get dropped off at OULED YANEG just over the causeway, and be left with a 2km walk.

Accommodation and Activities

Most places to stay are by the beach at **SIDI FREJ**. The first you come to is the *Hôtel Cercina* (☎81228) at 5TD per person b&b in rather poky "bungalows", or 8TD–13.5TD (depending on season) in small but passable rooms with own bathroom. Beyond the *Cercina*, the *Kastil* (☎81212) is basic but friendly and just 4TD per person b&b low season, 7TD high, for square little huts posing as bungalows. The *Residence Club Vacation Village* further up is closed until 1993, and past that are two hotels catering for (mainly British) package tourists. They're both more expensive but correspondingly plusher than the *Cercina* or the *Kastil*. The *Hôtel Farhat* (☎81236) has rooms with garish orange and yellow decor for 17.5TD/22TD b&b low season, 26.5TD/40TD high, and the *Grand Hôtel* next door (☎81266) is more soberly decorated at 14TD/22TD b&b low, 26.4TD/42TD high. Notices in the *Grand*'s lobby warn that "It is pure sunlight on the island" and advise you to "ensure that you wear suntan lotion at all times."

As for **passing the time and enjoying yourself**, the *Grand* is bigger and noisier and in general offers more **facilities** than the *Farhat*, but between the two of them and the *Cercina*, you can windsurf (5TD/hr), ride horses or camels (6TD/hr), or go out in a fishing dhow (6TD/hr, crew included). You can **change money** in the *Grand* six evenings a week, and in the *Farhat* on three. The **beach** at Sidi Frej is not unparalleled but the *Grand* has the best piece of it. A good investment is to **hire bicycles** from the *Farhat* or the *Cercina* (the *Grand* charges twice as much), and explore the islands at will, perhaps taking in the **Borj el Hissar** – another ruined fort from the Aghlabid period, rebuilt by the Spanish, a couple of kilometres down a track from the hotel zone.

You can **eat** at all four Sidi Frej hotels and, if you're lucky, try local **Kerkennah specialities** such as *tchich* (a kind of octopus soup), and *melthouth* (something between pasta and couscous). The *Farhat* and the *Grand* do a 4TD set menu; otherwise you'll be paying around 7TD a head in the *Cercina* and slightly less in the *Kastil*. The *Cercina* is generally agreed to have the best food, but its service is second-rate. The best sugges-tion is probably to stay at the *Farhat*, eat at the *Cercina* and use the *Grand*'s facilities – so long as your budget is up to it and you don't mind waiting for ages to be served.

Remla

The main road continues along the southern shore to the islands' "capital", **REMLA**, which boasts the only other **hotel** – the *Jazira*, right on the main street (☎81058) with clean, if spartan, rooms at 8TD/12TD b&b. In dire straits, you could also stay at the **Maison des Jeunes** (☎81148) – 4TD a bed. Remla also has a **bank**, a petrol station, a **doctor** and a country–hours **PTT**. You can eat at the *Jazira* for 4TD-odd, or around the corner at the *Sirene Restaurant*.

Going fishing

Doing anything energetic on Kerkennah is really to defeat the object of coming here, but a popular **excursion** is to go out with one of the fishermen: they will take people out for a small fee, sometimes even cooking a meal of fresh fish into the bargain. The islanders use a curious fishing technique involving screens made of palm fronds set in V shapes in the waters all around the shore (see p.288). A trip in one of their small sail-ing boats, as the sun falls behind the palms and floods the sea a deep blood red, is one of Tunisia's most idyllic experiences. In Remla, Rachid at the *Jazira* will take people out at 10TD each for half a day, or ask around the fishing boats and come to your own arrangements.

Beyond Remla

From Remla, the road keeps straight on to end in the fishing village of **EL ATTAIA**, the most attractive place to stay if you're camping. A turning to the left leads through some small settlements before reaching an unlikely **museum** devoted to Bourguiba's dramatic escape from French custody in 1945, when he passed through the village: the boat he used, the house he sheltered in, and some of the letters he wrote from various international places of exile, have all been faithfully preserved. En route to El Attaia, you might try to find the meagre **Roman remains** near the village of EL ABBASIA.

travel details

Trains

FROM ENFIDA TO:
Tunis (5 daily, 1hr 30min); **Grombalia** (3, 45min); **Bir Bou Rekba** (5, 30min) connecting for **Hammamet and Nabeul**; **Sousse** (5, 45min); **Monastir** (2, 1hr 20min); **Mahdia** (2, 2hr 30min); and **Sfax** (2, 3hr 30min).

FROM SOUSSE TO:
Tunis via **Bir Bou Rekba** (8, 2hr 15min, all of which, except the midday service and 2 evening departures, connect for **Nabeul and**

Hammamet); **El Jem** (5, 1hr); **Sfax** (5, 1hr 50min); **Gabes** (2, 4hr 30); **Gafsa** (1, 6hr 30min) and **Metlaoui** (1, 7hr 15min); **Monastir** (metro from bd Mohamed V, hourly, 1hr 30min); **Mahdia** (4 direct, 1hr 40min, plus 3 on the metro, changing at Monastir).

FROM MONASTIR TO:
Mahdia via Ksar Hellal and Moknine (Mon–Sat 8, Sun 4; 1hr 10min); **Tunis** (3 direct, 3hr 10min); **Sousse** (hourly, 1hr 30min); **Enfida** (3, 1hr 20min); **Bir Bou Rekba** (3, 2 of which connect for **Nabeul** and **Hammamet** – 2hr).

FROM MAHDIA TO:
Monastir via Moknine and Ksar Hellal (Mon–Sat 8, Sun 4; 1hr 10min); **Sousse** (4 direct, 1hr 40min, plus 3 on the metro, changing at Monastir); **Tunis** (3 direct, 4hr).

FROM EL JEM TO:
Tunis (5, 3hr); **Sousse** (5, 1hr); **Sfax** (5, 50min); **Gabes** (2, 3hr); **Gafsa** (1, 5hr 10min); **Metlaoui** (1, 6hr).

FROM SFAX TO:
Tunis (5, 4hr); **Sousse** (5, 1hr 50min); **El Jem** (5, 50min); **Enfida** (1, 2hr 30min); **Mahres** (2, 40min); **Gabes** (2, 2hr 30min); **Gafsa** (1, 4hr); **Metlaoui** (1, 5hr).

Buses

FROM ENFIDA TO:
Sousse (hourly, 1hr); **Tunis** (regular, 1hr 30min); **Nabeul** via **Hammamet** (2 daily, 2hr).

FROM SOUSSE TO:
Tunis (5 daily, 2hr 30min); **Kairouan** (4, 1hr 30min); **Le Kef** (2, 3hr 45min); **Monastir** (frequent, 45min); **Mahdia** (frequent, 1hr 30min); **Sfax** (5 daily, 2hr 30min); **Gabes** (4, 5hr 30min); **Medenine** (5, 7hr); **Houmt Souk (Jerba)** (1, 6hr 45min); **Douz** (1, 7hr 15min); **Nabeul** via **Hammamet** (2, 2hr 15min).

FROM MONASTIR TO:
Sousse (frequent, 45min); **Tunis** (1 daily, 3hr); **Nabeul** (1, 2hr 30min); **Sfax** (1, 2hr); **Ksar Hellal** and **Moknine** (frequent, 30min).

FROM KAIROUAN TO:
Tunis (18 daily; 2hr 15min); **Sousse** (13, 1hr); **Sfax** (3, 2hr); **Gabes** (1, plus several nocturnal, 4hr); **Le Kef** (2, 3hr 30min); **Gafsa** (3, 4hr); **Houmt Souk (Jerba)** (2, 7hr).

FROM MAHDIA TO:
Tunis (1 daily, 4hr); **Nabeul** (1, 3hr 30min); **Sousse** (frequent, 1hr 30min); **Sfax** (2 daily, 2hr 30min); **Moknine** and **Ksar Hellal** (frequent, 30min).

FROM EL JEM TO:
Tunis (2 daily – plus several late night, 2hr 30min); **Sousse** (5, 1hr 15min); **Sfax** (5, 1hr 15min); none direct to **Kairouan**.

FROM SFAX TO:
Tunis (9 daily, 5hr); **Sousse** (5, 2hr 30min);

Kairouan (3, 2hr); **Mahdia** (2, 2hr 30min); **Monastir** (1, 2hr); **El Jem** (5, 1hr 15min); **Le Kef** (2, 4hr 30min); **Sbeitla** (1, 3hr); **Gafsa** (5; 3hr 30min); **Nefta** via **Tozeur** (1, 6hr); **Gabes** (9; 2hr 15min); **Houmt Souk (Jerba)** (2, 4hr 45min); **Medenine** (5, 3hr 30min); **Tripoli** (2 weekly, 12hr).

Louages

TO TUNIS DIRECT FROM:
Enfida/Sousse/Monastir/Kairouan/Sfax.

LOCAL SOUSSE–MAHDIA SERVICES:
Sousse–Monastir.
Sousse–Hergla.
Monastir–Moknine/Ksar Hellal–Mahdia.
Sfax (Bab Kasbah)–Mahres.
Mahdia–Ksour Essaf–La Chebba.

REGIONAL LOUAGE ROUTES (AND SOUTH):
Enfida–Sousse/Zaghouan/Nabeul.
Sousse–Kairouan/Gafsa/Mahdia/El/Jem/Sfax.
Kairouan–Maktar/Sbeitla/Sfax/Sousse.
Mahdia–El Jem–Sfax/Sousse.
Sfax (bd de l'Armée)–Sousse/ Kebili/Gabes–Medenine–Tataouine/Tripoli.
Sfax (Bab Diwan)–Gabes/Gafsa/Sidi Bou Zid/Tripoli.
Sfax (bd des Martyrs)–Mahdia.

Ferries

FROM SFAX TO:
Kerkennah Islands, 4 times a day in winter, 6 in summer (1hr).

Flights

FROM MONASTIR TO:
Tunis (1–2 weekly); **Jerba** (1–2); flights with Tunis Air to **Paris** (2 weekly); **Brussels** (1–2); **Luxembourg** (1); **Lyon** (1); **Nice** (1); **Rome** (1); **Frankfurt** (1); **Geneva** (1). Most of Monastir's air traffic is seasonal charters from Europe and the UK. It's sometimes possible to get a one-way ticket: try Tunis Air and the tour operators.

FROM SFAX TO:
Flights on a Tunisavia Twin Otter to **Tunis** (2); **Valetta** (1); **Tripoli** (2); Tunis Air/Air France to **Tunis** (1); **Paris** (2). All other flights are charters, including an occasional one to London.

PHONE CODES

Enfida, Sousse, Monastir, Mahdia, El Jem ☎03. Kairouan ☎07. Sfax, Mahres, Kerkennah ☎04.

CHAPTER FIVE

THE TELL

he Tell begins with **plains** – good, well-watered farming land – but rises quickly into the Dorsale mountains, the highest in the country, forming a barrier across from Zaghouan to Kasserine. Beyond lie empty and infertile steppes which fade towards the coast into the Sahel. The plains have been heavily populated since Roman times, though the southern parts, over the centuries, were steadily taken over by esparto grass and left to sheep and camel herds. The tribes that lived here in the nineteenth century were notorious for their banditry; the Hammama, centred on the tomb of Sidi Bou Zid, used to raid to the very gates of Sfax. During the Protectorate large areas of public grazing land were taken over by colonists and the tribes were left to fight over the scraps. Most of the population lived by working on colonial estates and gathering esparto grass. Ever since, **the economy** has been severely depressed and, even in larger towns like Le Kef and Kasserine, most people now leave to look for work in Tunis or the Sahel – often without success. The feelings of frustration which haunt the region found expression in January 1984 when the "bread riots" started in Kasserine, leading to the deaths of 80 people (see p.335).

Lack of attention from tourists contributes to this sense of neglect, though for those who want to get off the beaten track this is one of the most exciting parts of the country. The three great **Roman sites** of **Dougga, Maktar and Sbeitla** are the most obvious pull, but it's worth the effort to explore some of the towns, too. **Testour** is a small Andalusian market town, its heritage of tiled roofs and decorative brick walls preserved virtually intact. **Le Kef**, with its resonant history, striking mountainside position and friendly atmosphere, is a delightful place to stay and from here, you're also well poised for the Tell's most dramatic landscapes – the wide open spaces which include untouched ancient sites like **Haidra** and the mysterious mountain known as **Jugurtha's Table**.

MARKET DAYS	
Monday – Maktar, Tajerouine	Thursday – Teboursouk, Le Kef, Siliana,
Tuesday – Dahmani, Kasserine, Le Krib,	El Aroussa
Haffouz, Hajeb el Ayoun	Friday – Testour, Thala, El Houareb
Wednesday – Sbeitla, Sers, Menzel	Saturday – Sidi Bou Zid
Chaker	Sunday – Rohia

Approaching from Tunis: Testour and Ain Tounga

Approaching the Tell from Tunis, the main westward route splits at MEDJEZ EL BAB, where the northern fork climbs over the Teboursouk range and runs through the towns covered in Chapter Three ("Bizerte and the North"). The southern branch follows the Medjerda River into the Tell at Testour.

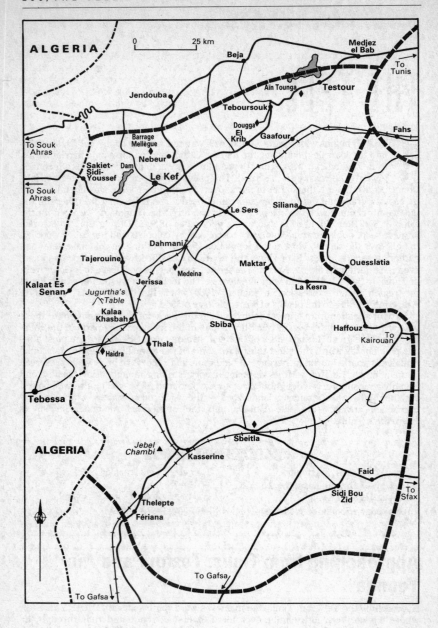

Testour

A cluster of tiled roofs on a mound above the River Medjerda, **TESTOUR** looks so Spanish that it's no surprise to find that it was built by Andalusian refugees in the seventeenth century. Its appearance and the local people's way of life have changed very little since, less perhaps than any other town in Tunisia. This, and the almost pristine rural feel of the place, give it a particular fascination, the more so if you can coincide with the **Friday regional market**. At all events, it's worth a stop en route from Tunis to Dougga and Le Kef: an easy enough road to travel by bus or *louage*.

Practicalities

There have been few incursions into the fabric of the old town – most of the straggle of **new development** flanks the main road going out, west, to Le Kef. One of the last of these buildings, the *Hôtel Ibn Zeitun* (☎68033) is currently closed and there doesn't look to be anywhere else to stay.

Buses stop at the defunct *Café du Transport*, near the hotel, and again (on the far side of town) below the hillside cemetery. They run hourly to Teboursouk and Le Kef, and to Medjez el Bab and Tunis.

Testour's growth and the Great Mosque

Some of the **Andalusian Muslims**, evicted from Spain in the wake of the Christian reconquest, were wealthy enough to settle in Tunis itself, where the Rue des Andalous is a reminder of their presence. Others had to petition the authorities for land, and in 1609 were granted the old Roman site of Tichilla, today's Testour. The new Andalusian communities were renowned throughout North Africa for their commercial abilities and hard work, and the citizens' bourgeois pride and culture found permanent expression in their mosques and public buildings.

The **Great Mosque** is only the largest and most beautiful of an extraordinary number of mosques built in the town in the early seventeenth century. It stands at the end of the main street, with its walls like crumbled biscuits, surmounted by a ribbed tiled roof. Inside, the delicate arcades of the two courtyards – one hung with white jasmine – are a marked contrast to the generally heavier local styles. Yet even here you find Roman blocks have been re-used and incorporated – doorframes, capitals, columns, oil presses in the paving; one corner column in the main court sports a milestone proclaiming "Carthage 66 miles".

Lesser mosques

Formerly, the whole town would come together in the Great Mosque for Friday prayer. Other mosques, built on virtually every side street off the main avenue, would serve the specific needs of local communities – business and municipal meetings as well as everyday prayer. One of the most striking is the **Çghair Çaia Mosque**, built by a local family with what looks suspiciously like a church bell-tower on top of its minaret.

At the opposite end of the main street to the Great Mosque is another graceful reminder of Andalusian culture, the **Zaouia of Sidi Naseur el Baraouachi**, built around his tomb in 1733. It begins in a lengthy passage, opening on to a tiny paved courtyard enclosed by an arcade and almost swamped by an orange tree. The tomb itself, covered by a stuccoed dome, is still an object of veneration – the stains on its far wall made by hands coated in henna to ward off the evil eye.

Traditional trades

From its foundation, Testour's economy centred on the agricultural activities of the region – for which it still provides an important market – but there were also skilled artisans among the immigrants. The town was long famed for its *chechias*, skullcaps made from the wool of local flocks. These have almost disappeared, but the other main trade – traditional tile production – has survived. A factory can be seen down by the river below the Great Mosque, one of only two left in all Tunisia (the other is at Tozeur), and the tiles it produces were used in the recent restoration of the Great Mosque. To make them, sand is mixed in troughs for 2–3 days with water and dung (which makes the tiles impermeable) before being shaped in moulds, heaped into the kiln, and fired for several days. Some 2000 tiles are produced in every week-long cycle.

The Maison de Culture
Most of the Andalusian immigrant communities established in Tunisia included Jews as well as Muslims, though many have left for Israel over the last decades. Anti-Semitic traditions, however, endure. The town's **Maison de Culture** (down one of the side streets north of the main avenue, just beyond a distinctive minaret with bands of faience tiles) is a good case in point. An old and elegant mansion, it was originally built for one Habiba Msika, a famous Tunisian *chanteuse*, by her wealthy Jewish husband. Moving in, she promptly murdered the man, and by all accounts seems to have lived happily ever after – performing, no doubt, in the purpose-built auditorium. Caretakers take delight in showing off some splendidly vampish photos, and in displaying the massive safe where the ill-fated husband kept his ill-gotten gains. Somehow, this tale of wealth and passion seems out of place in a town of honest, hard-working origins and very modest existence. Apart from the market the only event here is an annual **Festival of Malouf Music**, held towards the end of June in the large and hideous new café below the Great Mosque.

Aïn Tounga

At **AÏN TOUNGA** – nine kilometres west of Testour on the Le Kef road – is an ancient site which includes one of the most impressive **Byzantine fortresses** to be seen in Tunisia. Remains of its walls and towers, some half-buried but still enormous, loom over the modern road. Above an entrance to the southwest tower is a Latin inscription – which doesn't seem strange until you reflect that the Byzantines spoke Greek. The local people must still have spoken Latin after a century of Vandal rule, an interesting monument to the language as not just living but tenacious.

Above the fortress are the remains of Roman Thignica, a residential quarter crowned by a temple, with the outline of a theatre, baths and an arch hidden away in a garden below to the right.

Dougga

"Dougga very big city, monsieur" is what the hopeful guides hanging around the entrance will tell you, and they're right. **DOUGGA** (8am–5pm daily, 1TD plus 1TD to take photos) is both the largest and most dramatic of Tunisia's Roman sites, and it contains what some consider the most beautiful single Roman monument in North Africa. If you see only one Roman site in the country, it should undoubtedly be "these magnificent remains of taste and greatness, so easily reached in perfect safety by a ride along the Medjerda, as pleasant and as safe as along the Thames between London and Oxford", as James Bruce noted in 1765.

Teboursouk and Getting to Dougga

If you're travelling by bus from Tunis or Testour, the place you need to head for is **TEBOURSOUK**, an old and attractive farming town with a Thursday souk, just off the main road to LE KEF. **Buses** stop by a roundabout in the centre of town and **louages** stop opposite. The only **place to stay** in town is the *Maison des Jeunes* **youth hostel** (☎65095) close by, at 4TD a night. Otherwise, there's the 2* *Hôtel Thugga* some way below the town (☎65713), with various Roman artefacts tastefully arranged outside. It offers two styles of room, both at 14.2TD/24TD b&b.

Few tourists take the time to wander around the old town and **Byzantine fortress**, all dominated by a marabout clinging to the hill above. Dougga itself is 6km beyond, along a road which follows the wall of the valley up and around. It can seem like a long walk, but there's a good chance of a lift at least one way (coming back, you might prefer the downhill walk with its impressive views over the countryside). If you'd rather be sure, you should be able to arrange a round-trip deal with a taxi for about 6TD. Coming from Le Kef the bus runs through NOUVELLE DOUGGA, an unprepossessing collection of concrete bunkers 3km down from the old city along a mud track: *louages* from Teboursouk to Nouvelle Dougga can usually be persuaded, for a small consideration, to make a detour via the ruins. You could also walk up to the site from Nouvelle Dougga, which would probably avoid paying the entrance fee as there's no one on the gate that side of the site.

The Site

Dougga's name suggests non-Roman origins, as does its site high on the side of the valley: the Romans preferred flatter sites more suited to their standardised urban forms. Here they seem to have adapted well to a town which was described already in the fourth century BC as being "of an impressive size". By the second century BC it had become the seat of Numidian king Massinissa, whose support for Rome in the last war against Carthage gained much credit for the town. From the second century AD, 400 years later, and now under Roman administration, it began to enjoy a period of great prosperity. The Byzantines built huge fortifications and, after their departure, the local inhabitants remained among the ruins until excavating archaeologists forced them to move down the hill into the purpose-built modern village.

The theatre

The road to Dougga from Teboursouk winds into the site by a heavily restored **theatre**, almost at the top of the steep slope over which the grey remains are spread. Originally built in 168 AD, the theatre was one of a string of monumental projects of the second and third centuries financed with the money Dougga's leading families made out of the agricultural land it surveys: today it's used for occasional summer performances of the French Classics in May and June.

The temple of Saturn

Up on the hilltop behind the theatre are some early and peripheral odds and ends, beginning with the **temple of Saturn** whose skyline columns overlook the road. These columns formed the facade of a courtyard which in turn led into three inner chambers: the African pattern for a temple. This is not surprising, since underneath the second-century Roman remains were found traces of a pre-Roman sanctuary of Baal, the Carthaginian god. Look out in the paving opposite the central sanctuary chamber for a pair of mysterious footprints in the floor, remnants of some unknown ritual.

Around the temple of Minerva

On the summit of the hill are a few traces of the pre-Roman town, sited here for defensive purposes. A wall with two vestigial **towers** belongs to the Numidian citadel; beyond the towers are megalithic **dolmens**. Further in the same direction is a Roman **temple of Minerva**, and further still what can just be made out as the **hippodrome**: no more today than a long, flat field, unrecognisable until you pick out the semi-circular

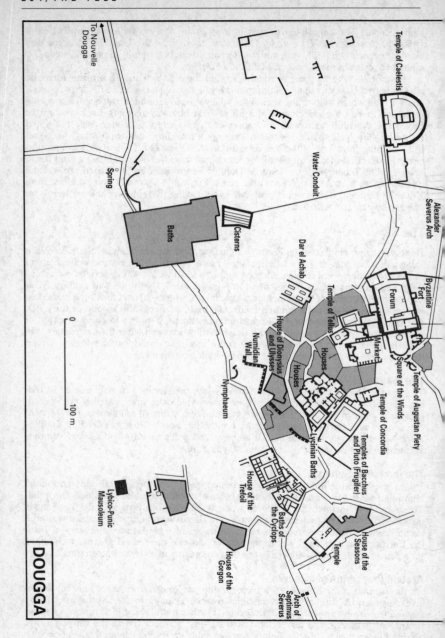

DOUGGA

To Nouvelle Dougga

Spring

Temple of Caelestis

Water Conduit

Alexander Severus Arch

Baths

Cisterns

Byzantine Fort

Dar el Achab

Forum

Temple of Tellus

Houses

Market

House of Dionysius and Ulysses

Numidian Wall

Houses

Temple of Augustan Piety

Temple of the Winds

Nymphaeum

Lycinian Baths

Temple of Concordia

Temples of Bacchus and Pluto (Frugifer)

House of the Trefoil

Lybico-Punic Mausoleum

Baths of the Cyclops

House of the Seasons

Temple

House of the Gorgon

Arch of Septimus Severus

0   100 m

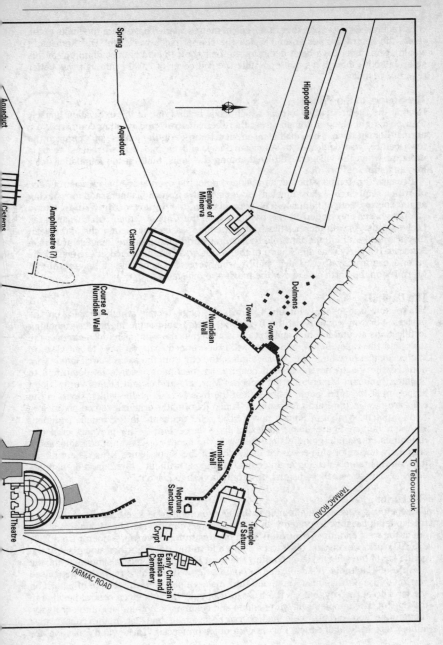

constructions facing each other hundreds of metres apart. These were the limits of the *spina*, the central barrier around which the chariot races were run. The Romans, it would seem, must have been dedicated to their sport to scratch a stadium out of this stony hilltop – though it's quite possible the soil cover of 2,000 years ago was better than that of today.

The Square of the Winds

Back at the theatre, follow a track which leads behind one of the excavation houses, then bear right along a Roman street that seems narrow and twisting compared to a normal Roman town. The small semi-circular **temple**, on the left as you approach the town centre, was dedicated to Augustan Piety, and beyond it is what used to be a **mosque** when the villagers still lived among the ruins, built on the foundations of a Roman temple of Fortune.

Because this temple stood at an oblique angle, the open space below was rounded off with a semi-circle – most unusual for conservative Roman planners, and introducing an unexpected note of intimacy. The plaza is called the **Square of the Winds**, after a compass-based inscription in the paving below the Capitol temple which names all twelve winds. As with mosaics illustrating the four seasons, or the months of the year, this is typical of the important role the natural world played in the imagery of Roman Africans. It's likely that the Square of the Winds was commissioned at the end of the second century by the Pacuvii family, who were also sponsors of the **temple of Mercury** on the north side and of the **market** to the south.

The Capitol

You're now face-to-face with the **Capitol**, the huge temple which appears on the posters – or you would be, if the Byzantines hadn't built some highly disorientating fortifications around it. The Capitol really is a magnificent sight as it looks out over the town and the valley below, and is so well proportioned that you have to get close to appreciate just how huge it is. It was a gift to the city from the same Marcii family who donated the theatre in the second century: an inscription records its dedication to "Jupiter, Juno and Minerva for the safety of Marcus Aurelius and Lucius Verus", joint emperors at the time. Some fragments of the massive cult statue which stood in the *cella* are now in the Bardo Museum in Tunis: this Jupiter originally stood six metres high, a potent symbol of Roman power. The relief sculpture in the temple pediment shows a human figure being molested by a large bird – the previous emperor, Antoninus Pius, undergoing his apotheosis at the hands (or claws) of an eagle, and a singularly uncomfortable reward it looks, too. In the 1780s James Bruce spent fifteen days on this temple making architectural drawings, "without", he remarked enigmatically, "feeling the smallest disgust, or forming a wish to finish it."

The Forum

The open space west of the temple is the **Forum**, modest in size because of the lie of the land, but lavishly decorated with columns of polychrome marble. Making your way out at the west end, the **Triumphal Arch of Alexander Severus** (emperor from 222–235 AD) lurks among the olive trees above and to the right. Further along, set in the gentle lap of the valley side, is possibly the most likeable of Dougga's monuments, the **temple of Caelestis**. It's dedicated to *Juno Caelestis* (Heavenly Juno), the Romanised version of the Carthaginian Tanit, and thus makes a pair with the temple of Saturn on the far side of the city; but it's the truly Roman cult which is given central position in the Capitol. The temple itself, with podium and columns, is nothing out of the ordinary, though the semi-circular colonnaded frame is, again, unusual in the conservative atmosphere of Roman Africa. Far away in other provinces (Turkey and Palestine, for instance) this sort of touch was commonplace, but in Tunisia innovation seems against the grain of the Roman designers.

An ancient residential quarter

Head back towards the city centre along a track which turns into a Roman street just below the Forum and runs past an imposing entrance to the right. This main street cuts through the centre of the town's most exclusive residential quarter. Large houses are crammed into all available space on the narrow side streets, and it's hard to imagine how it once looked when the walls stood to their full height. The main street follows the contour of the hill around, and one sharp left leads between houses to a **temple of Tellus** (Earth), recognisable by a small peristyle, and further along to the fortress-like remains of the **Licinian Baths**. You can get in from below, along a passage which is an original tradesman's entrance, though the official entrance was down some steep steps into a room with mosaics and columns still standing. The headless statue here is an eery reminder of the forgotten bourgeoisie which placed such store by this sort of facility: quite probably it even represented one of the Licinii family who donated the baths. The large central room was the *frigidarium*; a peristyle room reached through a vestibule was the *palaestra*, a sort of training room for athletes; and the *caldarium* (bathroom), above the tradesman's entrance, faced south to catch the sun.

The red light district

Continuing along the main street, then right and down at its end, the large **House of the Trefoil** has had its history censored: a staircase leads down to a wide courtyard surrounded by rooms, one in the clover-leaf shape which provides the building's name – a name that carefully avoids any suggestion of the house's original function. But the Romans were never so bashful: a stone with a relief of a phallus used to stand outside the door identifying the town brothel, until it was removed some 1800 years later by authorities concerned for tourist sensibilities.

Beside the brothel stood a small **baths complex**, now named after a Cyclopes mosaic found there. The baths were presumably connected with the brothel; they still contain a suspiciously well-preserved row of **toilet seats**.

The Arch of Septimius Severus

Heading down the hill past this elegant facility leads eventually to the **Triumphal Arch of Septimius Severus**, through which a track exited the city to join the main road below from Carthage. Septimius Severus, who came from Libya, was the founder of the dynasty of Roman emperors which ended with Alexander Severus (dedicatee of the Triumphal Arch near the Caelestid temple). It was Septimius's wife whose accent was notorious at Rome (see p.323); but not that of the Emperor himself, according to one tactful poet: "Your speech is not Carthaginian, nor your dress, nor is your spirit foreign: you are Italian, Italian...."

The Libyco-Punic Mausoleum

A track to the right, just before the arch, winds down to the **Libyco-Punic Mausoleum**, one of the few surviving examples of pre-Roman monumental building in Tunisia. Although it contains elements of the Graeco-Roman legacy common to all the Mediterranean world of the second century BC, it's more angular and oriental. Built for "Ateban, son of Ieptamath, son of Palu", the mausoleum managed to survive the Roman Empire intact, only to be destroyed in 1842 by Sir Thomas Reade, the British Consul, who was keen to get his hands on the bilingual inscription – which is now in the British Museum, the "inalienable property of the British people". The mausoleum has subsequently been rebuilt.

Le Kef (El Kef)

On the way to Le Kef, LE KRIB is frankly just one more farming town (with a Tuesday souk) along the road, but if you happen to be passing through it's worth backtracking a kilometre along the road towards Tunis to poke around the ruins of Roman **Mustis**: temples, houses, triumphal arches, a Byzantine fort, all sitting nonchalantly beside the road as if the Romans left only a few years ago. Look out for them anyway if passing through by road.

The first sign of the big centre of **LE KEF** is a rocky gleaming ribbon which twists round Jebel Dyr just below the mountain's summit, creating a shallow plateau to the southern tip of which clings the old town. It's a breathtaking setting – the more so in its isolation close to the Algerian border – and the kind of place where you feel involved just wandering round, contemplating the vistas below. But there's more than just views here: the town's long history has left a legacy of monuments, and it has also recently acquired one of the best museums in the country, devoted to regional culture.

Some history

Although still regarded as the unofficial capital of western Tunisia, Le Kef's historic predecessors enjoyed more prominence. The area was inhabited very early – Neolithic (new stone age) hunters left their tools nearby, and the Numidians built megalithic tombs – before the urban centre entered history as Carthaginan **"Sicca"** after the Second Punic War. Unable to pay its defeated mercenary army, Carthage packed them off here, to distant Sicca: a gesture which rebounded when the mercenaries rose in revolt to wage a four-year struggle in which they were only suppressed with the aid of yet more mercenaries. The war, of a legendary brutality, inspired Flaubert's blood and guts novel *Salammbô*, which includes a chapter entitled "Sicca". The town was annexed in 46 BC by the Romans who added the title "Veneria", giving it a rather dubious name. The Arabs, who took it in 688, called it Chakbanaria, but renamed it El Kef ("The Rock") in the seventeenth century.

Since the Islamic conquest, Le Kef's strategic position between the Tunisian hinterland and the Algerian interior has put it at the centre of so many inter-factional struggles that it has never quite regained its former eminence – a process accelerated in this century when the railway to Algeria was built through Jendouba and Ghardimaou to the north. Algerians have, however, had occasion to be thankful for Le Kef, which was the main base and command centre of the FLN (Algerian armed resistance) until 1962.

In the years since Independence the town has felt itself a victim of the national bias towards the Sahel region – feelings which erupted particularly strongly in the 1984 troubles. For a town of its size it is desperately short of recreational outlets and work. The townspeople are proud to have one of the largest schools in Africa, but the pupils which it educates find little employment.

Orientation and Practicalities

The old quarters of Le Kef huddle below the southern end of the mountain plateau; the new districts spill down the slope below. The **train station** is right at the bottom (come out of the station and turn right then left, or left then right), but the **bus** and **louage** stations stand about halfway up, leaving a short walk up past the modern administrative buildings to the town centre. The road at the top of the hill heads left towards SAKIET SIDI YOUSSEF, or right to **Place de l'Indépendance**. From there, **Avenue Bourguiba** follows the curve of the hill round to the right, a tremendous belvedere for the chequered plains below. The other way, **Rue Hedi Chaker** continues down past the **PTT** to meet the Sakiet Sidi Youssef road.

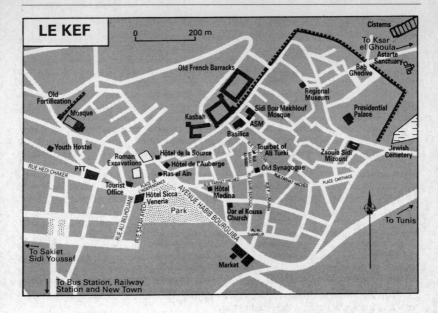

On the uphill side of av Bourguiba is the old town, with narrow cobbled streets winding up to the Kasbah at the cliff's edge. The Medina's main street is **Rue Farhat Hached**, which begins at av Bourguiba near pl de l'Indépendance; a third of the way along it is the old synagogue. Here rue Marakit Karama ascends to the Basilica in **Place Bou Makhlouf** and to the **Kasbah** beyond that, while rue Bahri Barbouch drops to pl Habib Thameur, just off av Bourguiba above the market.

Accommodation

Le Kef has several **hotels**, including one of Tunisia's most memorable abodes and a good mix of alternatives.

Hôtel de la Source, rue de la Source, just near the beginning of av Bourguiba (☎21397). Rather wonderful if a bit seedy, with a lovely air of fading decadence. It has a legendary room, the four-bed *chambre de famille*, where a huge double bed reposes under an ornate vaulted stucco ceiling; at 15TD this may be the nearest you'll come to sleeping like an eighteenth-century Tunisian bey, give or take the odd grubby sheet (check them first). Other prices vary – around 3–5TD/6TD.

Hôtel de l'Auberge, rue de la Source (☎20036), a couple of doors from the *Source*. Reasonably clean but a bit gloomy. 2.5TD/4TD

Hôtel Medina, 18 rue Farhad Hachad (☎20214). Newer than the *Hôtel de l'Auberge*, with clean, pleasant doubles at 6TD and a single for 3TD, but no hot water (there's a hammam up the street at no. 33).

Youth Hostel/Maison des Jeunes, 8 rue Mohamed Gammoudi (☎20424). Very friendly and right in town near the PTT. 4TD, as usual.

Hôtel Sicca Veneria, av Bourguiba (☎21561). Le Kef's most comfortable abode with all mod cons and a choice of bath or shower. 3* 13TD/20TD b&b.

Hôtel Nouvelle Ere, 59 rue Habib Karma. At the very bottom of the scale – extremely basic.

Hôtel du Marché off pl Habib Thameur. Also rock-bottom and closed on latest check.

Eating and drinking

For food, *Restaurant el Andalous*, in rue Hedi Chaker opposite the PTT, is good value at 2–3TD a meal, and highly recommended. They do salad with homemade mayonnaise, and great couscous. The *Restaurant de l'Afrique* two doors down, *Des Amis* on the steps by the *Hôtel de l'Auberge*, and *El Hana* in av Bourguiba above the market are all similarly priced.

For a smarter meal, try the *Hôtel Sicca*'s restaurant (around 8TD). Alternatively, if you've never had supper at a filling station, the *Esso Restaurant*, above the pumps in rue Hedi Chaker, fifty metres past the PTT, can arrange it for 7TD or so.

If you want to drink in the evening, try the *Hôtel de l'Auberge*'s bar (which does food too) – but don't expect instant service. There's also a cheap, unnamed bar/restaurant up behind the PTT at 4 rue Salya. The *Sicca*'s bar is only slightly more refined than these two.

The Town

Le Kef – or plain Kef as it's usually known – is a great place just to wander at random, catching glimpses, between houses or over the trees in the park, of the plains below. But it's full of historic interest too. The best way to begin a look around is by calling in at the **ASM office**, in pl Bou Makhlouf next to the Basilica and Sidi Bou Makhlouf Mosque (open 9am–2pm Mon–Sat). Le Kef's ASM is as much a social club as a cultural centre, thanks to the efforts of its energetic director Mohammed Tlili: if your French is good enough, and he has time to spare, he may be able to give you an introduction to the town. He wrote his doctoral thesis on its history, and most of the following architectural and historical detail is indebted to him.

Ras el Aïn and some Roman remains

A **spring**, *Ras el Aïn*, rises in the open space just below the *Hôtel de la Source*. It has always supplied the cities on this site – Roman blocks which channelled the water can be made out – and has received cult reverence through the centuries. Just next to the locked door of the spring proper is a small niche, a shrine to a supposed Islamic saint called Lalla Mna; in fact she was originally a Roman nymph, now renamed and Islamicised. Hers is still a living cult, and there are often recent offerings in the niche.

Back along rue de la Source, and just above it, is a confused area of ancient remains, including the entrance to a huge Roman **cistern** which fed the **baths** excavated across the street. The hexagonal building here was later converted into a church and marked the western limit of the Roman town.

Dar el Kouss Church

The larger and better preserved **Dar el Kouss Church** is round to the east: either take the first right off rue Farhat Hached immediately after it leaves av Bourguiba, or else continue along av Bourguiba past the beginning of rue Farhat Hached and take the first left; either way, the church is on the first corner. Dating from the fourth century, it has been restored for use as an open-air theatre, but is currently closed to the public. A small room in its far right-hand corner has a curiously carved lintel stone combining a Greek cross and a palm frond.

Ethnic communities

Rejoin rue Farhat Hached and turn right to meet rue Marakit Karama going up the hill and rue Bahri Barbouch going down it. With this street you take a leap forward to Turkish times when it was reserved for the **Jewish community**; the building on the corner of rue Marakit Karama is the former **synagogue**, due to be renovated and turned into a museum at some time, when the ASM can afford it. The Jews' traditional specialisation in jewellery lives on in the shops which still line rue Bahri Barbouch, but virtually all Jewish people have now departed for Tunis, France or Israel.

Racial segregation was formerly common in Tunisian and North African towns: the next street along used to be the centre of the **black community**. Formerly called rue des Nègres, the top end is now rue du Soudan and the bottom end rue Patrice Lumumba. Following the abolition of slavery in 1846, black people became a free community, but still specialised in certain trades, such as music. They also had their own patron saint, Sidi Hami, whose mosque still exists inside a private house in rue du Soudan. Nowadays, however, there's little difference in culture or lifestyle between black and white Tunisians.

The Tourbet of Ali Turki

It was during Turkish times, with the rise and internecine struggles of the Husaynid dynasty, that Le Kef was most directly involved in recent Tunisian history. The father of Husayn bin Ali, the dynasty's founder, is entombed just up the hill. You pass this somewhat derelict **Tourbet of Ali Turki** at the top of rue Bahri Barbouch and rue du Soudan. Carry on up and you will come to **Place Bou Makhlouf**, an open space below the Kasbah.

The Basilica

Pl Bou Makhlouf was the centre of the Roman town, and the **Basilica** under the walls of the Kasbah began life as an important Roman building. Later it was converted into one of the earliest mosques in Tunisia, serving (despite its lack of minaret) for many years as Le Kef's Great Mosque. It has only recently been secularised and turned into a **museum** (8–11am and 3–6pm daily, free) for antiquities discovered in the region.

The Mosque of Sidi Bou Makhlouf

The diminutive **Mosque of Sidi Bou Makhlouf** at the end of pl Bou Makhlouf, with the complex of streets around it, is one of the most captivating spots in Tunisia – all the charm of Sidi Bou Said and none of that resort's crowds. The mosque itself is a small masterpiece, the bare whitewashed courtyard leading into a domed prayer hall resting on antique columns and lined with white stucco work. On one side of the cobbled street leading up to it is a former *foundouk*, and opposite it the *Café of the Souks*, sadly now open only during the month of Ramadan, a place to sit and watch the changing patterns of light over the plains – magical under a full moon.

The Kasbah

Another place to admire the view is the **Kasbah** above, recently abandoned by the Army. The smaller and lower of the **forts** here is a legacy of the border struggles under the Beys: Hammouda Bey added it in 1813 to house a guard of ultra-faithful troops, stationed here to guard against Algerian designs on the town. The first entrance you reach, into the older, larger fort dating back to 1601, was converted into a prison for Tunisian nationalists. It's an absurdly melodramatic place, with its Beau Geste cells and French sentry box (once painted blue and yellow) and a Turkish gateway.

The Kasbah is now being renovated to house a **cultural centre** in the large fort, with cinema, open-air theatre and cultural archives, and a hotel and bar/restaurant in the small fort; the dungeons will become a small museum. All of which will no doubt be very twee – and is already viewed unenthusiastically in some quarters – but at the very least will increase Le Kef's recreational facilities. The project is due for completion in 1994. Meanwhile, the Kasbah is open to the public and entry is free.

The Regional Museum

Follow rue el Kasbah round above the Basilica and Sidi Bou Makhlouf to pl ben Aissa, where you'll find the worthy **Regional Museum** (9am–3.30pm Tues–Sun closed Mon; 0.8TD), housed in a restored *zaouia*. Exhibits concentrate on, and beautifully evoke, the way of life of the nomads whose tents are still to be seen on the surrounding plain. Put up in 1784, the building housing the museum was originally the headquarters of a Sufist religious brotherhood – the **Rahmania**.

The Presidential Palace and Zaouia of Sidi Mizouni

The old town walls run almost continuously from the Kasbah around to the east, finally encircling a **Presidential Palace**. This is something of a sore point in the town, as it occupies a prime site but is hardly ever used; a swimming pool beckons invitingly in its grounds, while the municipal pool in the park has never been opened. Just below the palace walls is the nineteenth-century **Zaouia of Sidi Mizouni** (or Zaouia of the Qadriya), whose garden must be among the most luxuriant this side of Hammamet. It's maintained by a friendly group of old men who will tell you that they knew Churchill when he was here during World War II. A perfect place to collapse.

Bab Ghedive

Bab Ghedive ("Gate of Treachery") gives entrance to the town just above the palace, not far from the museum. It earned its name in 1881 when the governor and town notables, having received no orders to fight, opened the gate to the French army on its "temporary mission" – even though the townspeople were prepared for a long siege. They surrendered the most important frontier defences without a shot being fired.

Out of Bab Ghedive

Once through the gate, the transition from town to country is startlingly abrupt. Just ahead, an iron ladder leads down into another vast **Roman cistern**: twelve gloomy chambers in length and one of the coolest places in Kef – but an alcoholics' den at night.

Over to the right from here, across the road, are more fragmentary remains, the first set of which may be the ancient **sanctuary of Astarte** so notorious for its erotic mysteries. Roman moralists professed shock that young Carthaginian girls of noble birth were forced to sacrifice their virginity here to the goddess, to ensure the fertility of the land on which Sicca depended, but it was the Romans who gave the town the suffix "Veneria", and sex still enjoyed a high profile here in Christian times.

The second area of remains, below the disused **Christian cemetery**, may have been the **Ksar el Ghoula Basilica** where there was once reputedly a magic mirror: men who suspected their wives of infidelity could look at the glass and find the face of their rival. Beyond it, a **Jewish cemetery** stretches all the way back to the wall, the part nearest to it being much older than the rest of the Jewish and Christian cemeteries.

Bab Aouaret

Back across town, the mosque in rue Souk Ahras, up behind the PTT, stands on the site of a series of religious and military buildings at Bab Aouaret. Next to it are the remains of a Turkish fortification, with a piece of the old city wall stretching off towards the Kasbah. This was once a Roman site, and some Roman remains are still lying around.

Moving On

The **autogare** is on the hill between the old and new towns, about halfway down on the left. All **buses and louages** leave from here, with hourly bus departures for Tunis and daily buses for destinations **all over the north and the Tell** – full details in "travel details" at the end of the chapter. **Louages** run to Tunis and Jendouba, and south to KALAA KHASBAH, KALAAT ES SENAM (for Jugurtha's Table), TAJEROUINE and EL KSOUR.

The **railway station** is right down the bottom of the hill, rather pretty and well-kept, but currently with only one very early departure to Tunis.

Le Kef Listings

ASM Their main office is next to the Basilica and Sidi Bou Makhlouf Mosque in pl Bou Makhlouf; open 9am–2pm Mon–Sat.

Banks Several around town, especially at the top of rue Salah Ayech and rue Ali Belhouane; others in av Bourguiba above the market, and opposite the bus station on the hill down into the new town. They run a weekend rota, so there should be at least one open Sat & Sun am.

Car hire *Hertz*, rue Salah Ayech (☎22059).

Cinemas *Cine Pathe*, av Bourguiba right next to the tourist office (not sign-posted and, in fact, not easily identified). *Cirta*, pl Carthage, up in the Medina on rue Farhat Hached.

Consulates The Algerian consulate is right down the bottom of rue Hedi Chaker at no. 3. You could try them for a visa but they will probably tell you to go to Tunis and apply there.

Market day Thursday.

Medical facilities The hospital (☎20900) is on the Sakiet Sidi Youssef road just past the top of the hill down to the *autogare* and new town. There is a night chemist in rue Souk Ahras (turn right just before the PTT in rue Hedi Chaker and it's 100m up on your left).

Passport photos In case you wangle an Algerian visa, places doing quick mugshots include one at the very top of the hill leading to the bus station and new town.

PTT Rue Hedi Chaker. City hours and international phones.

Supermarket *Monoprix* is 100m off to the left of the hill down into the new town, about half-way down, just above the bus station.

Tourist office Corner of av Bourguiba/rue Hedi Chaker (8am–6pm daily including weekends), run by the ASM. Little in the way of literature or maps, but happy to answer questions.

Around Le Kef

If the view across the plains around Le Kef tempts you, there are several good hiking possibilities and three particularly rewarding excursions – see the "South" section that follows.

Sidi Mansour

One of the best short walks is to **SIDI MANSOUR**, a small village 3 to 4km north of the town. Leave Kef by Bab Ghedive and scramble up the rocks below the TV mast. A rough path leads north through a small eucalyptus plantation and out on to the top of the plateau, opening on an immense view over the broken forests along the Algerian border and the glint of the lake behind the Mellegue Dam. The village, a small farming community, is soon reached; its spring water is locally reputed, but for what it's difficult to establish. Just to the west, beyond a deep river canyon, are wide caves gouged in the rock – a popular picnic spot and, incidentally, inhabited in prehistoric times. North of the village it isn't far to the other end of the plateau; or you can climb up to the east, then bend down and around and come back into Kef by the palace.

The Barrage Mellegue

The artificial **lake** visible, gleaming in the distance, from Sidi Mansour, was created by damming the river Mellegue. Buses go in this direction from Kef – to the attractive village of NEBEUR, below the northern tip of Jebel Dyr, and then on to BARRAGE

MELLEGUE, a small cluster of houses on the dam itself. The water crashing out at the bottom is the colour and, by all appearances, consistency of liquid chocolate (if you stand downwind you can see a thin coating of silt evenly applied). The reason for coming to the dam, though, is to walk back to Kef through open country – a five-hour hike, but a rewarding one. There's no danger of getting lost since Jebel Dyr is always in sight and, once you get to it, Kef is only 5km further on.

An alternative route to Sidi Mansour

If you aim for the top of the mountain, then head round its western face below the cliff edge, you should hit a winding **tractor track** which runs all the way to SIDI MANSOUR. At first it climbs through clumps of pines, foothills of the mountain proper, then emerges on to broader slopes which sweep up like waves against the rock. The scenery is tremendous, but it's only part of the value of the hike. Just as impressive is the insight you gain into the pace of life in the countryside of Tunisia, and above all the dominating need for **water**. When you set out on the walk, take as much as you can carry, but even so you'll probably need refills. For these you're dependent on the infrequent springs which the isolated local farmhouses rely on for all their daily needs. When you finally reach a small pipe you're usually surrounded by a group of children who have walked several kilometres with donkeys and cans to fetch the day's supply.

Hammam Mellegue

At the other end of Lake Mellegue, the restored Roman spa of **Hammam Mellegue** is at the end of a 12km piste. Hot spring water provides a communal bath (women in the morning, men in the afternoon), which is very popular with people from the surrounding villages. Walking is the only sure way of getting to it, though you might try sticking your thumb out just in case.

Sakiet Sidi Youssef: the frontier

West of Le Kef, **SAKIET SIDI YOUSSEF** is the last village before the Algerian frontier. The border post here is sometimes open, and accessible from Le Kef by *louage*, but you should check on this before setting out: the main crossing is 30km north at Ghardimaou (see p.147). The Algerian consulate in Le Kef might know the latest situation; on the other hand they might just feed you an unhelpful story with no bearing on reality when you actually get there.

There's little other reason for visiting Sakiet, although it does have a certain historical notoriety. It was here, in the midst of the Algerian War in 1958, that the French bombed the civilian population. The incident was denounced as a "new Guernica" and caused a rapid decline in relations between France and the newly independent Tunisia. One outcome was the Tunisian attempt to eject the French navy from their base at Bizerte.

South of Kef: Medeina, Kalaat and Haidra

The area **south of Le Kef** – before the fertile plains climb up onto bleaker steppes around KASSERINE – is right off the tourist routes. Yet, using Kef as a base, it's a quietly rewarding region to explore. The scenery, always impressive, becomes eerily compelling around the craggy mountain of **Jugurtha's Table**, and there are two unexcavated but well-preserved **Roman sites** at **Medeina** and **Haidra**. Each of these, but particularly Haidra, has an aloof grandeur in its remoteness, inspiring an excitement quite absent from the domesticated feel of the major sites.

Medeina

MEDEINA, Roman Althiburos, isn't the easiest site in Tunisia to reach. You have to get the bus to DAHMANI (also known as EBBA KSOUR), a small tree-shaded farming town, and then walk or hitch 7km down the JERISSA road: the turning to Medeina is on the left, and the site about a 4km-walk.

Despite its present remoteness, Medeina once stood on the main Roman highway from Carthage to Tebessa; today its ruins are attractive enough, rambling above a green river bed, though hardly extensive. The first glimpse is of a third-century AD **Triumphal Arch**, almost hidden in a field to the left. Beyond, reaching the centre of the site, the most distinctive building is the **Capitol**, just above the river bed: it stands to one side of the paved **Forum**, opposite the remains of a **temple**. A street ran southeast through the Forum, and following it you find a well-preserved **fountain** on a street corner. Further in this direction are the remains of a **theatre**.

Back in the Forum, alongside the temple opposite the Capitol, is the **House of Sixteen Bases**, whose name refers to the unusual reliefs on the bases of its inner portico. Some way north of here, over a stream bed, is the **Building of Asclepia**. No-one knows its precise function, but having begun life as a private house it seems to have become the home of some sort of cult connected with the healing god Asclepius. This explains the extraordinary number of baths found here, and the quality of the mosaics – most of them third or fourth century AD, and now removed to the Bardo Museum in Tunis.

Tajerouine and Jugurtha's Table

TAJEROUINE, first town of any size on the main road south from Le Kef, is quite a transport centre. The **bus** station in Tajerouine is in the middle of town on the main drag, with plenty of buses to Le Kef and SAKIET SIDI YOUSSEF. **Louages** stop nearby, down a road next to the mosque. Tajerouine has a **Monday souk**, and there are **banks** and a *Magasin Général* **supermarket** opposite the bus station, but **no hotel** and little character: it's hardly more than a roadside sprawl.

But beyond the town, you emerge on to the plains – vast open spaces with jutting **isolated mountains** that bob like ships on a calm sea. There is a good deal of mining on the plain: for example JERISSA, whose plant is visible from the top of the rock behind Tajerouine, is a major iron producer, and phosphates are extracted at KALAA KHASBAH.

Kalaat es Senam and up to Jugurtha's Table

The place to head for, however, to reap the best rewards of the scenery around here, is **KALAAT ES SENAM**, a small village at the foot of the mountain known as **Jugurtha's Table** ("Table de Jurgurtha"), a flat-topped mountain, like Jebel Dyr, but more sharply defined, with its tilting plateau standing out for miles around. *Louages* go to Kalaat es Senam either direct from Le Kef or with a change at Tajerouine. Stock up with water while you can, because it's a good two hours' walk from the village to the steps in the middle of the north side, though the steps themselves are an easy ascent.

The name Jugurtha's Table refers to the tradition that it was the stronghold of the Numidian king **Jugurtha** in his second-century BC struggles against the Romans; a role echoed in more recent times by the name of Kalaat es Senam – "Seat of Senam" – after a local bandit who made similar use of the mountain against the armies of the Beys. This dramatic past seems very close as you climb the steps to the summit, hacked into the rock and leading to a Byzantine gateway. The lunar-like surface is littered with remains which include troglodyte caves and a spooky marabout. Romance apart, the mountain also provides a magnificent **view**: if you have the equipment, it's an extraordinary place to spend the night. At the last visit, the only visible inhabitants were six overheated cows – how they got up there is a mystery.

Haidra

As with Medeina, **HAIDRA**'s remoteness has ensured that it is only minimally excavated; but it also means that the surviving monuments are exceptionally well preserved. Coming upon them you feel something of the awe early travellers must have experienced confronted with remains of a mysterious and magnificent past.

Getting there from Kalaa Khasbah

From Le Kef you can take any of the KASSERINE buses (or occasionally a *louage*) to **KALAA KHASBAH** (also known as Kalaa Jerda), an old Italian mining town still redolent of the colonial presence, with its tiled houses and profuse greenery. This, for some reason, is the terminal for passenger **train** services, and gets three trains to Tunis daily, via Sers, Gaafour and Fahs.

Hitching to the village of HAIDRA from Kalaa Khasbah is quite easy – there's only one road, so virtually everything that passes will stop. There are also **louages** from here and from Thala and Kasserine. Haidra has even more of a dead-end border feel than Ghardimaou, enlivened only by a grotesque railway station – with its extraordinary combination of Classical order and 1930s Deco this would look weird anywhere, let alone miles from nowhere on a North African frontier. There are no passenger trains nowadays. The **border post** here is usually open, but little used.

MAN BITES LION

The area was notorious among early European travellers for the lawlessness of its inhabitants. Although James Bruce, passing this way in 1765, managed to avoid mortal danger, he did have a curious gastronomic experience. A recent predecessor, one Dr Shaw, had claimed that the inhabitants of Haidra ate lions, but was promptly accused of "traveller's license" by the learned doctors of Oxford University, who "took it as a subversion of the natural order of things, that a man should eat a lion, when it has long passed as almost the peculiar province of the lion to eat man". Ever the vigorous empiricist, Bruce was not much impressed by expert opinion, and was glad to be able to report that he had "eaten the flesh of three lions – that is part of three lions – in the tents of the Welled Sidi Boogannim". He found the texture like old horse flesh, palatable except for a strong smell of musk. As for the locals, he sniffed, "a brutish and ignorant folk, they will, I fear, notwithstanding the disbelief of the University of Oxford, continue to eat lions as long as they exist."

The site

Ancient Haidra, Roman Ammaedara, was in its way a border post like the modern village, founded as a base for the Third Augustan Legion, whose job was to protect Rome's new province from hostile incursions. When the Legion was moved further west, the camp became an important town – but after the Islamic conquest reverted to its border role.

The outskirts of the Roman town (free entry) are marked by a **hexagonal mausoleum**, just outside the modern village by a tributary of the main river. The collapsed bridge just to the north carried the main highway from Carthage (via Medeina) west towards Tebessa in Algeria. Some way further along, dominating the main river bed, is the **Byzantine fort** – one of the largest in Africa and reputedly sponsored by the

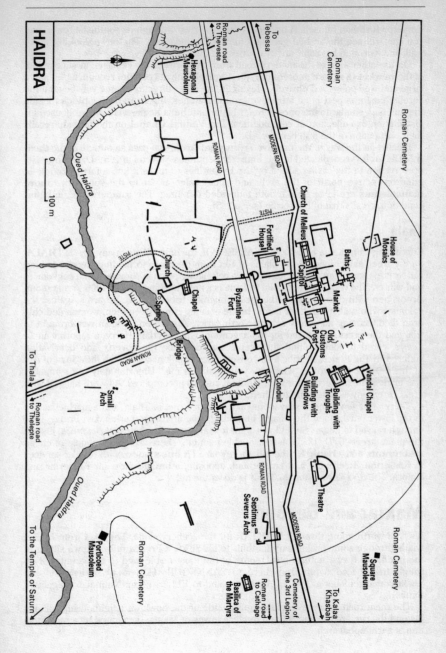

Emperor Justinian himself. A bridge crossed the river through its southeast tower, and you can still see the arched gate and tumbled foundations. The newer-looking north wall, and its round bastions, are by courtesy of the Turkish Bey.

On the other side of the modern road from the fortress are remains, in succession, of the **market** (a square depression), the **Capitol** (only its podium recognisable) and a large and well-preserved **church**. Moving in the other direction, some way beyond the derelict customs post is an attractive group of arches: the **trough-like blocks** inside the building, similar to the ones at Kef, Maktar and Bulla Regia, were probably used for distribution or collection of commodities. The **Vandal Chapel** on the far side recalls their occupation of the fifth century AD.

Finally, on the way to the massive **Triumphal Arch**, you pass an outline of the **theatre**. The arch was dedicated to the Emperor Septimius Severus in 195 AD, and owes its preservation to the casing added by the Byzantines to make it into a fort. A couple of hundred metres north of the arch, and about twice as far to the south, two **more mausoleums** are to be found, both four-sided this time. The southern one, in better condition, recalls that of Kasserine (see p.255).

Thala

Continuing from Kalaa Khasbah to KASSERINE, the only village of any size is **THALA**, on the steep slope dividing the plains of Kef from the more forbidding steppes around Kasserine – and, at an altitude of 1017m, a refreshing place in summer but a cold one in mid-winter. The village's only claim to fame is a notorious incident of 1906. A marabout, **Amor ben Othman**, inspired the local Fraichich tribes to take up arms against the colonists who had stolen their lands. In the ensuing riot sixteen men, women and children died, causing an outcry across North Africa. Amor Ben Othman was brought to trial and the press clamoured for his execution. Only Myriam Harry, a reporter on *Le Temps*, cared to look behind the scenes and describe the poverty and deprivation suffered by the Fraichich tribe as a consequence of colonisation. "Oh little Joan of Arc of this desert", she wrote, "what pity you inspire in me." Unfortunately her sympathy was inadequate protection for the marabout and his accomplices. All were hanged with great ceremony as a warning to others.

There are a few minor excavations on the main street in Thala, and a marble factory in the lower outskirts of the village, but, unless you arrive on market day, Friday, little enough reason to linger. Should you want to stay, however, the *Hôtel Bouthelja*, just off the main street (6TD/12TD) is reasonable enough. There are also a couple of cheap **restaurants** and a **bank**. Up the hill, there's an *STK* **bus station**, with regular services to Kasserine, Tajerouine and Le Kef and, opposite, a **louage stop** for Kasserine and Haidra. The *SNTRI* bus stop for Tunis is down the hill.

Maktar and Beyond

It's well worth going through **MAKTAR** for the scenery alone. The road from Le Kef winds through some preliminary foothills to LE SERS, a French railway town sitting in the middle of a vast natural bowl, some of the most fertile land in the country. Two rough tracks lead south from here to ZANNFOUR (6km away: widespread but unexcavated remains of Roman **Assuras**), and to ELLES (9km: Numidian megalithic tombs).

The main road goes on to climb up the side of the bowl: on neighbouring hilltops beyond the rim are the ancient and modern towns of Maktar, separated by a road junction at a triumphal arch.

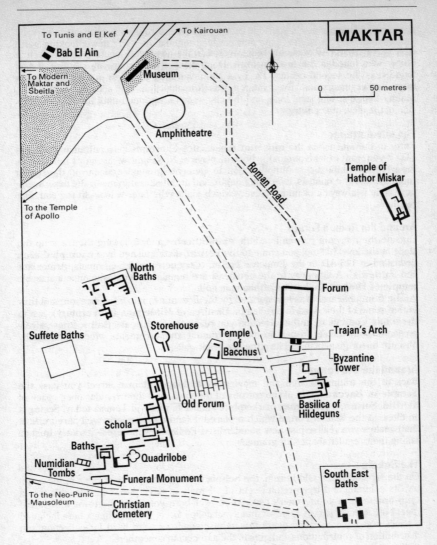

MAKTAR

To Tunis and El Kef
To Kairouan

Bab El Ain

Museum

To Modern
Maktar and
Sbeitla

0   50 metres

Amphitheatre

Temple of
Hathor Miskar

Roman Road

To the Temple
of Apollo

North
Baths

Forum

Storehouse

Suffete Baths

Temple
of
Bacchus

Trajan's Arch

Byzantine
Tower

Old Forum

Basilica of
Hildeguns

Schola

Baths

Numidian
Tombs

Quadrilobe

Funeral Monument

To the Neo-Punic
Mausoleum

Christian
Cemetery

South East
Baths

Modern Maktar: practicalities

Modern Maktar, across a ravine from the ancient town, is quite a tempting place to stay. At nearly 1000m altitude, the air is fresh, the scenery tremendous, and there's a relaxed feel to the town that can come as a welcome relief. **Market day** is Monday. **Buses** leave from a balustraded road at the bottom of the town and nearby is the unpretentious but perfectly adequate (5.5TD/9TD) *Hôtel Mactaris* (☎76014). **Louages** are to be found on the main street higher up.

Ancient Maktar

ANCIENT MAKTAR was only rediscovered in the nineteenth century by the French officer who founded the modern town. Dominating the surrounding country, it was founded in the second century BC by a Numidian king trying to protect his domain from Berber incursions. Even after it was Romanised in the second century AD, Maktar kept a strong local tone, and the city wasn't abandoned until the Hilalian invasion of the eleventh century.

The site entrance

Entry to the **site** is via the **museum** (open Tues–Sun 8am–5pm, entrance 1TD plus 1TD if you want to take photos), whose displays of Neo-Punic stelae show how enduring were local influences. Although Roman elements gradually appear on the stones (note the family emphasis, increasing depth, and architectural frames), the basic sculptural style is always a primitive naivety which makes the figures look, to the end, like rag dolls.

Around the Roman Forum

Outside the museum garden is a little **amphitheatre** and, following the track up the slope to the level hill-top, you come to the **Forum**, distinguished by a **triumphal arch** dedicated in 116 AD to the Emperor Trajan, "Conqueror of the Germans, Armenians and Parthians". A little way to the northeast are remains of what was once a sizeable **temple of Hathor Miskar**, a Carthaginian god.

The triumphal arch was transformed by the Byzantines into a fortification; and they buried some of their dead in the Vandal **Basilica of Hildeguns** (fifth century), just to the south. Continuing in this direction you reach the **Southeast Baths**, impressively preserved, but thanks in part to more Byzantine reinforcements which occasionally obscure the original plan and its attractive brick walls.

Around the Old Forum

Back at the triumphal arch and moving west along a Roman street you pass the **Temple of Bacchus**, one of the patrons of the town, and the irregular open space of the **Old Forum**, a pre-Roman marketplace similar to many in Tunisia today. Seeing it so close to the Roman Forum which replaced it (and a particularly well paved one at that) makes you realise just how standardised Roman towns were – it's easy to start taking their regular shapes for granted.

The Schola

On the far side of the Old Forum, the **Schola** is one of the prettiest ruins in the country, its columns and trees reminiscent of Olympia in Greece. Essentially, this was a **club-house** for a young men's association: well-born youths of the town who would meet both socially and as a sort of municipal police force. Their complex here included a basilica and the so-called *quadrilobe*, whose windows were used for collection and distribution of contributions and gifts to the association's members.

It was this sort of voluntary association, with its implicit faith in Roman order, that formed the backbone of the Empire. If it had been able to offer more to the rural Berbers as well as to the urban bourgeoisie, it might have lasted longer. A gravestone found at Maktar, belonging to the so-called "Maktar Reaper", is a rare case of **upward mobility**. The inscription tells the "local boy made good" story with relish – how the dead man worked his way up the social scale by the sweat of his honest brow. You too, it concludes encouragingly, can be a success: "Learn, mortals, to lead a blameless life. Those who have lived honourable lives have earned an honourable death."

Mausoleums and bathhouses

Look out in the Schola area for another funerary monument, a heavy tombstone inscribed with the name of the 18-year-old Julia Spisia. A small figure of the dead girl stands in a niche on one side of the stone, and the others are carved with unusual relief designs (one of them a tree with birds sitting in the branches). Behind the Schola, jumbled remains belong to a **cemetery** that was in use for 600 years: the earliest tombs were megalithic chambers, in widespread use before the arrival of the Romans and here well preserved. Some 500m further in this direction (there are gaps in the fence around the site) stands an oriental-looking **Neo-Punic Mausoleum** similar to the one at Dougga: the pyramidal roof and angular design are un-Roman, though they may in fact have been built during the Imperial epoch.

The **North Baths** date from Byzantine times, while the **Suffete Baths** were a second-century AD Roman facility later turned into a church. Standing in the makeshift aisle, you feel that the early Christians here must have been strengthened in their faith by the sight of so many relics of the dead culture they were replacing – a visual record of imperial obsolescence.

The route to Kairouan and other roads on

The most exciting way out of Maktar is the **road to Kairouan**, which runs through some of the most rugged scenery in the country. After about 10km you enter the vast **Forest of Kesra**, a blanket of bright green Aleppo pine named after **LA KESRA**, a Berber village clinging almost invisibly to a mountain face at an altitude of 1078m. The side road up to it is only 3km long, but it's a steep climb – worth it, though, for a fore-taste of the *ksour* in the south. The houses merge with the slope like bunkers, leaving no doubts about the defensive attitudes which built settlements like these. Soon after the village, the main road dives into a tunnel through a sharp ridge before continuing down a wide and lonely valley to meet the Kairouan–Sbeitla road. In a winding river valley just before this, look out on the left for remains of the **aqueduct** which carried water to Kairouan's Aghlabid Pools (see p.172).

Other routes away from Maktar can't compare. Along the **road to Fahs and Tunis**, SILIANA is an important centre, but a dull town (a track leads 9km west to Jama, site of the ancient **Zama Minor**, which is only for dedicated enthusiasts). While, heading **south to Sbeitla**, the only place of interest en route, SBIBA, has some remains of the ancient town of **Sufes**.

Sbeitla

Very little is recorded about Roman **Sufetula**. The town's one moment of abortive glory came in 646 AD when the Byzantine Prefect Gregory declared the African province independent here in anticipation of the coming Arab invasion. Much good it did him or the province: the Arabs won a famous victory here in 647, making **SBEITLA** the shortest-lived of all Tunisia's capitals.

The Modern Town: practicalities

SBEITLA, the modern town, is unexciting in the extreme, enlivened only on Wednesdays by the weekly **souk**. There is one **bank** in Sbeitla and the **PTT** (country hours) in av Farhat Hached, between the *autogare* and the town centre, is easily recognisable for some distance by the transmitter aerial sticking out of the roof. Altogether, it's not a very prepossessing place.

Still, **hitching out** again on the main road is generally good. The *autogare* is in rue Habib Thameur at the southern end of town (the train station behind it has no passenger services) with **buses** to Kasserine, Sfax, Gafsa and Tunis, and **louages** to Sidi Bou Zid and Kasserine.

Accommodation and sustenance

If you want to stay in Sbeitla, there are two 2* hotels; the *Bakini*, rue 2 Mars near a mosque (look for its octagonal minaret), which is clean and comfortable at 14.5TD/21TD b&b (☎65244); and the *Sufetula* on the Kasserine road beyond the site (☎65074), which caters mainly for organised tour parties and is a little pricier at 17.5TD/24TD b&b, but more spacious than the *Bakini* and with a view over the ruins and a swimming pool – which non-residents can use for a small charge.

For **food and drink**, the *Bakini* has a sedate bar and restaurant. Rather raucous by comparison, the *Hôtel Ezzohour* opposite the *autogare*, at the start of av Bourguiba, is no longer a hotel, but still dispenses beer. Basic food can be found in the *Restaurant des Ruines* at the other end of av Bourguiba, near the roundabout in the centre of town.

The Site

The **site** (open 8am–5pm daily, 1TD plus 1TD to take photos) lies along the Kasserine road, northwest of the new town. To get there, walk straight ahead out of the *autogare* up rue Taïeb Mehiri, and it's about half a kilometre. Touts hanging around outside sell "Roman" coins, some of which *may* actually be genuine, although worthless. A **museum** across the road is due to open some time: it will be included on the site entry ticket, but will be closed on Mondays. A **triumphal arch** to the right, a couple of hundred metres before the entrance, once signalled the site's southern limit, straddling the main highway east to Hadrumetum (Sousse).

The Forum

You enter between two solid-looking Byzantine **forts**, then turn diagonally left to reach the **Forum**, with its circuit wall and three temples side by side. It's unusual to find a Forum so well preserved, and it feels strange to be enclosed by the wall and massive presence of the temples (dedicated to Jupiter, Juno and Minerva). But this must be close to the original Roman conception of architecture used to assert domination.

Basilicas

Passing between the temples, head right to the next large group of remains, a series of **churches**. The first (on the right, with a palm tree standing next to a stretch of wall) is the three-aisled **Basilica of St Vitalis**; then comes the larger five-aisled **Basilica of Bellator** which probably served as the Byzantine town's cathedral. This was built on the site of a private house, and you can see on the floor two levels of mosaics, the lower ones belonging to the (possibly fourth-century) house, the others to the (maybe sixth-century) cathedral: the direct comparison of styles is interesting. On the northwestern side of the cathedral is a **chapel** dedicated to Jucundus, the Catholic bishop martyred by the Arian Vandals in the fifth century. Beyond the far corner of the cathedral is a baths complex that includes a cistern, and a row of seats forms the ever-present latrines.

The northern end of the site

In the distance, looking north, you should be able to see a **bridge** over the *oued*. Built by the Romans, the bridge is still in use (though admittedly heavily restored), providing access to a spring on the far bank whose water is pumped directly to Sfax. Just about level with the bridge, a solitary square ruin known as the **"Unidentified Temple"** stands over the northwest limit of the town. Look out here for the foundations of a

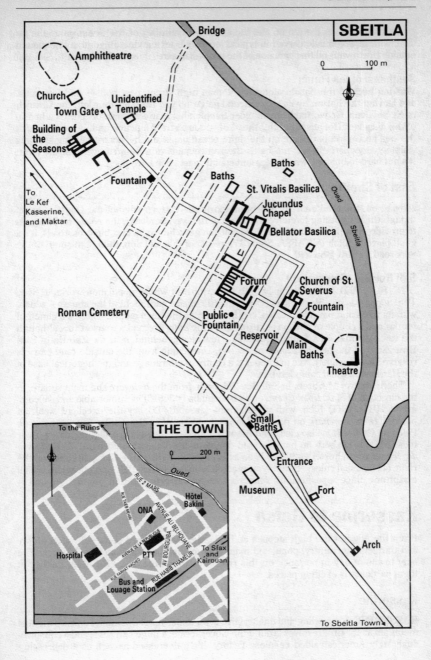

SBEITLA

0   100 m

Bridge

Amphitheatre

Church

Town Gate

Unidentified Temple

Building of the Seasons

Fountain

To Le Kef Kasserine, and Maktar

Baths

Baths

St. Vitalis Basilica

Jucundus Chapel

Bellator Basilica

Oued Sbeitla

Roman Cemetery

Forum

Church of St. Severus

Fountain

Public Fountain

Reservoir

Main Baths

Theatre

Small Baths

Entrance

Museum

Fort

Arch

THE TOWN

0   200 m

To the Ruins

Oued

RUE 2 MARS

RUE TAIEB HACHED

AVENUE ALI BELHOUANE

Hôtel Bakini

ONA

AVENUE DE LA REPUBLIQUE

AV. BOURGUIBA

PTT

Hospital

RUE FARHAT HACHED

RUE HABIB THAMEUR

Bus and Louage Station

To Sfax and Kairouan

To Sbeitla Town

triumphal arch over the street, and the attractive **Building of the Seasons** on the far side, with its colonnade carved in typical local style with a vine. Beyond, a low mound outside the town is all that remains of the **amphitheatre**.

Southeast of the Forum

Walking back to the Forum along the Roman high street, past houses and fountains, and leaving the Forum by its monumental gateway, you pass, on your left, the **Church of St Severus**. Converted from an older temple, this may well have been the cathedral of the dissident Donatist church. Ahead of you is a street junction and, directly over it, the well-preserved **baths** are on the right, paved pools and hypocaust heating systems visible everywhere. Below the baths the sad remains of a **theatre** overlook the river. It's not hard to imagine what a pleasant spot it must once have been.

East of Sbeitla

Moving on, the road **east to Kairouan** skirts the eastern edge of the Dorsale range, though there's nothing to entice a stop along the way. Similarly, the **route to Sfax** fails to provide even this limited interest. If you can get a lift to the first big crossroads, it's a good place to hitch to GAFSA. Some 17km east of this junction, then 8km south of the Sfax road, is **Sidi Bou Zid**.

Sidi Bou Zid (Gammouda)

SIDI BOU ZID is a notoriously drab town, most of whose population works in Sfax. The *autogare* is one block off av Bourguiba (the main road), behind the square – which, with its trees and pavement cafés, can be taken as the town centre. There's a clutch of **banks** and a couple of cheap **restaurants** by the *autogare*, and a **market** too, although the weekly **souk**, on a Saturday, is held a few blocks behind, near the **Zaouia of Sidi Bou Zid** and the nearby *zaouia* of his son. Unexciting from the outside (and entry is reserved for Muslims), this marabout is a centre of pilgrimage and the historical base of the Hammama tribal confederation.

There are two 1* **hotels** in Sidi Bou Zid, both, from the *autogare* and main square, in the direction of Sfax. *Hôtel Chems* on av Bourguiba (☎30515) is comfortable and welcoming at 10TD/18TD b&b, with a restaurant (around 4TD; try the excellent steak au poivre). *Hôtel Horchati*, on rue de Meknassy, 400m off av Bourguiba down the rue de Palestine(☎30217) is also clean and friendly, although the staff are slightly less on their toes (6TD/10TD b&b no bath, around double that price with bathroom). The *Maison des Jeunes* youth hostel (☎30088) is on av Bourguiba 200m in the Gafsa direction on the right (4TD, usual rules). Before you reach it, you'll pass the **PTT** on your right, with a **taxiphone** office opposite and a *Magasin Général* **supermarket** on your left.

Kasserine to Gafsa

From the edge of the high steppes at Thala, the GAFSA road passes through empty and unrelenting country, populated mainly by lonely shepherds and their flocks. The only towns of any importance on this road are **Kasserine** and FERIANA, neither of them particularly exciting places.

Kasserine

KASSERINE, a sprawling and unattractive town under Jebel Chambi (Tunisia's highest mountain at 1554m), revolves around the Governorate, a huge barracks, and a conspicuously ugly American-aided cellulose factory. It's a depressed as well as a depressing place; the bread riots of January 1984 began here. But it's the site of the remains of **Roman Cillium** and a large **Mausoleum** – and worth a dreary night for their sake.

Orientation and practicalities

The main square that marks the town centre boasts trees and flowers, three **banks**, a couple of cheap **restaurants** and the *SNTRI* station. The *SRT Kasserine* and **louage** station is also on one side of the main square in front of the train station (no passenger service). **Louages** serve Tunis, Sbeitla, Feriana and Thala, but not Le Kef or Gafsa.

A left out of this *autogare* down av Bourguiba takes you after 1km past the **cellulose factory** on your left (watch the lorry loads of esparto grass arriving). A few minutes' walk further on the right is a big **hunk of Roman mausoleum** and, after another 500m, a bridge over a large *oued*. Fork right at the junction beyond (past the **Mausoleum of the Flavii** on your right), and you come to another junction after 100m or so, by the **hospital** (☎70022). The left fork here (sign-posted "Gafsa") takes you to **Cillium**, the hotel and ruins. Buses run between the *autogare* and the hospital every fifteen minutes.

Accommodation and eating

Food is available on the main square, and behind it in av Taïeb Mehiri, where there are several **patisseries**, **rôtisseries** and **cafés**. There are several **bars** on av Bourguiba near the main square: the *Hôtel de la Paix* has one, and there's another next door. Officially, there are only three **hotels** in Kasserine, but a number of other places to stay are available.

Hôtel de la Paix, av Bourguiba 50m from the main square towards Sbeitla (☎71465). The rooms are not bad but the "breakfast" included in the (unofficial) price is a joke. 5TD/7TD.

Hôtel Pinus,100m further (☎70164). A comfortable if rather officious establishment. 1* 9TD /14TD b&b.

Hôtel Cillium, right out the other end of town (☎70682), past the hospital and by the ruins of the same name. Huge rooms, nice views of the ruins and a swimming pool (open for non-residents). Definitely the friendliest hotel in town. 3* 18TD/25TD b&b.

Youth Hostel/Maison des Jeunes, 1km from the town centre on av Bourguiba, on the left going towards Cillium. The usual Colditz-style barracks. 4TD a night and as unwelcoming as you'd expect.

Hôtel du Golf, on the main square (☎71044). Definitely for men only. 2TD.

Hôtel Ben Abdallah , 40 rue H Thameur (☎70568), down beside the *Magasin Général*. 2.5TD.

Hôtel d'Algerie, av 7 Novembre (☎71876), 3 blocks behind the main square. 5TD/7.5TD.

Cillium and the Mausoleum of the Flavii

The **remains of Roman Cillium** are well out of town past the *Hôtel Cillium*. If you don't fancy walking all the way or taking a taxi, get a bus to the hospital and walk from there, taking a left 100m beyond the hotel. The ruins begin a short way up this path, and are spread out over quite an area. The most impressive feature of a not very outstanding site is the third-century **arch**. Nearby is a group of rather pretty white-washed **marabouts**.

On the way to Cillium, and more engaging than its rather limited remains, is the **Mausoleum of the Flavii**, the best-preserved example of its kind in the country, which stands three storeys high next to the main road, decorated with a 110-line poetic (well, just) inscription to the dead Flavius. Four lines sum up the Roman dedication to conspicuous consumption:

> *"Who could fail to be mind-blown as he stands here, who would not marvel at this construction and be staggered at the wealth which has caused this monument to rise to the heavenly skies…?"*

Jebel Chambi

For all its height, **Jebel Chambi** is strangely uninspiring, compared to Jebel Zaghouan, for instance. But it should be rather moving: in February 1943, American infantry units with little combat experience were assigned to hold the pass leading to Thala. In a fierce battle that left over 1000 American troops dead, Axis forces dealt them a severe defeat. In General Patton's words: "The boys' morale was so low it could have passed under a snake."

Onward to Gafsa and Tébessa

There's nothing to stop off for on the road between Kasserine and Gafsa, one of the bleakest in the country. The only town of any size is FERIANA, 5km after the minimal remains of **Thelepte**, which look more than usual as if someone has just scattered a handful of hefty blocks across the road. Basilicas, baths and a theatre may just be visible in the home town of Saint Fulgentius (467–532). A **road to Tébessa in Algeria** splits off at Thelepte, but hitching prospects are practically nonexistent. Like most of the western border posts, it's usually open but little used.

travel details

The Tell is rather a diffuse region and does not have a very integrated system of transport. Le Kef and Kasserine are the main transport centres, reasonably well connected to other parts of the Tell and of the country. Places on the edge of the region, however, often have better connections outside it. Sbeitla and Kasserine have railway lines but no passenger services.

Trains

FROM LE KEF TO:
Tunis (1 daily, very early, 4hr) via **Sers** (30min), **Le Krib** (1hr), **Gaafour** (1hr 30min) and **Fahs** (2hr 30min).

FROM KALAA KHASBAH (KALAA JERDA) TO:
Tunis (3 daily, 5hr 30min) via **Sers** (1hr 40min), **Gaafour** (2hr 45min) and **Fahs** (4hr).

Buses and louages

FROM TEBOURSOUK TO:
Tunis (hourly from 5am to 6pm, 2hr 20min) via **Testour** (20min) and **Medjez el Bab** (1hr); **Le Kef** (hourly from 5am to 6pm, 40 min); **Beja** (2 daily, 1hr) via **Thibar** (30min).
Louages to **Tunis**, **Nouvelle Dougga**, **Thibar**, **Beja**, **Medjez el Bab** and **Gaafour**.

FROM LE KEF TO:
Tunis (hourly departures, 3hr) via **Teboursouk** (40min), **Testour** (1hr) and **Medjez el Bab** (1hr 30min); **Beja** (3 daily, 2hr); **Jendouba** (6, 1hr

10min); **Kasserine** (5, 4hr); **Thala** (6, 1hr 45min); **Kalaa Khasbah** (6, 1hr 30min); **Sousse** (2, 3hr 45min) via **Fahs** (2hr); **Sfax** (2, 4hr 30min); **Kairouan** (2 daily, 3hr 30min); **Sakiet Sidi Youssef** (2 daily, 1hr); **Bizerte** (1 daily, 4hr); **Maktar** (1, 2hr); **Ras Ajdir (Libyan border)** (1, 8hr); **Nabeul** (1, 4hr); **Gafsa** (1, 4hr 45min); **Sidi Bou Zid** (2, 3hr).
Louages to **Tunis**, **Jendouba**, **Kalaa Khasbah**, **Kalaat es Senam**, **Tajerouine** and **El Ksour**.

FROM KALAA KHASBAH (KALAA JERDA) TO:
Le Kef (6, 1hr 30min); **Thala** (5, 2hr); **Kasserine** (5, 2hr 30min).
Louages to **Thala** and **Kasserine**.

FROM THALA TO:
Tunis (4 daily with SNTRI, 5hr); **Kasserine** (5, 45min); **Tajerouine** and **Le Kef** (6, 1hr 45min).
Louages to **Kasserine** and **Haidra**.

FROM SBEITLA TO:
Tunis (4 daily, 3hr); **Kasserine** (6, 30min); **Sidi Bou Zid** (4, 1hr); **Gafsa** (2, 2hr); **Sfax** (1, 3hr).
Louages to **Sidi Bou Zid** and **Kasserine**.

FROM SIDI BOU ZID (GAMMOUDA) TO:
Tunis (4 daily, 4hr); **Sbeitla** (4, 1hr); **Gafsa** (4, 2hr); **Sfax** (4, 2hr); **Kairouan** (5, 1hr 30min); **Le Kef** (2, 3hr); **Kasserine** (2, 1hr 30min); **Gabes** (2, 4hr 30min); **Tozeur** (1, 4hr 30min).
Louages to **Sfax**, **Meknassy**, **Gafsa**, **Tunis**, **Ben Aoun**, **Haffouz** and **Sbeitla** (none direct to Kasserine).

FROM KASSERINE TO:
Tunis (Bab Alleoua) (6 daily, 5hr) via **Maktar** (2hr) and **Fahs** (4hr); **Tunis (Bab Saadoun)** (1 daily, 5hr) via **Le Kef** (2hr); **Sfax** (2, 4hr 30min). Other services to **Le Kef** (5, 4hr) via **Kalaa** **Khasbah** (2hr 30min); **Sbeitla** (6, 30min); **Gafsa** (6, 1hr 30min); **Gabes** (4hr).
Louages to **Tunis**, **Sbeitla**, **Feriana** and **Thala**, but not **Le Kef** or **Gafsa**.

PHONE CODES

Le Kef, Maktar,Teboursouk, Testour ☎08. Sbeitla, Thala, Kasserine ☎07. Sidi Bou Zid ☎06.

CHAPTER SIX

THE JERID

R ich in the phosphates which play a major role in Tunisia's economy, the **Jerid**
is an arid land of bare pink hills punctuated only by mining towns and sporadic
oasis-villages built around springs and deep gorges. These take time to
explore, but are memorable places to experience the precariousness of oasis
life. In contrast, the oases at **Tozeur** and **Nefta** – both reached quite easily – are vast
folds of luxuriance, set right at the edge of the **Chott**, a bizarre **salt lake** of shifting
colours and mirages. Nefta is especially worthwhile: a longtime centre of Sufism whose
monuments add an intriguing dimension to its character. Across the Chott lie further

oases – the scattered centres of the Nefzaoua, under constant threat from the dunes of the Great Eastern Erg. **Kebili** and **Douz** are the two main towns, but what supplies the interest is the access they offer to smaller villages around.

Gafsa

For hundreds of years **GAFSA** has been inspiring the sort of comment quoted by the Edwardian traveller Norman Douglas from an old Arab song: "Gafsa is miserable; its water blood; its air poison; you may live there a hundred years without making a friend." On the face of it, Douglas agreed – "One dines early in Gafsa and afterwards there's nothing, absolutely nothing, to do." After a brief flirtation with tourist development, the town now seems resigned to its fate as a stopover for coach parties heading south. But it really isn't as bad as people like to make out, and worth a day or two for the scenery alone.

History Ancient and Modern

Gafsa's history is one of the longest in the Maghreb, let alone Tunisia. The prehistoric Capsian culture which spread all over Africa is named after implements found near the site of Roman Capsa. In 107 BC, the Roman town's Numidian predecessor was famously captured by the Roman general Marius from the troublesome Jugurtha: "Except the immediate neighbourhood of the town," wrote the historian Sallust, "the whole district is desolate, uncultivated, waterless, and infested by deadly serpents, which like all wild animals are made fiercer by scarcity of food, and especially by thirst, which exasperates their natural malignity." Not short on malignity himself, Marius sacked the town and slaughtered the population – giving the excuse that the inhabitants were a "fickle and untrustworthy lot". An important Roman colony, Capsa was heavily fortified by the Byzantines and renamed Justiniana after the Emperor – neither of which moves proved any deterrence to Oqba Ibn Nafi, who captured the city and took 80,000 prisoners in 668. Despite the Arab conquest, and large-scale conversion to Islam, El Edrisi reported Latin still being spoken here in the twelfth century.

Gafsa's most recent world headlines were in January 1980. On January 27 a mysterious group of unidentified soldiers took over the town in a night-time operation. It took several days for the army to evict them, after 48 deaths; of the 60 captured, 13 were hanged on April 17. To this day the incident remains shrouded in mystery. Rumour has it that the leader was a native of Gafsa who had fled to Libya in the wake of the Ahmed Ben Salah purges of 1969, and the one consistent element in suggested explanations seems to be that the men came from Libya. As to the object, however, nothing is clear: if the Tunisian south was expected to rise spontaneously and declare allegiance with Libya, its mood had been severely misjudged. But it is significant that Gafsa was chosen as the target. As the economic and administrative capital of the Jerid, whose phosphates play such a large part in the national economy, there is some resentment among the citizens that they don't benefit more from the industry. True or not, the common view in the town, that the profits all go to rich businessmen in Sfax, suggests considerable disenchantment.

> ## PUTTING THE DEVIL BACK IN HELL
>
> Gafsa has a literary claim to fame in Boccaccio's 1353 classic, the *Decameron*, being the home of Alibech, the innocent virginal heroine of the book's 30th and most infamous tale. Setting off into the desert to learn how to serve God, Alibech encounters the pious young hermit Rustico, who agrees to teach her. Rustico, however, soon gets other ideas and persuades her to join him in a rather unorthodox enactment of putting the devil into hell, thus coining a sexual euphemism current in the Italian of the time. In the story, when the women of Gafsa found out how Alibech and Rustico had been serving God out in the desert, "they burst into such laughter that they are laughing still". English translators, though, found it no laughing matter and, even into this century, they refused to put the crucial parts into English, and printed them untranslated. Their readers were left to fathom the finer points of Rustico's method from the original Italian text.

Practicalities

The centre of town is marked by a nondescript triangular garden tucked in between av Taïeb Mehiri, av 2 Mars and av 13 Février. The Medina lies to the west of this triangle, across av 13 Février, which continues round the edge of the Medina as **Rue Ali Belhouane**, where most of the cheap hotels are located. Across the triangle, **Avenue Taïeb Mehiri** is Gafsa's main thoroughfare; on it, close by, are the cinema and central market. On the other side of the Medina is **Avenue Bourguiba**, running from the **Roman Pools** up to the **PTT**. Off to the left there, av de la Liberté is the Tozeur road.

Arriving by train, you are left way out in the suburb of Gafsa Gare on the Gabes road to the southeast. Your best bet is to take a taxi into town (3TD or so), or walk (bear right opposite the station and straight on) up to the main road where there are more taxis – and some buses, but not early enough for the arrival of the morning train.

Accommodation

Most of Gafsa's **budget hotels** are on rue Ali Belhouane, and **upmarket hotels** too can be found close to the centre of town. This leaves mid-range accommodation a little thinner on the ground, but not impossible to find (try the *Khalfallah*, the *Moussa* or the *Lune*). Those near the centre are keyed on the map.

Hôtel Alaya Pacha (1), 4 rue Ali Belhouane (☎20231). Rooms are clean, bright and inviting, the management less so. 4.5TD/9TD.

Hôtel de la République (2), 28 rue Ali Belhouane (☎21807). Probably the best deal of the hotels on rue Ali Belhouane, with big rooms and friendly management. 3TD/4TD (plus 0.5TD for a shower).

Hôtel Bechir (3), 40 rue Ali Belhouane (☎23239). Friendly and clean but the rooms are small. 4TD a room.

Hôtel de l'Oasis (4), 7 rue Ali Belhouane (☎20097). The people who run it are great, but the rooms are dark and gloomy. 3TD/5TD.

Hôtel Ennour (5), rue Mohamed Khaddouma (☎20620). On a little road parallel with rue 13 Février and easier to spot from the back than the front. 3.5TD/6TD b&b.

Tunis Hôtel (6), av 2 Mars (☎21660). By the bus station. The rooms are clean, but they cram the beds in. 5TD/6TD, or 3TD for a bed in a shared room (0.3TD for a cold shower).

Hôtel Khalfallah (7), av Taïeb Mehiri (☎21468). A touch classier than the other budget hotels. 9TD/12TD b&b.

Hôtel Moussa, av de la Liberté (☎23333). Out on the Tozeur road, about 500m past the PTT. Clean and neat and run by a very jolly bunch of women. 4.5TD/9TD b&b.

Youth Hostel/Maison des Jeunes, rue Mongi Bali (☎20268). To get to it, take the Tozeur road past the *Hôtel Moussa*, then the next right and the first left, and it's the building on your right that looks like a factory with a blue roof. 4TD.

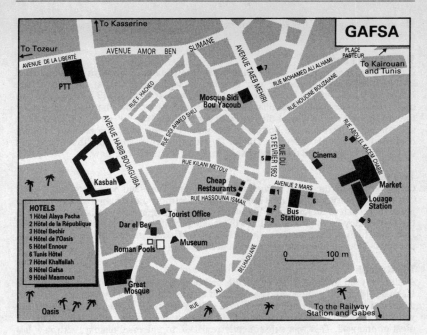

Hôtel Gafsa (8), rue Abou el Kacem Chabbi (☎22676). Classy in a discreet sort of way. 2* 19.5TD/28TD b&b.

Hôtel Maamoun (9), av Taïeb Mehiri (☎22433). The poshest gaff in Gafsa; for those who like their creature comforts. 3* 21TD/30TD b&b.

Lune Hôtel, av Taïeb Mehiri (☎22212). Not sign-posted and hard to find, 200m down from the *Maamoun* towards the edge of town, on the left past a housing estate. 15TD/22TD b&b.

Hôtel Jugurtha, Sidi Ahmed Zarroug (☎21300). Four kilometres west of town in a small oasis (see p.232). Was 3*, but closed for renovation: make sure it's reopened before you trek out there.

Eating

Most of the restaurants around the bus station and cheap hotel area are pretty bad value – overpriced greasy spoons basically. The exception is the *Restaurant de Carthage* beside the *Hôtel Tunis*. Otherwise, decent cheap eats can be found by taking rue Hassouna Ismail off rue Ali Belhouane by the *Hôtel de l'Oasis,* and then the second left, where there are three restaurants doing basic 2TD meals.

More sophisticated eating places include the rather sedate *Restaurant Semiramis* at around 8TD, the 4.5TD set menu at the *Gafsa*, and the rather pricier *Hôtel Maamoun* down the street.

Around Town

The town centre can have changed very little since Norman Douglas's day; Gafsa is still not a town for great sightseeing. Tourist attractions are mostly concentrated around the Roman Pools in the corner of the Medina at the bottom end of av Bourguiba. The skyline is dominated by the majestic minaret of the spacious **Great**

Mosque, overlooking the town from nearby, with, beyond it, the oasis and distant desert.

The Roman Pools

Gafsa's focal monument is the **Piscine Romaine** (Roman Pools), which every small boy will automatically assume you've come to see. A left turn at the end of rue Hassouna Ismail (off rue Ali Belhouane by the *Hôtel de l'Oasis*) will bring you to two open, rectangular pools in familiar Roman masonry. Apart from the fish, look out for the inscriptions on the side of the larger, upper pool, and the hot spring which you can see coming up through the bottom of the smaller, lower one. The arcaded building over the lower pool is called the **Dar el Bey** after the ruler who built this house, and on the far side steps lead down to a hammam using the pools' overflow.

Two museums

On the square by the pools, a small **museum** (open Tues–Sun 8am–noon and 2–6pm; closed Mon; entry free) exhibits mosaics from **Zammour**, an example of the Tunisian jigsaw approach to archaeology, but worth a look. A larger museum is due to open in the **Dar el Bey** by the lower pool. It will include part of the natural history collection of Philippe Thomas, the phosphate discoverer (see *Metlaoui and the Seldja Gorge* p.235), previously housed in a separate museum at Metlaoui.

The Kasbah

A little way up av Bourguiba stand the pinkly picturesque, crenellated walls of the **Kasbah**. It has had a chequered career: built by the Hafsids on a Byzantine foundation, it resisted a Turkish corsair's siege in 1551 only to surrender to the same opponent five years later. Its worst moment came in 1943 when an Allied ammunition dump blew out most of one wall. This was subsequently replaced, to universal dismay, with new law courts, and the Kasbah remains a rather soulless place until sunset, when the walls glow in harlequin shades of limpid colour.

The Gafsa oasis

Gafsa is situated at a transitional point between the last remnants of the central steppes and mountains to the north, and the incipient desert to the south: a position which has always made it an important place. The scenery is still the most striking feature, one long tongue of bleak hills passing behind the town to the west, another parallel in the southern distance. On the edge of this pocket is the **Gafsa oasis**, large but more diffuse than those of Tozeur or Nefta. If those oases are islands in the desert, then Gafsa is the big port on the shore.

Gafsa's significance as a desert "port" can be best appreciated by visiting two of its small satellite oases. Local buses leave regularly from the *Hôtel Tunis* for the **Lalla oasis**, 7km east of town. Stay on the bus until it turns around (at the end of its route) then walk on a bit further to a small café and two prolific springs. The stark contrast here between shady green and glaring pink hills really brings home the fragility of oasis existence. **Sidi Ahmed Zarroug**, the other oasis, lies 4km west of town and is now occupied by the luxurious *Hôtel Jugurtha*. If you're here in the winter – the only time of year suitable for energetic scrambling – the view out over the desert from the bald ridge which towers over the hotel is little short of magnificent.

A free-range zoo

If you find conventional zoos hard to stomach, there is an animal park at ORBATA a few kilometres out on the Tunis road where the likes of gazelles and ostriches roam about freely. It's open 8am–5pm daily and entry is just 0.1TD per person, or 0.5TD for a car or bus.

Moving On

The **bus station** is off av 2 Mars, right in the centre of town behind several cheap hotels, with seven buses a day to Tunis, four of them overnight, and others to Metlaoui, Tozeur and Nefta, and the phosphate areas of Redeyef and Tamerza. There are also regular departures for Sfax, Gabes, Kairouan, Le Kef and Kebili. Full details are given in "travel details" at the end of the chapter.

Louages for El Guettar (one of the nicest villages to visit around Gafsa; see below) hang out by the cinema on av Taïeb Mehiri, but for other destinations, you'll find them in a yard on the other side of the market, behind the Esso station, opposite the *Hôtel Maamoun*.

There is also a **railway station**, rather inconveniently located 3km down the Gabes road in the suburb of Gafsa Gare, a couple of dinars' taxi ride from town. There's a single overnight train to Tunis via Sfax and a less useful one, the other way, to Metlaoui, very early in the morning.

Listings

Banks There are several in av Taïeb Mehiri, and a couple by the cinema.

Car hire *Mattei*, 6 rue Mohamed Ali Alhami (☎20267), off av Taïeb Mehiri opposite Sidi Bou Yacoub Mosque.

Carpets Gafsa has its own style of carpet with designs quite unlike those found elsewhere. To check out styles and top prices, try the ONA shop off the Tozeur road.

Cinema In av Taïeb Mehiri, opposite the *Tunis Hôtel*, next to the central market.

Consulates The Algerian consulate behind 37 rue Houcine Bouzaiane (entrance in rue Abou el Kacem Chabbi, ☎21366) just *might* issue you a visa, but don't count on it, especially if packing a UK passport.

Festival The "Festival du Borj" is a series of theatrical and musical presentations in the Kasbah throughout August.

Hammams One can be found by taking the first left off rue Houcine Bouzaiane behind pl 13 Février: it's a blue doorway on the left without even a sign in Arabic, but an open door and two benches inside. Women in the afternoon, men mornings and evenings. The more renowned *Hammam Karaouani* is further afield (head up rue Houcine Bouzaiane to pl Pasteur and ask around), and there's also one by the Roman Pools, which uses their water.

International phone calls 17 rue Houcine Bouzaiane (off av Taïeb Mehiri at pl 13 Février). 7am–9pm daily.

Market day Wednesday.

Medical facilities The regional hospital (☎21200) is in rue Avicenne (up rue Houcine Bouzaiane to pl Pasteur, then right).

ONA crafts shop Off av de la Liberté (Tozeur road), first left coming from the PTT.

Passport photos Several places off av Taïeb Mehiri, including one by the cinema.

PTT On the corner of av Bourguiba and av de la Liberté (Tozeur road). City hours. No international phone services.

Tourist office ONTT (☎21664), in the square by the Roman Pools, open Mon–Thurs 8.30am–1pm & 3–5.45pm; Fri & Sat 8.30am–1.30pm; Sun closed.

Villages Around Gafsa

Some 20km east of Gafsa on the Gabes road is another oasis, **EL GUETTAR**, reached by bus or *louage* from Gafsa. It's nothing much in itself, a ribbon of modern concrete houses along the road, but the huge palmery is rarely visited and farmers still use old techniques, like the *noria*, a device to draw water from wells by animal power. The oasis is known for its pistachio nuts. At the end of the village, a road to the left leads to

Outsiders aren't that welcome in Sakket, Sened or Meich – as you arrive the women hide in their houses and the men gather into groups to discuss the *hawaja*, foreigner. Little has changed here in the past two centuries. As in Berber villages in the far south of the country, the villagers retain their distinct ethnic identity (though none have spoken Berber since the last century), and traditional dress and customs persist. Women wear the *bakhnug*, a shawl embroidered with geometrical patterns to shelter them from the eyes of strangers. Many of the men wear the knee-length trousers that used to be common before the last war. At the centre of each of the villages are marabouts' tombs, with rags and flags hanging from poles; the last place in Tunisia where you can see votive offerings to these village saints. The village oil presses are still animal powered and women grind their own flour by hand. In winter many people migrate into the pastures with their herds, and the villages are virtually deserted. Today, however, a different type of migration is slowly eroding the community, as many families abandon their villages for an easier life in the city.

the remote **Berber mountain villages** of SAKKET (14km), SENED (27km) and MEICH (42km) – highly worthwhile targets if you're prepared for a moderate adventure and to be a genuine visitor and not just another tourist (see box above).

Getting to these villages is difficult. It's possible to catch a bus to El Guettar but from there you'll have to walk, or, if you're lucky, get a lift. Ask at one of the cafés in El Guettar for directions. East of El Guettar, the main GP15 highway continues across the steppe to SIDI MANSOUR, a small village with an important marabout, and thence on to GABES (150km from Gafsa). Buses run both ways regularly.

Meknassy and Bou Hedma National Park

The road to SFAX takes you across the barren steppes between the Dorsale mountains to the north and the Chotts to the south. The only town of any size on this route is MEKNASSY, whose attraction is the nearby **Bou Hedma National Park** . This, alas,

The steppes cover a vast area of the centre of the country – from the southern foothills of the Dorsale ridge down to the Chott el Jerid. Most are degraded forests; it's a sobering thought that Hannibal probably got his **elephants** from this region a couple of few thousand years ago. Over the centuries, the wood has been felled and the land grazed by sheep, goats and camels, resulting in a landscape only barely productive for agriculture.

The steppes, and particularly the low hills and wadis rising up from them, are rich in unusual **small birds**. Worth special mention are crested larks, hoopoe larks (so called because of the long decurved bill and black and white wings), and the even more peculiar Temminck's horned lark, a striking bird with a black and white head pattern and, in breeding plumage, two distinct black "horns". In the rockier parts, look out for the trumpeter finch, a thick-billed pink bird with a weird nasal call. **House buntings** are common in villages and, as they're treated with some reverence by local people, are extremely tame.

Out in the wilder areas, you may see – with some patience and luck – some of the true **desert mammals**. Jerboas and gerbils are reasonably common, as are susliks, a sort of short-tailed ground squirrel with an upright "begging" posture. Most of the larger desert **antelopes** have been reduced to extinction by excessive hunting, but an ambitious reintroduction programme is underway at the **Bou Hedma National Park**, just south of Meknassy. Gazelle, oryx and addax are all being introduced, as well as ostriches, which were only exterminated from the south of the country this century.

is inaccessible by public transport. If you have a vehicle and want to visit it, you should first call in at the *Direction des Fôrets* office in Meknassy for a permit. For further information, see the wildlife box opposite.

Meknassy has a bank and hospital (☎35179) and *louages* out to Sfax, Gafsa and Sidi Bou Zid.

Metlaoui and the Seldja Gorge

In 1896 a French army vet and amateur geologist, Philippe Thomas, found phosphate deposits round **Metlaoui**. Previously known only for his work on goat diseases, the discovery made Thomas a national hero and turned an insignificant village into an important mining centre.

The transformation took little over a decade. Thousands of miners were recruited from Algeria and Libya, for local people were at first reluctant to work in the mining towns and were later excluded because the mine owners feared they would campaign for better conditions. Conditions were certainly bad: the companies provided no accommodation and huge *bidonvilles* grew up without any planning or services. At work there were few safety measures, and one third of employees had to retire because of injury, without compensation. Unions were discouraged by the companies' policies of maintaining a high turnover of personnel and by pitting one ethnic group against another; paying Algerians more than Libyans, and Libyans more than Sudanese. So tense were relations that fights used to break out between the groups, and on one occasion the Algerians burnt down a Libyan shantytown, killing over a hundred people. It was only in the 1930s that the unions managed to unite the workforce and direct their anger against their bosses rather than each other – and conditions then improved radically.

Despite its rather forbidding appearance and industrial history, Metlaoui still merits a visit: from the station you can take a train through the spectacular **Seldja Gorge** and on to REDEYEF, where there's transport to TAMERZA, first of the mountain oases.

Metlaoui

By 1899, phosphate from Metlaoui was being exported to France via the new railway to Sfax and other mines were being dug in the surrounding hills. The *Compagnie des Phosphates de Gafsa* was established after independence, and Tunisia is now the fourth largest phosphate producer in the world. Mining is problematic: the value of phosphate is unstable, the rock here is of poor quality, and wages are low. In 1977 the workers went on strike and their action led to the national crisis the following year that for a while threatened to overthrow the government.

METLAOUI itself is an odd jumble of French houses dwarfed by overhead phosphate conveyors and heavy mining equipment. Norman Douglas came here in 1930 and found "trim bungalows", an "air of neatness and well-being" and workers who "would slit your throat for a sou". All somewhat bizarre viewed from the perspective of the 1990s.

Orientation, accommodation and sustenance

The Gafsa road runs through the centre of town until it meets the TAMERZA/TOZEUR T-junction by a filling station and a disused cinema. Metlaoui's only **hotel**, the *Enassim* (or *Ennacime*) is 300m towards Tozeur on the left. A night here will set you back 8TD/12TD b&b. The rooms, if a bit gloomy, are presentable, and a new wing is about to open. You can also get a meal in the restaurant at 3.5TD for a set menu, and the hotel bar is one of only two places in town with beer. If you'd prefer a cheaper eating house, there are several along the Gafsa road.

The **PTT** is by the station and opens country hours. There's also a *Magasin Général* **supermarket** about 200m from the *autogare* towards town, but make sure you have enough cash to tide you over as there's **no bank** in Metlaoui at which to change money.

Transport and other practicalities

SNTRI **buses** to Tunis one way, or Tozeur, Kebili and Douz the other, stop by the main road junction. *SRT Gafsa* buses stop at the *autogare* a good half kilometre up the Tamerza road, with departures for Gafsa, Tozeur, Nefta, Redeyef and Tamerza, though you may have to change for the latter. **Louages** also operate from the same place and run to Tozeur, Redeyef, Gafsa, Tamerza and Tunis. If they don't find enough passengers at the *autogare*, they may cruise around town looking for them.

The **train** station is about a kilometre from the main junction on the Gafsa road, but services are sparse with one overnight train a day to Gafsa, Sfax, Sousse, and Tunis (you could also get to Gabes if you want to wait two hours at Sfax or Mahres for your connection). The other way, there's an afternoon service to Moulares and Redeyef, supplemented in the summer by the *Lezard Rouge* (see below).

The Seldja Gorge

If you take the Metlaoui–Redeyef train, it is possible to stop halfway at **SELDJA**, and return to Metlaoui an hour and a half later. Buy a ticket at the office in Seldja and wait around by the level crossing.

Seldja, a neat white signal box stuck in the middle of nowhere, was built by the French along with a remarkable series of bridges and tunnels. Previously, the Romans had diverted the water from these ravines, building an aqueduct to supply nearby agricultural land. Coming from Sbeitla, their caravans took a short-cut through here en route to Ghadames in present-day Libya. From the signal box you can walk back down the tracks to some of the more impressive parts of the gorge, its sheer sides worn completely smooth by the river. Norman Douglas nearly met his end in one of the tunnels, and phosphate trains do still pass at regular intervals, so watch your step. An alternative route to the gorge is by road from Metlaoui: a track leads out over the flat plain, too hot to walk, for 5km to a rock passage known as the *coup de sabre*, or sword thrust. Legend says that Al Mansour, a warrior, cut into the rock with one stroke, to prepare a bed for Leila, a princess escaping from her husband. There's a 4km path along the foot of the gorge to the signal box – if you walk it you'll see the wheeling silhouettes of birds of prey overhead.

Redeyef

REDEYEF, the last of the mining towns, is 17km further on and, like Metlaoui, has grown up around an old French community with its bungalows and church. The people who live here are surprised to meet tourists at all, for the very good reason that there's absolutely nothing to see. Nothing, that is, unless you're a train buff. During the summer months, the *SNCFT* lays on a tourist train, the *Lezard Rouge*, that runs between here and Metlaoui. Originally used by the Bey, the train consists of its original nineteenth-century carriages which have been restored in red velvet. The *Transtours/Lezard Rouge* office in Metlaoui (details on ☎40634) is about 100m into town from the train station.

If you don't want to wait for the train, you'll find **louages** to Tamerza from the square in the centre of town, or back eastward from the Moulares road on the edge of town. There are also **buses** to Tamerza, and to Gafsa and Tozeur via Metlaoui.

Tamerza and the Chott el Gharsa

West, beyond Redeyef, the towns lose their industrial ugliness and become a series of beautiful oases – some believe the most beautiful in the country. Certainly, their remoteness and inaccessibility leaves them unspoiled compared to places like Tozeur and Nefta; but it also means that facilities are few and public transport, beyond Tamerza, almost nonexistent. South of Tamerza, the recently ruined road to Tozeur (see p.244) crosses the Chott el Gharsa, a smaller salt-plain, giving a taste of the Chott el Jerid itself.

Tamerza

The road to Tamerza (on the right before you enter Redeyef) is unsurfaced, and the only transport connections are regular **louages** and a twice-daily **minibus** from Redeyef. At 7pm you can get a lift from the junction with a taxi which takes schoolchildren home and the customs officials out to their border post (around 1TD). Avoid the saloon cars which cruise along the road and charge well over the odds.

TAMERZA, with its high cascade and dense cultivation, is one of the least spoilt of all the Jerid oases. The oldest stone houses (to the south of the road from Redeyef) were abandoned after torrential floods in 1969, and the new village, a kilometre further on, is built in traditional Arab style with high blank brick walls facing the main street. Down a track to the left are the bamboo huts of the rather unfriendly and somewhat overpriced (8TD/13TD b&b) *Hôtel des Cascades*, above the waterfall and overlooking the oasis (☎45365). You might be allowed to camp next to the hotel and use its facilities – which don't include hot water. Surprisingly so, because below it, a **path** leads to the foot of the **cascades** – natural showers, one hot, one cold – then for several kilometres you can follow it back along the warm stream.

Mides

The mountain oasis of **MIDES** is best reached by mule from Tamerza; guides are available at the hotel – around 20TD each for a five-hour journey, not for those with tender bottoms. The mules follow a trail over the ridge opposite the abandoned village, then out across an open plain, occupied by the last remnants of a nomadic tribe.

The new Mides, by the customs post, and the older **Berber village** stand at opposite ends of the oasis, where the palms provide shade for pomegranates, which in turn shelter lemon and orange trees. Only from the top of the hill, above the ruins and the network of narrow paved streets, can you make out the spectacular position of the old houses, clinging to the sheer rock face of a deep gorge. This stretches for 3km around the southern side of the village, providing a natural defensive position. The guide can take you back to Tamerza by foot (ninety minutes' walk) along this valley floor: carry some water with you – it can be roasting hot.

From Tamerza to Tozeur

The road south beyond Tamerza leads across the Chott el Gharsa to EL HAMMA DU JERID and Tozeur, passing en route the small oasis of Chebika. There are no buses or taxis, and if you try hitching be prepared to wait. Flooding can render this road impassable to all but four-wheel-drive vehicles for months at a time, so check before setting out. The alternative is to go right back to Metlaoui and catch a bus or *louage* from there.

Chebika

CHEBIKA lies at the foot of the last range of hills beyond the desolate expanse of the Chott el Bahiri. Behind the new settlement by the road, the old village perches on a rock platform, bordered by palms and, on the far side, a steep gorge. As at Tamerza, a cascade falls from high up the cliff, feeding the streams and the agricultural land below. This was the site of the Roman outpost of *Ad Speculum*, from where signals were sent by mirror (*speculum*) describing the caravans en route to Tozeur. Because of its exposed position, the village was later named *Qasr el Shems* (Castle of the Sun). The springs are said to have risen up at a point where a wandering camel carrying the body of a holy man, Sidi Sultan, finally came to a halt; the marabout, attributed with the usual powers, is buried in the tomb near the ravine.

Since mining began, the villages of Chebika and Redeyef have been rivals, with the more wealthy miners able to buy land here in the oasis. Jean Duvignaud (see p.366) tells of an annual cathartic ritual which stood in for open warfare right up until Independence. The people of Redeyef used to go to a selected spot between the villages, lay out some bread and then hide behind a rock. The people of Chebika soon arrived on the scene and pretended to steal the bread. The owners would then run out and start a mock fight before both sides settled down to eat together. Throughout his book on Chebika, Duvignaud (see p.366) describes how similar traditions led to the destruction of the very community they were supposed to sustain. The men from here, for example, often married women from El Hamma, and ceded land from the oasis to the bride's father, depriving the village of its property and increasing the power of the absentee landlord. Agricultural production seldom increased, since the new owners (like the miners) were unskilled, and local families borrowed to survive.

The Chott el Gharsa and El Hamma du Jerid

Beyond Chebika, the road cuts across the corner of the **Chott el Gharsa**, a salt lake lying in a depression below sea level. Like the Chott el Jerid, it's not really a lake – though mirages easily suggest it must be – and the surface is inundated only in the wet season. On the other side of the Chott, **EL HAMMA DU JERID**, with its six springs and 110,000 palms, signals the beginning of the large oases around Tozeur. The waters of the Hamma, rising to a temperature of 38°C, were much favoured by the Romans; one later traveller compared the bath to a mustard plaster, and emerged feeling like a boiled lobster.

Tozeur

TOZEUR has always been the commercial and political centre of the Jerid, and for many years had greater regional power than the central government. This it owed to the date harvest, which made the town an important market and attracted caravans and merchants from the far south. Parts of the old fourteenth-century quarter still survive, but the oasis is the main feature.

Tozeur's history

After the first **Arab invasions**, the Berbers of Tozeur joined the Arab army which swept west through the Maghreb. By 900, however, Tozeur's radical **Kharijite sect** had begun to resist the rule of the Shiite Fatimids, and in 944 the legendary figure of Abu Yazid (or Abu Himara, "The man on the donkey") moved north from Tozeur to lay siege to the Fatimid capital at Mahdia. The rebellion failed and Abu Yazid was killed in 947, but the legend of "The man on the donkey" – the unruly southerner – became part of Tunisian mythology. Over the next centuries, Tozeur continued to be a centre of revolt; the Almoravids found strong support here when they tried to overthrow the Almohads, and the town's rebelliousness was only finally suppressed by the Hafsids in the fourteenth century.

Thereafter Tozeur lost its military might but developed as the major trading post for southern Tunisia. When Dr Shaw arrived in 1757, he noticed the "great traffick" in slaves, brought from as far away as the Niger river; the exchange rate was "one black" for two or three quintals of dates. James Bruce, heading for the Nile in 1765, reported that Tozeur was used by merchants from Timbuktu and other Saharan oases, dealing in sufficient wool and dates to load 20,000 camels each year. But by the middle of the nineteenth century, the Saharan trade had dwindled to one or two small caravans each year, and the oasis was thrown back on its own, still plentiful, resources.

Until the French occupation the town had a strangely ambivalent relationship with the Beys. Although there was a governor, a *caid* who usually lived in Tunis, the town was actually administered by its own council of elders. Every winter the Bey had to send a *mahalla*, a military expedition to force the town and surrounding tribes to pay their taxes and allow the *caid* to carry out his administrative duties. After a couple of weeks the *mahalla* would leave and the town once again became autonomous – until the following winter.

Practicalities: orientation, accommodation and food

Tozeur's backbone is its main street, **Avenue Bourguiba**. Lined with tourist souvenir shops, it can feel like a gauntlet of eager merchants trying to sell you carpets and sand roses. About two thirds of the way down is the central **Place Ibn Chabbat**, flanked by the **market**, **PTT** and **Palais de Justice**.

At the northern end of av Bourguiba, **Avenue Farhat Hached** is the main Nefta–Kebili road. This is where you arrive if **coming in by bus or louage**. The airport road branches off right about 500m towards Nefta. Should you happen to **arrive by air**, there's no public transport into town except taxis (around 3TD), although *Interrent/Europcar* have a desk at the airport if you want to hire a car immediately.

From av Bourguiba the other way along av Farhat Hached, towards Kebili, the road to Metlaoui and Gafsa branches off to the left, as av de la République, after a few hundred metres. Between av Farhat Hached and av Bourguiba at this point is the ancient **Ouled el Hadef** quarter.

The other end of av Bourguiba is the beginning of **Avenue Abou el Kacem Chabbi**, which runs westwards parallel with av Farhat Hached alongside the Zebda and Chebbia quarters, passing the ONTT tourist office and various turnings into the **oasis**. At the end of av Abou el Kacem Chabbi, the tarmac turns a corner by the Dar Cheraiat Museum to meet up with av Farhat Hached near the airport turn-off. Straight ahead, off the tarmac, is the road out to the **Belvedere** p.244.

Accommodation

As a popular tourist centre, Tozeur is blessed with quite a selection of pleasant hotels: you should have no trouble finding a place you like, whatever your budget. And women on their own need have no worries, even in the cheapest of these.

Hôtel Khalifa, av Bourguiba (☎50068). More than adequate, but ask for a room with an outside window. 5TD/10TD b&b (plus 0.8TD shower).

Résidence Warda, 31 av Abou el Kacem Chabbi (☎50597). Clean and bright with large breakfasts. Recommended. 6.3TD/9.6TD b&b.

Hôtel Essada (☎50097). Off av Bourguiba opposite the market. The cheapest place in town, but not for the fussy: the beds are so soft you almost sag to the ground. 2.5TD per person (plus 0.5TD shower).

Hôtel Aicha (☎50988). On the Nefta road, towards the airport turn-off. A neat, spotless 1* place. Most rooms have showers. 8TD/14TD b&b.

Hôtel Splendid (☎50053). Behind the PTT on the edge of the Ouled el Hadef district. A decent enough 1* place. But far more splendid than the rooms is the collection of banknotes in reception (one of the best in the country). Ask for a room with a shower and outside window. 9.1TD/13.2TD b&b.

Hôtel el Jerid, av Abou el Kacem Chabbi (☎50488). This is where they stick tour groups whisked in from Hammamet and Monastir on quick jeep "safaris" of the south. 1* 16.5TD/23TD b&b.

Hôtel Continental, av Abou el Kacem Chabbi (☎50411). A more deluxe version of the *Jerid*. 3* 22.2TD/34TD b&b low season, 24.9TD/37.4TD high; HB and even FB, very little extra.

Hôtel de l'Oasis, pl des Martyrs (☎50522). At the junction of av Bourguiba and av Abou el Kacem Chabbi. Rather a classy joint, but friendly with it. 3* 33TD/46TD b&b.

Hôtel Hafsi (☎50966). Out in the oasis beyond the Dar Cheraiat Museum. 3* 30TD/41TD b&b.

Hôtel Ras el Ain (☎50811). As far out of town (past the *Hôtel Hafsi*) as its prices are out of order. 3* 38TD/52TD b&b.

Youth Hostel/Maison des Jeunes, av de la République (☎50235). A couple of hundred metres up the Gafsa road from its junction with av Farhat Hached. Up and out by 8.30am; and curfew at 10pm. Only 3TD per person. Camping possible.

Belvedere Campsite, up by the Belvedere. Basic facilities are due to be installed some time; until then, it's friendly but primitive with hot and cold springs nearby, places to bathe and plenty of trees. 1.5TD per person including tent.

Food

There are a number of cheap restaurants along av Bourguiba and av Farhat Hached. On Bourguiba, the *Restaurant el Faouiz*, opposite the main square by the *Hôtel Khalifa*, does pretty standard fodder for about 3.5TD, as does the *Restaurant de la République*, a few metres further down. The *Restaurant du Paradis*, just by the *Hôtel Essada*, is even better value at around 2.5TD for large helpings of good food, and another good place is the *Restaurant des Amis* on av Farhat Hached opposite the bus station. Otherwise you could try the cheap, nameless eatery about fifty metres towards Kebili on the other side of the road, or the *Restaurant el Amal* about the same distance the other way. On av Abou el Kacem Chabbi, the *Hôtel el Jerid*'s restaurant does a 4.5TD set menu. There's also a cheap place on the same street at no. 60 and the slightly more refined *Restaurant Diamanta* at no. 74, opposite the road to Bled el Haddar. A meal in the *Restaurant du Soleil*, at no. 48 opposite the *Résidence Warda*, will set you back about 3.5TD. Across the street at no. 29, next to the *Warda*, is a patisserie which does delicious fresh orange juice in season. If you are on the way to the Belvedere, the Dar Cheraiat Museum's air-conditioned "Moorish café" is a handy refreshment stop. For a beer, your best bet is the bar of the *Hôtel Splendid*.

Around Town

The most interesting part of Tozeur is the **Ouled el Hadef** quarter, where the architecture, like the lives of its people, is very traditional. The **modern town**, though *sympa*, contains less of obvious tourist interest, the quarters of **Zebda** and **Chabbia** having been less zealous about preserving their traditions than Ouled el Hadef.

Ouled el Hadef

The oldest part of the town, the fourteenth-century **Ouled el Hadef**, backs onto the *Hôtel Splendid*, its entrances marked by plans of the quarter. As at Tamerza, its high walls are faced with small rectangular bricks, presenting a blank exterior to the narrow streets. The windowless walls ensure the privacy which is prescribed in the Koran: the Arabic word for a house, *maskin*, is related to *sakina*, which means "peaceful and holy". A fifteenth-century legal ruling of one Sidi Khalil, brief and to the point, states that "anyone may climb up his date palm but only if he previously informs the neighbour into whose house he might obtain a view". Only traditionally made bricks are used and the brickwork in the quarter is almost unique in Tunisia: the only other place it can be

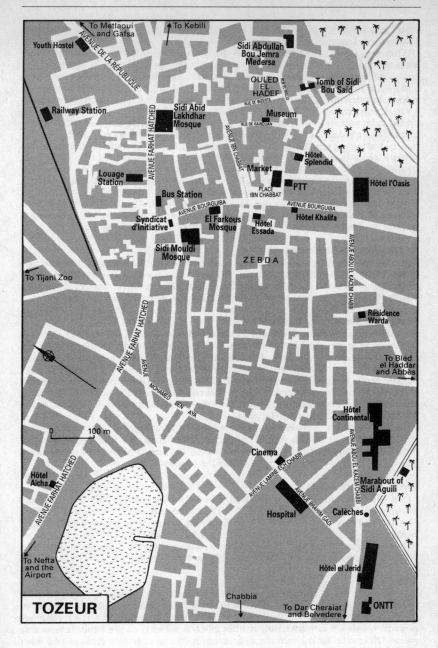

TOZEUR

found is in neighbouring Nefta. The bricks themselves are made near the Belvedere. For more on Tozeuri brickwork, see p.248.

The main street of the quarter, **Rue de Kairouan** (left off rue des Jardins) runs from one side of it to the other. On the right is the **tomb of Sidi Bou Aissa**, now converted into a **Museum of Popular Art**. In theory it is open Mon–Sat 8am–noon and 3–6pm (0.5TD), but you may have to get a child to go and fetch the caretaker to open it for you. Among the exhibits are objects from the traditional marriage ceremony – the wooden chests for the bride's clothes (paid for by the dowry), an Egyptian silk dress, and ornamental green and yellow pottery (green for the palm, and yellow for the dates). There is also a collection of manuscripts, including a timetable for the distribution of water through the oasis; this was devised by Ibn Chabbat in the thirteenth century as a way of ensuring equal supplies for every landowner and only put in print by the French. In the courtyard, amongst miscellaneous statuary, are two of the huge doors once fitted to the old houses. Men, women and children each had a different door knocker, with its own tone, to announce their arrival.

At the far end of rue de Kairouan, two right turns will take you down rue de Bizerte. The rue el Walid, on your left, leads to the **Medersa of Sidi Abdullah Bou Jemra**. Nearby, the finely carved **tomb of Sidi Bou Said** bridges the narrow street.

Avenue Bourguiba's mosques

The mosques on av Bourguiba are of limited interest. The **El Farkous Mosque** with its tall, slender minaret is attractive, and distinctive, but not very ancient. The **Mosque of Sidi Mouldi** down the road by the Syndicat d'Initiative has a minaret in a similar style, restored in 1944, but you probably won't be allowed up it to admire the view.

Along Avenue Abou el Kacem Chabbi

Avenue Abou el Kacem Chabbi is named after a Tozeuri poet whose shrine is tucked away by the ONTT tourist office. With the northern edge of the oasis on one side, it also skirts the quarters of Zebda and Chebbia. **Zebda** borders av Bourguiba, across which it glared angrily at Ouled el Hadef, the two in a state of mortal feud until the last century. **Chabbia**, a little further along, was one of the last places in Tunisia where the bride in a marriage ceremony still rode in a camel-borne litter. The camel still joins the procession, but nowadays the bride walks alongside it. If you want to see the real thing, you'll have to go to Jerba.

Behind the *Hôtel Continental*, near where the camel and *calèche* hirers hang out, is the little **marabout of Sidi Aguili**; nothing very special about it really, except that it's remarkably photogenic and appears anonymously on numerous postcard depictions of "the South". See how many you spot around the country.

Dar Cheraiat Museum

At the end of av Abou el Kacem Chabbi, by the Belvedere turning, is the **Dar Cheraiat Museum** (open daily 8am–midnight, 2.5TD), a kind of upmarket version of Dar Ben Abdallah in Tunis or Dar Jellouli in Sfax. Expensive it may be, but it's well laid-out, with explanations in English and lots of scenes from Tunisian life as well as treasures formerly belonging to the Bey, and other fascinating antiques. If you so desire, attendants dressed up like the Bey's servants will escort you round.

Tijani Zoo

Animal lovers will probably want to avoid the **Tijani Zoo** – left from av Bourguiba into av Farhat Hached, then sign-posted (right) after some 150m and off to the left a few hundred metres up (open daily 8am–5pm, 1TD). Once a **snake** farm, the reptiles are nowadays a very minor attraction, neither labelled nor easy to see beneath their wire gauze. Otherwise it's the typically depressing spectacle of **bears, jackals** and other miserable beasts pacing back and forth frustratedly in their undersized cages. Only the **domestic animals** lighten the atmosphere – but frankly even they are most enjoyable if you tag on behind a coach party and watch them watching the inmates.

The Oasis

The main attraction of Tozeur, its vast **oasis**, covers around ten square kilometres planted with some 200,000 palms and fed by 200 springs, its water channelled along dykes, or *seguias*, and controlled by a series of sluices. At the time of Ibn Chabbat, these streams were blocked with sections of palm trunks, which were opened and closed by orders of the warden.

For a **guided tour** through the oasis, look in at the Syndicat d'Initiative at the top of av Bourguiba. The standard rate is 3.5TD per person per hour by camel or horse-drawn *calèche*. Most tours leave by the *Hôtel Continental* on av Abou el Kacem Chabbi.

DATES AND DATE FARMERS

Deglat en nour dates

Of all the 70 species of date palms, the finest is the *deglat en nour*, or "finger of light", so called because of the translucent quality of the ripened fruit. Tozeur and Nefta produce 1000 tonnes of these dates every year, and most are exported to Europe for Christmas. They even have their own legend: a poor village woman died before she could make the pilgrimage to Mecca and was buried with her humble string of beads, made from date stones. The tears of the Prophet, shed in sympathy, germinated the stones and created not only an oasis but also the new variety. The palms are artificially pollinated in April and June each year, and the fruit harvested by hand at the beginning of winter: one tree is expected to yield some fifteen or twenty clusters of dates, each weighing about ten kilos.

Palm wine, the notorious *laghmi*, is simply the sap of the palm, collected from the top of the trunk or through incisions in the bark. It only takes twenty-four hours to ferment, but needs to be treated with caution: it's unpredictably potent stuff. *Laghmi* is generally available between April and October – ask around in the oasis. As for buying the dates themselves, in season the market is as good a place as any.

The sharecroppers' tale

Most of the palms are owned by wealthy, and often absentee, landlords who employ labourers as sharecroppers. Instead of a salary, they each receive a share of the harvest. Out on the plains where the main crop is barley, this share is about one-fifth – a share that gives them their name, the *khammes*. In the oases, however, the figure falls to one-tenth, sometimes even less, because the date harvest is so valuable.

Without capital of their own, and being paid only at the end of the agricultural year, the *khammes* have to borrow from their employers to tide them over. Paying high rates of interest on these loans forces them into heavy debt, which after a poor harvest, they are often unable to repay. And so they fall into a sort of debt bondage, bound to the employer in perpetuity because they cannot pay the ever-increasing loans. Since Independence the government has tried to improve their status by introducing a union to combat the employers. Strangely enough the *khammes* have remained apathetic. They see the weather, the cause of poor harvests, as the source of their condition and not the employers' ruthless exploitation of their poverty.

Bled el Haddar

The main road into the oasis starts in av Abou el Kacem Chabbi by the *Hôtel Continental*. Just over half a kilometre along it is the village of **Bled el Haddar**, site of Roman Tusuros, where a heavily restored brickwork **minaret** stands on a course of

Roman stonework in a square on the right of the main road. Also in the square is the **Great Mosque**, built around 1190 by the Almoravid Ibn Ghaniya who, like so many others, came to Tozeur to start a rebellion. Its beautiful stone mihrab, all the more striking in this plain interior, was the work of Andalusian craftsmen from the Balearic islands. As in many Islamic buildings the mosque exploits sunlight which, during the afternoon, shafts through the narrow windows down the central nave to the mihrab. The classic minaret above begins as a circle, develops into an octagon and ends up square: the bird's nest is a later addition. On the other side of the tower a path leads to the reconstructed **tomb of Ibn Chabbat** (first built in 1282), who devised the complex irrigation and cultivation system used in the oasis.

Abbès: a marabout, jujube tree and paradise

The road continues through some of the oasis's best cultivated land and comes, after a couple more kilometres, to the little village of ABBÈS. Just beyond it is the **marabout of Sidi Bou Lifa**, overshadowed by a huge **jujube tree** planted by the saint himself; both are reputed to be over 700 years old. Jujube trees, which originate from China, bear fruit which can be eaten fresh or dried, tasting a little like dates.

A few hundred metres past the tree and marabout is a garden and zoo, unassumingly called **Paradis** – a somewhat untended version, sadly (open 8am–6pm daily, 1TD). The menagerie has gazelles, several tormented baboons, snakes, and a family of lions, all kept in overcrowded captivity. If you arrive at the same time as a tour group, you can also see performing scorpions. More interesting, though overpriced, are the pistachio, rose, violet and pomegranate syrups made from plants in the garden and sold at the entrance.

The Belvedere

The road and sand track to the left follow the main water course out to the sign-posted **Belvedere** – a grandiose name for several large boulders which are, none the less, big enough to give a beautiful view over the oasis if you climb up them. You can make out the precise boundaries of the cultivated land, hemmed in by sand. During the Ottoman period the protecting bamboo fences were removed and the oasis went to ruin, blown by the south winds.

A hundred metres or so past the Belvedere, shards on the ground like broken glass glinting in the sun are in fact **rock crystals**. The nearby traditional **brick factory** is similar to the one in Nefta (see p.246).

Moving On from Tozeur

Tozeur is no longer served by any passenger **train** services and transport along the **direct road north to Tamerza** can be a problem. That road, washed away recently by flash floods, will take some time to put back in action. Until then, only four-wheel-drive vehicles can do the run (traffic was scarce anyhow), so check before you try hitching. If the road is still out and you don't want to go round the long way via Metlaoui, you could ask at the *Hôtel el Jerid* to see if any of the jeep tours will take you.

Tozeur's **bus station**, which is run by *SRT Gafsa*, is on av Farhat Hached very near the end of av Bourguiba (turn right at the end of av Bourguiba and it's on your right). There are several buses every day to Gafsa, Redeyef, Metlaoui, Kebili and Sousse, and one each to Douz, Kairouan, Gabes, Sfax and the Algerian frontier at Hazoua. Regular blue buses do a shuttle service to Nefta. *SNTRI*'s office is across the road; their westbound buses stop opposite it, the eastbound ones by the Agip station fifty metres east. They run five buses a day to Tunis (two of them overnight), plus two to Nefta and one to Douz.

Louages leave from a yard a few doors down from the *SNTRI* office, opposite the bus station. You should have no trouble getting a vehicle from here to Tunis, Nefta, Metlaoui, Gafsa, Kebili, Degache or El Hamma du Jerid.

Tozeur's **airport** (☎50388), 3km out of town, is not connected to Tozeur by any public transport except taxis, so you'll either have to take one of those, or walk (take a right off av Farhat Hached about 700m from av Bourguiba towards Nefta).

Listings

Airlines *Tunis Air*, av Bourguiba by pl Ibn Chabbat (☎50038).

Banks Two on av Bourguiba, and two more just round the corner in av Farhat Hached.

Car hire *Avis*, *Hertz*, and *Interrent/Europcar* all have offices on av Farhat Hached. *Avis* (☎50547) is not far from the junction with av Bourguiba. *Hertz* (☎50214) and *Interrent/ Europcar* (☎50119) are both a few hundred metres west towards the airport turn-off; *Interrent/Europcar* also have a branch at the airport (☎50388).

Cinema Av Lamine ech Chabbi (off av Abou el Kacem Chabbi opposite the *Hôtel Continental*) about 100m down on the right, at the corner of av Brahim Gadi.

Festival Every year around December, modelled on the Douz festival, a series of camel races and Bedouin spectacles on a site 500m off av Abou el Kacem Chabbi (turn off by the ONTT tourist office).

Hammams There is one three doors away from the *Hôtel Essada* (men 5–10am & 3.30–7pm; women 10am–3pm). The door is in the traditional red and green, but you may have to go in the back way, which is harder to find. Another hammam is behind the Syndicat d'Initiative (men 5–10am & 4–9pm; women 10am–3.30pm), and one more 50m up av Mohamed ben Aya (off av Farhat Hached opposite the zoo turn-off).

International phone calls In the PTT's back entrance (open PTT hours), or opposite it (look for the sign – open daily 7.30am–7.30pm). You can also use the phones at the *Hôtel Splendid*, at "reasonable" times, or any time if you're staying there.

Market day Sunday.

Medical facilities The Regional Hospital (☎50400) is on av Brahim Gadi (off av Abou el Kacem Chabbi opposite the *Hôtel el Jerid*).

Newspapers British papers are available at 30 av Abou el Kacem Chabbi.

PTT In pl Ibn Chabbat, just off av Bourguiba. City hours, changes cash. Phones at the back.

Supermarket *Magasin Général*, av Farhat Hached out towards the airport turn-off (open Tues–Sat 8am–12.30pm & 3–7pm; Sun 8am–1.30pm; Mondays closed).

Swimming pool If you don't fancy the oasis pools, best of which is the cold cascade by the Belvedere, the hotels *Jerid*, *Continental* and *Oasis* have pools you can use for a couple of dinars.

Tourist offices Tozeur has two, both friendly and knowledgeable. The ONTT office (☎50503) is on av Abou el Kacem Chabbi by the *Hôtel el Jerid*, open Mon–Thurs 8.30am–1pm & 3–5.45pm; Fri & Sat 8.30am–1.30pm; closed Sun. The Syndicat d'Initiative (☎50034) is more conveniently located, at the northern end of av Bourguiba by the corner of av Farhat Hached, open Mon–Sat 10am–noon & 3–6pm, sometimes Sun. They can arrange camel and *calèche* tours of the oasis at 3.5TD per person per hour.

ARRIVING FROM ALGERIA

If you're heading **from El Oued to Nefta**, keep enough Algerian dinars to pay for the *louage* between the two border posts. There are no exchange facilities on the Tunisian side, so your best bet is to arrive when the banks are open: *louages* from the border will take you to one.

Nefta

Coming from Tozeur, through almost totally barren and dusty land, the oasis at **NEFTA** is quite a shock. You don't notice it immediately – the drab buildings on the edge of the town shield its beginnings – but suddenly its extent becomes clear, as does that of the *Corbeille*, a unique crater-like depression densely planted with palm trees. The site of Roman Nepte, Nefta, according to the legends, was settled by Kostel, "son of Shem, son of Noah", at the place where water boiled for the first time after the flood. It is now one of the most important religious centres in Tunisia, traditionally linked with the mystical brotherhoods of **Sufism**: the ridge above the Corbeille is cluttered with simple white-washed domes and the old quarters somehow manage to pack in twenty-four mosques and over a hundred shrines.

THE SUFI TRADITION

Sufism, *Tasawwuf* in Arabic, is the Divine Wisdom which is contained within the *Tariquah*, the spiritual way or path laid down in the Koran. Participants are called *faqirs* or dervishes, meaning "poor", and strictly speaking the Sufi is one who has reached the end of the path, which is a direct personal experience of the Unity of God. A Sufi teacher, variously called a *faqir*, *sheikh*, or *murshid*, prescribes the chants, recitations and body exercises which have made this sect so famous. Besides the Koran and the *Hadith* (sayings of the Prophet), the Sufi looks to the *Hadith qudsi* in which God speaks in the first person through the Prophet. "My slave", reads one typical verse, "comes ever nearer to me through devotion of his free will, until I love him, and when I love him, I am the hearing with which he sees and the hand with which he fights and the foot with which he walks."

Sufism has often had an awkward relationship with orthodox **Sunni Islam**, threatening to usurp religious law and to substitute mysticism for the knowledge of the truth contained in the Koran; a problem partially resolved as early as the eleventh century by saying that Sufism was a way of "apprehending reality", not of finding new facts about God. In Tunisia Sufis have held considerable power; with the breakdown in the control of central government (from the Almohads in the thirteenth century onwards) the *sheikhs* had great influence in rural areas, setting up *zaouias* which provided shelter and teaching and administered justice. In the twentieth century Tunisian liberals as well as the French attacked their autonomy and what they considered an obsolete code of conduct. Many devout Muslims, however, continued to practise the **hypnosis**, trance-like **meditation** and **saint worship**, or *maraboutism*, with which Sufism had always been linked.

Practicalities

Avenue Bourguiba, the main road from Tozeur to the Algerian border, splits the town neatly in two. Coming in from Tozeur, it descends into the **Corbeille**, which it bridges at the narrowest point. North of the bridge, the Corbeille bends around to the west, spreading into a wedge that takes out a large chunk of town. To the south it becomes the **oasis** proper. The area to the south of av Bourguiba before the bridge is **Ouled ech Chrif**, one of Nefta's old quarters, at the heart of which is **Place de la Libération**.

Over the bridge at **Place de la République**, there are three roads to choose. A right turn up **Avenue des Sources** takes you along the edge of the Corbeille and then crosses it into the Ez Zaouia quarter. The first left off it takes you into **El Bayadha**, another of the old quarters, passing the brick kilns and the most important mosques. Bearing, rather than turning, right from pl de la République, av Bourguiba separates El Bayadha from **Beni Ali** to its south. Bearing slightly to the left from the *place*, the "route touristique" continues on its way towards Algeria. South of it is the oasis, and beyond that the silvery gleam of the Chott, which really does look like a sea from here.

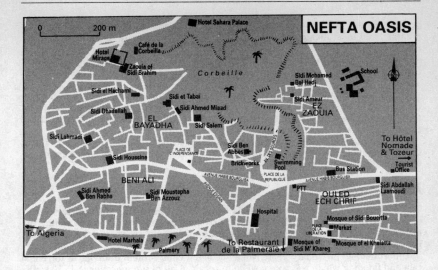

Accommodation

Nefta doesn't have the widest choice of **accommodation** in Tunisia, but you can find hotels in all categories, and their number is increasing as Nefta limbers up to become an overnight stop for tour groups "on safari" from the beach resorts.

Hôtel de la Liberté, Ouled ech Chrif. Also known as "Hôtel Mahmoud" after its genial manager, it can be found from the path off av Bourguiba by the PTT. Take the second left off that and it's on your left. Alternatively, ask around pl de la Libération – everybody knows it. Opinions are divided but those of a hippyish disposition generally like the place. 3TD per person (plus 0.5TD for a cold shower).

Hôtel Marhala, route touristique (☎57027). Clean and friendly. 7TD/11TD b&b, more for a room with shower. You can also **camp** here for 1.5TD and use the hotel's facilities.

Hôtel Habib, pl de la Libération (☎57497). Quiet and nicely located. 9.5TD/14TD b&b.

Hôtel le Nomade, av Bourguiba (☎57052). On the Tozeur road close to the edge of town. A pricey alternative to the *Marhala*, with pool, private bathrooms and primitive air-conditioning. 10.5TD/15TD b&b.

Hôtel Mirage (☎57041). 1*. At the Corbeille's northwestern corner. Currently closed as it divides, amoeba-like, into two hotels, the *Mirage* and the *Halaam*, opening, they hope, in 1992.

Hôtel Sunoa Caravanserail, route touristique (☎57355). Opposite the *Marhala*. Rather refined with all mod cons. 3* 38TD/50TD b&b. Another 3* package palace is being built next door and others nearby.

Hôtel Sahara Palace (☎57046/7/8). If money is no object, follow the likes of Brigitte Bardot and friends at Nefta's most chic hostelry, perched on the Corbeille's northern edge. 4* 60TD/70TD b&b.

Eating and drinking

There's a dearth of **restaurants** outside the hotels, but *La Source* in av Bourguiba by the tourist office is worth trying. Also recommended is *Mamma Restaurant* on the other side of the tourist office, although its opening hours are a bit sporadic. Best of all is a **nameless café/restaurant** near the Mosque of Sidi M'Khareg. This is only open in the evening and is hidden away in the oasis, so the best way to find it is to follow the groups of men sloping off among the palms. The **bar** is the focus of the town's nightlife, and most men come here to drink, which they do with an enormous gusto. But the food is good as well, if a little difficult to order, and in the party atmosphere everybody makes a great fuss of unexpected guests. Other belly-filling stations include *Restaurant Les Amis* in pl de la Libération and a couple of basic places opposite the bus station.

Of the **hotel restaurants**, the *Marhala* has probably the cheapest, doing a set menu for 3TD (2TD for guests). The *Nomade*'s restaurant is also quite reasonable, but tends to be monopolised by groups in season. If you feel like splashing out, a meal at the *Sahara Palace* will set you back about 9TD.

The best place in Nefta to have a cup of tea is probably the **Café de la Corbeille** at the northwestern corner of the Corbeille, from where you get the best view of the town. It is, however, rather touristy.

Around Town

The most rewarding pastime in Nefta is **wandering round the old quarters**, especially El Bayadha and Beni Ali, each a maze of small passageways. You can admire the distinctive local architecture, and through the ancient doorways see the looms and rugs which provide a living for most of the people.

Unfortunately, in January 1990, Nefta sustained considerable **damage** in torrential rain and flooding which will take a while to repair. A lot of the mosques in El Bayadha were affected, as was Sidi M'Khareg on the edge of the oasis. Houses in the old quarters also suffered, especially in Beni Ali and El Bayadha, a chunk of which fell into the Corbeille. The good news is that most of them are being rebuilt in traditional style using traditional methods.

El Bayadha

Some of the most important monuments in Nefta are near the *Café de la Corbeille*, at the Corbeille's northwestern tip. Just down the road is the **Zaouia of Sidi Brahim**, a complex of tombs, courtyards and teaching rooms. Followers of the Sufi faith are often buried here near the saint himself. Beside the *zaouia*, a track leads round a ridge over the Corbeille, past five **mosques**, all small, simple in design and packed closely together. The first you come to is the **Sidi el Hachani Mosque**, then the **Mosques of Sidi et Tabaï and Sidi Ahmed Miaad**. The oldest is the **Mosque of Sidi Salem** (sometimes called the Great Mosque), approached through an unobtrusive doorway off the narrow street; apart from one strip of carving around the walls, the fifteenth-

---

BRICKWORK IN TOZEUR AND NEFTA

The **building style** of the houses in the old quarters of Nefta and Tozeur is unique in Tunisia. Constructed of yellowish handmade bricks, they are picked out in relief with ornate geometrical designs. The ornamental shapes and motifs made with the bricks, unique in Tunisia, are repeated on local carpets and shawls. It's a decorative technique, first used in Syria and Iraq during the eighth century, that was carried west by the Arab invaders in the tenth. The only other place where it can can be seen is in Iran.

Although the archways and covered passages have been extensively restored, the materials are usually traditional: local clay and sand are mixed, soaked in water and left to mulch for a day. Then the mixture is shaped in a wooden frame and left to dry in the sun. Finally, the bricks are baked in a kiln for three days, at temperatures of up to 1000°C. The industry is on something of an upturn at the moment as people are returning to locally made bricks – which provide better insulation against extremes of temperature than breeze blocks.

century courtyard is completely unornamented. Finally comes the **Mosque of Sidi Ben Abbes**, the smallest. The nearby **brickworks** (see box opposite) are a large open space behind the mosque, where the workers will be pleased to see you. The road continues from here to come out on av des Sources near pl de la République.

Don't take it personally if the **guardians** of the *zaouia* and mosques turn you away. Nefta is considered a religious city, and local people generally don't like tourists wandering around their monuments. If you can't get in by yourself, you may be luckier with a Syndicat d'Initiative guide.

The Corbeille

There are several paths down the hillside from the mosques to the **Corbeille**. Beneath the café, hidden by the palm trees, is an open-air bath. Women generally use it in the mornings, men in the afternoons. It's obviously not a good idea to intrude on the opposite sex, and beware of going there at night – there's no lighting and there have been one or two cases of muggings. The springs rise below the *Hôtel Sahara Palace*, pride and joy of the local tourist board. The best way through the Corbeille is to walk by the hot stream, which saves trampling on the cultivated land and leads from the west to the east end of the valley. Look out for the local eccentric Mohamed, who lives in his garden by the hot stream. There he grows henna, tobacco and bananas, and sells tobacco pipes.

Norman Douglas liked the Corbeille so much that he wanted to make another at Tozeur – "all the elements are present", he explained, "it only requires a few thousand years of labour, and what are they in a land like this?"

The Nefta Oasis

The **oasis** proper, on the other side of the main road, extends, like Tozeur's, for some ten square kilometres. In addition to over 100 natural springs, new wells were drilled here in the 1960s, and seem to have reduced the flow from the springs in both the oasis and the Corbeille. Numerous tracks lead through the palm groves, all best explored on foot. Set right in the heart of the oasis is the **Marabout of Sidi Bou Ali** – follow a path past the PTT to the **Mosque of Sidi M'Khareg**, then turn right and left and continue for half a kilometre. This is a major place of pilgrimage, particularly on the third day after the Aid el Kebir (for an apprcximate date, see *Public Holidays*, p.29). For this reason the marabout is closed to non-Muslims, but you can walk through the passage by the door, and the tomb and courtyard, to glimpse the old pool adjoining the sanctuary. It's worth this short walk just to get among the surrounding gardens and to see the other, smaller marabouts along the way. Sidi Bou Ali was born in Morocco and came to Tunisia in the thirteenth century, hoping to resolve the religious disagreement which had divided the area. The legend that he planted the first palm trees in the Jerid (bringing the plants from Touggourt in Algeria) doesn't seem very likely, since Ibn Chabbat had already reorganised the oasis at Tozeur.

Many of the **pools** are used for bathing, women in the early morning and men in the afternoon. As ever, avoid intruding on the opposite sex, but otherwise the bathers are very welcoming. Running around barefoot, as local kids do when swimming, is inadvisable too – the oasis is infested with scorpions. If you do get stung you might do worse than follow the advice of Shaw in 1757: either bury your patient up to the neck, to make them "perspire" or, in "less serious" cases, apply hot ashes or powder of henna, with two or three slices of lemon. In practice a sting hurts like hell, but is rarely fatal.

Moving On from Nefta

The **bus station** is on av Bourguiba, 300m towards Tozeur from the bridge, on the left. *SNTRI* run two daily buses to Tunis, and there are loads of other buses to Tozeur, some of which continue to Metlaoui, Gafsa, Redeyef, Sfax and Kairouan. The other way, three buses (only one on Sunday) run to Hazoua. For all other destinations including Kebili and Douz, change at Tozeur. **Louages** leave from pl de la République, and serve Tozeur and the Algerian frontier at Hazoua.

If you are making **for Algeria**, the border crossing at HAZOUA is generally routine. En route, 10km out of Nefta, is a daily market specialising in **sand roses**, those bizarrely shaped crystals of pink gypsum, dissolved out of the sand by dew over the years and found by nomads deep in the dunes. *Louages* cross the four or five kilometres to the Algerian post, from where there are frequent buses to El Oued. You can buy Algerian dinars at the border post, but only for cash.

Nefta Listings

Banks Two on av Bourguiba, one opposite the bus station, the other between there and the PTT. When they're closed, you might be able to persuade the *Hôtel Sahara Palace* to change some money for you.

Hammams If the baths in the Corbeille and the oasis are not what you seek, there's a hammam in pl de la République (men 5–11am & 5pm–midnight; women 11am–5pm), but it has been known to overcharge tourists (should be 0.5TD). The *Hôtel Marhala* recommend a hammam near them in Beni Ali (men 5am–noon & 5pm–midnight; women noon–5pm).

Market day Wednesday.

Medical facilities The regional hospital (☎57193) is first left off av Bourguiba heading west from pl de la République.

PTT On av Bourguiba just by the bridge on the southern side (country hours). International phone calls and cash exchange facilities available.

Swimming pool Municipal pool on av des Sources near pl de la République. Closed in winter and when water supplies run low. Hotels like the *Caravanserail* and the *Sahara Palace* charge non-guests 5TD to use their pools (free in the latter if you eat there).

Tourist office The Syndicat d'Initiative (☎57236) is on av Bourguiba, out towards Tozeur on the left, about 300m past the bus station (open in theory 8am–5pm daily but don't count on it). It hires out camels at 2.5TD/hour, and donkeys at 1.3TD, both with a compulsory guide at 3TD/hour. You can also just hire the guide, who may be able able to smooth your way into some of the monuments.

The Chott and Kebili

The **Chott el Jerid** was once called the "Lake of Marks" – after the palm trunks planted across its normally parched surface to guide trading caravans. Here in 1885 Sir Lambert Playfair was shown a circular platform in the middle of it, called the "Middle Stone", where the camels could pass the night. Although the Chott can be crossed on foot at virtually any point for ten months of the year, tradition has it that leaving the recommended path can be fatal. Tijini, the fourteenth-century Arab historian, recounts the apocryphal story of the death of a thousand camels and their attendants in black mud beneath the thin salt crust. Now the Army has built a causeway and road right across, and daily buses from Tozeur to DOUZ via KEBILI have been introduced, making this once lengthy journey quick and easy.

Villages north of the Chott

On the way to the edge of the salt lake the bus passes through several small villages. At **DEGACHE**, 10km out of Tozeur, there is a **campsite** if you feel like staying, as well as basic facilities such as a bank, PTT (country hours), hot springs and municipal swimming pool. A couple of kilometres beyond, at **ZAOUIET EL ARAB**, a ninth-

ROUDAIRE AND PLOUGHSHARE: PLANS FOR THE CHOTT

In 1876 one **Captain Roudaire**, working for the French Ministry of War, put forward a plan to dig a canal from the coast at Gabes to the Chott el Fejaj (a finger-like extension of the main Chott pointing eastwards towards the coast). The sea water, he supposed, would flood the entire area of the salt lakes, creating a huge inland sea. In part this scheme was prompted by legends from the past; Roudaire thought the Chott was the site of the ancient **Bay of Triton**, birthplace of Poseidon, crossed by Jason with the Argonauts, and a Roman galley had been found on the northern shores. The Bey would not agree to "so dangerous an experiment" but once the French had occupied Tunisia, engineers no longer had to worry about his opinion. The project looked set to go ahead and Ferdinand de Lesseps, architect of the Suez Canal, became involved. At that point, to general embarrassment, preliminary surveys revealed that the Chott was, in fact, above sea level.

If Roudaire's project sounds daft then still worse was to follow. In 1962 the American Atomic Energy Commission set up the benignly named **Ploughshare Program** to enquire into "the peaceful use of nuclear explosions". In an associated paper, a leading scientist explained how the radiation would be just an "operational nuisance, quickly localized and easily controlled". For some unknown reason he couldn't put his finger on anywhere in the USA worthy of detonation, but the Bay of Triton seemed like an ideal place. With the mighty atom, the whole of the south and parts of the Sahara could be turned into a lake, open to mineral exploration and tourism. Like the programme itself, the idea was quietly cast aside.

century minaret, like that at Bled el Hader, stands on an old Roman brick base. Turning to the southwest at **KRIZ** the road begins to drop down towards sea level as you cross the Chott, giving a perfect view of the pale expanse of salt and sand, marked only by a single black tarmac strip. To the east the mountains gradually march into the distance and the crystal surface, on every side, is concealed by shimmering **mirages**. In the heat, water always seems to begin a few hundred yards ahead of you and the shore constantly recedes. This is a surreal land, the optical effects dreamlike and reminiscent of a Tanguy painting.

Smaller Nefzaoua Oases

The southern side of the Chott, the region called **Nefzaoua**, is an area full of oases, smaller but more frequent than those further north, with lonely clumps of palms standing among the dunes or on the salt flats.

Most of the **oasis villages** are stretched out along the road from Tozeur. They are decrepit, with little to recommend them, but if you want to see traditional oasis agriculture it's interesting to roam around the palmeries: the villagers will proudly show you their plots and present you with fruit straight from the trees. Just get off the bus or ask the *louage* to stop at any point: the road is busy so you should be able to get a lift on to KEBILI. There's a lively Sunday souk at **MENCHIA** – along with a few cafés – and **MANSOURAH**, just off the road 10km further on, has the remains of two Roman pools where you can swim – the village itself is famous for its melons. About a kilometre further, you reach **TELMINE**, now a compact place whose oasis was reputedly planted by conquering Egyptians. It was one of a series of outposts used by the Romans to guard against insurrection, and later became a thriving city – which the Almohads destroyed in 1205. The houses, crowded around narrow streets, still give it a medieval look, and a couple of Roman reservoir pools still survive.

On the peninsula of higher land that juts out into the Chott, the water comes from tunnels, called *foggara*, dug up the slope to reach high aquifers. Teams of workers dig

---

THE NEFZAOUA AND THE BEY

Ibn Khaldoun, writing in the fourteenth century, describes the Nefzaoua as an independent group of Berbers mixed with the nomadic Arabs, and in the twelfth and thirteenth centuries they played an important part in the Almoravid rebellion. During the Turkish administration, the Nefzaoua was ruled first from Tripoli and then, in the sixteenth century, from Tunis. Temple visited in 1835 and found the people quiet after another bout of insurrection. To punish their "rude conduct" the Bey had imposed a fine of 15,000 piastres – much more effective, Temple saw, than the "cutting off of heads: for, as they remark, 'what signify a few heads more or less? We have plenty of them but very few piastres.'" When Kebili became the centre of another revolt twenty years later the Bey had clearly had enough: he gave orders that the village was to be evacuated and its residents exiled to Cap Bon. Four years later he relented, but only after the villagers had bought back their lands at an extortionate price.

---

holes along the course of the *foggara* and excavate the earth and rock. As you drive along the road these circular pits, some of them 30 to 40m deep, are all you can see and, close up, the amount of work that has gone into the miles of tunnels below becomes evident. But these are only small. In Iran, where the idea came from originally, some of these *qanat*, as they term the *foggara*, extend for hundreds of kilometres.

Kebili

KEBILI, an important market town for slaves until the last century, is now the administrative centre of the Nefzaoua. Modern Kebili is essentially a military camp and only a few buildings from its past survive, by the mosque on the road out towards Douz. Among them is a substantial building, the **caïd's house**, named after Ahmed ben Hamadi, the village's first administrator appointed by the French. A cruel opportunist, Ahmed raced across the Chott to surrender to the French while the elected village *sheikh* vacillated. His reward was command over his fellow villagers whom he ruled tyrannically for three terrible years. His house was built of the stones from his neighbours' homes, which he had destroyed. His palace, as he liked to call it, is worth a visit to see what the village must once have been like.

Orientation, transport and other practicalities

The road from Tozeur brings you to a roundabout by a *Total* filling station at the bottom of a hill. At the top of the hill the **bus station** is just to your right, with plenty of departures to Gabes and Douz, and some to Tozeur, Sfax, Tunis and Gafsa. Following the road round to the left, the **louage station** is an open space by the road where you can pick up transport to Tozeur, Douz and Gabes. Beyond the *louage* station is av Bourguiba, heading left towards Gabes, or right towards Douz. If you're **hitching** out in the direction of Gabes, walk past the *Esso* garage at the main roundabout in the north of the town. With luck you can get a quick lift all the way. There is also a road across the Chott el Fejaj, which brings you out on the Gafsa–Gabes road about 19km east of El Guettar.

The town's main square, **Place de l'Indépendance**, is about 200m down av Bourguiba from the *louage* park in the Douz direction. There you'll find two **banks** and the **PTT** (city hours, international phones in the side entrance open the same hours).

Other practical information: Kebili's **regional hospital**, should you have the misfortune to need it, is on the edge of town out on the Gabes road (☎90461/2). In more upbeat vein, Kebili's regular **market day** is Tuesday and there's a **date harvest festival** here at the beginning of November. If you need some **booze** to celebrate it with, there's a warehouse on the BLIDET road (southwest) where you can buy wine and beer at wholesale prices. And to wash it all away the next morning, **hot springs**, on the left of the Douz road, about 1km out of the town centre, provide natural **baths** in the open air. The men's pool is by the road, the women's behind it on the way to the *Fort des Autriches* hotel. If you prefer the same bath in an indoor hammam, you'll find it 50m further along the road, on the left – women mornings, men afternoons.

Sleeping and eating

You may want to get straight on to the Saharan outpost of Douz but if you have, or want, to stay in Kebili there's a pleasant 2* hotel, the *Fort des Autriches* (☎90233), near the oasis to the east of town, sign-posted to the left just along the Douz road. It's named after an unsuccessful attempt to reintroduce ostriches into the region before World War I (the fat was reputed to be good for the health). The hotel (12TD sing/18TD dbl b&b) has a pool, reasonable food and impressive views over the edge of town. If the prices seem steep, the best alternative is a *Maison des Jeunes* **youth hostel** (☎90635) behind the *Total* station where the Tozeur road begins (4TD). The only other place to stay is the rather grotty *Hôtel Sahara* off on the left about 100m on towards Tozeur, charging 4TD/6TD. **Restaurants** (all very simple) and a **café** are located around pl de l'Indépendance and opposite the *louage* station. For something with a bit more class, try the *Fort des Autriches*.

South to Douz

The **road south from Kebili** takes you along the edge of the **Grand Erg Oriental**, the Great Eastern Sandy Desert, where the dunes reach hundreds of metres in height. Here at its northerly extent they are a touch less impressive, but you can at least get the feel of the desert. And to add a little local colour, scattered around are date palms fed by small springs and several nondescript hamlets.

En route: Jemna

It's worth stopping at **JEMNA**, the largest of the villages on the Kebili–Douz road, just for a drink. The public fountain at the roadside gushes gallons of delicious water a second – when you've tried it, it's easy to understand what desert explorers mean by sweet water. People come from all over the region to fill up their jerrycans to take home. Natural **hot baths** are open to both sexes (separately) 6am–11pm.

The *Hôtel Grad*, 4km beyond Jemna, 3km off the road, is used mainly by tour groups and charges 8TD/12TD b&b low season, 10TD/15TD high, with some accommodation in what are described as Bedouin tents.

Douz

With some justification, **DOUZ** calls itself "the gateway to the Sahara" and, as such, has become the tourist centre of the region. However, it's remarkably unspoilt by crass tourism – the people are an amiable lot and their town is a pleasure to stay in. It is also a good base from which to explore the isolated oases to the south.

A lot of people here are descended from slaves of west and central African origin who were once bought and sold in neighbouring Kebili. Many black families in Douz have maintained their musical traditions from across the Sahara. Both black and white people will tell you, however, that racial discrimination is a thing of the past, while intermarriage, frowned on in both communities until only twenty years ago, is now quite normal.

SAHARAN ADVENTURES: THE MRAZIG AND THE TOURISTS

Douz is the centre for the **Mrazig**, one of the nomadic peoples, numbering about 15,000, who still live in the Nefzaoua. With the promise of schools, medical facilities and housing, many of the nomads have abandoned the life which led them to three different areas every year. Some of the people still move south in spring, though, when the rains have provided pasture for the sheep and goats; during April the sheep are sheared and the women work on the rugs later sold in the large towns; by the summer the community has largely returned to the comparatively cool oasis and, while the men look after the land and dates, the women again prepare food for the winter. Two months later, the animals are taken north to fresh lands near Gabes or Gafsa and the people set up their tents nearby. At the beginning of winter they return to pick dates or press the olives, and to spend the cooler months around their home base.

The official brochure, **"Sahara Adventure"**, asks "will modern man understand the values of a world where dignity and honour mean what they say?" Well, no, modern man isn't really concerned about that sort of thing – and that goes for the tourist board as well, and the annual 80,000 trippers. Tourists here are not only packaged but hermetically sealed, shuttled from air-conditioned coach to plush hotel. And what of "Blessed solitude", "infinite space", the "warmth of meeting"? Sadly, this is mass entertainment pure and simple. The *Hôtel Saharien* regularly offers real-life Bedouin musicians and a sort of Oriental minstrel show.

Orientation

The centre of Douz is its **market square**, where the Thursday **souk** takes place, and the cheap hotels are all nearby. Arriving by road, the bus and louage stations are both nearby on **Avenue Taïeb Mehiri**. West of the market square is **Place des Martyrs**, site of the Syndicat d'Initiative **tourist office**, as well as the *Maison de la Culture*, which doubles as museum, theatre and cinema. Roads into the oasis from here take you to the bigger hotels.

Accommodation

Most of the budget hotels are near the market square, with more upmarket places out in the oasis. If none of these appeal, however, or if you yearn for the vastness of the open desert, you could opt instead to stay at the hotels in the nearby oases of Zaafrane or El Faouar (see p.257–8).

Hôtel 20 Mars, rue 20 Mars (☎95495). In the street behind the market square café of the same name. Not luxury by any means, but one of the nicest in the whole country. Great people run it, they play music and dance every night – with guests joining in – and the multi-bedded rooms are clean and pleasant. 2.5TD per person (plus 0.5TD for breakfast).

Hôtel Essada, rue Ghara Jawai (☎95019). Clean with hot water and friendly but rather eccentric management. 2.5TD per person, 1.5TD on the roof (plus 0.5TD for breakfast).

Hôtel Bel Habib, av Bourguiba (☎95309). Clean and friendly, but rooms are on the small side. 2.5TD per bed in rooms, 2TD on the roof (with reductions for food if eating in).

Hôtel du Sahara, av des Martyrs. At the junction of av Taïeb Mehiri near the PTT. Best try elsewhere first. 2.5TD per person.

Hôtel Roses des Sables (☎95484). Take the second left off av des Martyrs after the tourist office, and it's 200m down on the right. This is pleasantly silvine, with private bathrooms, heating in winter and sporadic air-conditioning in summer. 9.5TD/13TD b&b low season, 10.5TD/15TD high.

Hôtel Saharien (☎95337/9). Left off av des Martyrs before the tourist office and about 500m down on the left (*Hôtel Marhala* opposite is well and truly closed). Mostly bungalows, with bathroom, winter heating and summer air conditioning. A student card may get you a reduction. 12.5TD/17TD b&b low, 14.5TD/19TD high.

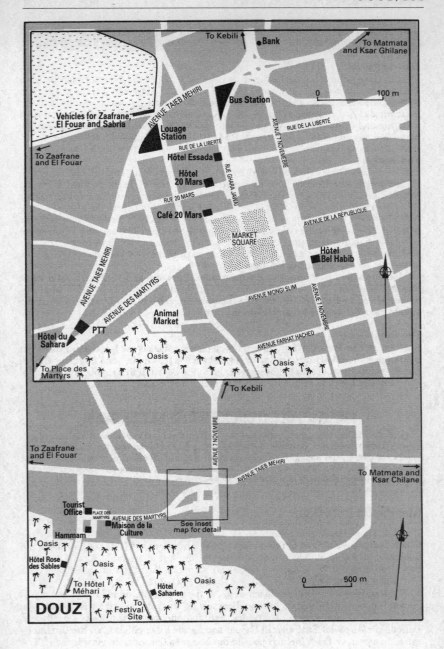

To Kebili · Bank
To Matmata and Ksar Ghilane

0   100 m

Vehicles for Zaafrane, El Fouar and Sabria

AVENUE TAIEB MEHIRI

Bus Station

Louage Station

To Zaafrane and El Fouar

RUE DE LA LIBERTÉ

Hôtel Essada

Hôtel 20 Mars

RUE DE LA LIBERTÉ

AVENUE 7 NOVEMBRE

RUE GHARA JAWAL

RUE 20 MARS

Café 20 Mars

AVENUE DE LA RÉPUBLIQUE

MARKET SQUARE

Hôtel Bel Habib

AVENUE TAIEB MEHIRI

AVENUE DES MARTYRS

AVENUE MONGI SLIM

AVENUE NOVEMBRE

Hôtel du Sahara

PTT

Animal Market

AVENUE FARHAT HACHED

Oasis

Oasis

To Place des Martyrs

To Kebili

To Zaafrane and El Fouar

AVENUE 7 NOVEMBRE

AVENUE TAIEB MEHIRI

To Matmata and Ksar Chilane

Tourist Office

PLACE DES MARTYRS

AVENUE DES MARTYRS

Maison de la Culture

See inset map for detail

Hammam

Oasis

Hôtel Rose des Sables

Oasis

Oasis

To Hôtel Méhari

Hôtel Saharien

To Festival Site

0   500 m

DOUZ

Hôtel Méhari (☎95145). Well out of town, a couple of kilometres past the *Hôtel Roses des Sables*. The only hotel with stars (3*) so far, but probably the first of many. 34TD/48TD b&b.

Food and drink

Most of Douz's cheap hotels double up as eateries and offer the likes of couscous, stew and chicken for a couple of dinars. The *Bel Habib*, *20 Mars* and *Essada* are all safe enough bets. Otherwise, there's the *Restaurant du Sud* by the *louage* station, and the *Restaurant el Acil* near the *Hôtel 20 Mars*. A cut above these is the *Restaurant el Kods* up at the end of av des Martyrs, on the left just before pl des Martyrs. You'll be hard-put to find any upmarket eating in town: the oasis hotels are the most promising.

The market

On Thursdays Douz is transformed by the weekly **market**. Townspeople, nomads, village people and tourists pour in to participate in one of Tunisia's most engaging souks. It says something for Douz that the presence of tourists seems to add to rather than detract from the whole affair. The centre of activity is of course the market square itself. Here you can find many of the traditional goods (jackets, leather shoes and slippers) which end up in the cities. You can also buy souvenirs like petrified wood or the inevitable sand roses, or get desert shoes made to measure overnight (in the square's southeastern corner, for example). In season, you'll find the region's famous *deglat en nour* dates for sale on the market's southern side.

Most of the tourists, however, are here to see the **camels**. These are not the most important livestock commodity, but you will find them on sale with the other animals – mainly sheep and goats – if you take the western exit (av des Martyrs) out of the square, then the second left and follow the throng.

The Great Dune

Another popular attraction for tour groups on one-day visits is the **large sand dune** out of town past the *Hôtel Roses des Sables*. It's a chance to play in the sand for those without time to get further out into the desert – or go to the beach. If this is you, you should of course ignore the rumour that the dune was built with the aid of bulldozers.

THE FESTIVAL OF THE SAHARA

At the end of December the **Festival of the Sahara** celebrates everything from popular pottery and a traditional marriage, to camel fighting (camel v. camel that is), sand hockey and even greyhound racing. It all takes place at a special **Festival Site** out beyond the *Hôtel Saharien*. Associated cultural activities such as music, singing and poetry contests take place in the *Maison de la Culture* in pl des Martyrs.

Moving On from Douz

Bus and *louage* stations are both on av Taïeb Mehiri, the **buses** at the end of rue Ghara Jawai (the road out of the market square's northern side). As well as buses and minibuses to Kebili, of which there are plenty (the last at around 4.30pm), two daily buses run direct to Tunis (one via Gafsa and Kairouan, the other through Gabes, Sfax and Sousse) and others to Gabes, Tozeur and EL FAOUAR.

The **louage** station is just a block away, at the end of rue de la Liberté and rue el Hanine, opposite the Zaafrane turning. Basically, all the vehicles are for Kebili, but you may be lucky, especially on market day, and find one going on to Gabes or Tozeur. Various **pick-ups** for Zaafrane, El Faouar and Sabria leave either from the turning by the cemetery in av Taïeb Mehiri opposite the *louage* station, or from outside the PTT.

Lastly, if you're tempted to try the **road across the desert** to MATMATA or KSAR GHILANE, you'll need four-wheel drive or a dromedary. For the former, the *Desert Club* in Douz's market square organise overnighters at Ksar Ghilane. As for camels, try contacting Tahar at the *Hôtel 20 Mars*, or ask at the *Hôtel Essada*.

Listings

Banks *Banque du Sud* is on av 7 Novembre, just north of the junction with av Taïeb Mehiri.

Cinema At the *Maison de la Culture* in pl des Martyrs (Wed & Fri).

Excursions A guide called Tahar does trips by camel (or jeep if you prefer) for about 20TD per person per day. He can usually be found at the *Hôtel 20 Mars*. The *Hôtel Essada* organises similar tours, as do one or two places in Zaafrane.

Hammams There's an unmarked one opposite the *louage* station by *Café 7 Novembre* (men 5–11am & 6–10pm; women 11am–6pm), but far better are the natural hot-spring baths found by taking the first left off av des Martyrs past pl des Martyrs (sign-posted "*Hôtel Roses des Sables*"). Just round the bend on the right, these are open 6am–noon & 3.30pm–midnight for both sexes (separate entrances) and offer the choice of bath or pool.

International phone calls If the PTT's hours are inconvenient, try the *Hôtel Saharien*.

Market day Thursday.

PTT Av des Martyrs, between the market square and pl des Martyrs (look for the transmitter aerial). Country hours, changes cash. International phone calls are possible – call then pay, no pay-phones.

Tourist office The Syndicat d'Initiative (☎95351) is in pl des Martyrs (open Mon–Thurs 8.30am–1pm & 3–5.45pm; Fri & Sat 8am–1.30pm; Sun closed) are very helpful and sell services such as camels at 3TD/hour and *calèches* at 1.8TD.

Trips Out West of Douz

The road out of Douz to the oases of **Zaafrane**, **El Faouar** and **Sabria** is now tarmac all the way. As well as the three daily buses from Douz, pick-ups do the run cheaply enough (see *Moving On*, opposite). Remember that transport back to Douz dries up around 4pm, so head back by 3.30 or so if that's where you plan to spend the night.

Zaafrane
ZAAFRANE is the real gateway to the Grand Erg Oriental. The village lies close to the main through track and is surrounded on one side by endless dunes, on the other by a cool oasis. Life centres around the café, a grocery store and the main well, while a small brickworks provides employment. Most of the houses are off to the left and many have been built for the nomadic **Adhara**, who still migrate to Ksar Ghilane during the spring. Their large black tents, often pitched nearby, are made from long strips of wool and goat hair, supported by two wooden poles. Paths lead from the main road to the sand dunes at the far edge of the village. From here the desert stretches into the distance beyond the remains of old stone houses, washed over by the sand. If you would like to follow the Adhara's migration route, *Berber Voyages* are among the people here who run **excursions**, offering a one-week round trip to Ksar Ghilane by camel for 250TD all-inclusive.

There is a hotel here, the *Zaafrane* (☎95074), which is not a bad old place, mostly bungalows with bathroom and heating or fan (depending on time of year), and Bedouin tents between March and October. Prices are 9.5TD/15TD b&b. They usually allow **camping** in the grounds too. A set menu in their restaurant is 2.5TD, they have a bar if you're in need of a cold beer, and they don't normally charge for use of their pool.

Whether or not you take the bus to Zaafrane you'll probably end up hitching back to Douz or on to El Faouar; most passing vehicles will pick up hitchhikers – expect to pay a small sum.

El Faouar

Beyond Zaafrane there are still pick-up trucks going to Sabria and El Faouar and it's no problem getting a lift. The main attraction is simply the drive through the desert. The road divides after 25km and most traffic goes straight to **EL FAOUAR** (also called Sabria el Faouar) with its Friday souk. This is the home of the **Ghrib** who, until recently, were a wholly nomadic community breeding cattle and sheep. A small group of stone houses stand below the *Garde Nationale*, and around the edge of the oasis are the huts, made from mud and palm fronds, used in preference to tents during the summer. There are other, smaller **oases**, unmarked on any of the available maps, between El Faouar and Zaafrane. If you're hitching, you might be dropped off on the way, but there will always be shade and an occasional car later in the afternoon.

El Faouar's hotel – the *el Faouar* (☎95085) – should be a horrendous monstrosity but, especially when not too swamped, is a pretty reasonable place. Off on the left as you come into the village from Zaafrane, it has a bar and restaurant (set menu 3.3TD) and a free pool; it also lends out sand skis gratis. The rate is a set 8TD per person b&b, whether in air-conditioned rooms with bathrooms, wooden shacks with shared facilities, or Bedouin tents. Behind the hotel, the dunes begin. While not as huge as the dunes deeper into the erg, the sand mountains round here still stretch immensely to the horizon and satisfy most visitors' desires to be, at last, really in the desert.

Sabria

SABRIA is the centre for the people of the same name, Arabised Berbers who are part of the larger Ghrib confederation. It's 3km off the El Faouar–Zaafrane road, turning off 7km east of El Faouar. Spectacular views over the desert greet you when you climb up some of the high dunes around Sabria – a vast expanse of sand stretches in every direction, dotted with little green oases.

Sabria is one of the few places where the "dance de la chevalure" is still authentically performed. On the first night of the marriage ceremony, the women remove all their jewellery and woollen head coverings and parade before the assembled men and musicians. To the beat of the tambour, and encouragement of the crowd, each dancer whirls her long hair round her head faster and faster. Over several hours the women gradually drop out, and the dance ends when just one is left on the floor.

North of Zaafrane and El Faouar

With your own transport, you might consider going round back to Kebili via **BLIDET**, a small village with a ruined *medina* on a hill flanked by minor oases, which can be reached from either Zaafrane or El Faouar. A hired car should be able to tackle the unpaved roads, but remember where you are and take appropriate precautions (see box p.314).

Between Zaafrane and Blidet, **NOUAIL** (also accessible by four-wheel-drive on a track that leaves the Zaafrane road 4km west of Douz) is used as a camping site by some of the Land Rover tour groups. It's not a campsite in the normal sense – "authentic" Bedouin tents await the happy Hilton hoppers – but they may allow you to pitch your own tent there. Food is basic but the campfire singsongs can be fun.

Coastwards: from Kebili to Gabes

For Shaw in the 1750s, the area east of Kebili to the coast was a "lonesome and uncomfortable desert, the resort of cut-throats and robbers." He recalled, "We saw the recent blood of a Turkish gentleman, who, with three of his servants, had been murdered two days before by these assassins." Nowadays there's no blood and little of interest until El Hamma. At **SAIDANE** the old French fort, once a hotel, is now a *Garde Nationale* post, so resist the temptation to photograph it as you pass. What may pass the time is looking out for the desert birds and mammals that can be spotted along the road.

El Hamma

EL HAMMA DE L'ARAD is 50km east of Saidane. Its hot baths, which have long attracted visitors from far and wide, gave it the name Aquae Tacapitanae, and there is still a **hammam festival** in March. Leo Africanus was less keen, noting somewhat irrelevantly, "the hot water tastes like brimstone so that it will in no way quench a man's thirst."

The open-air **baths** (0.6TD) are in a modern building, based on Roman foundations, opposite the marketplace; the entrance on the left is for women, men go round the corner to the right. The spring water rises at 47°C and heats up still further in the sunlight, and you sit on submerged stone seats in a shallow pool. If you don't have your own towel, you pay slightly extra for the wrap-round towels worn in the water (as ever, it's all very discreet). El Hamma also has two **banks** and a *Magasin Général* **supermarket** and, on Mondays, an additional attraction to the baths is the **weekly market**.

In the sixteenth century, unlikely as it may seem, El Hamma was a substantial town and a **major staging post** in the trans-Saharan trade. Then, in the 1630s, the Matmata who lived here refused to pay their taxes to the Bey, and the town was razed to the ground and its citizens expelled. A fort, the remains of which can be seen beyond the spring, was built to ensure Turkish sovereignty and the Beni Zid nomads were allowed to settle in place of the recalcitrant Berbers. Today there is nothing of the old town left and the modern buildings that have been built on the site are uninspiring to say the least. The **tomb of Rabbi Sidi Youssef** is the scene of an annual Jewish pilgrimage around December but you would need a certain dedication to coincide and participate in any way.

Most people, after taking a bath, will want to move on to **the coast** and GABES.

travel details

Trains

FROM METLAOUI TO:

Tunis (1 daily, overnight, 10hr) via **Gafsa** (1hr), **Mahres** (4hr 30min; change for **Gabes**, total journey time 9hr 20min), **Sfax** (5hr 15min), **El Jem** (7hr), **Sousse** (8hr) and **Bir Bou Rebka** (9hr; change, with 2hr 10min wait for **Hammamet and Nabeul**); **Redeyef** (at least 1 daily, 1hr 30min) via **Moulares** (1hr 20min) and the **Seldja Gorge**, leaving Metlaoui afternoons, departing Redeyef 30min after arrival to get back to Metlaoui well in time for the evening departure to Tunis. There *may* be extra summer services along the Redeyef route, including the *Lezard Rouge*.

FROM METLAOUI TO:

Tozeur, services suspended indefinitely.

Buses and louages

FROM GAFSA TO:

Tunis (8 daily, 4 of them overnight, 7hr);

Metlaoui (9 daily, 7hr 30min, 5 continuing to **Tozeur**, 1hr and **Nefta**, 1hr 30min, the other 4 to **Redeyef** and **Tamerza**); **Sfax** (5, 3hr 30min); **Feriana** and **Kasserine** (6, 1hr 20min, 2hr); **Gabes** (4, 2hr 30min); **Kairouan** (3, 4hr); **Le Kef** (1, 4hr 45min); and **Kebili** (2, 2hr).

Louages to Tunis, Tozeur, Metlaoui, Redeyef, Meknassy, Sidi Bou Zid, Sfax, Sousse and Gabes (none to Kasserine or Sbeitla).

FROM METLAOUI TO:

Tunis (6, 7hr 30min); **Tozeur** (5, 45min); **Nefta** (5, 1hr 15min); **Gafsa** (9, 30min), **Redeyef** (5, 1hr) and **Tamerza** (2, 2hr) though you may have to change at Redeyef for Tamerza.

Louages to Tunis, Redeyef, Tamerza, Gafsa and **Tozeur**.

FROM TOZEUR TO:

Tunis (5 daily, 2 of them overnight, 8hr); **Gafsa** (5, 2hr); **Metlaoui** (5, 45min); Redeyef (5, 1hr 45min); **Kebili** (4, 1hr 30min); **Nefta** (regular shuttle, 30min); **Hazoua/Algerian border** (morning bus, 1hr 30min); **Sousse** (2, 7hr); **Douz** (1, 7hr); **Kairouan** (1, 6hr); **Gabes** (1, 4hr 30min); and **Sfax** (1, 5hr 30min).

Louages to **Tunis, Gafsa, Nefta, Metlaoui, Kebili, Degache** and **El Hamma du Jerid**.

FROM NEFTA TO:

Tunis (2, 8hr 30min); **Hazoua/Algerian border** (3 daily, 1 on Sun, 1hr); **Tozeur** (frequent, 30min, changing for **Kebili and Douz**); **Metlaoui** (5, 1hr 15min); **Gafsa** (4, 2hr 30min); **Sfax** (1, 6hr); **Kairouan** (1, 6hr 30min).

Louages to **Tozeur** and **Hazoua/Algerian frontier**.

FROM KEBILI TO:

Tunis (3, 9hr); **Gabes** (9, 2hr 30min); **Gafsa** (2, 2hr); **Tozeur** (4, 1hr 30min); **Sfax** (3, 5hr); **El Faouar** (3, 1hr 30min); **Douz** (plenty, including hourly minibuses, 30min).

Louages to **Tozeur, Douz, El Hamma de l'Arad** and **Gabes**.

FROM DOUZ TO:

Kebili (plenty, the last at around 4.45pm, 30min); **Tunis** (2 daily direct, 9hr 45min, 1 via **Gafsa** and **Kairouan**, 1 via **Gabes, Sfax** and **Sousse**); **Gabes** (2, 3hr); **Tozeur** (1, 2hr 15min); **El Faouar** (4, 1hr).

Louages to **Kebili** and occasionally to **Gabes**. Pick-ups to **Zaafrane, El Faouar** and **Sabria**.

EL FAOUAR TO:

Douz (4 daily, 1hr, 3 continuing to **Kebili**, 1hr 30min, and 1 to **Gabes**, 4hr).

Flights

FROM TOZEUR TO:

Tunis (3 weekly), **Jerba** (2 weekly), **Paris** (weekly). Also one or two charters to Europe.

PHONE CODES

Gafsa, Metlaoui, Tozeur, Nefta and all northern districts in the Jerid ☎06. Douz, Kebili, El Hamma and districts south of the Chott el Jerid ☎05.

CHAPTER SEVEN

GABES AND MATMATA

The towns of Gabes and Matmata lie in a tract of land that swoops below the belly of the Sahel. For the most part nondescript, it is punctuated by fecund emerald oases and hemmed by mile upon mile of coast along the gulf. Almost every traveller heading south passes through **Gabes**, but few take the time to explore its central mosque and adjacent oasis – both remnants of a turbulent era in Tunisia's past, when the extensive oases were important staging posts for caravans from the other side of the Sahara.

Better known – and decidedly more spectacular – are the weird lunar landscapes and troglodyte villages around **Matmata**, a town blown to fame by the filming there of scenes in *Star Wars*. Sometimes the demands of tourism seem disturbingly overbearing in this region, geared to – indeed springing from – the film's success. Outside the tour groups, however, it's none too easy to make your way around without a car. If you've got one, or are going to hire one, or are willing to hitch, the most genuine experiences are to be found some way off the beaten track – at **Haddej** for example, where the underground way of life continues unaffected, or at the isolated, barely visited town of **Toujane** on the plain.

Gabes

In 1886 a French administrator arrived to take up a post at **GABES**, the coastal town billed as the port of the Sahara. "Imagine my surprise", he wrote to his superior, "when I had to disembark onto the beach and walk up the dusty path that is the main street to reach the only building, my office." Today Gabes has grown in size, but is still rather a disappointment. The busy new town, rebuilt after World War II, stretches for miles away from the coast and, though the palm groves reach to the sea they're largely inaccessible at this point, surrounded by the port and industrial complex. On the other hand, Gabes's pivotal position betwen the sea and the *chotts* ensures that virtually all traffic between the south and centre of the country passes through here – and there are things worth stopping for. Tucked among the alleys of the old quarters are several fascinating **mosques**; the well preserved **markets** are as alive with daily commerce as they ever were; and the long, sandy **beach** has the benefit of being almost undeveloped. Most alluringly, away from the main streets, parts of the vast **oasis** really are a classic haven of peace and shade.

Arrival and Practicalities

If it's open yet, a gleaming new terminus waits to greet travellers **arriving by bus**, opposite the *calèche* stand at the western end of town. From here, two main roads head east through the city centre, with services and shops all concentrated along them. Rue Lahbib Chagra branches northeast to become **Avenue Bourguiba**, which curves thorgh the **Jara** district and past the main market before turning a sharp bend to continue seawards past several of the town's best hotels and restaurants. Gabes's other main artery, **Avenue Farhat Hached**, follows a more-or-less straight line towards the sea, past the old bus station,and the PTT, whose enormous aeriel is a landmark visible all over town. If you're **arriving by louage**, this is the area where you'll be dropped. **Coming in by train**, you find yourself bang in the middle of town, and not a long walk from the beach.

Accommodation
Gabes has a wide choice of budget **accommodation**, including a very good – and extremely convenient – youth hostel. Among more expensive hotels there is less choice, with nothing over 2* bar a couple of package-type places by the beach. Apart from these, most hotels are in the centre of town around av Bourguiba and av Farhat Hached.

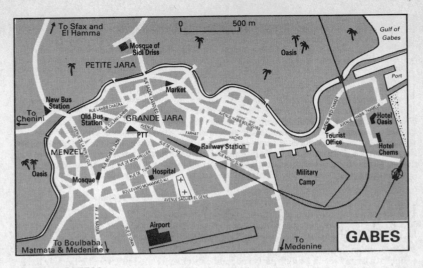

BUDGET HOTELS

Hôtel de la Station, av Farhat Hached, opposite the *louage* station. Extremely basic and basically male. 2TD per person.

Hôtel de la Poste, 116 av Bourguiba (☎70718). A bit on the dodgy side but friendly. Most women on their own will want to steer clear. Outside windows in short supply. Named after a post office that used to be across the road. 3.5TD per person.

Hôtel Salama, 262 av Farhat Hached (☎72233). At the corner of rue Sadok Lassoued. The management are friendly and the rooms adequate if slightly grimy. 4/7TD.

Hôtel Mourad, 300 av Bourguiba (☎70513). Above the UIB bank. Clean, quiet, mainly Libyan clientele. Most upstairs rooms have bathrooms. 4TD per person.

Hôtel Ben Nejima, 68 rue Ali Jemel (☎71591). On the corner of av Farhat Hached. Clean rooms and not bad for the price. 4TD per person.

Hôtel Regina, 138 av Bourguiba (☎72095). An old favourite whose French billiard table offers a change from pool. The only minus point is that windows all open onto the interior patio. 5TD per person low season, 6TD high.

Hôtel Keilani, 134 av Bourguiba (☎70320). Two doors down from the *Regina*. Once popular, currently closed.

Hôtel Marhaba, av Farhat Hached. Opposite the bus station. Not the first choice that springs to mind but perfectly adequate. 5/6TD.

Hôtel Medina, rue Haj Jelani Lahbib (☎74271). In the Menzel quarter, between av Farhat Hached and av de la République. Clean and pleasant rooms with bath. 6.8/9TD.

Hôtel M'Rabet, rue Ali Zouaoui (☎70602). Off bd Mohamed Ali, sign-posted from av Farhat Hached at rue Ali Bou Khalifa. Nice and clean, most rooms have showers, some a loo and balcony. 8.5/12TD b&b.

YOUTH HOSTELS

ONET Youth Hostel, 101 rue Sadok Lassoued. The YHA hostel, and a very fine one: friendly, central, well-run. 2.5TD, 0.7TD for large breakfast, 0.3TD shower.

Centre des Stages et des Vacances, rue de l'Oasis (☎70261). In Petite Jara, sign-posted from the market in av Bourguiba. The *Maison des Jeunes* hostel, and subject to the usual rules, regulations and chilly reception – but they do allow camping. 4TD per person in dorms, 2TD camping.

A HISTORY OF GABES

First occupied by the Phoenicians, Gabes was later a major port of **Roman Africa**, its name, Tacape, meaning a wet and irrigated place. In medieval times it was the terminus for many of the Trans-Saharan **caravans**, while the main *haj* caravan (carrying pilgrims on their obligatory trip to Mecca) passed through on its way to Tripoli and Cairo before reaching the holy city itself, bringing along with it thousands of merchants and their goods. Gabes was also famed for its **silk**, made from silk worms raised on mulberry bushes in the oasis. But even in those times the oasis had its seamier side. The tenth-century traveller Ali Mahalli complained that the oases were "the home of plague and death" and advised others to avoid the place or stay as short a time as possible.

Like Jerba, Gabes fell easy prey to seafaring European states, with the Aragonese first to arrive in 1279. Equally, when central government was weak and there were no Europeans about, Gabes was quick to reassert its **independence**. It did this during the Hilalian invasions and, later, whenever the Hafsids were too busy fighting among themselves to do much about it.

By the time of the Ottomans the city was divided into three separate quarters: **Jara**, with a large Jewish community, in the north, **Menzel** in the west and **Boulbaba** a couple of kilometres south. According to Leo Africanus, the entire region was surrounded by a dyke which could be flooded in times of war – though for much of the time, the city quarters expended their energies fighting one another. Their quarrels came to a head in **1881**, when Jara sided with the French, inciting their neighbours to attack. Without the help of a large French landing party and gunboats offshore the Jews would inevitably have been massacred. As it was, Menzel and Boulbaba were fined heavily and denied permission to hold a market, so forcing local trade into the hands of the **Jews**. The communities' rivalry and mutual loathing simmered throughout the Protectorate period, exploding again in 1942 when anti-Semitic riots, encouraged by the Germans, persuaded most of the Jews to leave for Jerba.

Under the French, Gabes became the key garrison point of the south, and a massive **fort** was built on the outskirts of the town in readiness for a tribal revolt or Italian invasion. Today the region remains strategically sensitive, and the town is full of Tunisian conscripts. Their presence is also partly explained by the fact that the Gulf of Gabes has considerable reserves of **oil**, which have been claimed by both Tunisia and **Libya**. The dispute was finally settled in 1981 and relations between the two countries, often tense, have improved somewhat since then.

MORE EXPENSIVE HOTELS

Hôtel Atlantic, av Bourguiba, junction of av Farhat Hached (☎20034). An enormous white French building with cavernous rooms. Well regarded. 1* 8/12TD low, 12/18TD high, b&b.

Hôtel Tacapes, 55 av Bourguiba (☎70700/1). Comfortable, courteous and central. 2* 16.5/24TD b&b low, 19.5/30TD high.

Hôtel Nejib, av Farhat Hached, junction of bd Mohamed Ali (☎71636). It may not have the most stars, but this is the classiest hotel in town. 2* 17/24TD low, 21/31TD high, b&b.

Hôtel Chems, (☎70547). By the beach. Massive bungalow complex. 2* 16.5/24TD low, 24/38TD high, b&b.

Hôtel Oasis, (☎70381). Down by the beach. Expensive but rather ordinary 3* place. 20/28TD low, 23/32TD high, b&b.

Chella Club, (☎27442). A tacky "vacation village" out in the oasis near Chenini. 10/13TD low, 14.5/21TD high, b&b.

Eating and drinking

Food certainly isn't one of Gabes's high points. With one or two exceptions, its restaurants are at the lower end of the market, though the first couple of places on the list, serving standard Tunisian fare, are a cut above the others in that price range.

La Bonne Bouffe, 62 av Bourguiba. A good feed for around 3.5TD. Recommended.

Restaurant Amori, 84 av Bourguiba. 2.5TD–3TD. Similar to the *Bonne Bouffe:* the food is as good but the atmosphere a little more downmarket. Watch French TV while you eat.

Hôtel Tacapes, 55 av Bourguiba. 4.5TD set menu. Not a bad place to eat, although the *Amori* and the *Bonne Bouffe* across the street are better value.

Restaurant Pizzaria el Khalij, 9 rue 9 Avril (on the corner of av Farhat Hached). Around 3.5TD, with a wide range of pizzas.

Restaurant la Pacha, 36 av Farhat Hached. Rather more finesse than most of Gabes's restaurants, for around 7TD.

Hôtel Nejib, av Farhat Hached (at the junction of bd Mohamed Ali). Around 11TD for a very reasonable French/Tunisian meal.

Restaurant de l'Oasis, 11 av Farhat Hached. Gabes's top restaurant. 12TD should buy you a first-class meal here.

If your budget is really tight, try the *Restaurant el Fath* opposite the railway station in av Mongi Slim or the cheapies (the *du Sud*, the *Dinar* and the *Voyageurs*) opposite the bus station. There are also some *gargotes* in av de la République and around the market. Otherwise try the *rôtisseries* which abound near the port.

Around Town

Gabes is not primarily a seaside resort. The swimming and the long sandy **beach** are reasonable, but no match for Kerkennah and still less for Jerba. Indeed, while the fishing port to the north can get quite lively, it almost seems the beach has been stuck on the eastern end of town as an afterthought. The town itself has all the **facilities** you would expect from such a pivotal communications centre but its places of real interest are concentrated in the **old quarters** of Jara, Menzel and Boulbaba.

Jara

Jara is divided into two parts. The larger, **Grande Jara**, extends outwards from the western end of av Bourguiba. Its main attraction is the **market**, open every day except Monday. To the north of the main street, lined with cheap cafés and *gargotes*, a covered passage leads through to a marketplace once crowded with caravans from Ghadames and Algeria. Around its entrance stand bulging panniers, filled with the henna for which Gabes is renowned. This area, being near Jara's Great Mosque, is reserved for "clean" goods – mainly clothes, rugs and poor-quality leather. Among the adjoining shops are the gold- and silversmiths, while the cobbled street leading down to the river is the territory of the so-called "dirty" crafts pursued by blacksmiths, knife-sharpeners and metalworkers. By the river itself is the unhygienic cattle market, well away from the mosque.

Although the Great Mosque is quite recent, there are a couple of older ones nearby – the mosques of **Sidi Haj el Nasf**, just a little further down av Bourguiba, and **Sidi Bou Ali** around the corner. Both are worth a look for their period exteriors.

The other part of the quarter, **Petite Jara**, is across the rue de l'Oasis bridge (rue de l'Oasis is a continuation of rue Sadok Lassoued). The **Sidi Driss Mosque** (rarely open) was built here in the eleventh century by an Arab prince of the Banu Jami, descendants of the Banu Hilal invaders. The prayer hall, like much of the Jara, has been built with old Roman columns and stone. Many of Jara's historic mosques, however, have disappeared, along with its old synagogues and most of its **Jewish heritage**.

Menzel

Menzel is the area around av de la République, and can also be reached by taking av Bechir Dziri off av Farhat Hached by the PTT. Menzel's monuments, such as they are, seem to have survived rather better than Jara's. The **Great Mosque**, in a square just west of av de la République, and the **Zaouia of Sidi Bnei Isa**, down a side street on the other side of av de la République, are both relatively outstanding, while a stroll down rue Bechir el Jaziri will take you past the **Zaouia of Sidi Haj el Nasf**. Even without tracking these all down, however, Menzel is the only quarter of Gabes that really retains its ancient feel, and is definitely the best part of town for a good, aimless wander. It also has its own market, on rue Omar el Mokhtar.

Boulbaba

The third of Gabes's historical quarters, **Boulbaba**, is somewhat removed from the town centre, down at the end of av de la République. But it's worth heading out to as Gabes's most important religious monument, the **Mosque of Sidi Boulbaba**, is there. To get to it on foot, take av de la République to the roundabout where it meets bd Mohamed Ali and continue straight on down av J A Nasser for another 500m over the *oued* to the next roundabout. The Medenine road branches off right here, but you want to follow the Matmata road (rue 6 Octobre) left for 200m and the Mosque is off on the left (look for the tall minaret). Bus #3 or #3b will also get you here from the town centre – ask the driver for Sidi Boulbaba.

The older mosque is not the one with the tall minaret, but on the opposite side of the square, and contains the tomb of the saint who was Mohammed's barber (not to be confused with the Mosque of the Barber in Kairouan p.173). Its courtyard is particularly beautiful, surrounded by colonnades and decorated with tiles. Boulbaba arrived here in the seventh century and, like many holy men and marabouts in the south, united warring factions to bring prosperity to the town – of which he is now the patron saint. The surrounding village, which took his name, stood on the site of Roman Tacape and was closed to local Jews and Christians. Non-Muslims may now enter the courtyard of the mosque, but not the prayer hall.

Next to the mosque is an imposing old *medersa* built in 1692, now a **Museum of Popular Arts and Traditions** (open Tues–Sun 9am–noon & 2–5pm, closed Mon, 0.6TD). The people who run it are welcoming and pleased to show you around. The pink stone building is really more interesting than the exhibits, although these include objects from daily life, textiles, a Punic ossuary and a little garden planted with henna, pomegranates, bananas and grapes. Some locally excavated Roman artefacts decorate the grounds.

Gabes Oasis

One part of the Gabes **oasis** starts behind the Petite Jara, leading along to the Sfax road and, in the other direction, to the sea. There are 300,000 palms here, but many are in poor health, spoiled by the damp sea air. The land has changed little since the days of Roman writer Pliny: "Here", he wrote, "in the midst of the sand, the soil is well cultivated and fruitful. Here grows a high palm and beneath that palm are olives and under that a fig tree. Under the fig tree grows a pomegranate and beneath that again a vine. Moreover, beneath these there are sown corn, then vegetables or grass." This tiered intercropping continues today, allowing farmers to cultivate an astonishing range of crops, some 400 varieties in total, including henna and spices as well as food produce.

Chenini

The main oasis villages are on the other side of the Sfax–Gabes road. Most worthwhile – although also most touristed – is **CHENINI**. A bus to here leaves every hour from opposite the school near the *Hôtel Medina* on rue Haj Jelani Lahbib, or go by taxi. Alternatively, you *could* walk (past the *calèche* stand, taking the road to the left of the new bus station) – but it's a long, hot trudge.

The small direct road winds around the irrigation ditches in a swirl of right-angle bends and ends up at EL AOUADID. If you turn left here, the road continues past a small café in the palm trees to a **Roman dam** – several layers of stone holding back a small reservoir. Next door is a **crocodile farm** (honest) and a rather unimpressive **zoo**. A path behind the dam goes on to the *Chella Club* and finally to impressive **gorges** at the southwest tip of the oasis. This is where the springs rise, but the club has concreted parts of the rock to erect a swimming pool. The road along the top leads past the **Marabout of Sidi Ali Bahoul** and on to Chenini itself. To the right is the turning for El Aouadid: the way ahead passes through NAHAL, back to the main Sfax road.

Moving On from Gabes

Gabes is the big transport link of south-central Tunisia, with loads of connections – though some of them at rather inconvenient hours. If you're pushed for time, however, it's worth knowing there are currently **no flights** out of Gabes. To cover some of the more inaccessible parts of the south with ease, you might consider a **tour**. Several Gabes operators offer Land Rover safaris (see "Listings" p.268).

The **bus station** is currently on av Farhat Hached, about 100m west of the PTT, but is set to move to a gleaming new building a couple of hundred metres further west beyond the *calèche* stand. As well as *SNTRI* and Gabes's own *SRT* (called *SOTREGAMES*), three other *SRT*s also operate from here. Between them, they run eight services a day to Tunis and frequent buses to Matmata (the last around 6.30pm), Sfax, Medenine and the Libyan frontier at Ras Ajdir, with several to Sousse, Tozeur, Houmt Souk (Jerba), Zarzis, Kebili, Gafsa and Tataouine. Many of these leave around midnight on their way between Tunis and places south, arriving early morning. Similarly, all except one of the buses serving Kairouan run at night, and will drop you in the holy city at a most inconvenient hour.

Louages leave from the open ground by the main PTT, and are often very crowded – be prepared for a scramble. They go all over, but surprisingly, there are none to Matmata; instead, *louages* leave from near the bus station for Nouvelle Matmata, where there are onward connections by pick-up.

The **railway station** is nearby, off rue Mongi Slim. There are only two daily trains, one of them overnight, to Tunis via Mahres, Sfax, Sousse and Bir Bou Rekba. If you take the night train, you can change at Mahres or Sfax for Gafsa and Metlaoui, but it makes for a long journey.

Gabes Listings

Airlines *Tunis Air*, 1 av Bourguiba (at the junction with av Farhat Hached, ☎71250).

Banks Several on av Bourguiba, including four near the Gabes Centre and one at no. 300 under the *Hôtel Mourad*. There are three more on av Farhat Hached near the corner of rue 9 Avril.

Books *Librairie Nefoussi*, 16 rue 9 Avril between av Farhat Hached and av Bourguiba, has a few pulps in English and *Librairie Africain*, 144 av Bourguiba, also sells the odd English title.

Car hire *Avis*, 4 rue 9 Avril (☎70210); *Budget*, 57 av Farhat Hached (☎70930); *Express*, 145 av Farhat Hached (☎70041); *Hertz*, 30 rue Ibn el Jazzar (near the corner of av Farhat Hached, ☎70525); *Mattei*, Immeuble CTAMA, at the western end of av Bourguiba by the *calèche* stand (☎74648).

Cinemas *El Khadra*, rue Abou el Kacem Chabbi (near the corner of av Farhat Hached); *El Jaouhara*, 288 bd Mohamed Ali.

Hammams The most central is in rue de Palestine, off rue Sadok Lassoued (men 5am–noon & 5–9pm; women noon–5pm).

International phone calls Apart from the PTT, there's a taxiphone office on av Farhat Hached opposite the *louage* station (open 8am–midnight daily), and one at 304 av Bourguiba, near the *Hôtel Mourad* (open 7am–9pm daily).

Medical facilities The Regional Hospital is in rue Romhdane Ali Dhari, off bd Mohamed Ali (☎72700). There's a night chemist at 234 av Farhat Hached.

Newspapers *Librairie Nefoussi* at 16 rue 9 Avril carries the *Herald Tribune*. A place at 240 av Bourguiba, near the bend, has British papers.

ONA crafts shop Av Farhat Hached, opposite the PTT (Mon–Sat 8am–noon & 3–6pm).

PTT In av Farhat Hached on the corner of av Bachir Dziri by the *louage* station. Has phones, changes cash, its huge transmitter aerial is visible all over town (handy if you get lost). Surprisingly, keeps country hours.

Supermarkets *Magasin Général* have two branches, one in Menzel at the corner of rue Omar el Mokhtar and rue Bechir el Jaziri (open Sunday but closed Monday), the other at the junction of bd Mohamed Ali and rue Mongi Slim. Otherwise, there's *Epicerie Fine* at 25 av Bourguiba, near the *Hôtel Atlantic*.

Swimming pool The *Hôtel Chems* charge 4TD for the use of theirs.

Tour operators If you can afford it, you might consider one of the **tours of the south** offered by companies in Gabes. Most of these are Land Rover trips, carrying up to 12 passengers, and they can cover a lot of ground that's hard to get around on your own. Probably the best of the companies is *Voyages Najar Chabbane*, who run a week-long trip to El Oued in Algeria as well as more local itineraries. They have an office close by the youth hostel.

Tourist office The Syndicat d'Initiative (☎70254) is on the corner of av H Thameur and av Hedi Chaker, open Mon–Thurs 8am–1pm and 3–5.45pm; Fri & Sat 8.30am–1.30pm; closed Sun. They are not incredibly informative, but they keep a reasonably current list of hotels and their tariffs posted up outside, along with a more out-of-date one of bus departures.

Matmata and Around

Like the Romans of Bulla Regia once did, the Berbers of **MATMATA** live underground, in **caves and courtyards** dug into the soft, crumbly sandstone. In Iraq and Iran people escaped from the intense heat by building wind towers, a primitive kind of air-conditioning which forced any breeze down into the living rooms. At Matmata, as at Bulla Regia and Gharian in Libya, the natural insulation of the earth was even more effective in providing cool temperatures during the summer and warmth in the winter. Sadly, the **travelling coach tours** and the three large **underground hotels** have completely changed the local way of life. The attempt to exploit custom and tradition now threatens their very existence, and the use of Matmata as a location for the *Star Wars* movie proved another nail in the town's coffin. You'll get repeated invitations into people's houses and you should be prepared to buy the local handicrafts in exchange for a quick peep. This is tourism at its most voyeuristic, and barbed wire and dogs around many of the pits demonstrate that not everyone in town is happy about it. Stardom and hussle aside, however, Matmata remains interesting in its own right and useful as a base from which to explore the other villages of this remarkable region.

The Gabes–Matmata road

On your way to Matmata, look out for the pentagonal bunker 5km out of Gabes, by a milestone to the left (east) of the road. Dated "le 28.1.36", it is part of the **Mareth Line** mentioned at the end of this chapter (p.273).

The bus from Gabes stops briefly at NOUVELLE MATMATA before climbing to the top of the Demer mountains: the old town lies in the valley on the other side but, with the virtual absence of any buildings, the place looks deserted. In fact, 5000 people live in the "craters" which come into view as you head further down the road.

The Matmata Berbers

The Berber tribe of the **Matmata** once lived near the hot springs of El Hamma, but were pushed back into the mountains by the Beni Zid (nomadic, northern Arabs) in the sixteenth or seventeenth century. While some Berbers did join the Hilalian armies which swept westward into Morocco, the tribe preserved its autonomy until the end of the seventeenth century. The Ottomans always had trouble collecting taxes in this area, and Mohammed Bey was forced to build forts at El Hamma to the north and Bir Soltane in the desert to the west to keep the Matmata under control. By the eighteenth century, however, these forts had been abandoned and military expeditions remained the only means of asserting government authority, sometimes with success, sometimes ending in humiliating failure. In 1869, for instance, General Osman led his army into the foothills only to be surprised at night and forced to flee leaving behind his artillery and richly adorned tent.

Under the French, the Berbers maintained their own **tribal court**, called the *miad*, which settled questions according to Berber law. In common with all the villages in the south, Matmata was still ruled by a *sheikh* or administrator of the community, answerable to a *khalifa* (deputy governor) and the *caid* (governor) at Gabes. The system continued until Independence, and the French officers of the *Service des Affaires Indigènes*, who supervised tax collection and public works, usually kept away from village affairs. Yet although they enjoyed some autonomy the government presence was still strong, as the fort on the outskirts of town, now an army base, testifies.

Matmata house design

Many of the houses and hotels in Matmata follow a regular **design** some 400 years old. Each is based around a circular pit with vertical walls, some seven metres deep by ten in diameter. A small, covered passageway, lined with recesses for animals and their fodder, leads from ground level down to the sunken courtyard, which is surrounded by small rooms and cisterns dug into the sandstone. Holes in the ceiling allow grain to be poured from ground level straight down to the lower storerooms. The largest houses have two or three pits linked together.

The ancient settlement: a note and a warning

Before the bulk of the Matmata tribe moved in here in the sixteenth or seventeenth century, a very much smaller community lived in ancient Matmata, around the *kala'a* – fortress – just discernible on the heights above Matmata. Their homes, built into the mountainside, have been abandoned in favour of pit dwellings, and trying to climb up there – as people occasionally do – is most inadvisable since the *kala'a* overlooks the army camp (ex-French fort) on the road to Toujane, and an appearance on its ramparts is likely to lead to trouble.

Practicalities in Matmata

The staff at the Syndicat d'Initiative **tourist office** in the centre of town (Mon–Thurs 8am–1pm & 3–5.45pm; Fri & Sat 8.30am–1.30pm; closed Sun) are very amenable, but you may have to track them down in the *Ouled Azaiz* café opposite. They can sort out the hire of camels, donkeys and other such rustic means of transport.

Other practicalities: there are **no banks** in Matmata (the nearest are in Gabes and Mareth) so bring enough dinars to see you through. If you fancy a swim, the *Hôtel Matmata* charges 2TD for the use of its **pool**. Matmata has its **souk** on Mondays and a **festival** every year at the beginning of November, featuring folk bands, a traditional wedding and something called a "poetic trilting mach".

Seven daily **buses** do the run to Gabes, with an evening *SNTRI* departure to Tunis and a midday bus to TAMEZRET and TAOUJOU, returning four hours later (there's an evening one too, but you wouldn't be able to get back). A minibus does a loop to BENI AISSA, NOUVELLE BENI AISSA, NOUVELLE MATMATA and back every morning. **No louages** serve Matmata, but you should be able to hitch or get on a pick-up to Nouvelle Matmata (about 1TD), from where there are *louages* to Gabes. It is said that the road to KSAR GHILANE is passable in a two-wheel-drive hire car but you ought to take pains to check this out locally before embarking.

Accommodation

Three of Matmata's four hotels are **converted pit-dwellings**, so staying in one is a good way to become familiar with the design of a traditional Matmata home, naturally warm in winter and cool in summer. Matmata's **youth hostel** is closed, but there is talk of reopening it in a converted pit-dwelling some time.

Hôtel Marhala, out on the road to Toujane (☎30015), is the most popular place. Location of the famous *Star Wars* disco scene. Tourists troop along here to eat, but many return to Gabes in the evening; still, the usual folk-dancing carries on long after dinner. 4.1/7TD b&b, (0.6TD extra for a room with shower).

Hôtel les Berbères, off the Tamezret road (☎30024). Smaller, friendlier and more recent. 4TD per person b&b.

Hôtel Sidi Driss (☎30005) is larger, nearer the centre of the village and not especially friendly. They cram each room chock-full of beds. 3.5TD per person b&b.

Hôtel Matmata, near the centre on the Toujane road (☎30066). Spacious, spotless rooms and a pool, but not a traditional pit-house. The only starred hotel in town (2*). 18/26TD b&b.

Eating and drinking

Your best bet for food is to try one of the hotels: all do set menus, the *Matmata* at 4.5TD, the *Sidi Driss* and *Marhala* at 3.5TD and the *Berbères* at 3TD. The alternative is the *Ouled Azaiz Café Restaurant* in the very centre of town, where you'll be paying about 4.5TD for a meal anyway. As for **drinking**, the obvious place to take your custom is the *Hôtel Marhala* – though the company down in the bar isn't as lively as you may recall from *Star Wars*.

Haddej and Tijma

To get some idea of what Matmata must once have been like, it's worth back-tracking to **Haddej**, formerly the region's most important village and home of the *khalifa*. The Syndicat d'Initiative in Matmata may be able to sort out transport if there are five or six of you: failing that, it's a question of walking or hitching 4km along the main road to **Tijma**. There you turn right for Haddej (sign-posted), about 3km up into the hills. A direct footpath also exists between Matmata and Haddej but it isn't easy to find.

Fatima's at Tijma

The **House of Fatima** in **TIJMA** has always been owned by a woman of that name. Due not least to its atypically sanitised condition, this house is now on the coach route and the current Fatima, plus daughter, receives the hordes with much aplomb. A bedroom with its *dukkana* (a sort of bench used as a bed) and a kitchen, with pots and postcards, are both open to view.

Jessour terraces

Walking through the valleys from Tijma to Haddej, the luxuriance of the olive, almond, and fig trees contrasts with the barrenness of the slopes. The trees flourish on hidden reservoirs of water stored in the thick soil of terraces, called *jessour*. Huge quantities of earth have been piled up behind barriers built across the valley floors. Winter storm waters soak into these "gardens", augmented by water channelled off the valley sides by shallow ditches and walls, to be stored for the long dry summer, helping olive and fig trees thrive in the inhospitable environment. The work involved in building these *jessour* was formidable – a garden of one quarter hectare (30m by 80m) behind a barrier 30m long would take about six months' work for one person – and so it's hardly surprising that they're no longer built, nor even repaired. Most of the men work in the cities and agriculture has been neglected, with the result that the region's terraces, its agricultural capital, are literally being washed away.

Haddej: olive pressing and wedding rites

A primary school among the palm trees marks the centre of **HADDEJ**, and the pit dwellings lie up ahead. As soon as you arrive, the village children will appear, offering to show you around (for a little backsheesh, of course). It's a good idea to take them up as the buildings are even better concealed than those at Matmata. Many of the pits were abandoned after the floods of 1969, when the water covered the courtyards for a week, but an underground **grain store** at the top of the slope is in remarkably good condition. Two tiers of interlocking, arched storerooms have been built into a rock, like the *ghorfas* which dominate the landscape further south.

On the left side of the path, just opposite, is the village **olive press**, also dug into the ground. At the centre of a small domed chamber is a circular stone, connected by a wooden shaft to the ceiling; a stone roller fixed to an axle is pulled around this shaft, crushing the olives spread out on the slab. The skins are taken from the stone and pressed again, by a heavy palm trunk fastened at one end to the wall. Oil runs through a series of esparto mats into a jar, and the underground location provides the warmth, in the winter, needed to separate the waste, which is fed to camels. In a final room the olives are fermented to give the oil the rancid taste the people of the south appreciate.

Nearby is an underground **marabout**, occupied only by its custodian. Another pit house, to the left of the olive press, was used for the village's **marriage ceremony**. Seven days before the wedding, the bride's family went into the large underground room to prepare the feast. On the marriage day the bride was brought here on a camel and taken into a small room, reached by the steps leading up from the basement (take some matches if you visit). The husband, who was staying in a cell further inside the rock, went through to see the bride and to sign the marriage contract. Taking a back staircase up to ground level, he was led round to the front door to be formally received. When the feast was over, bride and groom would be led into an airless cave, at the far end of the house, to remain in conjugal seclusion for several days. Meanwhile the celebrations went on outside with a company of African comics, jesters and dancers.

Villages north and west of Matmata

From the *Hôtel Les Berbères* in Matmata a new road leads to the remote mountain village of **Tamezret**. Getting there may be a problem: there is only one practicable bus from Matmata and cars are few and far between; a walk there and back will take the best part of a day (10km each way). In the vicinity, though, is a fair scattering of hamlets and villages that are every bit as interesting.

Beni Aissa

Neither easy to find, nor to get to (there's a daily minibus from Matmata and Nouvelle Matmata), **BENI AISSA** is a lovely little village where the people live in the same sort of homes as in Matmata. About one and a half kilometres out of Matmata, an unpaved road leads off right. Some 4.5km up it is another turn-off (left), and a couple of kilometres along that, you come into the village. A hired car will cover the route with no   difficulty.

Look out for the group of **marabouts** 100m or so beyond the school, bus stop, shop and post box that mark Beni Aissa's centre. Courtesy and consideration for local people make a big difference to how you'll feel about the village, and how the villagers view you – the importance of privacy in Islamic society is hard to overstress, and Beni Aissa is a far cry from Matmata.

Sidi Meta

The **main road** west to Tamezret, meanwhile, skirts the edge of a valley cultivated using the system of *jessour* (see p.270). About halfway between Matmata and Tamezret, set a kilometre back from the road to the right, is the village of **SIDI META**. The first you see of it is a white *koubba* high up on the hillside, all that remains of the old village. At some time in the last two centuries the villagers moved down into the valley below where, as at Matmata, they dug houses into the soft soil. Like Beni Aissa, Sidi Meta is rarely visited by tourists – and the people, as a result, are more accommodating. There's an oil press and an underground mosque that are worth seeing and the village also has a shop where you can buy bottled drinks.

Tamezret

TAMEZRET, built above ground, is packed around several steep slopes, topped by a mosque. One path between the tumbledown houses will take you to the **café** at the summit, the village's main tourist trap, where you can get a "traditional" cup of almond tea and climb onto the roof to see the next village of Zeraoua in the distance. Tamezret – and the villages around – is known for its woollen shawls, the ceremonial *bakhnoughs*, with striking geometrical designs identical to the facial tattoos sometimes seen on older women. Be sensitive, especially if you have a camera: tourism is creeping in, but so far it is not too obtrusive.

Zeraoua and Taoujou

The tarmac road continues as far as **TAOUJOU**. Beyond it is the village of **ZERAOUA**. Both are walkable from Tamezret – 4km and 7km respectively – but neither have accommodation (although someone may take pity on you and put you up), so try to arrange to get there and back in a day. The views across the plateau and into the desert are stupendous, as are the villages – tightly knit communities living in compacted houses that look like a continuous wall from a distance. If you have reliable four-wheel-drive transport and are rash – or confident – enough to want to cross the desert, a track leaves Tamezret for Kebili. It also goes direct to Douz (take a left after 26km).

Southeast from Matmata to Medenine

An alternative route from Matmata, starting out from by the *Hôtel Marhala*, leads to Metameur (55km) and Medenine (both covered in Chapter Nine, "The Ksour") by way of TOUJANE (23km). There are no buses at all in this direction and the bad surface makes it difficult to cover in a car without four-wheel drive or to hitch (if you want to try, walk out beyond the military zone). Alternatively, there's an easier approach to Toujane from Mareth on the Gabes–Medenine road (see opposite).

The Marabout of Sidi Moussa

About 3km from Matmata, the road begins to flatten out, revealing the **Marabout of Sidi Moussa** on a peak to the left. In the early summer this is the scene of an ancient *ziarad*, a tribal pilgrimage atttended by thousands of villagers from Matmata, and on the rocks around the tomb you can see the blood stains of animal sacrifices. Some 8km further along, just off the road, is the village of TECHNINE, known for its furniture, made from branches covered with clay, plaster and whitewash.

Beni Zelten

A further 4km – 15km from Matmata – a turn-off on the other side of the road winds for 8km down an incredibly steep gorge and out onto the plains to reach **BENI ZELTEN**, perched, like Tamezret, on the top of a small hill. Here though, the hill-top village has been deserted in favour of troglodyte dwellings and houses in the valley floor. Nevertheless it remains a remarkable site, and one that's unknown to most visitors. The road beyond the village continues to Nouvelle Matmata.

Toujane

Ignoring these detours and continuing along the (steadily deteriorating) Medenine road, you cross a series of deep gorges and then pass along the escarpment with spectacular views of the plains below. Suddenly the road drops again, this time giving a bird's-eye view of **TOUJANE**. The old town – not to be confused with Nouvelle Toujane down below – is one of the most isolated and untouched of the Matmata villages and, like Tamezret, populated by Berbers. It is also the most dramatic, spreading across two sides of a deep gorge and built around the foot of a mountain, from whose heights rear two brooding *kala'a* (fortresses).

If you're appproaching Toujane from the coast, read on.

Mareth

Midway between Gabes and Jorf, **MARETH** has long suffered from its important strategic position – commanding the narrow coastal plain between the Gulf of Gabes and the mountains. In 1936 the French army built a **defensive line** here to withstand a possible attack by the Italians in Libya. The line was first taken by Rommel and in 1943 it blocked the Allied advance from the east; in the ensuing battle, and Allied capture, the line and Mareth itself were virtually destroyed.

Around town

Apart from the busy **Monday market** the new town is not wildly interesting, but if you're staying anyway the options are the *Hôtel el Iman* (☎36035), on the main road, left just past the *louage* station as you go south (5TD a room), or, better and cheaper, the *Hôtel du Golfe* 100m further on the right (☎36135), a friendy place that only lacks hot water (2TD per person). You could stop at either hotel for a drink and a bite to eat.

Near ARRAM, 3km south of Mareth, you meet the remains of the wartime **Mareth Line**. The main road crosses a *oued* on a zig-zag bend and, to the east of the road, on the *oued*'s north bank by an obelisk in memory of the Free French forces, are a couple of half-buried **concrete block houses**. Watch out for some fierce dogs if you go up for a closer look.

To Toujane

If you're **heading for Toujane**, going via Mareth is the simplest approach, with a regular bus and possibilities of car hire or hitching (though most traffic only goes as far as the new town of Toujane, some way distant from the old). To hire a car, approach anyone in Mareth with a pick-up truck, particularly round the new café near the bus stop, or by the *Esso* garage, and you'll get an opening price of around 15TD, which with luck might be bargained down a little. This is, however, for the whole car, and the round trip does take three hours.

The road to Toujane is little more than a track across the plain – bumpy and often buried in sand – and in the hills, with the steep gradient and sharp bends, things get worse. The tracks are difficult to negotiate in a Peugeot and might bring a swift end to any smaller saloon car; there's a scattering of shops en route, one selling local rugs. It was this path that allowed the Eighth Army, advancing during a single night, to outflank the German lines.

Moving on from Mareth

Leaving the area, there are **buses** out of Mareth north to Gabes and sporadic ones south to MEDENINE or HOUMT SOUK. **Louages** go to Gabes and Medenine, but not Houmt Souk. However, it is not difficult to hitch to JORF, from where you can pick up the ferry to **Jerba**.

travel details

Trains

FROM GABES TO:

Tunis (2 daily, 1 overnight, 7hr), via **Mahres** (2hr, change for **Gafsa**, 7hr 20min and **Metlaoui**, 8hr 10min, including 2hr wait), **Sfax** (2hr 40min), **El Jem** (4hr), **Sousse** (5hr) and **Bir Bou Rekba** (6hr, change for Hammamet and Nabeul, long connection, easiest by road).

Buses and louages

Gabes is the main transport link between the south and the centre of Tunisia, and almost everything passes through here. It is therefore a very good place to pick up connections all over the country. Note, however, that many buses heading south have come from Tunis and arrive in Gabes around midnight, reaching their final destinations very early in the morning.

FROM GABES TO:

Tunis (8, 5 of them overnight, 6hr – choose *confort* or *normal* – 2 continuing to **Bizerte**, 10hr); **Matmata** (frequent, the last around 6.30pm, 1hr); **Sfax** (9, 2hr 15min); **Mareth** (frequent, 30min); **Medenine** (5, 1hr 15min); **Ras Ajdir/Libyan border** (4, 3hr); **Sousse** (4, 5hr 30min); **Kairouan** (1, plus several overnight, 4hr); **Tozeur** (1, 4hr 30min); **Houmt Souk (Jerba)** (7, 3hr 30min); **Zarzis** (2, 2hr); **Kebili** (9, 2hr 30min); **Gafsa** (4, 2hr 30min); and **Tataouine** (1, 2hr 30min).

Louages to **Tunis**, **Tripoli**, **Sfax**, **Mareth**, **Houmt Souk (Jerba)**, **Zarzis**, **Medenine**, **Tataouine**, **El Hamma** and **Kebili**, with the odd one direct to **Douz** (none to Matmata, but *louages* leave from near the bus station for **Nouvelle Matmata**, whence there are pick-ups onward).

FROM MATMATA TO:

Tunis (every evening, 9hr); **Gabes** (7, 1hr); **Taoujou** (2 daily, 30min) via **Tamezret** (20min); morning minibus loop to **Beni Aissa** (15min), **Nouvelle Beni Aissa** (20min), **Nouvelle Matmata** (30min) and back to **Matmata** (45min).

No louages, but pick-up connections to **Nouvelle Matmata**, thence out of the district.

FROM TAOUJOU TO:

Matmata (2 daily, 30min) via **Tamezret** (10min).

FROM MARETH TO:

Gabes (frequent, 30min); **Medenine** (5, 45min); **Houmt Souk** (7, 3hr).

Louages to **Gabes** and **Medenine** (but not Houmt Souk)

Flights

There is an airport at **Gabes** (entry via the military base), from which *Tunisavia* were running two weekly Twin Otter flights to Tunis, but this service has been suspended.

PHONE CODES

The code for the whole region is ☎05.

CHAPTER EIGHT

JERBA AND THE SOUTHEAST COAST

The island of **Jerba**, joined to the mainland by a causeway since before Roman times, perches at the southern end of the Gulf of Gabes, enclosing the smaller **Gulf of Bou Grara** between island and mainland. Eastwards, the coast dips past the modern town of **Zarzis** and the Bahiret el Biban lagoon before disappearing over the border into Libya.

This sun-soaked corner of Tunisia boasts some of the country's prime **beaches**, so it is hardly surprising that it has become a serious centre for seaside holiday resorts. The package industry has set up a ghetto in the northeast corner of Jerba, and beach hotels are beginning to spread, too, along the mainland parts of the coast around Zarzis. In midsummer it's probably a good idea to seek nirvana elsewhere.

There *are* deserted beaches if you have the means to get to them. On the **west coast** of Jerba and **southeast of Zarzis** are strands where you won't see another tourist, and not many Tunisians either. Do, however, check with the local police or National Guard before heading to potentially sensitive areas close to the Libyan border.

MARKET DAYS

Monday – Houmt Souk, Zarzis	Friday – Zarzis, Midoun
Tuesday – Sedouikech, Sedghiane	Saturday – El May, Ben Gardane
Wednesday – Ajim, Guellala, Mouansa	Sunday – Ajim, Guellala
Thursday – Houmt Souk	

JERBA

On the tenth [day] we made the country of the Lotus-Eaters, a race that live on vegetable foods....I sent some of my followers inland to find out what sort of human beings might be there, detailing two men for the duty with a third as messenger. Off they went, and it was not long before they were in touch with the Lotus-Eaters. Now it never entered the heads of these natives to kill my friends: what they did was to give them some lotus to taste, and as soon as each had eaten the honeyed fruit of the plant, all thoughts of reporting to us or escaping were banished from his mind. All they now wished for was to stay where they were with the Lotus-Eaters, to browse on the lotus and to forget that they had a home to return to. I had to use force to bring them back to the ships, and they wept on the way, but once on board I dragged them under the benches and left them in irons. I then commanded the rest of my loyal band to embark with all speed on their fast ships, for fear that others of them might eat the lotus and think no more of home. They came on board at once, went to the benches, sat down in their proper places, and struck the white surf with their oars.
So we left that country and sailed on sick at heart.

Homer, The Odyssey, book IX

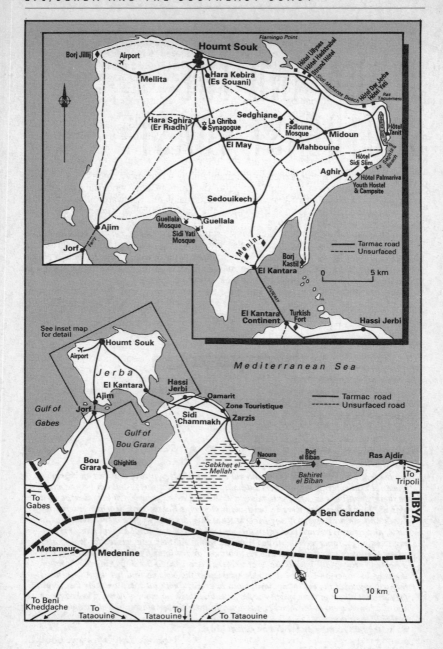

Flamingo Point

Borj Jillij

Airport

Houmt Souk

Hôtel Ulysse
Hôtel Haddrubal
Strand Hôtel

Mellita

Hara Kebira
(Es Souani)

Sidi Mahares Beach

Hôtel Dar Jerba
Hôtel Yati

Ras Taguermess

Sedghiane

Hara Sghira
(Er Riadh)

La Ghriba
Synagogue

Fadloune
Mosque

Hôtel
Tanit

Midoun

El May

Mahbouine

Aghir

Hôtel
Sidi Slim

Hôtel Palmariva
Youth Hostel
& Campsite

Sedouikech

Guellala
Mosque

Guellala

Sidi Yati
Mosque

Ajim

Meninx

Jorf

Ferry

Borj
Kastil

Tarmac road
Unsurfaced

0   5 km

El Kantara

El Kantara
Continent

Turkish
Fort

Hassi Jerbi

See inset map
for detail

Houmt Souk

Jerba

Airport

El Kantara

Ajim

Mediterranean Sea

Hassi
Jerbi

Qamarit

Zone Touristique

Tarmac road
Unsurfaced road

Jorf

*Gulf of
Gabes*

Sidi
Chammakh

Zarzis

*Gulf of
Bou Grara*

**Bou
Grara**

Ghighitis

Naoura

Borj
el Biban

Ras Ajdir

*Sebkhet el
Mellah*

*Bahiret
el Biban*

LIBYA

To
Gabes

To Tripoli

Ben Gardane

Metameur

Medenine

To Beni
Kheddache

To
Tataouine

To
Tataouine

To Tataouine

0   10 km

Jerba, like Minorca and Majorca, is said to be the legendary land of the **Lotus-Eaters** and – low-lying, semi-desert island that it is – it makes good territory for such myth and fantasy. Sandy beaches completely encircle the coast while, inland, the unique mosques and houses are scattered among palm groves. Its history and culture are to some extent different from the mainland; its architecture is quite distinctive, its ethnic background more diverse. Unfortunately, its seductive packageable charms, and easy access through the international airport, have also brought **tourism** on a big scale. A dozen hotels line the northern coast, which the government has declared a "zone touristique," and many of the people who come to stay here see the island as nothing more than a beach in the sun. And indeed Jerba is an excellent **beach resort**; the palm-rustled strands themselves are wonderful, the sea warm and limpid, the mood relaxed and the general scene idyllic. Moreover the hotels here are some of the country's best and more than adequate by any standard. If all you want is sun and sand, it's just the place to come: on the other hand, if that is all you want, you're missing out.

The island's intimate, farm-divided **interior** exudes a certain magic you won't find anywhere else, a district of country lanes through date and olive groves with the sea never far away. The beautiful whitewashed, fortified mosques are unique in Tunisia and the island also boasts three historic forts and scattered Roman remains, so far unexcavated. It's a big enough area (a little larger than the Isle of Wight) to explore in a genuine sense but small enough to do so by bicycle or even, with some effort, on foot.

Arrival and practicalities

Jerba's **airport** is at MELLITA, 6km west of Houmt Souk, and a further 12km from the heart of the hotel strip. Three daily buses head into Houmt Souk, from where there are buses to the hotel zone. If you don't have transport laid on by a hotel, and if the buses fail to connect with your arrival, you will have to take a metered taxi, which costs about 2TD to Houmt Souk and about triple that to the hotel zone, depending on where exactly your hotel is. After 9pm, a fifty percent surcharge comes into force. If you want to hire a car immediately on arrival, *Avis*, *Hertz*, *Europcar* and *Mattei* all have desks at the airport (☎50233).

By road, Jerba can be reached easily enough from the south or north. From the south, most buses take you straight through to Houmt Souk, via Zarzis and the causeway. Coming from Gabes and the north, it's faster to use the Jorf–Ajim ferry, although many buses still go the long way round via Medenine and Zarzis.

Note **if you are driving** that Jerba has a 70km/hr (43mph) maximum speed limit, rarely obeyed but sometimes enforced. Jerbans seem to know where the police are waiting to pounce; tourists are better off keeping within the limit.

Houmt Souk

Although **HOUMT SOUK** is increasingly commercialised, the *Association pour la Sauvegarde de l'Ile de Jerba* has made great efforts to preserve its distinctive architecture over the last decade. The island's capital, and its one real town, Houmt Souk remains a lively and interesting place and, at only 1500m from end to end, a very easy one to find your way around.

Practicalities

Most services and shops are on two main north–south roads, **Avenue Bourguiba** to the west and **Avenue Abdel Hamid el Kadhi** to the east. The town's network of tiny alleys and shaded squares lies between the two, along with its **main souk** (the town's

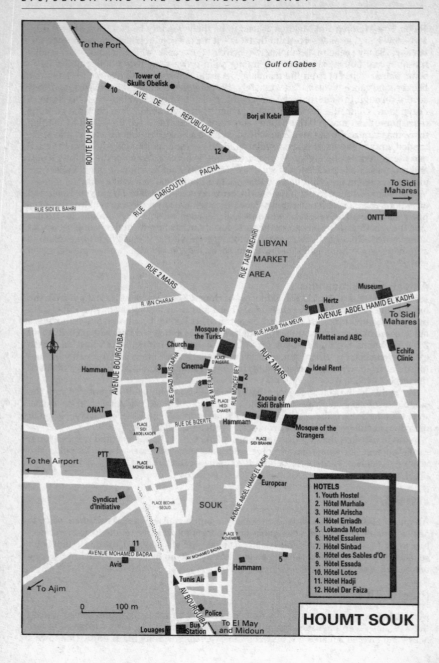

To the Port

Gulf of Gabes

Tower of Skulls Obelisk

10

AVE. DE LA REPUBLIQUE

ROUTE DU PORT

Borj el Kebir

RUE DARGOUTH PACHA

12

To Sidi Mahares

RUE SIDI EL BAHRI

RUE TAIEB MEHIRI

LIBYAN MARKET AREA

ONTT

RUE 2 MARS

R. IBN CHARAF

Museum

Hertz

9

AVENUE ABDEL HAMID EL KADHI

To Sidi Mahares

RUE HABIB THA MEUR

AVENUE BOURGUIBA

Hamman

Mosque of the Turks

Church

RUE GHAZI MUSTAPHA

Cinema

PLACE D'ALGERIE

3

8

RUE M FERJANI

RUE MOKTEB BEY

2

Garage

RUE 2 MARS

Mattei and ABC

Ideal Rent

Echifa Clinic

ONAT

4

PLACE HEDI CHAKER

1

Zaouia of Sidi Brahim

RUE DE BIZERTE

Hammam

PLACE SIDI ABDELKADER

Mosque of the Strangers

PLACE SIDI BRAHIM

PTT

7

PLACE MONGI BALI

To the Airport

AVENUE ABDEL HAMID EL KADHI

Europcar

Syndicat d'Initiative

PLACE BECHIR SEOUD.

SOUK

PLACE T. NOVEMBRE

11

AVENUE MOHAMED BADRA

AV MOHAMED BADRA

Avis

5

To Ajim

0   100 m

Tunis Air

6

Hammam

AV BOURGUIBA

Police

Louages

Bus Station

To El May and Midoun

HOTELS

1. Youth Hostel
2. Hôtel Marhala
3. Hôtel Arischa
4. Hôtel Erriadh
5. Lokanda Motel
6. Hôtel Essalem
7. Hôtel Sinbad
8. Hôtel des Sables d'Or
9. Hôtel Essada
10. Hôtel Lotos
11. Hôtel Hadji
12. Hôtel Dar Faiza

HOUMT SOUK

name means "marketplace", and everything is built outwards from the old souk). On each side is a main square – **Place Bechir Seoud (Farhat Hached)** on av Bourguiba, and **Place Sidi Brahim (7 Novembre)** on av Abdel Hamid el Kadhi. From the latter, opposite the Strangers' Mosque, **Rue Moncef Bey** leads to the Mosque of the Turks, from where av Taieb Mehiri leads seawards to the Borj el Kebir, where **Avenue de la République** crosses it, going left to the port and the other way towards the hotel zone.

Accommodation

Unless you're **camping** (the only two campsites are not in Houmt Souk but at Aghir, or you can camp wild at Flamingo Point, Ras Taguerness or on the west coast) or you want to stay by the beach at Sidi Mahares or Aghir, you'll probably end up in one of Houmt Souk's **hotels**. Four of these (including the town's excellent youth hostel) are old converted **fondouks** or *caravanserais*, once offering food and shelter to itinerant merchants and pilgrims. They share a common plan, with a large open courtyard surrounded by arches or colonnades. At the centre camel trains would be tethered by the well, their goods securely stored on the ground floor.

THE FOUNDOUKS

Youth Hostel (*Auberge de Jeunesse*) **(1)**, 11 rue Moncef Bey (☎50619). Off pl Hedi Chaker. Probably the best youth hostel in the country: very friendly and well-run, with double rooms and a distinct lack of rules and regulations. 2TD per person.

Hôtel Marhala (2) , rue Moncef Bey (☎50146). Next door to the youth hostel, and run, like its namesakes in Nefta and Matmata, by the Touring Club of Tunisia. Pleasant though rather basic rooms, and the best bar in town. 5.5/8TD low season, 6.5/10TD high, b&b .

Hôtel Arischa (3), 36 rue Ghazi Mustapha (☎50384). Near the church. Most attractive of the old *foundouks*, its court festooned with vines and enclosing a shallow pool. 1* 5/8TD low, 7/12TD high, b&b.

Hôtel Erriadh (4), 10 rue Mohamed Ferjani (☎50756). Off pl Hedi Chaker. Rooms have bathrooms but windows open only onto the central patio. 2* 9/15TD low, 13/20TD high, b&b.

THE OTHERS

Lokanda Motel (5), passage de la Municipalité (☎51513). Friendly, with a choice of old grotty rooms or newer cleaner ones. 2–3TD per person.

Hôtel Essalem (6), rue Redama (☎51029). Off pl 7 Novembre. Big comfy rooms. Terrace sleeping negotiable in summer. 5.3/6.6TD low, 6.6/8.8TD high, shower 0.7TD.

Hôtel Sinbad (7), pl Mongi Bali (☎50047). If the prices have any logic to them, they are too high for this place anyhow. 6/6.5TD low, 6/7.5TD high.

Hôtel des Sables d'Or (8) , 30 rue Mohamed Ferjani (☎50423). Not a *foundouk* but an old palatial house built around a central patio. The rooms are clean with a shower but shared loos. 6TD per person.

Hôtel Essada (9), 6 rue Habib Thameur (☎51422). Near the museum. Light airy rooms with balcony and bathroom. 9/13TD low, 12.5/18TD high, b&b.

Hôtel Lotos (10), 18 rue de la République (☎50026). Opposite the tower of skulls obelisk. Large clean rooms with bathroom. Run by the same people as the nearby *Hôtel Dar Faiza*, whose pool and tennis courts are open to *Hôtel Lotos* guests. 9.2/13.4TD low, 13/21TD high, b&b.

Hôtel Hadji (11), 44 av Mohamed Badra (☎50630). Rather formal with all mod cons. 1* 11/17TD b&b.

Hôtel Dar Faiza (12), rue de la République (☎50083). Up near the Borj. A well-run place with a small pool and almost family atmosphere. 1* 11.4/16.7TD low, 18.5/30TD high, b&b.

FURTHER OUT

These three places are down av Bourguiba towards the hospital.

Hôtel Nozha, 150 av Bourguiba (☎50381). Clean, pleasant and friendly. Rooms have balcony and bathroom. 1* 11/17TD low, 15.5/24TD high, b&b.

Hôtel Ben Abbes, 158 av Bourguiba (☎50128). Self-catering apartments, each with its own kitchen. 20–35TD low, 25–40TD high.

Hôtel Laroussa, av Bourguiba (☎50788). Just before the hospital. Unfriendly and over-priced. 8.5/12TD low, 11/16TD high, b&b.

TAP WATER

Jerba's tap water is slightly saline and, due to the island's high water table, not as safe to drink as in the rest of the country. You won't catch anything serious, but those with delicate digestive systems should stick to the mineral water.

Eating, drinking and hanging out

For **breakfast**, the café on pl Bechir Seoud is a cut above the rest, with fresh croissants and loads of pastries. The one on pl Hedi Chaker is more ordinary. If a continental breakfast isn't enough for you, the grocer's on pl Farhat Hached will do sandwiches with which to supplement it. **Fruit juice** is widely available – a place at the eastern end of av Mohamed Badra does it cheaper than anywhere else. As for **main meals**, many of the **tourist restaurants** are gathered around pl Hedi Chaker and pl Sidi Brahim. **Cheaper places** are tucked away around town.

CHEAP EATS

Restaurant Populaire, 29 av Mohamed Badra. Only around 3TD, but rather a greasy spoon.

Restaurant Essalem, 21 av Mohamed Badra. Similar basic fried fare to the *Populaire*.

Restaurant Tunisien, in the central souk. 3.5TD-odd for a good feed. Fish is especially recommended. Open lunchtime only.

Restaurant Les Palmiers, pl d'Algerie, at the end of rue Mohamed Ferjani, near the church. Solid Tunisian food for under 4TD.

Restaurant Sportif, 147 av Bourguiba. Good value at around 3TD a go. Try the excellent liver.

Restaurant Central, 128 av Bourguiba. Near the *autogare*. 3TD will fill you up here. Their couscous is pretty good.

There's also a **gargote**, 153 av Abdel Hamid el Kadhi (pl 7 Novembre), about 2.5TD a meal.

POSHER NOSH

Restaurant du Sud, pl Sidi Brahim. Better than most of the tourist traps; 5TD should see you satisfied.

Restaurant Neptune, pl Sidi Brahim. A reasonable alternative to the *du Sud* (but steer clear of the *Baccar* opposite).

Tokyo Restaurant, off rue Habib Thameur behind *Hôtel Essada*. A Japanese restaurant when they can get the necessary supplies in. Otherwise, a pleasant upmarket Tunisian eatery at around 8TD a meal.

La Princesse d'Haroun, an excellent fish restaurant down at the harbour. Around 10TD.

As for **hotel restaurants**, the *Dar Faiza* is probably the best for a meal.

As to **drinking**, most places, as usual, close by 8pm. The *Hôtel Marhala* has Houmt Souk's liveliest bar; the *Arischa* offers somewhere quieter and sometimes stays open later in summer. After closing time, your best bet is to find a restaurant where you can

A HISTORY OF JERBA

The **Carthaginians** who first settled on Jerba called it Meninx – "land of the receding waters", a reference to the highest tides anywhere in the Mediterranean. With its virtually landlocked gulf it was an ideal haven for any sheltering fleet, and quickly gained a reputation for trade and commerce. The **Romans** built an extensive city on the southern shores, exporting cloth (dyed imperial purple by the murex shellfish) throughout the Empire.

Under the **Arabs**, Jerba was a centre of almost permanent revolt as it constantly struggled to assert its independence from its overlords. The island strongly supported the **Kharijite rebellion** in 740 and, when the Aghlabids retook the north of Tunisia, Jerba became part of the Rustamids' Kharijite state (it is still one of Kharijism's last strongholds). Later, Jerba supported **Abu Yazid**'s 944 Kharijite rebellion against the **Fatimids**, and also rose up unsuccessfully against their successors, the **Zirids**. Throughout the centuries leading towards French domination, it remained a hotbed of defiance, never at peace for long.

From the twelfth century, Jerba came under serious threat from the Christian kingdoms, especially whichever one had control of Sicily just across the water. Like Sicily, Jerba's strategic position made it an object of Muslim–Christian rivalry. In 1135, Sicily's Norman king **Roger II** invaded Jerba, massacring or enslaving much of the population. The island resisted with little success and, a century later, suffered much the same fate under **Roger de Lluria** of Aragon. When Jerba again rose up in 1310, Aragonese troops under **Ramon de Muntaner** murdered or enslaved three quarters of the island's population and strangled its economy with punitive taxes. Even returned to Muslim rule by the **Almohads** in 1159, Jerba made repeated attempts to regain its autonomy. The Christians tried to retake it several times, but local resistance rebutted them. For much of the fifteenth century, at least, Jerba under the **El Samumni** family was virtually independent.

Piratical **merchant–sailors** wrought havoc in Jerba in the sixteenth century. The corsair Aruj **Barbarossa** made his base here in 1510, as did his protégé **Dragut** in 1535. Dragut, trapped with his fleet by the flotilla of Charles V of Spain in 1551, made a famous and daring **naval getaway** (see p.287). Later putting himself at the disposal of the Turks, Dragut returned to Jerba with an **Ottoman** fleet to set up shop in 1560, and completely trounced the coalition of European forces under Philip II of Spain which attempted to drive him out.

Under the **Ottomans**, Jerba became a centre of silk and wool production and its economy thrived. It was also a major terminal for trans-Saharan goods until the main commodity, African slaves, was banned in 1846. European merchants preferred to trade here rather than with the unpredictable mainland – if there was an uprising on the mainland, business could go on as usual on the island. This is just what happened in 1881; the islanders, fearing that Jerba would be occupied and sacked by the rebellious tribes on the mainland, welcomed the **French** invaders, gaining for themselves the lasting gratitude of the conquerors.

get away with ordering only beer, and perhaps a snack to go with it. Otherwise, you'll have to get a taxi out of town to a hotel such as the *Strand*, where you can drink till late. Make sure you can arrange transport back if you do this.

Around Town: Sightseeing

With a history as stormy and an identity as strong as Jerba's, it is hardly surprising that its capital is full of interest. Houmt Souk's nooks and crannies are gradually being pedestrianised, and its cottage industries are giving way to shops and restaurants that are hardly there for the benefit of Jerbans. But in spite of this onslaught, it still has loads of charm and remains one of the country's most pleasant towns. While you can't, unfortunately, enter any of the **mosques** or **zaouias**, the **fort and museum** are open to the public, and both are well worth investigation.

The souk

At the very centre of the town is its souk, with two **qaysarriya**, arched and covered passageways where traditionally the most expensive goods were sold, such as prized Egyptian cloth and filigree silver. Coral and jewellery are now the market's pricey mainstays, but the leather goods are often pretty shoddy. Be ruthless when you barter – it's often not unreasonable to make an initial offer of a tenth of the quoted price. In the less tourist-oriented part of the souk, the daily **fish auction** is interesting to visit.

Mondays and Thursdays are the souk's busiest days, with traders coming in from around the island. The market is then full of people selling straw baskets and mats, along with **musicians** from Midoun (see p.288) selling and playing their instruments.

The Zaouia of Sidi Brahim

Next to the souk, the **Zaouia of Sidi Brahim**, with its heavily buttressed walls, is typical of the ascetic Ibadite style of architecture (see box p.292) and looks much more military than religious. Once used for worship, teaching and as a rest house for travellers, it contains the tomb of the saint and his followers. Building was begun in 1674 but only completed thirty years later by the Bey, Mourad Ben Ali. A small door into the courtyard is usually open, but non-Muslims are not allowed to enter.

The Mosque of the Strangers and the Mosque of the Turks

Across the road is the extravagant **Mosque of the Strangers**, whose contrast with the *zaouia* could hardly be greater – covered with domes and topped by an extravagantly carved minaret. Again, sadly, it is closed to visitors.

Avenue Moncef Bey, just opposite, leads to the smaller **Mosque of the Turks**, really the most interesting of all Houmt Souk's mosques. It was originally Sunni Hanefite and is now Sunni Malekite, but the distinctive minaret was built by followers of Ibn Abdul Wahab, an eighteenth-century Islamic reformer from Arabia who introduced a fundamentalist and staunchly nationalistic brand of Islam. The unusually shaped minaret was first dubbed "phallic" by the Victorian polymath Sir Harry Johnston – a contentious epithet that has rather stuck. Johnston was convinced of "an unrecognised system of phallic worship throughout the south, and on Jerba all but the most recently built mosques have a phallic emblem on the summit of the minaret".

European buildings

Just round the corner in a quiet cul-de-sac, the **Catholic church** offers no such mysterious symbols for interpretation. But it's a strange baroque building which was once the centre of a thriving Christian community on Jerba. From the 1840s Greeks, Italians and Maltese came to the island for the sponge-fishing. Some stayed on and, by the 1890s, several thousand Europeans were living on the island. With Independence, however, most left and the church fell into disrepair, eventually to be turned over to more secular uses: today it's a gymnasium.

Opposite the *Hôtel Marhala* is another reminder of the island's European links, the **Maltese fondouk**, where merchants and sponge-collectors once stored their goods.

The Borj el Kebir and Libyan market

From the Mosque of the Turks, rue Taieb Mehiri leads to the fort, variously called the **Borj Ghazi Mustapha** or **Borj el Kebir** (open Mon–Sat 9am–5pm, closed Sun, 0.8TD plus 1TD to take photos). The site was originally occupied by the Romans, but a fort was first built here by the Aragonese King of Sicily, Roger de Lluria, in 1289. Its most famous moment came in 1560 when, after Philip II of Spain's armada was wiped out by Dragut's Ottoman fleet, his men retreated inside the fort, only to be massacred by the Turks. The skulls of the Spaniards (by various accounts numbering 500 or 5000) were piled up in a great tower – which stood until European powers prevailed on the Bey, despite strong local opposition, to bury them in 1848. All that remains now of this **tower of skulls** is a discreet obelisk marking the site 100m over towards the port.

The fort has been excavated but the site is hard to interpret for the untrained eye: for clues, look towards the new bridge over the ditch on the east side which leads first into a hall (*skifa*) and then into a courtyard between two perimeter walls. On the far side, the tomb of Ghazi Mustapha (who rebuilt the fort under the Turks) stands on the site of a thirteenth-century mosque. The west wall, with its four massive towers, is original.

On your way to the Borj el Kebir, and especially on Mondays and Thursdays, the **"Libyan market"** spreads itself along av Taieb Mehiri, with bargains and goods brought in from across the border. Most of the traders are Libyan and rarities include European jams, gummed cigarette papers, Nescafé.... At any rate, the market is well worth a browse, and is fast becoming one of Houmt Souk's main attractions, even if the tourist offices don't mention it in their literature.

The museum

For more concrete historical evidence than that offered by the obscure remnants of the fort, take a look at the concise **Museum of Arts and Popular Traditions** on the eastern edge of town, along av Abdel Hamid el Kadhi (Sat–Thurs 9am–noon, in summer 3pm–6.30pm, in winter 2pm–5.30pm; Fri closed; 0.8TD plus 1TD to take photos).

The museum's **first room**, once the Zaouia of Sidi Ameur, contains costumes worn on various occasions and in each part of the island. Search out in particular the old *fut'a*, a wrap-around garment worn by Berber women, and the traditional shawl or *bakhnug*. The long ornamental brooches in the cabinets are worn to indicate tribal allegiance: a Malekite would wear such a brooch on the left, a Berber in the middle and a Bedouin on the right. As in all the regions of the south (and much more than the north), Jerba has its own **marriage rituals**, now threatened by increasing costs and the demand for high dowries from the bride's father. The ceremonies begin six weeks before the wedding day, when red or yellow eggs are sent as invitations to the guests. During the week before the marriage the bride will receive presents from her husband and his family, including jewellery and ceremonial dress of the kind on display in the museum. She must also apply henna (on two different occasions) to the whole of her palms, fingers and feet; a Berber, though not a Malekite, might use a black paint called *ouchi*. At some stage, both the man and woman will be led in procession around a fertile olive tree, striking their companions with a branch to hasten other marriages taking place in the village. On the Friday before the wedding the bride is formally presented and unveiled to her family, who traditionally throw money at her feet. Finally she is carried to the groom in the privacy of a **palanquin**, a screened canopy placed on the back of a camel.

The museum's **second room**, the former shrine of Sidi Zitouni, has an original pottery roof (although the stucco work on its walls has been restored). Display cases contain ornamental jewellery made by the island's Jewish community. Downstairs is a reconstruction of an old pottery workshop of the sort still used at Guellala (see p.291). A room across the next courtyard was once used as a kitchen by pilgrims staying at the sanctuary. The large "Ali-Baba" jars are used as marriage chests, since there's little wood on the island. As you leave the museum, have a look at the weaver's hut, the *harout*, with its triangular front and sunken external buttressing; like the *houch* (see p.289), these are unique to Jerba.

Houmt Souk transport: around the island and moving on

For travelling around the island, **taxis** are probably your best bet. These are metred and can be picked up in av Bourguiba at the junction with av Mohamed Badra, on the traffic island in front of the *Tunis Air* office. You'll get one more easily in the morning and, with luck, you should be able to share with someone. Failing that, remember that

hitching is very easy in Jerba (you may have to resort to it to get back to Houmt Souk anyway), and, depending on the heat, even **walking** is not out of the question for getting around parts of the northwest of the island.

Houmt Souk's **bus station**, run by *SRTG Medenine*, is in av Bourguiba just south of the town centre. **Local buses** serve the hotel zone of Sidi Mahares (#11) and Midoun (#10) eleven times a day. There are also seven buses a day to Sedouikech (#16) and to Hara Sghira and Guellala (#14), five to Ajim (#12) and three to the airport (#15). El May is served by buses #10 and #16; for Aghir, take a bus to Midoun and change there. For transport between Houmt Souk and the hotel zone with the maximum possible delay, there's a **tourist mini road train** every two hours at 2TD.

As for **inter-city buses**, Gabes is easy enough to get to, but others are often full and need booking in advance – especially the two every day to Tunis. There are also night buses to Kairouan and Bizerte and one service daily to Sousse. Limited buses go direct (but not non-stop) to Zarzis, Medenine, Tataouine, Ben Gardane, Sfax and El Hamma de l'Arad, while **louages** – not within Jerba but to Tunis, Gabes, Zarzis and Medenine – leave from next to the bus station.

The **airport** (☎50233) is 6km west of Houmt Souk near Mellita. Three buses a day head out there, and a taxi should cost around 2TD (3TD at night). Jerba has some reasonably inexpensive **flights** back to Tunis. There are also various flights to Tozeur, Monastir and several European cities (more in summer, plus a number of charters).

Houmt Souk Listings

Airlines *Air France*, 131 av Abdel Hamid el Kadhi (pl 7 Novembre) (☎50239); *Tunis Air*, av Bourguiba (☎50159).

Banks There are six spread out along av Bourguiba and on pl Farhat Hached.

Belly-dancing classes Suat, who works at the *Ettabsi* restaurant in av Abdel Hamid el Kadhi, gives lessons.

Car and motor bike hire Houmt Souk is one of the best places in the country to hire a car as so many firms operate here, though prices are, as usual, high. Shop around and compare, but take into account the age and condition of the cars and the small print conditions and extras. *Hertz*, for example, offer discounts at various hotels and restaurants around southern Tunisia (and their cars are new); ask to see their list.

Companies include *ABC*, av Abdel Hamid el Kadhi at rue H Thameur (☎51067); *Avis*, 51 av Mohamed Badra (☎50151); *Ben Jemaa*, 1st floor, 4 av Mohamed Badra (☎50340); *Budget*, rue 20 Mars (☎50185); *Express*, av Abdel Hamid el Kadhi (☎50438); *Hertz*, 10 rue Habib Thameur (☎50196); *Intercar*, 173 av Abdel Hamid el Khadi (☎51155); *Interrent/Europcar*, 161 av Abdel Hamid el Kadhi (☎50357); *Mattei*, av Abdel Hamid el Kadhi (at rue H Thameur) (☎51367); *Topcar*, 19 rue 20 Mars (☎50536).

Some of the touring companies such as *Atlas Voyages* and *Tunisie Voyages* in av Bourguiba will hire out their Land Rovers in winter. The place to hire motor bikes is *Holiday Bikes* (☎57169) out of town by the *Hôtel Sirene* and *Jerba Yasmina* (they also do bicycles). *Ideal Rent* in av Abdel Hamid el Kadhi opposite the *Shell* station (☎50303) hire out bicycles at 1TD/hr or 6TD/day, and mopeds at 4TD/hr or 18TD/day. *Hertz* do mopeds at similar daily rates. They are supposed to be for island use, though if you're persistent it's sometimes possible to negotiate a weekly rent for use around the south.

Car repairs If you have a Land Rover, try the garages around the bus station.

Cinema Pl d'Algerie opposite the Mosque of the Turks. Specialises in kung fus, masalas, and similar lurid extravaganzas.

Festivals There's a biennial "touristic" Ulysses festival every other July, and a September sand yacht regatta at Houmt Souk port.

Gymnasium The old colonial church in rue Mustapha Ghazi is now a gym, charging around 1TD/hour for a workout.

Hammams The oldest, friendliest and most central is by the *zaouia* at 17 pl Sidi Brahim (men 5am–1pm; women 1–7pm). The Hammam Ziadi at 93 av Bourguiba is cleaner but dearer and less friendly (men 6am–noon; women 1–6pm). There is also a rather grubbier one at 117 av Abdel Hamid el Kadhi.

Market day The Libyan market and the central souk are active every day, but Mondays and Thursdays are the busiest.

Medical facilities The regional hospital is at the southern end of av Bourguiba (☎50018). There's also a private clinic behind the Mosque of the Strangers, charging 7TD for a consultation, and another (the *Echifa*) near the museum (☎50441), where a consultation with a specialist will set you back 10TD. The night chemist is at 166 av Bourguiba.

Newspapers British papers are available at 127 av Bourguiba, near the PTT.

ONA crafts shop Av Bourguiba, near the PTT.

PTT Av Bourguiba opposite pl Mongi Bali. City hours. Payphones open until 7.30pm weekdays.

Supermarket *Magasin Général* at the corner of rue Tahar Battikh and av Abdel Hamid el Kadhi. There's another in pl Mongi Bali at the entrance to the souk.

Tourist offices Both of the following are friendly and helpful with lots of information, maps and brochures. ONTT, rue de la République, on the road to the "zone touristique" (☎50016), Mon–Thurs 8.30am–1pm and 3–5.45pm, Fri & Sat 8.30am–1.30pm, Sun closed. Syndicat d'Initiative, av Bourguiba, opposite pl Mongi Bali (☎50915), Mon–Sat 9am–12.30pm & 3.30–6pm, Sun closed.

Tour operators If you're short on time, Houmt Souk has a number of companies offering **tours of the south**. Land Rover trips can be good value and worthwhile but avoid the coach tours, which stick only to main roads and routes. *Carthage Tours*, by pl Bechir Seoud, are among the best. *Holiday Bikes*, out in the hotel zone, do bike and jeep expeditions as far as Agadez, across the Sahara in Niger, but for that you would want to book well in advance and probably, like most of their customers, from France (see "Car hire").

JERBAN SOCIETY

Jerban society is quite distinct in many ways from that of mainland Tunisia. Its population forms a patchwork of different **ethnic and linguistic groups** – Arabs, Berbers and black Africans, Muslims (both Ibadite and Sunni) and Jews – who vary markedly in their traditions, style of dress, the names they bear and the way they speak, though these differences generally pass unnoticed by foreigners. However, all these people share a common Jerban identity: their traditions differ from those of the mainland as much as from each other, and each has a place in Jerban society.

Today, however, with the present **tourist influx**, it seems no exaggeration to talk of a **crisis** in Jerba's identity. Nowhere in Tunisia is there such an obvious and direct clash between a still very traditional society and the demands of a foreign culture. Services have become strained, prices inflated, and local culture and agriculture increasingly ignored. If you consider that the average package tourist gets through more meat and dairy products in a week than the majority of Tunisians consume in an entire year, it's easy to see just how drastic recent changes have been.

Even more serious a threat to the Jerban way of life is **emigration**, with traditional communities disrupted by the departure of Jews to Israel and of young men off to seek their fortunes elsewhere, usually by opening corner shops (known in Tunisia simply as *Jerbans*). Through the centuries the business acumen of its people – especially the Ibadites and Jews – has been of lasting importance to Jerba. People from the island now work as grocers all over Tunisia, and there are Jerban communities throughout Europe and as far away as Brazil. Following Independence, the government attempted to introduce national cooperatives in order to modernise the shops and to stop tax evasion and profit hoarding: but the islanders would have none of it, and the scheme eventually had to be abandoned.

The Beaches

Jerba's **beaches** are some of the best – arguably *the* best – in the Mediterranean. Only relatively short stretches of the almost continuous blaze of soft fine sand have been swamped by large-scale development. The worst build-up has been limited to the island's northeastern corner along **Sidi Mahares** beach and round to **Aghir**. Even here, the beach is plenty wide enough for all, and there are two campsites and space for camping wild. For the real desert island setting, however, you want the island's **west coast**.

Flamingo Point

Just before the hotels begin, the low sandy peninsula of Ras Rmel – known as **Flamingo Point** – stretches lazily out into the sea. Between November and March, you'll see a lot of the pink waders here, and often **dolphins** too, just a few yards offshore. A lot of Tunisians and Libyans **camp** out here in summer, as they do at the other end of the hotel zone, and there is no reason why you shouldn't join them.

Sidi Mahares – the Jerba package strip

A #11 bus from Houmt Souk will take you out along **SIDI MAHARES BEACH**, past the tourist complex and the string of hotels along eight kilometres of beach and surf until you reach the lighthouse at Ras Taguerness. The bus stops at most of the hotels en route, and you specify which one you want as you buy the ticket; the first on the beach is the *Hôtel Ulysses*. Prices for staying at these hotels – unless you're pre-booked on a package – are very inflated, especially in summer, though most are good and easily bear comparison with their equivalents in say Greece or Spain. Only a few operators – among them *Panorama* and *Tunisia Bureau Travel* (p.7)– offer package holidays here from the UK.

Sidi Mahares hotels include the following:

Strand Hôtel av rue (☎57430). The most economical of the beach hotels. 1* 5/10TD low, season, 23/32TD high, b&b.

Hôtel Sidi Yati (☎57016). Currently closed. Furthest from Houmt Souk, and formerly quite competitively priced. 2*.

Hôtel Dar Jerba (☎57191). An enormous complex more like a village than a hotel, with a choice of different kinds of rooms, and all the facilities anyone could want; you could spend your whole holiday inside this place. 2*/3* from 17.7/27TD low, 27.6/42.6TD high, b&b.

Hôtel Beau Rivage (☎57130). A friendly little *pension* near the *Dar Jerba*. 8/12TD low, 18/28TD high, b&b.

Hôtel Hadstrubal (☎57657). If only the best will do, this is the newest, the most expensive and the most luxurious hotel on the island. 4*L 40/50TD low, 60/110TD high, b&b.

Ras Taguerness

The **lighthouse** opposite the *Sidi Yati* hotel at the end of Sidi Mahares beach, near the cape called **Ras Taguerness**, is sometimes open to the public. More obvious local attractions include the **kart track** and, every Saturday evening, a **German-style barbecue buffet**.

Across from the lighthouse begins a **sand spit** enclosing the **Sebkha Sidi Garous** lagoon. In summer, *camping sauvage* is the order of the day here, as Tunisian and Libyan families pitch tents or sleep out on the beach. Some 5km down the spit is the 2* *Hôtel Tanit* (☎57132), one of the best hotels around here and, like many of the hotels, with waterskiing and windsurfing facilities (14.5/24TD b&b low, 35/52TD high). The spit continues for another 2km beyond the hotel. Look out for **flamingos** and other birds in the lagoon behind.

La Seguia

Around the point, on **La Seguia beach**, is a carefully restricted *Club Med* with two branches (*"Jerba la Fidèle"* and *"Jerba la Douce"*). A couple of kilometres down the beach is the 2* *Hôtel Sidi Slim* (☎57021/3), where the sands narrow and palm trees provide shade right down to the water (13/21TD low, 26.5/46TD high, b&b). There's a **campsite** too, at 1.5TD per person with use of showers, toilets and hot water (the hotel restaurant does a 4TD set menu and windsurfing is 4TD/hour).

Aghir

A little further, the beach at **AGHIR** is not Jerba's best. It's often covered in seaweed, and, after storms, the water tends to be infested with jellyfish. The rather pricey 3* *Hôtel Palmariva* (☎57830) is locally best known for its mixed hammam, after 7pm each evening (25/42TD low, 58/92TD high, FB). Next door, near the Midoun/El Kantara junction, is the *Centre des Stages et Vacances* **youth hostel/campsite** (☎57366). Friendly, if a bit run down, it charges 4TD in four-person dorms, or 2TD per person camping plus 0.5TD per tent; cheaper huts are also available. There are hot showers (and separate women's loos), and you can hire bicycles for 0.5TD/hr or 2TD/day, and use the *Palmariva*'s facilities (their disco for example).

Public transport doesn't extend to Houmt Souk, but there are ten hourly **buses** a day from Aghir to Midoun – two of them via Sidi Mahares. From Midoun, you can get anywhere on the island.

El Kantara

A single road leads south from Aghir to **EL KANTARA**, passing some deserted beaches on the way. Over to the left, a track heads over the sand and out along a strip of land to the fort of **Borj Kastil** – a long way to walk if you're not driving (8km) so hire a bike from the *Centre des Stages*. The fort was built by Alfonso V of Aragon during his brief mid-fifteenth-century tenure of the island. The surrounding rocks are said to be good for underwater fishing.

It was the Carthaginians who created the **causeway** which stretches 7km from El Kantara to the opposite shore. In 1551, Dragut the pirate, trapped with his fleet by the flotilla of Charles V of Spain between the causeway and the fort of Borj Kastil, made his famously daring **naval getaway**. To gain time, he barricaded himself in the fort and held off the Spaniards while his men, under cover of darkness, dug through the causeway, enabling his fleet to escape into the Gulf of Bou Grara. Although it could still be forded in the intervening period at low tide, the causeway was not repaired for over 400 years, finally reopening in 1953.

Across the causeway, EL KANTARA CONTINENT has nothing special to commend it except a ruined **Turkish fort** gazing languidly at Borj Kastil across the water. From here, there are two roads to ZARZIS, a coastal road via HASSI JERBI passing the tourist hotels and beach zone and a less scenic but more direct route via Sidi Chammakh.

Meninx

The site of ancient **MENINX** is spread around the road junction by El Kantara. Very little now remains of the city – established by the Phoenicians and rebuilt by the Romans – but if you want to explore, there are two patches of **unexcavated remains**. One area is spread up the Aghir road for 2km or so on both sides, the main area of blocks and fallen columns being about 1km from the causeway on the seaward side of the road. The other patch of remains is about 100m north of the piste to GUELLALA, less than 1km from the causeway (just before the date palms begin). Roman debris then lines the piste for another 200m beyond that. There is nothing spectacular to be seen, but the site is good for a stroll, and there's a number of nooks and crannies that repay closer inspection.

The West Coast

Long and wild, virtually uninhabited and empty of tourists (it's not as postcard-pretty as the other coasts) the **west coast of Jerba** is the place to really get away from it all – if you can get there, that is. At its northern end is the island's airport; to the south, Ajim, Jerba's main port; and in between no transport at all. If you stay, anywhere along this 20km shore, you're down to looking after yourself, camping or just sleeping out – no hardship so long as you have suitable supplies of food and water.

Mellita and Borj Jillij

Two roads run out to Jerba's **west coast** from Houmt Souk. The first leads past the radio tower to the **airport** (for details of departures, see p.296). **MELLITA**, the village nearby, has some of the oldest *menzels* on the island. The road continues (as a track) to the eighteenth century fort of **Borj Jillij**. The west coast is the best part of the island for **fishing**, and a series of *zribas*, traps made from palm fronds, stretch in a line away from the shore. The fish are caught by the current in a triangular enclosure and then swim into a smaller trap called an *achoucha*. A hole, which looks like an escape route, leads into a net, or *drina*, which can be lifted from the water.

From Borj Jillij you can drive or cycle back along a track by the sea to Houmt Souk, a distance of about 11km.

Ajim

The main Houmt Souk–Gabes road leads through dull countryside to the fairly dreary port of **AJIM**, the most important centre for sponges, which are still taken from the sea floor by divers – now mainly Tunisians but originally Greeks and Maltese. Ajim is also a centre for the local date harvest, though compared with the *deglat* variety of Tozeur the crop here is poor – three varieties of palm provide nothing edible at all and are kept only for *laghmi*, or palm wine (see p.21). Chances are it was this powerful, natural brew that knocked out Ulysses's companions; it merits respect. Be careful too if you go swimming here – the channel swarms with large jellyfish, constantly chewed up in the ferry propellors. The channel is also full of octopuses and all along the quay are stacked piles of **octopus traps** – ceramic pots laid on the sea bed in the evening. The creatures, looking for hiding places at the end of a night's foraging, crawl into them only to be hauled out in the morning.

The Ajim–Jorf **ferry** runs every half hour between 6am and 9pm, and every hour or two through the night. Foot passengers go free, cars pay 0.6TD. If you need to change money, Ajim has a bank – but there are no hotel or restaurant distractions.

Inland Jerba

Even today, Jerba is not really an island of towns and villages, but of individual homes. The only villages as such are the two Jewish "ghettos" of Hara Sghira and Hara Kebira. Houmt Souk, once just a marketplace (which is what its name means), only became a town this century. Other places marked on maps – Midoun, Mahboubine, El May, Guellala – really are little more than markets. People shop and work in them, but few people live in them.

Midoun

MIDOUN, the island's second town, is really little more than a row of **souvenir shops**, a pair of **banks**, a few **restaurants** and a **covered market**, but it's quite a lively place during the Friday souk. The other event of the week is a mock Berber

---

HOUCH AND MENZEL – JERBAN HOMES

Jerban homes, spread around the countryside, take the form of a *houch* (traditional house) inside a *menzel* (piece of land), each one belonging to a different family. From the outside, a *houch* looks like a small square fortress, with blank white walls and a small tower at each corner. Like the mosques, these houses were designed in response to numerous invasions from the eleventh century onwards, and it's been suggested that the basic plan was taken from the Roman forts, or *limes*, on the mainland. Three large rooms surround the central courtyard, each used by one section of an extended family. The parents in each section sleep in the tower, called a *ghorfa* or *kouchk*, often crowned with a dome. This is the only part of the house with external windows, traditionally placed higher than a man on horseback, but the breeze is fed down below through holes in the floor. Near the house is a simple guest room (usually facing east) and a threshing floor. The distinctive Jerban well is flanked by two upright supports for a system of pulleys operated by camel or mule; a system you see all over the island.

---

wedding put on for tourists every Tuesday afternoon. Otherwise, in practical terms, there's an **ONA crafts shop**, a **hammam**, at least one all-night **chemist**, and a very reputable **doctor**, Dr Massabi, the mayor's wife.

The *Restaurant de l'Orient* on the main roundabout does cheap and filling Tunisian food (around 2TD); the *Restaurant el Guestile*, just up the souvenir shop street, is more tourist oriented, and does good seafood at about 7TD a meal. Eating is likely to be the most you'll do in Midoun, but if you should want **to stay**, the *Hôtel Jawhara* (☎57363) is clean and pleasant at 8/12TD in the low season, 10/16TD high – but ask for a room with a window.

Midoun's underground **oil-press** (*massera*) is worth a look. It is in the centre, less than 50 metres from the main roundabout and police station. As at Haddej and Matmata, underground air ensures humidity throughout the winter, necessary to separate the oil. A mule or camel used to turn the stone roller around its base, crushing the olives, but the press is now motor-driven. After pressing, the skins are transferred to a sieve (*chamia*) which is squashed by the weight of a palm trunk, hinged at the wall; the oil and vegetable water drip through into a jar and separate. Around the main room are storage chambers, used by each family for their olives.

Frequent **buses** run to Houmt Souk via Mahbouine and El May, and there are also plenty of buses to Aghir and the hotel zone. **Taxis** wait for custom by the main roundabout.

From Midoun to Houmt Souk

The direct road from Midoun to Houmt Souk is largely uninteresting, but there are a couple of mosques en route worth breaking the half-hour journey for. The **Fadloune Mosque**, 3km out of Midoun on the south side of the road, appears anonymously on numerous postcards of the island. It is no longer used for prayers so you should be able to go in and look around. Another couple of distinctive Jerban mosques appear about 8km further to the north of the road.

Mahboubine and El May

A more picturesque route from Midoun to Jerba is by way of Mahboubine and El May through the vineyards and fruit and olive groves. All along this road, behind the high banks (or *tabia*) are the traditional Jerban houses (*houch*) each commanding the *menzel* or estate of a different family. All the sand tracks here to the north of the road lead past one *menzel* after another – a district best explored by bicycle from Houmt Souk.

MAHBOUBINE itself has little more than a central square, a couple of cafés and a nineteenth-century mosque inspired by the Blue Mosque in Istanbul. Rather more distinctive is **EL MAY**, 8km further on, with its typical Jerban **Mosque Umm et Turkia**. Like the Zaouia of Sidi Brahim in Houmt Souk, the low walls of this fortified building are supported by thick buttresses, the minaret a squat, rounded stump. Around its walls a Sunday **market** takes place; other signs of business include two banks and a PTT. Buses pass through here regularly between Houmt Souk and Midoun or Sedouikech.

Hara Sghira (Er Riadh)

Two kilometres from El May, in the direction of Houmt Souk, the road turns off left for Guellala. On the way is a **Jewish settlement** called **HARA SGHIRA** ("Small Ghetto"), now officially Er Riadh. Buses pass through seven times a day each way between Houmt Souk and Guellala.

Er Riadh's **synagogue of El Ghriba** (the "miracle") is a kilometre and a half out of the village down a well sign-posted road. It is a place of pilgrimage for Jews from all over North Africa on *Lag be Omer*, the 33rd day after Passover, and a large new hostel for pilgrims reflects the importance of the site. The present building is covered inside with rather garish tiles and dates only from 1920. The original synagogue was apparently constructed at the place where a holy stone fell from heaven: an unknown woman arrived, "miraculously", at the same time, to direct operations. If the Jews ever leave Jerba, it is said that the synagogue's silver key will be thrown back to heaven. An inner sanctuary contains several manuscripts, including one of the oldest Torahs in the world. One plaque on the wall offers a benediction for the Supreme Combattant,

---

THE JEWS OF JERBA

Opinion is divided about when **Jews** first came to Jerba: possibly 566 BC, following the fall of Jerusalem to Nebuchadnezzar, or 71 AD when the city was taken by Titus. The island community today numbers about 1500, some of whom have evidently returned here after emigrating to Israel. Historically, Jewish **artisans** have worked as jewellers, playing a considerable part in developing the island's commercial reputation.

Jerban **Jewish colonies** sprang up over much of the south, often made up of shop-keepers or itinerant blacksmiths. But while they established small communities in remote villages, they kept their bonds with Jerba, returning to the island during the summer and for important religious festivals.

To begin with Jews were tolerated, but only while they kept to their own community and traditional occupations. **Under the French** their position improved, but they remained second-class citizens relative to the Europeans and European Jews. Their own attitude helped maintain this position: for while other communities took advantage of the educational and financial resources of world Jewish organisations, the Jews of Jerba rejected aid, preferring to keep their strict and distinctive form of Judaism untainted. Consequently they won a reputation as intransigent **traditionalists**, gained far less from the Protectorate than other communities, and became the target of French and Arab anti-Semitism.

The new state of Israel offered an opportunity to make a new life in the Promised Land, and by the early 1950s many Jews were leaving. After Tunisian Independence the trickle of emigrants became a flood and the community shrank. Despite Bourguiba's attempts to encourage integration, anti-Semitism remains a problem – albeit a relatively minor one: "We have nothing against Tunisian Jews, it is only the State of Israel we object to." And it is **anti–Zionism** that provokes occasional outbursts of hatred. As recently as 1985 a policeman, apparently incited by radio broadcasts from Libya, burst into the Ghriba in Hara Sghira and killed three worshippers before he could be restrained.

Bourguiba, and another asks for **donations** (these are not optional – less than 0.5TD and you will be promptly shown the door).

Hara Kebira (Es Souani)

The other Jewish village, **HARA KEBIRA** (now officially Es Souani), near Houmt Souk, is rather more workaday than Hara Sghira. It boasts no less than eleven synagogues, but none as interesting as El Ghriba. On the other hand, if you want to have some jewellery made up, Hara Kebira is full of workshops and you should find prices here lower than in Houmt Souk.

IBADITES AND BERBERS

From the earliest Arab invasions, Jerba became a centre for the **Kharijites**, an ascetic Islamic sect hostile to the Damascus Caliphs who ruled the Arab empire, and with a considerable following among the Berbers. With the fall of the Kharijites' capital of Tahirt (Algeria) to the Fatimids in 909, Jerba, along with the Mzab in Algeria, the Jebel Nafusa in Libya, and the island of Zanzibar in Tanzania, became one of their last refuges.

Ibadites, as they are known today, form nearly half Jerba's Muslim community and are concentrated in the south and west of the island. They are extremely strict in their religious practice, and follow the dictates of the Koran even more scrupulously than other Muslims. They also differ from Sunni (orthodox) Muslims in certain details of their religious rituals. The austerity of their religion is best expressed in their architecture, and they built the most simple and severe of all the 300 mosques and marabouts around the island. In times of war these semi-fortified buildings would serve as a place of refuge for those outside the *houch* or *menzel*, the country houses in the interior (see p.289).

Most of Jerba's dwindling minority of **Berber-speakers** are Ibadites. They live in the south of the island, especially around Ajim, Guellala and Sedouikech. Because they speak a different language, they tend to be at a social disadvantage (getting a job is always a problem for example), and the low social status of Berber is the main factor behind the decline of the language.

Guellala

GUELLALA rivals Nabeul in Cap Bon as a centre for handmade, mass-produced **pottery**. The clay is dug out of the hillside on the road to Sedouikech (the one prominence on the island), then bleached and cleaned in the sea. All the products were once exported from a port down the road, and people used to travel around the markets near Tataouine selling their goods. The staple of the industry, large *terracotta* vessels used for storing and cooling water and oil, went to markets as far afield as Benghazi and Constantine. Workshops line the main street, though of the ones operating, only one is still in the original style, partly underground and insulated with stone and soil to protect the drying clay from the heat and wind. The 300 kilns in the village are constructed with special bricks, made from earth which has been washed with alluvial deposits. Most of the glazed ware is garish and geared to the market in cheap souvenirs, though the Berber bowls, baked at the lowest temperatures, are more authentic and interesting. A Guellala speciality nowadays is the "magic camel", a water jug in the shape of a camel with a hole in the base through which it's filled. When placed the right way up, the water miraculously fails to escape from this hole and pours only from the mouth. (If you need to change any money to invest in a bit of pottery, Guellala has a **bank**.)

Guellala has an underground oil press (through the shop with the ceramic map on the door), but the **oil press** in use today, out on the edge of town by the El Kantara road, is actually much more interesting – a wonderful piece of vintage Science Museum technology – ecpecially so if you manage to call in when it's being used.

Out of town, along the shore, are a couple of interesting mosques and a few bits of Roman masonry. The **Guellala Mosque**, by the beach, dates back to the fifteenth century. Half a kilometre westwards up the beach, you'll find the odd piece of Roman wall. There is more underwater just offshore, and local farmers often turn up pieces of marble and mosaic in their fields. In the other direction, 1500m east along the coast, the **Mosque of Sidi Yati,** even older than the Guellala Mosque, stands disused and crumbling by the shore.

If you get the **bus** to Guellala, timings are such that the last bus back to Houmt Souk is easily missed. A **taxi** to Houmt Souk costs about 2.5TD, but it's easy enough to **hitch** a lift via either Sedouikech or Hara Sghira.

THE MAINLAND SOUTH OF JERBA

The **mainland behind Jerba** basically consists of the small towns of Jorf and Bou Gara and, on the country's remote southeast coast, the nascent resort of Zarzis and the route into Libya via Ben Gardane. With most people heading for Jerba's lotus-eating shores, this corner is still a very little visited part of Tunisia – but it's a region that's likely to become increasingly the subject of tourist development over the next few years so long as Tunisia's giant neighbour continues to assent.

Jorf and Gightis

JORF, the mainland ferry terminal, is not the most inspiring town in Tunisia. However, the ferry services ensure that you won't be stranded for long. There are fairly frequent *louages* to Gabes and to Medenine, though you may have to push for a place. Between Jorf and Gabes the only town is MARETH (see p.273), from where adventurous travellers can strike off to TOUJANE. En route to Medenine you could stop off at BOU GRARA to visit the Roman port of GIGHTIS – though as passing *louages* tend to be full, it can prove difficult to continue on afterwards.

Gightis

GIGHTIS was established by the Phoenicians and became a trading post under the Carthaginians. The Gulf of Bou Grara could provide shelter for a large fleet and, recognising its strategic importance, the Romans attacked the city during the first two Punic wars. After the campaign of Julius Caesar, from 46 to 40 BC, the Romans assumed control and for the next 200 years Gightis flourished as a major port of Africa Proconsularis and Byzacenia. The Roman trade route went from Carthage via Hammamet, El Jem and Gabes to Gightis and then on to Oea, Leptis Magna and Ghadames in Tripolitania. The city was later sacked by the Vandals, but the Byzantines thought it worthy of restoration. With the Arab invasion of the seventh century, however, the port was destroyed and the site covered over until excavations in 1906.

The site

The larger central square, the **forum**, dates from the reign of the Emperor Hadrian (117–138AD) and is overlooked by a **temple** dedicated to Serapis and Isis. A long flight of steps leads up to the top of the red sandstone podium, but little remains of the columns or interior walls. The stone-flagged road, down to the port, begins by the arch at the other end of the forum and passes, on the left, the **temple of Bacchus**. Behind the portico, where only the fragments of columns remain, is an underground passage and several small rooms, their purpose unknown. The **port** has long since been silted up but a partly submerged row of stones marks the site of a **jetty**, once 140m long. Stone foundations by the road also give an idea of the town's extent – stretching to the Capitol Temple, at the top of a slight hill, towering above the shops and houses. On the right-hand side of the Forum (as you face the sea) are the **baths** and several scraps of mosaic. Walking through the baths, away from the square, the **market** is ahead and just to the right; built in the third century, it consists of a central courtyard surrounded by a walkway, fitted out with shops. Nearby are the remains of villas and a temple of Mercury.

Bou Grara

The new village of **BOU GRARA** is a kilometre up the side road, past the ruins. From the rock, on the right of the site, there's a sweeping view of the inland sea, mud flats and the older fishing port down below. Although French naval architects believed they could build a second Bizerte in this natural harbour, the modern port never quite lived up to the promise of its ancient predecessor: the water was far too shallow to accommodate heavy military vessels and the plans were scrapped.

On to Zarzis and the Libyan Frontier

There isn't much to see around **Zarzis**. Like Sfax, the town is surrounded by olive plantations, most of which were planted this century. Until recently, few travellers ever bothered to go further east, but since Libya has tentatively started allowing entry to tourists, BEN GARDANE and RAS AJDIR are slightly more on the beaten track.

Zarzis

Halfway down the coast that nearly encloses the Gulf of Bou Grara, **ZARZIS** has a good, long beach with new hotels, though it pales in comparison with Houmt Souk and much of Jerba. Even so, French officers considered it the cushiest posting in the south, a paradise after the parched heat of the interior. It was also the only place south of Gabes that suffered colonisation by the French. Unfortunately, the soldiers and the colonists didn't get on: the officers feared that if too many colonists arrived they would lose their holiday resort to the civil administration, and did everything they could to make their lives difficult. The colonists, in turn, sent frequent complaints to the government, claiming that the army ruled with "the sword and the bull whip rather than any legal code". In the end, Independence arrived before the military could be persuaded to abandon the town.

Orientation

Avenue Mohamed V is the main road in from Jerba. At **Place de la Jeunesse**, the town's central roundabout, it meets **Avenue Farhat Hached**, the road to Medenine. The third exit from pl de la Jeunesse is rue Hedi Chaker, leading to **Place 7 Novembre** by the **Great Mosque**. From there, roads lead off towards the port and towards Ben Gardane.

The "Plan de Zarzis", issued by the Tourist Board, looks promising enough, with a seaside restaurant and a fishing port, but the coastal road leads through a large unmarked military camp – hardly designed for an evening stroll – while the restaurant is closed.

Practicalities – and diversions

There are **banks** around pl de la Jeunesse and pl 7 Novembre, while the **PTT** (country hours) is just off pl 7 Novembre, and the **cinema** opposite. There's an **ONA crafts shop** at 1 av Farhat Hached, a *Magasin Général* **supermarket** next door at no. 3, and a **night chemist** down the road, just past the *SNTRI* station.

Taxis leave from the Shell garage by pl de la Jeunesse, louages (to Medenine and Houmt Souk) from av Farhat Hached down on the right, opposite the *Hotel l'Olivier*. The *SRTG Medenine* bus station is just past the *louage* station, with seven buses a day up to the beach hotels (see below), two to Gabes, five to Houmt Souk, and four each to Medenine and Ben Gardane. Opposite is the *SNTRI* stop, with one daily bus a day starting here, and several passing through.

Market days in the souk are Mondays and Fridays, and there's a livestock market on Wednesdays at Mouansa, 5km out of town. On other days there is little of interest in Zarzis, although there is a small museum of traditional clothes and artefacts, currently closed for renovation, in rue de la Confédération du Grand Maghreb. Zarzis celebrates a sponge festival in the last week of July every year.

Accommodation in town

The hotels by the sea are all expensive and the ones in the town not too great.

Hôtel de la Station, av Farhat Hached (☎80661). By the *SNTRI* station. Very adequate rooms, many with bathroom. Probably the best deal in town. 3.5/7TD.

Youth Hostel/Maison des Jeunes, rue d'Algerie. The usual set-up. 4TD per person.

Hôtel Karim, off rue Hedi Chaker by pl de la Jeunesse (☎81009). Grubby but quite comfortable. 4/7TD.

Hôtel du Sud, 20 av Farhat Hached (☎81340). Reasonably clean and pleasant but ask for a room with an outside window. 5/8TD.

Hôtel Afif, av Mohamed V, on the Jerba road (☎81639). Friendly, clean and bright. 5.5/8TD low season, 6.5/10TD high.

Hôtel du Port, rue de la Confédération du Grand Maghreb (☎80777). On the road down to the port. 6/8TD low, 7/10TD high, b&b. There are also six-bed self-catering bungalows at 20TD low, 25TD high.

Hôtel l'Olivier, av Farhat Hached opposite the *SRTGM* bus station (☎80637). A homely sort of place. 7/10TD.

Hôtel de la Ville (aka Hôtel Medina), off av Farhat Hached (☎81861). The best in town. Rooms are big and airy and women have a separate loo. 11/14TD low, 15/18TD high, b&b.

Eating in Zarzis

There is a souk in the middle of the town, just inside whose entrance (opposite the *Shell* garage) is the best place to eat, the *Restaurant de Caravans*. Avoid the pricey *Palmier* on the other side of the square – possibly the worst place in Tunisia. Cheap eateries in av Farhat Hached include the *Restaurant des Pyramides* at no. 27, the *Restaurant Zarzis* by the *Hôtel l'Olivier* and the *Restaurant de la Station* next to the hotel of the same name: you can fill up for less than 3TD in all of them.

The tourist zone: beach hotels and seaside practicalities

Four kilometres north of town is the *zone touristique*, with three hotels known as the "les trois zeds".

Hôtel Zephir, the first you come to (☎81026/7/8). A 3* place, this caters for a mainly German crowd, who put up with some of the most relentless musak ever piped. 18/30TD low season, 33/52TD high, b&b.

Hôtel Zarzis, along the beach and round the headland. Also 3*(☎80160), this is a slightly classier joint than the *Zephir*, but its customers are also mainly German sun-seekers. 18/30TD low, 32/50TD high, b&b.

Hôtel Zita, just past the *Zarzis*, and a lower-key, 2* place that closes out of season (☎80246). 22/34TD b&b.

A new and cheaper hotel, the *Hôtel Er Rachid*, is being built and should be open by now. Nearby, the *Restaurant Boualya* claims to offer "Lebanese specialities" such as felafel or foul at 1TD a plate, but in fact specialises in hamburgers (0.8TD).

On the main road outside the hotels are the **car hire** offices of *Avis* (☎81706), by the entrance to the *Zephir*, and *Hertz* (☎80284) and *Interrent/Europcar* (☎80562) nearer the *Zarzis*. There are also **buses** and **taxis** into town, an ONTT **tourist office** (open if you're lucky), and a taxiphone office for **international calls** (8am–noon & 3–7pm daily).

The **beach** at the *zone touristique* has the best swimming in the Zarzis area, and the *Zarzis* and *Zita* have new pools, reputed to be the best in Tunisia. Barriers at the hotels' entrances prohibit roaming Tunisians, but tourists should be able to get in. There are good value watersports here: windsurfing at the *Zephir*, for example, is 3.5TD an hour.

Oamarit

Some 9km further north at **OAMARIT**, two "hotel clubs" aim to provide everything you need – fortunately, as they're in the middle of nowhere. The 3* *Hôtel Club Oamarit* (☎80770) (22.5/32TD low, 49/78TD high, b&b) has just about all the **sports** facilities you could want including a body-building centre (5TD a session), waterskiing (7TD a tow), parascending (10TD) and wetbikes (10TD/15min). If you're not staying, you can eat in the restaurant (pizzas 2.5TD) and use all of these – but remember not to go swimming on a full stomach. The *Oamarit* also boasts a "semi-Olympic swimming pool with its basin for children" and "various restorative services" intriguingly available from reception. You can hire a car from *Budget* or *Express* inside the hotel, or *Mattei* (☎81266) just outside. The 3* *Sangho Club* next door (☎80124) is more *Club Med* in style and altogether more exclusive than the *Oamarit*, although slightly cheaper (33/ 47TD low, 52.5/89TD high, FB only).

East of Zarzis

The road south towards Ben Gardane (there are buses and regular *louages*) skirts the **Sebkhet el Mellah**, a large salt flat which used to be the site of a mustard gas factory during World War I and today contains a massive salt mine. From CHABAKA a path leads along the coast to the old Turkish fort, **Borj el Biban**, right at the end of a spit that once marked the border with Libya. The fort is now in a sad state of disrepair, but the views along the deserted beach are real tourist brochure stuff.

Ben Gardane

The only attraction at **BEN GARDANE**, the end of the route, is its Saturday **market** – very lively and far more agricultural than others in the south. Off the beaten track for many years, it is the last main town before the Libyan frontier, and now a staging post on the route to Libya. If you have to stay here, there are four hotels in town, although the largest, the *Pavilions Verts*, is now closed. The others, spread out down the main road, include the *Hôtel el Ouns* (☎65920), the *Alger* (☎65279), the *el Amen* and the *Essada*. There are also two **banks**, a **PTT** and a *Grand Magasin* supermarket.

SNTRI run two **buses** a day to Tunis. There are several others to Medenine, Tataouine, Zarzis and Houmt Souk, plus regular shuttles to the Libyan frontier. **Louages** run to Medenine, Zarzis, and Ras Ajdir.

Onward to Libya

If you're striking out for **Libya***, the Tunisian frontier post is at **RAS AJDIR**, 33km east of Ben Gardane, but you'll encounter several police checks on the way. At Ras Ajdir, the prevailing atmosphere is one of complete chaos as you get out of your vehicle to go through the various **formalities**, which include filling out a departure card and getting your passport stamped. There are 24-hour **exchange facilities**, but you

---

* For further information about Libya, see p.382.

should avoid using them unless desperate (apart from the queues, the rates are bad and they may decide on a whim not to change travellers' cheques).

Buying Libyan dinars is quite easy on the road to the frontier. Money changers line the road all the way from Medenine waving their wads of bills at passing cars. Ascertain the going rate before you start haggling (it's usually about three times the official rate). Remember that it is officially illegal to import or export Tunisian currency in Tunisia, or to import Libyan currency in Libya.

There are always plenty of vehicles at the border, and you should have no difficulty finding **transport** to Tripoli, 196km away. Note that *louages* in Libya are called *taxi binasser*, or service taxis. Once over the border, the first thing you notice will probably be the improved state of the roads. At present there is no customs or immigration on the Libyan side and the police check your passport further along the road. If the cross-border tourist traffic grows, this is likely to change.

travel details

Buses and louages
FROM HOUMT SOUK TO:

Tunis (3 daily, 8–10hr); **Bizerte** (2, 10hr); **Sousse** (1, 6hr 45min); **Kairouan** (2, 7hr); **Sfax** (2, 4hr 45min); **Gabes** (6, 2hr 30min); **Medenine** (4, 2hr); **Tataouine** (2, 3hr); **Zarzis** (5, 1hr); **Ben Gardane** (2, 2hr).
Louages to **Tunis**, **Gabes**, **Zarzis** and **Medenine** (none to places on Jerba).

FROM ZARZIS TO:

Tunis (2, 9hr); **Medenine** (4, 1hr); **Houmt Souk** (5, 1hr); **Ben Gardane** (4,1hr); **Gabes** (2, 2hr).
Louages to **Houmt Souk** and **Medenine**.

FROM BEN GARDANE TO:

Tunis (2, 9hr 30min); **Zarzis** (4, 1hr); **Houmt Souk** (2, 2hr); **Medenine** (3, 1hr); **Tataouine** (1, 2hr); **Ras Ajdir/Libyan frontier** (regular shuttle, 40min).
Louages to **Medenine**, **Zarzis** and **Ras Ajdir**.

FROM RAS AJDIR TO:

Tripoli (frequent, 4hr); **Tunis** (daily, around 4pm, 10hr), but it might be faster to do the run by *louage* in stages, rather than wait for the bus.
You should have no difficulty finding **transport** to **Ben Gardane** and thence to **Medenine**, **Zarzis**, **Gabes** or **Sfax**.

Ferries
FROM JORF TO:

Ajim and back (service every half-hour, dropping to every hour or two at night).

Flights
FROM JERBA TO:

Tunis (daily, or more frequent, 45min–2hr 10min, some via **Tozeur**, 40min); **Monastir** (twice a week, 40min). Current fares to Tunis: 23.6TD one-way, 37TD midweek return, or 46TD weekend return, cash only. One or more flights weekly on *Tunis Air* to **Brussels, Frankfurt, Geneva, Lyon, Marseille, Paris, Zurich**; *Air France* to **Paris**.

PHONE CODES

The code for the whole region is ☎05

CHAPTER NINE

THE KSOUR

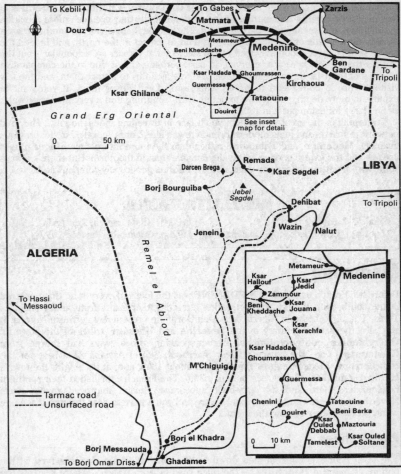

O f all Tunisia, the **South**, the region that dips down towards the border with Libya and Algeria, is the most exciting and the most remote. It has long been this way: in the Middle Ages, Arab travellers avoided the region because the tribes were notorious for their lawlessness and banditry. It was a reputation that passed on to later generations, for during the eighteenth and nineteenth centuries few

European travellers entered the region, and only three are known to have visited **Medenine**, still the largest and most important town of the area. Even the intrepid James Bruce, who went on to discover the source of the Nile, preferred to take the boat from Gabes rather than risk his neck with these tribes. When the French army invaded in 1881 they too gave the region a wide berth; it was many years before it was fully integrated, and it remained under military administration until 1956.

With their steep escarpments, the south's arid mountains are impressive in themselves, but even more striking are the **ksour** (*ksar* in the singular), the fortified communal granaries, and the mountain villages of **Douiret**, **Chenini**, and **Guermessa** that they hide. Strange and extraordinary as monuments, they are even more remarkable as living settlements in so barren a land. The people themselves are another reason to visit: there's little of the hassle that you tend to expect in the north, and indeed the coolness of your reception may lead you to suspect that visitors are unpopular – but the truth is that people here are reserved. In part, perhaps, this is due to the comparative absence of tourists: there are few hotels and few facilities to attract them, and the few visitors who do come tend to be on whistlestop Land Rover tours. If you want to explore in more depth, you'll have to put up with "roughing it in a very moderate way", as Sir Harry Johnston put it in 1892.

Transport is the greatest problem you'll face in travelling independently. The road network is sparse, and joins modern French towns like **Zarzis** (covered in the previous chapter), **Medenine**, and **Tataouine** rather than the more interesting villages. Buses are few and the *louage* service is less dependable than in the north. But there's always some way of getting where you want, and the effort is generously compensated.

MARKET DAYS

Monday – Tataouine	Friday – Ghoumrassen, Ksar Jedid
Thursday – Beni Kheddache, Tataouine	Sunday – Medenine, Remada

Medenine

Before the French occupation, **MEDENINE** was the focus of everything that mattered in the south, with a huge weekly market attracting merchants from as far afield as Tunis, Tripoli, Tebessa in Algeria, and even Bornu, in present-day northern Nigeria. It was also the central granary of the **Touazine** and **Khezour**, tribes of the powerful **Ouerghamma confederation** of Berber-speaking tribes, who had moved from Ghoumrassen on the advice of their marabout, Sidi el Assaibi. As a base for the confederation, Medenine grew rapidly from about 1800, and, at its height, the town's *ksar* had some 8000 *ghorfas* (see box on p.300). The French established their southern headquarters here and its jerry-built appearance hasn't improved much since. Nevertheless the town is the regional centre and you'll have to pass through it at some point, probably even staying the night.

Practicalities

The town centre is concentrated down by the *oued* at **Place des Martyrs**, at the bottom of **Avenue Bourguiba** – the main road in from Gabes – where it meets the Tataouine road (av 2 Mai), the Jorf road and the road to Ben Gardane (av Abdel Hamid el Kadhi). About 100m towards Jorf is the town's **main roundabout**. From here, **Rue des Palmiers** continues on to Jorf and **Rue 18 Janvier** heads uphill past the **bus and louage stations** to join up with av Bourguiba. Off av Bourguiba, just above this

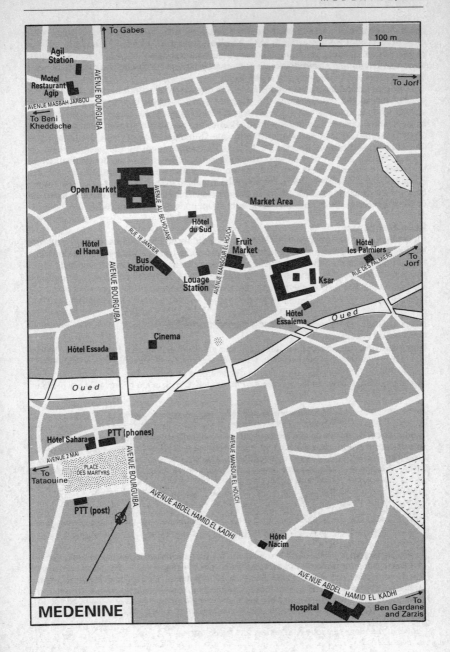

junction, is an open market, built by the French in 1912; but it's a low-key affair with most of its produce going straight to Gabes. The main **market area** is the other side of av Mansour el Houch, including a covered fruit market at no. 64, which leads through to a more traditional street market in the area up behind the **ksar**. Souk day is Sunday but there are stalls out every day of the week.

Other practical matters: the PTT is on pl des Martyrs, its postal section (open city hours) across the square from the **phones** section (open country hours). To call abroad when it's closed, ask at the *tabac* just fifty metres up the Tataouine road past the *Hôtel Sahara* (it's open daily 7am–9pm). **Banks** are mostly by the main roundabout or on av Bourguiba up above its junction with rue 18 Janvier. One of them should be open on Saturday and Sunday mornings. There's a **cinema** down by the *oued* between av Bourguiba and rue 18 Janvier, and **hammams** the other side of av Bourguiba just by the *oued* (men 5am–noon and 6pm–midnight; women 1–6pm), and at 26 rue des Palmiers (similar hours). Lastly, for essential supplies, there's a *Grand Magasin* **super-market** at 18 av Bourguiba, and a **night chemist** further up at no. 46. The **hospital** (☎40830) is on the Ben Gardane road, about 400m up from pl des Martyrs.

Accommodation

Medenine's hotels are generally lousy: nothing even approaches luxury, and the budget places tend to be dingier than usual (and some have no phone). If you don't like the look of any of the following, the closest alternative is at Metameur (see p.301).

Hôtel les Palmiers, rue des Palmiers, 50m past the *ksar* (☎40592). Clean rooms, hot water and overall the best deal among the cheapies. 2.5TD per person.

Hôtel Essada, 87 av Bourguiba (☎40300). Rather spartan, not especially friendly and few rooms have outside windows. 3TD per person.

Hôtel el Hana, av Bourguiba (☎46190). Up past the *Essada*. Rather stuffy, but okay for one night. 3.5TD per person.

Hôtel du Sud, rue Abderrahim Ibn Khaldoun, off av Ali Belhouane. Basic and not recommended for women. 3TD per person in a shared room, or 8TD for a room with a double bed.

Youth Hostel/Maison des Jeunes, rue des Palmiers (☎40338). Unsign-posted, in a group of white buildings about 500m past the *ksar* on the left. Check-in after 5pm. 4TD per person.

GHORFAS, KALA'A AND KSOUR

Throughout the south people stored their grain in **ghorfas**, small stone cells (the Arabic word means room – you ask for a *ghorfa* in a hotel) a couple of metres high and five to ten metres long. The cells were generally constructed on top of one another and side by side, at times reaching to eight storeys. Individual units were always built in the same way: grain sacks filled with earth were placed between the two side walls to act as a support during the construction of the roof. A layer of matting was placed over the top of these sacks, in the form of an arch, and then covered with clay, mortar and gypsum. When the plaster had dried, the clay was chipped away, the net removed and a palm door fitted at the front. The rough inner walls were covered with plaster, usually with stucco figures such as handprints or fish to ward off the evil eye, sometimes with inscriptions or geometrical patterns.

In the first years of the Arab invasion, the Berbers retreated inland to the high mountain tops, building **forts** (or *kala'a*) near their cave dwellings. Once the Arabs had occupied the fertile land the Berbers were forced into peace treaties and the *kala'a* was replaced by the **ksour** (singular: *ksar*), fortified granaries belonging to each tribe. The outer defensive wall consisted of the back of these *ghorfas*, presenting a blank facade to the would-be assailant. The **shape of the perimeter** was dictated by the site, whether along a hilltop, as at Ksar Jouama, on a hillside as at Ksar Ouled Soltane, for example, or down in the more spacious river valley, like Medenine.

Hôtel Essalema, 85 rue des Palmiers. Opposite the *ksar*: get a room with a view over it. 5TD per person.

Hôtel Nacim, av Abdel Hamid el Kadhi, the Ben Gardane road (☎41563). The rooms are clean but bare with shared showers in the loo. Overpriced at 8TD per room.

Hôtel Sahara, rue 2 Mai, next to the PTT phone office (☎40007). Clean and friendly and the nearest thing to luxury in Medenine. Small rooms, but more spacious accommodation is being added on the top floor. 9/12TD b&b, or HB and FB options if you're staying longer.

Motel Restaurant Agip, av Bourguiba (☎40151). Next to the *Agil* (sic) filling station at the top of av Bourguiba. A 2* place, recently closed for renovation but, if it reopens, air-conditioned and rather more expensive than the *Sahara*.

Food and drink

Medenine is not exactly for gourmands, and even **cheap eateries** are thin on the ground. Probably the best of them is the *Restaurant Malouf* on av Bourguiba up by the *Banque du Sud*, and the *Restaurant Carthage* opposite the bus station in rue 18 Janvier will also plug a gap for around 3TD. In the same price range, you could try the *Chez Habib* or the *Restaurant Paris*, on av Bourguiba at no. 35 and 85 respectively. Your only option for more **refined meals** is the *Hôtel Sahara*.

The ksar

Sadly, Medenine's **ksar** has gradually been demolished since the beginning of the century when the tribes began to store their grain in silos near the fields rather than carry it all the way into town. One large courtyard remains, right in town on the rue des Palmiers. With its *ghorfas* converted into curio shops, coachloads of holiday-makers are bused in to look at it (nearby cafés double their prices for anyone looking remotely like a tourist). There are some more *ghorfas* behind it, mainly abandoned, but up to three storeys high and giving a much better idea of the original construction. On the whole, the *ksar* is a disappointment, but it forms an introduction to those to the west and further south, which, although originally far smaller, are much better preserved.

Moving on

Bus and louage stations face each other about halfway up rue 18 Janvier. **Buses** head for Tunis three times in the morning and once overnight and there are also regular services for Tataouine, Gabes, Sfax, Houmt Souk (Jerba) and Zarzis. There are three daily buses to Ben Gardane, one of which continues to the Libyan frontier at Ras Ajdir (en route, at the Zarzis turn-off, look out for the signpost to "Cairo 2,591km").

Local services include several daily to Beni Kaddeche, Ghoumrassen and Metameur. Most of these destinations are also served by **louages**: remember a group of four or five may find it economical to negotiate a deal with a *louage* driver for a day-trip round some of the *ksour*.

Metameur

The 600-year-old **ksar** of METAMEUR has a dramatic silhouette, standing isolated in the plain. Though quite small, with three courtyards and *ghorfas* that reach only three storeys, it's remarkably well preserved and hasn't been converted wholesale to tourist use. It's a short bus ride 6km along the Medenine–Gabes road or an easy enough hitch from the top of av Bourguiba in Medenine to the turn-off (1km walk to the village).

The village was founded around the thirteenth century by a local marabout, **Sidi Ahmed ben Adjel**, who set up shop in a cave, and the local nomads who followed him. Today the village is still occupied by Sidi Ahmed's descendants, the **Temara**, and the descendants of his followers, the nominally Berber **Harraza**. At one time each Harraza family paid their Arab Temara masters in wheat, barley, oil and the much-prized local wood. In autumn and winter the *ksar* is barely used by the Temara and Harraza tribes-people as they're out in the plains with their herds: the *ksar* is at its busiest in summer. The **mosque of Sidi Ahmed Ben Adjel**, housing the saint's tomb, also draws a congregation on Fridays, mostly nomads from the surrounding pastures.

Practicalities

The best preserved of the *ksar*'s courtyards is now the *Hôtel les Ghorfas* (☎40294) where (for 5TD per person b&b, or 8TD HB) you can stay in a *ghorfa* and still enjoy such modern luxuries as tea and hot running water. The owner is very knowledgeable about local culture, and happy to converse on the subject for as long as you let him. In winter it's a good idea to arrive early as he sometimes gives up and goes home around nightfall if there are no customers.

When you're ready for **moving on**, apart from the **bus** back to Medenine, you could head north by walking up to the main road and seeing what will stop for you (a bus isn't necessarily more likely to do this than a private car). There's also a piste from Metameur to TOUJANE and MATMATA, 56km west, which you could try hitching down – but you'll need luck on your side. You can no doubt cover the piste in a hired car without four-wheel-drive, but progress is slow, and it's faster (and probably safer) to go the long way round via Gabes.

South of Medenine: over the Jebel Haouia

Although there's a main road (P19) south from Medenine straight to Tataouine, it goes through the plain on a route that's uniformly dull. A spectacular alternative is to make a detour to the west via **Ksar Jouama** and **Beni Kheddache**, straight through the rugged mountains of **Jebel Haouia**, where the most impressive of the *ksour* sit perched on mountain spurs.

If you plan on doing this, take note that it's not easy: **public transport**, and asphalt, run southwest from Medenine as far as Beni Kheddache, and strike north from Tataouine up to Ksar Hadada, but making the connection between the two roads, if you don't have your own wheels, involves hitching the 22km of dirt track which link Beni Kheddache with Ksar Hadada. As the easiest way to get to Ksar Hadada is therefore from the *south* – from TATAOUINE – that part of the Jebel Haouia is covered in detail later in the chapter, on p.308.

Medenine to Beni Kheddache

Three minibuses daily run up the road from Medenine to Ksar Jouama and Beni Kheddache, but if you don't happen to coincide, you could try hitching: start in av Masbah Jarbou (left off av Bourguiba up at the top of the hill by the *Agil* station).

After you leave Medenine the minibus stops briefly at **KSAR JEDID** ("New Ksar"), built in the 1890s when the security imposed by the French army allowed the mountain tribes to store their grain safely in the plains. It was the first stage in the process of abandonment for, within thirty years, the tribes had stopped using *ksour* altogether, keeping their grain in unprotected silos near the fields.

Ksar Jouama

From Ksar Jedid the road climbs the escarpment to **KSAR JOUAMA** and the modern village. The *ksar* is just visible on the crest of a steep hill to the right, and there's a path from the road, a little walk back from the bus stop and village shop, which leads past a deserted mosque to the bottleneck of the *ksar* and its entrance gate. An inscription gives its Islamic date as 1174 (1764 AD), but the *ksar* was almost certainly here before then. Decades of disuse have taken their toll – the outer wall is now crumbling and some of the *ghorfas* have collapsed – but it still makes a strong impression.

If you've taken an early bus, it's possible to stop off at Ksar Jouama and catch the next one – if you can catch the driver's attention. Or try hitching – it's a busy road.

Beni Kheddache

BENI KHEDDACHE is 11km further, a large village that used to be another mountain *ksar*. Reginald Rankin, who came here in the 1890s, described it as "a sort of Saharan Windsor" with walls sixty feet high and a hundred yards long and a courtyard covering twenty thousand square yards. Unfortunately it was demolished by the French, just before the last war, to make way for a market. However, a few *ghorfas* survive behind the mosque, whilst the *ksar* has become a settlement – a village and market centre for the surrounding tribes. Souk day is Thursday.

There are no hotels in Beni Kheddache, though in cases of severe hunger there is a **restaurant** opposite the mosque serving cheap, unappetising set meals. So you'll want to leave before long: if you don't have your own **transport**, the last bus back to Medenine goes about 6pm. There are also *louages* and pick-ups to Medenine and Ksar Hallouf, but none south to Ksar Hadada. You could try **hitching** down there, but start early as the road is very quiet. The road way out west to KSAR GHILANE (see p.313) is pretty well impossible to go down unless you have your own four-wheel-drive vehicle.

Back to Ksar Jedid via Zammour and Ksar Hallouf

An alternative route back from Beni Kheddache to Medenine (or a detour if you prefer) heads north over 2km of tarmac to **ZAMMOUR**, where a track to the right leads up to the *ksar*. Small and largely ruined, it compensates with great views.

Beyond Zammour, 12km of piste brings you to **HALLOUF**, a small thirteenth-century *ksar* overlooking a fertile valley, itself overlooked by a ruined *kala'a*. It's worth climbing up for the views of the plain, with Jerba visible in the hazy distance. In the *ksar*, there's now a **Relai** (☎47037) where you can spend the night in a *ghorfa* for 6TD b&b or 8TD HB. Sleeping conditions are a bit basic at present, but should improve as it gets going properly. If you don't want to stay there, you could just stop off for a 3.5TD couscous dinner.

Pick-ups run a shuttle service to Beni Kheddache and there's a Land Rover which stops in Hallouf on its way between Beni Kheddache and Medenine. The piste from Zammour to Hallouf is passable in a normal two-wheel-drive car, and continues for another 8km to BHAIRA, where it meets the paved road to Ksar Jedid and Medenine.

The Jebel Haouia and Ksar Kerachfa

The road south over the plateau – towards Tataouine via Ksar Hadada and Ghoumrassen – turns off the Medenine road just outside Beni Kheddache. Unsurfaced beyond the first kilometre (though passable, with care, in any ordinary car) it winds across the hillocky plateau of the **Jebel Haouia**, through dense plantations of olive and figs that use the same *jessour* technology as Matmata (see p.269). General Jamais, commanding a punitive expedition into the region in 1883, called it "a true paradise in the desolation of the south", and the contrast with the desert plains is, indeed, staggering.

The plateau is the home of the **Haouia**, intractable enemies of the French. Part of the Ouerghamma confederation, they are one of the few communities who still practise **transhumance**, the seasonal movement from pastures in the desert to the coastal plain. In the winter months they camp in the plain or in the *Dahar* (the arid plateau to the west of the mountains), returning to their fields in summer for the fig and olive

harvests. Since the beginning of the century, however, the Haouia have abandoned
their *ksour* and now live in scattered houses and cave dwellings among their fields.

Ksar Kerachfa
One of the most impressive of the old *ksour*, **KERACHFA**, can be reached along a turning to the left (east) 10km down the road from Beni Kheddache. After looping 4km
down a rugged, winding track you turn a corner to be faced by a ruin of startlingly
gothic appearance on a spur overlooking the plain. Most of the *ghorfa* have collapsed,
but outside the main gate is a fitfully used **underground mosque**. Follow a path
around the spur and you come to two abandoned oil presses, still in good repair.

Back on the main track, you continue south over the plateau and, crawling along an
appalling surface, eventually sight the white minaret of KSAR HADADA (see p.310)
and regain the tarmac.

Tataouine (Foum Tataouine)

FOUM TATAOUINE – the full Berber name means "the mouth of the springs" –
evokes an image of the desert outpost, a palm oasis surrounded by drifting sand. This,
at any rate, is the tourist blurb's pitch. Reality is rather different, for the town is new,
busy and drab, built by the French administrators on an empty site. Yet though it has
nothing of historic interest in itself, within a radius of 25km are some of the most
impressive sites in Tunisia. Tataouine, with Tunisia's southernmost hotels and banks,
is more of a base for exploration than Medenine, with enough accessible goals to its
north and west (**Ghoumrassen, Guermessa, Ksar Hadada, Chenini** and **Douiret**)
to fill a week or more, while to the southeast of the town there are interesting *ksour*
within walking distance, and further south the well-preserved *ksar* of **Ouled Soltane**.
Tataouine itself, despite its lack of any historic depth, has a certain inexplicable charm
– don't be surprised if you find yourself making up excuses to delay leaving. In April
the **Festival of the Ksour** enlivens the town, in pale imitation of Douz's Saharan
Festival, with "traditional marriages" and a "pop concert".

Arms and trade
Tataouine was built as the far south's administrative centre and **garrison town** and
the military presence is still strong. As late as 1950 the soldiers outnumbered the 300-
odd civilians by three to one. Most of these troops were members of a penal battalion
of the French army and the French Foreign Legion, and for the most part they were
German. Indeed in the 1930s German was the town's third language.

The town's other function was as a **market centre**. At the turn of the century the
French had great expectations of this market as the focus of Saharan trade. It was not
to be: trade had already dwindled and what was left passed through Tripoli, where
ivory and gold could be sold openly. In 1896, commerce dried up completely after a
French nobleman, the Marquis de Morès, was killed by Tuaregs while gun-running for
the Mahdi's forces holding out against British imperialism in Sudan.

Tataouine's modern **marketplace**, off av Bourguiba in pl Ali Belhouane, is lively,
and it's worth trying to coincide with the souk held on Mondays and Thursdays. The
Place fills with merchants from all over the south buying sheep, in the early summer,
olives, in the autumn, and locally made blankets at any time. Other merchants, mainly
from Jerba, sell groceries and dubious plastic knicknacks. It's always very colourful,
with tribespeople coming in from distant villages and nomadic encampments, and
peddlers stocking up with the goods they sell from their camels' backs to people in the
remotest communities.

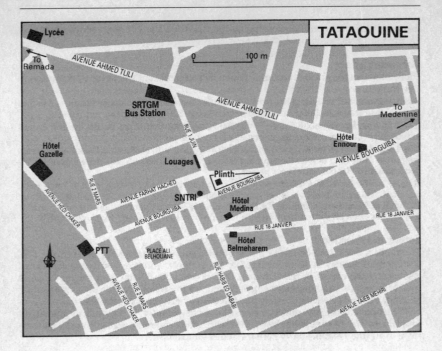

Practicalities: orientation, accommodation and eating

Tataouine's main street, **Avenue Bourguiba**, is a continuation of the main road from Medenine. About halfway down it stood a statue of Habib Bourguiba, but this has now been removed and only the **plinth** is left. It remains to be seen how many other Tunisian towns will follow Tataouine's example and – anti-Stalin-style – start pulling down statues of the supreme combattant. In the meantime, don't expect to see any signs indicating the street's name – it will probably change to Avenue 7 Novembre. Some 300m towards Medenine from the plinth, the **Remada road** (av Ahmed Tlili) branches off left. In the other direction, av Bourguiba finishes at **Avenue Hedi Chaker** in front of the **PTT**. A right here takes you down to the Remada road, passing a number of miliatary camps whose personnnel can be suspicious of tourists and don't take kindly to people climbing up on the rocks behind for the view – which also gives you a vantage point over the camps.

Practical details

International phone calls can be made from the PTT or from taxiphone offices nearby at 5 av Bourguiba, and at the other end of av Bourguiba, opposite the *Hôtel Ennour* (both open daily 8am–8pm). There are several **banks** in town, a couple of **cinemas** and a clutch of **hammams.** Two of these are near the bus station: one directly opposite it on the Remada road, only for men (5am–6pm) and the other down a side street by the *Mobil* station a few doors away: bear left after twenty metres and it's at the end of the street (4am–9pm for both sexes; separate entrances). For supplies, the *Grand Magasin* **supermarket** is by the market in pl Ali Belhouane, and there's also a **night chemist** at 2 av Bourguiba, opposite the PTT. For more serious matters, the **hospital** is in rue Pasteur (☎60114).

Accommodation

There isn't a huge choice of accommodation in Tataouine, but what's on offer is reasonable enough.

Hôtel Ennour, 107 av Bourguiba (☎60131). Stuffy rooms, few with outside windows. On the grotty side of adequate, but the cheapest place in town. 2.5TD per person.

Hôtel Belmeharem, pl 18 Janvier (☎60104). Charming staff make up for the somewhat rudimentary rooms and sporadic hot water. 3TD per person.

Hôtel Medina, pl 18 Janvier (☎60999). A gem of a place, with staff as bright and pleasant as the rooms. Hot water only in the morning (shower early or shower cold) is a small sacrifice. Recommended and only 3.5TD per person.

Hôtel Gazelle, av Hedi Chaker (☎60009). Phone ahead or arrive early as it is often fully occupied by tour groups. This is not only Tataouine's top address, but also the base hotel of the hotel at Ksar Hadada and the *Relai* at Chenini, so you can enquire about them here and maybe even get a lift out to Chenini if you coincide with staff transport. 2* 13/19TD b&b.

Eating and drinking

There are a few cheap eateries on and off av Bourguiba and av Farhat Hached. The *Restaurant Ennacim* at 49 av Bourguiba, for example, and the *Restaurant des Jeunes* just around the corner in rue Habib ed Dababi will both fill you up for under 3TD. If you really want something more sophisticated, try the *Hôtel Gazelle*'s set menu for not much more. The *Gazelle* is the only place in town where you can get a beer.

A Tataouine speciality, now common all over the country, is the **kab el ghezal**, or *corne de gazelle*, a sweet pastry horn filled with honey and nuts, available at any patisserie in town (the *Palestine* on av Farhat Hached for example).

Moving on: Tataouine transport details

Buses operated by *SRTG Medenine* run from the bus station 200m down the Remada road and only a couple of blocks away from the empty plinth in av Bourguiba. From here, there are five departures daily to Medenine (the last at about 2.30pm) with limited continuation services to Gabes, Ben Gardane and Houmt Souk (Jerba). There is now only one bus a day down to Remada and the Libyan frontier at Dehibat. *SNTRI*'s office is at 67 av Bourguiba and two buses a day leave for Tunis from across the road by the plinth – one morning and one evening. **Local bus services** run several times a day to Ghoumrassen, Ksar Ouled Debbab and Maztouria, but it's better to pick up the latter at the *lycée* (100m west and across the street), as the driver usually turns the bus there without taking it into the terminal.

Louages park between the two bus companies in rue 1 Juin (off av Bourguiba by the plinth). Medenine and Ghoumrassen are the obvious destinations, but you'll also find vehicles to Remada and Dehibat, and direct to Tunis.

There are also **pick-ups** and Peugeots around the region to be found in rue Hammadi Khdir, the street opposite the *Cafe PTT* (22 av Bourguiba) and around the corner in av Farhat Hached. These are cheap but tend to dry up after **midday**, so set out early. And, as in Medenine, if there are three or four of you, you may want to negotiate a deal with a **taxi** to one or more of the local *ksour* and Berber villages (try a *louage* if there are five in your group). Taxis can usually be found in pl 18 January or near the *louages*. Expect to pay around 5–8TD each way to places like Chenini, Douiret and Guermessa, plus around 5TD an hour for the driver to wait while you look around.

Alternatively, you could **hitch** out to the villages from the Remada road, or walk or take a bus to the appropriate turn-off and hitch from there.

Ksar Ouled Soltane and the Jebel Abiadh

To the east and south of Tataouine stretches the mountain range of **Jebel Abiadh**, home of the most powerful tribe in the south, the **Ouderna**, part of the Ouerghamma confederation, and of several smaller **Berber** communities. Though their *ksour* and villages litter the mountains, the sites aren't as dramatic as Douiret and Chenini to the west of Tataouine (see p.310); even so, they're still pretty impressive, and have the great advantage of being free of tourist parties.

The Berbers living in these mountains lacked the independence enjoyed by the larger communities at Douiret, Chenini, and Guermessa. Most shared their village with semi-nomadic groups who claimed Arab origins, or else the village was closely linked to a neighbouring nomadic tribe's *ksar*. French anthropologists used to maintain that the Ouderna, the dominant tribe, had Berber serfs who paid them olives, figs, and wool in return for "protection". It was, they claimed, "a veritable slavery such that the Ouderna can spill the blood of his Berber client without fear of the law". This was fantasy: in reality there were bonds between the nomads ("Arab") and the sedentary villagers ("Berber"), but these represented an exchange of services; in return for agricultural produce the nomad guarded a sedentary neighbour's herd, gaining access to widely dispersed pastures without the trouble of a lifestyle on the move.

Ksour near town

KSAR MEGALBA is the easiest to reach of these *ksour*. Just head down the Remada road for about a kilometre and then turn right, cross the *oued* and head up towards the mosque straight ahead. It's well preserved, with three-storeyed *ghorfas* and the remains of storage racks and broken pottery. From the smell and the look of the place, however, most visitors have left their mark.

There's another *ksar* on a hill to the left of the Remada road, opposite the turn-off – one of a number called KSAR DEGHAGHORA – but it overlooks a military camp of some sort and they don't like you up there, especially not with a camera.

Just south of Ksar Deghaghora, a paved road to the left (east), sign-posted BENI BARKA, takes you up into the Jebel Abiadh – "White Mountains" – proper. This road passes a large number of *ksour* in varying states of repair, though you'd need to be a serious *ksar* enthusiast to want to visit all of them. The first is **KSAR GURGA**, on your right after 1km, wonderful and deserted, and still within walking distance of Tataouine.

Beni Barka

After another 4km, you'll be able to see the village of **BENI BARKA**, also on your right, pitched atop the escarpment as you approach along the valley floor. You'll have to stop the bus and walk up the steep track to the top. Formerly an important market, the centre of a thriving Berber community linked to the Arab community of Ksar Ouled Debbab, most of it is now in ruins: even so, the entrance gate, dating from the fourteenth century or before, is still spectacular, standing on the very edge of the cliff and offering good views across the plain. The village has been deserted in favour of the many new cave-dwellings in the surrounding slopes, some of them excavated eight metres into the rock. As you walk up to the old village, look out for ripple marks in the rocks and fossils of ammonites and sea molluscs, proof that this area has not always been desert.

Around Maztouria – Abandoned Ksour

The road now passes a number of desolate *ksour*. KSAR ZOLTANE is up on the right, about 1km past Beni Barka. A couple of kilometres further, a road branching off left takes you to KSAR TOUNKET. And 7km beyond Beni Barka is the new village of **MAZTOURIA**, where many of the surrounding people have settled near a spring.

Ksar Kedim

As you enter Maztouria town, you pass two more abandoned *ksour* (KSAR OULED AOUN and KSAR AOUADAD) up on your right. More interesting is **KSAR KEDIM** (or Ksar Zenetes), also on the right overlooking Maztouria. According to an inscription, it was built in 1091 AD, shortly after the Hilalian invasion, and is usually ascribed to the Zenetes, the Berber ancestors of the region's tribes. Its huge stone gateway and outer wall are quite unlike the other *ksour*, more like a fortress in appearance. Also unique is the **underground well**, reached by a tunnel. Ksar Kedim is currently being restored, which may not bode well for its survival outside the needs of the tour operators. Beyond it, and also on the right, the next *ksar* is called KSAR DAHAR (known also as Ksar Deghaghora).

Transport in the Jebel Abiadh

Maztouria is the transport focus for the district and the terminus of **bus** services, with five a day to Tataouine (the last around 7pm). If you're coming from Tataouine, you pick up the bus outside the lycée. After midday, Maztouria is also the furthest any pick-up will go, but there's enough traffic on the road to make **hitching** easy. A baker's van goes most days from Maztouria to Ksar Ouled Soltane, and has room for a couple of people. It leaves at around 9am and can take you beyond Ksar Ouled Soltane to a scattered desert settlement with a small shop and a well: it's even possible the villagers here may allow you to sleep in the local school.

Tamelest

From Maztouria, the route continues to the village of **TAMELEST** (6km), also built to settle the region's nomads. Overlooking the village is the *ksar* of the same name, the thirteenth-century granary of the Ouled Chehida, the Ouderna's most powerful group. In 1915 their *sheikh* led the only full-scale tribal revolt against the French. Although they managed to overwhelm the telegraph stations in the south, the French garrisons held out and within a month the Ouderna were defeated by a column from the north, and forced into Libya as refugees. Much of the damage done to this *ksar*, and others in the Jebel Abiadh, dates from this period.

Ksar Ouled Soltane

The road splits 2km beyond Tamelest, where the left fork leads, in 3km, to **KSAR OULED SOLTANE**. You may have to walk most of the way, although people do occasinally get lifts. It should be easier on a Friday, though you may be lucky any day: Monday and Thursday mornings pick-ups and other vehicles drive down to Tataouine for the souk and come back early afternoon.

The *ksar* at the end of the road is the best preserved in the south, with the outer wall still intact. Ksar Ouled Soltane was built by the Ouled Chehida (the Ouled Soltane are a lineage of that group) on low land where it can be seen for miles around, a tribute to their confidence in those troubled times. To get to the entrance, walk around the top of the hill, past the mosque and next to the shops and café. The two courtyards inside (one fifteenth and the other early nineteenth century) are connected by a passage made from palm wood. *Ghorfas* rise four storeys high and are still used to store grain and olives. On Friday afternoons the courtyards function as meeting places for the community, the majority of whom spend most of the year out in the pastures with their herds of sheep, goats, and camels. Thus, not only is the *ksar* intact but so is the way of life that goes with it. The explanation for this situation, unique in the south, lies in the Ouled Chehida's reluctance to migrate to the cities along with the *ksar*'s continued isolation from mass tourism. It's a community with a strong identity and a traditional lifestyle, one of the few left in Tunisia.

Ghoumrassen and Beyond

The P207 road north to **Ghoumrassen** begins 2km south of Tataouine, on the Remada road (1km past the Beni Barka turn-off). This is the "back" route to Medenine via **the Jebel Haouia** and **Beni Kheddache** (see p.302) and the easiest way to get to **Ksar Hadada** – where the asphalt ends. You also need this road, initially, for **Guermessa** and **Chenini**, two of the the area's ruggedly scenic, traditional Berber villages (the other is **Douiret**, covered on p.311–313).

Ghoumrassen

After turning off the Tataouine–Remada road, you branch right after 3km (the left fork goes to Chenini). Some 12km beyond the fork, the road passes the large but unimpressive KSAR EL FERICH, whose two storeys of *ghorfas* lie flat on the plain and are still in use. The guard posted there is happy to show people around.

GHOUMRASSEN, squeezed into a sharp-sided valley, 8km further north, is an ancient settlement: French officers found traces of a Roman fort nearby, with inscriptions now lost in a museum somewhere. In the fourteenth century, the historian El Tijani, accompanying the Hafsid ruler of Tunis on the *haj*, stopped at Ghoumrassen for three months. He describes a community at war with its Arab neighbours, living in the shelter of a fortress, the Kala'a Hamdoun, in caverns within the rock.

The *kala'a* has now gone, its site marked only by a thin wall, a path cut into the side of the spur overlooking the main part of the town and the white tomb of the marabout Sidi Moussa Ben Abdallah (the near-legendary figure who united the Ouerghamma). But the cave dwellings, the **ghar**, remain, cut into the softer strata at the base of the spur. Most consist of a single room, a cooking area (near the front) and a raised living quarter behind, but some of the larger *ghar* have several rooms separated by massive pillars of stone. A walled courtyard called a *houch* at the front provides a private living area; the outer wall is usually a raised *ghorfa* used for storage.

Each of the five spurs on the northern side of the mountain shelters a separate part of the community, another group living at Ksar Hadada. These have long been at odds and, during the French occupation, when they were brought under the command of a single *sheikh*, there was frequent fighting. With the construction of the new town in the valley in the 1890s, however, the community was brought together and peace finally achieved. Few families now live in the *ghar*: they are considered dangerous because rocks frequently fall from the cliff faces onto the courtyards below. As you wander round you can see the devastation these rockfalls have caused: take care.

Practicalities

Ghoumrassen is now a market town and very lively during the Friday souk, which attracts tribespeople from Nefzaoua in search of the region's esteemed olive oil. Most of the town shops are located on the long main street. There are lots of **cafés**, and **patisseries** selling the Ghoumrassen speciality, *ftair* (doughnuts), but no hotel, so you'll have to go on, or back, to Ksar Hadada or Tataouine. If you need a **bank**, however, you'll find two, plus a *Grand Magasin* **supermarket** and a **PTT** (country hours) where you can make international phone calls. You can also make them from a call box opposite the *STB* bank.

Moving On: Visits to Guermessa and Ksar Hadada

If you're driving, the most **direct road to Medenine** commences at the eastern end of the main street. Roads to Tataouine, Guermessa, and Medenine via Ksar Hadada branch off at the other end of town. The **bus station** is a block from the main street towards the eastern end of town, with several daily buses to Tataouine, Medenine, Ksar Hadada and Guermessa. **Louages** leave from the middle of the main street, serving Medenine, Tataouine and Tunis. **Hitching to Guermessa** shouldn't be too much of a problem: the tar road branches off the main Tataouine road just out of town.

Guermessa

GUERMESSA is less troubled by tourists than its sister villages of Douiret and Chenini to the south, perhaps because it was rather difficult to reach until recently. Even now, despite the newly surfaced road and apart from the two daily **buses** to Ghoumrassen, it's not exactly well connected and has few facilities.

Guermessa is built around a spur with a ruined *kala'a* on its peak up to which leads a distinctive paved **pathway** from the valley below, no mean engineering achievement, considering the size of the slabs. Although still inhabited, the construction of a new village in the plains is gradually drawing families away, and within a decade or so it too will likely face abandonment.

Ksar Hadada

From Ghoumrassen north towards Beni Kheddache and Medenine, the tarmac runs for 6km as far as **KSAR HADADA** (sometimes called Ghoumrassen Hadada). The old *ksar* here is no longer used for grain storage and half of it has been abandoned. The other half is now occupied by the **Hôtel Ksar Hadada** (☎69605). Run by the same management as the *Gazelle* in Tataouine, it's a bit of a fleece-the-tourists affair (b&b for 8.5/12TD), but the only place to spend the night between Tataouine and Medenine. If you specifically want to spend a night in a conveted *ksar*, this is probably not the one to choose (those at Metameur and Ksar Hallouf are better). Still, the rooms have showers and toilets, and meals in the **restaurant** are very reasonable, at 3TD for the set menu.

When it's time to move on, the only **public transport** is the four-times-daily bus service to Ghoumrassen, whence you change for points beyond. If you're planning to head **north of Ksar Hadada**, you really need your own vehicle. There are 22km of very rough piste – just passable, but slowly, without four-wheel-drive – before the resumption of a good surface at Beni Kheddache and the road to Medenine. You could try hitching but there isn't much traffic. For details of this route – and of the wonderful-looking *ksar* of Kerachfa, 12km out of Ksar Hadada – see p.303.

Chenini

Most people approach Chenini directly from Tataouine on the paved road. You can **take a taxi** (5TD each way; bargain them down from 15–20TD) or **hitch**, which is easiest on market days (Mon & Thurs) when trucks return to Chenini at noon. During the summer season, staff of the *Relais* restaurant in Chenini, who live in Tataouine, wait at the turn-off on the Remada road (2.5km out of Tataouine) and you may get a lift with them. And there's a supply van to the *Relais* from the *Hôtel La Gazelle* every day.

The village

CHENINI is best seen from a distance. The village is built around a peak surmounted by a ruined *kala'a*, with a white mosque resting on a crook of the spur, the whole ensemble intensely dramatic in its size and desolation. From the distance each row of dwellings fronted by their *ghorfa* seems to cling to the steep mountainside. Reginald

Rankin, travelling in the 1890s, was mightily impressed: "I have seen nearly all the so-called wonders of the world and unhesitatingly say that the cave dwellings of the Saharan troglodytes seem to me the most wonderful thing of all." An inscription in one of the *ghorfas* gives the date 1143 AD, but the village is certainly older than that.

As at Ghoumrassen the *ghar*, most of which are still inhabited, are dug into soft strata on the slopes below the fortress, but here several levels of cave dwellings form bands around the spur joined by steep walkways. You can visit a working camel-drawn oil press, an underground communal bakery, and even enter some of the houses, but you'll usually be charged, so fix a price before you enter. This is increasingly a problem at Chenini: it has suffered from over-exposure to parties of tourists, most of whom arrive in the morning. If you want the place more to yourself, go later.

While Chenini itself is something special, the **views** from it are also quite outstanding. For a leisurely **walk** with brilliant vistas, follow the path up from the mosque in the village, along the hillside above the underground mosque (see below), down to a spring where the villagers collect their water.

The underground mosque and the story of the seven sleepers
Even older than the village around the *kala'a* is an abandoned village a kilometre along the escarpment. Here only the **underground mosque** (ask for the *Jemaa Kedima*, the old mosque) survives. Below the leaning minaret are two interconnected rooms, one housing the tomb of a marabout, the other that of the **Seven Sleepers**. According to folk legend – quite a common one in the region – seven Christians were imprisoned in this underground hiding place during the Roman occupation. Four centuries later, when their cell was opened, they awoke as if they had been asleep. All that time, however, their bodies had continued to grow, so that they were now twelve feet tall. Only when they had been converted to Islam did they die, and their bodies were buried here in these long tombs.

Practicalities
Chenini has a *Relais* **restaurant** with a good 3TD set menu, and even **beer**. In the summer, you may be able to **stay** for 2.5TD, but in the evenings the restaurant is closed so you'll have to bring your own food. For more details, call the *Hôtel Gazelle* in Tataouine (☎60009), who run it.

There is **no public transport** from Chenini. If you don't have your own wheels, it shouldn't be too difficult to hitch out. The very rough **back route to Guermessa and Douiret** is just about passable in a hired car if you go slowly, though a four-wheel-drive vehicle is preferable. For the intrepid there's an 8km **footpath to Douiret** over the mountain, which is supposed to be easy enough to follow, though the help of a guide would be a sensible idea.

To Douiret and Beyond

Douiret is probably easier to reach than Chenini from Tataouine. The Douiret road turns off the Remada road at KSAR OULED DEBBAB, 8km south of Tataouine. Ouled Debbab (four buses a day or pick-up van from Tataouine) is the largest *ksar* of the **Ouled Debbab** tribe and now abandoned. They claim an exotic Arab Hilalian line of descent but probably share the indigenous Berber origins of neighbouring Douiret.

Douiret

DOUIRET, 11km down the paved road (hitch or walk), is utterly Berber and immediately impressive: a ruined *kala'a*, perched on peak some a 700m high, with a white

THE BERBER VILLAGES: A LIFESTYLE UNDER THREAT

Life in the Berber villages of Ghoumrassen, Guermessa, Chenini and Douiret has traditionally revolved around **agriculture**. Considerable effort has been put into the construction of *jessour* (agricultural terraces) and cisterns so that trees can be planted in the arid landscape. Although sheep and goats were once raised here, too, they were a small part of the economy and the villagers never participated in the transhumance of their nomad neighbours. Each village had a specialist profession: the Douiri and Guermessi worked as vegetable market porters, the Ghoumrassini sold their doughnuts, and the Chenini newspapers. Young men worked in the city for a few years and then returned to their village, spending the money they had saved on **brideprice** or a new *jessour*. Today, however, the young men go to **France and Libya**, stay away longer and marry outside the community. Many do not return. As you look round the villages, women vastly outnumber men, most of whom are old: migration is killing the community. This is doubly sad, since with these villages will die the last of Tunisia's Berber culture.

THE BERBER LANGUAGE

Although **Berber** was the predominant language in Tunisia under the Romans, it was quickly overtaken, after the Arab conquest, by Arabic – the language of the new religion, of law and government. Only in the communities of the south did Berber survive, and here too it was in a gradual decline. By the end of the nineteenth century Berber was only spoken as a first language in Douiret, Chenini, and Guermessa and, with the French occupation, the extension of government to the south and the imposition of Islamic law, Arabic finally made inroads here, too. However, migration and the consequent dispersal of the Berber population was the death blow. Now, only women speak the language and cling determinedly to the old traditions; the men, forced by education and work in the cities to adopt Arabic as the *lingua franca*, will soon become fully assimilated, swamped in the dominant Arabic culture.

Ironically, the French made every effort to separate the Berbers from their Arab neighbours. French **anthropologists** claimed that they were in fact Europeans who had migrated to North Africa at an early date. While the Arabs were caricatured as lazy, sly, and tyrannical the Berbers, in contrast, were supposedly industrious, honest, and democratic (all considered evidence of their purported European origins), and for these reasons worthy of a privileged place in Tunisian society. In reality the French were trying to divide and rule, and the Berbers, on the whole, refused to play the game. While accepting many of the privileges offered by the government, including an independent administration and large tracts of Arab land, they remained just as hostile to the French as their Arab neighbours.

mosque on the slope setting off the soft colour of the bare stone. If you climb to the top and onto the precarious rubble of the *kala'a*, the panoramic views over the surrounding desert are stunning. The village is much like Chenini, though the *ghar*, inhabited in the nineteenth century by 5000 people, are mostly unoccupied. A new village was built on the plain in the 1960s, and many Douiri have set up home there or gone to Tunis.

Wandering around Douiret you can find oil presses (three of them in use), bakeries, and inscriptions – all in remarkably good condition. On the plain below is an old graveyard with the whitewashed tombs of revered marabouts, and a small building, the office of the French officer sent to administer the community in 1888; it was abandoned after two years when the French base was moved to Tataouine. The only part of the old village still in use is on the other side of the spur. If you stray into this quarter women quickly disappear into their houses, so be especially tactful if you have a camera. There's an interesting mosque here as well, with an inscription in archaic Berber script (the only example of it known) but non-Muslims are rarely allowed in to see it.

To get **back from Douiret** you have to wait for a pick-up, most easily located at the new "shopping area". Alternatively, there are tractors, with the ubiquitous trailers, who will usually give people lifts.

Ksar Ghilane

If you have a **four-wheel-drive** car there is a sign-posted route from the Douiret–Chenini track to **KSAR GHILANE** (47km), a Roman fort on the edge of the sandy desert. It's a frighteningly desolate place, but there's a well here, and such was its importance that a **fort** was built to defend it: one of a chain, the *limes*, that extended the full length of the Roman frontier. The main attraction is, however, the journey across the **Dahar** (a desolate and arid plateau that used to be the haunt of *fellaga*, or bandits) and an opportunity to see the desert **gazelles and antelopes** that used to be found all over the south. Ksar Ghilane is linked traditionally with the Nefzaoua area south of the Chott el Jerid, in particular with the village of Zaafrane, whose Adhara people still spend part of the year at Ksar Ghilane with their flocks. Apart from the odd Roman remain, the only specific item of interest here is a **monument** to the column of Free French troops under General Leclerc who, in 1943, made an epic march of well over 2000km from Lake Chad to join Montgomery's British and Commonwealth troops in an assault on the Mareth Line (see p.273).

There are two **places to stay** in Ksar Ghilane, both *campements* – put up for the benefit of jeep tours from Gabes and Douz – where you sleep in traditional-style Berber tents (3TD or 4TD per person b&b; if you have your own tent, you may be able to pitch it for less). Just how authentically Berber all this is can be gauged from the fact that the Ministry of Tourism have been asking the police to move on real Berbers in case their untidy presence upsets the chic clientele from the coastal resorts.

DESERT WILDLIFE

Predictably, the **stony desert** or *hammada* that covers much of the southeast of Tunisia has a sparse wildlife population. The sand desert in the southwest has, if anything, even less. Neither habitat owes very much to Mediterranean influence, with the huge Sahara to the south dominating the ecosystem. **Plants** are thin on the ground, but the wonder is that they can survive at all. They do this by special adaptation, their leaves often reduced to thin strips to reduce water loss to a minimum. Another strategy evolved by some plants is to have swollen leaves which can store water; cacti are best known for this, but many other plants do it too.

The small **desert mammals** are almost entirely nocturnal, feeding on plants and seeds in the cool of the night. The big ears of the jerboas are not just for acute hearing – they may also serve a temperature control function in the same way as an elephant's ears do. On the other hand, **lizards** are mostly active by day – though hard to see easily since they have a surprising turn of speed.

Birds fall into two groups – those that concentrate **around the oases**, and the true desert dwellers which live out in the inhospitable wastes. In the **oases** themselves **palm doves** are common: this is their "home" habitat, and they've spread to the rest of Tunisia's towns in much the same way as the collared dove has done in northern Europe. If you're truly devoted, rubbish tips are worth exploring for scavenging ravens. Out **in the desert** and away from the villages and oases, you'll come across many of the steppe birds – larks, wheatears, cream-coloured coursers, shrikes and so on. Lurk around any area of oasis water in the early morning and the reward may be a flock of fast-flying **sandgrouse** coming in to drink. Tataouine is a good base for seeing desert wildlife, with the full range of species. This was the last region in Tunisia where ostriches were found, though any sighting today of a large long-legged bird with a black and white neck is likely to be the **Houbara bustard** – a little-studied rarity.

DRIVING IN THE DESERT

Driving in the desert is a potentially hazardous business and claims victims every year. You should not drive in desert regions, let alone think of leaving the main surfaced roads, without taking all the necessary precautions. Don't assume everything will be fine; consider what may happen if you break down in the middle of nowhere with little chance of anyone passing for hours, or even days.

First, make sure your vehicle is up to the terrain. Do all the usual fuel, oil and water checks and make sure you're carrying tools and a jack and spare tyre, preferably two. Take spare fuel if possible, and carry at least **five litres of water** per person at all times. Don't forget, either, to take high-factor suntan lotion, a sunhat and sunglasses and appropriate clothing, including warm clothes for nighttime, when the desert can get bitterly cold, especially in winter. A shovel is invaluable (even a tarmac road can get covered in drifts), and steel sand ladders or mats will help you get unstuck too. A compass is a very good idea.

Always inform the National Guard of your arrival and departure at every post on your journey. Tell them where you're going and when you expect to arrive (occasionally you may be refused permission). If you can't find the Guard, tell the police or gendarmes instead. Keep to well-defined pistes as much as possible and in open desert always travel in convoy, never alone.

If you get stuck in a sandstorm, stop. Point your vehicle downwind and wait until the storm abates. This will avoid damage to your engine. And if you break down or get lost there's one fundamental rule that's more likely to save your life than any other: **stay with your vehicle**. Don't go wandering off into the desert alone: dehydration, sunstroke and heat exhaustion can strike amazingly quickly, and a car is a lot easier to find than a person wandering around alone.

The *Sahara Handbook*, by Simon and Jan Glen (*Lascelles*) contains much timeless good advice on preparing and driving a vehicle in the desert.

Remada and the Extreme South

REMADA, 70km south of Tataouine, is yet another garrison town imposed on the south by the French and has nothing of great interest. When the French arrived, there was a small oasis and the remains of a **Roman fort** nearby, part of the *limes*, now incorporated into the army base. The army continue to dominate the region: it's a "military zone" and first line in the defence against Libya. The border is now open and tensions have decreased in the last few years, but you may still get some strange looks and will still have to show your documents time and time again: seven "terrorists" were caught crossing the border in 1986, and everybody is on the look-out for more.

There's **no hotel** in Remada, and nowhere to stay: your best bet is to return to Tataouine by bus or *louage* before they dry up around 3pm. If you get stuck, you'll just have to throw yourself on the mercy of the local police – who knows, they may have a spare cell for the night. The only **restaurant** in town is very basic, and you're just as well off buying food from one of the shops. Bring enough dinars with you as there's **no bank** either. **Market day** is Sunday. If you were hoping to get to **Ksar Segdel**, on a track to the east of town, it's only possible with a four-wheel-drive vehicle.

West to the Jebel Segdel

The most feasible trips out from Remada are to the villages in **the Jebel Segdel**, 8km out on the road, west, to Borj Bourguiba. It's an eight-hour walk over a flat plain followed by a scramble up a steep escarpment: you may be able to find a guide at the *Maison du Peuple* beyond the marketplace on the Borj Bourguiba road. The area is completely deserted; only the collapsed ruins of the villages and the **eroded landscape** of their *jessour* remain of a once-flourishing economy. Between the sixteenth and eighteenth centuries, the tribes abandoned a total of 25 villages between Douiret and Dehibat. Why they left is still a mystery: the French blamed the expansion of the Ouderna people, though climatic change and plague epidemics may also have played a part. Today the only residents of these ruins are, so the locals claim, **jackals**.

Borj Bourguiba

BORJ BOURGUIBA is accessible only by Land Rover and with a permit from the *Gouvernorat* in Tataouine – which you're most unlikely to be granted. This military prison and settlement takes its name from the ex-President, who was interned here under the Protectorate (when it was called Borj Le Boeuf). Ironically enough, the prison held many of Bourguiba's own political enemies in the 1970s and 1980s.

South to Dehibat and the Libyan Frontier

There are two buses a day to **DEHIBAT**, on the Libyan border, and it's a fairly regular run by *louage*. The village has again been taken over by the Army but the old *ksar*, now a barracks, is still there. From the 1880s until 1911, sovereignty over this town was in dispute between the French and the Turkish administration of Libya. The Dehibi had deserted the village to live in Matmata and Douiret a century earlier, but the French paid them to return in order to substantiate their claims. Eventually, when the Italians invaded Libya, the French forced them to concede the village and its lands. Today's military presence indicates Tunisia's continued insecurity over the district, although **smuggling** is another possible reason for it.

There's **nowhere at all to stay** in Dehibat, though you're only likely to be here if you're self-sufficient and equipped for desert travel – or you intend crossing the border.

Onwards into Libya

Dehibat is the southernmost point of **entry into Libya**, the only other authorised crossing being at Ras Ajdir on the coast. Border formalities are taken much more seriously down here, and you can expect more thorough customs searches on both sides. From Dehibat, there is transport over the 18km to the Libyan border post at Wazin, and beyond that to **Nalut** 47km away, where there are connections to the rest of Libya.

Southwest of Dehibat

Travelling **south from Dehibat** requires a pass from the *Gouvernorat* in Tataouine, which they are unlikely to grant. If you go, this is **gazelle** country, so keep your eyes peeled. South of Dehibat are the border posts of JENEIN (120km from Remada) and M'CHIGUIG (225km). **BORJ EL KHADRA** (also called Borj el Hattaba, and formerly Fort Saint) is at the southernmost tip of Tunisia, where the borders of Libya and Algeria meet. Even if you were allowed to cross, there's nothing very exciting on the **Algerian side** (the nearest important town being the oil terminal at Hassi Messaoud, 500km northwest), though in a convoy you could head south to Borj Omar Driss, over pistes to Tamanrasset and into West Africa. On the **Libyan side**, the ancient and fascinating former caravan terminus of Ghadames beckons. At present, however, the only way to get there is via Nalut.

PHONE CODES

The code for the whole region is ☎05, as in the rest of the south

travel details

Transport in this region – by road only – can be very irregular and you may have to resort to hitching, arranging a lift or hiring a taxi. There is always more transport in the morning and it often dries up completely by the afternoon, so the earlier you set out the better. Market days (see p.298) can be good for travel if you get up early enough. Transport usually heads out to a market first thing in the morning, returning late morning or afternoon.

Buses and louages
FROM MEDENINE TO:

Tunis (4 daily, 7hr); **Metameur** (7, 15min); **Beni Kheddache** (3, 45min); **Ghoumrassen** (4, 1hr 30min); **Sousse** (5, 5hr); **Sfax** (5, 3hr 30min); **Gabes** (5, 1hr 15min); **Tataouine** (5, 1hr); **Houmt Souk/Jerba** (4, 2hr); **Zarzis** (4, 1hr); **Ben Gardane** (3, 1hr 30min).

Louages to **Tunis, Tataouine, Ghoumrassen, Beni Kheddache, Houmt Souk (Jerba), Gabes, Zarzis** and **Medenine**.

FROM TATAOUINE TO :

Tunis (2, 8hr 30min); **Medenine** (5, 1hr); **Ghoumrassen** (4, 45min); **Maztouria** (5, 20min); **Ksar Ouled Debbab** (4, 20min); **Dehibat** (1, 3hr); **Houmt Souk (Jerba)** (2, 3hr); **Ben Gardane** (1, 2hr); **Gabes** (1, 2hr 30min).

Louages to **Tunis, Medenine, Ghoumrassen, Remada** and **Dehibat**, plus **pick-ups** to **Maztouria, Ksar Ouled Soltane, Ksar Ouled Debbab** and **Douiret**.

FROM GHOUMRASSEN TO:

Medenine (4, 1hr 30min); **Tataouine** (4, 45min); **Ksar Hadada** (4, 10min); **Guermessa** (2, 20min). **Louages** to **Tunis, Medenine** and **Tataouine**.

PART THREE

THE

CONTEXTS

THE HISTORICAL FRAMEWORK

Tunisia has a long, dense and complicated historical record. The region was host to some of the earliest tool-making human cultures and was the centre of the still dimly understood Carthaginian empire. The Romans left a clear mark and Islam arrived early in the faith's history at the end of the seventh century. Modern Tunisia is a comparatively recent creation, but the roots of the country in its present shape go back to the eighth century. What follows is the briefest of outline introductions to Tunisian history from the year dot to the end of 1991.

PREHISTORY

Around a million years ago, **early hominids** were living in North Africa's tropical climate, hunting with the primitive tools known as "pebble culture". These gradually gave way to heavy hand-axes, until about 50,000 years ago the discovery of fire encouraged what was by now almost *Homo sapiens* to live in fixed settlements. A culture known as **Aterian** began to make smaller, more specialised tools, and the next step forward was the arrival about 10,000 years ago of Caucasoid Proto-Hamites from western Asia. These people were probably fair-skinned, buried some of their dead, spoke a language related to ancient Egyptian, and made the most sophisticated tools yet: barbed arrows and long, thin blades which have been found near Gafsa and which have given their name to the influential culture (Capsian Man) found as far away as Kenya.

The blades found at Gafsa have been dated to around 6000 BC, and for the next 4000 years **Capsian people**, perhaps with some infiltration from further east, continued to live in caves and survive by hunting and gathering. About 2000 BC the introduction of metals from Sicily brought Tunisia into the Bronze Age, but it was still a relatively small-scale society of nomadic hunters which the Phoenicians encountered when they arrived at the beginning of the first millennium BC. Contemporary Greek accounts consistently distinguish "Libyans" from "Ethiopians" in North Africa, and the so-called Libyans were descended from the Proto-Hamites, fair-skinned in contrast to the Ethiopians, and still speaking their remote Libyc language. The Greeks called them *barbaroi*, a name originally attached to any people who did not speak Greek and which found its final form as **Berbers**. Pure Berbers, of whom there are very few in Tunisia (most live in remote areas of Algeria and Morocco) are the descendants of these Proto-Hamites.

THE CARTHAGINIAN EMPIRE, 814–146 BC

The **Phoenicians** were originally drawn to North Africa from their home in the region of modern Lebanon because they needed staging-posts for the long haul across the Mediterranean. Traders supreme of the ancient world, they were already heavily involved in exploiting the resources of Spain and beyond (principally metals), and the towns they founded (such as Sousse, Utica and Bizerte) were important transit points.

Traditionally, the earliest of these ports were founded around 1100 BC, **Carthage** itself in 814. Part of this ancient tradition is the myth of the foundation of Carthage (Qart Hadasht: New City) by Queen Dido (or Elissa) and a band of exiled nobles from the Phoenician homeland. The myth may reflect a genuine influx of the Phoenician ruling class, caused by Assyrian pressure at home in the ninth century BC; but it may just be a later rationalisation of Carthage's supremacy among the cities in North Africa. There is little archaeological evidence to support the gap between the foundations, and ninth-century dates all round may be more accurate.

At first, the Phoenician trading posts were more or less isolated enclaves on the coast. Links with the homeland were strong, and there was no reason to use the hinterland for more than immediate needs. Towards the end of the seventh century BC, however, a rival for Punic (Phoenician) trade domination appeared as **Greeks**, based in southern Italy and Sicily, began to extend their reach through southern France and eastern Spain. Conflict was inevitable, and the Phoenician cities amalgamated for security under Carthage – though the relationship was never to be easy. Fighting through the sixth century went Carthage's way, but in 480

BC the Battle of Himera in Sicily resulted in a decisive Greek victory. Forced from now on to fight its own battle for survival in the western Mediterranean, Carthage became increasingly independent of the homeland and simultaneously extended its control over the Tunisian hinterland: the Carthagian Empire was born. The year 396 BC saw another bad defeat in Sicily followed by domestic upheavals; then in 310 BC the Greek king of Syracuse, Agathocles, boldly eluding a Carthaginian army which had landed in Sicily, descended on Cap Bon and for three years devastated North Africa.

This episode was the last to involve Greeks against Carthage. The young and vigorous Italian city of **Rome** had been gradually superseding the Greeks in Italy and Sicily, and henceforth Carthage's struggle for domination of the Mediterranean basin and Europe was with this formidable opponent. The first of three famous **Punic Wars** (263–241) consisted mainly of naval skirmishes around Sicily, but also included one episode of war on land which became enshrined in Roman national legend. The Roman general **Regulus** landed with an army in Africa and had some success before being defeated and captured along with his force. He was allowed to return on parole to Rome to plead before the Senate for acceptance of Carthaginian terms, but when this was refused he kept his word as a man of honour and returned to certain death and a place in the pantheon of Roman national heroes. Roman versions of the story dwell with loving detail on the grief of his family and the brutality of his death at the Carthaginians' hands.

Carthage finally lost the war and had to accept Roman terms, surrendering its fleet and agreeing on spheres of influence in Spain. It was to Spain, however, that the Carthaginians soon turned their attention. After preliminary manoeuvring by both sides, the Carthaginian general **Hannibal** deliberately moved over the agreed border in 218 and proceeded to make his legendary march (with elephants) through France and over the Alps. Although he won initial victories at Trasimene and Cannae, he remained isolated in Italy for several years with no support, either locally or from home, which would enable him to take Rome. This was in part because the Roman Scipio had been tying down Carthaginian forces at home, and in 202 Hannibal was finally compelled to return.

Scipio defeated him at the **battle of Zama** in central Tunisia, winning the official title "Africanus". Hannibal fled to Asia Minor – and to his own place in Roman legend as a dreaded but respected opponent.

Carthage had to surrender its fleet again, and to refrain from training elephants. Although Carthaginian power had now been effectively nullified, for many Romans a threat remained as long as the city physically existed. The arch-conservative Cato used to end every speech in the Senate, on whatever subject, with the phrase "Carthage must be destroyed". A story goes that one day he came into the Senate and deliberately spilled some ripe figs on to the floor. Questioned, he replied that these were Carthaginian figs – the implication being that a Carthage this healthy was one Carthage too many.

The hawks won the day, and in 150 BC a third war was provoked, culminating in the final, apocalyptic **sack of Carthage** in 146 BC. Descriptions of this are predictably lurid, and the ruins were ploughed over with the proverbial salt to ensure that they remained barren. The Carthaginian Empire was well and truly obliterated, and the Romans set up the province of Africa in northern Tunisia.

CARTHAGINIAN CIVILISATION

The Carthaginians have always aroused hostility; by the seventh century BC Homer was describing a typical Phoenician as "grasping and well versed in deceit". Unfortunately, so little has survived of their civilisation that we are forced to rely almost entirely on Greek and Roman accounts, which deserve the same caution as modern western descriptions of, say, Libya. "Phoenician faith" was a proverbial Roman term for dishonesty, and Roman mothers told their children "Hannibal's coming" to make them be quiet.

But the Carthaginians do seem to have succeeded in antagonising many of the people they came across. Hannibal crucially failed to secure any local support during his long stay in Italy, and the Romans later claimed to have had little difficulty in persuading North Africa's Berbers to transfer their allegiance. A simplistic explanation for this might be found in the Carthaginian **commercial vocation**. Their exploits in pursuit of profit were legendary. Two of these – fifth century BC voyages west round the coast of Africa and north as far as Brittany – may be so legendary as not actually to have taken place, but at the very least they reflect Carthaginian interest in distant markets.

The competitiveness which made them such successful traders left them ill-equipped to get on with others, or even among themselves. The **Truceless War** (241–237 BC), which inspired Flaubert's novel *Salammbô*, is a graphic example. Carthage had always relied on its naval strength, recruiting mercenaries whenever a land army became necessary. When peace was made at the end of the First Punic War, there were no funds to pay the mercenaries. The authorities tried to get rid of the problem by sending the mercenaries off to Sicca (Le Kef), but with the support of the oppressed Berbers they turned on their erstwhile masters and a four-year struggle of unrelieved brutality ensued. After hiring yet more mercenaries, the Carthaginians finally won – but the episode indicates a reliance on wealth rather than loyalty, manifestly an unsuitable policy for a country aspiring to Great Power status.

From what can be gathered of **Carthaginian society**, it was oligarchical and conservative and permanently divided into jealous factions which prevented any unified policy being carried out. Power was concentrated in the hands of the ruling aristocratic families (or whichever one had the support of the Army), and although many of the native Berbers were technically free, in practice the tribute demanded made them resentful of their effective subjection.

Characteristically for such a society, **religion** and **art** remained essentially anti-humanistic. The most important gods were **Baal** and his consort **Tanit**, and their worship included child-sacrifice – a practice which, somewhat hypocritically, made the Romans throw up their hands in horror. But details of the less lurid aspects of their religion are barely known. At first the gods were worshipped at *tophets* (holy places), just a sacred area with perhaps a small shrine to hold a divine effigy, but gradually under Greek influence these became more substantial, with a monumental porch and a courtyard attached. By the fourth century BC some Greek cults were even introduced, though in modified form.

Carthaginian art was almost all derived from foreign sources – Egyptian, then Greek – and much of what little there is consists of incompetent attempts to reproduce what had been seen elsewhere. There are few original characteristics, and the most distinctive Carthaginian image – the symbol of the goddess Tanit, a bare circle balanced on stick legs – only proves the **anti-humanist trend**.

So few archaeological remains have been found that it is impossible to say what **Carthaginian towns** looked like. Only domestic housing has yet been uncovered, at Kerkouane and Carthage, with none of the great public buildings which characterised Graeco-Roman civilisation. Under Greek influence, though, more regular civic planning may have come in. Outside their cities the Carthaginians eventually adapted very successfully after their early disinterest. Their expansion into the Sahel and the Medjerda Valley after the fifth century BC was successful enough to be mentioned by Agathocles' expedition of 310 BC, and the theoretician Mago wrote a treatise on farming which was so well considered that the Roman Senate ordered it to be translated in 146 BC.

ROMAN AFRICA, 112 BC–439 AD

The immediate attitude of the **Romans** to their acquisition in Africa was less than positive. The destruction of Carthage had been a preventative measure designed to protect the Straits of Sicily and ensure the safety of Italy: there were no plans for colonisation, and the province of Africa consisted of no more than the Carthaginians had controlled, roughly everything east of a line from Thabraca (Tabarca) to Thaenae (Sfax).

Even so, Romans seem to have moved to Africa on their own initiative. In 112 BC it was the native king **Jugurtha**'s misguided slaughter of Romans living at Cirta (Constantine in Algeria) which forced the Senate to intervene in Africa against his rampaging, and presumably these were traders who had moved in to exploit the new territory. Jugurtha was king of Numidia, the native kingdom that stretched west from the Roman border through Algeria. He was the grandson of Massinissa, a Numidian king who had provided invaluable support for the Romans against Carthage in the second century BC; now that the Carthaginian threat had gone, however, there was no more incentive to support the Romans than there had been to support Carthage previously. The Romans had created a power vacuum in their province which they were eventually going to have to fill.

Jugurtha was finally defeated in 105 BC, and a few veterans were settled in the north of the province. It was only in 46 BC, however, when Julius Caesar finally won the Roman Civil War against Pompeii at the battle of Thapsus (near Mahdia), that **colonisation** really took off. The existing province was extended in the west by a line running south from Hippo Regius (Annaba in Algeria) and in the east by the addition of Tripolitania (western Libya), and renamed Africa Proconsularis. As a symbol of the Roman presence, **Carthage** was refounded in 44 BC.

Under the Empire (from 30 BC) growth in Africa was phenomenal, made possible by a combination of political and economic factors. Politically, Africa was for two centuries one of the most stable provinces of the Empire. Where a small part of France needed four Roman legions (of 6000 men each) to maintain its defences, the whole of Africa needed only one. Its base moved steadily further west during the first century AD, from Haidra on the Tunisian border to Tebessa in Algeria, and Lambaesis near Batna; and a line of frontier forts was established, running westwards from the Chott el Jerid, and east from Ghadames at the southern tip of Tunisia. Within the province, the characteristic network of Roman roads grew, but they were designed to facilitate trade instead of the usual defence.

The **agricultural trade** in question was the basis of Africa's economy. In the first century AD, Africa is said to have provided two thirds of Rome's grain requirements, to Egypt's one third. As Rome's population swelled, the supply of grain grew to be of supreme importance: this is the era when Juvenal coined the phrase "bread and circuses", and when bad weather one year kept the grain ships from sailing there was panic in Rome. Accordingly the Romans invested a great deal of time and expertise in developing the province's infrastructure, maximising the potential which the Carthaginians had only touched on – they had had only themselves to feed, after all. In the second century AD olive oil production began to be encouraged in the Sahel, and other products included a gaudy yellow marble (from Chemtou); purple dye; wild animals for amphitheatre displays; coral; wood; and plain domestic pottery, which by the second century was being exported all over the Empire.

Throughout the first two centuries AD there was hardly an interruption in Africa's steady increase in prosperity and importance. By about 200 AD as many as one sixth of Roman Senators were of African origin, and in the Severans from Tripolitania, Africa provided a dynasty of Emperors. In 180, however, there was a portent of things to come. The Proconsul of Africa tried twelve Christians and executed them when they refused to recant their faith. The rise of **Christianity** in Africa, signalled also by the polemical writings of Tertullian, was a symptom of the problems threatening the Empire throughout its unwieldy expanse.

In 238 Thysdrus (El Jem) was the scene of a revolt which spread over the Empire and ushered in half a century of great unrest. The golden age was over, and while commitment to the imperial way of life steadily dropped, Christianity became more widespread. In 312 the Emperor Constantine was converted and the Empire officially became Christian. Constantine was trying in effect to restore the Empire to the hearts of its people, but in Africa he was foiled by the **Donatist** schism in the local Church. This was caused by Christians unwilling to accept priests who had renounced their faith in the face of persecution; to avoid being "tainted" by such priests, they formed their own communion. One famous supporter of the official Church, who spent his life trying to heal the rift, was Saint Augustine of Hippo (Hippo Regius, in Algeria).

Through the fourth and fifth centuries the Empire gradually crumbled in the face of internal tyranny and external aggression. One such tyranny in Africa, under Gildo (386–98), put Rome in a quandary: whether to put the upstart down, risking disruption of the all-important grain supply, or just to cut their losses. In the end, Gildo and his 70,000 men were suppressed. The external problem, raiding by local tribes, was equally serious. One pleasant theory holds that the tribes had discovered a secret weapon which decisively increased their combat strength – the camel; more likely, internal dissension was too great for organised resistance on any scale. Donatist supporters probably aided the Vandals, a Germanic tribe which invaded North Africa from Spain in the 420s. Their capture of Carthage in 439 put an end to the Roman era, and effectively cut the area off from Western Europe. From now on, the region's loyalties would lie in a different direction.

IMPERIAL ROME

African society under the **Roman Empire** settled to two levels: a wealthy, urban, Romanised middle class, and a poorer, rural native culture. A good deal is known about the rich, because they left the material remains which can be seen everywhere in Tunisia today. The life of the rural Berber population will always remain obscure, because their poverty produced only a meagre material culture. Although limited opportunities did exist for social advancement, the essential gap between the social classes was never eradicated, and the alienation of the less privileged Berbers was to be an important factor in the eventual disintegration of imperial culture.

To be fair to the Romans, most of the better-off were of local origin: when one speaks of "Romans", this is usually a reference to Romanised Africans. The opportunity was there for imperial citizens to make good – as never under Carthage – and many of them made the most of it, as the African senators and emperors show. It's certainly difficult to imagine the equivalent happening in the British Empire. Other things sound more familiar, though: Septimius Severus, the first "African" emperor, had a wife who wasn't quite acceptable in smart Roman circles because of her strong accent.

The most striking fact about the **towns** where the middle class lived is that there were so many of them: literally hundreds. These smallish settlements of 5–15,000 inhabitants provided homes for farming landlords, markets for their produce – and a perfect environment for one-upmanship. In the absence of any external pressures, wealth was diverted into civic and private rivalry: local plutocrats put their money into buildings and facilities on which their names would be prominently displayed. The ensuing prestige translated itself without too much difficulty into political office.

The basic aim was **Romanisation**, and this meant building institutions which fostered Roman values. The spiritual heart of any self-respecting town was the **Forum**, a regular paved space enclosed by colonnades and surrounded by administrative and religious buildings. The most important of the town's religious buildings, the **Capitol**, was almost always on the Forum: it was dedicated to the Capitoline trio of Jupiter, Juno and Minerva, patrons of the Empire. Other temples and shrines served cults which were a curious mixture of Roman and local influences; the Carthaginian goddess Tanit, for instance, was given a Roman name, Caelestis (Heavenly One), and worshipped all over Africa Proconsularis. Priesthood was a temporal matter, open only to those of a certain social status and thus closely tied to political authority.

Baths may not seem like an obvious imperial building type, but in fact they became almost synonymous with Roman civilisation. They were magnificent buildings, their soaring vaulted ceilings impressive products of Roman engineering expertise, but it was the activity they housed which made them so central to imperial life. Surrounded by mosaics and statuary, citizens of all ranks could go for a small fee and spend hours there. Actual bathing was only a small part of the full ritual, which also included exercising in gymnasia, reading in libraries or just sitting around. Other public facilities such as theatres and amphitheatres were usually set on the outskirts of the town, not far from the vast cemeteries of ostentatious mausoleums which lined approach roads. By 250 AD, the countryside was criss-crossed by 20,000km of roads, aqueducts and bridges.

In material terms Roman Africa was a great success, though historians have tended to exaggerate Rome's achievement, not least the French who, in their eagerness to put down the Arabs, mistakenly attributed many of their engineering works to Rome. Culturally Roman Africa, best known for its lawyers, was less spectacular. Nevertheless the **mosaics**, used to decorate private homes and public buildings, reached heights in Africa almost without equal – perhaps partly because there was so little other artistic activity. The greatest name in **literature** was Apuleius, author of the *The Golden Ass* (see p.364), who was born in modern Algeria; others were Tertullian and Saint Augustine, the Christian writers. But these Christian names are a reminder of how briefly the Empire flourished. Once its citizens lost their faith in the imperial dream, from the third century onwards, the physical fabric also began to crumble. No great Roman buildings were erected after 250, and those already standing went unrepaired. The only new constructions were churches, often built in the ruins of older temples and baths, and the **Vandals** that came later inherited a way of life that was only a shadow of its former incarnation.

THE VANDALS, 439–533

One of the northern tribes which harassed the Roman Empire to its end, the **Vandals** were a Germanic tribe of Aryan Christians who worked their way through Spain into Africa. If the Donatist Berbers hoped that they would be rewarded for their support against the Romans, they were sadly mistaken. Religious persecution continued – including the destruction of religious and other images which was the Vandals' main characteristic. If half the Roman statues in the Bardo, for example, seem to have had their noses and penises knocked off, that is down to the Vandals.

Religion apart, the conquerors found what remained of Roman luxury fatally congenial – there are reports of a great pleasure palace south of Carthage. They never got any further than northern Tunisia, and after the death of **King Genseric** in 477 a succession of weak rulers tried unsuccessfully to levy extortionate taxes from the ever-rebellious Berbers.

THE BYZANTINES, 533–646

After little more than a century, the Vandals offered a tempting target to the resurgent eastern half of the Roman Empire, now established in Byzantium (modern Istanbul). The great Emperor Justinian had grandiose plans for recovering the lost realms of the western Empire, and to this end dispatched **Belisarius**, his general, in 533. Belisarius sailed with his army to Sicily, now held by the Ostrogoths, hoping to exploit their differences with the Vandals. In the event, the landing and conquest were so easy that this was unnecessary.

The same cannot be said for the next century of **Byzantine rule**. As virtual absentee landlords, hoping to exploit the territory, the Byzantines found themselves no more able than the Vandals to control the insurgent Berbers of the west and south. They made a more concerted effort, building massive fortresses whose ruins are almost the only reminder of their presence, but the Berbers were gradually proving that they could not be ruled by force alone, and Tunisia was too remote from Byzantium to be a prime concern. In 646 the Prefect Gregory declared the province independent of Byzantium, but this new state lasted only a year before falling to the **Arabs**.

THE FIRST ARAB RULERS, 647–800

When the first wave of **Arab invaders** hit North Africa from the east and defeated and killed the Byzantine Prefect Gregory at Sbeitla in 647, their new religion of Islam was less than 50 years old. After victory at Sbeitla, the first invaders stayed long enough only to collect their share of the rich booty distributed. It was the third Islamic wave, led by **Oqba Ibn Nafi**, which finally put down roots, making Tunisia part of a vast Arab empire ruled by the **Ummayad Caliphs** from Damascus. Ibn Nafi founded Kairouan as regional capital in 670. The rest of the seventh century was taken up with quelling the last of Berber resistance, led most famously by a legendary Jewish queen, Kahina; but in the eighth century it was with Berber converts in their army that the Arabs advanced to Spain (and ultimately as far as Poitiers in central France).

However, as with Donatism 400 years earlier, the Berbers turned to heresy as a way of asserting their independence. It took the form of **Kharijism**, a movement hostile to central government which denied any need for the Caliph to be an Arab, and advocated his election from among all true believers. This idea became very popular among the Berbers, who rose in rebellion under its banner. First defeated outside Kairouan in 742, they went on to conquer the city in 757 but were driven out four years later and their movement pushed into the south of the country, which remained part of a Kharijite state until 909. The Ibadites of Jerba are all that remains of it today, but paradoxically, it was Kharijism which brought Islam to almost all Berbers, making Islamicisation of North Africa far more lasting than Romanisation ever had been. Disaffection continued but the Berbers now broadly shared a faith with their rulers.

THE AGHLABIDS, 800–909

By the end of the eighth century, the **Abassid Caliphs** – who had usurped the Ummayads in 749 and moved their capital to Baghdad – were finding it ever harder to hold onto Spain and North Africa. When Ibrahim Ibn Aghlab put down a military rebellion and declared himself governor in 800, Tunisia became independent in all but name. For a century his descendants, the **Aghlabids**, controlled the whole country bar the Kharijite south. Unpopular in religious circles because of their dissolute lifestyle, the Aghlabids tried to make up for it by constructing and embellishing religious buildings throughout their domain. They also built a series of walled cities and *ribats*, most importantly Sousse, from where, in 827, they launched an invasion of Sicily. The island remained in Islamic hands until the eleventh century, and in 846 an Arab raiding party even managed to attack Rome and sack Saint Peter's.

The Aghlabids' building programme, their conquest of Sicily and raids on Italy, and their concern for irrigation and agriculture, made their reign something of a **golden age** for Tunisia. Their effect on culture was also strong: by the time their emirate fell, more people in Tunisia spoke Arabic than Berber.

FATIMIDS AND ZIRIDS, 909–1156

Meanwhile, yet another heresy was finding fertile ground in North Africa. The **Ismailis**, a Shiite faction, sent one **Abu Abdullah** to Algeria as a missionary for their cause. He soon converted a number of formerly Kharijite Berbers who joined him to invade the Aghlabid state in 903. When they took Kairouan, six years later, the Syrian Ismaili leader **Obaidallah Said** decided to come to Tunisia and take over, but was imprisoned en route by Kharijites in Sijilmasa (Morocco). Abu Abdullah struck west and attacked the Kharijites, destroying their Tahirt-based state which controlled Jerba and the south of Tunisia. On his liberation, Obaidallah declared himself *Mahdi* (see p.372) and took political power. Claiming descent from the Prophet's daughter Fatima, he began the **Fatimid dynasty** and built a new capital at Mahdia. He showed his gratitude to Abu Abdullah by having him assassinated.

Obaidallah and his successors made themselves highly unpopular through their attacks on the orthodox **Sunni** faith of most of their subjects – they had a distinguished lawyer flogged in the Great Mosque at Kairouan and various prominent Sunni theologians assassinated – and the extortionate taxes they levied to finance overseas military exploits. It was the Kharijites, however, who rose up against them. Led by **Abu Yazid** ("the Man on the Donkey") from Tozeur, they beseiged Mahdia in 944 and Kairouan the following year. The revolt was not crushed until 947.

In fact, the Fatimids were never primarily interested in Tunisia: they had their eyes on Egypt, and then the Caliphate itself. Obaidallah launched an abortive **campaign against Egypt** in 914–15 but, driven out by an army from Baghdad, had to be content with consolidating his power base and establishing control of Morocco and Sicily. In 961, however, his great-grandson El Muizz seized an opportune moment and finally achieved the long-desired conquest of Egypt, founding the forerunner of modern Cairo. The Fatimids ruled Egypt until overthrown by Saladin in 1171. They left Tunisia in the charge of their nominees, the **Zirids**.

The arrangement lasted until 1046, when the Zirids, under pressure from their subjects, withdrew their allegiance to the heretical Fatimids, transferring it back to the Sunni Caliphs in Baghdad. The Fatimids responded by unleashing against their former representatives the **Banu Hilal**, a hostile nomadic tribe who had been causing them trouble in Egypt. The Hilalians descended on Tunisia in an orgy of destruction – Ibn Khaldoun compared them to a swarm of locusts – which may in reality have been more the culmination of an already advanced process of disintegration. At any rate, they were more than a match for the Zirids, who abandoned Kairouan and holed up in Mahdia, leaving cities such as Tunis, Sfax, Gabes and Gafsa virtually independent, and the countryside under the control of **nomads** who had little use for the **infrastructure** of a settled society. This infrastructure, which had, since Roman times, helped to keep the region unified, fell into disuse. The country reverted to the fragmented, dark-ages condition of early Phoenician times – a few isolated coastal centres, and an unproductive stateless interior.

ALMOHADS AND ALMORAVIDS, 1159–1229

This disarray was exploited by maritime Europeans: the **Normans** recaptured Sicily in 1072, then took Jerba and ports on the east coast, and finally Mahdia in 1148, thus ending the last remnants of the Zirid state.

They were evicted by the **Almohads**, a religious movement from Morocco which followed the teachings of a revolutionary preacher named Ibn Tumart, whom they had declared *Mahdi*. After driving the ruling **Almoravids** out of Morocco and Spain into a final refuge on the Balearic Islands, the Almohads turned their attention eastwards to Tunisia. They took Tunis in 1159 and Mahdia the following year, and came to control an area stretching from Spain to Libya, uniting the Maghreb under a regime based in Marrakesh.

The Almohads' rule saw a massive growth in **Sufism** and an atmosphere of religious turmoil, but their biggest threat in Tunisia came in 1184 when they tried to subjugate the Balearic Islands. Pre-empting attack, the Almoravids under **Ibn Ghaniya** launched an invasion of Tunisia and set up a base in the Jerid. From there, they went on to conquer most of the country; but just as Tunis fell to them in 1203, an Almohad force captured their home base of Majorca and cut off their armies.

THE HAFSIDS, 1207–1574

Having regained Tunisia, the Almohads left it in the hands of a governor whose family, the **Hafsids**, ruled it from then on, declaring independence in 1229 when the Marrakesh regime repudiated Ibn Tumart's teachings. Many saw the Hafsids as the Almohads' legitimate heirs.

The Hafsids made **Tunis** their capital and gave the country the new orientation it needed. Contact with Europe was re-established after a gap of several centuries, and the trading state created by the Hafsids is recognisably the direct ancestor of modern Tunisia.

Mediterranean relations were both friendly and hostile, both mutually threatening and beneficial. The Hafsids sent ships to Valencia in 1238 to help the Muslim citizens defend themselves against the Christian kingdom of Aragon; but with Valencia's fall, they opened trading relations with Aragon. These grew to such an extent that eventually a large number of Christians were able to live in Tunisia under Aragonese protection, and were even allowed to preach their religion.

This did not prevent a **crusade** (the eighth crusade) being led against Tunisia by Louis IX of France. Louis's expedition was prompted by a desire to convert the Hafsid Sultan El Mustansir and by debts owed to French traders in Tunis; but after taking Carthage, the French king died suddenly of plague (he was later canonised).

Trade was now booming in the Mediterranean, and Tunis was exploiting it more successfully than anyone. Complex agreements were signed with European states such as Venice, Pisa and Genoa. There was also trade across the desert with West Africa, and in 1262 an embassy even arrived from Norway.

Hand in hand with trade went piracy – the two were often indistinguishable – and the **corsairs** of **Barbary** (as North Africa was now known in Europe) became the legendary scourge of Christian merchants, plundering their goods on the high seas and selling their crews into slavery. Christian corsairs were just as efficient as their Muslim counterparts, and Genoa and Pisa had their own **slave markets**. Credit arrangements between Barbary and Europe included provisions for ransoming captured merchants and sailors.

With the proceeds of these activities, **El Mustansir** (1249–77) created a kingdom in Tunis that was recognised as the leading monarchy in the Islamic world. Cultural life flourished and building programmes established what became Tunisia's classic style of architecture, influenced by the Andalusian artisans who were encouraged to immigrate from Spain.

After El Mustansir's death, however, the Hafsid state was riven with internal strife and became so weak that Tunisia began to disintegrate into small **city states** once again, Gabes, Gafsa and Tozeur being the main ones. Christians from Sicily occupied Jerba in 1284 and the Kerkennah Islands in 1286, and the region was twice split with rival sultans in Tunis and Bougie (Algeria). But in 1370, the Bougie sultan, **Abul-Abbas**, captured Tunis, took control of all the city states and islands, and reunited the country, beginning a Hafsid revival that lasted another century. In 1390, he even saw off a joint European expedition against Mahdia.

The Hafsids continued to rule until 1574 although their state was in decline, losing any real power in 1534. Even so, they had presided over a settled and prosperous era lasting more than three hundred years, one to which Tunisians still look back with some pride.

EARLY ISLAMIC SOCIETY

Although **Islam** reached virtually all the Berbers, largely through the medium of rural marabouts, society was little more homogeneous than it had been under the Romans. The rulers, whether Aghlabid, Fatimid or Zirid, had little in common with most of their subjects. The resentment of the ever-oppressed Berbers was felt even at the most apparently stable periods – hence, for example, the secluded palaces built by the Aghlabids outside Kairouan. Occasionally it found focus in a leader such as Abu Yazid, "The Man on a Donkey" from Tozeur, and the rulers were forced to defend themselves.

Urban society, however, flourished. Scholarship, law and education centred on mosques and the religious tradition (see p.349), and in the first centuries Arab culture here, as elsewhere, was able to absorb and disperse the knowledge it acquired during its rapid expansion. A specific example in Tunisia was the introduction around Gabes of silk culture, which had first been encountered in China. **Ibn Khaldoun**, a truly original thinker, was born in Tunis in 1332 and lived through an eventful 74 years which took in scholarship, exile and high political office. His best-known work, *Al Muqaddimah* (see p.364), set out historical principles several centuries ahead of its time. He saw history as a cycle reflecting the relative power of desert tribes and an urban state. The tribes were strong because life in the desert was harsh, they were constantly at war with their neighbours, and shared *assabiya*, solidarity that derived from their common descent and interests. The cities (and the states they supported) were, by contrast, weak because the luxury of urban life corrupted their bodies and their society. Tribes, such as the Hafsids in the thirteenth century, that were greedy for the wealth that control of a city offered, could defeat and take over a state that was internally weak. But as the new rulers settled into the same mould they also succumbed ultimately to another tribe. And so history unfolded in a cycle of dynastic rise and fall, but not progress.

The physical breadth of Arab culture played a large part in spreading knowledge. The geographer, **Ibn Battuta**, was born in Tangier in 1304, and is estimated subsequently to have travelled 120,000km. Even in early centuries, before the advent of the Ottoman Turks, it was a surprisingly cosmopolitan society – much more so than the bloodthirsty and intolerant image cherished by its Christian opponents might suggest. The Fatimid general Jawhar ("Pearl"), who captured Egypt in 970, had been a Christian eunuch slave in Sicily, which was itself a remarkable example of its period: when the Normans recaptured Sicily for Christendom in the eleventh century, they found the Arab culture so congenial that they happily made the most of it while at the same time raiding the Tunisian coast. In 1270 Louis IX's expeditionary force at Carthage found itself fighting against the army of Frederick of Castile, who had been engaged by the Sultan.

Islamic art, however, took a very different form from European. The ban on human and animal images removed at a stroke the narrative core of representative art, leaving an emphasis on disembodied form that came to be seen in **architecture** as well as in the **decorative arts**. For all their surface brilliance, Islamic buildings are distinguished most by their manipulation of space, whether in a courtyard or in a dome. In a Christian cathedral, large spaces are intended to be filled; but while spaces in mosques – courtyards or prayer halls – sometimes are filled, it is while they are empty that they have most significance, symbolising the all-embracing nature of Islam as a religion. Early architecture in Tunisia – the Great Mosques at Kairouan, Sousse, Tunis and Sfax – illustrates this aspect particularly well, and is outstanding in any company.

Later buildings, from the Hafsid period onwards, became locked into a more conservative and provincial style, with an emphasis on decoration rather than space. The classic elements of Tunisian architecture are the horse-shoe arch (a more restrained version than elsewhere in the Maghreb) and internal stucco decoration, a skill first brought by Andalusian artisans. Along with other features – tiles, doorways, relief patterns on minarets – these make for a tradition that is at its best extremely elegant, at its worst trivially pretty – a sort of classical Rococo. Certainly the majesty of the early buildings was lost when the Fatimids took their skills to Cairo in the tenth century.

SPANISH-TURKISH RIVALRY, 1534–1574

The sixteenth century in the western Mediterranean was glamorous but violent. Moorish civilisation in Spain was being toppled by the resurgent Christians and, encouraged by the capture of Granada in 1492, the Spanish launched naval raids on the ports of the Maghreb with some success. Opposition to these Christian corsairs arose in the form of the **Barbarossa** brothers Aruj and Khair ed Din, who based themselves on Jerba and set about winning back the Maghreb for Islam. After Aruj died in 1518 Khair ed Din petitioned the **Ottoman Turks** for support: still exhilarated by the capture of Constantinople in 1453, they needed no second invitation to contest such a vital region with the infidels, and Tunisia became the front line of an east–west confrontation, a sort of medieval Vietnam.

In 1529 Barbarossa took Algiers, then in 1534 he expelled the now abject Hafsids from Tunis, at the same time taking control of the east coast and Kairouan. This was too much for the Spanish, who sent a massive army in 1535 and restored the Hafsid **Moulay Hassan** as a puppet ruler. Events continued at this sort of pace for the next half-century, with Spain, France, Turkey, Naples and other powers all disputing the North African coast. In 1536 Francis I of France allied himself secretly with the Ottoman Sultan against their common enemy, Charles V of Spain. Fully supporting the Pope's denunciation of this unholy pact, Charles tried to make his own arrangement with the real regional power, Barbarossa, under which Barbarossa would become Spanish viceroy of the North African coast in return for helping to crush France and Turkey. This eventually fell through, however, and in 1544 Charles and Francis managed to resolve their differences in another treaty which nullified at a stroke the previous two.

Fighting in the field was fierce – the pyramid of skulls which stood on Jerba until 1849 was the result of one clash between Turks and Spanish – but the Turks were gradually gaining the upper hand. **Dragut**, a pirate who had been enslaved by the Spanish and ransomed by Barbarossa, extended his control from Jerba as far as Kairouan by 1557, and a flurry of activity at Tunis brought the war to a close. Taken from the Spanish in 1569 by an Algerian Turk, it fell to Don John of Austria in 1573, and then for the last time in 1574 to the combined Ottoman forces of Algiers, Tripoli and Turkey itself.

EARLY OTTOMAN RULE, 1574–1704

Tunis (like Algiers) was made a **Regency** of the Ottoman Empire, governed by a complex system which only helped to intensify internal strife. Power was divided between the **Bey**, a civil administrator in charge of the taxes levied from every town, the **Dey**, a military commander with access to the proceeds of foreign trade and piracy and the **Pasha**, the Ottoman Sultan's representative. At first it was the Deys who controlled the country: Othman Dey (1598–1610) and Youssef Dey (1610–37) were two commanders who left their mark on the architecture of Tunis, and by building up the fleet to renew its activities in the Mediterranean. In 1604 Jerba was brought back under Tunis's control. But while the Deys were busy with foreign and military affairs, Murad Bey and his son Hammouda Pasha (who combined the offices of Bey and Pasha), were strengthening their grip on domestic power, starting the first line of hereditary Beys, known as the **Muradids**. Firearms and the professional Turkish army allowed them to hold power far more effectively than any previous government and, unlike the Hafsids before them, they faced no threat of a tribal coup.

As the century wore on **European traders** were allowed back into the country. The first permanent French Consulate was built in the Tunis Medina in 1659, and an agreement was signed with England in 1662. Not that trade was any more tranquil than it had been before – in 1654 the English Admiral Blake bombarded and destroyed the pirate base of Porto Farina (Ghar el Melkh). But contact with the outside world boosted the opportunities for trade and began a short period of relative prosperity.

THE HUSSAYNIDS, 1704–1881

The Muradid line of Beys came to an end at the beginning of the eighteenth century when an Algerian invasion had to be repulsed. The successful commander was **Husayn Bin Ali**, a Turkish soldier of Greek origin based in Le Kef, who now took control of the country on the basis of his success. Despite his Ottoman ties he came to identify more and more with internal Tunisian interests, and from this time on the Ottoman connection, never very strong, was little more than nominal.

Such problems as Husayn had were closer to home. Having groomed a nephew, Ali, to succeed him, Husayn produced a son who naturally replaced Ali as heir. Ali responded by rebelling against his uncle, enlisting the support of the ever-hopeful Algerian Turks. Husayn was defeated once near the border at Le Kef in 1735, then killed at a battle near Kairouan in 1740. Now Husayn's sons in turn obtained Algerian support against the usurper: they too were defeated near Le Kef (1746), but ten years later succeeded in expelling Ali Pasha from Tunis. After seeing off (with some difficulty) their over-enthusiastic Algerian supporters, **Ali Bey** (1759–77) and **Hammouda Bey** (1777–1813) made Tunis once again a secure, prosperous and independent power in the Mediterranean.

But whatever their success in international politics the Beys failed to bring Tunisia fully under their control. Even at its apogee under Hammouda Bey, the Husaynid state only governed the cities, the Sahel, and the Tell. In the steppes of central Tunisia and in the far south the tribes were virtually autonomous. They paid their taxes irregularly, when forced to by a *mahalla* (military expedition), and though they might admit the Bey's sovereignty as commander of the faithful they would not allow him to intervene in their affairs.

The **early years of the nineteenth century** were the turning point of Tunisia's modern history. Under Hammouda Bey the economy and the state were strong, but in the following years both collapsed under an assault from the west. Cooperation between European navies after the Treaty of Aix-la-Chapelle in 1816 effectively put an end to Mediterranean piracy, an important source of revenues for the Beys. To make up the loss they increased taxes on trade and agriculture, putting a heavy burden on the economy. At the same time industrialisation gave European manufacturers a competitive edge that enabled them to subvert Tunisian products, first in the Mediterranean and then the domestic market. By the 1840s Tunisia's balance of trade surplus had become a deficit.

Tunisia was also beleaguered politically. In 1830 France had seized the Beylik of Algiers on the feeblest of excuses, and in 1836 it

signalled its interest in Tunisia by sending a fleet to discourage a Turkish invasion. To secure foreign protection without falling under the control of any one power, the Beys had to offer trading concessions to each of the European governments in turn, thereby aggravating the country's economic decline.

Ahmed Bey (1837–55) attempted to strengthen the state through internal reform — extending his control of local government and founding a **European-style army**. But this failed. The government could not afford these expenses and had to increase taxes and borrow from abroad. Furthermore, by employing French military advisers and going on a state visit to France in 1846, Ahmed Bey brought Tunisia firmly into the French camp, and once they had a grip they would not let go. Ahmed's successors, Mohammed Bey (1855–59) and Mohammed es-Sadok Bey (1869–82), were less dedicated to government reform than to a life of luxury. Their reckless expenditure on palaces and neglect of the administration brought the country to the brink of collapse. Not only did they contract debts at disadvantageous rates but, in 1864, the doubling of the **poll tax** led to a widespread revolt. At one point the European consuls, fearing that the capital would be overrun, packed their bags and were ready to leave. In the end the revolt fizzled out when the government backed down and the tribes fell out with each other. But by then the government's weakness was clear to all inside and outside Tunisia.

Unable to increase taxes, the Tunisian government was virtually bankrupt. Trying to keep itself afloat, the country borrowed at ever-increasing rates from European (mainly French) banks in a spiral enthusiastically encouraged by the European powers. By 1869 Tunisia's main creditors — France, Britain, and Italy — feared the Tunisian government would be unable to service these debts and that this might serve as a pretext for one of the powers to invade. In a rare moment of international cooperation they set up an **International Financial Commission** that effectively supervised every act of the Tunisian administration. Behind the scenes, however, the powers were jockeying for position. They fought among themselves to secure the contracts awarded by the Bey — the TGM railway in Tunis for instance — and influence at court.

The only Tunisian who came close to arresting this decline was **Kherredin**. As a minister in Mustapha Khaznader's government (1857–64) he had masterminded a form of constitutional monarchy that guaranteed the **civil rights** of Tunisian and foreign citizens (the name of which, *destour*, meaning "constitution" in Arabic, lives on in the modern **Destour Party**). But jealousy at court and his unpopular pro-Turkish policy had led to his dismissal in 1862. When he returned from retirement in 1869 to head first the International Financial Commission and then the Bey's government he realised that Tunisia's only hope was to play off one power against another while strengthening Tunisia from within. He reformed the administration, local government, and the legal system and seemed set to restore government control over the tribes and their finances. A rapprochement with Turkey enabled him to oppose the British and Germans, who did not want the ailing Turkish Empire broken up, against the French and Italians, who did, and so postponed the threatened French invasion.

Sadly Kherredin's government was short-lived (1870–77). Despite his reforms the economy was still weak and when he tried to embroil Tunisia in Turkey's war with Russia, as a loyal country of the Ottoman empire, the French Consul, **Theodore Roustan**, was able to galvanise opposition at court and have him overthrown. Without his directing hand the administration foundered. Worse still, the French were able to secure an agreement on the division of the Ottoman Empire with Britain and Germany at the Congress of Berlin in 1878. In return for Cyprus, Britain gave France a free hand in Tunisia. And so Tunisia's fate was sealed. France's only rival in Tunisia was now Italy – a new nation eager to join the colonial powers – and when the Italians appeared to be getting the upper hand at court the French decided to act.

In **1881** France announced that 9000 Khroumir tribesmen had raided Algeria, an action they had encouraged as a pretext, and that it was compelled to defend its territory. A force of 30,000 men was sent across the border, occupying first Le Kef and then Tunis where in May the Bey signed the **Treaty of Ksar Said**, ceding to the French all control over foreign affairs "to ensure the re-establishment of security and order along the frontier and the coast".

The Bey had given in without a fight, ordering his garrisons to surrender; in the words of a Tunisian song "he sold his people like vegetables". Even so, resistance continued piecemeal among the tribes, led by a former *caid* (provincial governor), **Ali ben Khalifa en-Naffati**. But when **Sfax** fell in July 1882, bombarded into submission by nine ironclads and four gun boats, and then **Kairouan** in October, many of the tribespeople submitted. The remainder (100,000 people, one tenth of the population) fled to Libya as dissident refugees. There, disappointed by the Sultan's indifference and starving in squalid camps, they gradually gave in. By 1885 there were probably fewer than 1000 dissidents left.

Having defeated all opposition, the French secured their control of Tunisia. In 1883 the **Treaty of the Bardo** recognised the Bey as the nominal ruler but forced him to comply with any "suggestions" made by the French Resident General. Thus whilst Tunisian administrators retained executive powers the French alone made policy.

THE FRENCH PROTECTORATE, 1881–1956

Colonial policy in Tunisia was less aggressive than it had been fifty years before in Algeria. There the French controlled the country directly and, following repeated rebellions, soldiers evicted Algerians to make way for colonists. In Tunisia the French were more clandestine, advancing the same policies under the cover of reforms to Tunisian law, usually with spurious claims to Islamic legitimacy. But the results were very much the same.

Large colonial estates were established in the Tell and Sahel by dispossessing Tunisians who lacked titles to their land. Tens of thousands of independent farmers were reduced to landless day-labourers. Iron, lead, and phosphate mining concessions were granted to French companies. Taxation increased markedly but government expenditure only met the needs of the colonists. A Tunisian-sponsored colonisation fund was established in 1897 to encourage **French immigration**. Roads, wells and dams were built to facilitate colonisation, not local development. Railways and ports were provided for the export of Tunisian resources to the metropole. Markets and advantageous tariffs allowed French goods to flood Tunisia, swamping local industry and draining precious local capital. In short, colonisation destroyed the Tunisian economy.

Within less than twenty years European settlers made up almost five percent of the population: 25,000 were French, but they were outnumbered by some 70,000 Italians. Most of the French colonists were government officials. They monopolised the higher echelons of the administration; few Tunisians achieved higher rank than a clerk. The **Italians**, fleeing impoverishment in southern Italy, set up small farms and businesses. Competition between the two communities was rife, occasionally violent. Eventually the French, fearing that their colonists would be overwhelmed by the militant Italians, many of whom were fervent supporters of Mussolini (and his fascist designs on the country), had to restrict their immigration to redress the imbalance.

There was little Tunisian **resistance**, at first, because Tunisia's urban elite, always cosmopolitan, was not over-resentful of the French presence. Life for them, particularly those around the Bey, was still very comfortable, and the resentment of the poorer classes had no outlet beyond sporadic outbreaks of violence. Those who sought reform, moreover, were admirers of France's material and economic power. These **young Tunisians** wanted co-operation with "mother France", not confrontation: they wanted to learn before seeking full independence.

Unfortunately, the French were by no means as conciliatory. Led by the newspaper publisher de Carnières, a strong colonial lobby opposed every reform. They saw **education** as a particular threat because it would make Tunisians unsuitable for the role they were born to fill, that of servant and labourers Their efforts were rewarded by cuts in the education budget and restriction of primary education to less than ten percent of the population.

Elitist and intellectual, the Young Tunisian movement could not rally popular support. Nor, despite demands for a wide range of constitutional rights, could its successor, the **Destour Party**, formed in 1920. Dominated by members of Tunisia's small professional and entrepreneurial middle class, they too were out of touch with the grass roots of Tunisian society, those who really suffered from colonisation. Their nationalism came across as a peculiarly ineffectual blend of nostalgia and legal hairsplitting rather than an active and broadbased campaign for independence.

Throughout the 1920s, however, growing resentment was fuelled by the economic depression. Violent demonstrations against French containing measures gave it some expression, but there was little organisation. Ever more reactionary, the Destour had nothing to offer, and a new organ was needed to channel popular nationalism. It was to meet this need that a group of rebels formed the breakaway **Neo-Destour Party** in March 1934 in Ksar Essaf. Their Secretary-General was **Habib Bourguiba**, whose life history epitomised the ideals of the new party. Born in 1903 into a lower-middle-class Monastir family, Bourguiba managed to make his own way by exploiting the few opportunities allowed Tunisians. He won a scholarship to the Sadiki College in Tunis, then another to study in Paris where he became a lawyer and married a French woman, returning to Tunis in 1927. His political activism did not fully begin until 1932, when he started up a newspaper, *L'Action Tunisienne*; two years later the new party was formed.

With his background, Bourguiba was able to identify and give voice to popular aspirations in a way that the old Destour party never had, and – for the first time in Tunisia's history – ordinary people acquired some (albeit outlawed) political muscle. Bourguiba was a formidable populist politician, and the Neo-Destour immediately drew massive support for its aims of **self-determination and a return to Islamic culture**. Ever the pragmatist, Bourguiba could be heard in these years advocating a return to the veil for women.

The French were quick to spot the threat posed by this new opponent. Six months after its foundation, they declared the party illegal and, for the first of many times over the next two decades, arrested Bourguiba. But their insecurity, and popular unrest, continued through the 1930s, fuelled by the situation in Europe and the growing ambition of **Mussolini**'s Fascist Italy. Having helped themselves to Libya in 1912 (taken from failing Turkey), and Ethiopia in 1936 – to the horror of the ineffectual League of Nations – the Italians' hopes of a new African Empire were rampant, and they had always felt cheated of Tunisia. The French built the **Mareth Line** – an

African Maginot Line – south of Gabes, and when Bourguiba was arrested after another violent demonstration in 1938 he was quietly interned in France to avoid any suggestions of weakness in Tunisia.

WORLD WAR II IN TUNISIA

Ironically, when France fell in **World War II** the **Italians** took Bourguiba to Rome, hoping for his support in their claim. Since, however, he trusted neither the Italians nor the Vichy French (nor much more, perhaps, the Free French), he consistently supported the Allies even when the **Germans** landed in Tunisia in November 1942.

The Germans had invaded in response to a double Allied advance: the British across the desert from Egypt (after El Alamein), and the Americans from Algeria following the **Operation Torch** landings of November 1942. The Allies needed Tunisia as a base to invade Italy, "the soft underbelly of Europe"; the Nazis needed it to control the Sicilian Channel and cut off Allied shipping from Egypt and India. By the end of the month the Allies had the west of the country, but as winter set in, they found the going harder than anticipated and, in February, **Rommel**'s retreating forces found a weak spot in the Americans' defences at **Kasserine** and inflicted a serious defeat. In spite of this setback, American forces held the line before the Algerian border as Commonwealth troops streamed into Tunisia from the east. By this time too, the Allies were able to decode Rommel's most secret messages, enabling them to obtain details of his plans and to identify and sink his supply ships.

The Germans held the **Mareth Line**, designed to prevent the Italians invading from Libya, now used against the Allies. By stealth, however, and using routes thought impassable by the Germans, **Montgomery**'s Eighth Army managed to get round the line, and had control of it by the end of March 1943, linking up with the Americans to the west. Over the next month, the Allies advanced through the country, their toughest battle being at **Takrouna**, which fell to New Zealand troops on April 19. On May 7, the Allies took Tunis and Bizerte, leaving the Germans only Cap Bon, for which a fierce battle was expected. In the event, however, German forces in Cap Bon surrendered only two days later.

The campaign fought in Tunisia is little known compared with the "glamour" of Tobruk and El Alamein, but the Allies alone left **15,000 dead**. Without Tunisia, moreover, it would have been impossible for them to invade Europe.

THE STRUGGLE FOR INDEPENDENCE, 1945–1956

After the end of the war, colonisers and colonised took up much where they had left off, and the only permanent reminder of this violent interlude are the **war cemeteries** dotted around the country. To all appearances, Bourguiba's political support for the Allies, and the military support of the many Tunisians who had fought for them, had very little effect on relations – but French intransigence would almost certainly have been hardened still further if the Tunisians had supported the Axis. Even so, **Bourguiba** had to make a hurried exit from Tunis in 1945 to avoid arrest. He went to Cairo, and spent the next few years travelling world capitals to drum up support for his country's cause, with considerable success. A born showman, he took to the stage of world politics with some panache.

Back at home, popular nationalism was growing steadily. The **UGTT**, a Tunisian-only Trade Union federation formed in 1946, became an important vehicle of resistance in Bourguiba's absence. A strike in Sfax in 1947 was put down violently. By 1950 the French were ready to talk, and even accepted Bourguiba as a negotiator. After he put forward proposals in Paris which included safeguards to French interests in Tunisia, a government was installed in 1951, headed by **Mohammed Chenik**, who had led a nationalist administration against the Axis occupation. But in a pattern that was to be repeated later in Algeria, the first signs of concession from the French home government produced a sudden hardening in the resistance of the Tunisian French. Under pressure from them, the French government reversed its policy. Bourguiba was exiled to Tabarca, then France, and **violence** escalated. In December 1952 **Farhat Hached**, Secretary-General of the UGTT and a close friend and ally of Bourguiba, was gunned down in Tunis by the **Red Hand**, a group of French settler terrorists.

This only succeeded in promoting international sympathy for the Tunisians: the Latin

American countries had succeeded in October 1952 in getting their problems on the UN agenda, and a resolution was passed calling for the resumption of **French-Tunisian talks**. There were those in France and Tunisia who thought the issue could be squashed, including a repressive French Resident General immortalised for his statement that "There can be no question of putting Monsieur Bourguiba on trial. Tunisians, who are apt to forget easily, have already almost forgotten his name." But if there was no legal outlet for nationalism, the guerrilla gangs who began to appear in the hills showed that it could not be simply ignored. In 1954 France suddenly reversed its policy, worried by recent disasters in Indo-China and fearing that, if they did not come to an agreement with Bourguiba, more radical politicians might gain the upper hand. Pierre Mendes-France came to Tunis with plans for internal self-government. After many months of talks, agreement was reached in June 1955, and Bourguiba returned to Tunis to an ecstatic welcome.

The agreement reached, however, only gave Tunisia limited internal autonomy – foreign policy and some aspects of the economy were still to be controlled by France – and this gave Bourguiba's traditional opponents an angle of attack. They claimed that he had compromised and betrayed the Tunisian nation – this was the time in the 1950s when pan-Arabism, inspired by Nasser in Egypt, was running strongly. Bourguiba's leading opponent, **Salah Ben Youssef**, defeated politically in December 1955, took to guerilla warfare with Egyptian and Algerian support. By 1956, though, his revolt had been suppressed; Ben Youssef escaped to Cairo, and five years later was murdered in Frankfurt.

Bourguiba always retained the support of the people, and he was well aware that full independence was within his grasp; on March 20, 1956, soon after Morocco, Tunisia became an independent state.

TUNISIA UNDER HABIB BOURGUIBA 1956–1987

In the years following **Independence** Bourguiba set up the political and legal framework for the kind of state he had envisaged. Almost immediately **elections** were held for the National Assembly, the result virtually a clean sweep for Bourguiba's **Front National**. By 1959 the Constitution had been passed in the Assembly. It gave Bourguiba wide powers as President, including nomination of government and civil service personnel, and initiation of legislation. Since all members of the Assembly were nominees of the Party (re-styled the *Parti Socialiste Destourien* or **PSD**), government really was Bourguiba's personal fiefdom. The small Communist Party was dissolved in 1963, to leave what was in theory a one-party state – in practice, a benevolent dictatorship under the Supreme Combattant. With the political framework in place, Bourguiba immediately set about bringing in the sweeping **social reforms** he had long sought. While in opposition, circumstances had dictated that he should call for a return to the Muslim veil for women, but now marriage laws were framed giving women a more powerful voice, and outlawing polygamy (though this had never been very widespread). Women were given the franchise, equal pay made statutory, family planning introduced on a wide scale, and education for women strongly encouraged (see p.354).

Another area of planned reform was more narrowly **religious**, and here Bourguiba had to tread very carefully to avoid alienating the religious establishment. He downgraded the great Zitouna University in Tunis to a theological faculty of the modern university, and in a still more daring step attempted to end the tradition of the Ramadan fast (see p.347). Working from within the Islamic tradition, Bourguiba obtained official support for the following ingenious argument: those engaged in a *jihad* (holy war) are excused from Ramadan; Tunisians are engaged in a *jihad* against underdevelopment; therefore Tunisians are excused from observing Ramadan. What is remarkable about this attempt is not the ingeniousness of the argument or the fact that it eventually failed, but Bourguiba's audacity both in challenging such a basic thread in the fabric of Tunisian life, and in getting official support for his challenge from the Mufti of Tunis. The main centre of resistance to change was the holy city of **Kairouan**, which had previously also opposed the enforcement of monogamy; the citizens pointedly observed Ramadan a day early, simultaneously with Cairo, in a gesture of Arab solidarity.

period of mixed success. It took several years to hive off the last remnants of the **colonial presence**, occasionally at some cost. The first of these problems was the naval arsenal at Bizerte, where the French had stayed on after independence because of NATO's decision that it was a vital link. To begin with there was no antagonism, but then in 1958 French planes from Algeria bombed the border village of **Sakiet Sidi Youssef**. This incident, at the beginning of the Algerian War of Independence, was denounced as "a new Guernica", and the newly independent colony understandably felt strongly about it. Tunisia demanded the evacuation of Bizerte, the French refused, and the Tunisian Army went into action for the first time. Some 1300 Tunisian lives were lost in a symbolic and drawn-out action before the French agreed to leave by 1963. Another moment of colonial tension came in 1964 when Bourguiba, under the influence of the young left wing of his party, suddenly **nationalised** the land of remaining settlers. Given his determination to maintain close relations with France relations were soon back to normal, helped by Bourguiba's unusually repentant tone in conceding a lack of experience.

During this decade Bourguiba set his pragmatic style in **foreign policy** – a pragmatism that could at times seem paradoxically radical. In 1965, during a visit to the Middle East, he referred to the existence of Israel as a "colonial fact", implying that the Arabs should negotiate over the Palestinian question. At a time two years before the June War when Arab rhetoric, led by Nasser, was more concerned with driving the Israelis into the sea, this was not a move calculated to improve solidarity. Indeed, Bourguiba's relations with Nasser remained explosive, partly because Bourguiba felt that he had been upstaged by Nasser as the leading man of the Arab world. Bourguiba's western orientation – in 1966 he actually voiced approval of US bombing in Vietnam – was another stumbling block, and in 1968 Tunisia boycotted the Arab League because of what it felt were pro-Soviet tendencies.

At home Bourguiba had his own problems of orientation, caused largely by the career of **Ahmed Ben Salah**. Once a leader of the UGTT trades union organisation, Ben Salah had been forced out in 1956 after daring to claim an

equal role for the unions in government. However in 1961 the President switched course, appointing Ben Salah as Minister of Planning, and began to direct the country along an increasingly leftist course. Collectivisation was introduced, particularly in agriculture, with cooperatives being formed out of the old peasant smallholdings. Bourguiba went around the country on well-publicised outings where he was shown riding through prickly-pear fences, a traditional symbol of the smallholder's pride. But in 1969, Bourguiba decided that collectivisation was a failure. Ben Salah and his policies were purged, and the country was given a violent twist to the right.

The Ben Salah affair was typical of Bourguiba's avowedly autocratic **style of government**: guided by the demands of the moment rather than by any long-term overriding principles, yet somehow still carrying the vast majority of the population. By appointing a **Prime Minister** to deal with executive matters – from 1969 – and so putting himself somewhere above everyday politics, he made himself a figure of almost royal detachment. When mistakes were made he could sacrifice a subordinate, such as Ben Salah, and enhance his own reputation by appearing to correct misjudgements that were ultimately his own responsibility. Ever a master of political infighting, as well as the wider stage, Bourguiba resisted an attempt at the beginning of the 1970s to reduce his influence within the Party, and in 1974 he was elected President for life.

As the 1970s wore on, however, Tunisia's international reputation for political stability and contentment in the developing world was being threatened. Early in the decade the government began to legislate against strikes, and the country's **human rights** record brought it mentions in the reports of Amnesty International. Deteriorating relations between the government and unions eventually came to a head when a strike in the mining industry in 1977 was followed in January 1978 by the first **general strike** since Independence, called by the UGTT. The strike was violently suppressed by government forces and arrests were made; in June the Socialist Democratic Movement was (illegally) formed. On the second anniversary of the general strike the mysterious **"Gafsa incident"** (see p.229), possibly a Libyan-backed coup attempt, was clearly an attempt at destabilisation, however badly calculated.

By now, though, the government was making promises of **political liberalisation**. In 1981 other political parties were legalised – providing, that is, they were representative, constitutional, "preserved national gains", and rejected fanaticism, violence, and foreign dependence. This, in effect, meant that the government could choose and manacle the opposition by rejecting the applications for legalisation made by parties that they considered too popular. As it was, the PSD/UGTT federation won all 136 seats in the November 1981 **election**, the first free election since 1956, prompting complaints of electoral malpractice from the recently formed Socialist Democrats and Popular Unity Movement.

Even more serious was the question of **Islamic fundamentalism**. Like every moderate Arab state, Tunisia was worried by the prospect of the Iranian Revolution spreading to its own shores and, as early as 1979, the government had banned the fundamentalists. In 1981 two religious movements appeared, the *Mouvement de la Tendence Islamique* (**MTI**) and the *Rassemblement Nationale Arabe* (**RNA**), only to be banned in July, before the elections. Soon after, over 100 of their leaders were summarily arrested and sentenced to long prison terms – arrests which presaged a new era of repression.

Meanwhile, discontent was fuelled by high **unemployment** (14 percent according to government statistics, but more realistically 20 percent and up to 40 percent among the young), by **poverty** (average income was only £1.25 per day), and **repression** administered by the police and the Destour Party's unofficial militia. There was little chance of an organised popular opposition because of the government's crackdown on dissidents. Consequently, when Tunisia's youth eventually exploded in January 1984, following the government's announcement that it would remove the **subsidy on bread** (Tunisians have one of the world's highest bread consumptions), **rioting** was spontaneous. It began in the south and west, the poorest regions, and quickly spread to Tunis. After ugly street battles with the police, in which at least eighty people were killed, Bourguiba went on television to announce that the subsidy had been restored, and the riots ended almost as suddenly as they had begun.

At a government level there was some doubt as to who would be sacrificed – there being no question that Bourguiba, though head of state, would relinquish responsibility . After a brief period of uncertainty the Prime Minister, **Mohammed Mzali**, survived, and **Driss Guiga**, the Interior Minister, was made scapegoat. Yet although the government soon settled down to its austerity programme and raised the price of bread again within a couple of months, everyone knew that the riots had shaken the leadership. This tacit understanding in turn hardened government attitudes towards the opposition – and encouraged the regime's opponents to redouble their efforts.

The UGTT under **Habib Achour** quickly dissociated itself from the electoral alliance of three years before and began to campaign rigorously on the government's economic and human rights records. Achour, a rival of Bourguiba's since the 1950s, set himself up as the unofficial leader of the opposition in the hope that he could rally the young behind a socialist flag and overthrow the government. He had little chance. In January 1986 he was arrested and imprisoned with twenty other Union leaders on trumped-up charges.

With the unions now under the government's thumb it was the **fundamentalists** who represented the greatest threat. For a short time the government appeared conciliatory and accorded the banned MTI's *emir*, **Abd el Fateh Morou**, a sort of semi-recognition. But after continued student unrest and a series of bomb attacks on ministry buildings it clamped down harder than ever. **General Ziadine Ben Ali**, the officer who commanded the riot troops in 1984, was appointed Minister of the Interior in May 1986. In the following month police appeared on the campuses, 1500 students were arrested, a publishing house with fundamentalist sympathies was closed down, and a purge of the civil service and armed forces began.

Bourguiba, who had virtually retired in the early 1980s, feared that he was losing control and began to reassert his authority throughout the administration. Early in 1986 he divorced and expelled his wife, Wassila, a formidable woman who had political aspirations of her own, and, under the guise of an anti-corruption campaign, arrested her relatives and minions. In June he appointed the 90-strong Central Committee of the Destour Party, a body that was usually elected by party members. Then in July, as a *tour de force*, he dismissed Mzali, whom he had publicly named as his successor only a month before, and replaced him with the economist, **Rachib Sfar**.

Mzali, a liberal with dreams of opening up the electoral process, was a danger to Bourguiba and his continuing control of power. It was no surprise, then, that the **elections of November 1986** were a sham, even boycotted by the recognised opposition parties. As for the fundamentalists, Bourguiba became even more determined that they should be eliminated. They were, he stated in private, a menace to the very nature of the secular state he had created and to destroy them would be the last great service he could render his country.

Early in 1987 the police began arresting suspects on the streets and by the end of April more than 2000 people had been jailed, among them **Rachid Ghannuchi**, the new leader of MTI. The Tunisian League of Human Rights complained about torture and detention without charge, only to find its offices closed and its leader under arrest. Men shaved off their beards to avoid suspicion and women took off their chadors. In March the government broke off relations with Iran, claiming that Iranian diplomats were inciting political unrest and providing the fundamentalists with arms. Shortly afterwards Rachid Ghannuchi and ninety other fundamentalists were charged with promoting terrorism and conspiring with Iran to overthrow the state.

Far from frightening the fundamentalists into submission, the campaign of repression sparked off a series of retaliatory **demonstrations and bombings**. And in August the fundamentalists showed that they were willing to strike at the government's Achilles heel: the economy. Bombs planted at four hotels near Monastir injured twelve tourists and threatened to mar Tunisia's reputation as a safe holiday resort. With **tourism** the country's most important source of foreign exchange and an employer of one in ten of the population, this would be a severe blow.

Fortunately, the government backed down from further confrontation. At the end of September only nine of the fundamentalists on trial were sentenced to death and five of them were sentenced *in absentia*. Then at the beginning of November – amid rumours of Bourguiba's ill health – Rachid Sfar resigned as Prime Minister to be replaced by **General Ben Ali**. Within a week (on November 7, 1987, a date commemorated in the names of many streets) Ben Ali had seized power in a **palace coup**. Bourguiba was diagnosed as senile, not surprisingly given his decrepit appearance in the previous months, and forced to retire. Ben Ali's opponents and rivals were placed under house arrest and a new administration was formed.

TUNISIA TODAY

Most Tunisians sighed with relief. Despite continuing affection for Bourguiba, particularly among older Tunisians who remember the French occupation, he was considered too old and out of touch to govern effectively. The question of succession had, moreover, created a great deal of uncertainty over the previous decade and its settlement was seen as a sign of returning stability.

Once in power, Ben Ali pursued a policy of **national reconciliation**, releasing 5000 political prisoners over the next six months, including MTI leader Rachid Ghannuchi. He reduced government interference in the internal politics of the UGTT trade union federation and began to introduce **political reforms**, banning imprisonment without trial, relaxing political censorship and putting the presidency up for election every five years.

In February 1988, Ben Ali announced that the ruling PSD was to change its name again, henceforth being known as the *Rassemblement Constitutionnel Démocratique* (Democratic Constitutional Assembly, or **RCD**). Limited freedom of political activity was also introduced, with opposition parties allowed to operate, and recognised by the state, so long as they were not anti-constitutional, religious, ethnic or regional. A number of opposition parties were legalised – though not the fundamentalist MTI.

At the RCD's first conference in July 1988, Ben Ali promised free expression and free **elections**. The latter materialised in April the following year, and resulted in the RCD taking all the seats and, apparently, eighty percent of the votes. Their main challengers were Islamic fundamentalists who, banned from fighting the election as a party, fought as independents and obtained up to a quarter of the vote in some areas. The MTI, now called **Ennahdha**, dismissed the elections as fraudulent and Rachid Ghannuchi moved to Paris where he felt freer to speak out.

Political **liberalisation** continued through 1989, with more amnesties and talk of legalising Ennahdha, but when this proved to be little more than talk, Ennahdha began to step up its activities. In December, a group of fundamentalist students began a hunger strike in protest at government attempts to close the faculty of theology at the Zitouna University in Tunis. Allegations of government inaction following the **January 1990 floods**, which killed thirty people and left thousands homeless, added fuel to the movement, together with a strike by municipal workers, riots in Nefta and Sidi Bou Zid, and clashes in Sfax and Kairouan between police and students associated with Ennahdha. The alarm bells really started ringing when fundamentalists scored a massive victory in **Algerian municipal elections** in June 1990. Arrests began in September as **repression** set in. Twelve opposition publications were closed and Ennahdha's student organisation banned. Meanwhile, moves were made to bring the legal opposition into the establishment fold. Legal opposition parties were given free seats in 1991 by-elections, and guaranteed **handouts** from the pork barrel. The illegal opposition were portrayed as "terrorists", with allegations of bomb-making and coup attempts. Since then, the **human rights** situation has deteriorated, and **Amnesty International** has expressed its concern. In October 1991, three fundamentalists were executed for the murder of a security guard in a raid on RCD offices.

TUNISIA'S FOREIGN RELATIONS

Ben Ali's problems don't stop at home. **Relations between Tunisia and its neighbours**, especially Libya, have had their ups and downs. In the late 1970s Tunisia accused Libya of interfering in its internal affairs, and it was generally believed that Libya had backed the "Gafsa coup" in 1980. After Tunisia lost a border dispute settled at the International Court of Justice, tension increased. In March 1985 the Libyan "Voice of Vengeance Radio" called on Tunisians to massacre their Jewish community and in the same month police

arrested seven suspected "terrorists" crossing the border. Then, at the beginning of August 1985, Libya expelled 31,000 Tunisian workers, most of them illegal immigrants. Libyan troops began to mobilise on the border and Habib Bourguiba said privately that he was ready to go to war. Arbitration by Kuwait managed to avert such drastic measures, but relations between the two leaders remained sour.

Since Ben Ali took power, however, there has been a dramatic improvement. The **Great Arab Maghreb**, based on a 1983 treaty between Tunisia and Algeria, has been gradually widened to include Morocco, Mauritania and, since June 1988, Libya. Libya has compensated the workers expelled in 1985 and opened its frontier with Tunisia, while the two countries have agreed freedom of movement between them, the right of their citizens to live and work in both countries, and the amicable settlement of a dispute over Mediterranean oil fields. The February 1989 establishment of the **Arab Maghreb Union**, an EEC-like organisation of the five Maghreb states, has helped to normalise relations further.

Ben Ali has also been successful in maintaining good **relations with the West**, in particular with France and the USA. America was the first country to recognise independent Tunisia and so it is not surprising that bonds between the two countries have been solid. There are **Peace Corps** workers and American military advisers, and in 1986 the Tunisian and American armies carried out a joint exercise. Many Tunisians believe that Ben Ali, who was trained in the USA, came to power with America's tacit support if not positive blessing. Certainly Tunisia makes a valuable United States ally: not only does it lie between Algeria and Libya, but the naval base at Bizerte is one of the best in the Mediterranean.

Relations with the West, however, came under great strain during the **1991 Gulf crisis**. Following Iraq's invasion of Kuwait, the USA and its allies, including Egypt and Saudi Arabia, sent troops and attacked Iraqi forces. In Tunisia, public opinion was massively behind Iraq's leader Saddam Hussein, who was seen as a champion of the Arab nation against Western interests, a kind of latter-day Nasser. Fortunately, the fundamentalist opposition, funded largely from Saudi Arabia, was unable to capitalise on this feeling and Ben Ali successfully outflanked them, opposing American intervention, but not strongly enough to alienate his Western friends. Tourism, accounting for over ten percent of Tunisia's GDP, suffered badly but has now returned to normal, while elsewhere, with fundamentalism so far contained, Tunisia seems to have settled back into "business as usual".

PROSPECTS FOR THE 1990s

The **economy** is still shaky after the ravages of high inflation in the 1970s, but the IMF-imposed austerity programme introduced in 1987 has stopped the growth of Tunisia's huge national debt and brought inflation down to manageable levels – officially, at least, less than ten percent. Inevitably, this has involved unpopular measures such as an **earnings freeze** for public employees (the state is Tunisia's biggest employer), **devaluation of the dinar**, and **abolition of food subsidies** – only this time gradually to avoid serious repercussions like those of 1984.

The future is, however, far from certain for Ben Ali and Tunisia. As Bourguiba's heir, Ben Ali has a hard act to follow in many ways.

When future generations look back they will judge Bourguiba as the father of his country. Following independence he provided Tunisia with the framework for a constitutional and secular democracy, even if the reality did not quite live up to the ideal. His self-identification with the country's destiny gave Tunisians a national cohesion lacking in many developing countries. The standard of living is one of the highest in the developing world, with little of the extreme poverty experienced in Morocco and Egypt. All Tunisians have access to education as far as university level, and to health services. Actual social progress may have lagged behind the radical legal framework introduced nearly 40 years ago, but it is a mark of just how far Tunisia has come that it tends to be judged – not least by Tunisians themselves – by western standards and not those of its 1950s contemporaries.

The tradition of secularism and development seems safe enough in Ben Ali's hands, and yet as the country returns to **political repression and fundamentalist unrest**, the question remains: how many of Bourguiba's vices may Ben Ali have inherited along with his virtues?

ARCHITECTURE

Seeing the sites in Tunisia inevitably takes you to mosques – which, unlike those in Morocco and much of the Islamic world, are often open to non-Muslims. They follow the same basic plan, whatever their size, style, and age, the most important model in Tunisia being the Great Mosque of Kairouan (for a plan, see p.171).

Besides this religious architecture Tunisia has a wealth of domestic architecture which, unadvertised and often hidden, can say more about Tunisia than any mosque or beylical palace. The best way to see domestic architecture is just to wander around the medinas and the villages. Although you can walk into many of the semi-public outer courtyards, you should be sensitive – like most people, Tunisians get upset if strangers walk uninvited into their houses.

This brief account is an attempt to introduce and explain the design, development and function of Tunisian buildings.

MOSQUES

All mosques face **Mecca**, the birthplace of Islam, the site of the *Kaaba*, the place of pilgrimage, and, most important of all, the direction of prayer. In the mosque this direction is shown by the **mihrab**: a shallow alcove in the *qibla* (literally, the facing) wall. This is not an altar. The direction, not the niche, is sacred and representations of the *Kaaba* are often placed there to emphasise this point. The mosque is built around the axis passing through the mihrab and at right angles to the *qibla* wall, so that the whole building faces Mecca. (Incidentally, toilets and beds are usually aligned at right angles to the axis so as not to profane.)

The mosque is a place of worship and a sanctuary, its separation from the world outside guaranteed by high, and often windowless, walls and strong gates. Inside, large mosques usually have a courtyard like a house. The parallel is important, for Islam considers its adherents a family. At the *qibla* end of this courtyard, nearest Mecca, is the **prayer hall** – broad rather than long because the front row of worshippers receives greater *baraka*, blessing from Allah, than those behind. What restricts their breadth is the ability of worshippers at either end to hear the calls to prayer and so act in unison with the rest of the congregation.

The prayer hall has to be ritually pure, so it is usually separated from the remainder of the mosque by a step or balustrade – before entering worshippers must take off their shoes so that no dirt is carried in. The worshipper must also wash before prayer – either partially or totally depending on their state of ritual impurity – and a **washing fountain**, a well leading to the cistern below, is often provided in the centre of the courtyard (as at Kairouan's Great Mosque) or in a washing room to the side (as at the Jema'a Zitouna in Tunis).

Inside the prayer hall there is very little **religious furniture**. The **imam** leads the prayer and preaches from a **minbar** – a pulpit, usually a flight of steps in ornately carved wood, occasionally a permanent structure in stone. The imam sits on the second step from the top, the highest step being reserved for the prophet. In the days before loudspeakers the imam's voice was amplified by the *muezzin* sitting on a raised wooden platform, the *dikka*, and then relayed through the congregation by strategically placed respondents, the *muballighun*. Today the only other piece of furniture is the *kursi es-sura*, the wooden lectern, usually placed next to the *minbar*. This is important because recitation, *tawliq*, considered a great art in Islamic society, is the basis of the service. Otherwise the prayer hall is bare. There are no pews (the congregation sitting instead on a floor covered with **carpets** in the richer establishments and alfa matting in the poorer), no elaborate screens, and no paintings.

Other rooms or buildings may be added to this basic design according to the size and function of the mosque. There is usually a **minaret**, the most distinctive feature of the mosque on the skyline, from where the *muezzin* calls the faithful to prayer. Some mosques have tombs, often crowded against the *qibla* wall, sometimes as the centrepiece and *raison d'être* of the building. Others have dormitories for pilgrims or students, or a school room and library. But all these are appendices to the basic plan, for, in essence, the mosque is simply the *mihrab* and the prayer hall. Most of the **masjid** – mosques used for daily prayer – are just that. It is only the larger congregational mosques used for Friday prayer, the **jema'a**, that have all the features.

Stylistically one can trace a gradual move towards lighter construction and more ornate decoration. The first mosques, those of the **Aghlabids**, used heavy columns, frequently of Roman origin, massive construction, and little or no decoration. The prayer halls were, consequently, dark, and much more impressive in their size than in their style of construction. Later the Zirids introduced the first domes and so gave prayer halls extra light and a sense of space. With brighter interiors artists were able to develop finer and more sophisticated decoration. Under the **Hafsids** these trends continued: domes became larger, covering more and more of the prayer hall, and decoration became more detailed and sumptuous. Then, during the **seventeenth century**, Turkish architects revolutionised styles. The dome was extended to cover the whole prayer hall, the superstructure was reduced to a minimum, allowing for more windows, and **Ottoman** and **Italian** decorative features (the keel arch, painted tiles, and stucco plasterwork) were adopted. Prohibitive construction costs prevented the architects of less monumental mosques adopting the massive domes seen at the Jema'a Sidi Mehrez in Tunis, but more modest Ottoman ornamental features spread throughout the country. Since then, styles of construction have changed little, except that modern mosques are built in reinforced concrete and their tiles and arches are more likely to be mass-produced than handcrafted.

DOMESTIC ARCHITECTURE

For Tunisians **the home** should be genuinely private. Walking around the *medina* in any city you are immediately struck by the lack of windows looking out onto the narrow streets. Those that exist have heavy bars or ironwork grills, and doors leading into the houses are made of thick wood reinforced with iron studs. Tunisian houses look in towards the family, not out towards the wider world.

Traditionally, family life took place within a **courtyard**, the *wust al-dar*, a private place where visitors are rarely admitted. Here women could go about unveiled, protected from the prying eyes of strangers. Between them and the outside world was a **hall**, the *driba*, with benches built against the wall, or a second courtyard, the *wust el-dwiriya*, a sort of antechamber to the house where the men of the

family could entertain visitors. Within the living quarters rooms were arranged around smaller covered "courtyards" so that a single building could accommodate numerous related families.

In contrast to the plain and anonymous outside walls of Tunisian houses these courtyards and the living rooms behind them displayed **extravagant decoration**. Since the Middle Ages floors have been made of tessellated slabs (termed *keddal*), designs of black and white marble (from the Jebel Ichkeul) in the wealthiest houses. In the seventeenth century handpainted **tiles** from Qellaline and Nabeul became popular (to be replaced by cheap Italian factory-made copies in the nineteenth century), and most houses have tiles up to shoulder height on the walls. A fashion for ornate geometrical **stucco work** also developed in the seventeenth century, and in the houses of wealthier Tunisians this delicate tracery begins above the tiles and continues over the vaults. During the nineteenth century, **paintwork**, abandoned in the fifteenth century, regained favour, particularly on the wooden ceilings and rafters of upper floors. Consequently the houses of wealthy families were full of colour and ornamentation.

Architectural features changed with the fashion. During the seventeenth century, when North Africa was opened up to mediterranean, particularly Italian, influences, a **loggia** was often added to the courtyard, usually three "moorish" arches on classical columns. More substantial houses had peristyle courtyards, a balcony supported on vaults with ornate wooden balustrades. Twin windows were yet another Italian import.

Yet whatever changes of detail fashion might impose, the basic structure of the town house remained unchanged until the early years of the twentieth century. Not only did this design suit the social context, it was also functional. The inner courtyards made the living rooms light and encouraged a through draught that made the rooms cool in summer. Some of the houses were **foundouk** (merchants' "hotels"), those of the European merchants doubling up as consulates; the lower floors, readily accessible through the courtyard, provided *makhzen*, storage space and stabling. The courtyard itself covered a cistern, *madjus*, containing the rainwater that fell on the marble floors and the roofs, or storage cellars.

Urban houses were crammed into the limited space inside the city walls, making housing densities very high (about the same as early Manhattan in the case of the Tunis Medina). For this reason the city "streets" were narrow, convoluted, and seemingly chaotic. Yet chaotic they certainly were not. Within the city each ethnic group occupied its own **fariq**, or quarter. In Tunis, for instance, the Jews were segregated in the Hafsia and surrounded by a wall, the Europeans down near the Bab el Bahr. Early on in the indigenous quarters there was no segregation by class or wealth; instead, the households were grouped in loose ethnic or family groups. Many of the streets were impasses, sometimes called **darb**, hidden from major thoroughfares by sharp bends. Family groups lived around these *darb* which still bear their names. The street provided a sort of outer courtyard used by the wider family group.

This urban structure and building style began to change when the **French** arrived. The new grid cities they built – the **Villes Nouvelles** – became the favoured quarters of wealthy Tunisians, who gradually abandoned the *medinas*. Their new houses or, more often, apartments, reflected their aspirations to French culture and their assimilation of a new individualistic social order. Boulevards and segregation by wealth replaced the equality of the **medina**'s narrow streets; isolated houses replaced the intimacy of the *darb*; and the smaller house of the nuclear family replaced the huge segmented house of the extended family.

Independence accelerated rather than reversed the process of westernisation. The new Tunisian middle class soon assimilated the social values and tastes of their European predecessors and with that their architecture. Expensive **suburbs**, much like those around any southern European city, gradually surrounded the larger towns. Today some of the architects are returning to the details of traditional housing, using arches, painted (though factory-produced) tiles, and even stucco plaster, but the inspiration and the design remain fundamentally European.

The departure of the wealthy inhabitants has inevitably led to the **decline of the medinas**. Houses have been divided up into one-room apartments, *oukala*, where families live in appalling conditions of overcrowding. Without an influential political lobby some of the *medinas'* residents go without electricity, water, or mains drainage. The fabric of the buildings has also suffered from lack of repair, unsympathetic modifications and dangerous extensions on roofs and walls. Faced with deteriorating conditions and soaring rents, many of the original residents preferred to move out, if only to a *bidonville* shanty town on the outskirts of the city, leaving the *medina* to recent immigrants.

A UNESCO-funded project to save the Tunis Medina's architecture is in full swing but the fruits are yet to be realised. If it is to be a success it will not be enough just to refurbish the buildings: money needs to be injected to revitalise the Medina's economy and change social attitudes so that it once again becomes a desirable place to live.

Rural domestic architecture has undergone the same transformation as urban architecture in the last century. Houses, usually of reinforced concrete and following the same pseudo-European design, are squeezing out traditional styles (see especially "The Ksour", Chaper Nine). Tunisia's architectural diversity is being replaced by a rather tacky and depressing homogeneity.

A CHRONOLOGY: MONUMENTS AND EVENTS

Tunisian buildings often bear a plaque stating the date of construction, or sometimes of restoration or additions to the building. Although the numerals and calendar are unfamiliar, if you treat this as a puzzle to solve, it's not difficult to translate.

١	٢	٣	٤	٥	٠	٦	٧	٨	٩	.
1	2	3	4	5	6	7	8	9	0	

The 1 and the 9 are easy enough and the others don't take long to become familiar. As for the years, the Islamic calendar began with the Hegira, Mohammed's flight to Medina in 622 AD (which was thus 1 AH). Moreover, the Muslim year is a little shorter than the western. To convert AH to AD, you add 622, then subtract the original AH year multiplied by 3/100, ignore anything after the decimal point and you have the AD year in which that AH year began. Thus, for example, 1412 AH (date) = 1412 + 622 - [3/100 x 1412] and therefore began in 1991 AD.

10,000–6000 BC	**Capsian Man** appears throughout North Africa	Implements found near Gafsa give name to this culture
2000	Introduction of metals from Sicily begins Bronze Age	
1100	Earliest Phoenician settlements	
c.800	**Carthage** and other major Phoenician ports founded	
600–300	Increasing conflict in western Mediterranean between **Carthaginians** and **Greeks**	
310	Expedition of Agathocles from Syracuse into Carthaginian territory	**Carthaginian civilisation** almost completely lost, thanks to Romans and overbuilding. Some houses at Carthage and Kerkouane; many funerary artefacts; occasional monuments (Maktar, Dougga, etc)
263–41	First Punic War between Carthage and Rome, including Regulus expedition	
218–02	Second Punic War – Hannibal crosses Alps from Spain with elephants	
150–46	Third Punic War – Carthage sacked in 146	First informal Roman settlements in new province
112–05	Jugurthine War in province of Africa	
46 BC	Caesar defeats Pompeii at Battle of Thapsus: Roman Civil War won, Carthage refounded	
1–200 AD	Almost uninterrupted growth in prosperity of Africa as rich province of **Roman Empire**; control gradually extended west to Morocco, south to Chott	**Roman** town plans and buildings imposed throughout province: theatres, baths, temples, forums, amphitheatres, bridges, aqueducts

193	**Severan** dynasty of African Emperors from Libya	
235	Uprising at Thysdrus makes Gordian briefly Emperor – end of the Empire's golden era	El Djem amphitheatre possibly built now, but after 250 AD fewer and fewer Roman monuments.
312	Empire becomes officially Christian, but Donatist schism in Africa is vehicle for disaffection with imperial rule	**Churches** built in ruins of old Roman buildings
429–535	Carthage falls to **Vandal** invaders from Germany (429), who rule in province for a century	Vandals leave minor monumental marks: Basilica of Hildeguns at Maktar and chapel at Haidra
535	**Byzantine** invasion, inspired by Justinian and led by Belisarius, drives out Vandals	Many **fortresses** indicate fragility of Byzantine control
647	**Arab invaders** defeat Byzantine Prefect **Gregory** at Sbeitla	
670	Third wave of invasion under **Oqba Iba Nafi** settles and founds Kairouan as capital	First **mosque** built at Kairouan on site of present Great Mosque
800–900	Prosperous **Aghlabid** dynasty rules Tunisia from Kairouan; Sicily captured 835	Aghlabids build **Great Mosques** at Kairouan, Tunis, Sousse, Sfax, and **ribats** along the coast. Simple forms
909–70	Heretical **Fatimids** rule from Mahdia, resisting **Kharijite** revolt led by Abu Yazid (940), then move to Egypt, from where they unleash destructive Banu Hilal invasion	Fatimids build Great Mosque at Mahdia, make additions to Great Mosque at Sfax
1059–1159	**Khourassanid** dynasty rules principality of Tunis during Hilalian invasions – **Normans** and other Christians raid east coast	Hilalians destroy much vital infrastructure throughout the country. Ksar Mosque built in Tunis
1236–1534	**Hafsid** dynasty establishes Tunis as capital; a century of great prosperity and prestige, followed by gradual decline	Tunis **Kasbah** and **medersas** built. Influx of **Andalusian** artisans brings Moorish techniques such as stucco-work. Hafsid architecture becomes the "classic" style of the country. First great souks in Tunis
1270	Abortive invasion (Crusade) by Louis 1X (St.Louis) of France	
1300–1400	Mediterranean trade and Christian attacks, domestic insecurity	
1534–81	**Hispano-Turkish** struggles for control of Tunisia and North African coast. Tunis taken by Turks (1534), Spanish (1535), Algerian Turks (1569), Don John of Austria (1573), combined Turks (1574)	Many Spanish and Turkish **forts** along the coast (La Goulette, Bizerte, Kelibia)

1580–1705	Regency of Tunis part of Turkish **Ottoman Empire**, ruled by Deys and Beys. Othman Dey (1584–1610) and Murad Bey (1612–31) secure power	**Hanefite** mosques built (octagonal minarets) in Tunis, Youssef Dey (1616) and Hammouda Pasha (1655). Increasing use of Italianate elements, but also pure Turkish Sidi Mehrez mosque in Tunis (1675)
1600–1700	**Trade** and **piracy** at their height. French Consulate established in Tunis 1659, agreement with Britain 1662. Porto Farina bombarded by British Admiral Blake, 1654	
1705	**Husaynid** dynasty established. Turkish connection increasingly nominal, internal struggles aggravated by Algerian Turks	Security and prosperity bring lavish building programmes: **Mosque of the Dyers** (1716) and **Mosque of Sahib At Tabaa** (1780s); **medersas** throughout Tunis Medina; **palaces** (Dar Ben Abdallah, Dar Husayn)
1700–1800	Tunisia's last great era before Independence under Ali Pasha (1759–82) and Hammouda Bey (1782–1814)	
1741	Expeditions against coral establishments at Tabarca and Cap Negre	
1784	French and Venetian fleets bombard Tunisian ports	
1830	**French** takeover in Algeria. Slave trade ends, leaving Tunisia in increasing economic straits. England, France and Italy all manoeuvring for position	Last luxurious buildings help to bankrupt the country. **Palaces** at Bardo, Mohammedia; **arsenal** at Ghar El Melkh
1860–64	**Kherredin's** constitutional reform	Kherredin's Sadiki College built in Tunis
1869	International Financial Commission takes over bankrupt country's finances	Pseudo-oriental **cathedrals** built at Carthage and Tunis
1869–77	Kherredin Prime Minister; administrative and judicial reform, diplomatic measures to prevent colonisation	
1881	**French invasion**, on spurious excuse of Khroumiri raids, and colonisation	**French quarters**, founded outside old *medinas*, become city centres. Vast estates created and farmhouses built in the countryside. Naval arsenal founded at Bizerte
1920	Nationalist Destour Party founded	
1930	Catholic Congress at Carthage helps inspire Bourguiba's nationalism	
1934	**Neo-Destour Party** founded and soon banned by French	

1942–43	Tunisian Campaign (WWII)	Commonwealth, French, Tunisian, US and German cemeteries stand as reminders
1952	Farhat Hached murdered by Red Hand terrorists; Tunisia problem discussed at UN	
1955	Bourguiba returns to Tunis with internal autonomy	
1956	Independence, March 20	
1957	Declaration of **Republic**	
1976	The first major strike, and demonstrations	
1978	The first general strike since independence sparks off a wave of government repression	
1980	Gafsa "coup" attempt	
1981	First free elections; parties restricted; accusations of vote-rigging	
1984	Bread riots start in the south and spread to Tunis	
1985	Conflict with Libya comes to the brink of war	
1987	Bourguiba overthrown by Prime Minister Ziadine Ben Ali	

ISLAM: THE BACKGROUND

Since many visitors to Tunisia will be new to Islam, a very basic background is given here: some theory, some history, and Tunisia's place in the modern Islamic world.

A NEW FAITH

The founder of Islam was the **Prophet Mohammed**, an Arab from the rich trading city of Mecca (now in Saudi Arabia). In about 609 AD he began to hear divine messages which were transcribed directly as the Koran. God claimed to have been misunderstood by earlier religions – Judaism and Christianity – and in Islam Jesus is only one of a number of prophets.

The main characteristic of the new religion Mohammed founded was its directness, a reaction to the increasing complexity of the established faiths: its essential tenet was simply "There is no God but God, and Mohammed is His Prophet." There is no intermediary between people and God in the form of an institutionalised priesthood or complicated liturgy, and worship, in the form of prayer, is a direct and personal communication with God. As well as the central article of faith, there are four other **basic requirements** in Islam: five-times-daily prayers; the pilgrimage (*hadj*) to Mecca; the Ramadan fast; and a religious levy.

The five daily times for **prayer** (bearing in mind that the Islamic day begins at sunset) are sunset, after dark, dawn, noon and afternoon. Prayer can be performed anywhere (literally), but preferably in a mosque. In the past, and even today in some places, a *muezzin* would climb his minaret each time and call the faithful. Nowadays the **call to prayer** is likely to be less frequent, and prerecorded; even so, this most distinctive of Islamic sounds has a beauty all its own, especially when neighbouring *muezzins* are audible simultaneously. The message itself is equally moving: "God is most great. I testify that there is no god but Allah. I testify that Mohammed is His Prophet. Come to prayer, come to security. God is great." In the morning another phrase is added, "prayer is better than sleep". The most easily recognisable phrase is *Allah Akhbar*, "God is great".

Prayer is preceded by **ritual washing**, and is performed with the feet bare. Facing towards Mecca (the direction indicated in a mosque by the mihrab – though prayer can be said anywhere), the worshipper recites the *Fatiha*, the first chapter of the Koran: "Praise be to God, Lord of the Worlds, the Compassionate, the Merciful, King of the Day of Judgement. We worship you and seek your aid. Guide us on the straight path, the path of those on whom you have bestowed your grace, not the path of those who incur your anger nor of those who go astray." The same words are then repeated twice in the prostrate position, with some interjections of *Allah Akhbar*. It is a highly ritualised

THE EVIL EYE

The superstition that envious looks bring **bad luck**, though disapproved of by strict Muslims, is ingrained in Arab culture. Even when admiring something belonging to a friend, formulae are uttered to ward off this **"evil eye"**. More unlucky than the remarks of friends, however, are the jealous glances of strangers.

For this reason, various charms are used against the evil eye. One of the most common is the so-called **"Hand of Fatima"**. The Fatima referred to is the Prophet's daughter, although what connection there is between her and the symbol of the hand remains obscure. It may be that the five fingers of the hand, like the five points of the pentagram star, represent the **five pillars of Islam** (declaration of faith, prayer, pilgrimage, charity and observation of

Ramadan). Certainly, the symbol is often combined with a Koranic quotation, or with the names of Allah and Mohammed written in Arabic calligraphy. Then again, the pentagram and the significance of the number five predate Islam and are often associated with Jewish mysticism. It is interesting to note that Jerban Jews share this belief in the evil eye, and use the same symbols to ward it off as do their Muslim neighbours.

Another charm against the evil eye is the **fish**. Again, its origins are obscure, though it's believed that it was originally a phallic fertility symbol. Whatever the truth, you'll see charms against the evil eye all over the place, in the form of car-stickers, hands and fish painted on houses, and cards on the walls of shops.

procedure, with the prostrate position symbolic of the worshipper's role as servant (Islam means literally "obedience"), and the sight of thousands of people going through the same motions simultaneously in a mosque (in a *jema'a*, rather than a *masjid*, "local mosque") is a powerful one. Here the whole community comes together for prayer, led by an imam, who may also deliver the *Khutba*, or sermon.

The **pilgrimage**, or *hadj*, to Mecca is an annual event, when millions come from all over the world to Mohammed's birthplace. Here they go through several days of rituals, the central one a sevenfold circumambulation of the *Ka'aba*, before kissing a black stone set in its wall. Islam requires that Muslims should go on *hadj* as often as is practically possible: for the poor, it may well be a once-in-a-lifetime occasion. In Tunisia from the earliest times to the French occupation pilgrims assembled at towns along a well-established route, passing through Kairouan and Gabes, to join the *rakeb*, a caravan numbering thousands of people. They would then make the journey to Mecca by foot or camel. The French made it a lot easier. They didn't want just anyone going on the *hadj* where they might pick up bad political habits like nationalism, so they restricted pilgrims to several hundred a year and laid on transport in the form of a special pilgrim boat. Now the government still helps many of the poor to make their *hadj* (by air) and the month when all the pilgrims leave for Mecca is still a great time of celebration in Tunisia. The story that seven visits to Kairouan equal one *hadj* to Mecca is really more apocryphal, expressing the unusual reverence in which the city is held.

Ramadan is the name of the ninth month in the Islamic calendar, the month in which the Koran was revealed to Mohammed. The custom of fasting is modelled directly on Jewish and Christian practice, and for the whole of the month believers must forgo all forms of consumption – food, drink, cigarettes, sex – between sunrise and sunset. A few categories of people are exempted: travellers, children, pregnant women and warriors engaged in a *jihad*, or holy war. Given the climates in which most Muslims live, the fast is a formidable undertaking, but in practice it becomes a time of some intense celebration as the abstinence of the day is more than compensated by huge consumption during the night.

Based on the five "pillars of faith", firmly underwritten by the Koran, Islam was an inspirational faith for the Arab people, and gained wide acceptance in the course of the Arab advance – particularly among the Berbers. The beginning of a new era was symbolised by the adoption of a new calendar: thus 1992 sees the start of the year 1413 in the Islamic calendar.

THE OLD BELIEFS

Whatever success Islam had during its early period of rapid expansion, it did not entirely eradicate **pre-existing religion**. Animistic beliefs in the powers of stones and trees (as at Fernana) and rites of ancestor worship were incorporated into the new faith, as was a belief in *baraka*, the power to work miracles given by God to some men. These "saints", or **marabouts**, formed a pantheon of intermediaries between people and God. Some had particular powers, to cure disease or generate rain, and prayers and sacrifices were made to them at their tombs for these services. Others acquired reverence as founder guardians of a tribe.

Baraka was not only embodied in tombs, it was also transmitted through blood, and the ancestors of these holy men enjoyed a particular respect – the *sharifs*, ancestors of the Prophet, more than any other. Some of them could even perform miracles. Ascetics and preachers might also acquire the status of a marabout, during their lifetime at least. In the fifteenth and sixteenth centuries, Tunisia was flooded with these holy men, most of them coming from Morocco. During a later time of crisis, in the nineteenth century, another wave arose, warning of the approaching Armageddon.

The dualism of the older faith was also retained as a belief in **bori**, evil spirits, and the evil eye. These led to rituals of exorcism, many of which were performed by Africans who were believed to be particularly powerful before the *bori*. You still see little bags of herbs around the necks of children to protect them against any harm, and the hand of Fatima is a widespread symbol (see box opposite) but today these beliefs are on the way out. They persist in remote rural areas where religious life still focuses on the marabout's tomb rather than the mosque.

ISLAM'S DEVELOPMENT

By **800 AD**, the new religion was dominant over an area stretching from Afghanistan in the east to Spain in the west. Given the rapidity of this expansion, it was inevitable that Islam would acquire some of the trappings of the older religions to which it had been a reaction, in the form of hierarchical and doctrinal disputes.

Like most religions, Islam soon developed its own institutions and with them particular interest groups. In the early years there was an understanding that consensus legitimised authority, the law, and religion. By the ninth century, however, the **ulema**, (the learned ones) – that is, the imam and the *sheikhs* of the religious colleges – had come to monopolise the interpretation of the Koran and the prophet's sayings. They became a religious establishment, wielding considerable power and controlling great wealth. Under their control the religion itself became increasingly intellectual and dogmatic. And so the scene was set for the division of the faithful.

The **first dispute** arose soon after the death of Mohammed, and has remained the biggest single split in the faith – equivalent to the Catholic–Protestant schism in Christianity. When the Prophet died, the spiritual leadership of the faith was the object of fierce contention among several Caliphs (rulers). A substantial minority felt that the new Caliph should be in direct descent from the Prophet, and their candidate was Ali, a cousin of the Prophet married to his daughter, Fatima. Eventually, Ali's supporters broke away from the **Sunni** mainstream to form the **Shi'a** sect.

Although the two groups agreed broadly in their respect for the Koran and its tradition (the *hadith*), the Shi'ites were forced into a more allegorical interpretation of the Koran in order to support their claims for a divinely inspired leader. Even the orthodox Sunnis found themselves increasingly unable to agree on points of legal detail (all law was taken from the Koran), and by the twelfth century, four **madhabs**, or schools of legal thought, had been established within the Sunni community: Hanefite, Shafite, Malekite and Hanbalite. Together with two Shi'a *madhabs*, these still account for the great majority of Muslims.

But there were also smaller and more radical sects. The **Kharijites**, or "Secessionists", were one of the earliest of these: puritanical in the extreme, they held that anyone guilty of serious sin deserved death. The rigour of this sect appealed particularly to subject peoples such as the Berbers in North Africa, alienated by the excesses of their new rulers.

Sufism, which remains a force in southern Tunisia, is not so much a breakaway sect as the name for a different emphasis within Islam, on the ecstatic and the mystical rather than the intellectual niceties of Koranic interpretation. It is a blanket term for the many different brotherhoods, often spread widely over the Islamic world, who evolved various practices in the attempt to attain some sort of mystic communion with God. The name Sufi derives from the word for wool, after the simple woollen clothes worn by early ascetics. During the eighteenth and nineteenth centuries, many of these Sufi brotherhoods spread throughout the Islamic world, with lodges as far apart as Yemen and Morocco linked by allegiance to their founder's teachings and, in some cases, a well-structured administrative hierarchy. They became institutions – in the case of the Senoussi of Cyrenaica, a government with a state.

The secret of the Sufi groups' success lay in their ability to meet the **religious needs** of the community ignored by orthodox Islam. Some, such as the Rahamania, became intellectual, placing great emphasis on learning. Others adopted more colourful practices in order to reach a state of **religious ecstasy**. The Aissouia, better known as the "whirling dervishes", used self-flagellation and music to induce a trance. Many of these brotherhoods are still active in Tunisia, though their secrecy, unorthodox practices, wealth, and ability to mobilise a large part of the population arouse great suspicion among the religious establishment and in the government.

With these basic institutions, Islam came to exert a profound influence over every aspect of life in one of the greatest civilisations the world has seen. Unlike Christianity, at least Protestant Christianity, which has to some extent accepted the separation of Church and State, Islam sees no such distinction. The **sharia**, or religious law, *is* civil law, and in a process of gradual accretion numerous layers have been added to the original code, the *Sunna* entrusted to the Prophet. Many controversial requirements, such as *purdah* (the seclusion of women), polygamy and slavery, have been declared not to be part of the original code – but it remains very much a question of interpretation.

Perhaps Islam's most fundamental role was in **education**, which was based almost entirely on the Koran. Young children (mainly boys) whose parents could afford it were sent to the *kouttab*, or primary school, where they learned to read and write by learning the Koran (all 6200 verses of it) off by heart. If they continued their studies, it would still be under religious auspices because the great universities, such as Al Azhar in Cairo (founded by Fatimids from Tunisia in the tenth century) and the Zitouna in Tunis, were based on mosques. Students might live and do some of their studying in *medressas*, or residential colleges, but teaching was based at the mosque, and the syllabus remained religious. Law, grammar, science, logic – all were subsidiary to the Koranic tradition as handed down from generation to generation. For several centuries Arab philosophers and scientists produced work that built on the Greco-Roman achievements they inherited, and was hundreds of years ahead of contemporary Europe – their role in transmitting this culture to the European Renaissance has gone generally unappreciated. Ibn Khaldoun, the great historian, politician and scholar born in Tunis in 1332, set out sociological principles which have only recently become current in the West.

DECLINE AND CRISIS

Despite its vigour, there was also a very static element in Islam and, as it developed, Arab culture became oppressed by the weight of a **religious tradition** increasingly hostile to free enquiry. Anything which threatened the authority of the religious establishment was gradually suppressed, and the dynamism which had taken the Arabs so far in so short a time was replaced by a static society unable to make the innovations that would keep them ahead of the fast-rising Europeans. Peter Mansfield (see p.365) quotes an example of this: the Arabs learned how to make paper from the Chinese when they captured Samarkand in 704, but refused for centuries to manufacture books mechanically because it was an invention unsanctioned by God and tradition.

At first this stagnation was relatively unimportant, because the Arab world was so far ahead of the European competition in every field. But as the pendulum began to swing in the other direction, there was no facility for adapting to match the Europeans. Napoleon's expedition to Egypt in 1798 was the beginning of a century in which almost every Islamic country came under the control of one or other of the European powers; a single exception – of which all the Arabs are aware today – was Saudi Arabia. Under **colonial rule**, Islam became the focus of opposition. In Algeria and Libya, Sufi brotherhoods led the resistance movement, drawing the support of the masses with a call to the *jihad*, a war to protect their faith as much as their country. Unfortunately, by the time it came to fight the battles, the wars had already been lost to the factories of Manchester and Lille.

It would be simplistic to blame this reversal of fortune on Islam alone. The Islamic nations were not, after all, the only ones to suffer the indignities of colonisation or mercantile exploitation. But because it is such an all-embracing religion, deeply rooted in every facet of the societies which hold to it, the nineteenth and twentieth century inevitably saw something of a **crisis** in religious confidence. Islam had once been the basis of a great civilisation which was now dominated by infidel foreigners: how should it react?

There were two alternatives: either Islam could try to adapt itself in some way to the essentially secular ways which had brought success to the West; or it could reject Western influence entirely; by purifying itself, it might rediscover its former strength. In practical terms, few Islamic countries under Western control were in a position at first to adopt either alternative – but these were the poles between which Islamic thought was operating.

Then, in the post-war period, self-determination suddenly came to the Middle East. First, the **decolonisation** process, accelerated in many countries by the contribution Islamic consciousness made to the nationalist movements, brought political autonomy. Second, and even more important, **oil** wealth brought economic self-sufficiency and the possibility of spiritual independence from the West. These two developments made the problem of identity suddenly immediate and real: in a situation where many of them could afford to reject Western values, how should Islamic countries now deal with the conflicts between their religion and secular materialism?

Some countries, notoriously to Western perceptions, have chosen to return to, or maintain, a more or less **traditional form of fundamentalist Islam**. To see this course, as many do in the West, as a deliberate return to barbarism is an egocentric failure to understand the context. A return to the totality of Islam is to choose one consistent spiritual identity, one that is deeply embedded in the consciousness of a culture unusually aware of tradition. Most people in the West would be outraged if they were suddenly told that they must give up many of the most fundamental rights and customs of their whole culture – yet this is what they blithely expect the Arabs to do.

Conflict with the West is another aspect of the return to Islam. Adoption of Islamic values signals a rejection of Western society's values – which are perceived as having been, and being, based on greed and exploitation. Traditional Islam offers a positivist brand of freedom, with substantial historical backing, which is clearly opposed to Western secularism. The most extreme Islamic fundamentalists are not passive reactionaries thinking of the past, but young radicals, often students, keen to assert new-found independence. Islam has in a sense become the anti-imperialist religion – hence the Black Muslim movement in America – and there is frequent confusion and even conflict between secular, left-wing ideals, and more purely religious ones.

But the rejection of all Western values does involve missing out on what the West sees as "benefits" of **development**. It may be begging the question in strictly Islamic terms to say that the emancipation of women, say, is a "benefit"; but in the more liberal countries, of which Tunisia is a leader, such steps are considered desirable, and simultaneously reconcilable with Islam (see "Women in Tunisia", p.354). The hope is that the supremacy of Islam, a vital part of national identities, can be maintained while shedding what are seen as its less desirable elements; most Islamic countries have now embarked on this formidable balancing act in their social and political lives.

ISLAM IN MODERN TUNISIA

For a country now so advanced in its liberalisation, **Tunisia** has always had a strong religious **tradition**. After Mecca, Medina and Jerusalem, Kairouan is the most holy city for

Muslims, still visited at the *Mouled* every year by visitors from all over the Islamic world. The university at Tunis's Great Mosque was long respected, and Tunisia's Malekite teachers still enjoy a high reputation. Yet at the same time there is a greatly revered Jewish shrine on Jerba (the *Ghriba*), and although the Jewish population has diminished over the last thirty years, tolerance is still unusually high.

The majority of Tunisians have always belonged to the **Malekite** school of the Sunni orthodoxy (their mosques easily recognised by square minarets). The Turks brought with them the teaching of the **Hanefite** school (these mosques have octagonal minarets), which still survives among Turkish-descended families; but there is little if any conflict between the schools, and since both are Sunni the two groups can use each others' mosques. Between them, these groups account for the vast majority of Muslims in Tunisia; for the outpost of **Kharijites** on Jerba, and the **Sufi** stronghold at Nefta.

Despite these long traditions, though, Tunisia – or at least Tunis itself – has always had a **cosmopolitan** element and therefore remained more open to innovation. Kherredin's attempt to introduce constitutional government in 1860 was a failure, but it was a move which several Islamic states have still to make more than a century later. Since Independence, Bourguiba had to tread a narrow path between secularisation and loyalty to Islamic tradition. With evidence of willingness to adopt Western values, vital Western aid and cooperation have always been abundant. At the same time the Islamic tradition has to be respected enough for the country to remain in favour with wealthier Arab countries, for both political and economic reasons.

After Independence, Bourguiba, broadly speaking, tried to **secularise** – as far as possible with the religious establishment's support – and with some success. During the 1950s and 60s religious observance dropped steadily, particularly in Tunis and among the younger generation. But in the 1970s and 1980s the trend reversed. Local and foreign funding boosted the number of mosques from 810 in 1960 to 2450 in 1986. What is more, the mosques are now full, with predominantly youthful congregations. Islam has had a revival that most Christian churches would envy.

Today Islam gives the young a sense of identity and solidarity in a world they see as hostile. It has also given them hope. The imams' calls for a **return to Islamic values** are interpreted by many as an indirect criticism of a government that has done so much to Westernise Tunisia and of the middle classes who live affluently amid poverty. Extremists, such as the *Mouvement de la Tendence Islamique*, have gone further, demanding that Islamic values and principles are applied in law and government. They would have an Islamic Republic along Iranian lines.

It is difficult to tell how many Tunisians would support such a radical constitutional change. Most have some sympathy with the fundamentalists' point of view but cling to their Westernised and materialist lifestyle. fundamentalism's most fervent supporters are among the **very poor** or the **frustrated lower middle class** who have gained little from Bourguibism. But to what extent their fundamentalism is a reaction to and expression of poverty and oppression or a genuine ideological commitment is unclear.

The government has tried to deflect criticism and return moderate fundamentalists to the fold of legitimate politics. It has proclaimed its Islamic credentials, stressing the pre-eminence of Islam as the official religion rather than the secular nature of the state. Ministers now make great show of their religious observance. Affronts to Islam, such as the sale of alcohol on Fridays, have been stopped, and the outward trappings of **Islamicisation** have been adopted. Arabic, for instance, is more and more important as the language of instruction at all levels of education.

These gestures may have appeased the moderates but the **extremists** remain unmoved. As their opposition became more vocal, Bourguiba, who feared fundamentalism as a threat to both the Destour Party and the secular nature of the state he had created, grew determined to root out what he saw as a danger. Confrontation escalated into violence through 1985 to 1987 and Tunisia seemed set to fall into a downward spiral of repression, dissidence, and terrorism. General Ben Ali's first two years in office don't suggest he has yet broken the chain, and recent executions of fundamentalists indicate his similar determination to keep state and religion apart. It would be a great achievement if, like Mubarak in Egypt, he could divert the radicals into parliamentary politics and thus institutionalise a revolutionary movement. The price the middle classes would have to pay for political stability – further, inevitable Islamicisation – might be worth paying.

TRADITIONAL SOCIETY

Traditionally, the family was the foundation of Tunisian society. Now, however, social life is changing and new allegiances and values are emerging that conflict with the old.

THE OLD TRADITIONS

In traditional society (which today means in rural areas and the poorer parts of the cities), the **extended family** was the fundamental social group. Tunisians spent much of their social life with close relatives and also tended to marry within the family unit (for a man, marriage to his father's brother's daughter was the ideal, even if it was rarely achieved), and mutual obligations meant that families were tied economically. Land in rural areas, for instance, was usually co-owned with brothers or cousins. If a man wanted to build a house or clear some land he would call on his relatives to help, on the understanding that he would reciprocate later. In the same way, if he had financial difficulties, or needed money to celebrate his daughter's wedding in proper style, he could rely on support from his close relatives.

Wider social groups were defined in the same family terms by means of descent from a common ancestor. In this way traditional Tunisian society was composed of a series of ever larger families: the nuclear family, the extended family, a lineage, a village or tribe. The frequency and intensity of social interaction declined as the size of the social group increased but, even at the scale of village or tribe, there were still communal rights and reciprocal obligations that unified the group.

Individuals were identified by their **genealogy**, a name chain in the Welsh fashion: Ahmed ben (son of) Mohammed ben Ahmed ben Slim etc. The name of a distant ancestor was usually used to identify the individual's lineage inside his community, but if he travelled to another village he would adopt the village name, if he went to a city, his tribe's name. There were no surnames that identified the individual definitively or transcended social context. People were always a member of such-and-such a family.

The family also created **honour** in the sense that reputation and good name derived from the achievements of ancestors and the length of an identifiable genealogy. People whose ancestors were *sheikhs*, marabouts, or even *hadjis* (those who have made the pilgrimage to Mecca) always identify them as such. The more esteemed the ancestor, the more detailed the genealogy. A *sharif*, for instance, will trace his ancestry right back to the prophet Mohammed.

Because honour was derived from descent and was shared by an extended group, attacks on individuals could escalate into a **vendetta**. A family shamed had to take appropriate revenge (an eye for an eye, a tooth for a tooth) if honour was to be saved, and reciprocal attacks could build up into long-lasting feuds. Most of these vendettas began with verbal or sexual attacks on women, for in this patriarchal society it was here that honour was most sensitive. Murder might be resolved by the payment of *dia*, blood-money, but never an attack on a woman.

BREAKDOWN OF TRADITIONAL VALUES

Now that Tunisians are moving to the **cities** this traditional society is breaking down. Migrants leaving the rural areas try to find accommodation near relatives or members of the same village community back home. The *bidonvilles* on the edge of Tunis and the *oukala* in the Medina are full of these transplanted rural communities. Many of the migrants also return to their home for the summer marriage season, the highlight of communal life, when social bonds are reaffirmed by complex webs of visiting and hospitality. But they're no longer temporary residents in the city, returning to their village when they have earned enough to get married and set up their own farm; they are now committed to an urban lifestyle and look at the village as their origin – not their goal.

After a couple of years in the city the migrant's visits home become, typically, less frequent, and social life begins to cross communal barriers, with **marriages** often taking place outside the community. Most important of all, income differentials among urban workers discourage the mutual aid that formerly united members of the same family. Gradually the **individual** with personal identity and interests emerges and distant family and community fade into the background.

Among these dislocated urban dwellers new allegiances and identities develop, those of **income and class**. A new ethos of personal advancement takes the place of the redundant ideals of the community and mutual aid, and with this emerge new conflicts between rich and poor. It is this struggle, expressed in the battle between the governing party and the secular middle class on the one side and the aspiring poor, newly educated and fundamentalist on the other, that characterises Tunisian politics today.

CUSTOMS AND CELEBRATIONS

As traditional society has been subverted by new social structures, so **customs** have been replaced by more "refined" mores. Tunisians still love celebrations, marriages in particular, but in the cities they have lost much of their social significance and zest. If you want to see Tunisian customs at their liveliest you have to go to the small towns and villages.

Every stage of the **life cycle** is associated with its own celebration and customs; birth, circumcision (in the far south, this includes some girls), marriage, and death. It is only at **marriage**, however, that strangers are welcome. Paradoxically enough in this patrilineal society, marriage, the social relationship that crosses patrilineages, is the most public of all social events. It is a matter of honour that the celebration is as splendid and well attended as possible. Most of the village turns out, and unexpected guests, even foreigners, are always welcomed.

Marriage ceremonies differ from region to region but they are always lengthy affairs taking several days, usually in the summer when migrants return home. The first days are spent in preparation. The bride has henna applied to her feet and hands and has all her body hair removed, before being taken to the groom's house where separate receptions are held accompanied by much music, usually performed by hired singers, drummers, and pipe-players, and ritual praise-singing. The ceremony and the communal celebration follow, usually a massive feast with more music and dancing. The consummation of the marriage is, however, the climax, and in rural areas sometimes a semi-public event, with the groom's mother present to check her daughter-in-law's virginity. More often the sheet is produced as evidence and, at this news, guns go off and the music starts all over again.

The other major celebration in village and tribal life is the **ziara**, a communal pilgrimage to the tomb of a marabout, usually the community's "patron saint" or eponymous ancestor, again a summer event. In the past everybody participated, even in nomadic communities where it was the only occasion in the year when everyone would camp together. As a communal, as much as a religious, activity it was important in reaffirming the bonds between members of the community. With everyone gathered around the tomb, visiting would take place, deals would be clinched and marriages arranged.

Pilgrims walked barefoot to the tomb, usually accompanied by music and singing, waving flags bearing religious slogans. There they made a communal prayer and then sacrificed an animal, sometimes a sheep but more often a bull. The **meat** was divided into scrupulously equal portions (symbolic equality being important in tribal life) and distributed to each of the families. The real celebration came afterwards with feasting and dancing.

Today, sadly, these festivals are becoming less and less common. The disintegration of village and tribal life, sapped by emigration and assaulted by affluence, is partly to blame, but the real cause is the expansion of **religious orthodoxy**. Tunisia's imams have no place for the marabouts next to God and so they lambast the old faith. As new mosques have penetrated the remotest villages, the marabouts' hegemony has been broken and their legitimacy undermined by the attacks of the educated religious establishment. The government encourages the trend. It doesn't want the people's religious allegiance scattered among a series of local saints, but wants it centralised instead where it is easier to control and manipulate. Consequently, schools throughout the country promote orthodox Islam and dismiss its local forms. As attendance at the mosques and schools increases, that at the *ziara* declines. Perhaps this is the last generation to participate and to see this manifestation of local Islam and tribal solidarity.

WOMEN IN TUNISIA

When still a young child, I told myself that if one day I had the power to do so, I would make haste to redress the wrong done to women.

Habib Bourguiba

Thirty years ago, Tunisian women shared the oppression experienced in most Arab countries. That their position has changed as much as it has is due largely to ex-President Bourguiba's personal vision and his ability to institute far-reaching reforms. Almost the first thing he did after Independence was to introduce the *Personal Status Code*, an attempt to improve the social position and treatment of women. Hitherto such issues had been controlled by the *sharia*, the Holy Law revealed by Allah through Mohammed and based on the Koran and Hadith.

This assessment of the position of Tunisian women is followed by two personal accounts by women travellers in the country.

WOMEN'S TRADITIONAL STATUS

In the eighth century the **Islamic code** had in fact improved women's status: the dowry (*mahr*) was paid to the bride instead of to her guardian, rights of inheritance and control of income were restored, albeit in a very limited sense. Divorce, though solely a man's right, was to be effective only after a three-month waiting period, the *'idda*, and the husband was supposed to maintain his wife (though the responsibility fell mainly on her brothers) and offer some explanation for his conduct. These limited reforms were, however, later ignored, and Mohammed's own conciliatory attitude (and that of Aysha, one of his wives) disappeared under the stern injunctions of the Koran itself.

Women were henceforth **veiled and segregated** to protect their virginity and reputation; **polygamy** remained common, **marriages** were contracted when the girl was young, and **divorce** proceedings became quite arbitrary. A man could repudiate his wife simply by pronouncing a formulaic saying, the *talaq*, three times in three months – but the three *talaq* were often all pronounced at one time, with no recourse for the woman and no *'idda* at all. Although it was possible to guard against polygamy by inserting a prohibition in the marriage contract, and to receive a portion of the *mahr* on divorce, such measures were seldom taken. A married woman lived in a patriarchal family and was expected to produce sons at regular intervals. Likewise the institution of **habous**, a legal entail excluding women, meant that they rarely received property through inheritance as was their right; and in the courts, a woman's word was worth less than that of a man.

Women, on the whole, enjoyed greater freedom in **rural areas** than in the cities. They were able to walk about within the village without the veil, and within the home they enjoyed considerable influence over their husbands, and power over their dependents. Most women had an independent income that came from the sale of artefacts or animal produce and they spent it as they wished. Divorce was rare, partly because parents consulted their children over the choice of spouse, and partly because of the social stigma attached. Moreover, the proximity of their own family afforded wives a certain protection and shelter. Nevertheless, their status was a far cry from Mohammed's concept of equality.

REFORM

It is against this background that radicalism of the **1956 Code** must be measured. In Turkey another great reformer, Mustafa Kemal

(Ataturk), had simply abolished the *sharia* and introduced the Swiss Civil Code. Bourguiba, helped in certain areas by the more egalitarian personal laws of Tunisia's Malekite legal school, justified his own reforms from within the original Koranic texts and thus secured the support of Tunisia's spiritual head, the *sheikh* of Zitouna. The marriage age was raised – to 19 for women, 20 for men – and informed consent made necessary. Polygamy was outlawed completely: Mohammed had stipulated that each wife should be treated equally and this was held to be impossible. *Sharia* and civil courts were merged together, divorce became a civil matter, and the formulaic *talaq* was abolished. The Koran itself states that arbitration is needed when there is marital discord: divorce, reasonably enough, is felt to be evidence of this. But although a woman can now sue for divorce on grounds of "mental incompatibility", alimony is not always granted. Bourguiba also encouraged people to think of the *mahr* as purely symbolic and gave his second wife a token one dinar. Custody of children has been restored to the woman at divorce, though only until the boy is 7 or the girl 9. Abortion rights were introduced over the next fifteen years, along with an extensive and effective family planning campaign. Legislation was passed on equal pay and, as the French left, opportunities for work were created. Women obtained the vote in two stages during 1956 and 1957.

Actual **social change** has been slow to follow these comparatively radical laws. A telling indication of the staying power of traditional attitudes is the assertion, frequently heard even from young and otherwise liberal men, that women now have "too much power". Despite the efforts of the *Union Nationale des Femmes Tunisiennes* (*UNFT*), formed in 1956 to introduce the reforms to the country, female **illiteracy** is higher than male, far fewer women than men have attended secondary school and university, and it is doubtful if the rural poor, especially the Berbers, are aware of their rights at all. Opinion polls amongst the lower classes in the ever-expanding cities, heavily affected by unemployment, show a decline in support for a woman's **right to work**; and the difficulty of finding somewhere to live (because women living alone are still considered immoral) can frustrate most of the independence that a job might otherwise have

brought. Work itself is thus no guide to emancipation. In fact, it has been argued that male authority may actually have increased inside the family as a result, because money earned is often paid directly to a husband or male relative, or used for the dowry – the goods which the bride herself brings to a marriage.

The economic recession, combined with events in Iran, may lie behind this reaction. Since 1979 increasing numbers of women, particularly in the cities, have taken to wearing the Iranian headscarf-like veil, or **chador**, instead of the traditional Tunisian *sifsari* – the white veil-cum-cloak often gripped between the teeth to hide the face. If the apparent backlash continues, the overall process of social change will be enormously complicated and women may find themselves caught between, on the one hand, the break-up of the extended family – which is already causing problems of isolation in the cities – and, on the other, new reactionary pressures.

WOMEN VISITORS TO TUNISIA

As briefly outlined on p.30, a woman traveller in Tunisia (either alone or with a female or male companion) faces certain, unavoidable difficulties. With the right approach, skill and luck, some of these can be overcome, but, as the following personal and very different accounts show, the problems are enduring ones. Further feedback and comments from women travellers – or Tunisian men or women – would be much appreciated for the next edition.

■ A SURFACE LIBERALISM
Linda Cooley taught in Tunisia for six years. The following article is reprinted from *Women Travel: Adventures, Advice and Experience* (a Rough Guide Special, Harrap Columbus; £6.95).

Tunisian women enjoy a measure of **freedom and equality under the law** unknown in many other Arab countries. Polygamy was abolished in the mid-1950s when Tunisia became independent. Divorce laws have been altered in women's favour. Most girls attend school. A reasonably large percentage of women are in higher education. Many women work outside the home. There are women in the professions and two women ministers in the government. An established feminist group exists, which holds regular meetings in the *Club Tahar Haddad* in the capital's Medina, and there is even a feminist magazine, *Nissa*.

But the presence of so many women in public can be misleading. It may lull you into a false sense of security when you first arrive and lead to false expectations of what you can and cannot do. If you walk around the capital (and remember, this is very unrepresentative of the rest of the country), you will see women in jeans and the latest fashions, sometimes sitting in cafés, even girls walking along holding hands with their boyfriends. But what you cannot see and should know is that these same fashionably dressed girls have fathers who expect them to be home by eight o'clock at the latest, who expect them to be virgins at their wedding and who often expect them to marry a relative chosen by the parents. The clothes may have changed in recent years, the amount of women at work may have changed, but, deep down, **social attitudes** remain unaltered. The Tunisian women you see in the streets are most often going to work or going home. The idea of a woman travelling abroad on her own, in this traditional Arab society, is understandably considered strange.

It is important to realise this before setting off on solo (or even two-women) travels. And to realise, too, how superficial are many of the Europeanised images – even in Tunis. **Bars** are not like those in France but exclusively male domains, and wandering in for a rest and a beer you will be stared at. Similarly, you can't expect to be able to chat to the man at the next table in the café about the best place to have lunch or the best time to visit the mosque, without your conversation being taken as an invitation to get more closely acquainted. **Western movies** have done an excellent job of persuading Tunisian men that all Western women spend their lives jumping in and out of bed with any willing male.

All this may sound somewhat off-putting. Yet in six years living in Tunis, I often travelled alone, I travelled with my son and I travelled with another woman. Perhaps I was lucky, but apart from the unwanted attentions of a few men, nothing happened to me. There is no part of the country that it is unsafe to visit – you can see everything.

But **travelling alone**, it is incredibly hard to get to know the people, and it is hard to relax, never being sure about how your behaviour will be interpreted if you do. I learnt to cope by avoiding direct eye contact with men, and above all never smiling at strangers. I once found myself being followed home because I inadvertently smiled at a man as we reached for the same tin of tomato sauce in the supermarket. It may irk you to keep your silence; not to answer like with like; not to show occasional disdain; but in the long run it will make your life more pleasant. After a while, the ignoring game becomes a reality; you really don't notice that anyone has spoken to you! If you cannot learn to ignore the hassle from men you will probably find yourself impatient to leave Tunisia after a very short time – it is an easy country for a woman on her own to dislike.

Travelling with a man makes it all much simpler. The stereotyped images on both sides (yours of pushy Arab men; theirs of loose foreign women) can be dispensed with and everyone can act naturally. Men will talk to you both as you're sitting in a café or waiting for a bus – and generally just for the pleasure of talking with someone different, nothing more. You may well get invited home to meet their families where you'll be able to talk to the women in the home too, as unlike in many other Arab countries, Tunisian women and men eat together.

You can also go to the **hammam** (public baths) with the women of the house. This is very worthwhile as it is the one place where women can meet traditionally as a group, away from all the pressures of a male-dominated society. Unless you speak Arabic, it is difficult to talk to the older women there, who rarely speak French, but they are more than willing to show you how to remove the hairs from your body, to henna your hair, to use *tfal* (a kind of shampoo made from mud) and to give you a thorough scrub with a sort of loofah mitten. You could, of course, go on your own to the hammam, but it's much better to go with a Tunisian woman, and introductions are almost exclusively made through men.

Another possibility is that if you express curiosity, you may well find yourself invited to a **wedding** (you don't have to know the bride or groom – hundreds of people attend Arab weddings who hardly know the couple), or some other traditional event. Total strangers can be very hospitable when it comes to sharing their customs and food with you. I once had the most beautiful couscous brought out to the field where I was eating my picnic of cheese sandwiches: but then, I was with my son and a male companion.

Alone or with another woman it is all possible. But you do miss a great deal of what is, essentially, Tunisian life. Hopefully through more contact between foreign women and Tunisians a greater understanding will ensue, on both sides, and the lone woman traveller will become more easily accepted. Meanwhile, ideas are changing — but very slowly.

■ PERSISTENT MYTHS
Lindsay Maginn travelled in Tunisia independently for two weeks with a female friend.

I had an idea that Arabs were a different lot, unfathomably religious in our eyes. Nobody seems to stop for prayer in Tunis, but they do stop for something else: Western women. Any chance to talk leaves men with immense interest and desire for you. They want to talk because they're interested and feel that somehow you need **protection and help**. They don't understand rejections of advice. One man offered us a lift in the most hospitable manner possible and then on the way to our destination asked if we wanted to sleep with him and his friend that night. Our attempts to explain when we refused seemed to perplex him.

Not much **communication** goes on openly in towns between Tunisian men and women, so appearing interested in Tunisian men can be seriously misinterpreted. Talking to men in **Tunis** won't get you into trouble but the cruising heroes in **Hammamet** are more aggressive in their approach, while arriving somewhere in the interior, like **Tozeur** for example, you find half the men (mostly older), regarding you, despite your appearance, with the same respect they would accord Tunisian women, and the other half seeming to imagine (or giving the impression they believe) you've just finished making your latest soft-porn movie for *Chaîne 2*. If you ignore their inviting comments, you're rude; if you're civil, that must mean you're interested in sex. This misunderstanding is frustrating for both sides because two weeks isn't really long enough to shatter the myth.

Tunisian men see **unmarried white couples** and can't understand why "If she'll sleep with him, why not me?" Unless he has travelled to Europe, a Tunisian man is going to find that question fairly impossible to answer. Trying to convince him of women's right to choose is a waste of breath: talking openly about sex is pretty unusual in Tunisia. As for **Tunisian women**, they are polite when you talk to them but they don't encourage conversation — and certainly not about private subjects.

To save yourself some degree of hassle, **cover up as much as possible**, at least neck to ankle. It might seem irksome to you but you'll get a better response from Tunisians. And try to travel in mixed-sex groups. The only question you may get then is "How much for the blonde?", a rather unoriginal joke.

LEGENDARY TUNISIA

Long before acquiring its present name, when it still belonged primarily to early Mediterranean civilisation, the land of Tunisia appeared in two of the greatest poems of European literature: Homer's *Odyssey* and Virgil's *Aeneid*. More than 2000 years later, it was this same remote past which drew many travellers to the French colony, among them the French writer Gustave Flaubert, whose novel *Salammbô* aimed to recreate one spectacular episode of the Carthaginian era.

In **Homer's** epic of wandering and survival the hero Odysseus, on his way home from Troy with a group of faithful but often foolish companions, is forced by hostile gods and goddesses to overcome a series of tests of his initiative before finally, after ten years, being allowed to return to his home on the island of Ithaca. Many of the episodes, such as the encounter with the one-eyed Cyclops, are now an integral part of European consciousness, and the **Land of the Lotus-Eaters** (see passage quoted on p.276) is among them.

There is an obvious and enduring fascination in the idea of a lifestyle emptied of cares by some mysterious substance, and it is hardly surprising that several places claim identity with Homer's idyllic land. Jerba's claim, however, is supported by very ancient tradition. While describing the peoples of North Africa, the fifth-century BC historian Herodotus comes to the Gindanes – a tribe, incidentally, whose

women wore a leather band around the ankle for each man they had slept with. "Within their territory", he continues, "a headland runs out into the sea, and it is here that the Lotus-Eaters dwell, a tribe which lives exclusively on the fruit of the lotus. It is about the size of a mastic-berry, and as sweet as a date. The Lotus-Eaters also make wine from it." The geographical similarity with Jerba (where the causeway connecting the island with Zarzis was probably built before Herodotus's time) is unmistakable, and anyone who has tasted Tunisian palm-wine (*laghmi*) will agree that it is a suitably primitive source of intoxication – which might well have been in use more than 500 years before Christ.

VIRGIL: *THE AENEID*

Like Odysseus, Virgil's hero Aeneas has difficulty in escaping the seductive charms of a part of Africa, but this episode from the Aeneid is much more emotionally and politically involved. On the face of it Aeneas's tragic love affair with Dido, queen and founder of Carthage (see p.000 for the background), is no more than that – but its implications go much deeper. Aeneas is forced to make a choice between his personal commitment to Dido and his public, divinely enforced commitment to founding a new Troy for his people – that is, Rome.

In the passage quoted here, the affair is almost at its end. Venus, goddess of love and implacable opponent of Aeneas, has made Dido fall in love with Aeneas in the hope that he will abandon the great Roman destiny planned for him by Jupiter, the king of the gods. Aeneas has duly returned Dido's feelings, their affair consummated al fresco to the accompaniment of thunder, lightning and nymphs wailing from the mountain-tops – but without making any formal commitment. Dido, herself committed totally, has alienated not only the neighbouring Numidian tribes (by rejecting marriage with one of their kings, Iarbas), but, through her infidelity to her dead husband Sychaeus, also her own Phoenician people. When Jupiter sends Mercury to remind Aeneas of his destiny, therefore, Aeneas knows that to abandon Dido will be to destroy her and the whole of her life. At first he plans to leave secretly, but Dido realises his intentions and, here, confronts him. Dido's eventual suicide on a funeral pyre symbolises the inevitable destruction of Carthage by Imperial Rome.

The end of the affair

At last Dido accosted Aeneas speaking first and denounced him:"Traitor, did you actually believe that you could disguise so wicked a deed and leave my country without a word? And can nothing hold you, not our love, nor our once plighted hands, nor even the cruel death that must await your Dido? Are you so unfeeling that you labour at your fleet under a wintry sky, in haste to traverse the high seas in the teeth of the northerly gales? Why, had you not now been searching for a home which you have never seen in some alien land, and had ancient Troy itself been still standing, would you have been planning to sail even there over such tempestuous seas? Is it from me that you are trying to escape? Oh, by the tears which I shed, by your own plighted hand, for I have left myself, poor fool, no other appeal, and by our union, by the true marriage which it was to be, oh, if I was ever kind to you, or if anything about me made you happy, please, please, if it is not too late to beg you, have pity for the ruin of a home, and change your mind. It was because of you that I earned the hate of Africa's tribes and the lords of the Numidians, and the hostility of my Tyrians also; and it was because of you that I let my honour die, the fair fame which used to be mine and my only hope of immortality. In whose hands are you leaving me to face my death, my Guest? I used to call you Husband, but the word has shrunk to Guest. What does the future hold for me now? My brother Pygmalion coming to demolish my walls, or this Gaetulian Iarbas, marrying me by capture? At least, if I had a son of yours conceived before you left, some tiny Aeneas to play about my hall and bring you back to me if only in his likeness, I might not then have felt so utterly entrapped and forsaken."

She finished. He, remembering Jupiter's warning, held his eyes steady and strained to master the agony within him. At last he spoke shortly:

"Your Majesty, I shall never deny that I am in your debt for all those many acts of kindness which you may well recount to me. And for long as I have consciousness and breath of life controls my movement, I shall never tire, Elissa, of your memory. Now I shall speak briefly of the facts. I had no thought of hiding my present departure under any deceit. Do not imagine that. Nor have I ever made any marriage-rite

my pretext, for I never had such a compact with you. If my destiny had allowed me to guide my life as I myself would have chosen, and solve my problems according to my own preference, I should have made the city of Troy, with its loved remembrances of my own folk, my first care; and, with Priam's tall citadel still standing, I should have refounded Troy's fortress to be strong once more after her defeat. But in fact Apollo at Grynium, where he gives his divination in Lycia by the lots, has insistently commanded me to make my way to Italy's noble land. Italy must be my love and my homeland now. If you, a Phoenician, are faithful to your Carthaginian fortress here, content to look on no other city but this city in far-away Africa, what is the objection if Trojans settle in Italy? It is no sin, if we, like you, look for a kingdom in a foreign country. Each time the night shrouds the earth in its moist shadows, each time the fiery stars arise, the anxious wraith of my father Anchises warns me in sleep, and I am afraid. My son Ascanius also serves as a warning to me; I think of his dear self, and of the wrong which I do him in defrauding him of his Italian kingdom, where Fate has given him his lands. And now Jove himself has sent the Spokesman of the Gods – this I swear to you by my son's life and by my father – who flew swiftly through the air, and delivered the command to me. With my own eyes I saw the divine messenger in clearest light entering the city gate, and heard his voice with my own ears. Cease, therefore, to upset yourself, and me also, with these protests. It is not by my own choice that I voyage onward to Italy."

Throughout this declaration Dido had remained standing, turned away from Aeneas but glaring at him over her shoulder with eyes which roved about his whole figure in a voiceless stare. Then her fury broke:

"Traitor, no goddess was ever your mother nor was it Dardanus who founded your line. No, your parent was Mount Caucasus, rugged, rocky, and hard, and tigers of Hyrcania nursed you.... For what need have I of concealment now? Why hold myself in check any longer as if there could be anything worse to come?... Has he spared a sigh or a look in response to my weeping, or has he once softened, or shed a tear of pity for one who loved him? Depth beyond depth of iniquity! Neither Supreme Juno, nor the Father who is Saturn's son, can possibly look with the impartial eyes of justice on what is happening now. No faith is left sure in the wide world. I welcomed him, a ship-wrecked beggar, and like a fool I allowed him to share my royal place. I saved his comrades from death and gave him back his lost fleet….The Furies have me now, they burn, they drive . . .! So, now, it seems, he has his orders from Apollo's own Lycian oracle, and next even the Spokesman of the Gods is sent by Jove himself to deliver through the air to him the same ghastly command! So I am to believe that the High Powers exercise their minds about such a matter and let concern for it disturb their calm! Oh, I am not holding you. I do not dispute your words. Go, quest for Italy before the winds; sail over the waves in search of your kingdom. But I still believe that, if there is any power for righteousness in Heaven, you will drink to the dregs the cup of punishment amid sea-rocks, and as you suffer cry 'Dido' again and again. Though far, yet I shall be near, haunting you with flames of blackest pitch. And when death's chill has parted my body from its breath, wherever you go my spectre will be there. You will have your punishment, you villain. And I shall hear; the news will reach me deep in the world of death."

She did not finish, but at these words broke off sharply. She hurried in her misery away and hid from sight, leaving Aeneas anxious and hesitant, and longing to say much more to her. Dido fainted, and fell; and her maids took her up, carried her to her marble bedroom and laid her on her bed.

taken from Book IV of the Penguin Classics edition, translated by W F Jackson Knight

FLAUBERT: SALAMMBÔ

*In the nineteenth century, Carthage's abrupt and tragic end made its fabulous past irresistible to the imaginations of many Europeans, among them **Gustave Flaubert**. But his decision to write a novel about ancient Carthage probably owed as much to the present as the past; on his first trip to the East in 1851 Flaubert had become obsessed with "the Orient", that mythical land created by feverish post-Romantic sensibilities. The letters which he wrote from the Middle East (you can find*

some of the best – and most lascivious – in Flaubert in Egypt published by Michael Haag) are a rich source for these Orientalist attitudes and in Salammbô are obliquely enshrined in fictional form. It seems extraordinary that anyone could ever have taken the historical aspect of this book seriously. Its plot, such as it is, deals with the War of the Mercenaries (241–37) – though with significant additions from the author's fertile mind, including the character of Salammbô, sex symbol supreme. Take away the plot and you in fact lose little: the bulk of the novel consists of Flaubert's attempt to recreate the atmosphere of Carthage as an ancient Orient, something of a cross between a Cecil B. deMille epic and a video nasty. It is also however, highly imaginative, not to say fantastic, and a whole generation did see the Orient in terms quite as excessive as Flaubert's. Eating, drinking, sex, violence, cruelty, beauty, wealth, poverty and nearly every human quality and activity was grotesquely exaggerated. In the episode included here, Hanno, one of the Carthaginian generals, is in Utica snatching in typical style a brief respite from the rigours of campaigning against the Mercenaries, or Barbarians.

Hanno takes a bath

Three hours later he was still plunged in the cinnamon oil with which the bath had been filled; and as he bathed, he ate on a stretched out ox hide, flamingo tongues with poppy seed seasoned with honey. Beside him, his doctor, standing motionless in a long yellow robe, had the bath heated up from time to time and two boys leaning on the steps of the pool rubbed his legs. But the care of his body did not interrupt his concern for the welfare of the state, and he was dictating a letter to the Grand Council and, as some prisoners had just been taken, wondering what terrible punishment to invent.

"Stop!" he said to a slave who stood writing in the hollow of his hand. "Have them brought in! I want to see them."

And from the back of the room filled with white steam where torches cast spots of red three Barbarians were pushed in: a Samnite, a Spartan, and a Cappadocian.

"Continue!" said Hanno.

"Rejoice light of the Baals! Your Suffete has exterminated the greedy dogs! Blessings on the Republic! Order prayers to be offered!" He noticed the captives, and then roaring with laughter: "Ha ha! My brave men from Sicca! You are not shouting so loudly today! Here I am! Do you recognize me? Where are your swords then? What terrible men, really!" And he pretended to try and hide, as if he were afraid. "You demanded horses, women, land, judicial office, no doubt, and priesthood! Why not? All right, I will give you land, and land you will never leave! You will be married to brand new gallows! Your pay? It will be melted in your mouths in the form of lead ingots! And I will set you in good positions, very high, among the clouds, so that you can be near the eagles!"

The three Barbarians, hairy and covered in rags, looked at him without understanding what he was saying. Wounded in the knees, they had been seized and bound with ropes, and the ends of the heavy chains on their hands dragged along the floor. Hanno was angry at their impassivity.

"On your knees! On your knees! Jackals! Dirt! Vermin! Excrement! So they do not answer! Enough! Silence! Have them flayed alive! No! In a moment! "

He was puffing like a hippopotamus, rolling his eyes. The scented oil ran out beneath the bulk of his body, and sticking to his scaly skin made it look pink in the torchlight.

He went on:

"For four days we have greatly suffered from the sun. Crossing the Macar some mules were lost. Despite their position, the extraordinary courage.... Ah! Demonades how I am suffering! Heat up the bricks and make them red hot!"

There was a clattering of rakes and furnaces. The incense smoked more fiercely in its large burners, and the naked masseurs, sweating like sponges, squeezed over his joints a paste composed of corn, sulphur, black wine, bitches' milk, myrrh, galbanum, and styrax. He was tormented by constant thirst; the man in yellow did not give in to this craving and, holding out a golden cup in which steamed a viper's brew:

"Drink!" he said, "so that the strength of the serpents, children of the sun, may penetrate the marrow of your bones, and take courage, reflection of the Gods! Besides, you know that a priest of Eschmoûn is watching the cruel stars around the Dog from which your illness derives. They are growing paler, like the spots on your skin, and you are not to die of it."

"Oh, yes, that is right," repeated the Suffete, "I am not to die of it!" And from his purplish lips escaped a breath more noisome than the stench of a corpse. Two coals seemed to burn in place of his eyes which had no eyebrows left; a mass of wrinkled skin hung down over his forehead; his two ears, standing out from his head, were beginning to swell, and the deep creases which made semi-circles around his nostrils gave him a strange and frightening look, like that of a wild beast. His distorted voice sounded like a roar; he said:

"Perhaps you are right, Demonades? In fact a lot of the ulcers have closed up. I feel quite robust. Just look how I eat!"

Then less out of greed than for show, and to prove to himself that he was well, he attacked cheese and tarragon stuffing, filleted fish, pumpkins, oysters, with eggs, horseradish, truffles and kebabs of little birds. As he looked at the prisoners he revelled in imagining their punishment. However he remembered Sicca, and fury at all his pains burst out in insults at these three men.

"Ah! Traitors! Wretches! Infamous cursed creatures! And you exposed me to your outrages, me! Me! The Suffete! Their services, the price of their blood, as they call it! Oh yes! Their blood! Their blood!" Then talking to himself: "They will all perish! Not one will be sold! It would be better to take them to Carthage! I should be seen... but I have probably not brought enough chains? Write: send me .... How many of them are there? Go and ask Muthumbal! Go! No mercy! Cut off all their hands, and bring them to me in baskets!"

But strange cries, at once hoarse and shrill, could be heard in the room, above Hanno's voice and the clattering of the dishes being set round him. The noise increased, and suddenly the furious trumpeting of the elephants broke out as if battle was starting again. A great tumult surrounded the town.

The Carthaginians had not tried to pursue the Barbarians. They had settled at the foot of the walls, with their baggage, their servants, their whole satrap retinue and they were making merry in their handsome pearl-edged tents, while all that remained of the Mercenary camp was a heap of ruins on the plain. Spendius had recovered his courage. He sent out Zarxas to Mâtho, went through the woods, rallied his men (losses had not been heavy) —

and furious at having been beaten in battle, they reformed their lines, when someone discovered a vat of paraffin, no doubt abandoned by the Carthaginians. Then Spendius had pigs collected from the farms, smeared them with pitch, set light to it and drove them towards Utica.

The elephants, frightened by these flames, took flight. The ground sloped upwards, they were assailed by javelins, and turned back — and with mighty blows of their tusks and hooves they ripped, smothered, flattened the Carthaginians. Behind them, the Barbarians were coming down the hill; the Punic camp, with no defences, was sacked at the first charge, and the Carthaginians were crushed against the gates, for no one would open them for fear of the Mercenaries.

Dawn was breaking; from the west appeared Mâtho's infantrymen. At the same time horsemen came in sight; it was Narr'Havas with his Numidians. Jumping over the ravines and bushes, they drove the fugi-tives like hounds hunting hares. This reversal of fortune interrupted the Suffete. He cried out to be helped out of the bath. The three captives were still before him. Then a Negro (the same one who carried his parasol in battle) leaned over to his ear.

"Well now . . . .?" the Suffete slowly replied. "Oh! kill them!" he added brusquely.

The Ethiopian drew a long dagger from his belt and the three heads fell. One of them, bouncing amid the debris of the feast, jumped into the pool, and floated there for a while, with open mouth and staring eyes. The morning light was filtering in through cracks in the wall; the three bodies, lying on their chests, were streaming blood like three fountains, and a sheet of blood covered the mosaics, which had been sprinkled with blue powder. The Suffete soaked his hand in this still warm slime, and rubbed his knees with it; it had remedial powers.

taken from the Penguin Classics edition, translated by A J Krailsheimer

BOOKS

Books designated *o/p* are currently out of print, but still worth tracking down secondhand or in libraries. Some will occasionally by reprinted or published in a new edition.

TWENTIETH-CENTURY TRAVEL WRITERS

Norman Douglas, *Fountains in the Sand* (1911, o/p). Douglas, one of the most famous early modern travellers, as well as a pederast and a bigot, nonetheless writes in a compelling style about his travels around the Jerid. He saw the Chott, like just about everything else in Tunisia, as a symbol for the "sterility of the Arab soul".

Aldous Huxley, *In a Tunisia Oasis* (in a collection called *The Olive Tree*, o/p). If you can disregard the snide racist tone, this is by far the best of a largely barren English tradition of travel-writing about Tunisia. Some things in Nefta have changed very little.

Jonathan Raban, *Arabia Through the Looking Glass* (Picador, 1987). Like *Eothen*, this has nothing to do with Tunisia itself, but it is an excellent travel book about the contemporary Arab world: one man's view of the reality that lies (some way) behind Western suspicions and prejudices.

Reginald Rankin, *Tunisia* (1930, o/p). Wholly eccentric and spiced with prejudice, arrogance and sheer stupidity, but still a good read in spite, or because of, all that.

Sacheverell Sitwell, *Mauretania* (1940, o/p). Written by the aristocratic brother of the more famous Osbert and Edith, a member of the pre-war international glamour set, who played a prolific but insignificant part in the era's travel-writing boom.

EARLY TRAVELLERS

Leo Africanus, *History and Description of Africa* (translated by J Pory, 1896). Written by a Spanish Moor who converted to Christianity after being captured at sea by Christian corsairs. He got his nickname from the Pope, who encouraged him to write about the Arabs of Barbary. Not surprisingly, there's more than a whiff of propaganda in some of the accounts.

James Bruce, *Travels to Discover the Source of the Nile in the Years 1768–73* (1790, facsimile by Gregg Int., 1971). Six volumes of some of the most entertaining travel writing ever published. An eccentric British Consul at Algiers, Bruce passed through Tunisia on his way to Cairo and Ethiopia (to which most of the book is devoted; the Tunisian section was actually deleted after the first edition). Bruce's egocentric and extrovert personality made other people's behaviour a source of fascination to him – a fascination brilliantly conveyed in blunt and lively style.

D Bruun, *Cave-Dwellers of Southern Tunisia* (1898, o/p). Bruun was one of the first Europeans to live with the people of Matmata and Haddej, and his sympathetic account is still interesting if you can find it in a library. Unfortunately, at the end of the book the author attempts to divest a wandering nomad of clothes for his museum back home.

Olfert Dapper, *Africa* (translated by J Ogilby, 1670). An encyclopaedic compendium of reports culled from many different sources, full of fascinating nuggets.

Alexandre Dumas, *Tangier to Tunis* (Peter Owen, 1959). Dumas is not at his best here, and the editing has shortened the chapters on Tunisia, but there are some amusing vignettes in this rare translation of one of the many French travellers – Dumas visited in 1846.

Sir Harry Johnston, *A Journey through the Tunisian Sahara* (Geographic Magazine, 1898, o/p). Johnston, though handicapped by a lack of basic knowledge, was one of the first Englishmen to make an effort, during his travels from Jerba to Matmata, to understand the people and their way of life.

A. W. Kinglake, *Eothen* (Century Travellers and OUP, 1982). Long treasured as one of the classics of travel writing, but only now gaining wider recognition. Kinglake's travels through Turkey and Palestine to Egypt in 1835 have little to do with Tunisia, but this is an extraordinarily witty book to have with you when travelling yourself.

Lt Col Sir R Lambert Playfair, *Murray's Handbook for Travellers in Algeria and Tunis* (Murray, 1891, o/p). Written by a British Consul at Algiers whose unimaginative outlook is redeemed only slightly by his erudition.

Dr Thomas Shaw, *Travels and Observations Relating to Several Parts of Barbary and the Levant* (1757, facsimile by Gregg Int., 1973). The author, an exceedingly dry Scot, spent most of his time in North Africa misidentifying and cataloguing every Roman site he could find.

Sir Grenville Temple, *Excursions in the Mediterranean* (1835, o/p). An early imperialist view of Tunisia. The author, something of an amateur Romantic artist, produced some unlikely versions of the monuments and scenery he encountered.

Herbert Vivian, *Tunisia and the Modern Barbary Pirates* (1899, o/p). Vivian, if anything even more unpleasant than Lt Col Playfair (they met in a Tunis hotel, an encounter mentioned in the book), seems to have been gathering a little intelligence in the new French colony.

TUNISIAN LITERATURE

If you read French, look out for the publications of **Editions Sindbad** *and* **Editions Salammbô** *in Tunisia. They produce translation and original work of contemporary writers. Tunisian literature in English is rare.*

Gisèle Halimi, *Milk for the Orange Tree* (Quartet, 1991). A Jewish civil rights lawyer in France, part of Halimi's autobiographical account paints a picture of her childhood in Tunisia.

Albert Memmi, *Colonizer and the Colonized* (Earthscan Publications, 1990); *The Pillar of Salt* (US, Viking Penguin, 1992). Tunisia's most distinguished novelist, whose main theme is the problem of identity for North African Jews such as himself. Other books of his in print in English include: *The Scorpion* (US, O'Hara, 1975) and *Jews and Arabs* (US, O'Hara, 1975).

Mustapha Tlili, *Lion Mountain* (US, Arcade, 1990). One of the few Tunisian novelists whose work is available in translation.

Ibn Khaldoun, *The Muqaddimah* (Routledge, 1978). A translation, by N J Dawood, of the masterpiece by Tunisia's great fourteenth-century historian, whose fascinating mix of sociology, history and anthropology was centuries ahead of its time.

ANCIENT HISTORY AND LITERATURE

Gustave Flaubert, *Salammbô* (Penguin Classic, 1977). Sex, violence, and more violence: it's all here in a nineteenth-century novel that anticipates Cecil B. deMille. Flaubert claimed to have written a historical account of Carthage's brutal civil war with its Mercenaries (241–37), but the book owes little to history and everything to its author's obsession with the fabulous Orient. An extraordinarily bad novel, but a very enjoyable read.

Sallust, *The Jugurthine War* (Penguin Classic, 1969); **Livy**, *The War with Hannibal* (Penguin Classic, 1970); **Polybius**, *The Rise of the Roman Empire* (Penguin Classic, 1979). These are the texts Flaubert used. Sallust's book is the shortest, but by far the most entertaining, with melodramatic accounts of African war and Roman morality. Livy and Polybius are rather too much to the historical point.

Peter Brown, *Augustine of Hippo: a Biography* (Faber, 1969); **Augustine**, *Confessions* (Penguin Classic, 1970). Brown's classic biography contains much interesting background material on the Africa of Augustine's time. *Confessions* is the saint's most accessible work, a spiritual autobiography.

Virgil, *The Aeneid* (Penguin Classic, 1991). Books I and IV of the great Roman epic poem tell the tragic love story of Queen Dido (founder of Carthage) and Aeneas (founder of Rome), an inspiration to artists of every age since. The first version is still the best: read it and decide whether you can have any sympathy for the careerist Aeneas – and to get an idea of the mystique of Carthage.

Apuleius, *The Golden Ass* (US, Harvard University Press, 1989). A native of Madaurus (Soul Ahras in Algeria), Apuleius (120–80) was educated as a lawyer at Carthage University

and wrote several works. This is the most entertaining fiction to come out of Roman Africa:
while on a business trip in Greece the hero
meddles with Thessalian witchcraft and gets
turned into a donkey. In this form he goes
through a series of low-life adventures before
finally being returned to human form by the
goddess Isis.

TUNISIAN AND ARAB HISTORY

Lisa Anderson, *The State and Social
Transformation in Tunisia and Libya, 1830–1980*
(US, Princeton University Press, o/p). Don't be
put off by the thesis-like title: it's a good review
of Tunisian and Libyan political and social
history.

E W Bovill, *The Golden Trade of the Moors*
(OUP, o/p). Hard to classify, this wide-ranging
book about trans-Saharan trade is full of intriguing details about a fascinating and little-
studied subject.

Karl Brown *The Tunisia of Ahmed Bey, 1837-
1856*, (US, o/p). A fascinating insight into nineteenth-century Tunisia and the problems faced
by an Arab government struggling to keep itself
out of European clutches. Available in most
university libraries.

Wifrid Knapp, *Tunisia* (Thames & Hudson, o/
p). The most worthwhile of several introductory
history-cum-background books that came out in
the 1960s and 1970s.

Peter Mansfield, *The Arabs* (Penguin, 1991).
By far the best introduction to the Arab world.
available. A general history of the region, from
Islam's beginnings to the end of the 1970s,
followed by a short section on each country and
two excellent final chapters: "Through
European Eyes" and "Through Arab Eyes".

Arthur Marsden, *British diplomacy and Tunis,
1875–1902* (Scottish Academic Press, o/p). If
you want to see how devious and calculating
the foreign powers were in dividing up the
Mediterranean, then this is the book – very
scholarly but never dry.

Charles Messenger, *The Tunisian Campaign*
(Ian Allan, o/p). A pictorial history of World
War II in Tunisia.

Magali Morsy, *North Africa 1800–1900. A
Survey from the Nile Valley to the Atlantic*
(Longman, 1984). An excellent history of North
Africa in a period of crisis, placing Tunisia in
the context of North Africa as a whole.

Jamil M Abun-Nasr, *A History of the
Maghreb* (Cambridge University Press, 1975, o/
p). An authoritative history of the region by a
distinguished Maghrebian historian, but not
exactly a light read.

W Perkins, *Tunisia: Crossroads of the Islamic
and European Worlds* (US, Croom Helm, o/p).
The best pocket history of Tunisia available.
Authoritative and a good read.

Norma Salem, *Habib Bourguiba, Islam and the
Creation of Modern Tunisia* (US, Croom Helm,
1985, o/p). Another political history – a bit too
much of a eulogy to be credible as a balanced
review, and occasionally dull, but a nonetheless competent biography of the great man.

ISLAM AND SOCIETY

The Koran (Penguin, 1990; OUP, o/p). The
word of God as handed down to the Prophet is
the basis of all Islam, and notoriously untrans-
latable. Though the full effect is still probably
lost, the OUP edition is the one to go for;
Penguin's is stultifyingly prosaic.

S. H. Nasr, *Ideals and Realities of Islam* (Allen
and Unwin, 1985). An excellent survey of Islam,
and sufficiently detailed to be convincing. The
chapters on the Koran, Hadith and Sharia give
especially clear explanations.

Edward Mortimer, *Faith and Power* (Faber &
Faber, o/p). A useful introduction to the
complex relationship between Islam and politics; general historical background is followed
by six case studies of countries ranging from
Iran to secularised Turkey.

Edward Said, *Orientalism: Western Concepts
of the Orient* (Penguin, 1991). A book that pulls
no punches, this radical analysis of Western
attitudes to the Arab world was received with
some hostility when it was published. Said, a
literary critic of Palestinian origin, approaches
the problem through the writings of nineteenth-
century travellers (such as Flaubert), developing
it into an attack on virtually every so-called
modern Western "expert" on the Arab world.
Some of the literary criticism, showing how the
myth of "The Orient" was created and fostered
by a dominant and arrogant Europe, is
extremely acute, and his accusations of modern

racism are hard to deny; but it's not true that these prejudices are shared by every Western specialist.

Ernest Gellner, *Muslim Society* (CUP, 1983). The most comprehensive and thought-provoking study available on its subject by a brilliant and well-established scholar. Certainly not easy-going, but thoroughly recommended.

Lucette Valensi and Abraham Udovitch, *The Last Arab Jews* (Harwood Academic publishers, 1984). The definitive study of the Jerban community, its history, sociology, and prospects. Good illustrations too. Lucette Valensi has also written *Tunisian Peasants in the Eighteenth and Nineteenth Centuries* (CUP, 1986).

N Minai, *Women in Islam* (John Murray, o/p). Combines a valuable historical survey with an interesting analysis of contemporary Arab society, looking at the changing status of women from the time of Mohammed, through the Caliphate, to the Ottomans, then describing the customs and traditions, in various countries, applied at each stage of a woman's life.

Minority Rights Group Report, *Arab Women* (MRG, 1983). A general survey of the status of women, country by country, through the Arab world. The small section on Tunisia is dated but still a good introduction.

Jean Duvignaud, *Change at Shebika* (Penguin, o/p). In the 1960s, a group of French and Tunisian sociologists spent a year living in this isolated village near Tozeur. This is an interesting, honest account of their contacts with the people, sometimes open but plagued with misunderstanding and uncertainty. Duvignaud describes the position of the women, families,

religion and their working lives; in part he is vague and impressionistic but the conclusion – that local customs were inadequate in a time of social change – seems fair enough.

ART AND ARCHITECTURE

Michael Rogers, *The Spread of Islam* (Phaidon, o/p). In a book about the whole geographical range of Islam there's relatively little about Tunisia alone; but this is much the best general survey around of Islamic society, art and architecture. Strongly recommended if you can get hold of it.

Derek Hill and Lucien Golvin, *Islamic Architecture of North Africa* (Faber & Faber, o/p). It's a sad comment that this is the best available introduction to the architecture. Intended originally as an artists' guide to Islamic patterns, the pictures are numerous but of variable quality; the fuller historical introduction and notes on individual buildings are useful.

Michael Brett, *The Moors* (Orbis, o/p). A glossy picture book on the western Arabs with an unusually well-informed text by an expert in the field. A good investment.

D. Mitchell, (ed), *Islamic Architecture* (Thames & Hudson, o/p). Along with Rogers, the best of the books on architecture, with interesting articles on domestic architecture and on regional styles.

T. Burkhardt, *Art of Islam* (World of Islam Festival, o/p). A highly conceptual and impressionistic account of the relationship between Islamic doctrine and its art. Some of the best illustrations around, even if the text is at times hard to grasp.

LANGUAGE

Arabic is a notoriously difficult language for Europeans to learn, and further complicated by the fact that it varies considerably from country to country within the Arab world, not only in pronunciation but in vocabulary. Fortunately, however, Tunisia is virtually bilingual, and in the remotest of places you will find someone who can also speak French. With even basic school-knowledge French you'll find you can get by quite well.

For all this, though, French was the language of colonialism and any attempt at Arabic — even the most stumbling — gives great pleasure. Included here are some very basic words and phrases; if you want to learn seriously, the Bourguiba School in Tunis (see p.74) is highly recommended and exceptional value.

GESTURES

Tunisians are great **gesticulators**. The classic motion involves joining thumb and fingertips and holding the hand upwards; thoroughly infectious, this sign can mean almost anything, depending on the circumstances. Waved fiercely it conveys impatience, held quietly it means wait, patience, and shaken deliberately in conversation it claims ultimate authority for what's being said. As elsewhere in the Middle East, and round much of the Mediterranean, the word "no" is accompanied by a click of the tongue and toss of the head — flourishes which can at first seem contemptuously dismissive, but aren't intended that way. Also apt to be confusing is "come this way": the beckoning hand pointing downward, it often looks as though you're being told to go away. Sex in general is indicated by cutting one hand against the other.

TUNISIAN ARABIC

The transliteration is highly approximate, and intended to function phonetically. "Kh" represents a sound like the "ch" in loch, while "gh" represents a sort of gargling sound like a French "r".

In theory, there are two singular forms of "you": inti when addressing a woman and inta when addressing a man. In most of Tunisia, however, inti is used for everyone (to the shocked surprise of non-Tunisian Arab men). A lot of words referring to "you" end in -ik; strictly speaking, when addressing a man this should be -ak.

BASICS

Yes	Ayi, Aiwa	We	Ihna
No	La	You (plural)	Intoo
Please	Minfadlik*	They	Hoom
Thank you	BarkAllahufik*, Shukran	There's, Is there?, There are, Are there?	Fee (?)
Excuse me	Samahanee	There isn't, There aren't	Mafeesh
I	Ana		
You	Inti, Inta*	Good	Behi
She	Hiya	Not good	Mish behi, Khayeb
He	Huwa		

GREETINGS AND FAREWELLS

Hello	*Assalama*	Good night	*Tisbah ala khir*
Good morning	*Sabah el khir*	Goodbye	*Bisalama, Filaman*
(response)	*(Sabah en nour)*	My name's...	*Ismi...*
Good evening	*Missa el khir*	What's your name?	*Sismik?**
(response)	*(Missa en nour)*	Where are you from?	*Mineen inti?, Mineen inta?**
How are you?	*Ashnooa ahwalik**	I'm from...	*Ana min...*
Fine thanks	*Labes elhamdulillah*	Bon voyage	*Treq salama*
And you?	*Winti?, Winta? **	See you later	*N'shoofik* minbad*

DIRECTIONS AND TRAVELLING

Is there a... near here?	*Fee... qareb min hina?*	Straight on	*Tul*
Where is the...?	*Fayn el...?*	Near	*Qareb*
Hotel	*Nezel*	Far	*Bayeed*
Restaurant	*Mataam*	Here	*Hina*
Bank	*Bunk*	There	*Radi, Hinik**
Train (station)	*(Mahata el) tran*	When?	*Waqtesh?*
Bus (station)	*(Mahata el) car*	First	*El uwel*
Toilet	*Mihath*	Next	*El jai*
Left	*Lisaar*	Last	*El akher*
Right	*Limin*	Could you write it please?	*Yoomkin tnajim tekta-bah minfadlik?**

SHOPPING AND ACCOMMODATION

Have you got...?	*Andik*...?*	(Too) expensive	*Ghalee (barsha)*
A room	*Bit, Ghorfa*	Still expensive	*Mazal ghalee*
A shower	*Doosh*	Have you got anything...?	*'Andik* haja...?*
Hot	*Skhoon*	...better	*...khir*
Cold	*Biird*	...cheaper	*...arkhis*
Can I have a...?	*Yoomkin wahad...?*	...bigger	*...akbar*
Can I buy...?	*Yoomkin ashtiri...?*	...smaller	*...asghar*
Can I see...?	*Yoomkin ashoofa...?*	I haven't got any	*Ma'andish*
How much is...?	*Kaddesh...?*	Open	*Ftouh*
This	*Hada*	Closed	*Msaker*
That	*Hadik**		

OTHER COMMON OR USEFUL EXPRESSIONS

Slowly	*Shwaya shwaya*	In the name of God	*Bismillah (used when starting a meal or journey)*
Go away	*Imshi, Barra*		
Later	*Minbad*		
Never mind	*Maalesh*	Money	*Floos*
The same	*Kif Kif*	Let's go!	*Yalla, Nimshi*
Praise be to God	*El Hamdulillah (used whenever mentioning any kind of good fortune, repeated in response)*	Chill out	*Wasa balek (lit: "lengthen your mind")*
God willing	*Insh'Allah (used in any reference to hopes or the future, repeated in response)*	Shame on you!	*Shooma!*
		I don't know	*Ma'arfsh*
		I don't understand	*Mefehemsh*

TIME AND DAYS

What time is it?	Kaddesh loweqet?	Now	El an
One o'clock	El wahad	Later	Minbad
Five past one	El wahad wa draj	Today	El yoom
Ten past one	El wahad wa darjeen	Tomorrow	Ghudwa
Quarter past one	El wahad warbo'o	Yesterday	El barah
Twenty past one	El wahad warba'a	Sunday	El had
Twenty-five past one	El wahad wa khamsa	Monday	El tneen
Half past one	El wahad wa nuss	Tuesday	El tlata
Twenty-five to two	El wahad wa sabaa	Wednesday	El arba
Twenty to two	El etneen ghir arba'a	Thursday	El khemis
Quarter to two	El etneen ghir arbo'o	Friday	Ej jemaa
Ten to two	El etneen ghir darjeen	Saturday	Es sebt
Five to two	El etneen ghir draj		

FRENCH ESSENTIALS

BASICS AND GREETINGS

Yes/no	Oui/non	Goodbye	Au revoir	Open	Ouvert
Good morning	Bonjour	Please	S'il vous plait	Closed	Fermé
Good evening	Bonsoir	Thank you	Merci	Go away!	Va-t-en
Good night	Bonne nuit	Could you?	Pourriez-vous?	Stop messing	Arrête de
Sorry, excuse me	Pardon	Why?	Pourquoi?	me about!	m'emmerder!
How are you?	Ça va?	What?	Quoi?		

DIRECTIONS

Where is the road for . . . ?	Quelle est la route pour . . . ?	Far	Loin
Where is . . . ?	Où est . . . ?	When?	Quand?
Do you have . . . ?	Avez vous . . . ?	At what time?	A quelle heure?
. . . a room?	. . . une chambre?	Write it down, please	Ecrivez-le, s'il vous plaît
Here, there	Ici, là	Now	Maintenant
Right	A droite	Later	Plus tard
Left	A gauche	Never	Jamais
Straight on	Tout droit	Today	Aujourd'hui
Near	Proche, près	Tomorrow	Demain
		Yesterday	Hier

BUYING

How much/many?	Combien?	Like this/that	Comme ceci/cela
How much does that cost?	Combien ça coute?	What is it?	Qu'est-ce que c'est?
Too expensive	Trop cher	Enough	Assez
More/less	Plus/moin	Big	Grand
Cheap	Bon marché	Little	Petit

THINGS

Bus	Car, autobus	Ticket (return)	Billet (de retour)	Post office	Poste, PTT
Bus station	Gare routière	Bank	Banque	Stamps	Timbres-postes
Railway	Chemin de fer	Key	Clef	Left luggage	Consigne
Airport	Aeroport	Roof	Terrasse		d'equipage
Railway station	Gare	Passport	Passeport	Visa	Visa
Ferry	Bac	Currency	Change	Money	Argent
Lorry	Camion	exchange			

ARABIC NUMBERS

1	١	Wahad	10	١٠	Ashara
2	٢	Zous, Etneen	11	١١	Ahdash
3	٣	Tlaata	12	١٢	Etnash
4	٤	Arbaa	13	١٣	Talatash
5	٥	Khamsa	14	١٤	Arbatash
6	٦	Sitta	15	١٥	Khamstash
7	٧	Sabaa	16	١٦	Sittash
8	٨	Tmaania	17	١٧	Sabatash
9	٩	Tissa	18	١٨	Tmantash
19	١٩	Tissatash	80	٨٠	Temaaneen
20	٢٠	Ashreen	90	٩٠	Tissaeen
21	٢١	Wahad wa ashreen	100	١٠٠	Mia
22	٢٢	Etneen wa ashreen	200	٢٠٠	Miateen
30	٣٠	Talaateen	300	٣٠٠	Tlaata mia
40	٤٠	Arabaeen	400	٤٠٠	Arba mia
50	٥٠	Khamseen	1000	١٠٠٠	Lef (often used
60	٦٠	Sitteen			for a dinar)
70	٧٠	Sabaeen			

GLOSSARY

ABBASIDS Dynasty of Caliphs who ruled the Arab empire from Baghdad 749–1258.

AGHLABIDS Arab dynasty, ruled northern and central Tunisia from Kairouan in the ninth century.

AH (After the Hegira) Islamic date, the equivalent of AD. Islamic years begin with Mohammed's flight to Medina (see p.342).

AÏN Spring.

ALMOHADS Religious movement from Morocco, which came to control the whole of the Maghreb, from Marrakesh to Tunisia, in the twelfth century.

ALMORAVIDS Dynasty which ruled Morocco in the eleventh century and invaded Tunisia in the twelfth.

ARIANISM Christian heresy followed by the Vandals, based on an attempt to reconcile Christianity with Germanic pagan religions.

ASM *Association de Sauvegarde de la Medina*. Organisations dedicated to preserving architectural heritage of old Arab towns.

AUTOGARE Bus and *louage* station.

BAB Door or gate.

BARBARY European term for North Africa in the sixteenth to nineteenth centuries.

BASILICA Roman building type with aisles, later used for churches.

BERBERS The non-Arab native inhabitants of North Africa since about 4000 BC, speaking their own language. Very few pure Berbers survive in Tunisia, though they form the majority in Morocco and Algeria.

BEY Ottoman official, in practice the ruler of Tunisia in the eighteenth and nineteenth centuries (the adjective is *Beylical*).

BORJ Fort.

BOURNOUSE Long woolen or camel-hair men's outer garment, often with hood.

BYZANTINE The continuation of the Roman Empire in the East, ruled from Byzantium (now Istanbul), which controlled Tunisia in the sixth century AD.

CALDARIUM Hot room in Roman bath.

CALÈCHE Horse-drawn tourist carriage.

CAPITAL Stone "cushion" at the top of a column or pillar.

CAPITOL Central temple of Roman town equivalent to a cathedral.

CARTHAGE Phoenican city founded about the ninth century BC, which became capital of the Carthaginian Empire finally defeated by Rome.

CELLA Inner sanctuary of a temple.

CHECHIA Red felt hat, like a soft fez.

CHICHA (SHEESHA) Café water pipe.

CHOTT Flat dry area; used for salt lakes and occasionally beaches.

CORSAIRS Pirates, Muslim and Christian, who operated in the Mediterranean from the thirteenth to the nineteenth centuries.

DAR House, palace.

DEY Ottoman military officer of junior rank. Their control of troops meant they effectively ruled Tunisia in the early seventeenth century.

DONATISM Fourth- and fifth-century dissident Christian church set up to avoid "contamination" by insincere Orthodox priests.

DRIBA Entrance hall.

ERG Sand dunes.

EL QUDS (EL QODS, EL QUODS, EL KUDS) Jerusalem, the third holy city of Islam.

ENNAHDHA Illegal fundamentalist political party, formerly the MTI.

FATIMIDS Dynasty of heretical Ismaili Muslims who ruled Tunisia, from Mahdia, in the tenth century, and Egypt in the eleventh.

FOUNDOUK Inn, storehouse and sometimes trading base, known as a *caravanserai* in the eastern part of the Arab world.

FORUM Enclosed open space at centre of Roman town.

FRIGIDARIUM Cold room in Roman bath.

GARGOTE Cheap restaurant or café.

GHAR Cave.

GHORFA Room – refers in particular to the cells used to store grain inside a *ksar*.

HAFSIDS Dynasty who ruled Tunisia, from Tunis, in the thirteenth, fourteenth and fifteenth centuries. Originally governors for the Almohads, they declared independence in 1229 when the Marrakesh regime ditched Ibn Tumart's teachings. Seen as the Almohads' true heirs, the Hafsids presided over Tunisia's golden age.

HAJ (HADJ) Pilgrimage to Mecca, or someone who has made this journey (older people are politely assumed to have done it, and so are addressed as *haj*).

HAMMAM (Turkish) bath.

HANEFITE One of the four schools of orthodox Sunni Islam, founded in the eighth century. Widespread in Anatolia and brought by the Turks to North Africa – whose mosques are distinguished by octagonal minarets. The school is less austere than the native Malekite school, laying some stress on commercial success.

HILALIANS (Banu Hilal) Nomadic Arabs who invaded Tunisia in the eleventh century, were outside the control of its Zirid rulers, and severely disrupted its infrastructure.

HOUCH Jerban house, looks like a small fortress (see p.289).

HUSAYNIDS Dynasty of Beys who ruled Tunisia from 1705 until (nominally) 1957.

HYPOSTYLE Hall supported by pillars as in many prayer halls of mosques.

IBADITE Member of the main branch of Kharijism.

IMAM Roughly the Islamic equivalent of a Christian priest, except that Islam has no real clergy.

IMPASSE Blind alley.

INFIRMERIE Clinic staffed by nurses for dealing with general medical complaints.

ISMAILI Shia splinter formed on the death of the sixth Shiite imam (equivalent to the Sunni Caliph), claiming that only descendants of his son Ismail could be given the title of imam.

JEBEL (DJEBEL) Mountain.

JEMAA (DJEMA'A) Great Mosque, or Friday Mosque (*Grande Mosquée*), the central place of worship in any town. During the week citizens may worship at *masjids*, smaller local mosques, but on Fridays they worship together at the *jemaa*, to hear the imam's homily.

KASBAH Administrative centre and/or fort of Arab town.

KEF Rock.

KHARIJITES The "Secessionists", an early heretical sect, still surviving in Jerba, which found eager adherents among the Berbers in the first years of the Arab conquest.

KHOURASSINIDS Dynasty of princes who ruled the Tunis region during the eleventh century.

KOUBBA Dome, the correct name for the tomb of a marabout.

KOUTTAB Koranic primary school.

KSAR Communal fortified granary built mainly in the south (plural *ksour*).

LALLA Female saint.

LIMES Chain of forts built along the frontier of the Roman Empire.

LOUAGE Service taxi (see p.13).

MAGHREB "West" in Arabic, used of the countries of the Maghrebian confederation (Morocco, Algeria, Tunisia, Libya and Mauritania), especially the first three.

MAHDI The last prophet, Islam's equivalent of the second coming. Various people have claimed to be the Mahdi. Three are mentioned in this book: Obaidallah, founder of Mahdia and the Fatimid dynasty; Ibn Tumart, founder of the Almohads; and Mohammed Ahmed, who liberated Sudan from the British in 1886.

MALEKITE School of orthodox Sunni Islam, founded at Medina (Arabia) in the eighth century and dominant in North Africa for many centuries, with mosques distinguished by square minarets. More rigorous than the Hanefite, many people consider it the purest school.

MALOUF Andalusian-based traditional folk music.

MARABOUT Holy man, and by extension his place of burial. The tombs, dotted all over the North African countryside, are often centres of cult worship. Marabouts played a vital role in spreading Islam among the Berbers.

MASJID Small local mosque, for everyday (rather than Friday) prayer.

MEDERSA (MEDRESSA) Residential college of Islamic education, usually in the form of a court surrounded by students' cells. These colleges spread throughout the Islamic world from the thirteenth century onwards, generally as state foundations teaching the local orthodoxy.

MENZEL Dwelling place – in Jerba refers to the family *houch* and the enclosure around it.

MIDHA Ritual washing and latrine facility attached to mosque.

MIHRAB Niche indicating the direction of Mecca (and of prayer).

MINARET Tower attached to mosque from which the *muezin* gives the call to prayer.

MINBAR Pulpit from which imam delivers homily at Friday prayers in a *jemaa*.

MUEZIN Singer who gives call to prayer.

MURADIDS The first hereditary line of Beys who ruled during the seventeenth century, nominally under the Ottoman sultan.

NADOR Watchtower.

ONA *Organisation National de l'Artisanat* The national crafts organisation, their shops are expensive but useful for pre-bargaining guidelines.

ONTT *Office Nationale de Tourisme et Thermalisme* (National Office of Tourism and Spas).

OTTOMAN Empire, based in Constantinople (Istanbul) from the fifteenth century to World War I, to which Tunisia belonged as a regency.

OUED (WADI) Seasonal river – may only have water in it for a few days a year.

PALAESTRA Roman gymnasium.

PERISTYLE Court enclosed by columns.

PHOENICIANS First great trading nation of Mediterranean history. Originally from what is now Lebanon, they founded trading posts (some of which became the Carthaginian Empire) along the southern Mediterranean coast.

PROTECTORATE The period of French control (1881–1956). The Beys stayed, and French rule was largely indirect and less repressive than in neighbouring Algeria.

PTT *Postes, Télécommunications et Télédiffusion*. Post office.

PUNIC Of Carthaginians and their culture.

QIBLA Direction of prayer, physically indicated by the mihrab.

RAS Headland or cape.

RCD *Rassemblement Constitutionnel Démocratique*. Ruling political party, formerly the *PSD*.

RIBAT Monastic fortress, a building type which sprang up on North African coast in the ninth century. *Marabout* originally meant an inhabitant of a *ribat*.

RUSTAMIDS Kharijite dynasty who ruled the south of Tunisia from Tahirt (Algeria) in the ninth century (see p.167).

SABAT Room built in vault over narrow street.

SAHEL Coast.

SEBKHA Salt-encrusted mud flat.

SHIA Schismatic Islamic sect whose split from the Sunni majority in the seventh century remains the biggest sectarian division in the faith. Shi'ites emphasised the spiritual side of Islam in reaction to the power of the Umayyad Caliphs (see p.348).

SIDI Lord, saint, title of holy men.

SIFSARI Light women's outer garment wrapped around the body, which can also be used as a veil if held between the teeth. Tunisia's answer to the sari.

SKIFA Narrow passage, entrance.

STELA Tombstone (plural *stelae*).

SOUK Originally a covered urban market, now used of any kind of market, but especially a weekly one.

SUFI Unorthodox sects in Islam which take their teaching, often with mystical associations, from one originating teacher. Some cults spread throughout the Islamic world, transmitted by *zaouias*.

SUNNI Islamic orthodoxy; the vast majority of Muslims are Sunni, though they belong to a particular school, such as the Malekite or Hanefite.

TAXIPHONE Public telephone for national and international calls.

TOURBET Islamic mausoleum.

TRICLINIUM Roman dining room.

TUAREGS Nomadic Saharan Berbers.

UMAYYADS Dynasty of Caliphs who ruled the Arab Empire from Damascus 661–749. The same family ruled Spain 756–1031.

VANDALS German tribe who sacked Carthage in 439 AD and ruled in Tunisia until 535 (see p.324).

WAHABISM (1) Islamic heresy following Abdallah Ibn Wahab founded in 782 AD, one of two branches of Kharijism. (2) Eighteenth-century, Islamic, anti-colonial movement founded by Ibn Abdul Wahab.

WHITE FATHERS Order of monks cloaked in white *bournouse*-style habits founded in 1870 and based originally in Carthage, later in Thibar. They left Tunisia in 1976.

ZAOUIA Religious cult based on the teachings of a particular marabout, a sanctuary around the marabout's tomb, or a seminary-type base for his followers.

ZIRIDS Dynasty that ruled Tunisia in the eleventh century. Originally governors for the Fatimids, they declared independence in 984, incurring the Fatimids' wrath. During the Hilalian invasions, they ruled not much more than Mahdia.

ZITOUNA Olive tree.

WILDLIFE

For a country a mere 800km long by 250km wide, Tunisia packs in an amazing variety of habitats. Although northern Tunisia will be familiar to anyone who knows the Mediterranean – a combination of lime-stone and sandstone hills, pine and cork oak forest, and agricultural land – as soon as you get south of the great Dorsale ridge of mountains that splits the country, you're into something totally different: steppe deserts north of the Chott el Jerid, and true rolling sand dunes to the south, with fertile oases punctuating both.

It takes some practice to learn to identify promising wildlife sites. Look for sites' variety of different **habitats,** such as a hillside with woodland, scrub and rocky gorges. **Fresh water** is invariably a magnet and always worth checking out. **Deciduous woodland** is terrific, but give the monotonous olive groves a miss. For flowers, look for **colour,** which often indicates richness, especially on hillsides. A site with a **wide variety of plants** will tend to be richer in insects, and hence small birds and reptiles too.

The **time of day** is important, too. While flowers, insects and reptiles can be watched right through the day and are best when it's hot, birds are most active at dawn and dusk. A walk through the woods at dawn or within the two hours afterwards can yield ten times as many birds as the same walk at midday.

CLIMATE AND HABITAT DESTRUCTION

Climate, as always, plays a major role in determining the distribution of plants and animals. Any visitor from northern Europe has to keep the lack of water firmly in mind – it's the dominant factor. Although Tunisia includes the wettest place in North Africa (the cork oak forests around Aïn Draham on the Algerian border), large areas of the south have an annual average rainfall of less than 50 millimetres. And average rainfalls are highly misleading; what actually happens is that there is no rain at all for years, and then a sudden deluge. This patchiness is common in the north as well.

This is confusing for the average naturalist. It means that animals and plants have adapted to become highly flexible and unpredictable in their appearances. While in Britain you can go to a wood and see the same orchids flowering year after year, you can't always do that in Tunisia. After a very wet year, parts of the desert will bloom in a blaze of colour, the *sebk-has* will flood and suddenly support huge popu-lations of wintering birds. After a very dry winter, annual plants may simply not germi-nate, some perennials will retreat into their bulbs or roots and not even flower, and the desert will remain devoid of vegetation.

Parallel with climate, **agriculture** is the other hugely important factor. The fertile north of the country has been used as an intensive agricultural belt from the first century BC right through to the French occupation, and agricul-tural pressures are no less intense now with Tunisia's population growing at 2.5 percent annually. This has meant that the original forests have long since been cleared, and many of the scrubby Mediterranean hillside regions have been converted to arable land or greatly modified by pressure of grazing.

Grazing pressure accounts for changes to the desert, too, with the familiar pattern of desertification being caused by a combination of overgrazing and climatic change. Many people who live in the south depend on wood for their cooking and heating; combine this with over seven million grazing animals and you can see why forests have degraded to scrubland and desert.

FIELD GUIDES AND TIMES TO VISIT

Despite the loss of habitat, Tunisia still has abundant **plant and animal life**, and much of it can be easily seen. One problem is the lack of **identification** books. Birds are fine – many of the standard field guides include North Africa – but **plants** are a problem since the only comprehensive guides to flora in Tunisia are highly technical, out of print, unillustrated, and in French. The following accounts therefore concentrate on species which can also be found in the northern Mediterranean, or which are covered in Oleg Polunin and Anthony Huxley's standard field guide, *Flowers of the Mediterranean* (Chatto, 1990). For general coverage of the wildlife sites of Tunisia and a detailed run-down of the species, Pete Raine's *Mediterranean Wildlife: the Rough Guide* (Harrap, 1990) is an invaluable companion to supplement the wildlife features in the *Rough Guide to Tunisia*.

Spring is a good time to visit. Not only are the hillsides in full flower, but this is also the best time for migrating birds passing through Tunisia in April and May on their way to breeding grounds further north. By **high summer** much of the country is burnt out, but good flowers are still to be found in the mountains and the coast, and breeding is in full swing for summer migrant birds from further south. **Autumn** sees the return migration of European breeding birds, as well as a late flowering of many species of bulbs. **Winter** is the best time to visit the deserts of the south, with many of the desert plants choosing this time to flower (water permitting), and the winter season also sees the build-up of birds from Europe and Russia with huge concentrations of wildfowl and waders.

BIRDS

Tunisia's **bird** population varies widely depending on the time of the year – it's more obviously affected by migration than countries further north. During spring migration, the country can seem like the avian equivalent of Piccadilly Circus in the rush hour: summer visitors like **bee eaters** arrive to breed from their winter quarters south of the Sahara; winter visitors, mostly **waders and wildfowl**, leave to migrate the thousands of kilometres to their breeding grounds in northern Europe, spring migrants such as **honey buzzards** pass through, sometimes in huge numbers; and the resident birds just stay where they are. In autumn, the same happens but in reverse.

FARMLAND

Farmland can be rewarding especially where the fields are small and broken up by trees or patches of scrub. Finches are much in evidence here – familiar **goldfinches**, **linnets** and **chaffinches** are joined by the yellow **serin**, a distant relative of the canary. **Nightingales** are a common summer visitor and the colourful and exotic **hoopoe** can be found wherever there are suitable old trees for nesting. Another abundant farmland species is the resident **corn bunting**, a heavy, brown bird with a monotonous song usually described as like the jangling of a bunch of keys. The song of the small resident **fantailed warbler** is no less monotonous, a repetitive "tsip" delivered in its undulating flight. Farmland attracts **migrating quails** and is often hunted over by **black kites** – long-tailed and with level wings – and **marsh harriers,** with equally long tails but wings tilted upwards. Black and white **great grey shrikes** are also found here, often perching on telegraph wires; they're joined in summer by their smaller, red-headed relative the **woodchat shrike**.

WOODLAND

Deciduous woodlands are really only found in the **Khroumerie** region in the northwest of the country, and are home to many birds which, though common in Europe, are rare in Africa. Look for **woodpeckers**, **jays**, **wrens** and **tits** all year round, with **warblers**, **nightingales** and **wrynecks** in summer. Coniferous woodlands are less exciting, although **finches**, tits and some warblers are common.

The **scrubby hillsides** of the north are rewarding for small species. **Sardinian warblers**, with their glossy black caps, red eyes, and scratchy song are abundant. One species found only in North Africa is **Moussier's redstart**, an extremely beautiful small bird, with a striking plumage of orange, black and white. **Stonechats** are resident in this type of habitat, and the same zones are widely used as feeding stations by migrating **wheatears**, **warblers**, and **wagtails**. **Barbary partridges**, another North African species, breed on these hillsides too.

Mountains, whether the forested hills round Aïn Draham, the limestone ridge of the Dorsale, or the barren massifs of the south, are the best place to see resident **birds of prey**. **Buzzards**, **eagles**, **vultures**, **kites** and **falcons** all use the rocks as breeding sites, gliding out over the surrounding plains in search of food. **Blue rock thrushes**, very like blackbirds but a superb powder-blue colour, are also found in mountains, as are **black wheatears** and **rock buntings**.

THE COAST

Tunisia's coastline varies from the rocky shore of the north, around Bizerte, to flat mudflats in the southeast. Predictably, this is the place for **seabirds**; a wide variety of gulls and terns spend the winter here, including the **slenderbilled gull** and the **Caspian tern**. The latter is the largest of the terns of the region, almost gull-sized and with a very stout, red bill. The islands off the north coast have colonies of two species of shearwater. But it's the tidal mudflats of the Gulf of Gabes that hold the most exciting birds, with huge wintering populations of **waders** (primarily **dunlin**, **sandpipers**, **stints** and **redshank**) along with large numbers of more exotic species such as **flamingos**, **spoonbills** and **avocets**.

DESERT BIRDS

Finally, the hills, *oueds* (dry stream beds) and oases of the **deserts** hold their own specialities. There is a truly bewildering variety of **larks** and **wheatears** around here, enough to tax the keenest ornithologist. One especially strange lark is the **hoopoe lark**, so-called because of its long, decurved bill and black and white wings. Its song starts on the ground with a series of repeated notes, slowly ascending in pitch until the bird culminates with a final flurry of notes as it takes off vertically and then spirals down to start all over again. Another desert bird with an extraordinary call is the **trumpeter finch**, locally quite common.

MAMMALS

Although the top-of-the-food-chain predators such as lion and leopard were finally shot out earlier this century, there are still exciting species such as **jackal**, **wild boar**, **porcupine**, **mongoose** and **genet**, a beautiful tree-climbing carnivore with a spotted coat and a long ringed tail. The cats are still represented by **wild cats** and (it is said) **lynx**. But ignore anyone who says it's easy to see mammals; they're shy and often nocturnal, with good reason considering the long history of hunting. But the wooded mountains of the Khroumerie hold a good range of species, as do some of the limestone mountains like Djebel Ichkeul.

Further south, small desert rodents are of interest. **Desert rats**, **gerbils** and **jerboas** lope around the desert at night, and a species of **suslik**, *Psammomys* (a sort of short-tailed ground squirrel with a characteristic upright "begging" posture) is common on the salt-marshes and *sebkhas* of the south. Most of the larger desert antelopes have been reduced to the point of extinction by disturbance and hunting, but an introduction programme of **gazelle**, **oryx**, **addax** (as well as **ostrich**, which has only been exterminated this century south of Medinine) is in progress at the national park of Bou Hedma, in the steppes near Maknassy. **Fennec foxes** (a beautiful desert fox with huge ears) certainly used to occur on Chott Djerid but may have disappeared by now.

One final **mammal** which may still exist on the shores Tunisia is the **Mediterranean monk seal**, which is down to its last few hundred, mostly in Greece and Turkey. Perhaps a few still hang on around some of the islands off the north coast.

REPTILES AND AMPHIBIANS

Throughout the country, reptiles and amphibians are much in evidence. **Lizards and skinks** are everywhere on the dry hillsides, small **geckos** come out in the evenings to pursue their useful insect-eating lifestyle on the walls and ceilings of older buildings and **frogs and toads** croak a deafening spring chorus wherever there is fresh water. The handsome **painted frog** is widespread, blotched in brown and green. In the desert, you sometimes see **desert lizards** running like the wind on their hind legs from bush to bush. **Tortoises** and **pond terrapins** are both, locally, quite abundant. A dozen species of **snakes** also occur; although only some are poisonous, they do include several species of **viper**, and you should be cautious when out walking on rocky hillsides – shorts and sandals are possibly not a good idea.

BUTTERFLIES AND INVERTEBRATES

Butterflies are the most obvious insects. In spring, huge numbers of the migrant **painted lady** cross Tunisia from further south, bound for Europe. It's a pretty extraordinary phenomenon, for although they breed in northern Europe the young insects are doomed, as they can only very rarely survive the northern winters in hibernation. **Clouded yellows**, a deep yellow with black wing edges, undertake a similar migration but in smaller numbers. A small yellow butterfly with orange wingtips is likely to be the **Moroccan orangetip**, very common in early spring. Three striking species are the **Cleopatra**, *Gonepteryx*, like a huge **brimstone** but with orange patches on its yellow wings, and two species of **swallowtail.** Early summer is probably the time when butterflies on the wing are at their peak. Other striking animals of the lower orders include **praying mantids**, harmless but unnerving assassins of the undergrowth and, of course, **scorpions**, which you are most unlikely to come across unless you go looking under rocks and bark.

MARINE LIFE

Finally, the **marine life** of the rocky northern coast is well worth mentioning. Some of the best snorkelling and diving in the Mediterranean is here around the **coral reefs** off Tabarca, Cap Serrat and especially off the marine national park of the Zembra isles. The coral is long dead, a memory of a time when the Mediterranean was a much warmer sea, but it holds extensive seaweed beds and numerous fish. Sadly, spearfishing is much promoted as a tourist activity.

On the other hand, the Tunisian **fishing** industry is one of the best regulated in the Mediterranean, with the National Fisheries Board (the ONP) doing a superb job in ensuring that offshore fishing remains at a sustainable level. Apparently the weight of fish per area in Tunisian waters is some twenty times the weight in the same area around Sicily, where trawling is notoriously exploitative. A trip round any fish market, and especially the big one in Rue d'Allemagne in Tunis, gives some idea of the range and quality of what can be caught.

FLORA

The **flora of Tunisia** stands at the crossroads between the Mediterranean flora of the north and the desert plants of the south. The forests of the Khroumerie have an almost northern European feel about them, with cork oak, flowering ash and even hawthorn growing above bracken, whilst only a few finely tuned species can survive in the waterless desert conditions.

FARMLAND

Farmland hosts a colourful mass of plants in spring and early summer, especially around the field margins. Characteristic plants include **scarlet pimpernel** (confusingly, bright blue in much of the Mediterranean region), **poppies**, **marigolds**, **daisies** and **campions.** The borage family is well represented; most plants of this family have hairy stems and leaves, and five-petalled flowers which are often pink in bud but blue in bloom. The **common borage** has nodding star-shaped bright blue flowers (which you can eat in salads, incidentally), the **forget-me-nots** are in the same family and so are the **buglosses.** There are a number of different bugloss species (*Echium*) in Tunisia, but they all have blue or purple trumpet-shaped flowers with protruding pink stamens. One common species in this family that breaks the blue-flowered rule is **honeywort** *Cerinthe major*, which has unusual chocolate-tipped yellow flowers hanging in a fused tube.

Various **convolvulus** species are common: there are pink varieties in early summer and, in spring, a colourful one is the aptly named *Convolvulus tricolor* – blue around the edge, yellow in the middle, and white in between.

Although the uncultivated field margins have most of the farmland species, an occasional field will have escaped the attentions of the herbicide spray, and here you can see a blaze of colour from miles off, including the bright yellow of *Chrysanthemum coronanum*, the scarlet of **poppies,** and sometimes the nodding pink of **wild gladioli.**

A plant to watch out for on grazed agricultural land is the **asphodel**, *Asphodelus microcarpus*. It grows up to a metre in height, with flowering spikes flung up from a narrow-leaved basal bulb; the flowers are pink with darker veins. It's the classic indicator species of **overgrazed land** since stock won't touch it, and it slowly takes over as other, more nutritious species are eaten away. In some parts of Tunisia the asphodel forms a virtual monoculture over large stretches of impoverished land.

One final group is the introduced species. **Mimosa** or wattle is widespread, with long pendant strings of yellow flowers in spring. It's an Australian species, and well adapted to a hot dry climate. So are the **eucalyptus** (gum) trees which have been widely planted both in forests and for roadside shade; it's hot enough for them to flower here, often very strikingly in a mass of yellow or red blossom.

On farms and around villages you're bound to see the **prickly pear**, a large cactus introduced to Europe, it is said, by Christopher Columbus. The **century plant** *Agave amencana* is another American species, brought over from Mexico in the eighteenth century; it produces a huge flowering spike up to ten metres high when it's ten to twenty years old, and then dies, although suckers round its edge may live on. Much smaller, but equally noticeable, is the **Bermuda buttercup.** A very common wayside plant, it flowers in spring in a sheet of absolutely brilliant yellow among bright green, trefoliate leaves. Despite its name it was introduced from South Africa, as was the **Hottentot fig** *Carpobrotus*. This last species now dominates sandy cliffs and banks by the sea, with its mat of fleshy leaves and psychedelic pink or yellow flowers.

THE COAST

The **coastal areas** also hold many of these farmland plants, and in fact was their original habitat in many cases. Field margins are continually being disturbed, and the plough creates an ecological niche similar to the effect of the sea and shifting sand. Three common plants around the Tunisian coast are all familiar to British gardeners. **White alyssum**, *Lobularia manbma*, beloved as an edging plant by bedding plant enthusiasts, grows sprawlingly with clusters of white **flowers**; **Virginia stock**, *Malcolmia mantima*, has tiny pink red or purple four-petalled flowers; and the everlasting **sea lavender** (still known as *Statice* although botanists have renamed it *Limonium*) has papery blue and white flowers. Saltmarshes are a common feature of the east coast, and inland where there are vast dry salt lakes (*sebkkas*). These are often dominated by

plants of the **glasswort** family – low shrubs with fleshy cylindrical stems and minute flowers. Only real plant freaks will want to sort them out down to species level as they're a very difficult group.

HILLSIDES AND MOUNTAINS

The scrub-covered **hillsides** of the north, and the slopes of the wetter limestone mountains of the centre, form perhaps the classic Mediterranean botanical habitat, equivalent to the *garigue* of France or the *matorral* of the Iberian peninsula. Here you can find the aromatic shrubs of **rosemary**, **sage** and **thyme** together with the **rockroses**, *Cistus*, with their profusion of flat white or pink flowers. Limestone hills tend to have a wider variety of ground flowers than the sandstone ones; peer under the bushes for many **orchid** species as well as **irises**, including the delightful, tiny *Iris sisyrinchium*, which only flowers in the afternoon after the heat of the sun has warmed it. A noticeable spring species here, also common on farmland is a small **valerian**, *Fedia cornucopiae* – low growing with clusters of pink tubed flowers. It seems to be unpalatable to goats; you see it flowering profusely where everything else has been grazed out. One plant which is heavily grazed is the **dwarf fan palm**, *Chaemerops humilis*, a low-growing relation of the ubiquitous date palm; on ungrazed hillsides (if you can find any) it can sometimes be dominant.

DESERT SPECIES

The **sand and stone deserts** south of the Dorsale mountains have a quite different flora. Plants are sparse, except in the oases where many of the farmland and hillside species mentioned above can be found, and they are highly adapted to the dry conditions. They survive in two ways. Sunlight is so abundant that they don't need big leaves to gather energy, so their leaves are reduced to **narrow stems** in order to reduce water loss by transpiration. The other technique is to try to store water, and some desert plants have fleshy swollen leaves for this purpose. Many desert plants and shrubs have ferocious **spines**, too, as protection against grazing animals, although there's not much that can protect against the camel, which will even browse on prickly pear.

ONWARD TRAVEL

Tunisia is a superb transit point, strategically sited at a crossroads between Europe, Africa and the Arab world. The most exciting options are the great overland routes. Crossing into Algeria you can head south to emerge on the far side of the Sahara – one of the few classic journeys left in the 1980s and certainly the closest to Europe. Alternatively, limiting your sights to the northern reaches of the Great Eastern Erg, there is the North African Loop – an exciting and satisfying circuit which can take in as much or as little as you like of Sicily, Tunisia, Algeria, Morocco and Spain. Though today a very disparate region, these countries once comprised a western Arab Empire and each of them – southern Spain above all – today bears impressive monuments of the age. Now too, it's becoming more feasible to head the other way through Libya to Egypt.

ALGERIA

Algeria, considerably less well known than either Tunisia or Morocco, has always been a more adventurous part of North Africa in which to travel. This it remains – a vast expanse with some quite extraordinary routes. And Algerians are themselves a major, positive factor: some of the most easy-going and hospitable people in North Africa.

Entry requirements vary from time to time, but most Western nationals now need a visa; exceptions are Scandinavians, Swiss, Italians, Maltese and Spanish. If you have Israeli or South African stamps in your passport, you can forget about a visa, and if you are Jewish, it's probably best not to say so. Visas are supposed to be issued in your **country of residence**, and this rule is at present being strictly applied in Tunis, probably in retaliation for racist immigration restrictions against Algerians in Europe. If you cannot prove you're a Tunisian resident, you will probably not be issued a visa there. If you forgot to get one back home or elsewhere (Commonwealth nationals, for example, seem to have no trouble getting them in London), or if yours has run out (they are valid for 45 days), you can apply by leaving 38TD and waiting a month. You will probably not get your visa, and you lose the money regardless. British travellers in particular, perhaps because of Britain's stance in the 1991 Gulf Crisis, stand very little chance, with 90 percent being refused. There are Algerian consulates in Le Kef and Gafsa which you could try. As a last resort, it is *just* possible that certain European nationals (such as Germans) can get one at the border, but it's not something to count on. If Morocco is your destination, you may either have to fly or travel via Europe.

As if the visa situation weren't bad enough, travellers are also required to change 1000 dinars (about £100 sterling) at the official rate whilst in the country. Black market rates, widely available, are greatly more favourable, but currency laws are rigidly adhered to: if you are caught inside Algeria with undeclared foreign currency, you're in trouble.

The number of **border posts** open between Tunisia and Algeria depends somewhat on the state of relations between the two countries. Currently you can cross at Babouch, Ghardimaou, Hazoua el Oued, Sakiet Sidi Youssef and Bou Chebka – the last two are sometimes suspended – and it should also be possible at Tabarca el Kala and Haidra Ras el Aioun. Babouch (see p.137) and Ghardimaou (see p.147) are your best bets for northern Algeria; Hazoua (see p.250) for the south.

Bus, *louage* and train connections are all detailed within the text. Be warned that the **Trans-Maghreb Express**, the most popular route across the border, is invariably crowded and in summer can be pretty horrific. You might consider flying part of the distance: student fares between Tunis and Algiers are good value. Within the country, buses are usually the most effective and comfortable form of transport, though there are also good train services in the north, and, because of the country's size, planes are worth considering, and often not much dearer than the bus.

The fastest route through Algeria cuts across the big **northern cities** of **Constantine**, **Algiers** and **Oran**. This is not in itself the most interesting part of the country though the mountain scenery is often spectacular. Making relatively short detours the rewards are greater. **Timgad**, almost completely preserved, is one of the most extraordinary Roman towns anywhere; any one of the roads between Batna and the immense oasis of **Biskra** will take you through dramatic canyons; the **Turquoise Coast**, west of Algiers, is a long series of mountainous and isolated coves; and right over in the mountains by the Moroccan border, **Tlemcen**'s Islamic architecture is among the most important and beautiful in North Africa.

If you have time to spare, though, even as little as a week, try to take in at least something of **the south**. The sheer size of the desert regions here is hard to grasp: **Tamanrasset**, near the Niger border, for instance, is further from Algiers than is Paris. Closer, and easily accessible from the north (either driving your own vehicle or hitching) are some of the most spectacular Saharan dunes — stretching between **El Oued**, so-called "City of a Thousand Domes", and the fantastic desert architecture of **Ghardaia**.

Getting around in the Sahara really does feel more like travel than tourism and it needs time and energy to explore the desert pistes. The two really compelling attractions are both **mountain ranges**: the **Hoggar**, to the north of Tamanrasset, rising over 3000m, and the **Tassili**, some way to the east with its exceptional prehistoric cave paintings. Further still, the trans-Saharan routes lead across the desert, the **Tanezrouft** route to Gao in Mali and the **Hoggar** route to Agadez in Niger. If you're heading this way and have your own transport, note that there is a short-cut from **Borj Omar Driss** to Tamanrasset, not very prominently marked on maps, but useful if

coming to or from Tunisia and navigable by any vehicle fit to cross the desert, though for safety you must always travel in convoy and inform the police of your route and departure.

The Saharan routes to West Africa are covered in detail in **West Africa: the Rough Guide** (Harrap Columbus), which is also the only serious guidebook to Africa's western bulge. Simon and Jan Glen's **Sahara Handbook** (Lascelles) is also useful for the practicalities of taking a car across the desert. The only guides to Algeria itself are in French: try a combination of the *Guide Bleu: Algerie* for cultural background, and the *Guide du Routard: Algerie–Tunisie* for budget practicalities (both published by Hachette).

Note that, as this book goes to press, the feasibility of the trans-Saharan routes is in doubt following attacks by Tuareg nationalist guerillas and bandits on a number of vehicles. The Tanezrouft is closed and the Hoggar may be open only to an official, armed convoy.

MOROCCO

Assuming you're in Algeria, crossing to **Morocco** is now straightforward following a rapprochement between the countries in spring 1988. There are two **points of entry**: **Figuig**, a beautiful oasis in the south, and the town of **Oujda**, not far from Tlemcen, a good base from which to head for Fes and Meknes. The Trans-Maghreb Express no longer goes all the way through — it stops at Maghnia, just beyond Tlemcen, where you take a bus to the border, and another on to Oujda (a further 15km).

Less westernised than Tunisia — and much poorer — Morocco can at first seem a difficult place to travel. Harassment here is a constant for women, and there is an additional factor to come to terms with in the country's unique brand of hustlers, masquerading in turn as students, guides or sellers. Once you've gained a certain confidence, though, this is probably the most interesting and memorable country in North Africa. Each of the great imperial cities of **Fes**, **Meknes**, **Rabat** and **Marrakesh** is worth taking considerable time to explore. So too — and much more relaxed in their attitudes — are the remote Berber villages of the High Atlas mountains in the south. For a full treatment of the country, **Morocco: the Rough Guide** (Harrap Columbus) is the obvious choice.

SPAIN, ITALY AND GREECE

From Morocco it's only a two-and-a-half-hour ferry ride to **Spain**, also covered in the Rough Guide Series (Harrap Columbus). Parts of Spain, notably Andalusia, were under Muslim control for nearly 800 years, and it was the arts centre of the Arab world. Parts of the classical culture of modern Tunisia have deep roots in Andalusian music and poetry but to see Andalusian architectural styles – the Great Mosque of **Cordoba** and the Alhambra at **Granada**, to name just the best-known examples – a visit to Spain itself is a must.

Taking the North African loop in the opposite direction, there are regular ferries from Tunis to **Sicily**, and beyond. Sicily is quite different in feel to the rest of Italy and enjoys a measure of autonomy from the mainland. Its convoluted history reads like a roll-call of civilisations – Greek, Roman, Arab, Byzantine and Norman – and each has left its mark. The capital, **Palermo**, is a frenetic blend of styles, Baroque churches leaning against elaborate Spanish palazzos, Norman chapels tucked into twentieth-century bombsites. In addition there are some outstanding classical sites, equal to, and occasionally surpassing, anything in Greece, the best known being **Agrigento**, with its line of preserved temples. The mountainous and isolated interior demands time, for example, to make the fascinating trip around the foothills and up the summit of Mount Etna, Europe's largest active volcano. Outside the main cities, and the two tourist resorts of Taormina and Cefalu, Sicily gets few visitors. But you can get away from it all completely by venturing on to the dozen or so offshore islets, of which the active volcanic Stromboli is the most spectacular. All the details are covered in *Sicily: the Rough Guide* (Harrap Columbus) and, with the rest of the country, *Italy: the Rough Guide* (Harrap Columbus).

From **Brindisi**, just across Italy's "ankle" from Sicily, there is access to **Greece**, also well covered in the Rough Guide series (*Greece* and *Crete*, Harrap Columbus). Ferries leave daily for the ports of **Igoumenitsa** and **Patras**, calling en route at Corfu where you can stop over at no extra charge if you have this written in on your ticket. Greece's capital, **Athens**, is one of the best places to get cheap air tickets for all points east.

LIBYA

For many years, **Libya** did not allow entry to tourists and its attractions remained inaccessible. Even now tourism is not encouraged, but it is possible to obtain a visa, and, while travel presents certain difficulties, the rewards more than repay the effort. In addition, Libya's eastern border is now open to Egypt. Forget any media preconceptions: Libyans are extemely friendly, and political differences between your government and theirs will not affect that. Libya is also a vast and fascinating country with huge potential for independent travel. If you haven't had your fill of **Roman ruins**, Libya has some that put Tunisia's in the shade, and are more professionally restored too.

The **visa situation** is always fluid, and may change with political developments, so keep your ear to the ground. Before applying for a visa, you have to get your passport stamped with a translation of the information from its first two pages into Arabic. Most Western embassies will do this for their nationals free of charge. At the latest check, the Libyan embassy in Tunis was not issuing visas to tourists, but the consulate in Sfax was providing them (valid from the date of issue, not the date of intended entry) without much trouble. It's best when you apply to say you are in transit to Egypt. You're required to state your religion when applying for a visa (don't put "none", "atheist" or "Jewish") and you won't get a visa if you have stamps from South Africa, Israel or the Israel–Egypt border.

Entering Libya, it's currently possible to cross between Tunisia and Libya in two places: **Ras Ajdir** on the coast (see p.295), and **Dehibat–Wazin** in the south (see p.315). The former is more hassle-free (you probably won't even see a Libyan border official), and has much better transport connections.

Tripoli, the capital, is a buzzing cosmopolitan city with an atmosphere a little hard to place, but plenty to see and do: above all, do not miss out on the Jamahawaria Museum, one of the best in Africa, housed in a palatial fortress called the Red Castle, with its entrance in Green Square. **Louages** (*taxi binasser*, or service taxis) to and from Tunisia are all based at the Tunis station (*mahata Tunis*) by the Medina wall. For Egypt and Sudan, and most parts of Libya, they leave from Meidan

Swahali, a large square nearby. With the **bus station** (*mahata utubus*) in Sharia el Ma'ari only a few hundred metres away, this is also the main area for **cheap hotels**, known in Libya as *funduq* (look for the sign فندق). They cost around 3–5LD, but most of them close their doors around midnight so try to arrive before then. The Youth Hostel (1LD; YHA card usually required but they may not insist) is at 69 Sharia Amar ben el A'ass, off Green Square. Other places with hostels include Khoms (for Lebda), Sabrata, Ghadames, Sirte, Benghazi, Shahat (for Cyrene), Sabha and Ghat.

Around the country, **Lebda** (Leptis Magna), on the coast 2km east of the city of **Khoms**, has an incredible four-way arch and baths in such an amazing state of repair you'll have no trouble imagining them as a giant, 2000-year-old hammam, while **Sabrata**, even closer to Tunisia, has a Punic mausoleum to compliment its sister at Dougga. The other important Roman site is at **Cyrene** in the east, between Libya's second city, **Benghazi**, and **Tobruk**, site of the famous World War II siege. The **Jebel Nafusa** range, stretching eastwards from the Tunisian border at Wazin, is, like Jerba, heir to the Kharijite tradition and full of fascinating little **mosques and** ksour even more impressive than those of Tunisia. **Nalut**, just over the border from Dehibat, has one of the best *ksour*, outdone only by the thirteenth-century *ksar* at **El Haj**. To the south, near the southernmost tip of Tunisia, the lovely old caravan terminus of **Ghadames**, famous for its beautiful Saharan architecture, is now the subject of a UNESCO conservation project.

There are one or two **possible problems** to bear in mind when visiting Libya. First, **money**: in theory all non-resident visitors to Libya must change US$500 at the official exchange rate. At the moment, this is not being enforced at land frontiers. In fact, changing money is not always easy with both banks and the black market often hard to find. In Tripoli at any rate, expatriates and other foreigners may be able to advise you. Second, **Arabic** is the only official language, and most signs are in Arabic alone. If you cannot read or speak it, you'll have difficulties; fairly few Libyans speak English. Finally, if you travel in southern Libya, you may encounter the **security police** who, although polite, like to check passports and ask questions about your parents' names and whether you've been to Israel. It's usually no problem, but people do occasionally find themselves locked in a cell for a few hours. Remember that foreigners are not often seen in the south and Libyans have genuine reason to be wary after 1987, when American jets attacked Tripoli, killing 37. Stay away from anything military, and keep your camera out of sight.

Unfortunately, there are no travel guides to Libya: the practical information here is as good as you'll get. Maps of Libya and Tripoli do exist, and are sometimes available at specialist travel bookshops (see p.362).

ONWARDS FROM LIBYA

It is now possible to travel right across North Africa from Casablanca to Cairo, and if you have the chance to go to **Egypt**, you shouldn't miss it. Cheap, easy-going and friendly, Egypt is one of the most fascinating countries in the world. It really needs no advertisement, but you do need a good travel guide; it's now covered by the first-class *Egypt: the Rough Guide* (Harrap Columbus). There's an open land frontier with **Israel** (another Rough Guide). Direct service taxis from Tripoli run to Cairo.

Heading south from Libya is more complicated. There is no public transport across the frontier with **Niger** and you risk a lot of trouble from the Niger authorities if you try to cross that way (you will almost certainly be sent back). You can, however, now cross into **Chad** (whose embassy in Tripoli is at 25 Sharia Mohamed Mussadeq, ☎43955).

INDEX

This index includes all the towns and villages covered in the guide, selected historical figures, as well as italicised references to other topics, and to subjects covered in *Basics* and *Contexts*. Place names sometimes spelt "Dj" are indexed under "J".

HELP US UPDATE

We've gone to great lengths to ensure that this first edition of **Tunisia: the Real Guide** is as up-to-date and accurate as possible. However, Tunisia is a fast-changing country and, if you feel there are places we've under-rated or over-praised, good hotels we've missed or others that have closed – or vanished – then please write. The latest details about your favourite restaurant or beach are as useful as letters about obscure desert *pistes*; if you want to take us to task on historical and cultural detail we'd be equally pleased to hear from you; and we always aim to improve our maps with each edition. Please locate places as accurately as possible – sketch maps are a help. We'll send a free copy of the next edition, or any other Real Guide if you prefer, for the most useful (and legible!) feedback.

Richard Trillo, Africa Editor (Tunisia 1st Edition), The Real Guides, Prentice Hall General Reference, A division of Simon & Schuster Inc, 15 Columbus Circle, New York NY10023